ROUTLEDGE HANDBOOK OF CONTEMPORARY CENTRAL ASIA

The *Routledge Handbook of Contemporary Central Asia* offers the first comprehensive, cross-disciplinary overview of key issues in Central Asian studies. The 30 chapters by leading and emerging scholars summarise major findings in the field and highlight long-term trends, recent observations and future developments in the region. The handbook features case studies of all five Central Asian republics and is organised thematically in seven sections:

- History
- Politics
- Geography
- International Relations
- Political Economy
- Society and Culture
- Religion

An essential cross-disciplinary reference work, the handbook offers an accessible and easy-to-understand guide to the core issues permeating the region to enable readers to grasp the fundamental challenges, transformations and themes in contemporary Central Asia. It will be of interest to researchers, academics and students of the region and those working in the field of Area Studies, History, Anthropology, Politics and International Relations.

Rico Isaacs is Associate Professor in Politics at the University of Lincoln, UK, and the editor of *Central Asian Survey*. His recent books include, among others, *Party System Formation in Kazakhstan* (2011), *Nation-Building and Identity in the Post-Soviet Space* (with A. Polese, 2016) and *Politics: An Introduction, 3rd edition* (with B. Axford, V. Browne and R. Huggins, 2018), also published by Routledge.

Erica Marat is Associate Professor at the College of International Security Affairs at the National Defence University, Washington, D.C. Her research focuses on violence, mobilisation and security institutions in Eurasia, India and Mexico. She is also the author of *The Politics of Police Reform: Society against the State in Post-Soviet Countries* (2018).

ROUTLEDGE HANDBOOK OF CONTEMPORARY CENTRAL ASIA

Edited by
Rico Isaacs and Erica Marat

LONDON AND NEW YORK

First published 2022
by Routledge
2 Park Square, Milton Park, Abingdon, Oxon OX14 4RN

and by Routledge
605 Third Avenue, New York, NY 10158

Routledge is an imprint of the Taylor & Francis Group, an informa business

© 2022 selection and editorial matter, Rico Isaacs and Erica Marat; individual chapters, the contributors

The right of Rico Isaacs and Erica Marat to be identified as the authors of the editorial material, and of the authors for their individual chapters, has been asserted in accordance with sections 77 and 78 of the Copyright, Designs and Patents Act 1988.

All rights reserved. No part of this book may be reprinted or reproduced or utilised in any form or by any electronic, mechanical, or other means, now known or hereafter invented, including photocopying and recording, or in any information storage or retrieval system, without permission in writing from the publishers.

Trademark notice: Product or corporate names may be trademarks or registered trademarks, and are used only for identification and explanation without intent to infringe.

British Library Cataloguing-in-Publication Data
A catalogue record for this book is available from the British Library

Library of Congress Cataloging-in-Publication Data
Names: Isaacs, Rico, editor. | Marat, Erica, editor.
Title: Routledge handbook of contemporary Central Asia / Rico Isaacs and Erica Marat.
Description: Abingdon, Oxon ; New York, NY : Routledge, 2021. | Includes bibliographical references and index.
Identifiers: LCCN 2021006267 | ISBN 9780367178406 (hardback) | ISBN 9781032050096 (paperback) | ISBN 9780429057977 (ebook)
Subjects: LCSH: Asia, Central--Handbooks, manuals, etc.
Classification: LCC DS327.5 .R68 2021 | DDC 958--dc23
LC record available at https://lccn.loc.gov/2021006267

ISBN: 978-0-367-17840-6 (hbk)
ISBN: 978-1-032-05009-6 (pbk)
ISBN: 978-0-429-05797-7 (ebk)

DOI: 10.4324/9780429057977

Typeset in Bembo
by Deanta Global publishing Services, Chennai, India

 Printed in the United Kingdom
by Henry Ling Limited

CONTENTS

List of figures	ix
List of tables	x
List of contributors	xi
Acknowledgements	xvii

	Introducing Central Asian studies *Rico Isaacs and Erica Marat*	1

PART I
History   **11**

1	Central Asia before the advent of Russian Dominion *Michael Hancock-Parmer*	13
2	Russian rule in Central Asia *Ian W. Campbell*	26
3	Collectivisation, sedentarisation and famine in Central Asia *Marianne Kamp and Niccolò Pianciola*	41
4	Development in post-war Central Asia *Artemy M. Kalinovsky*	56

PART II
Politics   **71**

5	Varieties of authoritarianism in Central Asia *David G. Lewis*	73

6 Informal governance, 'clan' politics and corruption 87
   Aksana Ismailbekova

7 Nation-building in Central Asia: Policy and discourse 101
   Dina Sharipova and Aziz Burkhanov

8 Unsettled space: Unfinished histories of border delimitation in the
   Ferghana Valley 115
   Madeleine Reeves

PART III
Geography **133**

9 Boundaries, borders and identities 135
   Vincent Artman and Alexander C. Diener

10 The history of water politics in Central Asia 154
    Christine Bichsel

11 Rethinking spectacular cities: Beyond authoritarianism
    and mastermind schemes 168
    Mateusz Laszczkowski and Natalie Koch

12 Politics of green development: Trees vs. roads 180
    Emil Nasritdinov

PART IV
International Relations **191**

13 Russia and Central Asia: Evolving mutual perceptions and the rise of
    postcolonial perspectives 193
    Marlene Laruelle

14 China–Central Asia relations: Re-learning to live next to the giant 202
    Nargis Kassenova

15 U.S. policy and Central Asia 218
    Charles E. Ziegler

16 Domestic sources of foreign policy in Central Asia 232
    Shairbek Dzhuraev

17 Military power and capacity 248
    Erica Marat

18 Globalisation and migration in Central Asia 263
    Caress Schenk

PART V
Political Economy **279**

19 Economic reform and development in Central Asia 281
    Richard Pomfret

20 Oil, capital and labour around the Caspian 303
    Maurizio Totaro and Paolo Sorbello

21 Corruption 319
    Johan Engvall

22 Modernisation and development in Central Asia 330
    Liga Rudzite and Karolina Kluczewska

PART VI
Society and Culture **347**

23 The nationalisation of traditions 349
    Svetlana Jacquesson

24 Thinking with gender about Central Asia 362
    Svetlana Peshkova

25 Contemporary art in Central Asia 377
    Alexandra Tsay

26 Language policy and language in Central Asia 391
    William Fierman

PART VII
Religion **409**

27 Islamic renewal in Central Asia 411
    Bayram Balci

28 Securitisation of religion in Central Asia   422
    Edward Lemon

29 Liberalism and Islam in Central Asia   437
    Galym Zhussipbek

30 Tengrism   451
    Rico Isaacs

Index   *461*

FIGURES

9.1	Map of Historical Regions of Central Asia. Source: Prepared by the University of Kansas Cartographic Laboratory, Modeled on Bregel 2003	136
9.2	Map of Russian Empire. Source: Prepared by the University of Kansas Cartographic Laboratory	137
11.1	President Nursultan Nazarbaev as the architect of Astana (statue at the Presidential Cultural Center, Astana). Photo by Mateusz Laszczkowski	169
11.2	Spectacular new architecture in Astana. Photo by Mateusz Laszczkowski	172
13.1	Kazakhstan, Kyrgyzstan, Tajikistan and Uzbekistan's approval of the Russian leadership, 2006–2017. Source: Gallup Worldwide Research Data	196
17.1	U.S. security aid to Central Asia. Source: Security Assistance Monitor (https://securityassistance.org/)	256
25.1	'Kyzyl Traktor' art collective, performance 'Dervish,' Prague 2003. Picture: courtesy of the artists	379
25.2	'You cannot run away from the truth' banner during Almaty marathon, April 21, 2019. Picture: Tamina Ospanova	382
25.3	Vyacheslav Akhunov and his work 'Alphabet of Socialist Realism,' 2003. Picture: courtesy of the artist	383
25.4	Gulnara Kasmaliyeva and Muratbek Djumaliyev, TransSiberian Amazons, installation, 2005	384
25.5	Alexander Ugay, 'A model for the assembly,' 2013, courtesy of the artist. Photo: exhibition view, 175 Gallery, Seoul	387
25.6	Alexander Ugay, 'A model for the assembly,' 2013, courtesy of the artist	387

TABLES

9.1	National Composition of Kazakhstan 1989, 1999 and 2009	141
13.1	Average Percentage Approval of Russian Leadership, Including 'Do Not Know' Responses, Gallup World Poll Surveys, 2006–2018	196
18.1	Remittance flows 2017, millions of US dollars	265
19.1	Initial Conditions: Republics of the USSR 1989/1990	282
19.2	EBRD Transition Indicators, 1999 and 2009	284
19.3	Growth in Real GDP, 1989–1999 (per cent)	286
19.4	Growth in Real GDP, 1999–2014 (per cent)	288
19.5	Macroeconomic Indicators 2015–2019	293
19.6	Economic and Social Indicators, 2018	295
22.1	Net ODA and Official Aid Received by Central Asian Countries (in million USD)	333
28.1	Table of Banned Extremist Groups in Central Asia	430

CONTRIBUTORS

Vincent Artman is a Fellow at the Havighurst Center for Russian and Post-Soviet Studies at Miami University. His research focuses on the intersection of religion, identity and the nation-state in Central Asia. He has published in Europe-Asia Studies, Central Asian Affairs, Geopolitics and Territory, Politics, Governance.

Bayram Balci is the director of l'Insitut Français d'Études Anatoliennes in Istanbul, Turkey, where his research focuses on Religion and Politics in Turkey, Central Asia and the Caucasus. He was between 2006 and 2010 the director of Institut Français d'Etudes sur l'Asie Centrale, IFEAC, based in Tashkent. A non-resident scholar with the Carnegie Endowment's Russia and Eurasia Programme from 2011 to 2014, he is affiliated with CERI Sciences Po in Paris, France. His main publications are *Missionnaires de l'Islam en Asie centrale: les écoles turques de Fethullah Gülen* (2003) and *Islam in Central Asia and the Caucasus Since the Fall of the Soviet Union* (2019).

Christine Bichsel is Professor for Human Geography at the Department of Geosciences of the University of Fribourg. Her research interests centre on political geography, environmental history and critical water studies. Christine is the author of 'Conflict Transformation in Central Asia: Irrigation Disputes in the Ferghana Valley' (Routledge, 2009).

Aziz Burkhanov is Associate Professor in the Graduate School of Public Policy at Nazarbayev University in Nur-Sultan, Republic of Kazakhstan. His research interests include nationalism and identity theories, and national identity politics, policies and practices, with a special focus on identity issues and their perceptions in the public narratives in the former Soviet area. He has worked in policy analysis and consulting as a Research Fellow at the IWEP, a think-tank advising the Kazakhstan government on policies, and as Senior Associate at IHS Cambridge Energy Research Associates (CERA). He has authored 'Kazakhstan's National Identity-Building Policy: Soviet Legacy, State Efforts, and Societal Reactions,' *Cornell International Law Journal* (2017), 'The Determinants of Civic and Ethnic Nationalisms in Kazakhstan: Evidence from the Grass-Roots Level,' *Nationalism and Ethnic Politics* (2017); and 'Kazakh Perspective on China, the Chinese, and Chinese Migration,' *Ethnic and Racial Studies* (2016); among others.

Ian W. Campbell is Associate Professor of History at the University of California-Davis. His first book, *Knowledge and the Ends of Empire: Kazak Intermediaries and Russian Rule on the Steppe*, was published by Cornell University Press in 2017. He is currently working on a transregional history of borderlands violence in the Russian Empire.

Alexander C. Diener is Associate Professor of Geography at the University of Kansas. His thematic interests include political, social and economic geographies, international relations and border studies. He has authored three books, edited three volumes and received funding from the NSF, SSRC, IREX, AAG, Fulbright and MacArthur Foundation.

Shairbek Dzhuraev is co-founder and director at Crossroads Central Asia, a Bishkek-based research institute. He previously served as deputy director at the OSCE Academy in Bishkek, and Dean of academic development at the American University of Central Asia. Shairbek's research interests include political regimes, international relations and foreign policymaking in Central Asia. He has a PhD in International Relations from the University of St Andrews.

Johan Engvall, PhD, is a researcher at the Swedish Defence Research Agency (FOI), and a non-resident senior fellow with the Central Asia-Caucasus Institute & Silk Road Studies Program. He is the author of *The State as Investment Market: Kyrgyzstan in Comparative Perspective*.

William Fierman, is an Emeritus Professor in Central Eurasian Studies in the Hamilton Lugar School of Global and International Studies at Indiana University. His research interests concern the politics of Central Asia, especially policies affecting language, Islam, and state identities. He is the author of numerous peer-reviewed articles, book chapters and books including *Language, Planning and Development: the Uzbek Experience* (Mouton Press, 1991) and *Soviet Central Asia: The Failed Transformation* (ed.) (Westview Press, 1991).

Michael Hancock-Parmer is Assistant Professor of World History at Ferrum College. He is researching comparative nationalist historiography and the exploitation of the early modern era for modern nationalist narratives, particularly in Eurasia. He is currently preparing his dissertation on nationalist historiography for publication.

Rico Isaacs is Associate Professor of Politics in the School of Social and Political Sciences at the University of Lincoln. His research interests lay at the intersection of authoritarianism, culture and political theory in post-Soviet states with a particular focus on the Central Asian Republics. He is the author of *Film and Identity in Kazakhstan* (2018) and *Party System Formation in Kazakhstan: Between Formal and Informal Politics* (Routledge 2011) and is also currently serving as editor of *Central Asian Survey*.

Aksana Ismailbekova is a member of the research project Kinship Universals and Variation at the Max Plank Institute for Social Anthropology. Her research interests include Kyrgyz patron-client relationships, rural development, informal economy, postsocialism and economic anthropology. She is an author of *Blood Ties and the Native Son: Poetics of Patronage in Kyrgyzstan* (2017).

Svetlana Jacquesson is a senior researcher at the Asian Studies Department of Palacky University, Olomouc. In her current research – conducted within European Regional Development Fund Project 'Sinophone Borderlands: Interaction at the Edges' under Grant CZ.02.1.01/0.0/0.0/1 6_019/0000791 – she focuses on UNESCO-driven heritage claims in Central Asia and their relationship to China's heritage boom. She has extensively published on 'history making,' or popular ways of re-emplotting history to support old and new identity claims as well as on the dynamics of collective identities in independent Kyrgyzstan.

Artemy M. Kalinovsky is Professor of Russian, Soviet, and Post-Soviet Studies at Temple University and PI of the ERC funded project *Building a Better Tomorrow: Development*

Knowledge in Practice in Central Asia and Beyond. He is the author of *A Long Goodbye: The Soviet Withdrawal from Afghanistan* (2011), and, *Laboratory of Socialist Development: Cold War Politics and Decolonization in Soviet Tajikistan* (2018), which won the Davis Center and Hewett prizes from the Association of Slavic, East European, and Eurasian Studies. Kalinovsky is also the editor or co-editor of a number of edited volumes dealing with Soviet history, the Cold War and globalisation, including *Reassessing Orientalism: Interlocking Orientologies in the Cold War era*, with Michael Kemper (Routledge, 2015) and *Alternative globalizations. Eastern Europe and the postcolonial world*, with Steffi Marung and James Mark (2020).

Marianne Kamp is Associate Professor of Central Eurasian Studies at Indiana University. In 1991, during her doctorate at the University of Chicago, she started doing oral history and social history research in Uzbekistan. Her publications focus on the history of collectivisation, and on women and gender in Central Asia.

Nargis Kassenova is Senior Fellow at the Davis Center for Russian and Eurasian Studies (Harvard University), leading its Program on Central Asia. She is also Associate Professor at the Department of International Relations and Regional Studies of KIMEP University (Almaty, Kazakhstan), where she created two centres – Central Asian Studies Center (CASC) and China and Central Asia Studies Center (CCASC). She holds a PhD in International Cooperation Studies from the Graduate School of International Development, Nagoya University (Japan). Her areas of research include Central Asian politics and security, Eurasian geopolitics, China's Belt and Road Initiative and governance in Central Asia, and history of state-making in Central Asia.

Karolina Kluczewska is a postdoctoral research fellow at the Käte Hamburger Kolleg/Centre for Global Cooperation Research, University of Duisburg-Essen in Germany. Her research investigates development aid and localisation of global governance frameworks in Central Asia, in particular in the field of migration and healthcare. She also has practical work experience in the development sector in Tajikistan.

Natalie Koch is Associate Professor in the Department of Geography and the Environment at Syracuse University's Maxwell School of Citizenship and Public Affairs. She focuses on nationalism, state power, identity politics and alternative sites of geopolitical analysis such as spectacle, sport, science and higher education, environmental policy and urban planning. Empirically, her research centres on the resource-rich states of the Arabian Peninsula and post-Soviet Central Asia. She has published in journals such as *Central Asian Survey*, *Central Asian Affairs*, *Eurasian Geography and Economics*, and *Political Geography*, and she is the author of *The Geopolitics of Spectacle: Space, Synecdoche, and the New Capitals of Asia* (2018), editor of the book *Critical Geographies of Sport: Space, Power, and Sport in Global Perspective* (Routledge, 2017), and co-editor of *Handbook on the Changing Geographies of the State: New Spaces of Geopolitics* (2020).

Marlene Laruelle is Research Professor of International Affairs and Associate Director of the Institute for European, Russian and Eurasian Studies (IERES) at the George Washington University. She is also Director of GW's Central Asia Program. She has recently authored *Russian Nationalism. Imaginaries, Doctrines, and Political Battlefields* (Routledge, 2018) and edited *The Nazarbayev Generation. Studies on Youth in Kazakhstan* (2019).

Mateusz Laszczkowski is Assistant Professor at the Institute of Ethnology and Cultural Anthropology, at the University of Warsaw. His work focuses on social and political change, the politics of infrastructure, space and place, state power, social movements and resistance. He has investigated these themes through empirical research in diverse settings: urban Kazakhstan and, more recently, Alpine Italy and rural Poland. His publications include articles in journals such as *Anthropological Theory*, *Ethnos*, the *Journal of the Royal Anthropological Institute*, *Social Analysis* and *Focaal*. He is the author of the monograph *'City of the Future': Built Space, Modernity and Urban Change in Astana* (2016), co-editor of *Affective States: Entanglements, Suspensions, Suspicions* (2018), and director of the ethnographic documentary film *The Site: Building Resistance*.

Edward Lemon is Research Assistant Professor at the Bush School of Government and Public Service, Texas A&M University, Washington, D.C. His research focuses on security, secularism, counter-extremism and authoritarianism in Central Asia. He is editor of the book *Critical Approaches to Security in Central Asia* (Routledge, 2018).

David G. Lewis is Associate Professor in International Relations at the University of Exeter. He held previous posts at the Department of Peace Studies, Bradford University, and with the International Crisis Group in Central Asia and in Sri Lanka. His current research is primarily focused on comparative authoritarianism and politics and governance in Russia and Eurasia. His most recent book is Russia's New Authoritarianism: Putin and the Politics of Order (Edinburgh University Press, 2020).

Erica Marat is Associate Professor at the College of International Security Affairs at the National Defence University. Dr. Marat's research focuses on violence, mobilisation and security institutions in Eurasia, India and Mexico. Her recent book, *The Politics of Police Reform: Society against the State in Post-Soviet Countries* (2018), explores conditions in which police reform projects succeed and why they fail in countries with recent authoritarian past.

Emil Nasritdinov is Associate Professor and Coordinator of Anthropology, Urbanism and International Development Master's program at the American University of Central Asia (AUCA). He is also the director of AUCA's Social Innovations Lab Kyrgyzstan (SILK). His main areas of research and teaching expertise are migration, religion and urbanism. He teaches undergraduate and graduate subjects and publishes in all three fields. In his research, he favours interdisciplinary approach, combination of quantitative and qualitative methods and extensive use of all forms of visual materials: from GIS maps to his own sketches. His interest in urban activism that motivated his contribution to this volume, started with the publication of a special issue in *Central Asian Affairs* titled 'Re-Claiming Bishkek' and co-edited with Philipp Schroeder.

Svetlana Peshkova is a mother and public educator. Trained as a socio-cultural anthropologist and a scholar of Islam and gender, she currently is Associate Professor of Anthropology, Core Faculty in Women's and Gender Studies Department, and a Coordinator of Native American and Indigenous Studies Minor at the University of New Hampshire (UNH, Durham, NH, USA). Svetlana is learning and writing about Muslim women leaders, gender, Islam in post-Socialist space, decolonialism and Indigenous heritage of New England (USA).

Niccolò Pianciola is Associate Professor of History at Nazarbayev University in Nur-Sultan, Kazakhstan. His research focuses on Russian and Soviet colonisation of nomadic Central Asia, the great famine in Kazakhstan, forced migrations in modern Eurasia, the environmental history of the Aral Sea and the opium trade between Russia, Central Asia and China.

Richard Pomfret has been Professor of Economics at the University of Adelaide since 1992. From 1979 to 1991, he was Professor of Economics at the Johns Hopkins University School of Advanced International Studies. He has acted as a consultant to the United Nations, World

Bank, OECD, IMF and Asian Development Bank. He has published over a hundred articles and twenty books, including *The Economies of Central Asia* (1995), *The Central Asian Economies since Independence* (2006), and *The Central Asian Economies in the Twenty-first Century: Paving a New Silk Road* (2019).

Madeleine Reeves is Senior Lecturer in Social Anthropology at the University of Manchester, where she works on the anthropology of politics, space and mobility. She is the author of *Border Work: Spatial Lives of the State in Rural Central Asia* (2014), as well as a number of edited collections, including *Affective States: Entanglements, Suspensions, Suspicions*, co-edited with Mateusz Laszczkowski (2017) and *The Everyday Lives of Sovereignty: Political Imagination Beyond the State*, co-edited with Rebecca Bryant (2021).

Liga Rudzite is a PhD student in Business Administration at the Tallinn University of Technology (Estonia). Her research engages in critical examination of the development cooperation management practices in Kyrgyzstan. In parallel to her PhD studies, Liga continues to be involved with civil society organisations and movements in Latvia and globally, working on strengthening synergies between academics and advocates for better social and global development policies and practice.

Caress Schenk is Associate Professor of Political Science at Nazarbayev University (Nur-Sultan, Kazakhstan) with teaching and research expertise in the politics of immigration and national identity in Eurasia. Her book is called *Why Control Immigration? Strategic Uses of Migration Management in Russia* (2018). Current research is funded by research grants from Nazarbayev University and the Tomsk State University competitiveness improvement programme. Previous research has been funded by the American Councils for International Education, Nazarbayev University and the Fulbright Scholar Program and has been published in *Demokratizatisya*, *Europe-Asia Studies* and *Nationalities Papers*, and in other edited volumes. Dr. Schenk is a senior researcher in the Laboratory for Social and Anthropological Research at Tomsk State University, a member of the Program on New Approaches to Research and Security in Eurasia (PONARS Eurasia) and a regional manager of the CoronaNet Research Project.

Dina Sharipova is Assistant Professor of Political Science in the Graduate School of Public Policy in Nur-Sultan, Republic of Kazakhstan. Her research interests include the issues of identity, identity politics and policies in Central Asia, security issues, as well as formal and informal institutions. She served on the Board of the European Society for Central Asian Studies and is a member of the Editorial Board of Central Asian Survey. She has authored the book *State-building in Kazakhstan: Continuity and Transformation of Informal Institutions* (2018) and published in such journals as *Nationalities Papers*, *Central Asian Survey*, *Nationalism and Ethnic Politics* and others.

Paolo Sorbello holds a PhD from the University of Glasgow. His research focuses on labour relations in Kazakhstan's oil sector. He is a research fellow at the Ca' Foscari University of Venice and works as a journalist in Kazakhstan.

Maurizio Totaro is a PhD student at the University of Ghent. His doctoral research looks at the relationship between socioeconomic transformations connected to oil extraction and changes in subjectivities and imaginaries in the Mangystau region, Kazakhstan.

Alexandra Tsay is an independent research fellow interested in conjunction between art and politics, art and memory and a curator based in Almaty, Kazakhstan. She is a founder of Open Mind project that aims to raise critical discussions around contemporary art in Kazakhstan through curated exhibitions and interdisciplinary academic research. She is interested in independent artistic agency and art practices that challenge the power and create new narratives and discourses in not so open societies of Central Asia. Alexandra is an alumna of the University of Warwick.

Galym Zhussipbek is an independent researcher based in Almaty. He is also a faculty member at the Department of Social Sciences, Suleyman Demirel atindagi Universitet in Kaskelen, Almaty, where he has courses related to human rights and nationalism. Zhussipbek has a PhD in International Relations (Ankara University, Faculty of Political Science). In recent years he has been engaged in projects related to the discrimination of human rights based on ethnic and religious grounds (a consultant to the Equal Rights Trust), liberalism and Islam, building inclusive institutions (Ministry of Education of Kazakhstan) and development of human rights in post-Soviet geography.

Charles E. Ziegler is Professor of Political Science and University Scholar at the University of Louisville. Ziegler is co-editor (with Judith Thornton) of *The Russian Far East: A Region at Risk* (2002); author of *The History of Russia* (2009), *Foreign Policy and East Asia* (1993), and *Environmental Policy in the USSR* (1987); and editor of *Civil Society and Politics in Central Asia* (2015). Ziegler was guest editor for a special issue of *International Relations* on the Responsibility to Protect (2016), and for a special issue of *Central Asian Survey* on authoritarianism in Central Asia (2016). Ziegler has published over 120 book chapters and peer-reviewed articles and presented over 100 papers at national and international conferences. He is Executive Director of the Louisville Committee on Foreign Relations and Faculty Director for the Grawemeyer World Order Award. He is currently working on a book on Russia as a Pacific power.

ACKNOWLEDGEMENTS

Much of this project was put together and written during the Covid-19 pandemic of 2020. We are grateful for the hard work, talent and effort of our contributors for submitting their excellent chapters despite the challenges presented by the pandemic. Our sincere gratitude also goes to Alexandra de Brauw and Dorothea Schaefter from Routledge for their assistance in putting this volume together. Finally, we are indebted to our families for their love and support.

INTRODUCING CENTRAL ASIAN STUDIES

Rico Isaacs and Erica Marat

Research of Central Asia has long been siloed between scholarly communities based in the West, Russia or Central Asia. After the long dominance of Russian academia in framing narratives on the region for an international audience, Western scholarship took over in the 1990s. More recently, that scholarship has expanded as more research by Central Asian scholars are published in Western outlets and academics reference their research and initiate joint projects. There is still deep inequity in research resources, especially in supporting and engaging with publications in native languages. But the ever more expanding dialogue between Western and Central Asian counterparts allows for a richer discussion that challenges rehashed orientalist notions of Central Asia as a backwater of the Russian empire or as lacking permanent significance in Western political interests. This change will only continue to enhance Central Asian area studies, as for the scholars who are from and based in the region, the local developments have never been obscure or unimportant.

This volume reflects the proliferation of scholarship in Central Asian studies which has emerged in the last three decades, from all the different disciplinary standpoints and diverse methodological approaches it has to offer. It is our attempt to draw on the expertise of a wide range of colleagues from within the field to offer a cross-disciplinary overview of key issues within contemporary Central Asian studies.[1] The volume only represents a beginning, and a tentative one at that, towards breaking the imbalance and structural inequalities present in Central Asian studies.

Situating the field of Central Asian area studies

The Central Asian space has been essential to the spread of Islam beyond the Arabian Peninsula, while fourteenth- and fifteenth-century Samarkand in modern-day Uzbekistan was a centre of Islamic scholarship, science and learning. The region was an important staging post on the Ancient Silk Road through which world trade passed. And was a central component of many empires, including the Mongol, Timurid, Russian and British empires, and the USSR. Central Asia remains at the heart of global politics, geographically sitting between Europe and Asia.

Kazakhstan, Kyrgyzstan, Tajikistan, Turkmenistan and Uzbekistan are now countries that define the boundaries of an eponymous people, but include dozens of other ethnic minorities. The modern boundaries of the Central Asian republics were a creation of the Soviet regime, envisioned by the Bolsheviks and elaborated with the help of ethnographic research regarding the indigenous population's physical features, language and lifestyle. The Soviet's 'divide-and-rule' approach to Turkestan, the territory between Eastern Siberia, Afghanistan and the Caspian Sea, was driven by the need to secure control over the region. The Bolsheviks drew on European understandings of the nation and state, imposing Marxist-Leninist ideology through propaganda and coercion (Kendirbai 2020; Kassymbekova 2016; Hirsch 2005). Today's national territories are largely the result of a 20-year effort in the 1920s and 1930s to define the Soviet territory and reflect Soviet collaboration with regional elites. Ultimately, the goal was to move towards the great communist future with clearly defined nations strongly linked to a specific territory.

The process of nation creation in Central Asia followed the pattern used by the Soviets in Belarus and Ukraine. The perceived lack of strong national identity among Central Asian peoples was compensated for by creating the standard attributes of a Soviet nation: defined territory, national flag, anthem, emblem, language, flagship economic sector (cotton, grain, industry), an academy of sciences and a national university. The territorialisation and ethnicisation of the population facilitated the assimilation of smaller ethnic groups under the umbrella of larger groups (Igmen 2012). Minorities that spoke a different language and differed in lifestyle but were linked to a Soviet Socialist Republic (SSR) had special schools set up by Moscow that offered education in their own language. However, Soviet propaganda penetrated every part of the region, including infrastructure, architecture, education and mass media, and these modernisation efforts were channelled through the collectivisation and industrialisation of local and republican economies.

The impact of Soviet nation-building from the 1920s to the 1950s is still evident in Central Asia, in terms of border delimitations, the structure of local languages and even in material cultural artefacts. Writing about Soviet state-building, Rogers Brubaker argues that 'no other state has gone so far in sponsoring, codifying, institutionalising, even (in some cases) inventing nationhood and nationality on the substate level, while at the same time doing nothing to institutionalize them on the level of the state as a whole' (1994: 29). The Soviet Union's institutionalised definition of nationhood continues to structure national identities in the successor states as well.

Today Central Asian studies uncovers a wider range of political, social and economic issues, offering compelling case studies for comparative research with other parts of the world. Contributions to this volume frequently reference theoretical categories developed in other areas or disciplinary studies. Nation-building is the most common theme which scholars have drawn their attention to. Scholars have sought to explore national-building policies and discourses perpetuated by political regimes in the region and associated questions related to ethnicity and identity (Akbarzadeh 1999; Bohr 1998; Roy 2000; Kurzman 1999; Mellon 2010; Dave 2007; Cummings 2010; Adams 2010; Kudaibergenova 2020; Kudaibergenova 2013; Isaacs and Polese, 2015; Burkhanov and Sharipova 2016; Rees and Williams 2017; Megoran 2017; Dadabaev 2015). Some of this literature, with its focus on ethnic complexity, was an effort to explain instances of ethnic conflict in the region from different disciplinary perspectives (Akiner 1997; Akbarzadeh 1996; Rumer, 1993; Fumagali 2007; McGlinchey 2011; Megoran 1999).

Another set of themes to emerge relates to the failure of democratisation and the establishment of authoritarianism. Research has reflected the all-encompassing power and personalities of the region's presidents and in some instance's personality cults (e.g. Turkmenistan) (Carlisle 1995; Gleason 1997; Kubicek 1998; Cummings and Ochs 2002; Cummings 2004; Huskey 2002; Lewis 2008; Schatz 2009; Peyrouse 2012). Given the dominant position of the region's presidents, such a focus on their power and agency was understandable. However, to explain the durability and underpinnings of authoritarianism some scholars turned to the role of pre-

Soviet informal, traditional politics, norms and organisations as explanatory factors (Schatz 2004; Collins 2006; Gullette 2007), while others rooted their explanation in the formal institutional legacy of the Soviet Union (Jones Luong 2002). Thus, Central Asian politics and society was predominantly understood through the perceived tension between informal and formal political relations (Isaacs 2011) in how it related to neopatrimonialism, clientelistic networks, political mobilisation (Tunçer-Kılavuz 2009; Radnitz 2010; McGlinchey 2011; Isaacs 2014) and how informality underpinned capitalist development in the region (Robinson 2013).

The informal–formal paradigm for studying Central Asia mostly operated at the macro-level, focusing on the state, its formal and informal institutions, the region's presidents and discourses used for legitimation. But anthropological studies have taken a different approach, concentrating instead on the everyday, providing a micro-level perspective. Based on extensive ethnographic fieldwork, anthropological studies have focused on a range of everyday practices, norms and relations, including, but not limited to, borders, identities and modernity (Finke 2006; Reeves 2014; Megoran 2017; Mostowlansky 2016); local customs, law and informal institutions and practices (Sadyrbek 2017; Werner 1999; Trevisani and Massicard 2003; Rasanyagam 2011; Beyer 2016; Ismailbekova 2017; Isabaeva 2021); gender (Tursunova 2014; Tlostanova 2010; Shreeves 2002; Kandiyoti 2003; Werner 2004; Fathi 2006); religion (Bukharbayeva 2019; Mastibekov 2014; Sultanova 2011; Khalid 2007; Sela and Levi 2009; McBrien 2017; Jones 2017); migration (Urinboyev 2020; Turaeva 2015; Sagynbekova 2016; Marat 2009; Blum 2017) and trade and bazaar politics (Spector 2017; Nasritdinov 2006). This plethora of anthropological studies has only deepened our understanding of the region. However, one issue with them is that it has disconnected them from other disciplines, missing the potential for greater synthesis, cross-referencing and theoretical innovations.

There have also been advances in the fields of political geography, history and International Relations. Scholars in geography have explored transformations in the urban environment and how it relates to authoritarian spectacle and regime legitimation (Satpayev 2019; Koch 2018; Sharipova 2018; Dagiev 2013), the politics of water (Menga 2017; Ziganshina 2014), urban resistance (Junussova 2020; Nasritdinov 2018; Marat 2018) and spatial politics (Schröder 2017). In the history field, the opening of archives, new documentary knowledge and loosening of previous taboo areas of Central Asian history has produced a wealth of work which has sought to re-assess our understanding of how Central Asian nations were created and the role of local elites in some of the harshest and most tragic events of the Soviet period such as collectivisation, sedentarism and famine (Khalid 2015; Dadabaev and Komastu 2016; Bustanov 2017; Cameron 2018; Kindler 2018).

International Relations too has developed its study of the region. It has moved beyond simplistic readings of the region as part of some New Great Game, to observe the agency of the Central Asian states themselves in the international context (Madiyev 2020; Toktomushev 2016; Cooley 2012), their centrality to corruption and high finance in the global political economy (Cooley and Heathershaw 2017) and how the Central Asian space can be better understood via the lens of postcolonialism, whereby outsiders are encouraged to avoid essentialising the region as one which is obscure, fractious and oriental (Dave 2007; Adams 2008; Heathershaw and Megoran 2011; Cummings 2012).

Thanks to the sum of these advances in knowledge, we know the intricacies of the region like never before. More archives have opened, more communities have been engaged with, and perhaps we understand the region on its own terms better than ever, freed as we are from the shackles of the normative and orientalist lenses of the past.

This volume includes studies with both deductive and inductive approaches. Work by Reeves, Laszczkowski and Koch, and Kalinovsky build theoretical explanation from extensive engagement in the field. Nasritdinov inducts his intimate observation of urban politics in Bishkek to broad theoretical categories of governance in public spaces. The chapters by Lemon, Ismailbekova and Peshkova, by contrast, deduct theoretical categories derived from other context in their research of religions, patronage and gender in Central Asia. Overall, all chapters connect rich findings from the field with theoretical elaborations derived from other fields. At the same time, Engvall's research of corruption and Dzhuraev's analysis of foreign policy formation in Central Asia also offer revised or new categories for comparative research in other area studies as well. Across chapters, qualitative research methods dominate, but include a rich variety of approaches ranging from ethnographic studies, in-depth interviews, archival research and analysis of political discourse.

As a form of area studies, Central Asia challenges notions of metrocentricity by offering new insights into the influence of material culture, as shown by Laszczkowski and Koch, patterns of economic liberalisation as demonstrated by Pomfret, and the significance of in/formal borders as explored in chapters by Reeves and Diener and Artman. The shifting line between the formal and informal can be seen in the studies of migration flows. Schenk explains how Russian government offers greater opportunities for employment to Central Asian migrants by opening borders, but the private sector prefers to hire foreigners informally to avoid taxation, thus forcing them into an illegal status.

Central Asian studies show how expressions of state power continues to shift: states try to control societies through physical infrastructure as demonstrated by Laszczkowski and Koch's chapter and informal politics of corruption and patronage, as argued by both Engvall and Ismailbekova. Countries inherited different infrastructures from the Soviet regime. Most evident disparities in economic and military developments are examples of how Soviet centralised planning strategies defined wealth and defence capabilities in the independence. In both areas, Kazakhstan and Uzbekistan received more industrialised economies and military capabilities. As Pomfret demonstrates in his chapter, Kazakhstan entered independence with the most promising economic conditions among the Central Asian countries and embarked on a rapid economic growth, while Kyrgyzstan and Tajikistan were unable to benefit from hydropower sector due to the conflict with downstream countries. Likewise, Marat writes that Kazakhstan and Uzbekistan inherited large military installations, with a greater degree of independent military production and available equipment; post-Soviet military equipment in Tajikistan was placed under the Russian control.

Geopolitically, both Laruelle and Ziegler find there is still division between Russian and Western influence, their policies are reactionary to their greater geopolitical interests and domestic developments. But the influence of external powers is shifting as well. Laruelle explains that Russia has moved away from pursuing natural resources in Central Asia and instead expanded the presence of Russian language media and education. The United States continues to disengage from Central Asia, focusing only on strategic security collaboration with Uzbekistan. External powers are much more powerful international actors, like China, as Kassenova shows. Central Asian countries are often forced to build relations unfavourable to their domestic interests. But Dzhuraev concludes international relations in Central Asia should be studied with the consideration of public opinion that often prioritises closer relations with Russia.

Contributors also notice dichotomies in both states' and societies' treatment of complex social issues. Lemon examines securitisation of Islam and division into 'bad' and 'good' Islam. The Soviet legacy of seeing religious practices as a political threat is now complemented by political leaders' justification of control over religion as a way of averting terrorism and violent extremism. Peshkova reviews how in scholarly work, political governance and development efforts by international donor organisations, gender is politicised as dichotomous – male and female categories – in Central Asia. This rigid approach to gender misses on the varieties of femininities, masculinities and other identities. Likewise, the securitisation of Islam misses out on many nuances of religious expressions in Central Asian societies.

In total, the authors in this volume provide an account of the complex and diverse ways in which social and political relations transpire and intersect in Central Asia and how such myriad of social forms are embedded in historical norms and lived experiences. While we would not suggest that this volume is completist in anyway, it does pull together many of the different strands within Central Asian studies to offer a general introduction to the field useful to students, teachers, academics and newly interested observers. Below we provide a brief excursion as to the book's organisation and content.

Organisation of the book

The *Routledge Handbook of Contemporary Central Asia* is divided into seven sections. Each section covers a broad theme within Central Asian studies: history, politics, geography, international relations, political economy, society and culture and religion.

Part I, 'History,' of the handbook reviews the history of Central Asia. It is difficult to grasp the processes, dynamics and challenges of modern-day Central Asia without an understanding of Russian colonialism and then Soviet rule, the legacy of which to this day is ever present in questions of borders, identities, culture and politics. The aim of the first two chapters by Hancock-Parmer and Campbell is to summarise pre-Tsarist and then Russian colonisation of the region. Chapter 3 by Pianciola and Kamp then moves to the Soviet period, offering an account of the processes of collectivisation and sedentarisation undertaken by the Soviet regime in the 1930s, two policies which not only tragically led to widespread famine in Kazakhstan but fundamentally reshaped society and culture in the region. In Chapter 4 Kalinovsky continues the discussion on the Soviet period by exploring the politics and practices of economic development in Central Asia between World War II and the collapse of the Soviet Union. In Kalinovsky's account, local populations negotiated and practised Soviet policies of development.

Part II, 'Politics,' analyses the most salient political issues the region has faced in the last three decades. Rather than seeing the regimes in the region as representing some homogenous type, the section begins with the chapter by Lewis offering an overview of their diversity as a set of authoritarian regimes. The chapter by Ismailbekova explores the phenomenon of clan politics through a concentrated examination of Kyrgyz politics, all the while with a keen critical eye on the concept given its ubiquitous use in the study of the region's politics. The next chapter by Burkhanov and Sharipova explores the policies and discursive strategies of nation-building among the five Central Asian republics in the effort to inculcate feelings of national solidarity and to build public support. It examines the multiple and contested narratives of national identity which have emerged in the region. Moving from the state to society, the last chapter in the 'Politics' section by Reeves centres on the densely populated Ferghana Valley region, where the borders between Kyrgyzstan, Uzbekistan and Tajikistan intermingle. Rather than focus on interstate disputes over borders and territory the chapter will instead explain how traders, farmers and border guards negotiate their livelihoods across these borders.

Part III, 'Geography,' shifts tension away from the political to explore the relationship between geography, politics and history in the region. Diener and Artman in their chapter explore the dynamic and ever-evolving nature of the 'geographical imaginary' of Central Asia and how the delineation of borders at different points in its histories has created different political and cultural geographies manifested in different identities. The following chapter by Bichsel then explores the historical trajectories of water politics in Central Asia. Water has been a fundamental source of both agricultural prosperity and contestation in the region. Bichsel traces the dynamics of water politics through an environmental political history of irrigation. Laszczkowski and Koch's chapter moves to explore the urban environment in Central Asia via an analysis of the spectacle of grand urban development project of Nur-Sultan in Kazakhstan (previously Astana). Rather than simply focusing on the regime's practices of the politics of urban design, the chapter instead focuses on the multiplicity of actors involved in the process of designing 'spectacular cities,' importantly including ordinary people and how their individual practices co-exist with, and develop in relation to, elite visions of cities. Nasrtidinov's chapter focusing on Bishkek presents an entirely different picture of power relations within a city. There is little glamour in urban activists' resistance against mayor's decision to cut trees in favour of wider roads. The contestation over the urban space is filled with despair and at times turns into physical resistance by residents against heavy machinery dispatched by the mayor's office to demolish the city's greenery.

Part IV, 'International Relations,' moves towards a macro perspective of the region, providing an overall analysis of the international relations of the five Central Asian republics. The chapters by Laruelle, Kassenova and Ziegler analyse broad trends and dynamics within Central Asian international relations, examining the region's governments' interaction and engagement with Russia, China and the United States and these powers' interest in the region, pertaining to hydrocarbons, transnational organised crime, democracy promotion and political Islam. Dzhuraev's chapter reviews foreign policy formation within Central Asia as a distinct process of managing international forces and domestic demands. Next, Marat assesses the institutions of the military and examines their influence on state and society in the contemporary period. Concluding the section on 'International Relations' is a chapter by Schenk who analyses the relationship between migration and globalisation in the region, examining how labour migration patterns, efforts of economic integration, transnational social relations and security threats are shaping migration patterns and state responses throughout the region.

Part V, 'Political Economy,' gives the reader an overview of the region's political economy. Pomfret provides an analysis of the different paths that each Central Asian Republic has taken with market reform, the influence of the resource boom on their economies, their need for economic diversification and the influence of domestic and international politics on economic reform in the three decades since independence. Totaro and Sorbello's chapter introduces the reader to the complexity of oil politics in Central Asia via a focus on the strategies of capital accumulation and labour governance in the region's oil industry. Engvall's chapter then switches the focus to the role of corruption in the region's political economy. Engvall argues that corruption in the region should not be understood as an indication of state weakness but rather as a specific form of political economy whereby public office provides agents with authority, resources and revenue collection. The final chapter in the 'Political Economy' section by Rudzite and Kluczewska provides an analysis of international development cooperation in Central Asia, examining the different external and internal actors involved, their varying programmes and imaginaries of development. The chapter focuses on Kyrgyzstan and Tajikistan, the states which are most foreign-aid dependent, and explores how local actors negotiate and relate to the norms and activities of development actors in the region.

Part VI, 'Society and Culture,' turns the reader's attention key issues in society and culture in Central Asia related to traditions, gender, art and language. In her chapter, Jacquesson discusses the concept of traditions and how they have been used in official regime discourse to nurture post-Soviet identity building. Focusing on everyday life-cycle celebrations, the chapter introduces the reader of how ordinary people practice and negotiate state-led regulations on traditions and what this reveals regarding the dilemmas of national identity formation across the Central Asian space. Peshkova's chapter offers the reader an overview of how gender has been ordered in Central Asia and been transformed through its various historical formulations. By using gender as an analytical lens, readers can survey the diverse ways in which people practice gender in the region and seek to contest its normative ordering. Tsay's chapter offers insights into contemporary art in Central Asia through case studies of artists in Kazakhstan, Uzbekistan and Kyrgyzstan. The chapter demonstrates how artists are using their medium to challenge regime discourses and narrative offering illustrating how art has emerged as a site for free expression and critical discourses in increasingly closed and non-democratic regimes. The section then concludes with Fierman's chapter which summarises language policy in the region. It will give the reader an insight into the challenges of promoting national languages in some states in the region, given the predominance of Russian, and how language policy is linked to nation-building efforts and regime legitimation.

Concluding the *Routledge Handbook of Contemporary Central Asia* is a section which deals with the question of religion. The first two chapters address the history, role and place of Islam in the region. The chapter by Balci explores domestic and international perceptions of the so-called 'Islamic revival' in Central Asia. Following this, Lemon analyses how regimes in the region have sought to securitise Islam to justify repression and co-option of religious groups. The following two chapters will then seek to go beyond the predominant paradigms of Islam in the region. The chapter by Zhussipbek examines the possibility of reconciliation between Islam and liberalism, by assessing the convergence between the Islamic school of Maturidi with its rationalist and anti-hegemonic orientation and the political liberalism of John Rawls with its concepts of fairness and overlapping consensus. Concluding the handbook is the chapter by Issacs which examines the pre-Islamic religion of Tengrism which has re-emerged in the last few decades as a religious identity which its proponents argue is the native religion of the region and which is central to the regional identity of the Turkic populations of Kazakhstan, Kyrgyzstan, Uzbekistan and Turkmenistan.

Note

1 A study of the Oxus Society in late 2020 counted over 170 volumes produced by scholars from the region publishing in both English and native languages.

Bibliography

Adams, L. (2008) 'Can We Apply Postcolonial Theory to Central Eurasia?,' *Central Eurasian Studies Review*, 7(1): 2–7.
Adams, L. (2010) *The Spectacular State: Culture and National Identity in Uzbekistan*. Durham: Duke University Press.
Akbarzadeh, S. (1996) 'Why Did Nationalism Fail in Tajikistan?,' *Europe-Asia Studies*, 48(7): 1105–30.
Akbarzadeh, S. (1999) 'National Identity and Political Legitimacy,' *Nationalities Papers*, 27(2): 271–90.
Akiner, S. (1997) 'Melting Pot, Salad Bowl – Cauldron? Manipulation and Mobilisation of Ethnic and Religious Identities in Central Asia,' *Ethnic and Racial Studies*, 20(2): 362–98.
Beyer, J. (2016) *The Force of Custom. Law and the Ordering of Everyday Life in Kyrgyzstan*. Pittsburgh: University of Pittsburgh Press.
Blum, D. (2017) *The Social Process of Globalization: Return Migration and Cultural Change in Kazakhstan*. Cambridge: Cambridge University Press.
Bohr, A. (1998) 'The Central Asian States as Nationalising Regimes,' in G. Smith (ed.) *Nation-Building in Post-Soviet Borderlands: The Politics of National Identities*. Cambridge: Cambridge University Press, pp. 139–166.

Bukharbayeva, B. (2019) *The Vanishing Generation: Faith and Uprising in Modern Uzbekistan*. Bloomington, IN: Indiana University Press.
Burkhanov, A. and Sharipova, D. (2016) 'Kazakhstan's Civic Identity: Ambiguous Policies and Points of Resistance,' in Mariya Omelicheva (ed.) *Nationalism and Identity Construction in Central Asia: Dimensions, Dynamics, and Directions*. Lanham: Lexington Books, pp. 203–226.
Bustanov, Alfrid K. (2017) *Soviet Orientalism and the Creation of Central Asian Nations*. Abingdon: Routledge.
Cameron, S. (2018) *The Hungry Steppe: Famine, Violence, and the Making of Soviet Kazakhstan*. Ithaca, New York: Cornell University Press.
Carlisle, D. (1995) 'Islam Karimov and Uzbekistan: Back to the Future?,' in T. J. Colton and R. C. Tucker (eds.) *Patterns in Post-Soviet Leadership*. Boulder: Westview Press.
Collins, K. (2006) *Clan Politics and Regime Transition in Central Asia*. Cambridge: Cambridge University Press.
Cooley, A. (2012) *Great Games, Local Rules: The New Great Power Contest in Central Asia*. New York: Oxford University Press.
Cooley, A. and Heathershaw, J. (2017) *Dictators without Borders*. Yale University Press.
Cummings, S. N. (ed.) (2004) *Oil, Transition and Security in Central Asia*. Abingdon, Oxon: Routledge.
Cummings, S. (ed.). (2010) *Symbolism and Power in Central Asia: Politics of the Spectacular*. London: Routledge.
Cummings, S. N. (2012) *Understanding Central Asia: Politics and Contested Transformations*. New York: Routledge.
Cummings, S. N. and Ochs, M. (2002) 'Saparmurat Niyazov's Inglorious Isolation,' in S. N. Cummings (ed.) *Power and Change in Central Asia*. London: Routledge, pp. 115–29.
Dadabaev, T. (2015) *Identity and Memory in Post-Soviet Central Asia: Uzbekistan's Soviet Past*. Abingdon, Oxon: Routledge.
Dadabaev, T. and Komastu, H. (eds.). (2016) *Kazakhstan, Kyrgyzstan, and Uzbekistan: Life and Politics during the Soviet Era*. London: Palgrave Macmillan.
Dagiev, D. (2013) *Regime Transition in Central Asia: Stateness, Nationalism and Political Change in Tajikistan and Uzbekistan*. Abingdon, Oxon: Routledge.
Davé, B. (2007) *Kazakhstan. Ethnicity, Language and Power*. London: Routledge.
Fathi, H. (2006) 'Gender, Islam, and Social Change in Uzbekistan', *Nationalities Papers*, 25(3): 303–317.
Finke, P. (2006) *Variations on Uzbek Identity: Concepts, Constraints and Local Configurations*. Oxford: Berghahn Books.
Fumagali, M. (2007) 'Framing Ethnic Minority Mobilisation in Central Asia: The Cases of Uzbeks in Kyrgyzstan and Tajikistan', *Europe-Asia Studies*, 59(4): 567–590.
Gleason, G. (1997) *The Central Asian States: Discovering Independence*. Boulder: Westview Press.
Gulette, D. (2007) 'Theories on Central Asian Factionalism: The Debate in Political Science and Its Wider Implications,' *Central Asian Survey*, 26(3): 373–87.
Heathershaw, J. and Megoran, N. (2011) 'Contesting Danger: A New Agenda for Policy and Scholarship on Central Asia,' *International Affairs*, 87(3): 589–612.
Hirsch, F. (2005) *Empire of Nations: Ethnographic Knowledge and the Making of the Soviet Union*. Ithaca: Cornell University Press.
Huskey, E. (2002) 'An Economy of Authoritarianism? Askar Akaev and Presidential Leadership in Kyrgyzstan,' in S. N. Cummings (ed.) *Power and Change in Central Asia*. London: Routledge, pp. 74–96.
Igmen, A. (2012) *Speaking Soviet with an Accent: Culture and Power in Kyrgyzstan*. Pittsburgh: University of Pittsburgh Press.
Isaacs, R. (2011) *Party System Formation in Kazakhstan: Between Formal and Informal Politics*. Abingdon, Oxon: Routledge.
Isaacs, R. (2014) 'Neopatrimonialism and Beyond: Reassessing the Formal and Informal in the Study of Central Asian Politics,' *Contemporary Politics*, 20(2): 229–45.
Isaacs, R. and Polese, A. (2015) 'Between "Imagined" and "Real" Nationbuilding: Identities and Nationhood in Post-Soviet Central Asia,' *Nationalities Papers*, 43(3): 371–82.
Isabaeva, E. (2021) 'Transcending Illegality in Kyrgyzstan: The Case of a Squatter Settlement in Bishkek', *Europe-Asia Studies*, 73(1): 60–80.
Ismailbekova, A. (2017) *Blood Ties and the Native Son: Poetics of Patronage in Kyrgyzstan*. Bloomington, IN: Indiana University Press.
Jones Luong, P. (2002) *Institutional Change and Political Continuity in Post-Soviet Central Asia*. Cambridge: Cambridge University Press.
Jones-Luong, P. (2017) *Islam, Society, and Politics in Central Asia*. Pittsburgh: University of Pittsburgh Press.

Junussova, M. (2020) *Cities and Local Governments in Central Asia: Administrative, Fiscal, and Political Urban Battles*. Abingdon, Oxon: Routledge.

Kandiyoti, D. (2003) 'The Cry for Land: Agrarian Reform, Gender and Land Rights in Uzbekistan', *Journal of Agrarian Change*, 3(1–2): 225–56.

Kassymbekova, B. (2016) *Despite Cultures: Early Soviet Rule in Tajikistan*. Pittsburgh: University of Pittsburgh Press.

Kendirbai, Gulnar T. (2020) *Russian Practices of Governance in Eurasia: Frontier Power Dynamics, Sixteenth Century to Nineteenth Century*. Abingdon, Oxon: Routledge.

Khalid, A. (2015) *Making Uzbekistan: Nation, Empire, and Revolution in the Early USSR*. Ithaca, New York: Cornell University Press.

Khalid, A. (2007) *The Politics of Muslim Cultural Reform: Religion and Politics in Central Asia*. Berkley, CA: University California Press.

Kindler, R. (2018) *Stalin's Nomads: Power and Famine in Kazakhstan*. Pittsburgh: University of Pittsburgh Press.

Koch, N. (2018) *The Geopolitics of Spectacle: Space, Synecdoche, and the New Capitals of Asia*. Ithaca, New York: Cornell University Press.

Kubicek, P. (1998) 'Authoritarianism in Central Asia: Curse or Cure?,' *Third World Quarterly*, 19(1): 29–43.

Kudaibergenova, D. (2013) '"Imagining Community" in Soviet Kazakhstan. An Historical Analysis of Narrative on Nationalism in Kazakh-Soviet Literature,' *Nationalities Papers*, 41(5): 839–54.

Kudaibergenova, D. (2020) *Towards Nationalizing Regimes: Conceptualizing Power and Identity in the Post-Soviet Realm*. Pittsburgh: University of Pittsburgh Press.

Kurzman, C. (1999) 'Uzbekistan: The Invention of Nationalism in an Invented Nation,' *Critique*, 15: 77–98.

Lewis, D. (2008) *The Temptations of Tyranny in Central Asia*. New York: Columbia University Press.

Madiyev, O. (2020) *Uzbekistan's International Relations*. Abingdon, Oxon: Routledge.

Marat, E. (2018) *The Politics of Police Reform: Society against the State in Post-Soviet Countries*. Oxford and New York: Oxford University Press.

Marat, E. (2009) 'Labor Migration in Central Asia: Implications of the Global Economic Crisis,' *Anthropological Quarterly*, 79(3): 431–61.

Mastibekov, O. (2014) *Leadership and Authority in Central Asia: The Ismaili Community in Tajikistan*. Abingdon, Oxon: Routledge.

McBrien, J. (2017) *From Belonging to Belief. Modern Secularisms and the Construction of Religion in Kyrgyzstan*. Pittsburgh: University of Pittsburgh Press.

McGlinchey, E. (2011) *Chaos, Violence, Dynasty: Politics and Islam in Central Asia*. Pittsburgh: University of Pittsburgh Press.

Megoran, N. (1999) 'Theorizing Gender, Ethnicity and the Nation-State in Central Asia', *Central Asian Survey*, 18(1): 99–110.

Megoran, N. (2017) *Nationalism in Central Asia: A Biography of the Uzbekistan-Kyrgyzstan Boundary*. Pittsburgh: University of Pittsburgh Press.

Mellon, J. (2010) 'Myth, Legitimacy and Nationalism in Central Asia', *Ethnopolitics*, 9(2): 137–50.

Menga, F. (2017) *Power and Water in Central Asia*. Abingdon, Oxon: Routledge.

Mostowlansky, T. (2016) *Azan on the Moon Entangling Modernity along Tajikistan's Pamir Highway*. Pittsburgh: University of Pittsburgh Press.

Nasritdinov, E. (2006) *Regional Change in Kyrgystan: Bazaars, Open-Air Markets and Social Networks*. Melbourne: University of Melbourne, Faculty of Architecture, Building and Planning.

Nasritdinov, E. (2018) 'Translocality and the Folding of Public Space in Bishkek', in Manja Stephan-Emmrich and Philipp Schröder (eds.) *Mobilities, Boundaries, and Travelling Ideas: Rethinking Translocality Beyond Central Asia and the Caucasus*. London: Open Book Publishers, pp. 319–347.

Peyrouse, S. (2012) *Turkmenistan: Strategies of Power, Dilemmas of Development*. Abingdon, Oxon: Routledge.

Radnitz, S. (2010) *Weapons of the Wealthy: Predatory Regimes and Elite-LED Protests in Central Asia*. Ithaca: Cornell University Press.

Rasanyagam, J. (2011) 'Informal Economy, Informal State: The Case of Uzbekistan,' *International Journal of Sociology and Social Policy*, 31(11–12): 681–96.

Rees, K. and Williams, N. (2017) 'Explaining Kazakhstani Identity: Supraethnic Identity, Ethnicity, Language, and Citizenship', *Nationalities Papers*, 45(5): 815–839.

Reeves, M. (2014) *Border Work: Spatial Lives of the State in Rural Central Asia*. Ithaca: Cornell University Press.

Robinson, N. (2013) 'Economic and Political Hybridity: Patrimonial Capitalism in the Post-Soviet Sphere', *Journal of Eurasian Studies*, 4(1): 136–45.

Rogers, B. (1994) 'Nationhood and the National Question in the Soviet Union and Post-Soviet Eurasia: An Institutionalist Account,' *Theory and Society*, 23(1): 47–78.

Roy, O. (2000) *The New Central Asia: The Creation of Nations*. New York: New York University Press.

Rumer, B. (1993) 'A Gathering Storm,' *Orbis*, 37: 89–105.

Sadyrbek, M. (2017) *Legal Pluralism in Central Asia: Local Jurisdiction and Customary Practices*. Abingdon, Oxon: Routledge.

Sagynbekova, L. (2016) *The Impact of International Migration*. New York: Springer International Publishing.

Satpayev, D. (2019) *Deformatisya Vertikali: Ot 'Anoninnyh Imperii' do Antilobbi*. Almaty: Print House Gerona.

Schatz, E. (2004) *Modern Clan Politics: The Power of 'Blood' in Kazakhstan and Beyond*. Seattle: University of Washington Press.

Schatz, E. (2009) 'The Soft Authoritarian Tool Kit: Agenda-Setting Power in Kazakhstan and Kyrgyzstan', *Europe-Asia Studies*, 41(2): 203–22.

Schröder, P. (2017) *Urban Spaces and Lifestyles in Central Asia and Beyond*. London: Routledge.

Sela, R. and Levi, S. (2009) *Islamic Central Asia: An Anthology of Historical Sources*. Bloomington: Indiana University Press.

Sharipova, D. (2018) *State-Building in Kazakhstan: Continuity and Transformation of Informal Institutions*. Lanham, Maryland: Rowman & Littlefield.

Shreeves, R. (2002) 'Gender and Development in Rural Kazakhstan', in R. Mandel and C. Humphrey (eds.) *Markets and Moralities: Ethnographies of Postsocialism*. Oxford: Berg, pp. 212–235.

Spector, R. (2017) *Order at the Bazaar: Power and Trade in Central Asia*. Ithaca, New York: Cornell University Press.

Sultanova, R. (2011) *From Shamanism to Sufism: Women, Islam and Culture in Central Asia*. London: Bloomsbury Publishing.

Tlostanova, M. (2010) *Gender Epistemologies and Eurasian Borderlands*. New York: Springer.

Toktomushev, K. (2016) *Kyrgyzstan-Regime Security and Foreign Policy*. Abingdon, Oxon: Routledge.

Trevisani, T. and Massicard, E. (2003) 'The Uzbek Mahalla: Between State and Society,' in T. Everett-Heath (ed.) *Central Asia: Aspects of Transition*. London: Routledge/Curzon, pp. 205–218.

Tunçer-Kılavuz, I. (2009) 'Political and Social Networks in Tajikistan and Uzbekistan: "Clan," Region and Beyond,' *Central Asian Survey*, 28(3): 323–34.

Turaeva, R. (2015) *Migration and Identity in Central Asia: The Uzbek Experience*. Abingdon, Oxon: Routledge.

Tursunova, Z. (2014) *Women's Lives and Livelihoods in Post-Soviet Uzbekistan: Ceremonies of Empowerment and Peacebuilding*. Lexington: Lexington Books.

Urinboyev, R. (2020) *Migration and Hybrid Political Regimes*. Berkley, CA: University of California Press.

Werner, C. (1999) 'The Dynamics of Feasting and Gift Exchange in Rural Kazakhstan,' in Ingvar Svanberg (ed.) *Contemporary Kazaks: Social and Cultural Perspectives*. London: Curzon Press, pp. 209–228.

Werner, C. (2004) 'Feminizing the New Silk Road: Women Traders in Rural Kazakhstan,' in Carol Nechemias and Kathleen Kuehnast (eds.) *Post-Soviet Women Encountering Transition: Nation-Building, Economic Survival, and Civic Activism*. Baltimore, Maryland: Johns Hopkins University Press.

Ziganshina, D. (2014) *Promoting Transboundary Water Security in the Aral Sea Basin through International Law*. Leiden, Netherlands: Martinus Nijhoff Publishers.

PART I

History

1
CENTRAL ASIA BEFORE THE ADVENT OF RUSSIAN DOMINION[1]

Michael Hancock-Parmer

[East of the Caspian] towards the sunrise there stretches from its shores a boundless plain as far as sight can reach. At that time, the Massagetae were ruled by a queen, called Tomyris, whose husband had died. The Persian Emperor Cyrus sent a message with a pretense of wooing her for his wife, but Tomyris would have none of his advances, well understanding that he wooed not her but her kingdom.

(Herodotus 1858: 344)
–Herodotus (c. 484–425 BCE)

If you have nothing to tell us, but that on the banks of the Oxus and the Jaxartes, one barbarian has been succeeded by another barbarian, in what respect do you benefit the public?

(Voltaire 1901: 93)
–Voltaire, François-Marie Arouet (1694–1778)

Central Asia is a region where history has left an oversized footprint.

(McChesney 1996: 1)
–Robert D. McChesney (b. 1944)

From the chapter title – 'Central Asia before Russian Dominion' – one may guess which portions of Central Asia are under review; namely, those that fell to the military conquest of the Russian Empire, the territory of the modern republics of Kazakhstan, Uzbekistan, Turkmenistan, Tajikistan and Kyrgyzstan. Sometimes called Western Turkestan or until 1991 Soviet Central Asia, these vast territories roughly equal the size of continental Europe. We may broadly divide the history of the region across three eras: the present back to the arrival of permanent Russian military settlement (ca. 1865–present), the Islamic period (beginning with the occupation of Merv and Herat in 651 CE) and the pre-Islamic period (stretching back to the Achaemenid Persian Empire in the sixth century BCE). This historical survey will summarise the history of the territory relevant to contemporary Central Asia from the earlier two eras.

DOI: 10.4324/9780429057977-1

Pre-Islamic period

Central Asia was home to both sedentary and nomadic societies long before the historical period. Following Richard N. Frye, the primary difference between the different groups of people indigenous to Central Asia was language or tribal affiliation, markers that leave no remains in the archaeological record (Frye 1996: 31). Reading potsherds allows archaeologists to track changing practices, but linking pottery decoration to a tribe, language or culture is speculative at best. In other words, unknowable languages were spoken by unknowable cultures, living in small and scattered populations.

The region is home to thousands of archaeological sites and some modern cities were first settled as encampments and villages in the prehistoric era. Agriculture arrived in the region around 7000 BCE, though restricted to oases, river valleys and arid zones watered using irrigation. By 6000 BCE, large mammal domestication included sheep, goats and cattle, though it was the domestication of horses after 4000 BCE that cemented the importance of the region in world history (Findley 2005: 23). No evidence has yet emerged of large towns prior to the first millennium BCE and around the time of the arrival of the Indo-European speakers.

The term 'Indo-European' refers to the language and not the ethnic or genetic markers of these people. This survey of the history of Central Asia includes a focus on the linguistic evidence, which should not be conflated with modern ethnic or national identity. This refers both to prehistorical languages like Proto-Indo-European and more recent languages preserved in the historical record.

While Caucasoid and Mongoloid anatomical features in skeletal remains have extended east and west across Eurasia since ancient times, their skeletons do not record their languages. Linguistic evidence suggests that the wide-ranging Indo-European speakers were acquainted with both agriculture and herding. These Indo-European speakers figure prominently in recent scholarship on the rise of the wheel, pastoral nomadism and mounted archery (Anthony 2007). Speaking of long-term cultural continuities in the region (not exclusive to Western Turkestan, of course), characteristics and practices 'misleadingly grouped together as shamanism' (Findley 2005: 25), including water taboos, animal art and cults of ancestral spirits, link the Saka, Scythians, Turks, Mongols and Tokharians, connecting Indo-European and Altaic cultures across the inland grassy sea. While the Indo-Europeans dominated Central Asia until the first century CE, archaeological evidence suggests that 'already by the second millennium BCE ... Mongoloid types had begun to expand westward' (Frye 1996: 35), with the population-multiplying consequences of the successful acquisition of animal husbandry and agriculture.

In the earliest historical era, interactions between pastoral nomads and their sedentary neighbours already marked Central Asia, as portrayed in the religious texts of Zarathustra (Zoroaster). A priest of the old Aryan religion, Zarathustra probably lived in Bactria, the most prosperous and populous part of the region, around the year 1000 BCE. He advocated reform by rejecting the glorification of violence and the worship of the vast pantheon of *deava*s. Zarathustra instead proclaimed the existence of one deity, Ahura Mazda, 'wise lord.' William McNeill suggested the possibility of the religion of Zarathustra maturing alongside the spread of sedentary populations in Persia and Central Asia, outlawing 'bloody sacrifices' in favour of ritual prayers and celebrations that later emerged as central to the religion itself, offering an intriguing parallel to the adaptations of Judaism and Christianity during the Roman era (McNeill 1963: 154). Many other religions later passed through Central Asia in the historical period, including the earlier expressions of Buddhism emerging from Afghanistan, as well as Judaism and Christianity. However, for longevity and impact, Islam remains the central religion of historical and contemporary importance. Its longevity of religious and political control began in the early eighth century, continuing with Islam's replacement of a rich tapestry of confessional diversity with a superficial, if vocal, majority. Even so, much evidence from the Islamic era suggests that older, indigenous religious practices and beliefs continued.

The first historical political power in the region that can be identified without speculation was the Medes, under whom the religion of Zarathustra spread from Mesopotamia to Anatolia, Persia and Central Asia. The Medes came to rule over the Persians in Fars and, together with the Babylonians, brought down the Assyrians by conquering Nineveh. The agriculturally settled Medes and Hittites of Anatolia spoke languages related to those of the nomadic Saka and Scythians of the Eurasian plains. However, arguing that these populations shared ethnic, cultural, religious or economic connections is more fraught.

One may usefully divide Central Asia roughly north from south. This creates two large geographic expanses: one dominated by pastoral nomadism (the north) and the other intensely cultivated amid nomadic herders (the south). In the time of the Medes, who ruled the southern agriculturalists, the northern inhabitants were recognised in Persian and Egyptian sources as the nomadic Saka. They divided the Saka into vague groups under evocative labels like the Hauma-brewing Saka, the Saka beyond the river, the Saka beyond Sogdiana, the Saka beyond the plains and the Saka beyond the marshes. None of these groups have been meaningfully connected to known archaeological sites, similar to the Massagetae of the Greek sources who lived east of the Caspian Sea, but unlike the Scythians of the Pontic steppe personally visited by Herodotus.

Persia and Alexander

The ancient armies of the Medes and Persians forged both alliances and deadly wars with their nomadic neighbours. Nomads and townsfolk have long worked and lived side-by-side, such that the attempts of anthropologists to meaningfully separate the two categories have often failed in practice, devolving into discussions of 'semi-nomads' and the like. The arrival from outside the region of powerful agriculturalists or pastoral nomads had echoing influences in the region; as the arrival of the Persians coincided with the growth of cities, so did the movements of the Turks and Mongols see the rise of gigantic pastoral societies. Speaking of the Persians, the two largest and important cities of the region at the time were Samarkand and Balkh (Marakanda and Bactra, respectively, to the Greeks), with the tertiary centre of Merv (Margiana) linking them to the Achaemenids and Medes in greater Iran. The Aramaic language used to run the Achaemenid Persian Empire became the basis for the earliest indigenous written languages of Bactrian, Sogdian and Khwarazmian – but they came later, after Alexander's conquest and the establishment of the Greco-Bactrian and other successor states. When Alexander died in Babylon in 323 BCE, the Greco-Persian Empire he had conquered dissolved and Central Asia passed to Seleucus I Nikator. The dynasty that survived Seleucus through his son Antiochus (by his wife Apama, daughter of the Sogdian Spitamenes) has not attracted a great deal of scholarly attention, but historians know it as Greco-Bactria. In the 1960s, archaeologists investigated a set of ruins known by its Turkic name Ay Khanum and found a recognisable Greek *polis* in northern Afghanistan. The inscriptions and materials attest to the spread of uncontaminated Greek language within the bounds of Central Asia. Moreover, the two de facto state languages of Aramaic (from the Achaemenids) and Greek appeared south of the Hindukush on the didactic Buddhist inscriptions of Ashoka (c. 304–232 BCE).

Parthia and the silk routes

The Seleucid dynasty maintained independence in southern Central Asia until the mid-second century BCE, despite increasing threats in the north and west. After Hannibal's decade-long occupation of the Italian peninsula in the Second Punic War, the Carthaginian Empire suffered a fatal reversal of fortune. Hannibal escaped east to the Phoenician heartland and Roman eastern expansion pushed him further east in the Parthian and Greco-Bactrian wars on the western fringes of Central Asia. Rule of the region passed entirely to the Parthians under Mithridates I (c. 171–138 BCE). Despite the advent of political unity, the Parthian rulers oversaw a period of increasing chaos following waves of nomadic incursions from the north.

A movement of nomadic people not unlike the massive migration of Germanic tribes into the Roman Empire thoroughly remixed the demographic makeup of Central Asia, beginning already in the second century BCE. The linguistic and cultural makeup of the northern steppe began to shift as the Finno-Ugric- and Indo-European-speaking populations gave way before the proto-Turkic-speaking. Where the influx of nomads among the sedentary inhabitants falls on the continuum between assimilation and extermination remains unknown. During this period (c. 200 BCE–200 CE), Central Asia existed on the periphery of larger states: Parthia to the north and west and the long-forgotten Kushan to the south and Han China to the East. In terms of cultural history, Mahayana Buddhism spread along the trade routes that blossomed in Central Asia connecting Rome, Parthia, Sogdia, India and China. This network was first labelled the Great Silk Route by the German Orientalist Ferdinand von Richthofen in 1877 in recognition of its most prominent luxury item, silk, being of profound commercial and diplomatic importance as a trade good.

The dynamic period of political shake-ups reflected an underlying demographic change, though understanding the change in terms of ethnicity, culture and language remains beyond the grasp of the surviving evidence. The Zoroastrian Sasanid state in Iran replaced that of the Arsacid Parthians in the 220s, while the Kushan fell to a nomadic invasion from the north in the mid-fourth century CE, the so-called Kidarite Huns, in turn, replaced by a more powerful nomadic confederation, the similarly Altaic Hephthalites, who passed through Central Asia into what is now Afghanistan before conquering large sections of northern India. The Turkicisation of the steppes continued, most famously as other relatives of the Xiong-nu of the Chinese sources invaded Anatolia and Eastern Europe, the Huns of the late Classical period. The Silk Roads flourished throughout this politically turbulent time, even into the sixth century CE. The Sogdian merchants that dominated trade began to establish colonies ever eastward, communities of Buddhists and eastern Christians.

Manichaeism, an extinct world religion, first thrived and then slowly dissolved in the period between the third and fifteenth centuries CE. The artist-healer-prophet Mani (216–277) was distantly related to the Arsacid royal family of the Parthian Empire and had his first religious revelation at the age of 12. Raised in an environment bestride Zoroastrian, Christian and Buddhist teachings, Mani utilised these thinkers of the (not-so-distant) past in describing a dualistic religion of good and evil, sinful and pure, the elect and the auditors (Tardieu 2009). Mani suffered a martyr's death, ensuring his philosophy would outlive him. Though there is no way to document the historic connection between the two, many have supposed that Manichaeism survived in Europe in the form of Catharism, so viciously exterminated in the thirteenth century during the Albigensian Crusade.

Another people emerged from northeastern Asia in the sixth century CE, the Göktürks (Celestial Turks) under their Qaghan, the title an etymological cousin of Khan. Thanks to the wide dispersion of their pastoral nomadic subjects, the Türk Qaghanates occupied truly massive territories throughout the Eurasian steppe belt. The memory of the Qaghanate survives in part thanks to their inscribing their political origins in violent rebellion from the Tang Dynasty in China on stone monuments found in Mongolia by the Russian Turkologist Nikolai Yadrintsev in 1889. By the end of the seventh century, the first Turkic state had splintered and fertilised numerous successors throughout and without the region, from the Khazars west of the Volga to the newly emerged Qarluqs of Central Asia proper.

Islamic period

It was this period (c. 670s–690s) in which eastern and western powers again encroached in the form of Tang China and the Umayyad Caliphate. The Arab conquest of Central Asia far exceeded that of the Chinese; from their base of operations established in Merv (Antiochia in Margiana to the Greeks, near modern Mary in Turkmenistan), the *ghazi* fighters and their *mawali* patrons first raided and then occupied most of southern Central Asia, inspiring a much more rapid, even zealous, conversion to Islam than that found in the Zoroastrian Iranian lands to the west. Just as Greek invaders and opportunistic local rulers shared control, the Arab conquerors received assistance from *mawali* counterparts and this model extends into the modern era with the Russian conquest, with the use of indigenous nomadic tribes. We will extend that model into the modern period, when the nineteenth-century Russian conquest similarly exploited local aid in the form of Kazakh tribes looking to achieve independence from their overlords in Kokand.

Islamic influence spread rapidly. Qutaiba b. Muslim, named governor of Khorasan in 704, began Islamic annexation of the region and the Muslim armies had reached the Syr Darya River (Seyhun) already by 751. In the same year, the Battle of Talas near the present-day border of Kazakhstan and Kyrgyzstan settled Islamic dominance of the area over that of the Tang Chinese dynasty. The Turkic Qarluqs, Oghuz and Qipchaq migrated ever westward into various pastures of Eurasia. Later scholars used the names of these three tribal confederations to create linguistic, ethnic and other conventional classifications of the diversity of Turkic languages and cultures. Roughly speaking, the Qarluqs lived in the east and middle (modern Uzbeks and Uyghur), the Oghuz in the west (modern Turkmen and Turks) and the Kipchak in the north (modern Tatar, Karakalpak, Kazakh and Kyrgyz).

In the ninth and tenth centuries, the border towns near the Syr Darya River between the steppe and sown, namely Farab (Otrar), Isfijab (Sayram) and Shash (Tashkent), witnessed the first large-scale conversions of Turkic speakers to Islam. It was at this time that the term 'Turkmen' (Turcoman, Türkmen) came to specifically refer to the western-most Turks, the Oghuz, largely to differentiate them from their non-Muslim neighbours (Golden 1992: 212–13). Around the year 985, a Turkmen notable named Seljuk fell out with the head of the Oghuz in Yangikent and fled a short distance to Jend in the delta of the Syr Darya (the ruins of which are in southern Kazakhstan). The Seljuk Empire originated in Central Asia but rose to power and historical importance only after its centre moved west into Persia. At its zenith, the territory of the Seljuks stretched from the Bosphorus to Afghanistan until its dissolution in the late twelfth century.

One of the curious problems of the arrival of Islam into Central Asia was whether and how to convert the native population. Scholars in the past have argued that Islam was ultimately, like most major religions, a culture of cities. This was certainly the case of temple-centred Judaism and even Christianity, its pretensions to pastors, sheep and flocks notwithstanding. Muhammad, however, spoke often and directly to nomads. The issue is far beyond the scope of this introduction, as the word *arab* itself carries the meaning of wandering like a nomad. Exceptions and explanations from Muhammad explained how the obligations of Islam could be met by both city dwellers and merchants, travellers and Arabs/nomads. Why, then, did religious conversion in Central Asia focus so heavily on the *mawali* of the cities?

Perhaps because the first Islamic dynasty in the region was Iranian, that is to say, a citified dynasty: the Samanids. The early form of the modern Persian language dates to this period, particularly and most indelibly etched by the pen of Ferdowsi (c. 940–1020), author of the Shahnameh, the Book of Kings and a colossal work of expressive historical fiction telling the mythical and historical past of Iran and Turan. That ancient phrase 'Iran and Turan' expresses both familiarity and contempt between the sedentary Iranians of the agricultural regions and Turan, which by then had come to mean the nomadic Turks beyond the Oxus River (Jeyhun). Curiously, however, the Samanids had already a century before Ferdowsi's time introduced the crucial institution of the ghulam, Turkic slave-soldiers who quickly became the core of the armies of Islam far beyond the bounds of Central Asia. The Samanids, then, founded at least two long-lasting institutions in the Islamic world: Turkic military slaves converted to Islam and Bukhara as a source of Islamic schooling and culture. It is no mistake that the so-called Golden Age of Islam rests on the laurels of thinkers with *nisba*s like Bukhari, Balkhi, Farabi, Khwarezmi and Biruni, although Central Asia's most famous son was likely the polymath Ibn Sina (c. 980–1037). As a physician, his fame relies on *al-Qanun fi'l-Tibb*, taught in Europe into the Early Modern era as *The Canon* and as a philosopher his works directly influenced scholasticism and its champion Thomas Aquinas (d. 1274).

When, around the year 1000, the Turks completed their 'infiltration of the oasis states,' they sealed the current cultural form with their defeat of the 'last Iranian dynasty to rule in Central Asia.' From then until now, Central Asia has split two ways: the west, leaning towards the Near East, and Iran, while similarly Muslim, bearing 'a thick [Chinese] veneer, which was penetrating ever deeper' (Frye 1996: 238). Bartol'd and his followers in Turkology differ on this pivot point and prefer to see modern Central Asia ultimately descending from the arrival of the Mongols in the thirteenth century.

The arrival of the Mongols

When the assembly of nomads in the steppes of northeast Asia declared Temujin (c. 1167–1227) as Chinggis Khan (Genghis Khan) in 1206, still long before the creation of the massive Mongol Empire enshrined in many history surveys, many territorial and regime changes were already afoot. The Khwarezm Shah's state centred in modern Uzbekistan faced incursions from the south, originating within the growing Ghurid Empire. In eastern Central Asia the Qara-Khitai, or Western Liao (Golden 1992: 185), oversaw a fusion of Chinese and nomadic imperial rule over a Turkic, Muslim population (Biran 2005). A group of Naimans, fleeing Chinggis Khan, follower their leader Kuchluk in an attack on the Qara-Khitai, with support from local Qarluqs. This blow to the Qara-Khitai opened the way to opportunistic war by the Khwarezm Shah. Kuchluk, a Christian convert to Buddhism who prohibited public Muslim worship in his realm, emerged from the chaos as the de facto ruler of the region. Muhammad, the Khorezmshah, satisfied that his eastern borders were secure, directly challenged the Abbasid caliph in Baghdad in 1217, though winter storms and Kurdish troops prevented the military sovereignty once enjoyed by the Great Seljuks in the eleventh and twelfth centuries. A powerful but recently humbled Khwarezm Shah likely did not see the nomads to his northeast as an existential threat; the two groups exchanged embassies in 1215 and 1218. Tensions rose, however, when one of his governors, in the city of Otrar on the northeastern fringe of his power, slaughtered a caravan under the protection of the Mongols and seized their goods. Chinggis Khan sent an ambassador, assuming a misunderstanding, but the Khorezm Shah ordered the murder of that ambassador. As a result, the Mongols retaliated with the goal of total annihilation. 'For Chinggis Khan in particular, war was a personal vendetta against wilfully defiant rulers ... which was justified in one of three ways' (Atwood 2004: 349): as vengeance for past attacks, as a punishment of those giving aid to his enemies or as retribution for those who executed Mongol envoys. The Khwarezm Shah had committed a capital crime and while Temujin did not invent this code, he brutally followed it.

Presciently, the Qarluqs had recently sworn fealty to Chinggis Khan before he passed through the ruined Qara-Khitai state and deposed Kuchluk, so that the Mongols were greeted as liberators by the Muslim population in eastern Central Asia. The remnants of the Qara-Khitai military joined the invasion of the Khwarezm Shah Empire and razed the bulk of its cities and populated areas between 1219 and 1222. The war was deeply personal and bound by a strict code of honour; entire towns might be spared, sold into slavery or slaughtered in service to the sense of Chinggisid justice. Great cities were torn apart, brick by brick, the smoking rubble ploughed into the ground: the region as a whole would recover, thanks to its central importance in the rising Mongol Empire, but many of the cities so destroyed never rose from the ashes. Mongol rule later stretched into Russia, instigating the so-called Tatar Yoke, but any such harness weighed much heavier on the shoulders of the people of Central Asia. After the initial conquest, Temujin's third son, Ogedei, pursued the remnants of their enemies west, seizing the steppe and forests of the Russian princedoms in 1237–1241. This effectively brought all of Central Asia from its southern boundaries in Afghanistan to its northern extremes in Bulgar within a single state.

Central Asia was unified for the first and so far last time in recorded history. The Mongol Empire was the largest contiguous land empire the world has yet seen, but it fragmented after three generations. Already before the end of the thirteenth century, the descendants of the sons of Chinggis Khan had shifted their centres of political power outside of the bounds of this survey: the heirs of Chaghatay to Eastern Turkestan (Moghulistan) and the house of Jochi to Sarai and Haji-Tarkhan (Astrakhan), the cities of the Golden Horde of the 'Tartars.' The territories of Jochi and Chaghatay saw their nomadic populations thoroughly Turkicise and adopt Islam – this is usually credited to Uzbek Khan (r. 1313–1341) for the Jochids and Baraq Khan (r. 1266–1271) for the Chaghatayids. The territory of Hulegu, another grandson of Chinggis Khan, included the southwestern marches of Central Asia. By the early 1300s, his progeny nominally controlled the region south of the Amu Darya River.

Not long after the death of the last of his dynasty in 1335, Central Asia splintered briefly into warring chieftains, only to be nearly entirely reunited first by the Chaghatayid Khan Toghluq-Timur and then more completely by his protege, Timur Bek (Amir Timur, Tamerlane, 1336–1405). Far more a military and charismatic force than a governor, Timur carved a Turco-Mongol state from the stretched and cracking hide of the deserts and oases while making use of Chinggisid charisma in the form of expendable puppet Khans. His was the foundational proto-gunpowder empire, as the three states recognised as such (the Ottomans with their Janissaries, the Mughals with their Sepoys and the Safavids with their Qizilbash) arose from the remnants of the Timurid Empire in the sixteenth century (Lincoln 1994: 41–7). Timur's military technology and repeat invasions engendered a level of cruelty that surpassed the Mongols, notably in Herat, Baghdad and Delhi.

The rule of Timur's descendants centred on the deserts and oases of southern Central Asia, while the Chinggisid charisma and pastoral nomadism continued in the north. Abu'l-Khayr, elected in 1428 as Khan of the house of Jochi in Western Siberia, conquered the Syr Darya region by the 1440s but in turn fell prey to the Oirats coming west from the Chu River. This cataclysmic encounter (or his own misrule) forever split the followers of Abu'l-Khayr into the Uzbeks (as his people had already been known) and the Uzbek-Qazaq. The Uzbeks moved south of the Syr Darya, while the Uzbek-Qazaqs, or Kazakhs, came under the patronage and protection of the last of Chaghatay's house on the steppe fringes of Moghulistan. They served as a buffer against continued Oirat expansion. When Abu'l-Khayr died in 1468, more Uzbeks joined the Kazakhs in the Seven Rivers region (Semirechie, Zhetisu, Yeti Su). Abu'l-Khayr's grandson Muhammad Shahi Bek remained on the Syr Darya. Muhammad, known as Shah-Bakht or more famously as Shibani Khan, followed the model of Tamerlane and through shrewd patronage and betrayal became 'the chief power in Central Asia' (Grousset 1970: 482), at the expense of the Timurid Sultan Ahmad Mirza. Uzbeks swelled his forces, allowing Shibani Khan to conquer Samarkand in 1500.

During this generation, poet-philosophers ruled Central Asia: Shibani Khan, Babur the founder of the Mughal dynasty in India and Ismail Safavi of Persia, all left impressive literary legacies. Religious controversies abounded, as the rise of the Qizilbash in Safavid Iran fomented violent advocacy of Shiism. The Uzbeks under Babur and Shibani Khan rendered many of them martyrs in the defence of the Sunnah. The rise of Shiism in Safavid Persia increased isolation in Central Asia, separating them from the rest of the Muslim world, or in the words of Sir Olaf Caroe (1892–1981), 'the curtain had fallen on Turkestan long before the days of Soviet rule, even before the Tsars' (Caroe 1953: 135).

Decline: Through globalisation or isolation?

The passing of the Central Asian Timurid dynasty in 1507 coincided with the advent of increased maritime trade in Western Europe around Ottoman middlemen, inadvertently producing New World European colonisation. 'The West' expanded economically and demographically at the expense of the 'the rest.' However, in the words of Robert McChesney, there remains 'strong evidence that Central Asia remained closely tied to the global economy after the maritime trade opened' (McChesney 1996: 42–3). For example, McChesney has noted the existence of a nascent tobacco industry cultivated in Bukhara already in the 1680s. There was an underlying superstructure made up of shrines, Sufi lineages and the webbing of a religio-economic managerial class of traders and shrine families dating to the Timurid. These same networks undergirded the so-called Gunpowder Empires in Mughal India, Ottoman Turkey and Safavid Iran. Perhaps the Gunpowder Empires might more accurately be labelled Shrine Empires, or Sufi, Empires? The great shrines of Central Asia sustained towns and flourished in major cities, diplomatically connecting religiously motivated nomads and with their sedentary neighbours, and peacefully redistributed some of the accumulated wealth of the region. It was this culture and economy, largely in place by the early fifteenth century, that the Russian Empire encountered when it seized control in the late nineteenth.

The existence of this Sufi shrine network of political and economic allegiances offers explanatory options to historians who struggled with big-picture views of the sixteenth through eighteenth centuries in the region. Its existence shows how the arrival of the exiled Jochid Khans fleeing the expansion of Muscovy in the late fifteenth and early sixteenth century succeeded in Central Asia because of their integration into the system. The network's prominence would also explain why the Oirat interludes, ostensibly interested in replacing the network of Sufi shrines with Buddhist ones, were so violently catastrophic in the region. I believe this organisation of shrines underlies the phenomenon observed by Professor Manz when she wrote that, despite the 'unnecessary cruelty of his campaigns [and] the confusion of his administration, ... what has struck me in my study of Temur's career is not failure, but success, not confusion but system' (Manz 1989: 19).

The arrival of Muscovy

The expansion of Muscovy southwards into the lands north of Central Asia indelibly marked the seventeenth century in the region, which splintered from pressures entering from the north and east. The Kazakh Khanate struggled to maintain control of pastures seized by the Buddhist Oirats while the Uzbek clans controlling the agricultural and merchant riches of the cities continued to subdivide among cadet branches of the Jochids, the Ashtarkhanids in Bukhara and the Arabshahids in Khorezm. There were periods of strife, but on the whole the 1600s in the southern half of Central Asia saw economic and social stability, illustrated by the literary production of Abu'l-Ghazi (1603–1663), the learned Khan of Khorezm (r. 1643–1663) who wrote *Shajara-i Turk* (*The Genealogy of the Turks*), appreciatively studied by European Orientalists since the eighteenth century.

Two migrations occurred between the Mongol Conquest of the thirteenth century and the Russian Conquests of the nineteenth century: the first and larger in the early sixteenth century with the arrival of the Uzbeks and the second and more destructive in the early eighteenth century with the arrival of steppe refugees fleeing the expanding Jungar-Oirat state. The first migration fomented the creation of the Khanates of Bukhara and Khiva, while the second the creation of the Khanate of Kokand in the Ferghana Valley. In the mid-sixteenth century, the modern ethnic identity of Central Asia came into focus: Turkmen in the south and west, Kyrgyz in the central mountain pastures, Kazakhs in the steppe roughly north of the Syr Darya and Uzbeks to the south, near the oases inhabited by Persianate Tajiks. From the sixteenth to the eighteenth century, first one and then another Khanate temporarily absorbed its neighbour or fell to outside interventions, but two powerful external forces entered the region that stymied any attempts to recreate Tamerlane's state: first from the east with the Jungar-Oirat state (1635–1755) and then from the south under 'the second Alexander,' Nadir Shah Afshar (1688–1747).

The Jungar rulers sought sovereignty over all the lands immediately east of Central Asia, from the Mongol steppe and the Tibetan plateau and vassal-tribute from their neighbours. Zealous defenders of the Dalai Lama in Tibet and so legitimised by Buddhist patronage rather than Chinggisid charisma, the Jungars followed a *khung-tayiji* whose title came from service to the Dalai Lama, the theocratic ruler in Lhasa. The armies of Galdan Boshugtu Khan (1644–1697) drove the Eastern Mongols into the arms of the Qing dynasty, seized the entire Tarim basin and raided deep into Central Asia, sacking the cities on the northern banks of the Syr Darya. Following the death of Galdan during a retreat in the wars with the Qing Empire, Galdan's nephew Tsewang Rabtan (1643–1727) more successfully avoided antagonising the Qing while violently punishing Lhasa, which he ordered sacked in December of 1717 – better destroyed than 'put at the service of China' (Grousset 1970: 533). Then, in response to the Kyrgyz and Kazakh raids into the heart of Jungar control in the Ili Valley, the Jungar forces launched a series of attacks in the 1720s, taking (or perhaps liberating) the cities of the Syr Darya from Kazakh control. Consequently, these actions of Tsewang Rabtan instigated a large refugee migration throughout the region: north towards the Oirats on the Volga (the Kalmyks), west towards Khiva, south towards Bukhara and east into the Ferghana Valley. It is an open question whether these Kazakhs returned to the steppe or integrated into the population of their adopted regions.

It was into this Central Asian context of reciprocal vying for territory between 1680 and 1730 that Peter the Great (1672–1725) sent two disastrous expeditions. First, the Bekovich party met their bloody end in Khiva in 1717 and secondly, the Bukhgol'ts expedition was turned back by Jungar military superiority in 1716. Hoping to regain prisoners and organise an alliance against the Qing, Peter and his successors sent peace envoys to the Jungars in the 1720s and 1730s, noting the presence of a cannon foundry and printing press, products of industrious

Swedish prisoners of war first captured by Peter at Poltava in 1709. Little was demanded (or could be taken by force), but much was promised by these Russian embassies, as witnessed by the nominal allegiance of the Kazakhs to similar Russian envoys in 1731 and 1740.

Several interregnums and succession crises marked this period: crises followed the deaths of Peter in 1725, the Kangxi Emperor of China in 1722, the overthrow of Safavid Persia by Mahmud Hotaki in 1722 and the violent interregnum in India between Shahid-i-Mazlum Farrukhsiyar (r. 1713–1719) and Muhammad Shah (r. 1719–1748). Within Central Asia itself, the death of Ubaydullah II, Khan of Bukhara (r. 1702–1711) was followed by that of the last powerful Khan of the Kazakhs, Tauke (Tawakkul, d. ca. 1717). Ubaydullah was succeeded by Abu'l-Fayz Khan (r. 1711–1747), whose long reign is best understood as a product of his impotence and willingness to take direction, whether from his own court of Uzbek tribal chiefs or that of Nadir Shah. The weakened condition of Central Asia, despite the persistence of traditional economic ties with its neighbours, allowed peripheral powers to increase their expansion into the region throughout the century. The Russian Empire ringed in the steppe along the northern rivers with Cossack fortifications, and the Qing annihilated the Jungars and brought Moghulistan (thereafter Xinjiang, New Borderland) and Tibet under their control. The Oirat-Jungars dispersed, those in the Central Asian steppe integrating into the Kazakh population with whom they had long maintained marriage relations. To the south, the Mughal Empire no longer reached the borders of Central Asia and was subsequently replaced by the Durrani Empire (a successor state of Nadir Shah) before the gradual expansion of British economic and administrative control of India.

The nineteenth century saw the arrival of the Russian administrative apparatus among the Kazakhs. Having abolished the Khanate, the Russians divvied up the pastures into faux provinces, each under a 'sultan-governor' from the family of Chinggis Khan with a small military detachment. These advances were not opposed: some Kazakh Chinggisids offered violence in return, most famously under Sultan Kenesari (fl. 1836–1847).

The phrase 'Great Game' is most evocative for many English speakers for this historical era, particularly readers of its chief populariser (for Americans, at least), the journalist and author Peter Hopkirk (1930–2014). Infelicitously for Hopkirk's readers, 'the clichés concerning the "Great Game ..." are much less innocent. They do not simplify; instead they deeply distort the past' (Morrison 2017). One traditional argument sees Russia invading Central Asia to restore prestige lost to Britain and France during the Crimean debacle and to restore its economy. Wonderful to behold in power-fantasies that reduce suffering and bloodshed to colourful maps and board games, when real-life political figures like George Nathaniel, aka Lord Curzon Viceroy of India (1859–1929), equated the region with a 'giant chessboard,' there were consequences beyond the players losing a point or winning a game. But it was a chessboard quite empty of pieces belonging to supposed puppet masters in St. Petersburg and London. The invisibility of indigenous military and religious cooperation and support (meaning Kazakh, Kyrgyz, Uzbek, Tajik and Turkmen allies in wrestling power from the Khan and Emir) is captured well in this typical statement: only 'about 40,000 [ethnic Russian] troops [were] stationed in the [region], which had a population of about six million souls ... [it was rather] the construction of railroads and of a telegraph network [that] proved an effective means of controlling the colony' (Soucek 2000: 204). While the keepers of maps in Europe held the population of Central Asia as little more than scenic backdrop in their power struggles, in fact Central Asia was conquered with Central Asian help and could not have been otherwise. Only recently has the role of the Kazakhs in the Russian Conquest begun to come more fully to light (Kilian 2013).

Individual inhabitants of Central Asia of power and means enjoyed a quid pro quo relationship with their Russian contemporaries; Russian fortifications, after all, survived best when supported by the local population which they guarded, protected or, at least, cowed. Even with tenuous local support, Russian imperial leadership could not find a silver bullet method towards control in the region. Russian imperial agents employed a multifaceted effort to control the local population, using coercion and adventure through mutual cattle-hustling raids with and against Cossack fortifications, religious inculcation through Tatar migrants and Christian missionaries, and bribery and coercion through new legal statutes and previously bought 'loyal' middlemen.

By the 1850s, the water-borne stratagems that saw the Caspian and the Aral as under-utilised Naval playgrounds had failed to pay dividends and were actually drained on resources, while attempts by Ignatiev to foster better diplomatic and trade relations with Bukhara and Khiva similarly fizzled, except to 'remove the fog' regarding the relative military strength of the adversaries. Ironically, the railroad and telegraph network were more useful to the Bolsheviks in taking control of the state apparatus than it was to the Tsarists in controlling the local population. It was with Kazakh assistance that the Russian Empire took the steppe and deflated the ambitions of the Khanate of Kokand; after the death of its last military commander of note, 'Alimqul ('Aliquli, c. 1833–1865), Kokand was a spent force (Tashkandi 2003: 7), and Russians completed their annexation in early 1876.

First the storming of Tashkent in 1865 and finally the acquisition of Merv in 1884 sealed the Russian conquest of Central Asia in blood. The Emir of Bukhara and Khan of Khiva became de facto vassals of the Tsar. Russia took pains to penetrate the high Pamirs in the 1890s, setting the border at the furthest extremes at the edge of Afghan sovereignty. Svat Soucek has placed these movements in the context not just of British India but also of French North Africa, where European colonisation 'presents an even closer parallel' (Soucek 2000: 200) in Algeria, Tunisia and Morocco.

In conclusion, when the agents and subjects of the Russian Empire arrived in Central Asia, in a trickle in the eighteenth century which increased to a steady flow by the mid-nineteenth century, they found a region with a longer, richer history than their own. Before Moscow or St. Petersburg had come into being, empires had risen and fallen into dust multiple times in the mountains and salt marshes, oases and steppes east of the Caspian Sea. With the Russians came a resurgence of postal routes, the likes of which had last crisscrossed the region in the Mongol era. More transformative was the graduated arrival of railroads, telegraphy, electricity, publishing houses and medicine capable of defending against smallpox, cholera and malaria. For one, no nomadic state has risen again since the promulgation of these technologies. These changes marked the entire world; the struggle to find continuities linking the eighteenth and twentieth centuries is the work of an entire field of historians studying the so-called Early Modern period. Electric lights and streetcars delighted and worried inhabitants of Moscow and Tashkent alike; the ease of movement from the Russian heartland to the colonial cantons in Tashkent and Vernyi (Almaty) increased contact and colonialist anxieties in ways recognisable to historians of the British, French and Spanish Empires. The indigenous population encountered by the pioneers of the Russian Empire were predominantly Turkic in language and culture, but still Persian survived across Central Asia, and even thrived in certain pockets across the region, given a

Persianate hue to the Turquoise cultural landscape. From this mixture arose one of the headaches of the Russian administration, the Sarts. A term applied to various groups of people for various reasons, the origin of that term was the loss (or lack) among some settled Central Asians of their historic identity: the Turco-Mongolic tribal lineages. In short, a Sart had no tribal identity, whether or not their ancestors had such lineages. For example, while the term was applied to some ancestors of modern Tajiks and Uzbeks, it was also used by the Russians to describe a small group of sedentarised Oirats (e.g. Sart Kalmyks) in Kyrgyzstan. There it gave the same sense of having lost touch with a nomadic life and lineage. In the next chapter, Ian Campbell lays out the finer details of growing Russian hegemony, including their attempts to define and control the usage of the term 'Sart.' Dr. Campbell illustrates the history of Russian Central Asia up to the sudden and violent arrival of Soviet rule in the winter of 1917–1918.

Note

1 This historical introduction would not have come together without the support of Devin DeWeese at the Research Institute for Inner Asian Studies (RIFIAS) at Indiana University in Bloomington. Thanks to a generous grant from Ferrum College, I was able to work within its holdings and write this new synthesis, an homage to Bartol'd and Bregel. If one cannot locate the time to read the translation of Vasilii Bartol'd's (1869–1930) dissertation *Turkestan Down to the Mongol Invasion*, Yuri Bregel's (1925–2016), *An Historical Atlas of Central Asia* provides the best and most complete précis of the region's history.

Bibliography

Anthony, D. (2007) *The Horse, the Wheel, and Language: How Bronze-Age Riders from the Eurasian Steppes Shaped the Modern World*. Princeton: Princeton University Press.
Atwood, C. P. (2004) *Mongolia and the Mongol Empire*. New York: Facts On File.
Barthold, W. (1968) *Turkestan Down to the Mongol Invasion*. Translated by T. Minorsky. Edited by C. E. Bosworth. 3rd edition. London: Luzac and Company Ltd.
Biran, M. (2005) *The Empire of the Qara Khitai in Eurasian History: Between China and the Islamic World*. New York: Cambridge University Press.
Bregel, Y. (2003) *An Historical Atlas of Central Asia*. Boston: Brill.
Caroe, O. (1953) 'Soviet Colonialism in Central Asia,' *Foreign Affairs*, 32(1), 135–144.
Findley, C.V. (2005) *The Turks in World History*. New York: Oxford University Press.
Frye, R. N. (1996) *The Heritage of Central Asia: From Antiquity to the Turkish Expansion*. Princeton: Markus Wiener Publishers.
Golden, P. (1992) *An Introduction to the History of the Turkic Peoples: Ethnogenesis and State-Formation in Medieval and Early Modern Eurasia and the Middle East*. Wiesbaden: Otto Harrassowitz.
Grousset, R. (1970) *The Empires of the Steppe: A History of Central Asia*. Translated by N. Walford. New Brunswick: Rutgers University Press.
Hancock-Parmer, M. (2017) 'Running Until Our Feet Turn White: The Barefooted Flight and Kazakh National History.' Ph.D. Dissertation (Indiana University).
Herodotus. (1858) *The History of Herodotus*. Translated by G. Rawlinson. Volume 1. New York: D. Appleton & Company.
Kilian, J. (2013) 'Allies & Adversaries: The Russian Conquest of the Kazakh Steppe.' Ph.D. Dissertation (George Washington University).
Kliashtornyi, S. (1986) 'Kipchaki v runicheskikh pamiatnikakh,' *Turcologica*, 1986, 153–164.
Lincoln, W. B. (1994) *The Conquest of a Continent: Siberia and the Russians*. Ithaca: Cornell University Press.
Manz, B. F. (1989) *The Rise and Rule of Tamerlane*. New York: Cambridge University Press.
McChesney, R. D. (1996) *Central Asia: Foundations of Change*. Princeton: Darwin Press.
McNeill, W. H. (1963) *The Rise of the West: A History of the Human Community*. Chicago: University of Chicago Press.
Morrison, A. (2017) 'Central Asia's Catechism of Cliché: From the Great Game to Silk Road,' *Eurasianet.org* [https://eurasianet.org/central-asias-catechism-of-cliche-from-the-great-game-to-silk-road].

Soucek, B. and Soucek, S. (2000). *A History of Inner Asia*. Cambridge: Cambridge University Press.
Soucek, S. (2000) *A History of Inner Asia*. New York: Cambridge University Press.
Tardieu, M. (2009) *Manichaeism*. Translated by M. DeBevoise. Champaign: University of Illinois Press.
Tashkandi, Y. D. (2003) *The Life of 'Alimqul: A Native Chronicle of Nineteenth Century Central Asia*. Edited and Translated by T. Beisembiev. New York: Routledge.
Voltaire. (1901) 'History,' in *The Works of Voltaire*. Translated by W. Fleming. Volume 5. New York: The St. Hubert Guild.

2
RUSSIAN RULE IN CENTRAL ASIA

Ian W. Campbell

The lands that today constitute the independent republics of Kazakhstan, Kyrgyzstan, Uzbekistan, Tajikistan and Turkmenistan gradually came under the rule of the Russian Empire during the eighteenth and nineteenth centuries, at times by agreement, at times by right of conquest. Tsarist rule in Central Asia was uneven, pragmatic and often fell short of its claims and aspirations. Still, it was a key source of social and cultural change, particularly as tsarist administrators began towards the end of the nineteenth century to make stronger claims on the subject populations of Central Asia and as the empire as a whole began to emphasise a model of belonging based on nationality rather than dynastic loyalty (Werth 2001). This chapter introduces readers to the institutions and policies the Russian Empire sought to introduce in Central Asia and explores their effects.

The incorporation of the Kazak hordes

Prior to 1731, the date historians most commonly give for the Russian Empire's formal involvement in Central Asia, Russia had some limited trade and diplomatic contacts in the region and had begun to construct fortified lines along the Ural and Irtysh Rivers. The territory near these rivers was occupied by the Kazak Junior and Middle Hordes, fleeing the expansion of the Jungar Mongol state, as detailed by Hancock-Parmer in the previous chapter of this volume. In 1731, then, Empress Anna Ioannovna accepted the petition of Abulkhair, khan of the Junior Horde, to become a Russian subject; the khans of the Middle Horde would follow later in 1731 and again in 1740. These were agreements that promised mutual benefit – protection from strong external enemies for the Kazaks, security for the new frontier lines for the Russians. But the two sides understood them differently. Kazak khans saw them as alliances, rather than permanent and binding oaths of subjecthood, nor were they speaking for all Kazaks of the Junior and Middle Hordes (compare Khodarkovsky 1992). Tsarist officials' expectation of a more fixed and lasting arrangement influenced their perception of what occurred during the subsequent decades, as indirect rule through Kazak khans left many matters outside their knowledge and control.

The situation on the steppe appeared chaotic to tsarist officials. Near the frontier line, there emerged a borderlands society characterised by cultural intercourse, mutual raiding and creolisation (Malikov 2011). The political situation appeared unstable, with results threatening to imperial interests. Dissatisfied with restrictions forbidding the use of pasture on the 'inner

DOI: 10.4324/9780429057977-2

side' of the Ural River and suspicious of Catherinian expansionism, Nurali, khan of the Junior Horde, briefly joined the Pugachev uprising of 1773–1774 (Bodger 1988; Olcott 1995: 36–9). Concerns about pastureland also inspired the revolt of Srym Batyr against Nurali in 1784. In the Middle Horde, khan Ablai skilfully manoeuvred between relationships with the Russian and Qing empires during his lifetime, maintaining a level of unity that did not outlive him (Noda 2016). A first attempt at changing the situation, developed by the Simbirsk governor-general Igelström in 1785, sought to introduce more direct rule by tsarist bureaucrats in the Junior Horde, but remained largely on paper (Abashin, Arapov and Bekmakhanova 2008). Part of the Junior Horde was granted permission to reside permanently on the inner side of the Ural River in 1801, forming the so-called Inner or Bukei Horde, but this too did not significantly change the situation in the Junior Horde proper (Olcott 1995: 50). Internecine strife continued in both the Junior and Middle Hordes at the dawn of the nineteenth century, while the Elder Horde remained part of the orbit of the khanates of Khiva and Khoqand.

Administrative reforms introduced during the 1820s sought to mitigate a situation that seemed increasingly unacceptable to tsarist officials. In the Middle Horde, Mikhail Speranskii introduced a set of 'Regulations on the Siberian Kirgiz'[1] that represented a significantly more interventionist approach to rule on the steppe – creating new fixed territorial divisions, investing power in officials formally chosen by the Kazaks (but subordinated to Russian officials in district centres and the regional centre in Omsk) and encouraging settlement on the land (Martin 2001: 36–9). The territory of the Junior Horde was divided into three areas, each led by a 'sultan-ruler' (*sultan-pravitel'*), with lower-level native administrators under them, all appointed by tsarist officials in Orenburg; 1844's 'Statute on administration of the Orenburg Kirgiz' refined and clarified this system, less direct and less interventionist than practices in the Middle Horde. There were some basic commonalities, though. In both hordes, the title of 'khan' was abolished, new forms of taxation appeared and some customs (including vengeance and mutual raiding, or *barymta*) brought under the auspices of imperial rather than customary law (Martin 1997).

The reforms, striking at the heart of older power structures and influential groups, could hardly pass unchallenged. Most famously, the 1837–1847 rebellion of Kenisary Qasimov of the Middle Horde, although in no sense a national liberation movement (Sabol 2003a), had a significant following and was a reaction to the growing economic and political constraints that new administrative measures, and the increased Russian presence that came with them, represented. Though unsuccessful, these revolts troubled administrators who sought control of the steppe and secure frontiers.

Indeed, there were several reasons why the empire's military presence in the steppe increased in parallel with the growth of its institutional presence, and that the fortified lines moved further south. A first set of new fortifications built in the 1820s, it was hoped, would provide a greater degree of control over subjects of whom new demands were now being made. Just as importantly, the Kazaks of the Elder Horde began to turn to Russia as a source of protection from the expansionist intentions of the khanate of Khoqand, at the zenith of its power during the first quarter of the nineteenth century (Levi 2017: 120–2). Much as their counterparts in the Junior and Middle Hordes had done in the face of the Jungar threat, they began to petition to become subjects of the tsar, starting in 1818 (Abashin et al. 2008: 44). Movement south brought Russians into contact with both Khoqand and the khanate of Khiva, both of whose interests conflicted with tsarist ideas of proper order in the steppe, trade interests and pretensions to great-power status in a region increasingly thought to be civilisationally inferior. It was the Khivan influence on the Kazaks considered (if dubiously) to be tsarist subjects and, especially, exaggerated reports of a thriving trade in Russian slaves in the khanate that inspired V.A. Perovskii, governor-general of Orenburg, to attempt a disastrously failed military campaign against it in 1839 (Morrison

2014d). In the wake of this humbling, extending the lines and maintaining more troops seemed, to convinced proponents of expansion like Perovskii, to be the only means of maintaining order and ensuring the success of expansion (Olcott 1995: 73). Thus, in the early 1850s tsarist forces began a pincer movement from the northwest and northeast. The movement from the northwest established a new fortified line along the Syr-Darya River and drove Khoqandian forces out of the northern reaches of their territory, most famously during the storm of Ak-Mechet' in 1853. The move from the northeast brought lands along the Ili River and in the foothills of the Semirech'e Alatau under imperial control, with the foundation of fort Vernoe (present-day Almaty) in 1854. It consolidated tsarist rule over the Kazaks of the Great Horde and brought some Kyrgyz, too, into the imperial fold. So, the situation would remain for several years, during which the Crimean War commanded the empire's attention. The movement south, and the conquest of Turkestan, would only resume in the 1860s.

The conquest of Turkestan

Contrary to popular belief, the movement to Turkestan had little to do with the initiative of 'men on the spot,' or with rivalry with Britain for control of Central Asia (*pace* e.g. Mackenzie 1974; Sergeev 2012). It was instead a matter of strategic imperatives internal to the Russian Empire (Morrison 2014a). The position of the tsarist lines had obvious strategic flaws. The far end of the western line (Fort Perovskii, the former Ak-Mechet') and far end of the eastern line (Vernoe) were more than a thousand kilometres apart, and the space between them lacked anything that looked, under imperial eyes, like a viable natural frontier; the Syr-Darya line itself was built in particularly unhealthy and impractical locations (Morrison 2014b). It seemed necessary to bring the lines together, establish a stable frontier and extend further 'protection' to Kazak subjects of the empire thought to need it. But despite the famous assurances of foreign minister A.M. Gorchakov that imperial expansion would stop on the unification of the lines, rather than continuing conflict with 'more regularly constituted states' (i.e. the khanates of Khoqand, Khiva and Bukhara), uniting the lines was only a prelude (Pierce 1960: 20). All three khanates were conquered little more than a decade after the movement to unite the lines had begun, with Khoqand the last to fall in 1876; the Transcaspian region (modern-day Turkmenistan) followed piecemeal in the 1880s, and with Anglo-British agreement on the border with Afghanistan in the Pamirs in 1895, Russian territorial control in Central Asia reached its fullest extent.

Forward movements by tsarist forces in the early 1860s brought them into further battle with Khoqandian forces, and by 1864, movement south (from Perovsk) and west (from Vernoe) to unite the lines was their chief objective (Morrison 2014c: 8). This seemingly simple objective proved indeterminate and difficult to control, as Alexander Morrison has shown, because of the absence of a suitable natural frontier. In 1864, as forces moving south under Col. N.A. Verevkin took the city of Turkestan, and a column under Col. M.G. Cherniaev moved west, taking Aulie-Ata and Chimkent, they moved through land where officials in St. Petersburg (especially Minister of War D.A. Miliutin) hoped to find such a frontier. They did not find it, but they found lands incomparably superior for provisioning and quartering troops to those through which the Syr-Darya line passed. Tashkent in particular recommended itself as the linchpin of the line – a major Khoqandian city, an important commercial entrepôt and the key to rich lands populated by sedentary agriculturalists. When Cherniaev tried unsuccessfully to take it in 1864, and succeeded in the attempt the following year, though he certainly wished to burnish his personal reputation in doing so, he was not straying far from the logic of his mission.

The conquest of Tashkent 'led to a direct collision between Russia and Bukhara' (Abashin, Arapov and Bekmakhanova 2008:74). The years 1866 and 1867 saw advances against Khoqand

and Bukhara, conquering the major cities of Khojent and Jizzakh; by 1867 sufficient territory south of the old lines was under tsarist control to necessitate the creation of a new political unit, the governor-generalship of Turkestan, with Gen. K.P. von Kaufman as its first governor-general. Kaufman concluded a treaty with Khudoiar, khan of Khoqand, early in 1868 that effectively neutralised the khanate, freeing him to direct his energies against Bukhara. The major Bukharan city of Samarkand was taken in May 1868, and a treaty signed less than two months later. Already, Khiva remained the only fully independent khanate in Central Asia, and Kaufman sent multiple columns against a polity he considered particularly impudent and unmanageable in 1873. It fell the same year, in a campaign that featured an as-yet uncharacteristic amount of bloodshed (Kaufman's massacre of several thousand Yomud Turkmen), becoming another vassal state of the empire.

Khiva and Bukhara retained their status as protectorates until the empire's end. Khoqand did not. Dissatisfaction with Khuodoiar's pro-Russian direction after 1868 prompted his Kyrgyz subjects to rebel against him repeatedly in 1873 and 1874; when the Kazak troops he sent to suppress the latter revolt instead joined the rebels, the situation became serious (Levi 2017: 204–8).[2] Under the leadership of Aburrakhman Avtobachi, a Kazak officer formerly part of Khudoiar's inner circle, this flared into an anti-Russian revolt that seized the Fergana valley. Kaufman himself, and especially Col. M.D. Skobelev, suppressed this anti-Russian movement with brutality, surpassing all previously accepted norms of the Turkestan campaigns. When the revolt was finally extinguished, the khanate of Khoqand was erased from the map, its remaining territory incorporated into the Russian Empire as Fergana oblast, with Skobelev as its first military governor.

Expansion left unresolved questions further to the south. Most notably, interest in securing the east coast of the Caspian and the conquest of Khiva brought the empire into conquest with the Turkmen tribes (most populous among them the Yomuds and Tekkes) who populated the deserts to the south and east of the Caspian. Movement into the desert consisted of largely ineffectual deep reconnaissance from the new coastal base of Krasnovodsk during the first half of the 1870s. Only rumours that the Tekkes, long notorious raiders, might become Persian subjects (thus creating a greater threat on the frontier) overcame St. Petersburg's reluctance to acquire further new and remote territory (Morris 1975: 530). Expeditions under Gen. N.P. Lomakin in 1877 and 1878, though, did little to change the situation, and when the Tekkes defeated the hapless Lomakin when he attempted to storm their stronghold of Geok-Tepe in 1879, official Petersburg thirsted for a decisive conclusion to the conflict. Skobelev, at the height of his fame in the aftermath of the Russo-Turkish War, returned to Central Asia at the head of a well-equipped expedition in 1880. Besieging the Tekkes at Geok-Tepe, he brought the conquest to a sadistic climax on 12 January 1881, killing 6,500 within the fortress proper and about 8,000 in cavalry pursuit after it fell (Campbell 2019a: 38). Turkmen lands further east, around the oasis city of Merv, entered the empire in 1884. The situation between the Russian Empire's southern frontier here and the British Empire's northernmost frontier in Afghanistan remained indefinite for another decade, which resulted in much sabre-rattling in the press of both empires and threatened war once, before final agreement on the border in 1895.

New territory and new laws

Uniting the lines and pushing further south prompted administrative changes. The steppe was now not a frontier but an internal province, and in Turkestan the empire had gained a population largely of sedentary agriculturalists, and a region with much more urban settlement than the steppe. Territorial reorganisation followed the early stages of the conquest, and a study commission under the guidance of F.K. Girs was dispatched to the Kazak steppe and Turkestan from 1865 to 1867 to undertake the research of local conditions believed to be necessary before new laws were written (Campbell 2017: 31–62). Two governing statutes emerged from this effort, the Turkestan Statute of 1867 and the so-called 'Provisional Statute' for the steppe regions of 1868. These remained the legal frameworks for most of the territory discussed in this volume until 1886 (in Turkestan's case) and 1891 (in the case of the steppe).[3]

The Turkestan governor-generalship was created in 1867 by separating the new territories in Turkestan from the governor-generalship of Orenburg, an administrative centre more than a thousand miles away from the new conquests, and initially consisted of the provinces of Semirech'e and Syr-Darya. Its administrative centre was at Tashkent, in the heart of the new territory, and many of the later conquests were added to its territory. The steppe regions were reorganised a year later. The oblast of the Orenburg Kazaks (populated mostly by Junior Horde Kazaks, and subordinated to the Orenburg governor-general) was divided into two provinces, Ural'sk and Turgai, and the oblast of the Siberian Kazaks (populated mostly by Middle Horde Kazaks, and subordinated to the governor-general of Western Siberia in Omsk) divided into Akmolinsk and Semipalatinsk Provinces. These four steppe provinces, populated largely by Kazak pastoral nomads, were all under the Provisional Statute even before they were unified into a single governor-generalship of the steppe in 1881. This statute differed from the laws governing Turkestan in several important respects, and these differences were driven by official perceptions of the particular local conditions in each region. Turkestan was populated by Great Horde Kazaks, Kyrgyz and 'Sarts' (in Russian administrative usage, a catch-all term for sedentary Central Asians who would now be referred to as Uzbeks and Tajiks), and by a mixture of sedentary agriculturalists, urban dwellers and pastoral nomads; laws and institutions meant to serve pastoral nomads could not be applied straightforwardly there.

Revisions to these governing statutes and territorial divisions ensued as a result of both the re-evaluation of earlier policy and the factional struggles among ministries and local administrators. The 1886 permanent statute for Turkestan reduced, to an extent, the power of its military leadership in favour of civilian ministries and officials, bringing it 'only slightly closer to the imperial system' as a whole (Brower 2003: 65). The Steppe Statute of 1891, on the other hand, largely tweaked, formalised and made explicit measures written into the earlier Provisional Statute; even without a change in principle, though, bureaucratisation and especially the development of the internal logic of earlier land law added up to massive change in the life of the steppe provinces. The following three sections will trace the most important developments in culture, governance and the economy in empire's Central Asian provinces during its last five decades of rule.

Law and governance

Power in tsarist Central Asia ultimately rested in the hands of governors-general. Governor-generalships were a characteristic institution for territories outside the Russian core of the empire (Matsuzato 2012: 83). The scope of the responsibilities of the men entrusted with them and the powers placed at their disposal were vast. Their chanceries were the central nodes of administration in the region, coordinating communication between the ministries of St. Petersburg and lower-level administrative instances. The chanceries dealt with a huge range of matters, including policing, taxation and personnel, while the governor-general's council debated policy and made recommendations. Some central ministries also had representatives in the regional administration, which at times functioned as a limitation on the governor-general's power and engendered confusion about administrative priorities (Martin 2001: 56–7). Governor-generalships consisted of several provinces (oblasts) each headed by a military governor, whose administration was essentially a microcosm of that of the governor-generalship (Pierce 1960: 66). The provinces, in their turn, were divided into multiple districts (*uezd*s), each with a commandant (*nachalnik*) heavily burdened with care for police matters, the judiciary, public health, education and more. Essentially, as Morrison (2008: 127) notes, the district commandants bore the responsibilities that *zemstvo* assemblies assumed in the core of the empire on top of the cares for order and security. Under the prevailing system of 'military-popular administration' (*voenno-narodnoe upravlenie*) these governors and district commandants were military men, generals at the gubernatorial ranks and officers in other senior bureaucratic posts (Morrison 2008: 126). (Some steppe provinces, like Akmolinsk and Semipalatinsk, later had their status changed, provided with civilian governors subordinated to the Ministry of Internal Affairs as well as, awkwardly, the governor-general.) These officials bore vast workloads, and many lacked the linguistic training necessary to communicate with locals or to understand the communities they governed on more than a superficial and stereotyped level (Morrison 2008: 146–51). The lack of finances and qualified manpower, combined with bureaucratic infighting on multiple levels, left tsarist administration in Central Asia much less powerful in practice than it was on paper. It combined life-and-death power and the ability to set new policies (and alter existing ones on the spot) with misapprehensions about native life and permanent blind spots.

Indeed, day-to-day governance depended strongly on the actions of low-level native administrators of cantons (*volost*s), and villages (*auls* and *kishlak*s for nomadic and sedentary populations, respectively). The cantons, the larger units, consisted of several *auls* or *kishlak*s, whose elders were supervised by the canton administrator (*upravitel'*). All of these were indirectly elected positions for salaried three-year terms: representatives of a set number of households acted as electors. The population's electoral power was not limitless, as their choices were subject to confirmation by the district commandant and could be removed from their posts in case of misconduct; elections could also be suspended in extraordinary circumstances, as after the Andijan revolt of 1898 (see below). These were positions that came with serious responsibility, including observation for signs of criminality or revolt, collecting taxes, convening elections and punishing petty crime; these responsibilities, and the power and potential revenue that came with them, made them very attractive, and elections could be highly competitive 'power contests among the village elites' (Morrison 2008: 183), rife with bribery and even violence. In the elections, elites whose power drew on sources predating tsarist rule clashed with new groups who derived power precisely from the social and economic change the empire created. The problems of the electoral system, and the unease with dependence on these native officials, prompted calls for reform aimed at greater supervision and Russianisation of local administration. In the end, though, the system remained roughly as it was, with its advantages (it was relatively cheap and demanded little manpower from the metropole, of which the Central Asian provinces were always short) and flaws, until 1917.

Central Asian subjects of the tsar existed under a patchwork of criminal and civil laws, and were subject to the jurisdiction of multiple officials, depending on the issue at hand. In the steppe provinces, the Provisional Statute continued a trend that Martin (2001: 50) argues dates to the Speranskii regulations more than four decades earlier. That is, it attempted to systematise and bring under bureaucratic control a system based on Kazak customary law (*adat*) adjudicated by traditional judges called *biy*s. Under the Provisional Statute these judges were elected by the population, confirmed by state officials and bound to set procedures. At the same time, the long-term goal remained the integration of the Kazaks to the general tsarist legal system, so they were given the right to have cases judged in Russian courts according to Russian laws; certain crimes were considered too serious to be adjudicated by the *biy* court at all. A similar parallel system with elected judges obtained in Turkestan but with still further variation. On the basis of a 'largely artificial' (Morrison 2015: 132) distinction between customary law and *shari'a*, nomads (largely Kazaks and Kyrgyz) were subject to the *biy* court, while sedentary natives (both agriculturalists and urban dwellers) were under the jurisdiction of the *qazi* court, based notionally on *shari'a*. It was a system rife with misunderstandings. Attempts to collect and codify *adat* were incomplete and, by definition, privileged some interpretations over others; *shari'a*, too, was 'more flexible than colonial administrators realized' (Morrison 2008: 245), and reifying it as though it was a unitary and unchanging object represented a significant change in the legal world of Turkestan's natives. Bureaucratisation and state supervision opened these legal institutions up to criticism and circumscribed their authority (Sartori 2017: 30). This was especially the case after revisions to the original Turkestan and provisional statutes in 1886 and 1891, which restricted the competency and discretionary powers of *qazi*s and *biy*s (Martin 200: 93; Morrison 2008: 264). The long-term effects of this blended system were paradoxical. On one hand, natives had to adapt and accommodate to the demands of a new legal system that, while it claimed to maintain traditional practices, often warped and changed them; on the other, they did not receive these changes passively but saw opportunities to advance their own moral and worldly agendas in the colonial legal system (Martin 2001; Sartori 2017). This was a plural legal system that aimed to tolerate a degree of local difference while maintaining bureaucratic control. It was far from fully integrated with the rest of the empire but still represented a significant change from the past.

Cultural and religious policy

The Turkestan and Provisional Statutes treated Islam and the institutions associated with it very differently. These policy differences, in turn, depended on divergent perceptions of Islamic practices in the sedentary societies of Turkestan and the nomadic communities of the steppe. The former's greater adherence to the formal rituals and institutions of Islam as tsarist orientalists understood things meant fundamentally different challenges for governance than steppe nomads who were believed to wear their beliefs lightly, if at all.

Tsarist observers of the nineteenth century considered Kazaks to be Muslims 'in appearance only, and only temporarily' because of their non-observance of certain rituals and the persistence of syncretic practices among them (Levshin 1832; Krasovskii 1868, v. 1: 391). This was not actually the case: much of the steppe was undergoing an Islamic revival during the tsarist era, and conversion to Islam was a fundamental part of their group identity (DeWeese 1994; Frank 2001). But imperial officials made policy on the basis of this supposed fact, although their priorities changed over time. During the Catherinian era and the first half of the nineteenth century, Robert Crews has argued, 'state elites associated Islam with civility' and promoted Islamic institutions as a means of governing and civilising the Kazaks and other unruly subjects (Crews 2006: 199). But as Islamophobia grew in the context of the Caucasian wars, this began to seem a less tenable strategy, and the idea that the inhabitants of the steppe were bad or temporary Muslims seemed to argue now for reducing Islamic influence on them, and with it a potential threat to imperial rule. Hence the Provisional Statute restricted the construction of mosques and the number of mullahs permitted (one per *volost*), while removing the steppe provinces from the jurisdiction of the Orenburg Islamic Spiritual Assembly, the Catherinian institution charged with regulating religious affairs in the Volga basin and the steppe. The Steppe Statute only reaffirmed these regulations, despite substantial criticism and resistance from the Kazaks and administrative misgivings about their efficacy. Official restrictions could not reduce the Kazaks' interest in Islamic education and observance – administrators knew too little, and their reach was too short for that – but they annoyed, antagonised and drove such observance further out of the state's view.

Turkestan, home to several major sites of Islamic learning, seemed to be another matter entirely. Here Kaufman, equipped with awesome powers, feared what he and others termed Muslim 'fanaticism' but also feared active attempts at conversion and persecution directed against a population vastly outnumbering imperial officials and soldiers (Brower 2003: 32–3). He favoured, instead, a policy of disinterest (*ignorirovanie*), which amounted to 'firm measures against Muslim religious institutions' while leaving private religious matters and *shari'a* untouched (Brower 1997: 119–20; Sahadeo 2007: 33). This contradictory and nominally uninterested approach, despite criticisms that it interfered either too much or too little in local religious life, survived Kaufman's death in 1881 and the revised statute of 1886 with little change. However, events on the ground ultimately lent weight to some critics' arguments. In 1898, a Sufi elder (*ishan*) named Madali led about 2,000 followers in an attack on an army camp near the city of Andijan in the Fergana Valley, killing 22 soldiers as they slept (Komatsu 2004). Though the badly armed rebels were quickly suppressed, the event had enormous resonance. The very fact that a religiously inspired rebellion had been conceived and carried out made Kaufman's disregard of Islam seem instead like dangerous ignorance. The new governor-general of Turkestan, S.M. Dukhovskoi, strongly advocated a more interventionist approach, most notoriously in a report, 'Islam in Turkestan,' presented to Nicholas II the following year. Dukhovskoi's report presented an 'apocalyptic vision of Islam in arms against the empire' (Brower 2003: 100) and demanded strict controls, including the ability to administratively discipline Muslim clergy and banning the pilgrimage to Mecca. Though Dukhovskoi's report and recommendations were mostly rejected in St. Petersburg, the Andijan revolt had a 'profound' (Morrison 2012: 260) impact on Turkestan's administrators for the last 20 years of imperial rule. The collection of materials on Islam that Dukhovskoi commissioned in its aftermath and circulated to local administrators bore the heavy stamp of the Kazan' Theological Academy, source of the most fearful and contemptuous thought about Islam in the empire (Campbell 2017:168–9). Anti-Muslim paranoia left administrators in Turkestan chasing shadows, pursuing conspiracies where none had existed (Morrison 2012), and implementing obnoxious policies in the face of official statements about religious toleration.

In education, too, tsarist officials intervened earlier and further in the steppe provinces than they did in Turkestan. Although both were home to a growing network of colonial 'Russo-native' schools by the turn of the twentieth century, the colonial school network was significantly more developed in the steppe. Well-born Kazak boys (most famous among them the ethnographer Ch. Ch. Valikhanov) attended the imperial cadet colleges (*kadetskii korpus*) in Omsk and Orenburg, and Orenburg was home to a school for Kazak boys from 1850 on. These institutions were to prepare a small cohort of children for imperial service, whether in the army or as low- to mid-level functionaries (administrators, scribes, clerks, translators). The later 'Russo-Kazak' schools on the steppe drew on these precedents but expanded both their ambit and the population they served. The Provisional Statute provided a modestly increased subsidy for education, and Turgai oblast took the lead in introducing schools, with the particular involvement of a Kazak trainee from the Orenburg boys' school, Ibrai Altynsarin (Campbell 2017: 74–80). The schools were inspired by the vernacular-language methodologies of the Kazan' missionary N.I. Il'minskii, who had pioneered the use of vernacular language alongside Russian and Cyrillic transcription in missionary schools in the Volga basin; here, though, the goal was not conversion but a general sort of Russianisation and cultural rapprochement, alongside the ongoing practical matter of training functionaries for the expanding colonial state (Dowler 2001: 120–1). This rapprochement meant acquiring some knowledge of Russian, arithmetic, geography and natural science, and doing so in more 'civilized' material surroundings. It did not, however, mean that basic Islamic catechistics were to be excluded from the curriculum – this was considered neither incompatible with gradual rapprochement nor suitable to convince parents to send their children to the new schools. In Turkestan, because of Kaufman's programme of *ignorirovanie*, colonial schools were only systematically introduced later, in the 1880s (Bendrikov 1960: 70–2). Central district schools were established first, with canton and village-level schools (sometimes mobile, among nomadic populations) coming later and teaching a reduced programme focused on literacy; several trade and professional schools were also opened, and a small number of graduates of the lower-level colonial schools would go on to enter gymnasia, technical schools and universities around the empire. In both the steppe and Turkestan, it was only a minority of the local population that ever visited these schools. Turkestan as a whole had only 3,000 students in its Russo-native schools in 1909 (Morrison 2008: 72), while in 1898 no steppe province enrolled more than 11 per cent of its school-age children in state schools (Tazhibaev 1962: 36–7). Much of the population continued, as before, to receive a basic Islamic education in the primary school (*mekteb*), with higher religious education available in the urban *medrese*. Still, the colonial school network sheds useful light on what imperial bureaucrats wished to do in Central Asia, on the sort of cultural development they wished to see. Moreover, even this small number of school graduates would go on to play an outsized role in the political life of the empire in its final years.

Tsarist cultural and educational policy engendered a range of responses among Central Asians, as the challenge that empire represented inspired new forms of cooperation and resistance aimed at adaptation and survival. Perhaps the best known of these was the Jadid movement, inspired by the Crimean Tatar Ismail Bey Gasprinskii and his new (phonetic) method of teaching Arabic literacy but, as Adeeb Khalid (1998: 93) notes, rooted in social conditions particular to Turkestan. The Central Asian Jadids focused on the idea of progress, especially scientific progress, arguing that secular knowledge of the world was both necessary and 'fully congruent with the 'true' essence of Islam' (Khalid 1998:113). Through their print organs and reformed primary schools, they admonished the Muslims of Turkestan, as a community, to abandon what they framed as ignorance and draw from Russian and European models so that they might survive. Some Kazak intellectuals engaged with the empire employed similar rhetoric to the Jadids of Turkestan, but there are important differences between the two groups. The latter were by and large products of Islamic educational institutions. The former had more commonly passed through tsarist schools, both the Russo-native elementary schools and institutions of higher learning; they were less likely to centre Islam and the Muslim community in their arguments. The Jadids saw the Muslims of Turkestan as the community they were addressing, while Kazak intellectuals viewed the Kazaks as a distinct community and articulated nationalist (or at least autonomist) visions for it. Still, Kazak nationalists, much like the Jadids, were 'committed ... to improving the social and economic status of the Kazak community through education, literacy, publishing, and political activism' (Sabol 2003b: 51–2).

Members of these groups were frequently strident critics of imperial cultural and economic policy, often falling afoul of the censor or of police organs. Still, they sought friendly interlocutors and shared some important assumptions of the 'civilizing' party among tsarist officials. Therefore, they made efforts to participate in and engage with imperial institutions. They strongly supported the post-1905 parliament, the Duma, and the Kazaks elected to it were mostly affiliated with the moderately liberal Kadet party; both groups would seek to rally society's support for the war effort from 1914 on. Yet the farcical elections to the Duma and P.A. Stolypin's electoral coup of 3 June 1907, made this participation difficult at the highest level, and the war effort too was fraught with tensions and difficulties (about which more below). Imperial institutions proved unable to keep the promises that some subjects believed they had made.

'Progressive' thought and a positive orientation towards secular knowledge were not the only, or even the most common, response to tsarist rule. Indeed, the common portrayal of older clerical and cultural elites as 'unreasoning obscurantists opposed to all positive change' (Khalid 1998: 5) owes much to the progressives' own rhetorical strategies. Rather, 'multiple modes of Muslim religiosity ... were prevalent before the Jadids, [and] were prevalent still during the time of the Jadids,' and Muslims in the steppe and Turkestan continued to address the concerns of their religious community after the conquest, and to adapt to the demands and structures it created (DeWeese 2016: 37–92). Rather, Muslims derided in some sources as stagnant and traditionalist engaged with the new world of print, cast a critical eye over their own schools and continued vibrant debates about jurisprudence and daily life (Eden, Sartori, and DeWeese 2016: 1–36; Frank 2016: 166–92). It was a small and self-conscious group of modernisers who came to the fore after 1917, but their victory and their dominant discursive position were far from foreordained. Much remains to be learned about the complexity of Islamic thought and practice in pre-revolutionary Central Asian society.

Economic change and resettlement

The colonisation of Central Asia under tsarist rule took two forms, official and unofficial. Official settlement was, initially, tightly restricted, as officials feared the disruptive potential of new arrivals from the Slavic core, who would require land and observation, and of whose 'civilizing' and economic potential they took a dim view (Remnev and Suvorova 2008). Colonisation by Cossacks was always part of imperial policy, from the establishment of the first frontier line; this population, organised in Central Asia into the Ural, Orenburg, Siberian and Semirech'e hosts, received land grants in exchange for military service, frequently hiring local labour or renting sections of land to locals (Kendirbay 2002: 2–13; Martin 2001: 62–5). Established Central Asian cities like Tashkent and Samarkand gained new Russian settlements, and new Russian military and administrative centres like Vernyi and Akmolinsk expanded, populated by state officials, soldiers, artisans, merchants and unskilled labourers (Morrison 2008: 46–50; Sahadeo 2007: 108–27). Officially sanctioned peasant settlement was limited, with groups of picked settlers forming small settlements in Turkestan (particularly in Semirech'e) during the 1870s. A large number of settlers during this period, especially to the steppe provinces, were irregulars, arriving without official permission. These were the so-called *samovol'tsy*, arriving in search of land that rumour had it was abundant and there for the taking, and fleeing land shortages at home; as Demko (1969: 51) has it, both 'push' and 'pull' forces brought them to the steppe. They were sometimes granted allotments; in other cases they rented lands from nomads, and in still others simply seized it from them (Kendirbay 2002: 14–15). Their numbers grew after the emancipation of the serfs in 1861, with the northern part of Akmolinsk oblast particularly favoured by would-be settlers.

This policy began to change in the 1880s, as a tsarist state fearful of migration sought to legalise it and bring it under state control. The year 1881 saw the approval of an experimental law permitting limited migration in hopes of reducing the problem of peasant land-hunger in some parts of the empire; this law was superseded by a less restrictive law offering aid to peasants who particularly needed to settle on new lands (Treadgold 1957: 76–9). This new direction intensified in the 1890s. The Steppe Statute of 1891 rendered explicit an idea that was implicit in the old Provisional Statute. According to the former, all pastures occupied by the Kazaks were officially state lands, which they used on rights of long-term rental. The Steppe Statute declared that any of these state lands, if found to be surplus to nomads' requirements (*izlishki*), could be seized for other state purposes.[4] At the same time, the wave of irregular settlers grew, spurred especially by the drought and famine of 1891–1892 in European Russia. Regulating and supporting this movement began to seem like sound policy – the movement of Slavic peasant agriculturalists to Central Asia appeared to serve both the Russianising agenda of Nicholas II and the programme of economic modernisation and railway construction favoured by Minister of Finances S. Iu. Witte. The local administrators responsible for welcoming these new arrivals and managing the strained relationships with locals that ensued did not consistently share this sanguine view of colonisation, and determined opponents sometimes succeeded in closing their provinces to resettlement for a period, but the overall vector of tsarist policy in this area is clear. The Committee on the Siberian Railroad alienated land for settlers near the railway line during the first half of the 1890s (Kendirbay 2002: 39–40). From 1896 on, a series of statistical expeditions to the steppe provinces and Turkestan attempted to determine precisely how much land a typical family of nomads needed for its survival, so as to subtract this number from the total acreage in a district or province and thereby determine its 'colonizing capacity' (*emkost'*), the number of settlers it could receive.

After the revolution of 1905, these calculations became particularly aggressive, as the Resettlement Administration responsible for colonisation and economic development on the imperial periphery was moved from the cautious Ministry of Internal Affairs to the more activist Main Administration of Agriculture and Land Management (Holquist 2010: 152). Under the government of P.A. Stolypin, attention and resources were lavished on this organisation, and the now-complete Trans-Siberian (1896) and Orenburg-Tashkent (1903) railroads facilitated the rapid circulation of people and goods. Semirech'e and the steppe, it was hoped, would be a second breadbasket for the empire, transporting food by rail to the core and for export. Turkestan, outside of Semirech'e, received comparatively few settlers during the tsarist era. However, with administrative encouragement, rural agriculturalists increasingly shifted their cultivation to American long-staple cotton for export to the textile mills of European Russia. This 'mitigated cotton monoculture' (Brower 2003: 77) only accelerated with the extension of the rail network. Russian colonisation here, then, assumed a supplemental role, which at times conflicted with the economic imperative of maximising acreage sown to cotton (Peterson 2018: 157).

Resettlement officials pinned high hopes on economic modernisation through colonisation, but it was fraught in practice. Both local activists (like the Kazak intellectual and Duma deputy A.N. Bokeikhanov) and official observers (most notably senator K.K. Pahlen, sent to inspect Turkestan in 1908–1909) criticised the deleterious effects of mass resettlement. The technocratic approach to colonisation concealed chaos: local resettlement officials, locked in a struggle with military and civilian administrators, abused their power; settler villages in the steppe disrupted pastoral nomadic migration; the water requirements of cotton cultivation came at the expense of cultivating staple foods. Yet such criticisms and observable problems did not significantly alter the momentum of resettlement policy. Between 1893 and 1912, more than a million souls settled in the steppe provinces and Semirech'e (Aziatskaia Rossiia 1914). The cumulative effects of this demographic and economic shift proved destabilising and transformative.

Revolt and collapse

In the summer of 1916, a revolt that seized several regions of Central Asia, including the oblasts of Semirech'e, Turgai, Fergana and Transcaspia, revealed the shortcomings of imperial rule. The demands of mobilisation for total warfare were incompatible with the grievances tsarist rule had created. The proximal cause of the revolt was a hasty and ill-considered edict from tsar Nicholas II of 25 June 1916 conscripting indigenous Central Asians for labour in the rear of the army (Uyama 2001: 80–3). The implementation of this order, Tomohiko Uyama (2019) has shown, was particularly disastrous in Central Asia because of the weakness of the state structures the empire had created. Metrical books (i.e. records of births, marriages and deaths) were not maintained here, meaning that who was actually subject to conscription was a matter of guesswork or arbitrary judgement. Compounding the situation, local people and tsarist administrators were both suspicious (sometimes with good reason) of the native administrators responsible for making these difficult decisions. It was this unusually chaotic implementation of an unpopular policy that fanned the flames of popular anger. Yet in some areas, especially Semirech'e, mass resettlement had long prepared the ground for revolt, as the presence of settlers put overwhelming pressure on land, water sources and migration routes (Happel 2010). Here, the Kazaks and the Kyrgyz revolted not just against conscription but against the threat to their way of life that resettlement represented.

In some areas, rebellion was quickly extinguished; in others it continued until early 1917, especially in Turgai oblast, where under the leadership of Amangeldi Imanov, up to 50,000 people took up arms, established some state structures and elected khans (Uyama 2001: 84–5). Tsarist punitive detachments sought to restore order with the overwhelming force that military governors believed the local population to require (Campbell 2019b). In Semirech'e, settler vigilantes committed terrible and indiscriminate reprisals against natives for violence committed against other settlers (Morrison 2019: 213–15). Perhaps 250,000 Kyrgyz fled this cycle of violence, crossing the border to China, with many perishing in the attempt. In total, more than 3,000 settlers and more than 100,000 locals died in the revolt, with enormous damage to crops, livestock and property. It is difficult to guess how tsarist officials would have addressed this situation and its underlying causes, although a reassertion of the primacy of the Russian nationality and of the rights of settlers in particular seems likely; A.N. Kuropatkin, an old Turkestan hand appointed governor-general in the summer of 1916, ordered more nomadic land opened to resettlement and the displacement of the Kyrgyz in areas that had witnessed violence against settlers to the arid, mountainous Naryn region (Brower 2003: 167).

But while revolt still smouldered in Turgai, and other regions dealt with its baleful consequences, the February Revolution brought new changes. Kazak intellectuals, for the most part, supported the early activities of the Provisional Government, but broke with it over the course of 1917 because of its failure to resolve the land question in a satisfactory manner; the opposition of liberal Russians to autonomy for the steppe also played a role (Sabol 2003b: 139–41). In Tashkent, at the heart of Turkestan's political life, a dual-power situation pitted supporters of the Provisional Government against the more radical Tashkent Soviet (Park 1957: 9). The Central Asian Jadids saw the era of revolution as 'an era of opportunity' and were enthused at the prospect of 'inclusion in the universalist order proclaimed by the Provisional Government' (Khalid 2015: 9, 59). The Bolsheviks' revolution in October 1917 changed the decision space for progressives and nationalists in the steppe and Turkestan alike, since it 'seemed to doom any aspirations ... concerning cultural political autonomy' (Sabol 2003b: 142). The Kazak nationalists, leading a political movement calling itself Alash Orda, created an autonomous political unit recognised by the anti-Bolshevik Siberian government in the summer of 1918; in Turkestan, progressives founded an autonomous state centred on Khoqand late in 1917. The Khoqand Autonomy was liquidated ruthlessly by Red Guards in less than three months. Alash Orda's cooperation with the Siberian government was always fragile, and it turned out that their new allies were no greater friends of national autonomy than the Bolsheviks were. As the tide turned against anti-Soviet forces, and central Bolshevik organs worked to find common ground with progressives in Turkestan in particular, seeking a modus vivendi began to seem the best and only viable way forward, despite the subordination and discipline inherent in such an arrangement (see Khalid 2015: 90–116). In rural areas, a struggle for control of local resources and power, fuelled by opposition to progressive and Muslim incursions, known as the Basmachi movement, continued into the mid-1920s. The years of conflict were accompanied by severe food shortages, creating a struggle for survival in both urban and rural areas (Buttino 2007: 211–38). The effort to establish meaningful Soviet power would thus take place in a setting riven with internal conflicts and grave doubts about the Soviet project.

Although Soviet rule in Central Asia, in many senses, came to represent a radical departure from the practices of the tsarist era, in other respects it exhibited important continuities with imperial rule (see Cameron 2018 and Peterson 2018, *inter alia*). While historians continue to debate the legacy of imperial rule to the Soviet era, it is clear that the changes wrought during this period significantly influenced the challenges and possibilities that the Bolsheviks faced as they came to power.

Notes

1. Both the present-day Kazaks and Kyrgyz were referred to as *Kirgiz* in pre-revolutionary Russian. I preserve this usage *sic* when quoting from period documents but employ the contemporary ethnonyms when using my own words.
2. These Kazaks were referred to as 'Qipchaqs' in local sources (Levi 2017: 29).
3. Transcaspia was governed under a separate (also 'provisional') statute from 1890, while Khiva and Bukhara retained the status of protectorates with restricted sovereignty after the conquest (Becker 1968).
4. The 1886 Turkestan statute also declared nomadic lands to be state property, but a law regulating the seizure of surplus lands was not passed until 1910, during the Third Duma.

Bibliography

Abashin, S., Arapov, D., & Bekmakhanova, N. (eds.). (2008) *Tsentral'naia Aziia v sostave Rossiiskoi imperii*, Novoe literaturnoe obozrenie, Moscow.
Marks, A. F. (1914) *Aziatskaia Rossiia: liudi i poriadki za Uralom*, St. Petersburg.
Becker, S. (1968) *Russia's protectorates in Central Asia: Bukhara and Khiva, 1865–1924*, Harvard University Press, Cambridge.
Bendirkov, K. (1960) *Ocherki po istorii narodnogo obrazovaniia v Turkestane*, izd-vo. Akademii pedgogicheskikh nauk RSFSR, Moscow.
Bodger, A. (1988) *The Kazakhs and the Pugachev uprising in Russia, 1773–1775*, Indiana University Press, Bloomington.
Brower, D. (1997) 'Islam and ethnicity: Russian colonial policy in Turkestan,' in D. Brower & E. Lazzerini (eds.), *Russia's orient: imperial borderlands and peoples, 1700–1917*, Indiana University Press, Bloomington, pp. 115–135.
Brower, D. (2003) *Turkestan and the fate of the Russian Empire*, RoutledgeCurzon, New York.
Buttino, M. (2007) *Revoliutsiia naoborot: Sredniaia Aziia mezhdu padeniem tsarskoi imperii i obrazovaniem SSSR*, trans. N. Okhotin, Zven'ia, Moscow.
Cameron, S. (2018) *The hungry steppe: famine, violence, and the making of Soviet Kazakhstan*, Cornell University Press, Ithaca.
Campbell, I. (2017) *Knowledge and the ends of empire: Kazak intermediaries and Russian rule on the steppe, 1731–1917*, Cornell University Press, Ithaca.
Campbell, I. (2019a) 'Bloody belonging: writing Transcaspia into the Russian Empire,' in K. Goff & L. Siegelbaum (eds.), *Empire and belonging in the Eurasian borderlands*, Cornell University Press, Ithaca, pp. 35–47.

Campbell, I. (2019b) 'Violent acculturation: Alexei Kuropatkin, the Central Asian Revolt, and the long shadow of conquest,' in A. Chokobaeva, C. Drieu, & A. Morrison (eds.), *The Central Asian Revolt of 1916: a collapsing empire in the age of war and revolution*, Manchester University Press, Manchester, pp. 191–208.

Crews, R. (2006) *For prophet and tsar: Islam and empire in Russia and Central Asia*, Harvard University Press, Cambridge.

Demko, G. (1969) *The Russian colonization of Kazakhstan 1896–1916*, Indiana University Press, Bloomington.

DeWeese, D. (1994) *Islamization and native religion in the Golden Horde: Baba Tukles and conversion to Islam in historical and epic tradition*, Pennsylvania State University Press, State College.

DeWeese, D. (2016) 'It was a dark and stagnant night ('til the Jadids brought the light): clichés, biases, and false dichotomies in the intellectual history of Central Asia,' *Journal of the Economic and Social History of the Orient* vol. 59, no. 1–2, pp. 37–92.

Dowler, W. (2001) *Classroom and empire: the politics of schooling Russia's Eastern nationalities, 1860–1917*, McGill-Queen's University Press, Montreal.

Eden, J., Sartori, P., & DeWeese, D. (2016) 'Moving beyond modernism: rethinking cultural change in Muslim Eurasia (19th–20th centuries),' *Journal of the Economic and Social History of the Orient* vol. 59, no. 1–2, pp. 1–36.

Frank, A. (2001) *Muslim religious institutions in imperial Russia: the Islamic world of Novouzensk district and the Kazakh Inner Horde, 1780–1910*, Brill, Boston.

Frank, A. (2016) 'Muslim cultural decline in imperial Russia: a manufactured crisis,' in D. Brower & E. Lazzerini (eds.), *Russia's orient: imperial borderlands and peoples, 1700–1917*, Indiana University Press, Bloomington, pp. 166–192.

Happel, J. (2010) *Nomadische Lebenswelten und zarische Politik: der Aufstand in Zentralasien 1916*, Franz Steiner Verlag, Stuttgart.

Holquist, P. (2010) '"In accord with state interests and the people's wishes": the technocratic ethos of imperial Russia's Resettlement Administration,' *Slavic Review* vol. 69, no. 1, pp. 151–179.

Kendirbay, G. (2002) *Land and people: the Russian colonization of the Kazak steppe*, Klaus Schwarz Verlag, Berlin.

Khalid, A. (1998) *The politics of Muslim cultural reform: Jadidism in Central Asia*, University of California Press, Berkeley.

Khalid, A. (2015) *Making Uzbekistan: nation, empire, and revolution in the early USSR*, Cornell University Press, Ithaca.

Khodarkovsky, M. (1992) *Where two worlds met: the Russian state and the Kalmyk nomads, 1600–1771*, Cornell University Press, Ithaca.

Komatsu, H. (2004) 'The Andijan uprising reconsidered,' in T. Sato (ed.), *Muslim societies: historical and comparative perspectives*, Routledge, London, pp. 29–61.

Krasovskii, N. (1868) *Materialy dlia statistiki i geografii Rossii, sobrannye ofitserami General'nogo Shtaba: oblast', Sibirskikh kirgizov*, St. Petersburg.

Levi, S. (2017) *The rise and fall of Khoqand, 1709–1876: Central Asia in the global age*, University of Pittsburgh Press, Pittsburgh.

Levshin, A. (1832) *Opisanie kirgiz-kazach'ikh, ili kirgiz-kaisatskikh, ord i stepei*, Karl Kraft, St. Petersburg.

Mackenzie, D. (1974) *The lion of Tashkent: the career of General M. G. Cherniaev*, University of Georgia Press, Athens.

Malikov, Y. (2011) *Tsars, Cossacks, and Nomads: the formation of a borderland culture in northern Kazakhstan in the 18th and 19th centuries*, Klaus Schwarz Verlag, Berlin.

Martin, V. (1997) 'Barymta: nomadic custom, imperial crime,' in D. Brower & E. Lazzerini (eds.), *Russia's orient: imperial borderlands and peoples, 1700–1917*, Indiana University Press, Bloomington, pp. 249–270.

Martin, V. (2001) *Law and custom on the steppe: the Kazakhs of the Middle Horde and Russian colonialism in the nineteenth century*, Curzon Press, Richmond.

Matsuzato, K. (2012) 'Intra-bureaucratic debate on the institution of Russian governors-general in the mid-nineteenth century,' in T. Uyama (ed.), *Asiatic Russia: imperial power in regional and international contexts*, Routledge, New York, pp. 83–101.

Morris, P. (1975) 'The Russians in Central Asia, 1870–1887,' *Slavonic and Eastern European Review* vol. 53, no. 133, pp. 521–538.

Morrison, A. (2008) *Russian rule in Samarkand, 1868–1910: a comparison with British India*, Oxford University Press, Oxford.

Morrison, A. (2012) 'Sufism, pan-Islamism, and information panic: Nil Sergeevich Lykoshin and the aftermath of the Andijan uprising,' *Past and Present* vol. 214, pp. 255–304.

Morrison, A. (2014a) 'Killing the cotton canard and getting rid of the Great Game: rewriting the Russian conquest of Central Asia, 1814–1895,' *Central Asian Survey* vol. 33, no. 2, pp. 131–142.

Morrison, A. (2014b) '"Nechto eroticheskoe,"' "courir apres l'ombre"? logistical imperatives and the fall of Tashkent, 1859–1865,' *Central Asian Survey* vol. 33, no. 2, pp. 153–169.

Morrison, A. (2014c) 'Russia, Khoqand, and the search for a 'natural' frontier, 1863–1865,' *Ab Imperio* vol. 2014, no. 2, pp. 165–192.

Morrison, A. (2014d) 'Twin imperial disasters: the invasions of Khiva and Afghanistan in the Russian and British official mind, 1839–1842,' *Modern Asian Studies* vol. 48, no. 1, pp. 253–300.

Morrison, A. (2015) 'Creating a colonial shari'a for Russian Turkestan: Count Pahlen, the Hidaya, and Anglo-Muhammadan law,' in V. Barth & R. Cvetkovski (eds.), *Imperial co-operation and transfer, 1870–1930: empires and encounters*, Bloomsbury Academic, London, pp. 127–149.

Morrison, A. (2019) 'Refugees, resettlement, and revolutionary violence in Semirech'e after the 1916 revolt,' in A Chokobaeva, C Drieu, & A Morrison (eds.), *The Central Asian Revolt of 1916: a collapsing empire in the age of war and revolution*, Manchester University Press, Manchester, pp. 209–226.

Noda, J. (2016) *The Kazakh khanates between the Russian and Qing empires*, Leiden, Brill.

Olcott, M. (1995) *The Kazakhs*, 2nd edn, Hoover Institution Press, Stanford.

Park, A. (1957) *Bolshevism in Turkestan, 1917–1927*, Columbia University Press, New York.

Peterson, M. (2018) *Pipe dreams: water and empire in Central Asia's Aral Sea basin*, Cambridge University Press, New York.

Pierce, R. (1960) *Russian Central Asia 1867–1917: a study in colonial rule*, University of California Press, Berkeley.

Remnev, A. & Suvorova, N. (2008) '"Obrusenie" aziatskikh okrain Rossiiskoi imperii: optimizm i pessimizm russkoi kolonizatsii,' *Istoricheskie zapiski* vol. 11, pp. 132–179.

Sabol, S. (2003a) 'Kazak resistance to Russian colonization: interpreting the Kenesary Kasymov revolt, 1837–1847,' *Central Asian Survey* vol. 22, no. 2/3, pp. 231–252.

Sabol, S. (2003b) *Russian colonization and the genesis of Kazak national consciousness*, Palgrave MacMillan, New York.

Sahadeo, J. (2007) *Russian colonial society in Tashkent, 1865–1923*, Indiana University Press, Bloomington.

Sartori, P. (2017) *Visions of justice: shari'a and cultural change in Russian Central Asia*, Brill, Leiden.

Sergeev, E. (2012) *Bol'shaia igra, 1856–1907: mify i realii rossiisko-britanskikh otnoshenii v Tsentral'noi i Vostochnoi Azii*, KMK, Moscow.

Tazhibaev, T. (1962) *Prosveshchenie i shkoly Kazakhstana vo vtoroi polovine XIX veka*, Kazakhskoe gosudarstvennoe izd-vo. politicheskoi literatury, Alma-ata.

Treadgold, D. (1957) *The great Siberian migration: government and peasant in resettlement from emancipation to the first World War*, Princeton University Press, Princeton.

Uyama, T. (2001) 'Two attempts at building a Qazaq state: the revolt of 1916 and the Alash movement,' in S. Dudoignon & H. Komatsu (eds.), *Islam in politics in Russia and Central Asia (early eighteenth to late twentieth centuries*, Routledge, London, pp. 77–98.

Uyama, T. (2019) 'Why in Central Asia, why in 1916? The revolt as an interface of the Russian colonial crisis and the World War,' in A Chokobaeva, C Drieu, & A Morrison (eds.), *The Central Asian Revolt of 1916: a collapsing empire in the age of war and revolution*, Manchester University Press, Manchester, pp. 27–44.

Werth, P. (2001) *At the margins of orthodoxy: mission, governance, and confessional politics in Russia's Volga-Kama region*, Cornell University Press, Ithaca.

3
COLLECTIVISATION, SEDENTARISATION AND FAMINE IN CENTRAL ASIA

Marianne Kamp and Niccolò Pianciola

Stalinism in rural Central Asia

Tsarist rule over Central Asia shifted herding and farming economies towards colonial integration with Russia. This integration was temporarily broken by World War I, the post-Tsarist Civil War and the early Soviet decolonising measures during the 1920s. Collectivisation of agriculture, or the expropriation of peasants and nomads and their concentration in state-controlled collective farms, was implemented from 1930 to 1935 and coincided with the creation of the Stalinist system in Central Asia. Stalin's ambition for rapid industrialisation in the USSR's heartlands entailed using Central Asian herders' and farmers' labour and products to support Soviet industry and the industrial labour force. It also involved the violent cultural and economic integration of the Central Asian population into an expanded and strengthened Soviet state administration. Collectivisation, as a policy, made possible the integration of a predominantly rural region into the first completely state-controlled economy in modern history, as well as the use of Central Asian economic resources for the benefit of the Kremlin's economic priorities. This led to a major famine in Kazakhstan in 1931–1933, as nomadic pastoralists had lost their herds to state meat and livestock requisitions between 1930 and 1932, when the Communist Party proclaimed their sedentarisation. For the other Soviet Central Asian republics, the trauma of collectivisation was less extreme, even in areas where nomads were subject to policies of forced sedentarisation. Those who farmed in Central Asia's irrigated zones were pressured to join collective farms, and to turn their efforts to raising ever-increasing amounts of cotton. This chapter provides an overview of Soviet collectivisation as a political-economy policy, and then explains how the herding and farming peoples of Central Asia lived and worked before collectivisation. The chapter then details collectivisation's course and impacts on herders and *dehqon*s (Central Asian peasant farmers). Finally, in the conclusion, the chapter outlines the main social and economic consequences of the collectivisation and sedentarisation policies in Central Asia.

Overview of collectivisation policies

In November 1929, Stalin decided to push the country towards total collectivisation of agriculture, with the aim of achieving three outcomes: to push the country closer to communism by eradicating

DOI: 10.4324/9780429057977-3

private property and trade in the countryside; to consolidate the 24.5 million Soviet peasant households into a much smaller number of collective and state farms so as to create economies of scale, mechanise production and increase productivity; and to simplify the state's compulsory extraction of peasant produce by subordinating peasants into collective units that had no choice other than to respond to government demands. The third, extractive, function was the most important, even though Bolshevik propaganda focused on the first two (Graziosi 2007: 257–74; Kotkin 2017).

While this was the overall logic of collectivisation, the Stalinist 'Great Turn' in the Central Asian countryside aimed to transform three main sectors of the region's economy. The first transformation was to increase grain production by extending the cultivated area, stimulating a new wave of peasant colonisation of the steppe, sedentarising the nomadic population, and effecting its partial transition from livestock breeding to agriculture. The second was to increase cotton production by displacing food production from irrigated to dry land, extending irrigation and creating large fields amenable to mechanisation. Cotton was already cultivated in the Ferghana Valley and several other regions of Uzbekistan and Tajikistan, as well as parts of Kyrgyzstan, Turkmenistan and in Kazakhstan's Syr Darya region; collectivisation brought cotton culture to farming areas where it had not previously been a specialisation. Soviet economic planners envisioned fully supplying the textile industry with cotton grown within the USSR (Vakhabov 1981: 55). The third sector was livestock breeding: here, Moscow aimed to increase state control over livestock breeding and meat production. Kazakhstan, as the main livestock-breeding area of Central Asia, was central to this purpose. The construction of a number of meat canning factories in the Soviet republic, with the largest in Semipalatinsk, linked livestock breeding to the nascent Soviet food industry (Pianciola 2009: 391).

These transformations were premised on increasing connectivity and interdependence between the two vast economic regions into which the State Planning Committee (Gosplan) had divided Central Asia. For Gosplan, the standalone Kazakhstan economic region had grain-growing and livestock-breeding economic specialisations. The rest of Central Asia constituted a farming-oriented economic region centred on Uzbekistan, where the priority was maximising cotton harvests. This distinction had a fateful connection with food policies: Moscow considered Kazakhstan a net food producer for grain and meat, while plans for the cotton-oriented economic zone, made up of Uzbekistan, Turkmenistan, Tajikistan and Kyrgyzstan, assumed that this region would be a net grain consumer. Grain and meat procurements were therefore extremely harsh in Kazakhstan, and much less so in Uzbekistan and the other Central Asian Soviet republics, where the demands for cotton, a technical crop, became extreme. Construction of new railroads served to increase economic interdependence and specialisation by facilitating the transport of produce between regions. During the First Five-Year Plan (1928–1932), railways were built in Central Asia, with repairs in the Ferghana Valley, new lines in Tajikistan and to Xorazm and, most importantly, new connections from Central Asia to Russia. The Turkestan–Siberia railway linked up Alma-Ata with the Russian network; it was fully operational by 1931 (Dakhshleiger 1953: 49; Payne 2001). Adding to the existing Orenburg–Tashkent line, these rail lines became the route by which Central Asia's enforced production quotas of grain, livestock and cotton were transported to Russia's industrial centres.

In practice, collectivisation was a process that began sometime between 1929 and 1935 in Central Asian sedentary farming communities, as well as among herders. Among sedentary farmers (*dehqon*), the process began when Communist Party activists or plenipotentiaries arrived in a rural community and called local residents to a meeting that was eagerly attended by some, unwillingly attended by others and avoided by many. The plenipotentiaries told meeting attenders to sign an agreement to transfer their fields, and perhaps their draft livestock and farm implements, to a newly formed collective and to farm those lands jointly with other members. Tiny collective farms elected their chairman (*rais*) from among those local *deqhon*s whom the Party deemed acceptable (Kamp and Zanca 2016: 60–8). The *rais* was responsible for organising collective farming. Members expected that on working days they would be paid in grain, much of which was sent from the northern Kazakh steppe and other grain-growing regions of the Soviet Union, and that they would be paid a share of the sale price after harvesting the shared crop and turning it over to the relevant state purchasing trust.

In reality, many kolkhozes were paper commitments, and fell apart as soon as plenipotentiaries left, or when members saw their own assets wasted, or when members did not show up for joint fieldwork, or when promises of bread for payment went unfulfilled, or when communities rebelled violently. This slowed the process of collectivisation in 1930, but the Party redoubled efforts, increasing coercion by raising tax levels on individual farmers and selecting the wealthier ones, the *bai*s, for something that the Party called liquidation or dekulakisation. Liquidation meant total dispossession of all property, and exile or arrest (Alimova 2006, Vol. 1: 225–6; 291–6). Properties seized from *bai*s were added to tiny kolkhozes, which grew in membership as their holdings became more attractive, individual farming became impossible, and holdouts witnessed the arrests, trials and disappearances of wealthy and influential community members. By 1935, most of Central Asia's irrigated farming zones and the *dehqon*s who farmed them were entirely collectivised.

Collectivisation in nomadic areas was largely analogous in terms of specific procedures: the initial dissolution of collective farms after the annual procurement campaigns; and the incremental character of the drive, with more households joining the kolkhoz after each annual collectivisation wave, until by the end of the 1930s all nomads were collectivised (Jacquesson 2010: 140). Collectivisation in nomadic areas differed from that in irrigated farming zones due to three factors: the legacy of settler colonialism, the sedentarisation campaign and the arrival of deported peasants from Russia. Slavic peasants, who comprised between one-fifth and one-third of the population in Kazakh and Kyrgyz lands, were placed under pressure from harsh grain requisitions and the threat of being arrested as kulaks and were forced into collective farms earlier than Central Asian pastoralists. When the Commissariat for Agriculture divided the USSR into three zones that were to undergo collectivisation at different paces, Kazakhstan, as a net grain producer, was included in 'Zone II,' in which 40–50 per cent of rural households were to be collectivised by the end of summer 1931 (Davies 1980: 284–5). Kazakh nomadic pastoralists were assigned both meat and grain procurement quotas. Plenipotentiaries sent from the cities to pastoralists' *aul*s mobilised the local poor as activists for collectivisation. Arrests, deportations and expropriation were instrumental in terrorising both peasants and nomadic herders into becoming kolkhoz members. On paper, only the rich would be repressed; in practice, this happened to anyone opposing collectivisation. In 1930, the political police (OGPU) were placed in charge of compiling the list of people to be deported, and carrying out deportations.

Among the Kazakhs and Kyrgyz, collectivisation was, on paper, paired with sedentarisation. The same plenipotentiaries for collectivisation would, in some cases, order the pastoral communities to build houses and settle in hastily chosen 'sedentarisation points,' corresponding to, or not far from, the area of the nomads' winter quarters. The nomads would resume their transhumance as soon as the plenipotentiaries left the village (Pianciola 2016). In the northern steppe, Kazakh pastoralists were displaced to make space for deported peasants from Russia. Up to 400,000 Russian peasants were forcibly moved or fled to Kazakhstan during the first half of the 1930s (Cameron 2018: 118–19), but many died en route or shortly after arrival. Across Kazakhstan, famine compelled many herders seeking survival to join collective farms.

Central Asian herdsmen before collectivisation

The lands of the Kazakhs and Kyrgyz contrast with the rest of Central Asia in a fundamental way: before World War I, herding lands were subjected to intensive Slavic settler colonialism. During the 1920s, peasant settlers from Russian and Ukraine constituted approximately one-third of Kazakhstan's population, while Slavic settlers made up one-fifth of the population in Kyrgyz lands. The majority of the settlers had immigrated to the region in a wave beginning in the 1890s and strengthening after 1905. The settler colonial character of the region had two main consequences. First, the steppe economy became agro-pastoral, although the relationship was not entirely symbiotic: herdsmen depended on grain for their subsistence more than the peasants depended on livestock-breeding products. Secondly, the violence of the 1916 anti-colonial uprising, and its subsequent repression, were harsher among nomads than in areas of irrigated agriculture. In some areas of Semirech'e/Zhetysu/Dzhety-Suu (corresponding to southeast Kazakhstan and northern Kyrgyzstan), Kazakhs and Kyrgyz had systematically massacred the Slavic settlers. The Tsarist army's subsequent repression, and the settlers' revenge, was particularly murderous against the Kyrgyz. After conquering the region in 1920, the Bolsheviks implemented a harsh decolonisation policy in the Semirech'e/Zhetysu/Dzhety-Suu area, razing dozens of villages to the ground and expropriating and expelling 30,000 settlers. Another 10,000 were expropriated in other regions of Turkestan, particularly Syr Darya and Ferghana (Pianciola 2008). The reform ceased in 1922 when the Bolsheviks became divided over policies targeting the Slavic settlers, many of whom had supported the Bolsheviks during the Civil War; this was also because, in 1922, grain-growers were needed in the fields given the widespread famine in Russia and the northern Kazakh steppe. Even though 'hard' decolonisation policies were discontinued, during the 1920s the immigration of new settlers was outlawed in the newly created ethno-national administrative units of Kazakhstan (designated an ASSR subordinate to the RSFSR in 1920) and Kyrgyzstan (as of 1924, an AO subordinate to the Kazakh ASSR). Priority access to land and water resources was granted to pastoralists over Slavic settlers in the region. These norms were not consistently applied, as conflict over lands and the illegal migration from Russia and Ukraine of tens of thousands of peasants resumed in the mid-1920s. However, early Soviet policies among the Kazakhs and the Kyrgyz had a clear post-colonial, compensatory character (Pianciola 2009: 193–280).

Towards the end of the 1920s, the Kazakh and Kyrgyz pastoral economy had not yet entirely recovered from the crisis that had spanned the period of World War I, the 1916 anti-colonial uprising and its repression, and the Civil War. Sparse data show that among the Kazakhs, about one-third of pre-war herds had been lost by the beginning of the 1920s. Among the Kyrgyz, where the disruptions and violence of the 1916 uprising and subsequent civil war had been harsher, approximately two-thirds of sheep and horses had been lost (Sitnyanskii 1998: 64). A number of regional famines had significantly reduced the population (Buttino 1990). The 1920s were a period of recovery from this crisis, but the official data pointing towards a total recovery of livestock numbers to pre-war herd size by 1928 were considered unreliable by agronomic expeditions working in the region at the time (Pianciola 2018: 104–5). The limited character of the recovery made both Kazakhs and Kyrgyz vulnerable to a new crisis in the pastoral economy.

First settler colonisation then the economic disruptions brought by wars and revolutions led to a shortening of animal transhumance among the Kazakhs, who practised 'horizontal nomadism' on long distances on the steppe. In 1926, one-quarter of Kazakh households moved further than 25 kilometres from their winter camps, 4 per cent moved more than 100 kilometres, while another quarter were fully sedentary, with only selected family members moving to herd livestock.[1] Kyrgyz nomadic paths also shortened as a consequence of the economic crisis of the late 1910s and early 1920s (Sitnaynskii 1998: 65). Many Kazakhs and Kyrgyz who had lost their livestock during the period of wars, revolution and famine settled temporarily. Despite this conjunctural crisis of nomadic pastoralism, both the Kazakhs and the Kyrgyz were still considered fully pastoral nomadic peoples. The Soviet state officially viewed sedentary life as the inescapable outcome of the economic and cultural modernisation projects that the Bolsheviks were committed to bringing to nomadic Central Asia. However, although sedentarisation was encouraged during the 1920s through fiscal incentives, compulsion was explicitly ruled out (Thomas 2018). Moreover, specialists on the steppe economy came to the consensus that in drier areas of Kazakhstan, nomadic pastoralism would continue to be the main economic activity for the foreseeable future, as the climate of those regions could not sustain agriculture (Cameron 2018: 45–69).

Communist administrators in Kazakhstan and Kyrgyzstan, as well as leaders in Moscow, believed that Kazakh and Kyrgyz societies still needed the kind of social revolution that had swept away the dominant class in the Russian countryside during 1917. Traditional leaders remained within herding communities, and the 'nativisation' of local administration was extremely low until the 1930s. The Kazakhs and Kyrgyz described their society as divided into patrilineal descent groups: they were what Western anthropologists called 'segmentary lineage societies.' Among the Kazakhs, three different kinds of lineages segmented society: Chinggisid noble lineages, 'commoner' (*qara*) lineages and holy *khoja* lineages claiming descent from local Sufi saints supposedly related to the family of the Prophet Muhammad or from the first four Caliphs (Frank 2019: 33–40). Soviet ethnographers and administrators applied Marxist schemes and identified a stratum of rich livestock owners (*bai*s) as the exploitative class within nomadic society. Starting in 1927 and continuing until 1929, policies of deportation were applied selectively to Kazakh and Kyrgyz elites. Rich herders, tribal leaders (*manap*s among the Kyrgyz), and former heads of districts (*volostnye upraviteli*) under the Tsarist Empire were deported. Within Kazakhstan, 696 households (approximately 3,000 people) were deported internally and 64 *manap* households were deported out of Kyrgyzstan (Ohayon 2006; Jacquesson 2010: 123–4; Loring 2008: 288). The 'small October,' as the head of the Party in Kazakhstan named this attempt at beheading local society, was aimed at subjugating local Kazakh and Kyrgyz communities to a state from which they remained largely extraneous. These deportations of community leaders were considered necessary for a revolution in the peculiar context of nomadic Central Asian societies: the absence of a previous social revolution, unlike in the Slavic regions, and the alleged social control exercised by tribal chiefs. These measures were parallel to land reform in sedentary Central Asia.

Central Asian agriculturalists (*dehqon*s) before collectivisation

In Central Asia's core zones of irrigated agriculture, Uzbekistan, Tajikistan and Turkmenistan, the most productive districts raised cotton. In 1910, after 15 years of commercially oriented cotton cultivation in Russian Turkestan, Russia's cotton textile industry sourced about 52 per cent of its raw cotton within the empire, primarily from Central Asia, and the remainder was imported (Stoklitskogo 1926: 37). During World War I, Russia's cotton imports dropped sharply, and Central Asia's significance as Russia's cotton supply rose. Early in the 1920s, while Central Asia was still a battleground between Red Army forces and anti-Soviet Basmachis, and cotton cultivation had shrivelled to a mere 10 per cent of its former scope, Soviet industrial trusts proposed that the Soviet Union should eventually become independent of cotton imports by producing all that was needed (Iuferev 1925: 1–7). The Soviet goal of cotton autarky drove the State Cotton Committee's plans throughout the 1920s, shaped the First Five-Year Plan (1928–1932), and when mass collectivisation began in 1929, dictated that cotton-intensive regions in Central Asia would be first to collectivise.

The organisation of farming life varied across the regions that became Uzbekistan, Tajikistan and Turkmenistan. Turkmens tended towards clan-based ownership of land and livestock, with extended families assigning members to raising cotton and grain on irrigated lands or to herding livestock in dryland and desert areas (Edgar 2004: 22–4, 176–7). Similar patterns were found in parts of the Bukhara Emirate. In the irrigated farming regions within Russian Turkistan, Bukhara and Khiva, most cultivators, or *dehqon*s, owned land individually, or were dependent share-croppers or day-labourers on lands owned by the wealthy. Starting in the 1890s, as Russia's textile industry distributed its preferred American upland cotton seed in Turkestan, *dehqon*s in the Fergana valley and in the Khujand region expanded cotton into 60 per cent of their fields and became dependent on imported grain to meet their food needs. In Russian Turkestan, cotton was a far more lucrative crop than any other except rice and tobacco, and *dehqon*s, from those who owned the smallest plots to the largest, went into debt to plant it (Penati 2010, 2013). *Dehqon*s in Tashkent and Samarkand Provinces raised a broader variety of crops, with grain and cotton in balance. In the Bukhara Emirate and Khiva Khanate grain was dominant. Cotton comprised a small proportion of farm production, and *dehqon*s continued to raise *g'o'za*, the short-fibre Central Asian cotton that was more labour-intensive and in lower commercial demand than American upland cotton (Penati 2016). Most *dehqon*s in Russian Turkestan were individual owners of their land. Extended family or clan ownership was more common in mixed herding and farming zones such as Turkmenistan, and Uzbekistan's Qashqa Darya and Surhon Darya Provinces.

In the early 1920s, after the Red Army defeated most of the anti-Soviet rebel (*Basmachi*) groups, Moscow's control over Central Asia deepened, even as Central Asians themselves were encouraged to join the Communist Party and become involved in government. Slavic settlers were far fewer in sedentary Central Asia than in Kazakh or Kyrgyz lands: they constituted less than 10 per cent of Turkmenistan's 1926 population, and less than 6 per cent of Uzbekistan and Tajikistan's population. Moreover, very few Slavs lived in rural areas. In 1924, National-Territorial delimitation reconfigured the sedentary farming areas of Central Asia into national republics: Russian Turkestan's Transcaspian District, joined to parts of the Khiva People's Republic (Dashauz) and Bukhara Emirate (Charjui) became the Turkmen Soviet Socialist Republic. The Uzbek SSR combined parts of the Khiva People's Republic (Khiva, Urgench, and surroundings) and the Bukhara People's Republic with the most populous and most intensively farmed provinces of Turkestan, namely Fergana, Tashkent and Samarkand. The mountainous areas of Eastern Bukhara were designated as the Tajik Autonomous SSR, subordinate to the Uzbek SSR until 1929, when Khujand was transferred and Tajikistan was elevated to Union Republic status (Khalid 2015: 266–315).

When combined with land reform, the new borders had immediate impact in sedentary farming regions. In 1925, Uzbekistan and Turkmenistan began implementing a land redistribution policy, known as Land and Water Reform. Local committees were told to assess the size of land holdings by household, to seize amounts of land that exceeded the local household norm and allot that land to the poor and landless. In the Turkmen SSR, the Party interpreted extended family ownership of large swaths of shared land as the means by which clan leaders exploited their kin, and they instituted a hasty dispossession of the kin-network leaders, and redistribution to individuals. Land reform drove many to flee across new and old borders. Tens of thousands of Turkmen households facing dispossession crossed into Afghanistan, but uncounted others resettled in Uzbekistan. Tens of thousands of *dehqon*s from Uzbekistan crossed into Tajikistan,

Kyrgyzstan or Afghanistan (Edgar 2004: 179–82; Abdullaev 2009: 259–60, 361). The leaders of the Tajik ASSR, where the Basmachi conflict lingered, focused their land redistribution efforts on appropriating lands abandoned during the fighting or otherwise seen as 'empty.' The Tajik ASSR began resettling tens of thousands of Tajik highlanders, and Tajik families coming from land delimited to Uzbekistan, and those returning from refuge in Afghanistan, into areas previously dominated by nomadic Uzbek Lokais, and into lowlands in river valleys targeted for cotton expansion (Kassymbekova 2016: 53–70). In Uzbekistan, land reform was premised not on movements or resettling but on norming land holdings within rural communities; *bais* (rich men) who lost the majority of their lands remained in their communities among the land's new owners (Kamp and Zanca 2016). When the anti-*bai* campaign raged in Kazakhstan in 1928, Party hostility in Uzbekistan focused more strongly on Muslim clerics and merchants. They were stripped entirely of their rural lands, many were arrested and others went into exile. The Party closed mosques and shut down private wholesale trade, including trade in cotton (Keller 2001: 118–206; Shamsutdinov 2003, 25).

Collectivisation in nomadic Central Asia

Calls to force an increase in the sedentarisation of the Kazakhs were made during the VII Kazakhstan Congress of Soviets in April 1929. They were linked to the reopening of the republic to agricultural colonisation from Russia and Ukraine, and the need to provide the new settlers with land. At this stage, sedentarisation was to be implemented only in the grain-growing areas of northern and, to a minor extent, southern Kazakhstan. The former nomads would have been settled in strips of land at the border between grasslands and the drier central area of Kazakhstan (Ohayon 2006; Pianciola 2009: 345). Total sedentarisation of the nomads in Kazakhstan was decreed later as a corollary of total collectivisation. Moscow made a formal decision on the issue on 16 February 1930, when the Council of People's Commissar of the USSR decreed that the sedentarisation of the nomadic population of Kazakhstan was central to the economic transformation of the republic (Sinitsyn 2019: 93). Sedentarisation plans were then extended to all Soviet nomadic populations. The Kazakhs were by far the most numerous largely nomadic ethnic group in the Soviet Union. Most of them lived in Kazakhstan, with other small groups in northern Uzbekistan and Siberia. The 1926 Soviet census had counted almost 4 million Soviet Kazakhs, more than five times the number of the second and third largest nomadic groups, the Kyrgyz and Turkmen, which had almost identical populations (approximately 763,000 individuals). Sedentarisation among the Kyrgyz was launched in 1931, although limited measures had been taken during the previous summer (Loring 2008: 339–44). Despite the fact that Kazakhstan and the Kyrgyz republic were central to Soviet sedentarisation plans, up until 1933 the sedentarisation measures at the local level had been either not implemented at all or limited to the construction of housing in 'sedentarisation points' deserted by the population fleeing procurements and famine. In Turkmenistan, part of the Central Asian economic region, collectivisation and sedentarisation of the nomadic population were linked to the expansion of cotton production, which dominated 30 per cent of the republic's cultivated acreage in 1931. However, widespread rebellions and a fall in livestock numbers led the Party to interrupt forced sedentarisation and collectivisation of the Turkmens temporarily in spring 1932 (Edgar 2004: 202–12). The policies of collectivisation and procurement also resulted in the eventual sedentarisation of other nomadic pastoralists, such as the Karakalpaks, the Uzbek Lokais in Tajikistan's mountains and the Uzbek Kungrats in the Surhon Dayro Province of Uzbekistan.

The attempt to extirpate pastoral nomadic practices was paired with 'cultural revolution' measures repressing religious practices such as pilgrimages to shrines. In Kazakhstan the anti-religious campaign and the closure of places of worship was a major factor in provoking violent resistance among the population (Pianciola 2009: 288; Frank 2019: 69–80). Hundreds of anti-state uprisings broke out in Central Asia between 1929 and 1931, especially among nomadic pastoralists subjected to policies of harsh meat and livestock procurements. It would be wrong to attribute a general pattern to the organisation of the rebellions. Some of them were led by former Tsarist district chiefs, while some adopted forms of Islamic legitimisation (Pianciola 2013). In some cases in southern Kazakhstan the uprisings had a marked anti-Russian character, but in other cases Russian and Kazakh communities fought together against the expropriations (Aldazhumanov 1998). The State repressed anti-collectivisation rebellions using political police troops (OGPU) and, unlike in Russia or Ukraine, regular Red Army units, in which Central Asians at this point served in very limited numbers. In 1926, out of the 45,000 Red Army soldiers of the Central Asian Military District, only around 2,000 were Uzbek, while other Central Asian ethnic groups were even less represented (Tarkhova 2010: 85, 91). Conscription of Central Asians into the Red Army began during the 'Stalinist Great Turn' at different times in the different republics: until 1928, when Kazakhs were first drafted, only the Slavic population of Kazakhstan served in the army.

Collectivisation harshly and indiscriminately impacted all rural communities in Central Asia, including Russian and Ukrainian peasants, but devastated Kazakh pastoralists in particular. Grain and meat procurements also hit both Europeans and Central Asians, though the pastoralists suffered more than the Slavic peasants from the repression of rural markets, as pastoralists depended more on purchased grains for consumption (Pianciola 2004). Although these policies led to generalised hunger, the massive famine at this time only engulfed the Kazakh pastoralists, leading to the deaths of one-third of the Kazakh population between 1931 and 1933. The specificity of Kazakhstan was twofold. Firstly, Kazakhstan was the only economic area of Central Asia that was considered a net producer of grain. In 1928, the Kremlin imposed high grain procurement quotas on the republic and did not relax these quotas during the famine years. Secondly, and most importantly, in July 1930 the Politburo in Moscow decided that Kazakh livestock should compensate the widespread demise of livestock in Russia due to collectivisation: everywhere in the Soviet Union, peasants had slaughtered their animals instead of handing them over to the collective farms. Between autumn 1930 and summer 1931, meat procurements were set at around one-third of Kazakhstan's livestock. During those 12 months, more than half of Kazakhstan's livestock disappeared due to procurements, mismanagement and epizooties.[2] Between the summer of 1930 and the summer of 1932, extreme procurement quotas for meat and livestock in Kazakhstan resulted in the requisition, export and waste by death of 90 per cent of the horses, cattle, sheep and camels owned by the Kazakhs. In summer 1932 the policy was discontinued in recognition that the 'reserve' of meat and livestock in Kazakhstan had been exhausted. The meat that was funnelled out of Kazakhstan was mostly used to feed Moscow, Leningrad, other Russian industrial centres and the Red Army (Pianciola 2018). Animals that were exported alive outside of the republic and did not end up in slaughterhouses were distributed among collective farms to be used for traction.

The Stalinist leadership's decision to turn Kazakhstan into an emergency reserve of meat and livestock to be used outside of the republic turned the already ongoing regional famine caused by collectivisation and procurements into a massive occurrence. The Party leadership in Moscow assumed that reported livestock numbers in Kazakhstan underestimated their real extent, and the decision was not overturned even when its tragic consequences became clear to the Kremlin (Pianciola 2018). A drought in some regions of Kazakhstan during 1931 made the impact of the famine worse, but it was not a major factor in causing it (Cameron 2018: 193–4). Kazakh livestock was targeted because the Kazakhs were by far the largest pastoral people of the Soviet Union and controlled the largest amount of livestock among the nomadic populations. Extracting meat and livestock from Kazakhstan was also easier than doing so from other, more remote, regions, as the Kazakh steppe was connected to Russia by two major railway lines. These specificities of Kazakhstan cause the policies implemented in the republic to stand out in comparison with those implemented in other nomadic areas. No other nomadic population suffered a comparable fate during collectivisation; among the Kyrgyz, for instance, the 1930 and 1931 meat and livestock procurement quotas reduced livestock by less than half and did not result in a major famine. A historian attributes approximately 26,000 deaths to starvation among the Kyrgyz during collectivisation, i.e. 4 per cent of the total Soviet Kyrgyz population (Batyrbaeva 2014: 222–4).

Collectivisation, procurements and famine in nomadic areas caused an exodus of herdsmen across the border to China. The flight was especially large from Kazakhstan; between 1930 and 1933 perhaps up to 200,000 people fled from the area to Xinjiang, many with their livestock (Cameron 2018: 233). In an attempt to prevent labour and economic resources from leaving Soviet territory, Soviet border guards fired on sight against migrants. In 1930, in the Ili Valley (the main gateway between Kazakhstan and Xinjiang) alone, more than 1,000 women, children and men were killed by border guards while trying to cross the border (Cameron 2018: 122–42). In the border regions of Central Asia, even more than in other regions of the Soviet Union, the upheaval brought about by collectivisation led to emigration of peasants and nomads. This in turn led to a strengthening of border controls and the weakening of ties in cross-border areas that had been socially and economically integrated up until the early 1930s. The control over the territory and the population made possible by collectivisation was instrumental to Moscow's policies of sealing the external borders of the Soviet Union, an aim that was only partially achieved during the second half of the 1930s (Shaw 2011; Dullin 2014). In some regions of Central Asia, this was also achieved by forcibly resettling population groups close to the borders (Kassymbekova 2016: 76–8).

Collectivisation in *dehqon* farming lands

Throughout the 1920s, there was little discussion of collectivisation in Central Asia's farming zones and far less implementation. *Dehqon*s who received land in Uzbekistan's land reform were encouraged, through advances and distribution of implements, to form land reclamation societies or artels for shared farming on newly distributed lands. More broadly, the agricultural trusts provided credit to *dehqon*s who joined purchasing or production cooperatives. Until Stalin's November 1929 announcement of mass, rapid collectivisation, the Central Asian Bureau of the Communist Party and Republic-level leaders repeatedly cited high membership levels in credit cooperatives as evidence that *dehqon*s, who all farmed individually, were making rapid strides towards socialism (Itkitch 1929). As of summer 1929, among Uzbekistan's rural population of 880,000 households, a negligible proportion, 24,250 households, belonged to some collective farming entity. Before mass collectivisation began, Uzbekistan's 500 or so artels, communes and societies for jointly working the land (TOZ) averaged 16 member households, and seven draft animals, oxen or horses (Berezovskii 1930). There was no evidence of any grassroots turn towards collectivisation, or that the Central Asia Bureau of the Communist Party regarded agricultural collectivisation as a priority. Until November 1929, political discussions of agriculture focused on expanding cotton planting and production by providing individual *dehqon*s with land, draft power and seed advances, and on dispossessing the wealthy *bai* or kulak, but not on reorganising small farmers into collectively owned farms.

In November 1929, when Stalin declared that mass collectivisation should begin in the USSR's key grain-producing regions, Central Asian Communist Party leaders, recently intimidated by purges of so-called nationalists, demonstrated a cultivated alacrity in volunteering cotton-growing districts for the same speedy transformation. The Central Asian Bureau declared target rates for collectivisation, with plans that 60 per cent of cotton districts would become collective farms within five years (Kamp 2019, 242). Where land reform had already provided lists of owners and properties, collectivising entailed drawing *dehqon*s to a meeting, calling on them to sign up for the kolkhoz, join their fields with others and donate a draft animal or farm implement. Recruits were offered access to new lands, promised priority for tractors or draft animals, and ordinary provisions, and were threatened with loss of seed advances. Although the Party had deferred collectivising grain lands until later, ongoing land reform efforts in grain-growing regions shifted from breaking up large holdings and redistributing land to individuals, to forming kolkhozes on newly appropriated land (Kamp and Zanca 2016). The Party recruited plenipotentiaries, sending them to kishlaks to organise *dehqon*s into collective farms. Unlike in Kazakhstan, this recruitment drew heavily on Central Asian Party members, Komsomol members and students, with advertisements noting that recruits needed to speak Uzbek.[3]

As elsewhere, initial efforts focused on attracting the rural poor to the kolkhoz, but a collective that was comprised of a minimal number of lands of the poorest households – those who saw most reason to join a kolkhoz – would be unsustainable to its members and unattractive to any *dehqon* who was not in need (Kamp and Zanca 2016). A harsh form of dekulakisation accompanied the drive to form kolkhozes. Plenipotentiaries found the remaining *bai* households, including those who had lost or redistributed some of their land already in reform, and strove to galvanise the poorest households against them. In February and March of 1930, hundreds of anti-collectivisation demonstrations arose. As the OGPU snuffed them out, they pinned local *bai*s with charges of counter-revolution (Alimova 2006, Vol. 1: 226–9, 240–1) Those who were designated as kulaks and counter-revolutionaries saw all of their lands seized and given to a nascent kolkhoz, instantly making the prospect of joining a kolkhoz mean access to additional fields (Kamp and Zanca 2016). Kulaks were sentenced to a variety of fates: those who were deemed harmless were assigned undeveloped land near their kishlak, leaving them in the community but severely reduced in wealth and status. Kulaks who were judged to be potentially nefarious were exiled to lands within their republic that were designated for new development. Those who were designated as posing an overt threat were exiled outside the republic (Alimova 2006, Vol. 1: 292). Kulaks and their families, numbering several tens of thousands, were sent from Uzbekistan to form new cotton-growing kolkhozes in Ukraine or the North Caucasus (Shamsutdinov 2001). As the collectivisation campaign continued and the Soviet political climate shifted to terror, repeated waves of dekulakisation dispatched to the Gulag those *dehqon*s who were accused of prior wealth, or of participation in the Basmachi movement. In addition to providing irrigated lands for kolkhozes and removing local status holders from their authoritative roles, dekulakisation strengthened Party and state control through arbitrary use of power that instilled fear. Kolkhoz formation invitations to households that considered their own lands and livelihoods adequate came against a background of sharply rising taxes on individual *dehqon*s and the constant threat of dekulakisation, making collectivisation proceed much more swiftly and thoroughly than planners had envisaged. For example, Uzbekistan's cotton-intensive regions were 70–80 per cent collectivised by January 1932, and its grain and herding regions were more than 50 per cent collectivised.[4]

Collectivisation meant that cotton cultivation could be mandated. In the 1920s, cotton planting and harvest levels rose rapidly, largely due to incentives: producer cooperatives provided low-interest seed loans and distributed crop advances based on an attractive, fixed purchase price. In 1928, the Soviet leadership adopted coercion and collectivisation as the solution to the 'scissors crisis,' when grain prices were low and peasants in the Soviet bread-basket regions held their harvests back against a hoped-for price increase. They began applying the same logic to cotton, even though as an inedible, commercial crop, cotton was not a harvest that *dehqon*s would hoard. The kolkhoz took planting decisions away from individual *dehqon*s. Newly formed kolkhozes across Uzbekistan were ordered to expand cotton planting to its upper limits. They were to grow cotton on nearly all irrigated fields, and plant grain only on dryland (unirrigated) fields (Kamp 2019). In regions of new irrigation, such as Tajikistan's zones of resettlement, or Uzbekistan's Bekabod, a place of kulak exile, those who arrived faced exceedingly difficult conditions, lack of housing and provisions and hard labour in digging the water channels to irrigate their quota of cotton. State control through kolkhozes turned cotton into a veritable monoculture across Uzbekistan, Turkmenistan and Tajikistan's low, irrigated lands, while grain cultivation was relegated to fields dependent on winter snows and spring rains.

Collectivisation's results for the *dehqon* farmers of Central Asia were not as deadly as they were for the Kazakhs. Dekulakisation and the dispossession of mullahs and other Muslim religious personnel removed tens of thousands of individuals and households from the Central Asian republics, exiling them to other regions of the Soviet Union, or driving them into exile abroad. Large-scale resettlements around Tajikistan's Vakhsh River irrigation projects made tens of thousands of households entirely reliant on the state's unreliable provision of food, housing and farming necessities (Peterson 2019: 276–83). The cotton-growing districts, which for decades had relied on grain provision from other regions, especially from Kazakhstan, became even less capable of meeting their own food needs due to their ever-increasing cotton mandate, and at the same time, more districts became cotton producers at the expense of their traditional grain crops. Although in Kazakhstan, collectivisation was a time of mass starvation, in Central Asia's sedentary republics it was a time of hardship and dearth, but not large-scale loss of life. In Uzbekistan, widespread failure of the spring grain crop in 1933 combined with shortfalls in grain imports from the rest of the Soviet Union, leading to famine that lasted for several months and that resulted in deaths that cannot be counted. Rural communities in Central Asia did not yet have Civil Registry offices (ZAGS) to record deaths (Kamp 2019). After this summer of starvation in Uzbekistan, although irrigation systems expanded haphazardly through projects that at the time were judged to be expensive failures, and Central Asian leaders were repeatedly chided for low-quality, low-yield cotton harvests, the Second Five-Year Plan showed that the State relented a bit on the cotton mandate (Obertreis 2017; Teichmann 2016). Kolkhozes were permitted to raise grain and lucerne for animal fodder on a proportion of their irrigated lands, and food supplies improved.

Unlike Kazakh and Kyrgyz lands, rural districts in Uzbekistan, Tajikistan and Turkmenistan remained largely unattractive to Slavic farming settlers, although throughout the 1920s and 1930s Russia was the source of immigration to Central Asian cities and district centres, often for Party work, administrative work or work in industry. There were exceptions: Khujand and Tashkent Provinces had hosted more rural Slav immigrants than did other provinces during the Imperial period, and this pattern continued during collectivisation.

Although there are many issues with Soviet census data, they clearly show that in Central Asia only the Kazakhs starkly declined in numbers during the 1930s. Between 1926 and 1939, Soviet Kazakhs went from approximately 4 million to 3.1 million, while Uzbeks increased from 3.9 million to 4.8 million. An absolute population growth was also recorded for the Kyrgyz, Tajiks and Turkmens.[5]

Conclusion

It is difficult to overstate the importance of collectivisation as a historical watershed in the history of modern Central Asia. This is particularly true for the Kazakhs, who lost one-third of their population, killed by a famine directly caused by the policies of livestock and grain procurements, which were inseparably linked to the logic of collectivisation. The entire Central Asian rural population experienced the traumatic changes of total collectivisation, with its manifold consequences.

First and foremost, collectivisation achieved the final subjugation of the independent peasantry in the Soviet Union, and total control over its produce and economic resources. The state now could determine what would be produced on farming and herding lands, and could extract the product at will. At the same time, this increased control was an 'etatisation' of Central Asian societies, especially in nomadic areas. It was an entirely new process of penetration and scale of expansion of state institutions into the countryside.

Secondly and relatedly, collectivisation achieved an unprecedented degree of institutional uniformity for the entire Soviet countryside, presented by the Bolshevik propaganda as the elimination of 'national inequality' (Zulkasheva 2018: 169). It forced peasants and pastoralists, who until then had lived under very different systems of social and legal relations, into a limited variety of productive and social units. Regardless of region or specialisation, there were three different kinds of collective farms, differentiated by the degree of socialisation of livestock and agricultural tools; there were also state farms or sovkhoz, where the land belonged to the state and the labourers were paid workers. Their duties vis-à-vis the state were formalised in the same terms from Karelia to Tajikistan, and from Kamchatka to Turkmenistan. In areas where nomads were sedentarised, isomorphism was extended to the built environment in the collective farms, where a very limited number of house models designed in Russia (typically bi-family houses) were erected from Kazakhstan to Siberia (Humphrey 1998: 283).

Thirdly, collectivisation and sedentarisation enforced an acculturation to a common Soviet culture through the repression of cultural practices linked to religious beliefs or healing practices and the introduction of Sovietising institutions, such as thousands of new rural schools, village clubs, stores and administrative structures (Michaels 2003; İğmen 2012). Although previously influential families retained or renewed their influence in some rural communities, it was more commonly the case that rural communities, stripped of their *bai*s or *manap*s and their mullahs, found new youthful leaders who joined the Komsomol and made their way up to positions such as kolkhoz chairman. More generally, the Soviet state discursively phased out identities related to specific economic practices and ways of life (such as 'nomad,' 'tribal' or 'clan' group names): everyone would be a collective or state farmer within the accepted number of Soviet ethnic nations. The new generations of rural dwellers, who became adults after total collectivisation, were integrated much more effectively into the socialising institutions (schools, the army) that operated the 'double assimilation' of local communities into the local specific ethnic nation and the wider Soviet people (Hirsch 2005).

Fourth, for the Communist Party, collectivisation was a step towards a socialist society. Collectivisation became a peculiar 'socialist modernisation' that would later be adopted as a standard measure in other communist states (Kligman and Verdery 2011). Socialist modernity required both the extirpation of 'backwardness,' as with the sedentarisation campaign in nomadic areas, and class war, i.e. the violent elimination of rural elites by imprisonment or deportation.

Fifth, collectivisation and sedentarisation entailed a comprehensive spatial reorganisation of economic activities, with an increase in regional economic specialisation and control over population movements. In Kazakhstan, the state proceeded with the administrative redistribution of famine refugees and their integration into different sectors of the economy, a process that lasted until the late 1930s (Ohayon 2006: 277–321). The construction of transport infrastructures connecting Central Asia to Russia facilitated this process, making possible the further economic specialisation of different areas in the region. With low investments in technology and high demand for hand labour, the quasi-monoculture in cotton served to prevent the *dehqons* from migrating (Abashin 2015: 315). The state asserted a new form of control in late 1932 by deciding not to distribute internal passports to peasants, creating a barrier preventing voluntary movement from the kolkhoz to the city.

Finally, and relatedly, the sedentarisation of the nomads and their settlement in collective farms was launched with the explicit aim of 'making space' for the last major wave of settler colonisation of Central Asia (Zulkasheva 2018: 180). During 1930–1933, hundreds of thousands of peasants from Russia were deported to Kazakhstan as 'special settlers.' Then, from the mid-1930s to the mid-1940s, the victims of the numerous waves of 'Soviet ethnic cleansing,' especially those in the Soviet borderlands, were also deported to Central Asia: primarily to Kazakhstan, but also to the Uzbek and Kyrgyz lands (Martin 2001: 311–43).

Collectivisation's primary objectives were the forceful subordination of Soviet rural peoples to state institutions, giving the state the ability to extract resources. The violent repression of rural elites was functionally crucial to these ends, removing those most likely to organise resistance.

For the other aims of collectivisation, there was space for compromise and relaxation. For instance, after collectivisation was achieved, nomadic practices were partially rehabilitated, while collective farms composed by a single clan, initially prohibited, were also accepted, provided that rural elites (*bais* among the Kazakhs, *manaps* among the Kyrgyz) had been removed (Jacquesson 2010: 138, 141; Kindler 2018: 218–36). Measures taken in 1932 allowing herdsmen to keep animals in private possession – all Kazakh and Turkmen livestock was de facto re-privatised – anticipated the new settlement between state and collective farmers across the entire Soviet Union, as regulated by the Kolkhoz Model Statute of February 1935. The statute left approximately 10 per cent of the land in personal possession of peasants ('family plots') and allowed them to own livestock as private property. Re-privatisation allowed livestock numbers to rebound; later, just before World War II, herds were targeted by a new campaign of socialisation. In 1941, only about one-third of Kazakh livestock was privately owned (Ohayon 2006: 336). Thus, the new collectivised system was stabilised, after healing the devastations brought by the total collectivisation campaign launched ten years earlier.

Notes

1 State Archive of the Russian Federation (GARF), A-374/16/88/44, V.G. Sokolovskii, "Main objectives, methods, research plan, and data elaboration plan of materials concerning the seasonal distribution and nomadic paths of the Kazakh population (under implementation by the Kazakhstan Statistical Office in the period 1927–1929)," 1928.
2 Russian State Archive of the Economy (RGAE), 4372/29/896/13, Plan for livestock procurements in 1930–1931, 19.08.1930.
3 Central State Archive of the Republic of Uzbekistan (UzSA), 196/1/49/24.

4 UzSA, R95/2/186/21-23.
5 For 1926 and 1939 census data, see Demoscope.ru (http://www.demoscope.ru/weekly/ssp/ussr_nac_26.php and http://www.demoscope.ru/weekly/ssp/sng_nac_39.php?reg=8, accessed 15 December 2019).

Bibliography

Abashin, S. (2015) *Sovetskii Kishlak mezhdu kolonializmom i modernizatsii*. Moskva: Novoe Literaturnoe Obozrenie.

Abdullaev, Kamoludin N. (2009) *Ot sin'tsiania do khorosana: iz istorii sredneaziatskoi emigratsii XX veka*. Dushanbe: Irfon.

Aldazhumanov, K. (1998) 'Krest'yanskoe dvizhenie soprotivleniya.' In *Deportirovannye v Kazakhstan narody: vremya i sud'by*, edited by G.K. Anes et al., 66–93. Almaty: Arys & Qazaqstan.

Alimova, D.A., ed. (2006) *Tragediia sredneaziatskogo kishlaka: Kollektivizatsiia, raskulachivanie, ssylka*. Three volumes, document collection. Toshkent: Sharq.

Batyrbaeva, S. (2014) 'Golod 30-kh gg. v Kyrgyzstane: novye materialy, novye podkhody.' In *Sovetskie natsii i natsional'naia politika v 1920–1950-e gody*, edited by N.A. Volynchik, 222–230. Moskva: ROSSPEN/Yeltsin tsentr.

Berezovskii, D. (1930) 'Kolkhozy UzSSR za 1928 i 1929 gody.' *Biulliten' Tsentral'nogo Statistichekogo Upravleniia Uzbekskoi SSR* 23: 3–31.

Buttino, M. (1990) 'Study of the Economic Crisis and Depopulation in Turkestan, 1917–1920.' *Central Asian Survey* 9(4): 59–74.

Cameron, S. (2018) *The Hungry Steppe: Famine, Violence, and the Making of Soviet Kazakhstan*. Ithaca: Cornell University Press.

Dakhshleiger, G.F. (1953) *Turksib: pervenets sotsialisticheskoi industrializatsii. Ocherk istorii postroiki Turksiba*. Alma-Ata: Izd. Akademii Nauk KazSSR.

Davies, R.W. (1980) *The Industrialisation of Soviet Russia Vol. 2: The Soviet Collective Farm, 1929–30*. Houndmills: Macmillan.

Dullin, S. (2014) *La frontière épaisse. Aux origines des politiques soviétiques (1920–1940)*. Paris: Editions de l'EHESS.

Edgar, A. (2004) *Tribal Nation: The Making of Soviet Turkmenistan*. Princeton: Princeton University Press.

Frank, A.J. (2019) *Gulag Miracles: Sufis and Stalinist Repression in Kazakhstan*. Vienna: Austrian Academy of Sciences Press.

Graziosi, A. (2007) *L'Urss di Lenin e Stalin. Storia dell'Unione Sovietica. 1914–1945*. Bologna: Il Mulino.

Hirsch, F. (2005) *Empire of Nations: Ethnographic Knowledge and the Making of the Soviet Union*. Ithaca: Cornell University Press.

Humphrey, C. (1998) *Marx Went Away, but Kark Stayed Behind*. Ann Arbor: University of Michigan Press.

İğmen, A. (2012) *Speaking Soviet with an Accent: Culture and Power in Kyrgyzstan*. Pittsburgh: University of Pittsburgh Press.

Itkitch. (1929) 'Khlopkovodcheskaia kooperatsiia Uzbekistana i ee perspektivy.' *Narodnoe Khoziaistvo Srednei Azii* 1: 95–118.

Iuferev, V.I. (1925) *Khlopkovodstvo v Turkestane*. Leningrad: RAN.

Jacquesson, S. (2010) *Pastoréalismes. Anthropologie historique des processus d'intégration chez les Kirghiz du Tian Shan intérieur*. Wiesbaden: Reichert.

Kamp, M. (2019) 'Hunger and Potatoes: The 1933 Famine in Uzbekistan and Changing Foodways.' *Kritika: Explorations in Russian and Eurasian History* 20(2): 237–267.

Kamp, M. and R. Zanca. (2016) 'Recollections of Collectivization in Uzbekistan: Stalinism and Local Activism,' *Central Asian Survey* 36(1): 55–72.

Kassymbekova, B. (2016) *Despite Cultures: Early Soviet Rule in Tajikistan*. Pittsburgh: University of Pittsburgh Press.

Keller, S. (2001) *To Moscow not Mecca: The Soviet Campaign against Islam in Central Asia, 1917–1941*. Wesport: Praeger.

Khalid, A. (2015) *Making Uzbekistan: Nation, Empire, and Revolution in the Early USSR*. Ithaca: Cornell University Press.

Kindler, R. (2018) *Stalin's Nomads: Power and Famine in Kazakhstan*. Pittsburgh: Pittsburgh University Press.

Kligman, G. and K. Verdery. (2011) *Peasants under Seige: The Collectivization of Romanian Agriculture 1949–1962*. Princeton: Princeton University Press.

Kotkin, S. (2017) *Stalin: Waiting for Hitler, 1929–1941*. New York: Penguin.

Loring, B.H. (2008) 'Building Socialism in Kyrgyzstan: Nation-Making, Rural Development, and Social Change, 1921–1932.' PhD dissertation, Brandeis University.

Martin, T. (2001) *The Affirmative Action Empire: Nations and Nationalism in the Soviet Union, 1923–1939*. Ithaca: Cornell University Press.

Michaels, P. (2003) *Curative Powers: Medicine and Empire in Stalin's Central Asia*. Pittsburgh: University of Pittsburgh Press.

Obertreis, J. (2017) *Imperial Desert Dreams: Cotton Growing and Irrigation in Central Asia, 1860–1991*. Göttingen: V&R unipress.

Ohayon, I. (2006) *La sédentarisation des Kazakhs dans l'URSS de Staline (1928–1945)* Paris: Maisonneuve et Larose.

Payne, M. (2001) *Stalin's Railroad: Turksib and the Building of Socialism*. Pittsburgh: University of Pittsburgh Press.

Penati, B. (2010) 'Notes on the Birth of Russian Turkestan's Fiscal System: A View from the Ferghana Oblast.' *Journal of the Economic and Social History of the Orient* 53(5): 739–769.

Penati, B. (2013) 'The Cotton Boom and the Land Tax in Russian Turkestan.' *Kritika: Explorations in Russian and Eurasian History* 14(4): 741–774.

Penati, B. (2016) *Hunt for Red Orient: A Soviet Industrial Trest between Moscow and Bukhara (1922–1929)*. Series: Carl Beck Papers Number 2406. Pittsburgh: University of Pittsburgh Press.

Peterson, M.K. (2019) *Pipe Dreams: Water and Empire in Central Asia's Aral Sea Basin*. Cambridge: Cambridge University Press.

Pianciola, N. (2004) 'Famine in the Steppe: The Collectivization of Agriculture and the Kazak Herdsmen 1928–1934.' *Cahiers du monde russe* 45(1–2): 137–192.

Pianciola, N. (2008) 'Décoloniser l'Asie centrale? Bolcheviks et colons au Semirech´e (1920–1922).' *Cahiers du monde russe* 49(1): 101–144.

Pianciola, N. (2009) *Stalinismo di frontiera: colonizzazione agricola, sterminio dei nomadi e costruzione statale in Asia centrale (1905–1936)*. Rome: Viella.

Pianciola, N. (2013) 'Interpreting an Insurgency in Soviet Kazakhstan: The OGPU, Islam and Qazaq "Clans" in Suzak, 1930.' In *Islam, Society and States across the Qazaq Steppe (18th - Early 20th Centuries)*, edited by N. Pianciola and P. Sartori. Vienna: Verlag der Österreichischen Akademie der Wissenschaften, pp. 297–340.

Pianciola, N. (2016) 'Stalinist Spatial Hierarchies: Placing the Kazakhs and Kyrgyz in Soviet Economic Regionalization.' *Central Asian Survey* 35(4): 73–92.

Pianciola, N. (2018) 'Stalinskaya "ierarkhiya potrebleniya" i velikii golod 1931–1933 gg. v Kazakhstane.' *Ab Imperio* 2: 80–116.

Shamsutdinov, R. (2001) *O'zbekistonda sovetlarning quloqlashtirish siyosati va uning fojeali oqibatlari*. Toshkent: Sharq.

Shamsutdinov, R. (2003) *Qishloq fozheasi: zhamoalashtirish, quloqlashtirish, surgun, o'rta osio respublikalari misolida*. Toshkent: Sharq.

Shaw, C. (2011) 'Friendship under Lock and Key: The Soviet Central Asian Border, 1918–34.' *Central Asian Survey* 30(3–4): 331–348.

Sinitsyn, F.L. (2019) *Sovetskoe gosudarstvo i kochevniki. Istoriia, politika, naselenie, 1917–1991 gg*. Moskva: Tsentrpoligraf.

Sitnyanskii, G.I. (1998) *Sel'skoe khozyaistvo kirgizov: traditsii i sovremennost'*. Moskva: Institut Etnologii i Antropologii RAN.

Stoklitskogo, A.V. (1926) *Khlopkovodstvo v SSSR i ego perspektivy*. Moskva: Biuro pechati i informatsii SNK i STO.

Tarkhova, N. (2010) *Krasnaia armiia i stalinskaia kollektivizatsiia, 1928–1933 gg*. Moskva: ROSSPEN.

Teichmann, C. (2016) 'Canals, Cotton, and the Limits of De-Colonization in Soviet Uzbekistan, 1924–1941.' *Central Asian Survey* 26(4): 499–519.

Thomas, A. (2018) *Nomads and Soviet Rule: Central Asia under Lenin and Stalin*. London: I.B. Tauris.

Vakhabov, M.G. (1981) *Formirovanie khlopkogo-promyshlennogo kompleksa v Uzbekistane*. Tashkent: Uzbekistan.

Zulkasheva, A.S., ed. (2018) *Tragediia kazakhskogo aula, 1928–1934. Tom 2: 1929-ianvar' 1932*. Almaty: Raritet.

4
DEVELOPMENT IN POST-WAR CENTRAL ASIA

Artemy M. Kalinovsky

Throughout the second half of the twentieth century, Soviet Central Asia was treated as a 'developing' region that needed investment, expertise and technology from the more 'developed' parts of the union to achieve similar standards of living. Although the term 'development' was not used in Soviet discourse in the same way that it came to be used in international organisations, among donors in the North, and post-colonial governments in the South, it was nevertheless central to the entire Soviet project. In Marxist ideology, history moved in stages, from feudal to capitalist to socialist. Once Central Asia was incorporated in the USSR, it too was expected to move from pre-capitalism to socialism.

The first decade of Soviet power changed little about economic relations in Central Asia, despite the emigration of many of the pre-revolutionary political and economic elites. The new Soviet state proclaimed that all parts of the country would achieve equal levels of economic development, although what that meant in practice was unclear. Moscow supported the creation of cooperatives and the spread of electrification, but for most of the 1920s these initiatives were marginal to economic life. It was with the First Five-Year Plan that the region was dramatically altered. The sedenterisation of nomads in Kazakhstan caused a massive crisis and the death of almost half of the Kazakh population (Cameron 2018; Hancock-Palmer 2019). Uzbekistan, Tajikistan and Turkmenistan were assigned the role of cotton production for the socialist economy; most investment was geared to irrigating lands to make that possible (Teichmann 2007; Reid 2016; Obertreis 1991; Peterson 2019). Industrialisation and widespread electrification would have to wait until the post-war period. In the years after 1953, the economic development of the region became tied up with overcoming the legacies of Stalinism. The wave of decolonisation taking place beyond Soviet borders underlined the need to prove the USSR had overcome the legacies of empire while Cold War competition forced Moscow to demonstrate development and equality.

While Central Asia is a diverse region geographically and demographically, there were a number of features that justified, for Soviet planners, its discussion as an economic region – a fact reflected in economic plans. One was topography: the mountainous republics of Tajikistan and Kyrgyzstan also hold the sources of the key rivers that irrigate the region, including the Vahksh, the Amu Darya and the Syr Darya. The climate of Uzbekistan, Turkmenistan and Kazakhstan is arid, with semi-desert and steppe lands and oases irrigated by the above rivers. From the 1960s onwards, demographers identified the region as sharing high demographic

DOI: 10.4324/9780429057977-4

growth, as compared to the European parts of the USSR, where population growth was rapidly slowing (Kalinovsky 2018).

Studying the development of Central Asia is useful not just for understanding the region's history in the twentieth century but also because it clarifies some of the problems internal to the Soviet Union, while also helping place Central Asia in a global context. Soviet approaches shared much with those originating in liberal and capitalist contexts. Moreover, the problems that Soviet planners hoped to solve in the post-Stalin era, especially the rural poverty exacerbated by the cotton monopoly, was itself a result of policies adopted from the late 1920s. The criticism of colonial 'underdevelopment' levied by scholars like Andre Gunders Frank and Walter Rodney against European powers could also be applied to the USSR (Frank 1966; Rodney 1973).

At the same time, we should not underestimate the role that ideology played in differentiating internal Soviet development from other development enterprises. In so far as Marxism was a rationalist ideology rooted in the Enlightenment, it certainly shared premises with development thought elsewhere. But the USSR's insistence on equality and mutual support, not only bound Moscow to projects of dubious economic rationality but also had a levelling effect, undermining the hierarchy implicit in the idea of designating Central Asia a region to be developed.

Development history has become a burgeoning field in recent years. Historians of development are interested in the attempt, which they trace, variously, to the inter-war period, the last decades of European colonialism or the early Cold War era, to help countries increase their economic capacity to the levels of Europe and North America (Lorenzini 2019; Unger 2018; Macekura and Manela 2018). Yet while some scholars have been working to integrate Soviet foreign aid into the story of twentieth-century development history, there is relatively little understanding of the domestic contours of Soviet development approaches (Engerman 2011; Kalinovsky and Kamp 2018). Throughout the period in question, however, it was to a large extent Central Asian economists, sociologists, and other specialists who developed and revised the models under discussion here, working with larger frameworks of state socialism. Some of these same scholars also articulated harsh critiques of Soviet development approaches in the 1980s, pointing to its shortcomings in terms of raising living standards and its social and environmental costs. (Umarov 1988; Olimov 1989) Contemporary Central Asian historians have not generally returned to these topics, but social scientists writing on contemporary development are increasingly interested in the Soviet roots of contemporary development initiatives. (Féaux de la Croix and Suyarkulova, 2015; Suyarkulova 2014; Doolotkeldieva 2016). Bridging the historiography of development with the re-evaluation of the Soviet experience and its consequences can prove fruitful for scholars across these fields.

Models

There were three main pillars for economic development in Central Asia. The first was energy. Expeditions carried out in the 1920s and 1930s had identified hydrocarbon reserves and enormous hydropower potential. The power of rivers like the Syr Darya and Vakhsh, whose sources were in Tajikistan and Kyrgyzstan, respectively, could be harnessed to provide electricity. Turkmenistan, Uzbekistan and Kazakhstan, meanwhile, were well endowed with oil and, especially, natural gas. Although the late Stalin era, in particular, had seen the construction of a number of dams at places like Kairakum in northern Tajikistan, these satisfied only local needs (Roberts 2018). The more ambitious idea, pursued by Central Asian planners and allies in central institutions, was a series of large dams whose electricity could be channelled into a grid covering not just their own republic but neighbouring ones as well. By the late 1950s, they had managed to secure support for a cascade of dams on the Syr Darya and the Vakhsh, the crown jewels of which would be the 300-metre and 3,000-megawatt Nurek Dam, as well as the 215-metre and 1,200-megawatt Toktogul Dam. The other three republics would meanwhile develop their gas reserves to power electricity production as well as provide heating to homes throughout the region. Since river flow was seasonal – much greater in the summer, when glaciers melted, than in the winter – planners envisioned a unified regional grid that would draw more on hydropower in the summer months and on hydrocarbon in the winter. The dams were not just supposed to be electricity producers. Their water could also be diverted to irrigate new areas for cotton and other crops. But for Central Asian planners the real draw was that the electricity they provided made it possible to envision the industrialisation of the republic (Kalinovsky 2018: chapters 1 and 3).

The second pillar was demography, namely the Central Asian republics' rapid population growth in the post-war period. During the 1950s, the notion of a 'dual sector' model took hold among development professionals and economists working in international institutions, Western academia and governments in developing countries. The economies of poor countries were characterized by excess labour in agriculture; that is, there were many more people than was necessary for production. This 'excess' labour could be used more effectively to staff new industries, which over time would lead to higher wages and higher standards of living. The model was associated with Arthur Lewis, a Trinidadian who earned his PhD at the London School of Economics and eventually won the Nobel Prize for his work. In fact, the model had echoes of Soviet debates in the 1920s about how to move the country into industrialisation (Lewis 1954). A similar premise lay behind the arguments of Central Asian proponents of industrialisation in the 1950s. The European parts of the USSR, devastated by the Civil War, the famine of the 1930s, and World War II, saw stagnating and even declining population growth in the post-war decades. Urbanisation contributed to this – not only did urban families desire fewer children than rural ones, but the shortages of houses in the cities meant that families often had fewer children than they ideally desired. The Central Asian republics (and parts of the south Caucasus), by contrast, were experiencing a baby boom. Rural families continued to desire large families, in addition to which, Soviet public health, however rudimentary, had succeeded in lowering infant mortality, meaning that more new-borns were surviving to adulthood. Central Asian planners and their allies in Moscow saw this as an opportunity. Whereas industries in the European USSR were facing the possibility of labour shortages, no such problem appeared on the horizon in Central Asia. People would move to industry because wages were higher; all that was needed was to build the factories and provide the training (Kalinovsky 2018: 72–4).

The third pillar was education. The new industries needed engineers, architects, and economists, to build factories and all sorts of skilled workers to run them. Higher education expanded exponentially in the post-war decades. All of the republics got their own universities, as well as polytechnic institutes. Moscow also invested in professional-technical schools (PTUs) which were supposed to provide skilled labour. The latter had trouble recruiting from indigenous populations, and the former turned out – for complicated reasons – to be better at producing specialists in the humanities and social sciences than ones in the natural sciences. Still, together they created a local intellectual elite who took the project of socialist construction and service to the nation seriously. Indeed, not only did many graduates of these institutions go on to work in new industries, but some became planners and social scientists who engaged in debates *about* development and economic management in subsequent decades.

Industrialisation did not mean that cotton-producing republics were not going to be freed from their obligations to provide the Soviet Union with 'white gold.' If anything, the attempt by Nikita Khrushchev and his successors to increase production of consumer goods only raised the importance of Central Asian cotton for the Soviet economy. But the assumption was that mechanisation would turn cotton production from a labour intensive enterprise to a capital-intensive one, thus freeing up yet more labour for industry and other sectors. This, after all, is what happened in the American south, and the USSR invested heavily in developing cotton-harvesting machines in the post-war decades (Pomfret 2002; Kalinovsky 2015).

Practices

It should not be surprising that these models failed to predict how people would behave. In fact, rural Central Asians proved reluctant to move to big cities, where industry was concentrated. Staffing the newly built factories thus meant bringing in workers from other parts of the USSR, something frowned upon by planners in Moscow who were facing perceived labour shortages in the industrialised parts of the country. And it was of course unwelcome from the point of view of Central Asian planners as well, who had counted on industry to raise the standard of living of their own populations.

Understanding why these dynamics took place – and what lessons Soviet planners took from the failure of their models – is itself revealing. Cotton production, for example, remained labour intensive. Although Soviet factories produced plenty of harvesters, farm managers proved reluctant to use them. One reason surely was that Soviet industry proved better at producing the machines than the technicians and spare parts to service them when they broke down. Farm managers found that they had to abandon the harvesters and mobilise labourers to take up the task. And with so many families willing to stay in the countryside in any case, and state agencies willing to mobilise additional help when necessary, it made more sense to rely on manual labour than to bother with unreliable machines.

With manual labour still needed in the collective farms, republic-level officials continued to rely on resettlement well into the 1970s. In many cases they seem to have been responding to the demands of farm managers in the valleys who promised to provide housing, plots and other facilities to families from the mountains. Although officials did not use the kind of force that their predecessors in the 1930s employed, they nevertheless relied on various pressure tactics to move reluctant villagers, such as closing village stores and cutting off supplies (Ferrando 2011).

At the same time, officials did not give up on mobilising the rural population into the labour force. Particularly at industrial sites located in rural areas, they relied on party activists to reach out to villagers and convince them to try out jobs in factories or on construction sites. Here, the role of ideology proved important. Construction managers often preferred to rely on more experienced labourers from outside the republic, but particularly at show-piece sites like the Nurek Dam or the Aluminium Plant in Tursunzade, party officials insisted that development was not simply about building infrastructure and factories but also about transforming individuals and societies. Managers thus had to not only recruit manual labourers but also take steps to train them. In the case of Nurek, this included setting up a local technical college which sent particularly promising students on to the Polytechnic Institute in Dushanbe; some of its graduates ended up assuming leading managerial roles in the dam's construction and operation.

While sites like Nurek or the Aluminium Plant did show successes in employing local men, they were far worse at recruiting women. There were never more than a handful of local women employed in the construction or operation of the Nurek Dam, for example, although the ones that did join the workforce were widely celebrated in the republic and beyond in the hopes that they would inspire other women. Planners also experimented with enterprises geared specifically towards employing women. At the construction site for the Nurek Dam, for example, planners opened a branch of a Dushanbe clothing factory to make use of female labour. Originally envisioned as a way to provide employment to the wives of workers who came from outside the republic, it became instead an experiment in mobilising local Tajik women for industrial labour. The idea was that the work required fewer skills, those that were required could be learned on the job, and it would be familiar enough to what women did in the home that they and their families would be more open to the idea. Activists from local party organisations partnered with the human resources department to conduct outreach among villagers. Although they were more successful here than with recruitment of women into heavy industry, the factory nevertheless never managed to fill all of its positions (Kalinovsky 2018: chapter 5).

How much these sites benefitted the local population depended on their function and the role they played in Soviet domestic politics and even foreign propaganda. Closed cities – such as nuclear sites in Kazakhstan or Chkalovsk outside Leninabad in Northern Tajikistan – offered a privileged life to those (mostly from elsewhere in the USSR, with some local political and technical elites) who lived within their confines. Few outsiders – let alone foreigners – were allowed to visit. Such cities received what was known as 'Moscow provisioning'; food and other goods from around the USSR were sent to these cities to keep their residents happy. Even if they relied on the surrounding countryside for food, interaction was limited (Guth 2018; Florin and Zeller 2018; Wooden 2018).

By contrast, cities like Nurek, while privileged, were also open. They served as a demonstration of Soviet technical achievements and friendship among Soviet nationalities; not only were outsiders and foreigners encouraged to visit as tourists, but some of them even worked on the construction site. Such cities existed in a kind of symbiosis with the surrounding villages, relying on them for food and labour, and even housing. The cities, in turn, were expected to help provide running water, health services and electricity, and assist with construction of schools and roads. None of this meant that the relationship between such cites (populated by people from outside the area) and the surrounding village was always harmonious. On the contrary, the relative material privilege of the cities, as well as the cultural differences between urban and rural life, combined with the proximity of one to the other, often led to discontent and sometimes even to violence (Kalinovsky 2016; Kalinovsky 2018, chapter 5).

One reason Central Asians may have preferred to stay on farms was the possibilities afforded by engaging in informal (but largely legal, or at least tolerated) agricultural practices. Members of state and collective farms were allowed to maintain private plots and to sell their surplus on the market. While the size of such plots was limited by law, farm chairmen could sometimes allow families larger plots in exchange for their work in the collective sector. The demand for fruits that grew only in Central Asia and the Caucasus also created opportunities for middlemen who brought these products to cities in central Russia, forming part of a tolerated shadow economy (Giehler 2011; Sahadeo 2019). Similarly, certain clothing items continued to be produced in the home rather than in state-organised workshops, even if these were later sold on the market or gifted as part of a 'ritual economy.' In both cases, however, we should be wary of seeing these kinds of economic practices as separate from socialist development. Farmers working on private plots used water, fertiliser and tools that came from the socialist sector; household producers similarly used inputs (including cotton) that came from socialised production.

Culture

Neither socialist nor capitalist development was simply about factories, roads and dams; both shared visions of creating 'new men.' In the US, for example, social scientists like Daniel Lerner and Alex Inkeles tried to identify traits that showed individuals moving from 'traditional' to 'modern' outlooks, which could mean, among other things, allegiance to nation rather than family or tribe, commitment to self-improvement, and faith in the power of science and technology (Lerner 1958; Inkeles 1969). In the Soviet tradition, the creation of new men was bound up with the notion of *kulturnost'*, or culturedness. The precise contours of culturedness varied but included a preference for edifying past-times, respect for knowledge and literature and proper comportment in an urban setting. At the same time, the Soviet Union from the 1930s onwards invested heavily in supporting and creating high culture that would be accessible to the masses and help create new socialist men and women. High culture and culturedness were thus symbiotic.

To a significant extent, the intellectual elites of the republics accepted the goal of creating cultured citizens, although they adapted the notion of high culture and everyday culturedness to their own (evolving) understanding of the nation. In practice, spreading culture meant investment not only in higher education and schooling but also in theatre, museums and concert halls, as well as orchestras, artists and performers. The connection between these institutions and development becomes obvious once we consider the importance placed on making the benefits of culture available in rural areas. Villages and collective farms were evaluated on the availability of services and facilities for culture and everyday life (*kultur'-byt*), which included schools, clubs, availability of newspapers and radio, stores, and facilities for extracurricular artistic activities. Together these were supposed to form the new Soviet person, whether rural or urban. In mountain areas, the difficulty of providing people with necessary cultural facilities was sometimes used as an argument for resettlement.

Soviet economists saw a direct link between culturedness and economic production. Working in factories helped shape modern men and women, who appreciated the power of science and technology but also learned to harness it for collective goals. Working on a dam or a canal was even more promising, as it allowed the worker to feel mastery over nature. Central Asian economists and social scientists, a relatively privileged and upwardly mobile group that identified strongly with the goals of the Soviet state, saw industrialisation as a way to speed up the acquisition of modern outlooks among the population. By the 1970s, the difficulty of getting rural Central Asians to join the industrial work force led some of them to suggest that the sequence had to be inverted. Rural residents seemed to be too traditional in outlook to move to cities and work in factories or pursue higher education. Rather than modernising individuals by bringing them into the industrial labour force, then, perhaps authorities should instead focus on modernising them in the countryside: that is doubling down on investment in facilities for culture and everyday life (Kalinovsky 2018L 80–1).

In practice, officials often adjusted their approach to their understanding of how local culture functioned. We see this, for example, in how labour was recruited at sites like Nurek, where a premium was placed on using local cadres. Socialist modernity was supposed to weaken the hold of the family, and particularly the extended family, on the individual. In fact, social scientists identified the patriarchal family as one of the 'pull' factors keeping Central Asian youth from migrating to cities. At the same time, local party activists recognised the importance of male elders in winning over support for recruitment, and would work to get their endorsement to facilitate recruiting younger workers. Similarly, to recruit women to the aforementioned clothing factory, they worked on men: promising them that women would work alongside other women, organising buses that would bring them to and from villages, and so on. Such compromises did lead to successes in recruitment, but they also reaffirmed the kind of authority socialist modernisation was supposed to undermine (Kalinovsky 2018, chapter 5; Kalinovsky and Pettina 2017).

We see something similar when we look at the construction of prayer spaces in the countryside, and the general tolerance for religious practice, especially after the 1950s. Formally, the

Soviet Union remained a state committed to overcoming religion, and placed severe restrictions on the numbers of churches, mosques and synagogues. In rural areas, however, officials often tolerated the use of 'clubs' as prayer spaces, and in some cases may have even supported their construction knowing that they would be used in this way. We also know that while members of the Communist Party in urban areas would be severely punished if they were found to be engaging in religious practice, it was somewhat more common in rural areas for even decorated party members to pray collectively and to keep the fast on Ramadan. We should not necessarily see such accommodations as simply a failure of Soviet ideology, however. Rather, tolerating and even facilitating such practices was a way for local officials to achieve their larger goals, such as recruiting workers, making sure girls went to school and so on (Dudoignon and Noack, 2011; Tasar 2017; Kalinovsky 2018: 137–8).

Cultural production was used to celebrate development, to shape modern individuals and, sometimes, to critique how development was carried out. Major infrastructure projects were celebrated in novels, songs, poetry and even theatrical productions (Bichsel 2017). As with other socialist realist works about industry, novels and movies about dams, factories and farm life celebrated individuals who attained mastery and pushed themselves to make the best possible contribution to the collective. Biographies of workers published in newspapers, pamphlets and in fictionalised accounts provided models of personal growth, and of movement from traditional to modern mind-sets. Both journalistic and creative works could also tweak the system, or show ways in which the system had to adapt to local realities. The novel *Voda k dobry snitsa*, otherwise celebratory of the Nurek Dam, begins with scenes showing the destruction of fences and trees belonging to peasants resettled in the area under an earlier development initiative (Khodzhaev 1982). Moritz Florin has shown how a documentary film made to be a celebration of the Toktogul Dam in Kyrgyzstan became instead a melancholy meditation on transformation of the river (Florin 2019). The 1978 Tajikfilm production *A schast'e riadom* [Happiness Is Nearby] celebrates the construction of the Nurek Dam, but also shows the hero taking a break from work to get advice from his father, a bearded shepherd in traditional clothes. Development is envisioned here not as a break with a traditional past but as co-existing alongside it.

Welfare

Though it may sometimes be hard to believe, Soviet officials took the welfare of the population seriously, particularly in the post-Stalin era. We can see the importance of welfare in discussions about industrialisation, resettlement and much else. Partially, this is connected to the way the welfare state as a whole was set up within the Soviet Union. Although healthcare was centralised through a USSR Ministry of Health (and republic ministries), actual services were often organised around or extended through industrial sites or collective farms. This was less obvious in larger cities, which would have numerous clinics, hospitals and other facilities, but much clearer in towns set up to service one factory or industry. To some extent, in other words, Soviet health care was inseparable from Soviet labour practices. At the same time, looking at the debates about welfare policies and actual practices of extending in Soviet Central Asia again reveals interesting tensions between Soviet universalism and its adaptation to local practices.

The USSR had already developed a rudimentary health network in the Stalin era, but in Central Asia in particular it was only in the post-war era that it penetrated deep into the countryside. The opening of new medical schools and nursing colleges in the late Stalin era helped to train thousands of new professionals who knew local languages and could be sent back to their home villages to set up practices and clinics. But what did bringing welfare services really mean? Soviet biomedical practice, derived from nineteenth-century European models, often contradicted local norms of propriety. The widespread use of hospitalisation, for example, which required the separation of sick individuals from their families, often led people to avoid treatment altogether (this was not unique to Central Asia, or even to rural areas, but the practice was naturally more shocking in places where it was newer). Similarly, there were issues of propriety: could a male doctor examine female patients? Was it appropriate for male medical staff to be involved in birth? How were officials to reconcile their goals of getting all births to take place in clinical settings, with the fact that such involvement went against local traditions? (Abashin 2015: 402–44).

It would be wrong to assume that people simply resisted the welfare state, or saw the establishment of biomedical practice as a wholly unwanted intrusion. Rather, communities sometimes demanded services while resisting the way these services are delivered. Local intellectuals, party activists and ordinary citizens petitioned to have welfare services extended; at the same time, many of the same people avoided practices they saw as improper or suspicious. Such resistance could be overcome by hiring practitioners who were themselves from the local community, employing female doctors and nurses to deal with all questions of women's health, and bending the rules on hospitalisation and family access if longer-term care was necessary. As elsewhere, people combined biomedical interventions with traditional practices.

One area where the relationship between universal commitments and local realities proved most difficult was on the question of demographics and family planning. From the 1930s onwards the Soviet Union had undertaken a number of policies to encourage childbirth, among them payments to women with more than three children. In the post-war Soviet Union, as demographic patters in Central Asia and the rest of the union diverged, the wisdom of such a policy started to come under question. If the point of such payments was to encourage women to have larger families, what was the point of this policy in places where women wanted to have large families anyway?

Yet Soviet officials found it difficult to consider a differentiated policy – one that would encourage childbirth in some parts of the country but not in others. A differentiated policy would come too close to the kind of racial differentiation the USSR was supposedly against. Only in the late Soviet era did a coalition of indigenous medical professionals and economists come together to support family planning in the region. For the economists, reducing family size was a way to raise the standard of living. Medical professional encouraged family planning to relieve the burden on rural women, whose health suffered from the expectation that they bear and raise as many children as possible while also working in the cotton fields. The proposals were attacked from a number of different corners, and had little practical effect at the time of the USSR's collapse (Kalinovsky 2018: 225–7).

The results of Soviet welfare policies were ambiguous. On the one hand, the rural health networks in particular clearly had an effect in terms of containing infectious diseases, improving childhood mortality and raising overall life expectancy when compared to earlier decades. More advanced treatment was available in larger cities, or, ultimately, in central Soviet cities like Moscow and Leningrad. At the same time, health officials themselves found the quality of health care lacking, and were sometimes aghast at the lack of training among front-line workers. Health outcomes, like other measures of development, fell behind the rest of the union, with internal disparities within the republics themselves. Most importantly, perhaps, some aspects of Soviet economic development did so much harm to people's health that no medical intervention could truly compensate. Industrial plants released pollutants into rivers. Cotton farming in particular relied on chemical fertilisers that made their way into drinking water, and was particularly harmful to women and children, who were used extensively in harvesting. In Kazakhstan, nuclear testing and the drying out of the Aral Sea both contributed to horrendous medical problems that continue to affect local residents decades after the USSR's collapse. These problems developed over decades but became heavily politicised during the perestroika era (Weiner 1999; Obertreis 2018).

Environment

By the 1970s it was becoming clear that development plans undertaken since the Stalin era, and particularly since the intensification of large dam construction and industrialisation in the 1950s, were doing serious damage to the environment. Some ecological effects were obvious. The air was becoming polluted, particularly in large cities and the urban centres that grew around major industrial sites. The mining of precious metals in parts of Kyrgyzstan and Tajikistan left its own environmental hazards, especially when these mines were haphazardly abandoned after the Soviet collapse (Wooden 2018). Others were less easily seen. For example, there would seem to be little connection between cotton farming and wild animals, but the intensive resettlement of people in valleys, the expansion of cotton farms and the resulting shrinkage of animal habitats brought people and animals into conflict, leading to a sharp decrease in wild animal life. At the same time, attempts to intensify animal production *after* collectivisation in Kyrgyzstan and Kazakhstan, limiting it to lands that could not be used for cotton, put further pressures on the arid steppe lands and led to increasing demand for fertiliser (Ohayon 2017).

The most obvious environmental damage was seen in the region's water systems. Large dams tend to 'clean' river water: what appears as dirty water upriver comes out as almost eerily clean downriver. But the silt carried by the river was also a source of nourishment for the soil; seasonal flooding would leave nutrients along the banks of the river that kept the soil fertile. Even without extensive cotton cultivation, farmers would have needed artificial fertiliser to make up for the loss of nutrients in the soil. But cotton cultivation, expanded far beyond traditional sites of agricultural production, in any case required extensive use of fertiliser. Runoffs from industry and chemicals used in agriculture were polluting the rivers and lakes so often proclaimed to be the lifeblood of the region. The more extensively the soil was used, the more chemical fertiliser it required (Kalinovsky 2018: 110–15).

The drying out of the Aral Sea was the most obvious, and eventually most symbolic, of the environmental disasters caused by development in the region. The causes pre-dated the post-war period. Already in the inter-war era, geologists argued that the waters spilling into the Aral Sea were 'wasted,' since the inland sea had little economic potential. Planners working on the irrigation of the Hungry Steppe after the Great Patriotic War, therefore, knew that what they were doing would ultimately lead to the sea's shrinkage, or even disappearance. As the sea shrank, fishing communities that had been set up on the Aral Sea littoral found themselves without a livelihood; the former sea floor dried out, became sand and polluted the air with pesticides and defoliants that had been deposited there over previous decades, making the area all but uninhabitable (Josephson et al. 2013: 232–3; Weiner 1999: 415).

It would be wrong to assume that Soviet planners were always indifferent to the ecological effects of their policies. On the contrary, both local actors and those based in Moscow sought ways to mitigate the damage caused by dam building, irrigation, cotton farming and industry. But with a system focused primarily on results – measured in terms of cotton harvested or goods produces – managers usually found it easy to ignore regulations, neglect filtration systems and generally avoid steps necessary to limit the environmental damage caused by their enterprises and farms. As officials acknowledged, they had created a system that farms were ill-equipped to use properly. Even the ministry officials themselves lost track of water channels. Older canals, some of them predating the Soviet period, were supplemented by newer ones, and both were sometimes repaired and modified without the changes being registered (Kalinovsky 2018: 110–15). A system that required up-to-date plans and records and specialists that could read plans and make them a reality failed because both were lacking.

In the case of the Aral Sea, however, the proposed solution was as bad as the problem. From the 1960s, a group of specialists began developing plans to refill the Aral Sea by using the water of Siberian rivers that flowed into the Arctic Ocean. The plans, which were being discussed publicly by the 1970s, involved a system of pumps and canals to move the water, as well as a series of underground nuclear explosions for the initial shift of water. The project had the support of a number of Central Asian specialists but drew opposition from Russian environmentalists, and was ultimately abandoned (Weiner 1999: 427).

Resistance

Few initiatives – whether they came from Moscow, from republic capitals or from local officials – were passively accepted. Still, the lack of any major resistance to policies that so clearly overturned people's lives requires some explanation. Certainly, the fact that most initiatives in the post-Stalin period came with at least some clear material incentives is important. So is the shadow that the Stalinist era cast over the decades that followed. The famine in Kazakhstan, the terror unleashed against intellectuals and political elites in the 1930s, and the willingness to use force against all enemies of the people undoubtedly had an effect on people's willingness to confront the regime, even when it was clear the regime was no longer prepared to resort to mass terror.

Resistance against development did take place, although its forms were more subtle than direct confrontation with the state. As we already saw, people sometimes welcomed the arrival of medical services, but not their intrusion into family life and violation of mores. One might also call the reluctance to join the industrial workforce, and to stay on the collective farm, where values and social control were more easily exerted and more easily hidden from the state, a form of resistance.

A clearer case for active, if sporadic, resistance would be the strategies highland villages adopted towards resettlement. In some cases, resettled villagers petitioned the state to allow them to return home, claiming that they were poorly suited for the hotter climate of the valleys. This worked in individual cases, particularly when such petitions came from elderly citizens. In other cases, villagers simply departed on their own –disappearing either during the resettlement process or after arriving at their destination. The problem was sufficiently widespread that officials developed blank forms for inspectors to use in trying to track down families who had disappeared after agreeing to be resettled. Many of these families apparently returned to villages where government services, including schools, had been abandoned, and government control was thus absent as well. It is difficult to estimate how many families managed to do this over the longer term, but the fact that thousands of families managed to live largely outside the view of the state, even during the period of developed socialism, is nevertheless remarkable (Kalinovsky 2015).

It was only in the perestroika era, however, that we see something like organised political resistance. Environmental issues, in particular, animated writers and scholars, some of whom had previously been reliable boosters of state approaches. In Tajikistan, the opposition of people like journalist Otahon Latifi and the poet Gulruhsor Sufieva helped put a stop to the construction of the Roghun Dam. But dissatisfaction with the results of Soviet development animated many of the political movements that sprouted during the late perestroika era, both in Central Asia and in the rest of the USSR. What was perhaps unique in Central Asia was that the failures of Soviet development were understood to be evidence not just that the planning system was inefficient but rather of colonialism (Scarborough 2018).

Revisions

By the 1970s, the seeming failure of agriculture workers to switch to industry and of young people to take advantage of educational opportunities pushed social scientists in Moscow and Central Asia towards micro-level studies of social processes to understand why populations did not conform to the patterns predicted by existing theory, leading them to factor in local traditions, culture and values. They also began to ask new questions: How was equality and standard of living to be understood? Was it simply a question of electricity or industrial production per unit of population? Such questions – and the shortcomings of the Lewis model of development – had already led Western experts and even the World Bank under director Robert McNamara to change their understanding of what was meant by 'development,' moving beyond indicators like GDP growth to focus on questions of poverty, inequality and eventually 'basic needs' (Finnemore 1997). In other words, just as the disappointment with the 1960s 'development decade' led to a paradigm shift in international development thought, the disappointment with the 'industrialization decade' in the USSR led scholars and planners to rethink their earlier assumptions and look for new tools to understand the causes behind the lack of change.

Studies undertaken by Soviet institutions of economic and labour research uncovered contradictory information. Scholarship that compared population growth to formal employment opportunities found a large and growing number of 'unemployed' in Central Asia; many studies treated all such people as dependents of wage earners. Closer observation revealed that many of these people were engaged in some combination of seasonal labour on collective farms, work on personal agricultural plots or other kinds of activity oriented around the home. Yet the tools of Soviet economics did not allow scholars to even estimate the possible income of these activities or their broader significance in terms of supplying the consumer market. Soviet economists studied the socialist economy; the kind of activity discussed above was usually discussed by legal scholars interested in determining the proper boundaries of such activity and the proper instruments for regulating it. But on the ground observations seemed to undermine these findings.

To make better sense of what was keeping Central Asians from moving from agriculture to industry and from rural areas to cities, planners also turned to sociology and even ethnographic studies. These studies showed that people, on the whole, did not want to move; few rural Central Asians seemed to find the idea of urban living or industrial work attractive. Women, in particular, seemed resistant to urbanisation, and continued to desire large families.

Some planners and scholars saw the problem as essentially one of placement. Rather than trying to move people to urban centres, the state should construct smaller enterprises closer to where people lived. Others, like the Uzbek economist and sociologist Rano Ubaidullaeva, went further. Industrialisation, they argued, had come up short in raising the standard of living and transforming the cultural life of rural Central Asians, particularly Central Asian women. At the same time, the economic activity they were undertaking on the margins of the socialist economy made it possible for rural Central Asians to have a higher standard of living than their urban counterparts, although this came at the cost of reinforcing patriarchal relations.[1]

From the late 1970s, a number of researchers in Central Asia and in Moscow began arguing for policies that more closely reflected how people lived, rather than how they *ought* to live. They suggested promoting home labour – that is, rather than encouraging women to join factories, they would be given the opportunity to work from home and be paid for piecework. According to regulations approved in 1981, they could even use their children in production. Home-labour was promoted across the USSR, but usually as a way to include pensioners and women of child-bearing age in the workforce on a temporary basis; in Central Asia it was meant to draw in people who were not part of the socialist economy at all, and to allow them to structure their work along supposedly 'traditional' lines. It was also an attempt to bring in practices from the shadow economy into the socialist sector. During the *perestroika* era, a number of other policies reflecting the importance of family in production were introduced as well, including a family-brigade and family subcontracting system for collective farms. Again, regulations made these new forms of labour organisation possible across the Soviet Union, but planners expected that they would have their greatest effect in Central Asia, where, they felt, the traditional family had survived intact.

Afterlives

By the time of the Soviet collapse the Central Asian republics were already trying to reorient their economies to deal with quickly changing realities. The Soviet Union had shifted to self-financing at the republican level in 1988. The republics were now expected to fund themselves internally, and to establish their own economic links with other republics and abroad. The loosening of central controls was welcomed by many local economists and planners, who hoped that greater local control would make it easier to adjust economic plans to local realities. Yet the spiralling crisis of the Soviet economy made this almost impossible; there was little demand for goods, and few resources for imports. By December 1991 all were facing a deep economic and even humanitarian crisis.

Despite the ferment of the late Soviet era and protests against the kind of infrastructural, industrial and agricultural development undertaken since that time, there has been substantial continuity in the kinds of projects undertaken by post-Soviet governments. Even as they shed aspects of state-socialism, the leaders of the newly independent states maintained many developmental goals, especially concerning industrialisation, urbanisation and female participation in the labour force. Yet they were doing so under dramatically new conditions. The unitary post-Soviet state existed no more. The 1990s was the heyday of the 'Washington Consensus,' according to which the best way for poor countries to become rich was to shrink the state and allow entrepreneurs to thrive; the role of development professionals was to prepare these conditions. The countries of the socialist bloc were declared to be in 'transition' from a failed socialist political economy to a liberal democratic order.

Yet we would be wrong to imagine a complete break with the socialist past, and not just because the people leading newly independent states were former Soviet cadres. First, structural elements (cotton monoculture, hydrocarbon production) continue to play such an important role in the region's political economy. Second, the problems of connectivity, infrastructure and energy production are still shaped by the Soviet inheritance, as is most dramatically evident in the commitment of Tajikistan to complete the Roghun Dam, construction of which had been suspended in 1990. Increasingly, China has stepped in to fulfil the ambitions of Central Asian states in these areas, transforming the region but also raising new questions about foreign domination of the economy (Hoffman et al. 2020). Third, labour migration to Russia and other countries, which plays such an important role in the economies of Tajikistan, Kyrgyzstan, and Uzbekistan in particular, has its roots in the Soviet era as well (Bahovadinova and Scarborough, 2018).

Finally, some of the continuities between the socialist approach to development and what came after can be explained by the role of knowledge production in the development process. After 1991, the newly independent republics turned to international development. But the organisations that came in also faced a problem: they knew little about the countries they were entering. Even as international organisations like the UNDP spoke of a break with the past, they came to rely on locals both to make sense of the situation and to implement policy. Many Soviet-trained economists and sociologists turned to doing research for international institutions or newly created independent think-tanks, while former activists started NGOs. At the same time, international officials came to see that their job was not just developing a 'brand new socio-economic system,' as an early UNDP assessment had it, but also preserving what had come before. There may have been little basis for a conversation between Soviet-trained specialists and international institutions when it came to macro-economic questions (Johnson 2016), but it is clear that when it came to understanding social and environmental problems international specialists and Soviet-trained ones understood each other quite well. Soviet specialists, many of whom had been involved in the revision and critique of Soviet development models in the 1970s and 1980s, became the eyes through which these international organisations 'saw' the countries they had come to help.

Note

1 See the research project carried out by Council on Productive Force, a research institute within GOSPLAN. Russian State Archive of the Economy Fond 399, opis 3, delo 1498, 18–20, 40–1.

Bibliography

Abashin, S. (2015) *Sovetskii kishlak: Mezhdu kolonializmom i modernizatsiei*. Moscow: Novoe Literaturnoi Obozrenie.

Bahovadinova, Malika & Scarborough, Isaac. (2018) 'Capitalism Fulfills the Final Five-Year Plan: How Soviet-Era Migration Programs Came to Fruition in Post-Soviet Eurasia.' in Marlene Laruelle (ed), *Eurasia on the Move: Interdisciplinary Approaches to a Dynamic Migration Region*. Washington, DC: George Washington University Central Asia Program.

Bichsel, C. (2017) 'From Dry Hell to Blossoming Garden: Metaphors and Poetry in Soviet Irrigation Literature on the Hungry Steppe, 1950–1980.' *Water History* 9(3): 337–59.

Cameron, S. (2018) *The Hungry Steppe: Famine, Violence, and the Making of Soviet Kazakhstan*. Ithaca: Cornell University Press.

Doolotkeldideva, Asel. (2016) 'Social Mobilizations, Politics and Society in Contemporary Kyrgyzstan.' PhD diss. University of Exeter.

Engerman, D. C. (2011) 'The Second World's Third World.' *Kritika – Explorations in Russian and Eurasian History* 12(1): 183–211.

Ferrando, O. (2011) 'Soviet Population Transfers and Interethnic Relations in Tajikistan: Assessing the Concept of Ethnicity.' *Central Asian Survey* 30(1): 39–52.

Féaux de la Croix, Jeanne, and Suyarkulova, Mohira. (2015) 'The Rogun Complex: Public Roles and Historic Experiences of Dam-Building in Tajikistan and Kyrgyzstan.' *Cahiers d'Asie centrale* 25: 103–132.

Finnemore, M. (1997) 'Redefining Development at the World Bank.' In Frederick Cooper and Randall Packard (eds), *International Development and the Social Sciences: Essays on the History and Politics of Knowledge*. Berkeley: University of California Press, 203–27.

Florin, M. (2019) 'Emptying Lakes, Filling Up Seas: Hydroelectric Dams and the Ambivalences of Development in Late Soviet Central Asia.' *Central Asian Survey* 38(2): 237–54.

Florin, M., and Manfred, Z. (2018) 'Soviet Transnationalism: Urban Milieus, Deterritorialization, and People's Friendship in the Late Soviet Union.' *Ab Imperio* 4: 131–46.

Frank, A. G. (1966) *The Development of Underdevelopment.* Boston: New England Free Press.

Giehler, B. (2011) 'Maxim Gorki and the Islamic Revolution in the Southern Tajik Cotton Plain.' In Stephane A. Dudoignon and Christian Noack (eds), *Allah's Kolkhozes: Migration, De-Stalinisation, Privatisation and the New Muslim Congregations in the Soviet Realm (1950s–2000s).* Berlin: Klaus Schwarz, 123–47.

Guth, S. (2018) 'USSR Incorporated Versus Affirmative Action Empire? Industrial Development and Interethnic Relations in Kazakhstan's Mangyshlak Region (1960s–1980s).' *Ab Imperio* 4: 171–206.

Hancock-Parmer, M. (2019) 'Flight and Famine: Interrogating Collectivization, Stalinism, and Genocide.' *Kritika: Explorations in Russian and Eurasian History* 20(3): 601–61.

Hofman, I., Oane V., and Kalinovsky, A. (2020) 'Introduction: Encounters after the Soviet Collapse: The Contemporary Chinese Presence in the Former Soviet Union Border Zone.' *Problems of Post-Communism* 67(3): 193–203.

Inkeles, A. (1969) 'Making Men Modern: On the Causes and Consequences of Individual Change in Six Developing Countries.' *American Journal of Sociology* 75(2): 208–25.

Johnson, J. (2016) *Priests of Prosperity: How Central Bankers Transformed the Postcommunist World.* Ithaca: Cornell University Press.

Josephson, P., Dronin, N., Mnatsakanian, R., Cherp, A., Efremenko, D., and Larin, V. (2013) *An Environmental History of Russia.* Cambridge: Cambridge University Press.

Kalinovsky, A. M. (2015) 'Tractors, Power Lines, and the Welfare State: The Contradictions of Soviet Development in Post-World War II Tajikistan.' *Asiatische Studien* 69(3): 563–92.

Kalinovsky, A. M. (2016) 'A Most Beautiful City for the World's Tallest Dam.' *Cahiers du monde russe* 57(4): 819–46.

Kalinovsky, A. M. (forthcoming) 'Exceptions to Socialism: Gender, Ethnicity, and the Soviet Central Asian Entrepreneur.'

Kalinovsky, A. M. (2018) *Laboratory of Socialist Development: Cold War Politics and Decolonization in Soviet Tajikistan.* Ithaca: Cornell University Press.

Kalinovsky, A. M., and Kamp, M. (2018) 'From Industrialization to Extraction: Visions and Practices of Development in Central Asia.' *Ab Imperio* 2018(2): 69–79.

Kalinovsky, A. M., and Pettina, V. (2017) 'From Countryside to Factory: Industrialisation, Social Mobility, and Neoliberalism in Soviet Central Asia and Mexico.' *Journal für Entwicklungspolitik* 33(3): 91–117.

Khodzhaev, M. (1982) *Voda k dobru snitsia* [Translated from Tajik by Valery Tal'vin.]. Moscow: Sovetskiy pisatel.

Lerner, D. (1958) *The Passing of Traditional Society: Modernizing the Middle East.* Glencoe: Free Press.

Lewis, A. (1954) 'Economic Development with Unlimited Supplies of Labor.' *Manchester School of Economic and Social Studies* 22: 139–91.

Lorenzini, S. (2019) *Global Development: A Cold War History.* Princeton: Princeton University Press.

Macekura, Stephen J., and Erez Manela (eds). (2018) *The Development Century: A Global History.* Cambridge: Cambridge University Press.

Obertreis, J. (1991) *Imperial Desert Dreams: Cotton Growing and Irrigation in Central Asia, 1860–1991.* Göttingen: V&R unipress.

Obertreis, J. (2018) 'Soviet Irrigation Policies under Fire: Ecological Critique in Central Asia.' In Nicholas Breyfogle (ed.), *Eurasian Environments: Nature and Ecology in Imperial Russian and Soviet History.* Pittsburgh: Pittsburgh University Press, 113–32.

Ohayon, I. (2017) 'Après la sédentarisation. Le pastoralisme intensif et ses conséquences au Kazakhstan soviétique (1960–1980).' *Etudes rurales* 200: 130–55.

Olimov, M. A. (1989) 'Etalon nekapitalisticheskogo razvitia?' *Narody Azii I Afriki* 4: 18–26.

Peterson, M. K. (2019) *Pipe Dreams: Water and Empire in Central Asia's Aral Sea Basin.* New York: Cambridge University Press.

Pomfret, R. (2002) 'State-Directed Diffusion of Technology: The Mechanization of Cotton Harvesting in Soviet Central Asia.' *Journal of Economic History* 62(1): 170–88.

Reid, P. (2016) 'Managing Nature, Constructing the State: The Material Foundation of Soviet Empire in Tajikistan, 1917–1937.' PhD diss., University of Illinois at Urbana-Champaign.

Roberts, F. (2018) 'A Controversial Dam in Stalinist Central Asia: Rivalry and "Fraternal Cooperation" on the Syr Darya.' *Ab Imperio* 2: 117–43.

Rodney, W. (1973) *How Europe Underdeveloped Africa.* London: Bogle-L'Ouverture Publications.

Sahadeo, J. (2019) *Voices form the Soviet Edge: Souther Migrants in Leningrad and Moscow*. Cornell: Cornell University Press.

Scarborough, I. (2018) 'The Extremes it Takes to Survive, and others on perestroika in Central Asia.' PhD diss., London School of Economics and Political Science.

Suyarkulova, Mohira. (2014) 'Between National Idea and International Conflict: The Roghun HHP as an Anti-Colonial Endeavor, Body of the Nation, and National Wealth.' *Water History* 6(4): 367–383.

Tasar, E. (2017) *Soviet and Muslim: The institutionalization of Islam in Central Asia*. Oxford: Oxford University Press.

Teichmann, C. (2007) 'Canals, Cotton, and the Limits of De-Colonization in Soviet Uzbekistan.' *Central Asian Survey* 26(4): 499–519.

Umarov, Hojamamat. (1989) 'Regional'nye osobennosti proiavleniia protivorechii sotsialisticheskoi ekonomiki," Izvestiia Akademii Nauk Tadzhikskoi SSR.' *Seriia: Filosofia, Ekonomika, Pravovedenie* 3: 29–37.

Unger, C. R. (2018) *International Development: A Postwar History*. London: Bloomsbury Publishing.

Weiner, D. R. (1999) *A Little Corner of Freedom: Russian Nature Protection from Stalin to Gorbachev*. Berkley: University of California Press.

Wooden, A. E. (2018) "Much Wealth is Hidden in Her Bosom': Echoes of Soviet Development in Gold Extraction and Resistance in Kyrgyzstan.' *Ab Imperio* 2: 145–68.

" # PART II

Politics

5
VARIETIES OF AUTHORITARIANISM IN CENTRAL ASIA

David G. Lewis

When Central Asian states gained independence in 1991, they did so in the context of two countervailing trends. On the one hand, they had no history of democratic politics and were emerging from a long period of Soviet rule. The instinctive reaction of political leaders was to use familiar mechanisms from the Soviet period – propaganda, a ruling party and repression – to stay in power, constructing modern forms of authoritarianism in newly independent states.

At the same time, these states emerged within the context of a global wave of democratisation. All Central Asian states joined the Organisation for Security and Cooperation in Europe (OSCE), which included commitments to human rights and democratic principles as part of a broad definition of security. The OSCE's Office of Democratic Institutions and Human Rights (ODIHR) dispatched international missions to observe elections and assess whether human rights were observed. Central Asian regimes maintained democratic processes, such as elections, but they served largely as a façade behind which political leaders constructed authoritarian regimes.

This interaction between domestic dynamics and international norms has produced different types of authoritarian regime in each country. But variation among different types of authoritarianism is difficult to categorise in existing typologies. According to Freedom House's annual 'democracy score,' all five Central Asian states are 'consolidated authoritarian' regimes. Yet it is obvious to anybody travelling between, say, Astana and Ashkhabad that the regimes in Kazakhstan and Turkmenistan differ markedly, even if both are evidently authoritarian in nature.[1] Existing theories of authoritarianism struggle to distinguish between these varieties of autocratic rule. They continue to categorise regimes according to the role of electoral institutions ('electoral authoritarianism' or 'competitive authoritarianism'), but this does not help to differentiate among consolidated authoritarian regimes (Schedler 2006; Levitsky and Way 2010). The lack of fully democratic elections is an important element of an authoritarian regime, but it is not sufficient to explain the different varieties of authoritarianism that have evolved in Central Asia. A more sophisticated understanding requires a deeper examination of state practices in different areas of social and political life and a more detailed understanding of how these regimes maintain their authoritarian rule. This chapter first outlines the evolution of democratic elections across the region, before examining a range of practices that set the Central Asian states apart from each other in significant ways.

DOI: 10.4324/9780429057977-5

Authoritarianism and elections

In the early 1990s, reflecting the democratic moment at the end of the Cold War, almost all the Central Asian states experienced some form of contested politics. In Tajikistan political disputes and electoral rivalries spilled over into civil war by 1992. In Kyrgyzstan political differences were channelled into peaceful, competitive elections for parliament and formed the basis for a fragile political pluralism. In Uzbekistan and Turkmenistan, on the other hand, any signs of internal dissension were quickly suppressed. In Kazakhstan the process took longer, but the result was the same: elections did not reflect changes in public opinion and played no role in choosing the executive. With the exception of Kyrgyzstan, these regimes tended towards a form of authoritarian political order in which elections played no role in choosing the executive – although they may have had other important functions such as mitigating elite fragmentation or constructing legitimacy (Isaacs 2011).

In Uzbekistan the transition from contested elections to consolidated authoritarian rule was rapid. Islam Karimov had been appointed as first secretary of the Communist Party in 1989 and was elected as president of the Uzbek SSR through a vote in the Supreme Soviet (legislature) in 1990. But when Uzbekistan held its first presidential elections in December 1991, he faced opposition from an avant-garde poet and dissident, Mohammed Salih. Karimov won the election easily with 87 per cent of the vote and Salih was forced to flee the country in 1993. Opposition parties were soon banned. Karimov avoided direct elections throughout the 1990s, instead having his term in office extended through a 1995 referendum, before finally facing a national poll for the first time in 2000. He was re-elected in 2007 and 2015 with over 90 per cent of the vote. No genuine opposition candidates were permitted to contest the poll. His successor, Shavkat Mirziyoyev, initiated a series of liberalising reforms, but his election in December 2016 was no more democratic than previous polls. No opposition parties were permitted to take part in parliamentary elections in December 2019, although there was more debate and competition among candidates than at previous elections.

Kazakhstan initially had a much more pluralistic political landscape, but also ended up with a carefully managed electoral system. In the first ever presidential election on 1 December 1991 Nursultan Nazarbayev won an uncontested poll, gaining 99 per cent of the votes. There was more competition at parliamentary elections in the 1990s, but in the 2000s the political space for any unsanctioned political activity closed rapidly. In 2007, the ruling party, Nur Otan, won all 98 elected seats in the new Mazhilis (legislature). The authorities allowed two other pro-Nazarbayev parties into parliament at the 2012 elections, but Nur Otan still dominated the legislature. The situation remained virtually unchanged after parliamentary elections in March 2016. Presidential polls produced overwhelming majorities for the incumbent. Nazarbayev won 91 per cent of votes in 2005, 96 per cent in 2011 and 98 per cent in 2015. None of these elections was judged to be free or fair by international observers. Hopes were raised by talk of reform under a new leader, Kassym-Jomart Tokayev, after Nazarbayev stepped down in 2019. As part of a carefully orchestrated transition, Tokayev won a snap election in June 2019 with a relatively modest 71 per cent of the vote, after a centrist opposition leader was allowed to compete, but there was no sign of further democratisation.

Tajikistan followed a very different trajectory, but also ended up with a highly controlled, non-democratic electoral system. The 1997 peace deal that ended the Civil War introduced multiparty democracy, with representation in government for opposition movements, including the Islamic Renaissance Party of Tajikistan (IRPT). But President Rahmon used the cover of the peace agreement to centralise power and gradually remove his potential opponents one by one. This process was completed in 2015, when the IRPT was first excluded from parliament at elections in March and later banned. Many of its members were arrested and imprisoned. All legal opposition disappeared from Tajikistan's parliament and the ruling People's Democratic Party dominated the legislature. At parliamentary elections in March 2020, although five other parties won seats, they were all completely loyal to the regime. The OSCE concluded that infringements of rights had 'left no space for a pluralistic political debate' and that all 'genuine opposition has been removed from the political landscape.'[2] Rahmon won his fifth presidential election in October 2020, with over 92 per cent of the vote.

Turkmenistan had been an outlier even among Central Asian regimes in its minimal adherence to democratic procedures. Saparmurat Niyazov, who had been Communist Party First Secretary since 1985, won a presidential poll in 1992 with 99.5 per cent of the vote, but there were no other candidates. In 1994 Niyazov extended his period in office indefinitely in a referendum, winning 99.9 per cent of the votes, and until his death in 2006 never again faced the voters. Elections to Turkmenistan's legislature did take place in 1994, 1999 and 2004, but they always had the same result: the country's only legal party, the Democratic Party of Turkmenistan (DPT), won all the seats (Bohr 2016). His successor, Gurbanguly Berdymukhamedov, held an election in February 2007 and won a more modest 89 per cent of the votes. At subsequent polls in 2012 and 2017 he returned to form with more than 97 per cent of the votes. In 2012, a Law on Political Parties was adopted allowing for a multiparty system to be established. When elections were held in December 2013, an artificial opposition party – the Party of Industrialists and Entrepreneurs – and state-sponsored organisations such as the Women's Union of Turkmenistan also competed for seats. Despite the changes in electoral processes, the Turkmen legislature remained powerless, with all political influence centralised in the presidential administration. The only articulated opposition to the regime came from opposition activists in exile publishing critical commentary online.

Paradoxically, having followed very different trajectories after independence, the four most authoritarian Central Asian states all ended up with similar electoral systems. Presidents held regular polls but faced no real opposition. Seats in parliament were divided among a ruling party and a small number of artificial, pro-government parties according to arbitrary and unwritten rules that had little to do with the voting process. Political parties did not reflect different social or ideological positions or interest groups, but were created in a top-down fashion to create a façade of democratic practice and to consolidate elites. These parliaments and elections were not unimportant: there is extensive research on the role of elections and political parties under authoritarianism (Gandhi and Przeworski 2007; Brownlee 2007; Gandhi and Lust-Okar 2009; Frantz and Ezrow 2011). But they had little in common with democratic political parties or democratic elections.

The exception was Kyrgyzstan, where elections were competitive but not fair – bribery and vote manipulation were rife, but that did not prevent different political parties from entering parliament. Successive Kyrgyz presidents attempted to follow the wider Central Asian authoritarian model and build ruling parties that could dominate parliament, but in each case their attempts to rig the system in their favour resulted in mass unrest. President Akaev established the Alga Kyrgyzstan party to run in the February 2005 elections, but he was forced from office by popular unrest. President Kurmanbek Bakiev founded the Ak Jol party in 2007 and sought to make it an effective ruling party at the December 2007 parliamentary election, when it won 71 out of 90 seats. He easily won a fraudulent presidential election in 2009, winning 77 per cent of the votes. But in 2010 he was also ousted after mass protests. After Sadyr Japarov was elected president in January 2021, after another outbreak of popular unrest, he introduced changes to the Constitution to strengthen the presidency at the expense of parliament, which were approved in a referendum in April 2021.

Authoritarian practices and authoritarian regimes

Central Asia offers a case study of regimes which share similar non-democratic electoral systems, but have very different types of authoritarian regime. To understand variation that is not reflected in electoral dynamics, it is useful to examine other political practices. Glasius (2018) suggests that because regime categorisation is now so confused between different versions of democracy and authoritarianism, it is much more productive to assess authoritarian practices, which may be encountered in all regimes, rather than democratic elections. Natalie Koch suggests thinking about a particular saturation of illiberal governance practices as a way of unpacking what authoritarianism means in contemporary politics (Koch 2016a: 442).

This approach opens up a shift from a mono-dimensional analysis ('how free are elections') to a multidimensional analysis – focusing on the state's various practices in different areas of public life (Polese et al. 2017: 3). One way to categorise this array of state practices is by using the tripartite framework developed by Lewis et al. (2018) to analyse authoritarian responses to internal armed conflicts. They seek to understand how authoritarian regimes manage internal rebellions by achieving hegemonic control in three domains: discourse; space; and political economy. This provides an alternative framework to examine how authoritarian regimes in Central Asia function in reality and how they maintain power. It seeks to explain authoritarian persistence by showing that authoritarianism is more than an absence of democratic elections, but represents a complex political order, which seeks to achieve control in multiple domains and to manage contradictions between them. By explaining different state practices in these three areas, we can gain a more nuanced understanding of varieties of authoritarianism that goes beyond the conduct of elections and the failure to develop democratic institutions.

Authoritarian discourse

Recent scholarship has examined ways in which Central Asian regimes achieve legitimacy, despite their lack of democratic credentials (Isaacs and Du Boulay 2019; Polese et al. 2017; Omelicheva 2016; Lewis 2016a; Matveeva 2009; Schatz 2008). Omelicheva discusses legitimacy in terms of discourse – an approach also developed in Lewis (2016a) and Lemon (2014), who use the concept of hegemonic discourse to explain how regimes maintain power. The state controls a hegemonic discourse – 'the dominant ideas, tropes, narratives and syntax that circulate in a society in ways that constrain the possibility of articulating alternatives to the political status quo' (Lewis 2016a: 422) – to ensure that alternative political ideas are excluded from the public sphere. Discourses are policed through overt censorship, prosecution of dissident voices and suppression of independent media, but also through more subtle linguistic games that resonate with existing social beliefs and norms. The more a government can rely on what Rampton calls 'deeper hegemony' – 'the gradual but incremental hegemonisation of the social field' (Rampton 2011: 254) – the less the state will need to rely on state coercion and violence to control discourse. In other words, discourses that have some resonance among a domestic population and with international actors are easier to maintain without recourse to repression than those that do not.

Kazakhstan was most successful in balancing discursive control with social and economic modernisation, because a central basis of its legitimacy was its economic performance. The result was a form of 'soft authoritarianism' (Schatz 2012), which prioritised agenda-setting and persuasion over coercion and state violence. The government argued that an autocratic regime was the most efficient and effective means to achieve social stability and promote economic prosperity. This technocratic authoritarianism explicitly cited East Asian models – Singapore's Lee Kuan Yew was a personal inspiration for Nazarbayev – in arguing that democracy and political pluralism were inappropriate distractions during a period when the focus should be on economic development. Antagonistic politics was viewed as undermining a socio-economic framework in which the state provides technocratic solutions, based on expertise and managerial competence. Elites embraced a 'cult of the knowledgeable manager,' who could ensure prosperity without being involved in divisive politics (Rustemova 2011: 37).

There was little difficulty in finding traction for this national discourse of technocratic performance with the international community, which was willing to overlook the lack of democratic elections in favour of economic prosperity and investment opportunities. Kazakhstan was able to find numerous discursive agents – public relations firms or senior Western politicians – to reproduce its own talking points in the international arena. Among the Kazakh population, a performance discourse also resonated, because for much of the population the government's claims of economic competence appeared to be reflected in policy outcomes. The Kazakh government used its high budget revenues from oil and gas sales to boost social spending and to invest in infrastructure. GDP per capita advanced from a low of just US$3,740 in 1995 to US$10,570 in 2016, producing a new Kazakh middle class – concentrated in Almaty and Astana – which experienced rapidly growing real incomes and had a vested interest in the preservation of the authoritarian political system. After 2014, when the economy faltered as energy prices fell, and reports of high-level corruption became more widespread, maintaining a performance discourse became more challenging and the government faced growing social discontent. At times the government responded by shifting to a discourse that blamed outsiders for internal problems, blaming exiled politician Mukhtar Ablyazov for the unrest in Zhanaozen in 2011, for example. But when Kassym-Jomart Tokayev – a diplomat and technocrat – took over the presidency in 2019, he continued to emphasise traditional themes of social stability and state-led economic growth.

In Uzbekistan the government developed a very different discourse which constructed legitimacy by focusing attention on internal and external threats and divided the population into friends and enemies. There was a genuine threat to the state from militant Islamist groups in the 1990s, but the challenge was often exaggerated and the state response was brutal. The government became one of the most repressive states in the world, with no independent media or political space for opposition groups. Torture of prisoners was systemic. In 2005 Uzbek troops killed hundreds of protesters, after the arrests of religiously inspired businessmen sparked an uprising in the eastern town of Andijan. Karimov portrayed the crackdown as a legitimate response to terrorism. Uzbek officials – with some success – referenced the wider global discourse of the 'global war on terror' to justify Uzbekistan's repressive practices to an international audience. Inside Uzbekistan the government attempted to resonate with traditional social structures and attitudes: the role of the president as 'protector' was often framed within traditional portrayals of male authority at the family level (Megoran 2008). Yet this discourse of a paternalistic authoritarianism had an obvious contradiction: as the state became the source of so much violence against society, it generated resentment and resistance, prompting further cycles of repression.

Uzbekistan's discourse of danger also damaged the economy because it empowered the security services – notably the National Security Service (SNB), which forcibly took over legitimate businesses and controlled both licit and illicit cross-border trade. When Islam Karimov died in 2016, President Mirziyoyev claimed that the SNB had been involved in major organised crime and expropriation of businesses. A crackdown on the SNB's role in the economy followed, as Mirziyoyev shifted the official discourse away from countering threats and in the direction of achieving economic growth and effective governance. In Mirziyoyev's annual state of the national speeches, the shift was very clear, with a new emphasis on technocratic and economic goals: tackling poverty, boosting regional trade and creating jobs. In terms of democratic elections, Uzbekistan remained largely unchanged. But the shift in legitimation discourse nevertheless had a very significant impact on state practices in the economy – and to a lesser extent in media and civil society.

Tajikistan's President Emomali Rahmon also constructed an authoritarian regime based on a threat-based discourse and the division of the population into friends and enemies (Lemon and Rahimi 2020). Few Tajiks believed that the government could solve the country's dire social and economic problems – people relied much more on their own individual, family and community efforts to find work, housing and education. Instead, the government advanced a legitimacy discourse that asserted its role as the bulwark against the threat of renewed Civil War and state collapse. These claims resonated with the international community – which supported Rahmon's version of the peace process and largely turned a blind eye to the regime's human rights abuses – and with much of the population, in which the popular trope – 'as long as there is no war' – became a justification for poor governance. Peace was widely understood in Tajik society in terms of a lack of division and antagonism – such as those cleavages represented by political parties and democratic politics – and instead as the result of hierarchical order, in which a leader was able to enforce a unity of views on society (Heathershaw 2009; Lewis 2016a).

The discourse of negative peace was accompanied by increased repression and media control. Tajikistan's media became progressively less free, critical websites were blocked and independent media closed. Its rating in an index of media freedom compiled by the NGO Reporters Without Borders declined sharply, from 115 out of 180 countries in 2014 to 161 in 2020.[3] Uzbekistan, on the other hand, was moving in a more positive direction, although from a low base, up from 166 in the world in 2016 to 156 in 2020. Uzbekistan's shift to a discourse based more on performance and less on security threats made it less necessary to maintain previous levels of repression against the press. Tajikistan was effectively travelling in the opposite direction.

In Turkmenistan the level of media freedom was even more dismal, rated by RSF as the second worst in the world after North Korea. Rather than relying on performance (most people's living standards remained extremely low) or on an internal or external enemy (it had no recent experience of internal conflict), Turkmenistan's discursive framing focused on a much simpler idea – a cult of personality. Kazakhstan, Uzbekistan and Tajikistan also had their fair share of veneration of the political leader, but the artificial creation of charismatic leadership was not the primary focus of state discourse. In Turkmenistan President Niyazov became a ubiquitous presence in the political landscape, his image visible everywhere, whether on a revolving gold statue in the centre of Ashgabat or the corner of every television screen in the country. He renamed the months of the year and wrote a book, the Ruhnama, full of folksy nationalism, which became required reading in all schools (Lewis 2008).

Turkmenistan's personality cults have often been portrayed as irrational and bizarre. But they served a political function, creating an iconic centre of gravity around which public life rotates and circulates (Rolf 2004). Niyazov's personality cult fulfilled a political purpose – to construct a nation in the context of a weak national identity and relatively strong sub-national identities, in a territory marked by rather uncertain and porous borders (De Leonardis, 2017). In that context, a political personality provided a centre of gravity around which the division of the population into friends and enemies could take place. The leader and the nation are one, and thus '[c]riticizing the leader … becomes coterminous with betrayal of the nation and is harshly persecuted' (Leese 2014; 4–5). This functional role of constructed charisma – as opposed to some inherent, genuine charisma in a leader – became clearer when President Gurbanguly Berdymukhamedov revived many aspects of the personality-based discourse after a short-lived period when he appeared to favour political reforms. The content of personality discourse is almost irrelevant.

Berdymukhamedov has promoted himself as a sportsman, a cyclist, a rapper and a horseman. In the personalistic regime, the person at the centre must dominate the national discourse – the content of that domination is less important than the feeling of ubiquity that personalistic legitimacy discourses demand. But in the absence of genuine legitimacy gained through the charisma of the leader, a personality discourse is weaker than one based on performance or external threat; consequently, the level of coercive control and repression is significantly higher. Turkmenistan's regime was involved in mass human rights abuses, and many individuals effectively 'disappeared' into its prison system, imprisoned for long sentences with no contact with the outside world.

Monopolising space

Democratic regimes are usually able to channel mass protests and regional discontent through mediating institutions – the media, parliament, peaceful demonstrations and elections. Where these mechanisms are absent or dysfunctional, any physical protests can be seen as highly threatening to regime stability. Protests and demonstrations represent challenges to the state's dominance of political and physical space – whether taking control of the streets or by promoting regional autonomies or separatism. These spatial challenges can be fatal for a regime; in several cases Central Asian governments have resorted to armed force to assert control in their spatial peripheries.

In Tajikistan, the regime gradually expanded its territorial control across the country during the 2000s. Government forces clashed with local armed groups in the eastern Rasht district in 2009–2011 in a struggle for political control that also meshed with disputes over business and contraband. A second round of internal conflict accompanied central government attempts to impose control on local elites in the remote Gorno-Badakhshan Autonomous Oblast (GBAO) in the summer of 2012, when more than 50 people are reported to have died in fighting between government forces and the supporters of local Civil War–era commanders. In Kazakhstan, regional tensions contributed to the conflict in the western town of Zhanaozen in December 2011, when a long series of peaceful protests by oil workers ended in clashes, in which police killed at least 14 people and injured many more. By contrast, regional divides in Kyrgyzstan were reflected in the country's public politics – no government was able to use force to impose full control on powerful clans in the south of the country – instead, regional divides often contributed to unrest and helped to mobilise protestors to overthrow incumbent presidents. Deep-seated regional affiliations laid the basis for political competition and made building an authoritarian state in Kyrgyzstan more difficult.

The Kyrgyz state was not only unable to control its regions but also frequently lost control of the streets of the capital, Bishkek. In 2005, 2010 and again in 2020, Kyrgyz presidents were forced from office by mass unrest on the streets. Protestors seized control of central squares and stormed government headquarters in a symbolic demonstration of the regime's lack of spatial control. By contrast, the Uzbek state maintained high levels of physical control and surveillance in its urban spaces. A highly coercive law enforcement system controlled public and private space in ways that were effective in preventing any physical mobilisation against the regime. Under Karimov, there were numerous physical police checks on vehicles, widespread surveillance of public places, an extensive informer network in both private and public environments, and strict controls on the internet. After 2016 the government relaxed some controls on mobility, but a Soviet-era registration regime continued to limit mobility inside the country. The state also used existing hierarchical forms in society to ensure spatial control, particularly in the traditional residential neighbourhoods known as the *mahalla*. Historically developed as units of self-government, *mahalla* committees worked closely with law enforcement agents to contribute to what Sievers terms 'grassroots absolutism' (Sievers 2002: 152). Indeed, the *mahalla* goes beyond the control of public space into private spaces. As Rasanayagam notes, the government 'attempts to use the mahalla as a medium for extending the presence of central government into the intimate spaces of the family' (Rasanayagam 2011: 110–1).

Kazakhstan also refused to allow any cession of control over the streets. Kazakhstan is leading the way in Central Asia in installing digital surveillance and 'Smart City' technology supported by Chinese technology (Jardine 2019). But much of its control still uses traditional methods. When thousands protested after Nazarbayev's chosen successor Tokayev won a snap election on 9 June 2019, there were more than 500 arrests by police. In response to international pressure, the government reformed the restrictive legislation that limited scope for streets protests, but a new law adopted in May 2020 still effectively restricted any demonstrations to spaces decreed by the government. The Prosecutor General's Office outlawed a new group called *Koshe Partiyasy* (Party of the Street) as extremist on the grounds that it was linked to Mukhtyar Ablyazov's banned Democratic Choice of Kazakhstan party. The authorities were nervous of any nexus between political activists in exile and political activists on the street inside Kazakhstan.

Spatial control is also achieved through architecture and the built environment. Kazakhstan's most striking piece of spatial politics was the construction of a new capital at Astana – later renamed Nur-Sultan. The shift of the capital asserted a new spatial identity for the nation and sought to overcome regional fractures (Köppen 2013). The northern geographic location of Astana shifted the centre of political power away from the commercial capital Almaty, but the new city also marked a sharp break with the Soviet past and the construction of a state that had global aspirations. Buildings designed by international architects such as Norman Foster contributed to a new identity for the Kazakh state. In all the Central Asian authoritarian regimes, the rebuilding of the state is producing new cityscapes, landscapes and architecture, which in turn construct new legitimacy discourses and spatial realities. In Tashkent a similar process has erased memorable central spaces in favour of new cityscapes that involve resettlement and displacement of local residents and promote a global aesthetic that asserts the powerlessness of the population in the face of local authoritarian practices and global capital (Akhmedov 2018).

Architecture and memorialisation played a particular role in the construction of Turkmenistan's authoritarian order (Koch 2016b). The reconstruction of the capital Ashgabat deliberately destroyed symbols of the Soviet period and any historical epochs prior to the Niyazov era. Instead, the landscape is dominated by modern luxury buildings – symbolising the supposed prosperity and wealth that independent Turkmenistan has achieved – and a series of monumental sculptures that in one way or another represent the personality of the president. There are prominent statues of President Berdymukhamedov, including one with his favoured Akhal-Teke horse. In November 2020 he unveiled a golden statue of the Alabay breed of dog. These monuments are often mocked in international media, but they serve a purpose in marking out political space and reinforcing the sense of ubiquity of the political leader. They symbolically exclude the possibility of space being used by other political forces: the president is always present, even when represented only by his animal friends. Consequently, citizens – whatever they think of Berdymukhamedov – are required to act in response to these statues and memorials as if they believe in his claim to be a charismatic leader, observing external ceremonies of loyalty regardless of their personal beliefs.[4]

Authoritarian regimes also seek to control spaces beyond their borders, concerned about plots among political exiles, facilitated by ease of communications in cyberspace and international finance. The Kazakh authorities pursued political exiles abroad with obsessive zeal, none more so than opposition politician and banker Mukhtyar Ablyazov, a banker and opposition leader. In early 2009 he fled to the UK, leaving behind the failing BTA bank, in which the

Kazakh authorities claimed to have uncovered a multi-billion-dollar fraud. The Kazakh authorities pursued Ablyazov and his associates in multiple jurisdictions abroad, winning civil proceedings in the UK courts, but failing to win his extradition from France (Cooley and Heathershaw 2017). The Kazakh government also pursued other former insiders, such as Rakhat Aliev, who had been married to Dariga Nazarbayeva, the president's eldest daughter, before falling out of favour in 2007. The Kazakh authorities sought his extradition from Europe, but in February 2015 he was found dead in a cell in Vienna, having apparently committed suicide.

In Uzbekistan and Tajikistan, repressions at home forced many political opponents into exile, but these states continued to reach beyond their borders to control the diaspora. Uzbek security agencies conducted extensive operations abroad, including surveillance, intelligence-gathering and threats against exiles. The Tajik authorities used a range of legal mechanisms – including Interpol – to attempt to detain individuals abroad, and cooperated with security services in Russia to kidnap exiles and bring them back to Tajikistan to face long terms of imprisonment. There were also credible allegations that the Uzbek security forces were involved in assassination attempts on Uzbeks abroad. In October 2007 in Osh, in southern Kyrgyzstan, a gunman shot dead Alisher Saipov, a young journalist who had been critical of the Uzbek authorities. In February 2012 Obid-kori Nazarov, a well-known Uzbek cleric who had gained political asylum and lived in the remote northern town of Stromsund in Sweden, survived an assassination attempt after a gunman shot him in the doorway to his block of flats (Lewis 2015).

Controlling the political economy

Different state practices in controlling discourse and space help us to differentiate varieties of authoritarianism in Central Asia. Equally important are state and corporate practices in a third domain – that of political economy. Practices in political economy are not merely about balancing resources between the population (to avoid unrest) and loyalists (to avoid defection), while maintaining international credibility (Tumutlu 2016). They are also about shaping and controlling elites through legal and economic mechanisms – what Slater (2010) calls 'ordering power.' An array of formal and informal practices – gatekeeping mechanisms – serves to maintain the strategic heights of the economy in the hands of a small, hand-picked elite. Central Asian authoritarianisms can be usefully compared by examining the exclusiveness of this group of business elites, the mechanisms used to exclude and suppress new elites, and the extent to which political control trumps the need for economic competence and business investment, including foreign investment. The most successful systems ensured political control of economic resources, while allowing foreign investment and trade to stimulate the economy. In other cases, the control of the authoritarian state over business effectively stifled competition, reinforced inequality and embedded widespread poverty.

Kazakhstan provides the clearest example of this complex balance of political control and economic prosperity, in which a process of economic consolidation for a narrow elite was balanced against the need to improve the business environment for investors. The process of consolidation began in the energy sector, culminating in 2002 with the merger of several companies to create a new giant, state-owned company KazMunayGaz, with Nazarbayev's son-in-law Timur Kulibayev appointed as First Vice-President. Second, business groups close to the regime reportedly gained control of much of the construction sector, which became a lucrative area for investments during the construction of a new capital in Astana (Peyrouse 2012). Third, groups linked to the Nazarbayev family gradually established informal control over much of the mining sector (Global Witness 2010). The mining giant ENRC was also controlled by close allies of the president. Following the arrest and imprisonment in 2009 of Mukhtar Dzhakishev, the head of the Kazakhstan uranium company Kazatomprom, media reports suggested that other elites were now able to assert greater control over the uranium mining sector (Lillis 2009). Finally, entrepreneurs close to the regime gained direct or indirect control of key private banks following a banking crisis in 2008–2009. This informal extension of control over each sector of the economy was matched and supported by a formal reassertion of state control of strategic sectors of the economy through the country's sovereign wealth fund, Samruk-Kazyna.

Kazakhstan had to balance this concentration of power in strategic business with the need to promote small and medium-sized business and to advertise a positive business environment to foreign investors. Paradoxically, as the regime consolidated formal and informal control over many sectors of the economy, Kazakhstan also rose rapidly in international ratings on the ease of doing business, reaching 25th in the world in the World Bank's index in 2020. This outcome was not only the result of a flawed ratings system that focused primarily on formal indicators. It also reflected a genuine effort in Kazakhstan to improve the business environment for small business, while restricting access to the major business sectors that had political importance. According to a Kazakh analyst, Dosym Satpaev, there is a 'ceiling beyond which no one is allowed to go. [I]f you own something that is worth more than those in the inner circle own, that is dangerous' (cited in Junisbai, 2010: 250). New emerging elites faced informal measures to constrain their business below this 'ceiling.' Informal gatekeeping practices restricted high-level business to a small club of the well-connected and politically loyal actors. However, as long as the informal ceiling remained relatively high, this system still offered scope for many smaller businesses to thrive and for different economic and social actors to benefit. The danger of such a dual system is that the mechanisms used to maintain hierarchical control of the economy in strategic sectors risk entrenching poor governance throughout the system. Authoritarian practices in the political economy help to ensure political control but require a careful balancing act to maintain the performance-based legitimacy discourse that underpinned the regime.

In Tajikistan the regime achieved political control over business but struggled to leave sufficient space for economic growth and business development. The presidential family reportedly came to control the most lucrative branches of the economy (Eurasianet 2019). The small scale of the economy left limited space for other actors to thrive. Those who challenged this narrow control of major businesses – or attempted to convert business success into politics – faced extreme reprisals. In 2013 businessman and former government minister Zaid Saidov was arrested after he attempted to set up a New Tajikistan Party. He was subsequently sentenced to 29 years in prison on charges widely believed to be politically motivated. The economic impact of this narrow control seemed clear. In 2017 some 40 per cent of Tajiks aged 15–24 were neither working nor studying (Putz 2017). In the absence of business opportunities at home, migration to Russia remained the only viable option for most people to find work.

In Uzbekistan, Islam Karimov was opposed to the emergence of any 'oligarchs' – business elites that Karimov feared could challenge his monopoly of political power. In theory the state retained control over much of the economy, but in practice a small circle of elites dominated by the presidential family and the security services informally controlled many businesses and were involved in hostile 'raiding' against both foreign and domestic business (Lewis 2016b). The 'ceiling' at which business attracted the attention of state elites became very low, with law enforcement and other officials acting as predatory agents against small and medium-sized business. State control of agriculture forced many farmers to grow cotton and sell it to the state at low prices, often using low-cost forced labour. State-linked elites benefited from the export of cotton, but much of the rural population lived in poverty. After 2016 the government embarked on significant economic reforms. Behind the rhetoric, the process has attempted to ensure that political elites retain control over key sectors of the economy, while space is created for new small and medium-sized businesses to emerge and stimulate economic growth and employment opportunities. But small networks of elites and oligarchs still dominated many business sectors, making it difficult for new entrants to compete.

There was no sign of a shift in policy in Turkmenistan where the president and his close allies dominated the most significant financial flows and business sectors – there was almost no scope for any significant independent business to operate at any scale except as an adjunct to the state. Turkmenistan was ranked at 170 out of 180 countries in terms of economic freedom.[5] Where private sector expertise was required, both presidents Niyazov and Berdymukhamedov used foreign business and non-Turkmen advisers to avoid the development of an indigenous business elite that might demand a role in the country's governance. The system survived because Turkmenistan had extensive gas reserves, which the government exported to China, and used the revenue to fund its extensive apparatus of repression. This allowed the regime to operate without creating a better environment for domestic business or for foreign investors. But the model was under increasing strain by 2020, with reports of social unrest and food shortages (Eurasianet 2020).

Conclusion

There were numerous factors that contributed to the emergence of authoritarian regimes in Central Asia after 2001, including historical, cultural and contingent factors in the post-Soviet period. Initial periods of political contestation in the early 1990s were followed in most cases by a consolidation of political control around a single leader. By the third decade of independence, Central Asian states – with the partial exception of Kyrgyzstan – had coalesced around an authoritarian model in which electoral processes were undemocratic and played only a limited role in determining policies and personnel. This shared rejection of democratic elections disguised a wide variation in state practices in different social domains that determined how effective they were at meeting social needs and how much they resorted to repressive measures to ensure political control.

First, they varied in their development of different types of legitimacy discourse, focused on performance, threat or personality. When states sought legitimacy through performance, they relied less on coercion and repression, and produced better governance outcomes. Threat-based discourses required extensive repression and downgraded economic performance and social needs. The personality discourse that was central to Turkmen politics was the least effective for society and the most repressive.

Second, each regime used multiple techniques to prevent political opponents from occupying physical space – in Uzbekistan, Tajikistan and Kazakhstan this struggle resulted in the use of force against the population – shooting civilians dead to assert government control. Other techniques – from cyber surveillance to changes in the built environment – provided non-violent ways for regimes to achieve social and political control over urban spaces. States also used covert operations internationally to police and repress political activity among exiles.

Third, Central Asia's authoritarian regimes sought to consolidate and control their dominance of key business sectors, not only for personal self-enrichment but to prevent potential political opponents from using resources to challenge their political dominance. The trajectory in Kazakhstan and Tajikistan was towards growing consolidation of economic power around a small elite linked to the presidential family. But in Kazakhstan, the economy was sufficiently large to allow smaller business to find a niche. In Uzbekistan, the death of Karimov opened up some new opportunities for business, but a narrow elite still controlled large swathes of the economy. In Turkmenistan a rentier economy was easy for the regime to control, although poor governance and dependence on gas prices threatened to provoke a major socio-economic crisis.

Despite this variety in practices in these three domains, each Central Asian regime has enjoyed remarkable longevity and relative stability. Frequent predictions that Central Asian authoritarian rule would prove to be fragile and prone to state collapse have so far proved mistaken. Kyrgyzstan appeared to be an exception to this persistent authoritarianism. Its political life was marked by a plurality of discourses, contested physical spaces and a diverse business elite. The result was a pluralist society and state, but one that was also beset by fundamental political and economic problems. Central Asian authoritarianism was often highly repressive and did not meet the political, social and economic demands of Central Asian societies. But for many people in the region, Kyrgyzstan's political system also represented a warning that the existence of pluralism and diverse centres of power was not a guarantee that a sustainable form of democracy or economic prosperity would follow.

Notes

1 In Freedom House's ratings, the country scores range from Turkmenistan (0), through Uzbekistan (2), Tajikistan (3), Kazakhstan (5) and Kyrgyzstan – once described in the 1990s as an 'oasis of democracy' – scoring 16. By comparison, Estonia scored 85 and Armenia 33. These scores have been remarkably consistent over the last decade, with slight improvements in Uzbekistan after the death of former president Islam Karimov, and a worsening of Kyrgyzstan's political liberties.
2 'Republic of Tajikistan Parliamentary Elections, 1 March 2020. ODIHR Election Assessment Mission. Final Report, 27 May 2020, https://www.osce.org/files/f/documents/9/9/453243.pdf
3 https://rsf.org/en/tajikistan
4 Cf Lisa Wedeen's observation that 'Citizens in Syria are not required to believe the cult's flagrantly fictitious statements and, as a rule, do not. But they are required to act as if they do' (Wedeen 1998: 506).
5 https://www.heritage.org/index/ranking

References

Akhmedov, A. (2018) 'Dispossession and Urban Development in the New Tashkent,' *Open Democracy*, 21 December 2018. Available at: https://www.opendemocracy.net/en/odr/dispossession-and-urban-development-in-the-new-tashkent/, accessed 27.12.20.
Bohr, A. (2016) *Turkmenistan: Power, politics and petro-authoritarianism*. London: Chatham House, Royal Institute of International Affairs.
Brownlee, J. (2007) *Authoritarianism in an Age of Democratization*. Cambridge: Cambridge University Press.
Cooley, A. and Heathershaw, J. (2017) *Dictators without Borders*. New Haven, CT: Yale University Press.
De Leonardis, F. (2017) *Nation-Building and Personality Cult in Turkmenistan: The Türkmenbaşy Phenomenon*. London: Routledge.
Eurasianet. (2019) 'Tajikistan: National Air Carrier Becomes Presidential Family Plaything,' *Eurasianet*, 23 January. Available at: https://eurasianet.org/tajikistan-national-air-carrier-becomes-presidential-family-plaything, accessed 27.12.20.
Eurasianet. (2020) 'Turkmenistan: The Mirage of Bounty,' *Eurasianet*, 3 November. Available at: https://eurasianet.org/turkmenistan-the-mirage-of-bounty, accessed 27.12.20.
Frantz, E. and Ezrow, N.M. (2011) *The Politics of Dictatorship: Institutions and outcomes in authoritarian regimes*. Boulder, CO: Lynne Rienner Publishers.
Gandhi, J. and Lust-Okar, E. (2009) 'Elections under authoritarianism,' *Annual review of political science* 12: 403–22.
Gandhi, J. and Przeworski, A. (2007) 'Authoritarian institutions and the survival of autocrats,' *Comparative political studies* 40 (11): 1279–301.
Glasius, M. (2018) 'What authoritarianism is… and is not: a practice perspective,' *International Affairs* 94 (3): 515–33.
Global Witness. (2010) 'Kazakhmys: Risky Business: Kazakhstan, Kazakhmys plc and the London Stock Exchange,' *Global Witness*, 13 July. Available at: https://www.globalwitness.org/archive/risky-business-kazakhstan-kazakhmys-plc-and-london-stock-exchange, accessed 27.12.20.

Heathershaw, J. (2009) *Post-Conflict Tajikistan: The Politics of Peacebuilding and the Emergence of Legitimate Order.* London: Routledge.

Isaacs, R. (2011) *Party System Formation in Kazakhstan: Between Formal and Informal Politics.* London: Routledge.

Isaacs, R. and Du Boulay, S. (2019) 'Legitimacy and Legitimation in Central Asia: Cases of Kazakhstan and Turkmenistan,' in R. Isaaacs and A. Frigerio, eds. *Theorizing Central Asian Politics.* Houndsmill, Basingstoke: Palgrave Macmillan, pp. 17–41.

Jardine, B. (2019) 'China's Surveillance State Has Eyes on Central Asia,' *Foreign Policy*, 15 November. Available at https://foreignpolicy.com/2019/11/15/huawei-xinjiang-kazakhstan-uzbekistan-china-surveillance-state-eyes-central-asia/, accessed 24.06.21.

Junisbai, B. (2010) 'A Tale of Two Kazakhstans: Sources of Political Cleavage and Conflict in the Post-Soviet Period,' *Europe-Asia Studies* 62 (2): 235–69.

Koch, N. (2016a) 'We Entrepreneurial Academics: Governing Globalized Higher Education in "Illiberal" States,' *Territory, Politics, Governance* 4 (4): 438–52.

Koch, N. (2016b) 'The "Personality Cult" Problematic: Personalism and Mosques Memorializing the "Father of the Nation" in Turkmenistan and the UAE,' *Central Asian Affairs* 3 (4): 330–59.

Köppen, B. (2013) 'The Production of a New Eurasian Capital on the Kazakh Steppe: Architecture, Urban Design, and Identity in Astana,' *Nationalities Papers* 41 (4): 590–605.

Leese, D. (2014) 'The Cult of Personality and Symbolic Politics,' in S.A. Smith, ed. *The Oxford Handbook of the History of Communism.* Oxford: Oxford University Press, pp. 4–5.

Lemon, E. (2014) 'Mediating the Conflict in the Rasht Valley, Tajikistan: The Hegemonic Narrative and Anti-Hegemonic Challenges,' *Central Asian Affairs* 1 (2): 247–72.

Levitsky, S. and Way, L. (2010) *Competitive Authoritarianism: Hybrid Regimes after the Cold War.* Cambridge: Cambridge University Press.

Lewis, D. (2008) *The Temptations of Tyranny in Central Asia.* London: Hurst.

Lewis, D. (2015) 'Illiberal Spaces: Uzbekistan's Extraterritorial Security Practices and the Spatial Politics of Contemporary Authoritarianism,' *Nationalities Papers* 43 (1): 140–59.

Lewis, D. (2016a) 'Blogging Zhanaozen: Hegemonic Discourse and Authoritarian Resilience in Kazakhstan,' *Central Asian Survey* 35 (3): 421–38.

Lewis, David G. (2016b) *Tackling Corruption in Uzbekistan: A White Paper.* New York: Open Society Foundations.

Lewis, D.G., Heathershaw, J., and Megoran, N. (2018) 'Illiberal Peace? Authoritarian Modes of Conflict Management,' *Cooperation and Conflict* 53: 486–506.

Lillis, J. (2009) 'Kazakhstan: Business Climate Grows Gloomy Amid Arbitrary Arrest Controversy,' *Eurasianet*, 9 June. Available at: http://www.eurasianet.org/departments/insightb/articles/eav061009.shtml, accessed 27.12.20.

Matveeva, A. (2009) 'Legitimising Central Asian authoritarianism: political manipulation and symbolic power,' *Europe-Asia Studies* 61 (7): 1095–121.

Megoran, N. (2008) 'Framing Andijon, Narrating the Nation: Islam Karimov's Account of the Events of 13 May 2005,' *Central Asian Survey* 27 (1): 15–31.

Omelicheva, M.Y. (2016) 'Authoritarian Legitimation: Assessing Discourses of Legitimacy in Kazakhstan and Uzbekistan,' *Central Asian Survey* 35 (4): 481–500.

Peyrouse, S. (2012) 'Neopatrimonial Regime: Balancing Uncertainties among the 'Family,' Oligarchs and Technocrats,' *Demokratizatsiya: The Journal of Post-Soviet Democratization* 20 (4): 345–70.

Polese, A., Ó Beacháin, D., and Horák, S. (2017) 'Strategies of Legitimation in Central Asia: Regime Durability in Turkmenistan', *Contemporary Politics* 23 (4): 427–45.

Putz, C. (2017) 'More, Better Jobs: Tajikistan's Employment Problems', *The Diplomat*, 15 February. Available at: https://thediplomat.com/2017/02/more-better-jobs-tajikistans-employment-problems work, accessed 27.12.20.

Rampton, D. (2011) '"Deeper Hegemony": The Politics of Sinhala Nationalist Authenticity and the Failures of Power-Sharing in Sri Lanka,' *Commonwealth & Comparative Politics* 49 (2): 245–73.

Rasanayagam, J. (2011) *Islam in Post-Soviet Uzbekistan: The Morality of Experience.* Cambridge: Cambridge University Press.

Rolf, M. (2004) 'Working towards the Centre: Leader Cults and Spatial Politics in Pre-War Stalinism', in B. Apor, J.C. Behrends, P. Jones and A. Rees, eds. *The Leader Cult in Communist Dictatorships.* London: Palgrave Macmillan, pp. 141–57.

Rustemova, A. (2011) 'Political Economy of Central Asia: Initial Reflections on the Need for A New Approach,' *Journal of Eurasian Studies* 2 (1): 30–9.

Schatz, E. (2008) 'Transnational Image Making and Soft Authoritarian Kazakhstan,' *Slavic Review* 67 (1): 50–62.

Schedler, A. (2006) *Electoral Authoritarianism: The Dynamics of Unfree Competition*. Boulder: Lynne Reinner.

Sievers, E.W. (2002) 'Uzbekistan's Mahalla: From Soviet to Absolutist Residential Community Associations,' *The Journal of International and Comparative Law at Chicago-Kent* 2: 91–159.

Slater, D. (2010) *Ordering Power: Contentious Politics, State-Building, and Authoritarian Durability in Southeast Asia*. Cambridge: Cambridge University Press.

Tutumlu, A. (2016) 'The Rule by Law: Negotiating Stability in Kazakhstan,' in M. Laruelle, ed. *Kazakhstan in the Making: Legitimacy, Symbols, and Social Changes*. Lanham, MD: Lexington Books, pp. 3–28.

Wedeen, L. (1998) 'Acting "As If": Symbolic Politics and Social Control in Syria,' *Comparative Studies in Society and History* 40 (3): 503–23.

6
INFORMAL GOVERNANCE, 'CLAN' POLITICS AND CORRUPTION

Aksana Ismailbekova

Central Asia has been described by political scientists via the oversimplified notion of 'clan politics' (Collins, 2002; Schatz, 2004; Luong, 2002), one which assumes that strong kinship ties interfere with democratic processes. These debates describe the politics of the Central Asian countries as clan-dominated but give little attention to the organisation and functioning of kinship ties with respect to politics from a broad social perspective. Not only has the term 'clan' become popular in academic discourse, but it has influenced development organisations, journalists, and diplomats. Meanwhile, local scholars make equal use of other terms, such as 'tribalism', which equally carry negative connotations about the shape of democracy (Dzhunushaliev and Ploskih, 2000). In this regard, Radnitz (2010) argues that 'clan' is not enough to explain mass mobilisation and political loyalty; rather, the combination of economic opportunities, patron-client relationships and informal networks is important for understanding the dynamics of post-Soviet regime change in Central Asia.

In response to these recent accounts, anthropologists (Finke, 2002; Gullette, 2010; Hardenberg, 2009; Jacquesson, 2010; Ismailbekova, 2017) have criticised the concept of 'clan' as a misleading analytical term with no empirical basis. Though 'clans' (patrilineal descent groups) are an important feature of social organisation in Central Asia, it has not been possible to demonstrate that political loyalties can be transposed in any simple way onto 'clan' loyalties. Because political analysis premised upon clan identification obscures more than it reveals in post–Soviet Central Asia, scholars urged breaking the logical interpolation of clan politics with actual 'clans' and have proposed alternative analytical concepts for understanding local kinship systems. The prominent emergence of lineage associations over the past decade begs a further reconsideration of the anthropological perspective. Among their other effects, lineage associations openly tie political loyalty to descent group loyalty. The emergence of lineage associations appears to reflect a special moment of social change (Ismailbekova, 2018). While different forms of informal politics appear in both in practice and scholarly interpretation of all Central Asian Republics, in this chapter, as a way to introduce the reader to the phenomenon of informal governance and corruption, I focus solely on the case of Kyrgyzstan.

One of the most prominent works on corruption in Kyrgyzstan is Johan Engvall's (2016) *The State as Investment Market: Kyrgyzstan in Comparative Perspective*. Engvall argues that the state in Kyrgyzstan is akin to a marketplace where politicians and businessmen make investments in order to reap gains. For instance, by buying government positions and paying large sums

DOI: 10.4324/9780429057977-6

of money to political parties, elites enjoy unparalleled access to state resources and privileges. This, according to Engvall, has become the expected or normal behaviour in Kyrgyz politics as corruption 'is not only pervasive but also standardized and rationalized' (Engvall, 2016: 198). In contrast, I argue that state positions are not sold as a purely economic transaction but that acquiring such positions also necessitates that the recipients fulfil certain criteria concerning kinship, loyalty, obligation and hospitality (2017). In other words, investing in state positions in Kyrgyzstan should not be understood solely as being grounded in rational calculations of making a return on the initial investment, rather they are embedded in local values and expectations such as reciprocity and exchange.

Kyrgyzstan's political history since independence, in particular, demonstrates how in spite of popular upheavals and changes in leadership, high levels of corruption and patronage continue to persist. The chapter delves into informal practices that influence and often override formal systems of governance. The analysis focuses on the informal governance system, revealing the nature and emergence of the different informal power networks that have evolved under the different political regimes since independence in Kyrgyzstan (1991–2017). It also identifies key forces of the modus operandi of power holders: the first president, Askar Akayev and his family networks (1990–2005); the second president, Kurmanbek Bakiyev and his circle of trust (2005–2010); the fourth president, Almazbek Atambayev (2011–2017); and the fifth president, Sooronbai Jeenbekov (2017–2023). For the analysis, I will not include the third interim president Roza Otunbayeva (2010–2011) as well as Sadyr Japarov (from 2021), as Otunbayeva was in charge for only one year and Japarov became president in 2021. On the Japarov phenomenon, there are very valuable sources and analyses dealing with the issues of nationalism, populism, traditionalism and social media (Doolotkeldieva, 2021, Mamedov, 2021; Baialieva and Kutmanaliev, 2020, Ismailbekova, 2021). The analysis shows how the social upheavals and constitutional changes have brought about changes to the formal system but failed to uproot informal governance practices and high levels of corruption that persisted throughout all transformations.

The conceptual approach in this article was inspired by the work of Baez-Camargo & Ledeneva (2017) who identify three key patterns of informal governance, namely, *co-optation, control* and *camouflage*. Baez-Camargo and Ledeneva propose analytical tools and distinguish patterns of informal governance to enable a better understanding of authoritarian regimes. They highlight the roles of informal practices and norms adhered to by elite networks in systemically corrupt environments, whereby unwritten rules, rights, and obligations function to channel and steer political influence, sanctions, and resources. Therefore, like formal governance, informal governance has allocative functions distributing resources and power, and is used as the basis to decide on access to or exclusion from the benefits of distribution. The conceptual approach identifies three key patterns of informal governance – namely co-optation, control and camouflage.

These three modalities, however, are ideal types and are hard to demarcate in practice just as formal and informal channels of governance are deeply enmeshed. The case of Kyrgyzstan furthermore uncovers hybrid types. Similar analysis of formal and informal practices can be applied in other Central Asian countries.

Historical background: Kinship and (in)formal politics

Most ethnic Kyrgyz can trace their lineage to one of 40 lineage groupings, each with a common geographic origin and unique history and genealogy. During Soviet times references to one's lineages were prohibited by the state. In the post-Soviet context, kinship systems have flourished and function in part due to a more open political environment. The introduction of competitive electoral processes contributed to the strengthening of kinship networks. As political institutions were weak, kinship formed an important aspect of mobilising voters and gathering political support (Ismailbekova, 2017).

In a patrilineal society like Kyrgyzstan, a Kyrgyz man's identification is relational, meaning that he cannot be identified as Kyrgyz without being linked to other male relatives such as fathers, grandfathers and their forefathers. Most Kyrgyz view their lineage identity or ancestral belonging as a given or natural part of their identity; thus it cannot be changed, removed, or left out of any matter. In other words, it flows in the blood. In the modern context, kinship provides not only the base for an individual's identity but also a pathway for political loyalties. Correlation between kinship and political loyalty can promote accountability of the state by invoking "shame" and "honour" against political officials who fail to represent the interests of their kin.

Most importantly, these kinship-based patronage networks hold significant power to mobilise voters, control patronage and organise protests. They function as lobby groups or even rudimentary political parties that reach deep into local and regional institutions. At the same time, there is the emergence of kinship-based patronage networks, which are increasingly striving for formal recognition in Kyrgyz politics and society.

Revolutions and corruption in Kyrgyzstan

Since independence in 1991, Kyrgyzstan has experienced mixed developments oscillating between democratisation and semi-authoritarian rule. In comparison to other Central Asian regimes, Kyrgyzstan has a much more competitive political environment, having had a succession of four different presidents within 25 years. Unpopular political leaders were thrown out of power as a result of public protests organised twice: in 2005, known as the Tulip Revolution, and in 2010, and again in 2020. During all these times the changes seemed to take place in the name of 'people's power' and offered hope for democratic transformations in Kyrgyzstan. The source of people's discontent during the tenures of the first president, Askar Akayev, and the second president, Kurmanbek Bakiyev, was their blatant corruption, nepotism among political elites and the resulting poverty of the majority of the population. People's patience was exhausted due to high levels of unemployment, the privatisation of the business sector and the monopolisation of state positions on the part of the presidents' allies and family members. Both changes of power also presented ideal moments to consolidate anti-corruption forces and take over the expelled presidents and state officials (*chinovniki*).

However, although the political opposition played a big role in overthrowing incumbents twice, in both cases incoming political elites reverted to practices similar to those of the regimes they helped topple. A key reason was that old elites were able to silently block reforms out of fear of being removed from their traditionally privileged positions (Engvall, 2012). The opposition's attempts to reform corrupt institutions were thus offset by the old elites' countervailing efforts including the continued informal distribution of political offices (Ismailbekova, 2017). It is important to highlight the role of kinship in revolutionary movements that were recruited along the lines of kin solidarity and metaphors.

Co-optation

As an informal practice, co-optation refers to the recruitment of individuals into groups or networks. Among political elites, it is often expressed in the form of strategic appointments of allies and potential opponents, who are thereby granted impunity in exploiting the power and resources associated to public office in exchange of mobilising support and maintaining loyalty to the regime. Co-optation often involves corruption because it represents a mechanism to regulate access to rent-seeking opportunities and typically involves an informal redistribution of public resources. Co-optation can also be "horizontal" when political and business elites' relationships that are based on strong bonds of trust, reciprocity and loyalty, which enable and sustain a system of mutually beneficial exchanges.

Political family networks of Akayev

The increase in formal presidential powers allowed the first president Akayev to consolidate an informal network that gradually monopolised most sectors of the executive branch, parliament and private sector. His authority to appoint key positions enabled him to elevate his family members and relatives to the highest levels during the 15 years of his presidency. Apart from the family members' dominance in economy and politics, other influential groups surrounding the president emerged as well, each with varying degrees of influence on decision-making. The informal network of Akayev included key persons of regional groupings (kin members, lineage members, etc.) from the Northern region of Kyrgyzstan, influential business elites, his own students, known academics and family friends (Alymbaeva & Sharsheeva, 2015). These people were either in the state apparatus or in the business sectors, while others were businessmen-turned-state officials. Hence, there was a symbiosis of kinship, business and politics.

During Akayev's leadership, control over business reinforced political influence and vice versa. Family members were able to protect their investments by harnessing their influence in the regime in order to secure favourable political decisions. Therefore, belonging to Akayev's inner circle was key to facilitating informal financial flows as well as their concealment. Finally, under Akayev's regime, opposition parties remained weak and without clear alternative policy programmes. This was partly due to the fact that in practice they were part of the existing political system, a loyal opposition that would often enter agreements with the government. In fact, many of them maintained frequent contact with government officials and Akayev often resorted to *co-opting* opposing political parties and groups by inviting them to join the government and offering posts in the health, defence or security ministries (Respublika, 2004). These loyalists supported the government in exercising full control over the distribution of lucrative resources of the state, thereby contributing to regime stability and security.

Political-family networks of Bakiyev

Consistent with the thrust towards an ever more centralised regime, the second president Bakiyev (2005–2010) pulled more of his loyal supporters into occupying positions of power. His family members and relatives were soon found across government structures and in control of state resources and power. Indeed, the formal restructuring aimed only to strengthen the power of a small group of people who were loyal to Bakiyev (Pannier, 2009) and who related to the president through patterns of familial, affective and communal preferences. The Kyrgyz economy was controlled by an informal network around the president's son Maksim Bakiyev (Pannier, 2009), while law enforcement and the presidential administration were in the hands of Bakiyev's close family. Bakiyev's immediate family held high positions in Bishkek, while his distant relatives from the same lineage were in charge of governance on the village, rayon and oblast levels (Delo Nomer, 2009). Most of his kin openly showed their solidarity for their own 'native son' and secured support from local voters in both southern and northern parts of Kyrgyzstan

As a consequence, during Bakiyev's regime, the political elites that occupied the positions of most power and influence changed from mostly northern representatives to southern representatives. Within one year, there was not a single top-ranking official from the northern regions, including Naryn, Chui, Issik-Kul or Talas. Instead, Bakiyev filled key political positions in state administration, military and law-enforcement structures with close relatives and loyal supporters from the Jalal-Abad oblast. Thus, while power was transmitted from one political network to another, the governance mechanisms for exercising power worked in a similar manner under both Akayev and Bakiyev (Alymbaeva, 2013).

Bakiyev also established horizontal links with criminal groups, including that of a known criminal kingpin Ryspek Akmatbaev. As the southerner, Bakiyev needed support from business and political elites in northern Kyrgyzstan and Akmatbaev, being from Issyk-Kul oblast, extended him this authority. The kingpin's younger brother, Tynchtykbek Akmataliev, was elected into the parliament. Furthermore, by co-opting Akmatbaev, Bakiyev could counterbalance other criminal syndicates backed by other state officials. Competing criminal groups used threats and violence against state officials. As a result of this strategic alliance, Akmatbaev was able to enter politics, render himself immune to state prosecution, dictate his interests and even run for parliament (Marat, 2006: 91–93).

Party co-optation under Atambayev

Atambayev was elected as president of Kyrgyzstan in 2011. A result of the adoption of a new constitution that established a new parliamentary system, it became more difficult for regime incumbents to use co-optation because elections became more competitive. The president was no longer at the centre managing the informal governance of complex networks but rather political parties in parliament came to rely on the power of kinship. Additional political networks came from other influential groups, including three major political parties: Social Democratic Party of Kyrgyzstan (SDPK), Respublika and Bir-Bol.

Indeed, political parties became the heart of the political system in Kyrgyzstan (Engvall, 2017) with party lists populated mainly by wealthy and influential people. This meant that political parties became the vehicle whereby rich individuals sought power. Joining a political party became important mainly because access to financial resources and rent-seeking opportunities was now divided among the political parties that formed the coalition government. Parliament itself, rather than the presidency, became the rent-seeking system epitomising the state-business nexus. Thus, the parties within the coalition government divided not only major ministerial positions, agencies and services, but also lucrative enterprises in the mining, transportation and communication sectors (Engvall, 2017: 8).

Aspiring politicians invested a large amount of financial resources in order to join a party, ranging anywhere from $50,000 to $500,000. Parties spent money not only on political campaigning, but also on building one's capital once in the parliament. The quest for political power thus changed from simply courting the president to acceding to a seat in parliament, which provided a way to cabinet positions and thus significant power. For example: some party members got ministerial or embassy positions and protected their and others' business interests (Engvall, 2017: 9; Begalieva & Yntymakov, 2015). Atambayev became increasingly distrustful of many opposition leaders and used judicial power to jail his most prominent opponents. Unlike his predecessors, however, Atambayev did not bring his family members into politics. There were only a few important people in his circle that played a crucial role in Kyrgyz politics and supported the process of top–down co-optation of loyal supporters. These loyalists were key elites and held positions in the presidential administration, the government, parliament, law-enforcement and the court; as such they were granted large powers and access to resources.

Jeenbekov's informal networks

Jeenbekov, who has several brothers who have now occupied high posts, as well as some of his friends, altogether are trying to build a new power structure (Gostev, 2019). His brother Asylbek Jeenbekov was a member of parliament and may be playing a powerful role behind-the-scenes by influencing political decisions (Sputnik, 2018). The Organised Crime and Corruption Reporting Project (OCCRP) in collaboration with Kyrgyz journalists from Kloop and RFE/RL's Radio Azattyk have published their investigations in which they claim that Jeenbekov also has close ties to the family of Matraimovs, infamous for their wealth reportedly obtained through corruption and organised crime (Kloop, Azattyk and OCCRP, 2019). Iskender Matraimov, a member of the parliament, is likely closely connected to mafia and power structures of Kyrgyzstan and Tajikistan. The family is allegedly involved in drug trafficking and money laundering (Kloop, Azattyk and OCCRP, 2019; Sputnik, 2018). Many representatives of the legislative, executive, judicial authorities, law enforcement agencies in southern parts of Kyrgyzstan are reportedly also indebted to Matraimovs. The brothers allegedly earn $3 billion a year (Kloop, Azattyk and OCCRP, 2019; Sputnik, 2018).

Control

The second pattern of informality is control, which relates to how informal networks enforce discipline among their members. Control mechanisms are instrumental in managing clashes of competing interests and enforcing discipline within networks. Examples of informal control mechanisms include the discretionary enforcement of anti-corruption legislation against dissidents and peer pressure through rules of loyalty and reciprocity that tie network members together by creating obligations and responsibilities vis-à-vis the group.

Akayev's control: social sanctions, demonstrative punishment and selective law enforcement

Two modalities of informal control of the networks built by Akayev are worth noting. The first alludes to 'soft' enforcement mechanisms of discipline relating to how social reputation, status and trustworthiness are constructed in Kyrgyz culture, and a second group of 'hard' control actions associated with selective enforcement of the laws. With the first type of informal control, as noted above, kinship elements provided the social "glue" that bound informal groups together during Akayev's tenure. However, while the ideology of kinship dictates criteria for co-optation into the network, it also works as a mechanism of control for enforcing discipline because it hinges upon the unwritten imperatives of trust, obligation, loyalty and reciprocity vis-à-vis the group. Indeed, it can be said that kinship-affective values help to entrench informal practices because they combine emotions with rationality. The fundamental principles of Kyrgyz kinship include the duty to provide support in times of need (kinship security), the notion that blood relatives never betray or put each other into harmful situations.

Failing to uphold these principles leads to social sanctions in the form of shaming, which therefore motivates compliance with the social obligations associated to kinship membership. This simultaneously fuels the expectation that lineage leaders in positions of power and influence should "deliver" to the grassroots members of the lineage. For example, belonging to the Sarybagysh descent group, or to the Northern lineage groups more broadly, was one of the main informal mechanisms that ensured that unwritten contracts were adhered to and whereby loyalty was expected to be unconditional under Akayev. The resort to kinship identification as a criterion to accede to public resources and opportunities meant that genealogy was widely used and manipulated by politicians, businessmen and relatives alike as kinship links are still open to interpretation, manipulation and strategic deployment (Alymbaeva, 2013, Bolponova, 2015).

The second informal control mechanism involves resorting to the formal laws, usually the criminal code and anticorruption legislation, to selectively punish political opponents. Besides the opposition activists, several other radical opposition party members were taken out of the political race. There was also a strong informal opposition bloc, 'For the power of the people', consisting of parties and individual members from the South.

Bakiyev's control: social sanctions, demonstrative punishment, selective law enforcement and assassinations

Bakiyev maintained undisputed control over the regional arena by drawing on the concept of the 'native son'. He implied that it was important for everyone to be united under this umbrella concept as people who shared common lineages, ancestors and thus blood relations, with the implicit mechanisms of social control that come tied to this notion of lineage (Ismailbekova, 2017). In doing so, he created multifarious networks within and between different districts along kinship and provincial lines, rather than on the basis of administrative or professional lines. He manipulated identity to postulate the unity of the community and of the province based on patrilocal residence and belonging to the same places, namely, Osh and Zhalal-Abad in Southern Kyrgyzstan.

The unifying categories linking people at the village, district and oblast levels were shared ancestors and genealogical ties extending mainly to the descent groups of Teit, Avat, Sart, Tooke, Bargy, Cherik, Basyz, Munduz and Börü. Indeed, both people and leaders found creative ways of satisfying their own interests within the kinship system by manipulating genealogical identity for various purposes and cultivating the ideological basis for a ruling position (Ismailbekova, 2017). This ideology was widely used because each strong regional leader had a wide range of informal networks composed of kinsmen who were bound by both kinship and pragmatic criteria. The kin members were bound to the president on the basis of loyalty, mutual support in times of need and norms regarding honour and shame.

In contrast to Akayev's time, a strong opposition dominated the political landscape under Bakiyev's presidency. Many active opposition groups challenged the Bakiyevs and accused them of establishing family rule and maintaining ties with criminal groups (Marat, 2006: 91–93). It is important to mention the different types of social sanctions that Bakiyev and his family implemented. Bakiyev could directly control his own people through direct personal appointments which created a close circle of supporters who were dependent on him. However, informal control was also implemented beyond kinship by means of the collection of compromising material (a practice known as *Kompromat*), not just against opposition groups, but also against co-workers, friends, and allies. Fabricated criminal cases would also be brought against opposition leaders and, in some cases, control was executed through the most violent means. When the business could not be 'squeezed out' in a legal way or under the condition of insubordination, an administrative resource was used, by constantly sending financial auditors and inspectors to the companies for checks and controls (Kompromat, 2010).

Atambayev's control: Demonstrative punishment, selective law enforcement and kompromat

A new mechanism of informal control has been the use of state television channels to spread negative, unconfirmed information about opposition groups (Turgunbekov, 2013). If other mass media channels (such as Zanoza, Azattyk, Sentyabr TV and the online newspaper 24.kg) would criticise the actions of Atambayev, he would in return accuse the journalists of trying to destabilise Kyrgyzstan ahead of the presidential elections in November 2017 (Turgunbekov, 2013). The prosecutor general's office went even further and filed 26 million som claims against journalists of the Azattyk and Zanoza newsletters. The tension between the authorities and journalists increased after Atambayev publicly criticised Azattyk by saying that the journalists 'work for American money' and spread rumours about him (Irgebaeva, 2017).

Opponents of the constitutional changes advocated by Atambayev became the subject of criminal investigations. The main opponents were three members of the Ata-Meken party; a leader of the Ata-Zhurt party, Omurbek Tekebaev; the former justice minister, Almanbet Shykmamatov; and the former general prosecutor and current Member of Parliament, Aida Salyanova. They expressed doubts about the proposed changes of the constitution, claiming that the idea behind the modifications was to bolster the position of elites surrounding the president. Following these strong statements, prominent politicians were prosecuted.[1] It is important to highlight that in spite of the informal manoeuvring to weaken the president, this continues to be the key position of power in the country.

Jeenbekov's informal control: Demonstrative punishment, selective law enforcement using GKNB

Under the umbrella of fighting against corruption, Jeenbekov's government detained many well-known politicians and officials, including former prime ministers. According to Atambayev, Most politicians were convinced that Jeenbekov could put in prison anyone who did not follow his rule, especially when it comes to innocent people. And these politicians do what they are told to do, they cannot be blamed for it. It is understandable. (see more Irgebaeva, 2019b)

Atambayev's words say a lot about Jeenbekov, especially about his rules of the game, his intentions and his punishment when his followers break his rules.

Despite changes to the constitution in both 2010 and 2016 which ostensibly divested power from the president to parliament, president Jeenbekov has significant levers of informal control. This was neatly explained by one MP of the Kyrgyz Republic:

> The Constitution was changed in both 2010 and 2016, but people have not changed. People can change constitutions, but the changed constitution cannot change politicians. Instead of learning from the mistakes of former politicians, current politicians make the same mistakes. It is not parliament that controls it, but the president who controls us (parliament) like a TV remote control. We cannot control the government because most parliamentarians are dependent, fearful and uneducated. That was the main reason to bring in these obedient wealthy people because they are not protesting. This is very convenient for the government not to have their opinion. It is convenient for the president when parliamentarians have *fish mouths* that cannot speak or express their thoughts.[2]

The oligarchs in parliament are kept by the president on a short leash using the power of GKNB (security services). The GKNB is appointed by the president without parliamentary interference. Sometimes Jeenbekov makes an example of those who violate this informal rule by publicly punishing and enforcing criminal charges against those who dissent from his rule. If the MPs came to power to keep their business, they should keep following their own interests, instead of engaging in politics. Therefore, to protest against the president is to put at risk the personal business interests of parliamentary deputies, so the president uses parliament for his own needs. There are mutual interests between the two sides, which do not coincide and do not conflict. Therefore, the Kyrgyz parliament is often referred to as 'the oligarchic parliament'.

Camouflage

The third informal pattern is camouflage, which refers to the manner in which informal transactions take place behind an institutional façade of democracy and commitment to the rule of law. This often means that, in contexts with high prevalence of informal practices, formal rules are often manipulated, undercut, diverted or exploited for the sake of informal interests.

Akayev's camouflage: the illusion of inclusive democracy and charitable contributions

While the monopoly over positions of power and influence enabled Akayev's networks to amass personal fortunes at the expense of public resources, throughout his presidency, Akayev formally promoted the establishment of Western models of state governance characterised by fair elections and other principles of liberal democracy, including the protection of human rights, independent mass media and a pluralist society. He thus promoted the slogan: "We will develop democratically", expressing the intention to transform Kyrgyzstan into "the second Switzerland", an island of democracy in Central Asia, distinguishable from the other authoritarian countries in the region (Anderson, 1999). Akayev also resorted to populist appeals, asking support for his policies and initiatives from the electorate directly, reminding people of their Soviet past and demanding that they accept the Western style of democracy. Akayev claimed that he would secure democracy and freedom, unlike the Communist party secretaries, who used the "threat" as a tool to motivate people to work. He warned against the unfair privatisation processes, yet also defended the concept of private property.

But as his government systematically excluded substantial groups from positions of power and influence, Akayev embraced the idea of a plural society comprising diverse ethnic, religious, and racial groups through slogans such as "Kyrgyzstan is a multi-ethnic society" and "Kyrgyzstan is our common home" (*Kyrgyzstan – nash obshyi dom*) (Akzhol, 2005). He spoke about the importance of the Russian language, which was also the language of other large ethnic minorities in Kyrgyzstan. However, unlike in other Central Asian countries, the Russian language became the official state language as a sign of Kyrgyz nationhood. As a result of this tactic, he was successful in gaining public support during his first two rounds of elections and for changes to the constitution (Fumagalli, 2016). In this regard, Akayev could gain support among ethnic Russians and other ethnic minorities groups in Kyrgyzstan.

Bakiyev's camouflage: fabricating an image of elite consensus and party politics

When coming to power in 2005, Bakiyev claimed that he would work for the interests of the population, pledged not centralise power like his predecessor, and fight corruption. As a result, Kyrgyzstan would become a truly independent and successful state with a high quality of life. In order to achieve this, Bakiyev suggested, it was necessary to carry out reforms in the governance system, particularly in the law enforcement and judiciary sectors (International Crisis Group, 2008). He emphasised the importance of the party system and introduced his pro-presidential party Ak-Jol (Bright Way) in 2007, stating that the party would represent those citizens committed to the benefit of the people of Kyrgyzstan. After the parliamentary elections of 16 December 2007, Ak-Jol received the maximum number of seats: 71 out of 90. One of the strongest opposition parties, Ata-Meken did not overcome the 0.5 per cent barrier in each region of the country that it is necessary under the new law (Segodnya, 2007).

The main basis for the Ak-Jol party was Bakiyev and his informal inner circle since the party structure remained institutionally weak and subordinated to the leader, who exercised control over the party both formally and informally. One can think of this party in terms of a pyramid, consisting of three main levels: top, middle, and bottom (Bugazov, 2013). The close and distant relatives of the president comprised the top of the pyramid. Businessmen and Ak-Jol party leaders were in the middle of the pyramid. The bottom included supporters of the party from the regions. The middle and bottom levels members had a reciprocal relationship with the president: they were either loyal to the president or paid a lot to receive lucrative positions, access to resources and business immunity. Their relationships were based on mutual interests but not on common ideologies or political views (Bugazov, 2013). Members of parliament from the Ak-Jol party shared genealogical links, regional ties, and business interests.

Bakiyev and his informal networks commanded the real powers hidden behind the formal party system. Before elections, powerful individuals would be asked to collect votes from their region, but in the post-election period, some individuals would be removed and seats would be given to completely different people due to re-negotiations taking place behind the scenes. Rather than implementing the promises given to voters, the party was used as a machine to get parliamentary seats and distribute spoils among different cliques (Bugazov, 2013).

Atambayev's 'Anti-corruption' as camouflage

Atambayev started his presidency with the intention of establishing justice, cleansing political power from corruption and achieving economic prosperity (BBC, 2017). For this purpose, he launched several initiatives focusing on anti-corruption, democratic accountability and e-governance 'Taza Koom'. He enacted judicial reforms aimed at promoting better control of corruption. This included creation of the Anti-Corruption Service of the state national security committee with Rosa Otunbayeva serving as its head (UN, 2016). Also, in 2012, president Atambayev made headways with the development of an anti-corruption strategy. The coordinating body of this initiative was the defence council, but the bodies that carried out the measures were the state national security committee, the prosecutor general's office, the ministry of internal affairs and the state committee for state security. Following this, an anti-corruption law and strategy were adopted and measures to combat corruption were also reflected in the National Strategy for Sustainable Development 2013–2017 (NSSD, 2013).

The outcomes of the "war on corruption" were disappointing. While embracing the discourse of a commitment to anti-corruption and good governance, in practice Atambayev continued to simply enforce informal control, selectively investigating and prosecuting individual politicians and political enemies (Mazykina, 2012).

Jeenbekov's 'Anti-corruption' as camouflage

During the presidential election campaign Jeenbekov also promised to strengthen the fight against corruption. He even announced a list of 35 corrupt officials who would be held accountable (Asanov, 2018). In the first year of Jeenbekov's presidency, the main corruption cases focused on the accident in 2008 at the Bishkek Thermal Power Plant and the disclosure of corruption. As a result of the criminal investigation, Atambayev's associates, including former prime minister Sapar Isakov, chairman of the state customs Service Kubanychbek Kulmatov, mayor of Bishkek city Albek Ibraimov and deputy of Jogorku Kengesh, Osmonbek Artykbaev were detained.

Jeenbekov signed a law to strip the immunity of ex-presidents that allowed him to prosecute Atambayev who was accused of illegal land use and the release of the criminal authority of Aziz Batukaev from prison. Atambayev has repeatedly stated that all charges against him as well as his circle are political in nature (Selivanov, 2019). At the same time, Jeenbekov continues to support officials, such as the former top Customs official, Raim Matraimov, who has faced allegations of corruption (Irgebaeva, 2019a,b).

Conclusion

This chapter examined the dialectical relationship of formal and informal governance and their relation to and effect on corruption and patronage in Kyrgyzstan. Despite the changes of the formal political system from a presidential to a parliamentary style of government, the logic of informal governance and its rules and practices remained and were widely applied behind the facade of the formal frameworks. With the first president informality was exercised on the basis of personalised power, whereas with the second a presidential political party was instrumental and later under parliamentarism a plurality of political parties entered the scene. One would assume that it would be much more difficult for the president to pull all the strings under a parliamentary system. However, in Kyrgyzstan, the efficacy of the practices of co-optation and control did not decrease in any way following this constitutional change. Thus, practices related to informal governance are capable of adapting to different formal political systems due to their flexible and omnipresent nature. This contributes to regime stability and change; and has effects on corruption.

The camouflage of *democracy* and *anti-corruption campaigns* have been widely used by almost all presidents of Kyrgyzstan, although some used this rhetoric more than others, in order to manipulate their groups' interests and to persecute other political leaders. The analysis furthermore showed that every president, upon their appointment, immediately started the process of government restructuring, which aimed only at strengthening the power of a small group of people. Co-optation overwhelmingly revolved around close kinship ties, close friends and regional identity during Akayev, Bakiyev and Zheenbekov's eras. Atambayev followed a different pattern by balancing the South and North through appointments and going beyond the regional division and kinship to incorporate individuals personally close to him (such as his friends, party members, advisers and even drivers) to positions of influence. However, there is no co-optation without control; they are two sides of the same coin. All the presidents used top–down or direct control by demonstratively punishing and selectively arresting opponents and relying heavily on practices of horizontal control (which are more centred on intra-elite enforcement of discipline).

The question remains, however, whether kinship-based patronage should take on a more open formal role in Kyrgyz politics, or remain informal entities behind the scenes. As we have already observed that either way, it seems that they will not disappear from the political scene. If the informal practice of patronage is taken seriously, what is better for political stability in Kyrgyzstan: if these kinship-based patronage networks continued to operate behind the scenes, or if they were accorded a formal role in the political structure? There would be enormous risks of politicising informal networks by bringing them out into the open, so that the stability of Kyrgyzstan may in fact depend on the continued functioning of this duality with regard to the persistence of this informal politics (Ismailbekova, 2018). At the heart of these informal networks is their ambivalence, their informal practice, multiple identities and moralities, and acceptance of the 'informal ways of getting things done' in Ledeneva's (2018) terms. They are central to the functioning/changing of politics and contributing to the competitiveness of the political system in the post-Soviet context. Instead of pretending that this facet does not exist, imagine openly recognising and addressing, even accommodating politically, the functional role of kinship-based patronage networks in Kyrgyzstan and Central Asia more broadly. Perhaps it is time to turn away from rejection and put to positive use such networks (cf. Lewis, 2004).

Notes

1 The criminal cases against Almanbet Shykmamatov, Aida Salyanova and Omurbek Tekebayev.
2 R.M. interview with the MP of KR, Bishkek, Kyrgyzstan, 2019.

Bibliography

Akzhol, A. (2005) 'Dom kotoryi postroil Akayev'. 7 February. Available at: http://www.centrasia.ru/newsA.php?st=1107748500, accessed 01.03.2017

Alymbaeva, A. (2013) 'O strukture politicheskoi elity Kyrgyzstana', *Kabarlar.kg*. 2 July. Available at: http://kabarlar.org/news/13395-o-strukture-politicheskoy-elity-kyrgyzstana.html, accessed 30.03.2017.

Alymbaeva, M. and Sharsheeva, G. (2015) 'Razmyshlenie posle 10 let', *Gezitter.org*. 24 March. Available at: http://inosmi.ru/sngbaltia/20150324/227085237.html, accessed 01.03. 2017.

Anderson, J. (1999) *Kyrgyzstan: Central Asia's Island of Democracy?* London: Routledge.

Asanaov, B. (2018) 'God Sooronbaja Zheenbekova vo vlasti', *Radio Azattyk*. 15 October. Available at: https://rus.azattyk.org/a/kyrgyzstan_jeenbekov_one_year/29544009.html, accessed 15 October 2018.

Baez-Camargo, C. and Ledeneva, A. (2017) 'Where Does Informality Stop and Corruption Begin? Informal Governance and the Public/Private Crossover in Mexico, Russia and Tanzania', *Slavonic and East European Review* 95 (1): 49–75.

Baialieva, G. and Kutmanaliev, J. (2020) How Kyrgyz Social Media Backed an Imprisoned Politician's Meteoric Rise to Power, OpenDemocracy, 15.10.2020; https://www.opendemocracy.net/en/odr/how-kyrgyz-social-media-backed-an-imprisoned-politicians-meteoric-rise-to-power/

BBC (2017) *Kyrgyzstan Profile – Leaders*. 30 July. Available at: http://www.bbc.com/news/world-asia-16187957, accessed 23 March 2017.

Begalieva, Z. and Yntymakov, A. (2015) 'Million za mandat deputata'. 25 September. Available at: https://rus.azattyk.org/a/27269026.html, accessed 25.09.2015.

Bolponova, A. (2015) 'Political Clans of Kyrgyzstan: Past and Present', *Central Asia and the Caucasus* 16 (3–4): 50–62.

Bugazov, A. (2013) *Socio-Cultural Characteristics of the Civil Society Formation in Kyrgyzstan*. Washington, DC: Central Asia-Caucasus Institute Silk Road Studies Program.

Center1.com (2017) 'Omurnek Babanov – novyi politemigrant ili polituznik Kyrgyzstana'. 21 September. Available at: https://centre1.com/kyrgyzstan/travlya-babanova-glavnogo-sopernika-vlasti-na-vyborah-prezidenta-kr/, accessed 22.09.2017.

Crosby, A. (2017) 'Jeenbekov Wins Kyrgyz Presidential Election Outright, Preliminary Vote Count Shows', *RFE/RL's Kyrgyz Service*. 15 October.

Collins, K. (2002) 'Clan, Pacts, and Politics in Central Asia', *Journal of Democracy* 13 (3): 137–152.

Collins, K. (2004) 'The Logic of Clan Politics: Evidence for the Central Asian Trajectories', *World Politics* 56 (2): 224–261.

Delo, N. (2009) 'Semeistvennost zhivet i protsvetaet', *Novosti-kg*. 11 November. Available at: http://delo.kg/index.php?option=com_content&task=view&id=384&Itemid=60, accessed 30.03.2017.

Dzhunushaliev, D. and Ploskih, V. (2000) 'Tribalism and Nation Building in Kyrgyzstan', *Central Asia and the Caucasus* 3: 115–123.

Doolotkeldieva, A. (2021) Populism à la Kyrgyz: Sadyr Japarov, Nationalism, and Anti-Elite Sentiment in Kyrgyzstan. Illiberalism Studies Program Working Papers no. 4, https://www.illiberalism.org/wp-content/uploads/2021/02/ILL-papers-no-4-February-2021.pdf

Engvall, J. (2012) *Against the Grain: How Georgia Fought Corruption and What It Means*. Silk Road Paper, September 2012. Central Asia-Caucasus Institute & Silk Road Studies Program, 5–62.

Engvall, J. (2016) *The State as Investment Market: Kyrgyzstan in Comparative Perspective*. Pittsburgh: University of Pittsburgh Press.

Engvall, J. (2017) 'From Monopoly to Competition, Constitutions and Rent Seeking in Kyrgyzstan', *Problems of Post-Communism* 65 (4): 273–281.

Finke, P. (2002) 'Wandel sozialer Strukturen im ländlichen Mittelasien', in Andrea Strasser, Siegfried Haas, Gerhard Mangott, and Valeria Heuberger (eds), *Zentralasien und Islam/Central Asia and Islam*. Hamburg, Deutsches Orient-Institut, pp. 137–149.

Fumagalli, M. (2016) 'Semi-Presidentialism in Kyrgyzstan', in R. Elgie and S. Moestrup (eds), *Semi-Presidentalism in the Caucasus and Central Asia*. London: Palgrave, pp. 173–205.

Gullette, David. (2010) *The Genealogical Construction of the Kyrgyz Republic: Kinship, State, and "Tribalism"*. Folkestone: Global Oriental.

Gostev, A (2019) 'Hanskaya ssora. Krovoprolitnyi arrest eks-prezidenta i mir v Kyrgyzii', *Radio Svoboda*. 8 June. Available at: https://www.svoboda.org/a/30100033.html, accessed 09.06.2019.

Hardenberg, R. (2009) 'Reconsidering "Tribe", "Clan" and "Relatedness": A Comparison of Social Categorisation in Central and South Asia', *Scrutiny: A Journal of International and Pakistan Studies* 1 (1): 37–62.

International Crisis Group. (2008) *Kyrgyzstan: The Challenge of Judicial Reform*. Asian Reporter N°150, 10 April 2008. https://d2071andvip0wj.cloudfront.net/150-kyrgyzstan-the-challenge-of-judicial-reform.pdf

Irgebaeva, A. (2017) 'Atambayev obvili yhurnalistov v popytke destabilizirotvat situatsiyu pered vyborami preizidenta', *Kloop.kg*. 11 March Available at https://kloop.kg/blog/2017/03/11/Atambayev-obvinil-zhurnalistov-v-popytke-destabilizirovat-situatsiyu-pered-vyborami-prezidenta/, accessed 27.03.2017.

Irgebaeva, A. (2019a) 'Po Matrimovym i klanosty-daite fakty', *Kloop.kg*. 3 Novemeber. Available at: https://kloop.kg/blog/2019/11/03/po-matraimovym-i-klanovosti-dajte-fakty-chto-govoril-zheenbekov-na-vstreche-s-zhurnalistami/, accessed 03.11.2019.

Irgebaeva, A. (2019b) 'Chto govoril eks-president Atambayev na mitinge SDPK protiv korrupzii', *Kloop.kg*. 8 June. Available at: https://kloop.kg/blog/2019/06/08/chto-govoril-eks-prezident-Atambayev-na-mitinge-sdpk-protiv-korruptsii-pereskaz/, accessed 08.06.2019.

Ismailbekova, A. (2017) *Blood Ties and the Native Son: Poetics of Patronage in Kyrgyzstan*. Bloomington, IN: Indiana University Press.

Ismailbekova, A. (2018) 'Mapping Lineage Leadership in Kyrgyzstan: Lineage Associations and Informal Governance', *Zeitschrift für Ethnologie* 143: 59–84.

Ismailbekova, A. (2021) Native Son: The Rise of Kyrgyzstan's Sadyr Japarov. openDemocracy 28 January, 2021; https://www.opendemocracy.net/en/odr/native-son-the-rise-of-sadyr-japarov-kyrgyzstan/

Jacquesson, S. (2010) 'Power Play among the Kyrgyz: State versus Descent', in Isabelle Charleux (ed.), *Representing Power in Modern Inner Asia: Conventions, Alternatives and Oppositions*. Studies on East Asia. Bellingham, WA: Center for East Asian Studies, pp. 221–44.

Kloop (2019) 'Pochem vlastyam nado prekratit davlenie na telekanal aprel'. 10 August. Available at: https://kloop.kg/blog/2019/08/10/pochemu-vlastyam-nado-prekratit-davlenie-na-telekanal-aprel-ot-redaktsii-kloopa/, accessed 11.8.2019.

Kloop, Azattyk and OCCRP. (2019) 'Tenevye kurery. Kak milliony dollarov nalichnymi vyvozyat iz Kyrgyzstana', *Kloop*. 3 December. Available at: https://kloop.kg/blog/2019/12/03/tenevye-kurery-kak-milliony-dollarov-nalichnyh-pokidayut-kyrgyzstan/, accessed 04.12.2019.

Kompromat (2010) 'Bakiyev zlouptrebil vlastyu'. http://www.compromat.ru/page_29110.htm. Published 19.04.2010.

Ledeneva, A. (2018) 'Introduction: The Informal View of the World-Key Challenges and Main Findings of the Global Informality Project', in Alena Ledeneva et al (eds), *Global Encyclopaedia of Informality, Volume 1: Towards Understanding of Social and Cultural Complexity*. London: UCL Press, pp. 1–28.

Lewis, I.M. (2004) 'Visible and Invisible Differences: The Somali Paradox Africa', *The Journal of the International African Institute* 74 (4): 489–515.

Luong, P.J. (2002) *Institutional Change and Political Continuity in Post-Soviet Central Asia: Power, Perceptions and Pacts*. Cambridge: Cambridge University Press.

Mamedov, G. (2021) "Japarov Is Our Trump": Why Kyrgyzstan Is the Future of Global Politics. openDemocracy, 06.01.2021; https://www.opendemocracy.net/en/odr/japarov-is-our-trump-kyrgyzstan-is-the-future-of-global-politics/

Marat, E. (2006) *The State -Crime Nexus in Central Asia: State Weakness, Organised Crime, and Corruption in Kyrgyzstan and Tajikistan*. Silk Road Paper 2006, Central Asia-Caucasus Institute Silk Road Studies Program.

Mazykina, Y. (2012) 'Kyrgyzstan: Corruption. Akt i Bishkek', *24.kg*. 23 March. Available at: https://24.kg/archive/ru/community/124596-laquokyrgyzstan-korrupciyaraquo-akt-i.html/, accessed 01.10.19.

Nastoyashee vremya (2019) 'Byvshego presidenta Kyrgyzstan arresovaly po korruptzii'. 9 August. Available at: https://www.currenttime.tv/a/kyrgyzstan-atambayev-arest/30100957.html, accessed 10.08.2019.

Ministerstvo yustitsii Kyrgyzskoy Respubliki (2013) Natsional'naya strategiya ustoychivogo razvitiya Kyrgyzskoy Respubliki na period 2013-2017 gody from 21.01. 2013 г. n°11. –.2, п.2.5. Available at: http://cbd.minjust.gov.kg/act/view/ru-ru/61542.

Pannier, B. (2009) 'Bakiyev prodolzhaet politiku nepotizma, kotoryi byl prichinoi kraha Akayeva', *Azattykunalgysy*. 13 November. Available at: http://www.azattyk.org/a/kyrgyzstan_Bakiyev_and_his_son/1876167.html, accessed 12.03.2017.

Radnitz, S. (2010) *Weapons of the Wealthy: Predatory Regimes and Elite-Led Protest in Central Asia*. Ithaca, NY: Cornell University Press.

Respublika (2004) 'Iz poslednego doklada Mezhdunarodnoi krizisnoi gruppy'. Available at: http://kyrgyzby.narod.ru/archive/2004/recomend.htm, accessed 22.11.2020.

Schatz, E. (2004) *Modern Clan Politics: The Power of 'Blood' in Kazakhstan and Beyond*. London: University of Washington Press.

Segodnya (2007) 'V Parlament Kirgizii proshla lish partia Bakiyeva'. 17 December. Available at: http://www.segodnya.ua/world/v-parlament-kirhizii-proshla-lish-partija-Bakiyeva.html, accessed 22.11.2020.

Selivanov, E. (2019) 'Byvshemy presidenty Kyrgyzii predyavelny obvinennia v korruptzii pri modernisatsii TEZ Bishkeka', *OCCRP*. 18 June. Available at: https://www.occrp.org/ru/daily/9989-2019-06-18-15-18-54, accessed 18.06.2019.

Sputnik (2018) 'Korruptzionnyi klan Matraimovyh'. 10 December. Available at: https://ru.sputnik.kg/politics/20181211/1042380365/iskender-matraimov-kommentarij-statya-korrupcionnyj-klan.html, accessed 22.11.2020.

Turgunbekov (2013) 'Razvalitsya li vlast Atambayeva?' *Gezitter.org*. 23 November. Available at: http://3www.gezitter.org/politic/25807_razvalitsya_li_vlast_Atambayeva/, accessed 23.03.2017.

UN report (2016) Obshchaya Stranovaya Otsenka dlya Kyrgyzskoy Respublik. Available at: https://kyrgyzstan.un.org/ru/15703-obschaya-stranovaya-ocenka-dlya-kyrgyzskoy-respubliki, accessed 24.06.2021.

7
NATION-BUILDING IN CENTRAL ASIA
Policy and discourse

Dina Sharipova and Aziz Burkhanov

After the collapse of the Soviet Union in late 1991, countries of Central Asia had to establish a new identity-building policy upon which the new regimes could build their legitimacy. The way these countries dealt with it was different due to a variety of conditions existing across the region, depending on the demographic situation and the political openness of the regime. In this chapter we will briefly summarise the discourse about national identity-building in post-Soviet Central Asia by focusing on how these factors affected commonalities and differences across the region.

Scholarship of national identity issues in Central Asian countries expanded considerably after the collapse of the Soviet Union. The literature concentrated on several key areas, such as growing 'revenge nationalism', the relationship between various ethnic groups living in the region, the role of intra-elite and regional cleavages and continuity between Soviet policies and independent countries' approaches to language and identity (Brubaker 1996; Cummings 2006; Luong 2002; Commercio 2004; Chong 2006; Peyrouse 2008; Fierman 2000; Dave 2004; Oka 2006; Kolstø 1999; Luong and Weinthal 2010; Ó Beacháin and Kevlihan 2011). More recent work on national identity in Central Asia has been focusing on the role of state and policy instruments, such as the Assembly of People of Kazakhstan (Rees and Burkhanov 2018; Rees and Webb Williams 2017; Burkhanov and Sharipova 2014; Burkhanov 2017) and micro-level developments, arguing that multicultural approach of Kazakhstan remains more of an accidental choice rather than a cohesive policy (Sharipova et al. 2017; Burkhanov 2017). Survey-based studies on national identity have been expanding in the last few years. Rees and Webb Williams (2017) and Sharipova et al. (2017), among others, focus on mass surveys and interviews to highlight popular perception of national identity issues, as opposed to the earlier predominant approach in the scholarship that almost exclusively focused on 'top–down' state approaches and narratives.

This chapter is structured as follows: we will discuss identity politics in Central Asia by focusing on key identity narratives, discourses and an overview of nation-building policies in each of the Central Asian countries.

DOI: 10.4324/9780429057977-7

Kazakhstan

Background

Kazakhstan is the largest country in post-Soviet Central Asia. The country's population of 18 million people has also been most ethnically diverse in Central Asia due to demographic changes over the course of 20th century, including massive losses among ethnic Kazakhs during forced collectivisation as well as migration and deportation of various ethnic groups during the Soviet period. As a result of these changes, according to the last Soviet census of 1989, ethnic Kazakhs accounted for less than half of the population, though later this number had increased to 67 per cent in 2009 (Statistics Agency of the Republic of Kazakhstan 2000, 2010) and 70.2 per cent in 2019 due to the outflow of Slavic peoples, the return of ethnic Kazakhs from abroad and domestic demographic shifts (Vlast.kz 2019).

Policy overview

For almost the entire post-1991 period of Kazakhstan's history, the government's commitment to internationalist rhetoric and inter-ethnic friendship of the peoples living in the country has been a signature feature of domestic policies and a point of pride of the new regime. This has also been incorporated into the country's legal framework – for instance, both of Kazakhstan's post-independence constitutions, adopted in 1993 and 1995, respectively, emphasised the commitment of the state to 'develop the national cultures and traditions of all ethnic groups living in the country'. As such, each of the officially recognised ethnic minority groups was granted a so-called 'national-cultural centre', which is usually allocated some funding from the state and is overseen by an umbrella agency called the Assembly of the Peoples of Kazakhstan (Davenel 2012). From a legal point of view, the Assembly has the status of a consultative body in charge of ensuring interethnic harmony 'in the process of forming a civic Kazakhstani identity ... under the consolidating role of the Kazakh people'.[1] After the constitutional amendments of 2007, the political role of the Assembly has increased as nine members of the *Mazhilis*, the lower house of Parliament, are elected by the APK. Critics say, however, that the overall political importance and powers of the Assembly and national-cultural centres remain limited, as in most cases, these centres are just nominal bodies created to imitate a normal coexistence of diverse ethnic groups rather than actually resolving tensions (Schatz 2000).

The Constitution of Kazakhstan explicitly outlaws any discrimination on the basis of 'origin, social, official, and property status, as well as gender, race, nationality, language, religion, creed, and place of residence'.[2] Discrimination and other violations of human rights on the basis of ethnicity, race, language and religion are also mentioned in both post-1991 versions of Kazakhstan's Criminal Code, adopted in 1997 and 2014, respectively, and are punishable under the current Code by a fine of up to approximately $1,800 or a jail term.[3]

Yet, at the same time, while the regime tolerates people's manifestations of their ethnic identities during cultural celebrations and even at times encourages them, the government is also very concerned and suspicious about any potential political mobilisation of ethnicities. For instance, Kazakhstan's legislation prohibits creating political parties on an ethnic basis (Law on Political Parties 2002) and any politically charged activity by the ethnic minorities is closely monitored and controlled. However, at the same time, Kazakhstan largely relies on the Soviet approach of recording the ethnic background of its citizens and using it as an assigned category in domestic statistics and documentation. In continuation with Soviet practices, an individual's ethnic background is recorded and written on national ID cards.[4] This institutionalised ethnic identity is usually based on parents' ethnicity or, in the case of mixed marriages, is chosen by the child at the age of 16. It is also legally possible to change this ethnic identity record.[5]

Kazakhstan's current identity policy clearly demonstrates some of the government's concerns about the complex ethnic situation in the country. The regulations related to ethnic issues in Kazakhstan, as well as in other Central Asian countries, appear rather tolerant in comparison with those in some other post-Soviet states, especially the Baltics (Commercio 2010). For instance, citizenship in Central Asian countries was granted to anyone who lived in the republics at the moment of its independence regardless of ethnicity or language proficiency.[6]

Discourse

The latest policy initiatives and ideological statements from the government cement a vision that incorporates a multicultural, civic-nationhood vision of Kazakhstan. For instance, in 2016, the Assembly of People had adopted the 'Mangilik Yel' Patriotic Act,[7] which specifically outlines several key values of Kazakhstan's society and among them, mentions building up a 'Nation of Unified Future', 'Common History, Culture and Language'.[8] This ideological doctrine was also reincarnated in Astana's toponymics and landmarks – in 2011, a Triumphal Arch named 'Mangilik Yel' was opened and the main road connecting Astana Airport with downtown was also renamed Mangilik Yel avenue.

In 2017, the President announced another major ideological strategy called 'Rukhani Zhangyru' (commonly translated as 'Spiritual Modernisation'). While not directly touching upon matters of multiculturalism and identity, this program certainly includes several prominent and important sub-initiatives: 'Tughan Zher' [Homeland], a community-development program aimed at local and small projects in specific communities; 'Sacred Geography', which sponsors expeditions and research projects to the major yet understudied historical monuments of Kazakhstan; and '100 New Faces', a nation-wide online poll for finding prominent new figures in sports, business and academia. Other sub-initiatives include '100 new textbooks', a government-sponsored program of translating prominent Western university textbooks into Kazakh language, and finally, the switch to Latin alphabet.

In terms of broader discourse, various efforts by the Kazakhstan government to promote a new sense of identity have met different reactions from the media. The Turkic and Eurasian identity concepts, which the government has embarked on at a certain point, met a fairly cold response from the audience and were practically abandoned later. The third major attempt by Kazakhstan's government to develop a civic-based sense of identity, the 'Kazakhstani Nation' idea, has met the most hostile reaction and is by no means certain to succeed in the future (Kesici 2011). Instead, both Kazakh- and Russian-language media in Kazakhstan operate with the recorded ethnic-based identity terms. While the Kazakh-language press emphasises the 'Kazakhness' of the state, the Russian-language press tends to use a more inclusive term 'Kazakhstanis' (*Қазақстандықтар* in Kazakh; *Казахстанцы* in Russian) to accommodate Kazakhstan's ethnic diversity. The country's Russian-speaking domestic political discourse also uses such approaches as a marker of civic identity, which all ethnic groups seem to accept to a greater degree.

The regime in Kazakhstan has made several attempts to overcome existing cleavages and polarisations along the ethnic lines that exist in modern Kazakhstan society, having experimenting with *Kazakhstan as a Eurasian State* and *Kazakhstan as a Central Asian State* narratives, which, respectively, place Kazakhstan in broader Eurasian and Central Asian contexts. The term *Eurasian* for some time became a popular element of the public discourse in Kazakhstan; it emphasises exposure and closer connections to European culture, mainly via Russia, rather than Asia and explicitly emphasises that Kazakhstan is not an *Asian* state (Laruelle 2016). The references to the

Central Asian character of Kazakhstan are less frequent and are used predominantly in the context of news reporting about political relations with neighboring countries, such as Kyrgyzstan and Uzbekistan, although they play a similar role in demonstrating that Kazakhstan does not belong just to a traditional Asian cultural milieu; but, it makes a special case, together with the four other Central Asian republics, due to their common Soviet legacy.

Other narratives, such as *Kazakhstan as a Turkic State* and *Kazakhstan as a Muslim State,* rarely appear in the Kazakh-language discourse. It can be inferred that the Turkic unity idea, although more popular in the early stages of independence, turned out to be a disappointment and was gradually replaced by suspicions and prejudices against fellow Turkic peoples, such as Uzbeks, Uyghurs and Turks. Similarly, Islam is infrequently mentioned as a source of legitimacy or inspiration for the state-building in Kazakhstan rather fulfilling cultural and historical sphere (Bigozhin and Schwab 2016). Although Kazakh-language discourse acknowledges Islam's symbolic importance for Kazakhs by denouncing proselytising activities of Christian and other missionaries and criticising cases when Kazakhs convert to other religions, Kazakhstan itself is relatively rarely referred to as a *Muslim* state.

The public discourse on the national identity in Kazakhstan clearly demonstrates antagonism between the 'nationalising' 'state of Kazakhs' and a 'multiethnic state of Kazakhstan' vision of Kazakhstan. Kazakh-language newspapers tend to separate the society into Kazakhs and non-Kazakhs, while Russian-language audience remains disconnected from these debates and focuses on a multiethnic perception of the country. This antagonism remains one of Kazakhstan's key identity debates and policies.

Kyrgyzstan

Background

Kyrgyzstan's population is approximately 6 million in 2019 (an increase from 4.8 million in 1999). The largest ethnic groups are Kyrgyz, who comprise 70.9 per cent of the population (2009 census); other important ethnic groups include Uzbeks (14.5% of the population) living in the southern areas of the country and Russians (9.0%), who are mostly concentrated in and around the capital city of Bishkek in the North of the country (Statistics Committee of the Kyrgyz Republic 2011). Other small though but noticeable minorities include Dungans (1.9%), Uyghurs (1.1%), Tajiks (1.1%), Kazakhs (0.7%) and Ukrainians (0.5%). Similar to Kazakhstan, Kyrgyzstan has undergone a profound change in its ethnic composition since independence. The percentage of ethnic Kyrgyz increased from around 50 per cent in 1979 to nearly 70 per cent in 2007, while the percentage of European ethnic groups (Russians, Ukrainians and Germans) dropped from 35 per cent to about 10 per cent and Russians stopped being the largest minority.

Policy overview

The situation in Kyrgyzstan has been similar to Kazakhstan, although there are important nuances and distinctions. On the one hand, the country decided to change its name to the *Kyrgyz Republic* from the *Republic of Kyrgyzstan*, which some scholars labelled as a nationalist-influenced move to better reflect the idea of national statehood; on the other hand, statues and streets named after Lenin, Frunze or Komsomol still exist in many cities across the country (Lowe 2003). Kyrgyzstan was also the only country in the region to remove the famous 'nationality' graph inherited from the Soviet Union times in internal identification documents and to replace it by a phrase 'citizen of the Kyrgyz Republic'. Interestingly, for a certain time, due to nationalist protests, this graph was restored shortly afterwards, though later removed for good in the new ID cards issued starting from 2017, despite widespread support from ethnic Kyrgyz to keep the ethnicity data (Marat 2016).

Kyrgyzstan also experienced ethnic clashes in June 2010, after the overthrow of Kurmanbek Bakiyev's regime and while an interim government ruled the country. The period between April and June 2010 was marked by the lack of a legitimate state leadership, the provisional leaders' inability to control the regime's monopoly over the use of violence within the country's borders, as well as surviving pockets of support for the old regime in southern Kyrgyzstan (Marat 2016: 309). Violence occurred after an incident between young men at a local café in Osh escalated into one of the major outbreaks of ethnic violence in Kyrgyzstan's recent history. There were numerous reports of torture, rape, extortion and illegal arrests of Uzbek community members by a predominantly ethnic Kyrgyz police force (Marat 2016).

Discourse

Following the violence, societal discourse about national identity evolved towards further promotion of the ethnic Kyrgyz history and culture. Ethnic Uzbeks, the country's largest minority group, became a particularly frequent target for nationalist attacks (Marat 2016; Laruelle 2012). Nationalist discourse portrays ethnic Kyrgyz as a privileged group in the country and accuses ethnic groups, primarily Uzbeks, in lack of respect towards Kyrgyz language and culture. On the country-wide level, nationalism is expressed through specific policies, such as massive state-endorsed celebration of the 1000th anniversary of the Kyrgyz epic 'Manas' and its mandatory study in all schools across the country, celebration of the 2200th anniversary of the Kyrgyz statehood and the 1170th anniversary of the Kyrgyz kingdom (vesti.kg 2013). As Marat (2016) notes, knowledge of the Manas epic, the political legacy of Kurmanjan Datka, a Kyrgyz stateswoman, and the literary success of prominent Kyrgyz writer Chingiz Aitmatov have been so highly politicised that they drown out discussions of other elements of the Kyrgyz heritage.

Turkmenistan

Background

After the collapse of the Soviet Union, Turkmenistan has embarked on its own path of development. In 2018, the population of Turkmenistan was 5,411,012 million people. According to data for 2003, 85 per cent of the population are Turkmens, 5 per cent Uzbeks, 4 per cent Russians and 6 per cent other ethnic groups.[9] Turkmen society is divided into five main tribes – Tekke, Yomud, Ersari, Chowdur and Saryk – which are linked to specific regions of the country. Subethnic identities have survived the Soviet regime and continued to play an important role in self-identification of Turkmens during the post-independence period. The population of the country is predominantly Muslim (89%) and Christians (9%).[10] The majority of Turkmen population is Sunni, while a very small percentage is Shia. Ashgabat heavily controls religion and religious organisations to prevent extremism and opposition to authorities.

In terms of the political regime, Turkmenistan is the most authoritarian country among five Central Asian states. From 1991 to 2006, the leader of the country and an architect of state and nation-building policies was Saparmurat Niyazov. He declared independence and the policy of neutrality as the main achievements of the country. Building the cult of personality, Niyzov adopted the title of *Turkmenbashi* – the father of all Turkmen. After the death of Niyazov in 2006, Gurbanguly Berdymukhamedov became the leader of Turkmenistan adopting the title of *Arkadag*, the Protector. Although Berdymukhamedov partly dismantled the Niyzov's personality cult, he continued his predecessor's authoritarian leadership style (Polese and Horak 2015).

Policy overview

Nation-building policy in Turkmenistan is largely based on the cult of personality developed by Niyazov and then Berdymukhamedov. One of the pillars of nation-building, in addition to neutrality and independence, was Niyazov's *Ruhnama* book, *The Holy Book of all Turkmen* published in two volumes in 2001 and then 2005. The book served as one of the main foundations of the Niyazov's ideology and emphasised the historical role of the president in state and nation-building of Turkmen people in world history (Polese and Horak 2015). The book included historical, cultural and other aspects of Turkmen people and served as the basis for cultural and spiritual revival. *Ruhnama* was mandatory for schools and Universities' curriculum as well as for civil servants.

In terms of language policies, in May 1990, a new law 'On Language' was adopted that granted Turkmen language the status of the state language. All paper work in civil service and other organisations of the country was to be in Turkmen. Russian has remained the language of interethnic communication.[11] In 1993, the government created a Commission to work on transition from Cyrillic to the Latin alphabet. Starting with street signs, the government introduced the Latin script to the school and University curriculum and published textbooks in the Latin alphabet. Latinisation was done gradually and aimed to create distance from the Soviet past.

According to Article 10 of the Constitution, Turkmenistan does not recognise dual citizenship. The Law on Citizenship states that everyone who is born in Turkmenistan acquires citizenship of the country. The Constitution of Turkmenistan also declares that nobody can be forcefully deprived of citizenship of the country.[12] Anyone who can speak Turkmen language and has lived for five years on the territory of Turkmenistan can obtain Turkmen citizenship.[13] All human rights are guaranteed and protected by the state.[14]

Discourse

One of the important nation-building narratives was the creation of a unified Turkmen nation. Turkmens are divided into five tribes affiliated with five key administrative regions of the country. To overcome the sub-ethnic divisions and prevent possible inter-tribe conflicts among the Turkmens, the state rhetoric was about the uniqueness of Turkmen national history and unification of different tribes and regions in one nation with rich historical legacy (Kuru 2002). The official discourse focused on 'national revival' referring to a 5,000-year tradition of statehood that was forgotten and must now be restored to establish the powerful nation (Kehl-Bodrodi 2006).

As in other Central Asian states, nation-building in Turkmenistan was based on the revision of history and reference to a Golden Age and a glorious past – the Seljuk Empire (1040–1194). Historians searched for significant figures of the past who could serve as symbols of the Turkmen nation. One of those figures was Oghuz Khan, a mythological figure who lived in the third millennium BCE and now is considered the grandfather and founder of all Turkmen. Other historical figures included Sultan Sanjar, the khan who disseminated Turkmen culture in Asian and European countries and Magtymkuly, an 18th-century poet and philosopher, the founder of the Turkmen literature. *Turkmenbashi* emphasised the connections between himself and those historical figures, particularly with Oghuz Khan and proclaimed his rule as the Golden Age of Turkmen people (Polese and Horak 2015).

Niyazov's successor, Gurbanguly Berdymukhamedov, has introduced the concept of the 'Great/New Renaissance' defined as:

> a policy of spectacular, all-embracing reforms initiated by our highly valued President of Turkmenistan, Gurbanguly Berdimuhamedov, in order to strengthen and expand

the economic power of our homeland, increase the standard of living of the Turkmen people and develop all areas of the life of the state and society without exception. This means an emphasis on progressive thinking, professionalism and an innovative approach to everything touching on the interests of the people.[15]

However, the 'Renaissance Period' has been replaced by the 'Period of Might and Happiness', characterised as progress and innovation. In fact, those concepts also served to strengthen the cult of personality. Gradually, the role of *Ruhnama* as the basis of national revival disappeared from the nation-building agenda. In contrast to Niyazov, Berdymukhamedov has been more 'productive' in terms of publications producing more than 40 books on different topics. As with the case of *Ruhnama*, high school and university students must buy the president's books and then donate them to schools for public exhibitions organised on a regular basis.

The scholarly literature on nation-building in Turkmenistan is very much limited, which is explained by the difficulty to gain access to information on Turkmenistan. A number of scholars described the nation-building project in Turkmenistan explaining it mostly from a top–down perspective, i.e. how the state and the elites constructed the Turkmen nation. Many scholars emphasised the invention of tradition and the symbolic production of the Turkmen nation (Kiepenheuer-Drechsler 2006; Akbarzadeh 1999; Peyrouse 2012; Koch 2016). One of the latest interpretations of nation-building was provided by Polese and Horak (2015) who linked the cult of personality and nation-building processes in Turkmenistan. Scholars have argued that nation-building is not only constructed through traditional ways such as language, schools or reference to historical past but also through the figure of the president and his cult.

In conclusion, nation-building in Turkmenistan is a top–down project. Although some minor differences exist in nation-building projects between Niyazov and Berdymukhamedov, their policies are similar in that sense that the presidents defined those projects. Both presidents developed the cult of personality and used it to implement various projects and policies including nation-building. Due to the high level of authoritarianism in the country and the ideas of one single nation, neutrality and independence, Turkmenistan has largely avoided conflicts based on subethnic divisions.

Tajikistan

Background

Tajikistan is the only Central Asian country that had experienced civil war from 1992 to 1995. After the end of the conflict, the leadership embarked on building the state and Tajik nation. Tajikistan has about 9 million people, a majority of whom are Tajiks – 85 per cent; other ethnic groups living on the territory of Tajikistan include Uzbeks – 15 per cent or 1.2 million people, Russians and other ethnicities – 2 per cent.[16] Islam is the dominant religion in Tajikistan. Ninety-eight per cent of the Tajik population are Muslims. Tajik Muslims are divided into Sunni (95%) and Shia madhabs (5%).[17] Religion thus has not played a unifying role in Tajik society. Those who live in the Pamir region are mostly Shia, while others are Sunni Muslims. Only 2 per cent of the population confesses other religion in Tajikistan. Currently, more than 70 different religious non-Islamic organisations are registered.

In addition to religious differences, regional and local identities continue to play a crucial role in the politics and everyday life of Tajik nation. Regionalism is an important source of identity in Tajikistan (Kasymov 2013). These cleavages influence nation-building policies and create certain difficulties in constructing one Tajik nation.

Policy overview

As in Turkmenistan, the president of Tajikistan, Emomali Rahmon, and the leadership of the country play a leading role in the construction of the Tajik nation. In 2009, a new 'Law on the State Language of the Republic of Tajikistan' was adopted, according to which Tajik acquired the status of the state language.[18] The law states that Tajik should be applied in political, social, economic and cultural spheres of life. All paperwork and government documents have to be published in the Tajik language.[19] The duty of state authorities and local governments is to create favorable conditions for promotion and learning of Tajik.[20] Tajiks emphasise that their language is different from the Persian language. This is to stress the uniqueness of Tajik culture, history and the nation. Although Russian remains the 'language of interethnic communication', it has lost its privileged status since independence. However, the Russian Federation promotes and supports the Russian language in Tajikistan by building schools where instruction is in the Russian language exclusively.

According to the Law on citizenship, Tajikistan allows dual citizenship stipulated by international treaties. Tajikistan has an agreement with the Russian Federation regarding dual citizenship, according to which citizens of Tajikistan might also acquire citizenship of Russia.[21] Tajikistan is the only country in Central Asia that has an agreement on dual citizenship with the Russian Federation.

Discourse

In terms of discourse, the nation-building project of Tajikistan has similar features to those of other Central Asian states. The Tajik leadership promotes the myth about the ancient roots of Tajiks and supports the revision of history. 'The Glorious past' of Tajiks was associated with the Aryan civilisation and then with the Samanid Dynasty (819–999).

Another important theme of the nation-building discourse in Tajikistan is the search for a national idea. During the last twenty years, the Tajik authorities sought to develop a national idea but have not been successful. One of the disagreements has been between those who want to include religion into the national idea saying that Tajiks are Muslims. Others suggest forming the nation on the basis of Tajik national unity rather than Islam (Abdulloev 2019). Initially, the national idea was based on the Aryan civilisation, then the Samanid dynasty and finally some discuss the need to focus on religion, particularly the Hanafi madhab, as part of national idea and national identity. The lack of specific programmes to develop common national identity on the part of the government undermines the construction of Tajik national identity.

The discourse on language emphasises the ancient roots of the Tajik language that has a thousand-year history and, thus, serves as an important basis for national unification. This idea has constantly been reiterated in media discourse and presidential writings and speeches. President Rahmon often highlights that the Tajik language is one of the ancient languages on the earth and is a successor to Aryan languages along with those of Khorasan and Maverannahr and thus should be supported by the state. The idea of purity of the Tajik language is also promoted when authorities emphasise not to borrow too many words from other languages.

As other presidents, Rahmon also has written a number of books that have been introduced to the school and university curricula. Books such as *Tajiks in the Mirror of History: From the Aryans to Samanids* or *Wise Thoughts and Sayings of the President of Tajikistan – the Founder of Peace and National Unity – Leader of Nation Emomali Rahmon* discuss nationalism, national identity, history and Tajik language.

Conclusion

The creation of Tajik nation is far from complete. A unifying national idea would be an important step forward in nation-construction of the Tajik nation. However, the government should overcome the effects of regionalism that continue to impact Tajik society and national identity. As evidence suggests, nation-building in the country is based on a top–down approach with the leading role of President Rahmon.

Uzbekistan

Background

The population of Uzbekistan amounts to more than 30 million people. It consists of Uzbeks (84%), Tajiks (5%), Kazakhs (3%), Russians (2.3%), Karakalpaks (2.2%) and other ethnic groups.[22] Karakalpakstan was part of Kazakhstan; in 1936 it was incorporated into Uzbekistan. The population of Karakalpakstan amounts to about 1.7 million people.

Policy overview

Uzbekistan has conducted nationalising policies by promoting Uzbek language, history and traditions. The first Law on Language was adopted in 1989 granting Uzbek the status of state language. The Law stipulates that Uzbek is a nation-wide state language that should be used in the civil service, business, education and other spheres of life. The Russian language has been granted the status of 'the language of interethnic communication'. However, in 1995 the Law has been amended stating that 'citizens at their own discretion have the right to choose the language of interethnic communication'.[23] In September 1993, Uzbekistan adopted a law on the Introduction of the Uzbek Alphabet Based on the Latin Script. However, the transition has not been completed. As a result, two scripts – Latin and Cyrillic – are used in parallel. This situation has affected the population with younger generation mostly using Latin script and the older generation using the Cyrillic alphabet.

The government takes measures to raise the status of Uzbek language in the country. For that purpose, the Tashkent State University of the Uzbek Language named after Alisher Navoi was established. In October 2019 the president Mirziyoev signed the decree to widely celebrate the 30th anniversary of the Law on the State Language in Uzbekistan. In the autonomous republic of the Karakalpakstan region, however, there are two state languages – Karakalpak and Uzbek. As in other Central Asian states, Uzbek authorities have conducted the policy of renaming streets, districts, towns and toponyms.

In 2018, President Mirziyoev singed the decree on the concept of priority directions in policy on interethnic relations. The concept stipulates that the president determines the main directions of the policy and the government implements policy in interethnic relations. It regulates the relationship between the government and organisations of civil society. The concept identifies measures to regulate interethnic relations including provision of conditions for the preservation of cultural development, traditions and customs of different ethnic groups.[24] People can become citizens of Uzbekistan by birth. Any individual, who has lived in Tajikistan for five years, can speak Uzbek and is not a citizen of another country can obtain citizenship of Uzbekistan.[25] The amendments made to the Law on Citizenship in 2017 state that people who obtain citizenship of another state, serve in the army of a foreign state or work in security services, police, law enforcement bodies or other state bodies of a foreign state will be deprived citizenship of Uzbekistan.[26]

Discourse

The government has successfully developed discourse on the heritage of the Timurid civilisation (Dadabayev 2013). As in other Central Asian countries, Uzbek authorities have constantly referred to the glorious past and Golden Age of Uzbekistan, which is associated primarily with the empire of Amir Timur, a Middle Age ruler. Modern Uzbekistan is considered to be heir of that empire. The authorities support the myth by building the museum of Amir Timur and erecting monuments of Amir Timur in Uzbekistan.

The state rhetoric focuses on the idea of interethnic peace and agreement. State authorities emphasise the importance of the Uzbek language as a unifying force. Shavkat Mirziyoev, president of Uzbekistan said, 'Uzbek language is one of the most ancient and rich language of the world and is a symbol of national consciousness and independent statehood of our people'.[27] This rhetoric is used to show that the Uzbek language can unite all ethnic groups living on the territory of Uzbekistan. Recent concerns raised by Tajiks in regard to decreasing usage of Tajik language and Karakalpaks discussing the possibility to separate and join Kazakhstan or Russia cannot be neglected by the government. As a result, one of the main discourses in Uzbekistan is related to the development of civic identity. An individual ethnicity recorded in national ID cards has been a continuation of the Soviet practice. One of the suggestions made in 2018 was to get rid of ethnic identification in passports and national ID cards so that everyone could be identified as Uzbekistani. This initiative, however, has not received wide support from the Uzbek population.

Another important discourse on nation-building is that of transition to the Latin script. The debates on Latin and Cyrillic alphabets have been recently resumed. The supporters of the Latin script seek to expedite the shift to Latin alphabet and complete it as soon as possible. However, opponents believe that it is better to keep Cyrillic script as the main alphabet while using Latin as the second. The concern is about the loss of literary heritage and information that was written in Cyrillic. In addition, despite the fact that Latin script is currently used in schools and Universities, different versions of the Latin alphabet are still suggested and discussed. The debates are also raised in regard to the status of the Russian language. Some proponents of Russian suggest granting this language the status of interethnic communication that was taken away in 1995.

As in other Central Asian states, the nation-building process is under way in Uzbekistan. State leadership is responsible for the implementation of the nation-building project. Although Uzbekistan was able to avoid interethnic conflicts and is successfully building the Uzbekistani nation, it faces a number of problems related to ethnic minorities. The government has to address concerns raised by Tajiks in regard to the Tajik language and improve socio-economic conditions for Karakalpaks who cherish an idea to separate from Uzbekistan. Finally, the government has to complete the transition to the Latin script.

Conclusion

After the collapse of the Soviet Union all countries of Central Asia needed to build a new identity policy. The way these countries dealt with this challenge was different due to a variety of conditions existing across the region, depending on ethnic composition, socio-economic situation and political openness.

Kazakhstan and Kyrgyzstan, on the one hand, having less ethnically homogenous populations and more open political regimes, had debates about the ethnic component in every major sphere of state activity (Bohr 2016) and have also been the most advanced in terms of integrating populations by creating a new supraethnic identity, at least in public discourse. Yet, the civic-nationhood discourse had faced controversial reactions from both non-Kazakhs living in Kazakhstan and Kazakh nationalists. The Eurasianist and Turkic identity concepts, mentioned in the scholarship, also display the scope of debates over post-Soviet Kazakhstan's search for an identity.

Being significantly more homogenous countries with more autocratic regimes, Uzbekistan, Turkmenistan and Tajikistan followed a different path. The search for glorious ancestors, a common element for all Central Asian countries, was acutely promoted in these three states. For instance, Uzbekistan has integrated Tamerlane into its identity discourse and Tajikistan made the Samanids dynasty part of the official historical narrative of Tajik statehood. Similarly, the Islamic tradition has deeper roots in both Uzbekistan and Turkmenistan, and these countries display the crescent moon, a prominent symbol of Islam, on their national flags. The choice of Tamerlane as the glorious figure of Uzbekistan's history may be debatable from a historic point of view; yet, the idea of connecting the Temurid state with modern Uzbekistan was expected to dismantle all potential speculations that Uzbekistan was an artificial construction of the Soviet period.

Compared to other countries of the region Tajikistan was in a more difficult situation. The language could not be chosen as the main distinguished thing due to fear of submerging Tajik identity to a greater ensemble dominated by Iran, so the country's government finally chose the dynasty of Samanids as the connecting link between the modern state of Tajikistan and medieval statehoods. This general overview of identity building processes demonstrates differences in identity policies in Kazakhstan and Kyrgyzstan on the one hand, and Uzbekistan, Turkmenistan and Tajikistan on the other. As these examples demonstrate, there is a connection between the levels of ethnic homogeneity, the openness of the political system and the extent of the inclusivity of the country's identity policy.

Notes

1 Law of the Republic of Kazakhstan on the Assembly of the People of Kazakhstan.
2 Constitution of the Republic of Kazakhstan, Article 5, http://www.akorda.kz/ru/official_documents/constitution
3 Criminal Code of the Republic of Kazakhstan, 2014.
4 Law of the Republic of Kazakhstan on Personal Identity Documents.
5 Family Code of the Republic of Kazakhstan.
6 Law of the Republic of Kazakhstan on Citizenship.
7 *Kazakhstanskaia Pravda*, April 26, 2016
8 *Kazakhstanskaia Pravda*, April 26, 2016.
9 The CIA World Fact Book, https://www.cia.gov/library/publications/the-world-factbook/geos/tx.html
10 The CIA World Fact Book, https://www.cia.gov/library/publications/resources/the-world-factbook/geos/tx.html
11 Zakon Turkmenksoi Sotsialisticheskoi Respubliki, "O Yazyke" [The Law of Turkmen Socialist Republic "On Language"], http://medialaw.asia/node/259.
12 Konstitutsiia Turkmenistana, The Constitution of Turkmenistan, https://online.zakon.kz/document/?doc_id=31337929#pos=6;-155
13 Zakon Turkmenistana o grazhdanstve Turkmenistana, "The Law of Turkmenistan on Citizenship in Turkmenistan", http://www.turkmenistan.gov.tm/?id=4419.
14 Konstitutsiia Turkmenistana, The Constitution of Turkmenistan, https://online.zakon.kz/document/?doc_id=31337929#pos=6;-155
15 "Politika Novogo vozrozhdeniia i Velikikh preobrazovanii Prezidenta Turkmensitana". *Neitral'nyi Turkmenistan*, June 27, 2007.
16 CIA Factbook, Tajikistan, https://www.cia.gov/library/publications/the-world-factbook/geos/ti.html
17 CIA Factbook, Tajikistan, https://www.cia.gov/library/publications/the-world-factbook/geos/ti.html
18 Zakon Respubliki Tajikistan, "O gosudarstvennom yazyke Respubliki Tajikistan" [Law of the Republic of Tajikistan "On state Language of the Republic of Tajikistan"], https://online.zakon.kz/document/?doc_id=30514132#pos=0;0

19 Zakon Respubliki Tajikistan, "O gosudarstvennom yazyke Respubliki Tajikistan", [Law of the Republic of Tajikistan "On state Language of the Republic of Tajikistan"], https://online.zakon.kz/document/?doc_id=30514132#pos=0;0
20 http://base.spinform.ru/show_doc.fwx?rgn=29442
21 Zakon Respubliki Tajikistan, "O grazhdanstve respubliki Tajikistan", [Law of the Republic of Tajikistan "On Citizenship of the Republic of Tajikistan"], http://www.tajikemb.kg/index.php?option=com_content&view=article&id=323:law-of-the-republic-of-tajikistan-on-citizenship-of-the-republic-of-tajikistan&catid=45&Itemid=167
22 The World Factbook, https://www.cia.gov/library/publications/the-world-factbook/geos/uz.html
23 The Law on State Language of the Republic of Uzbekistan, http://base.spinform.ru/show_doc.fwx?rgn=770
24 Decree of the President of the Republic of Uzbekistan, "On adoption of the concept of priority directions in policy on interethnic relations", https://regulation.gov.uz/ru/document/1362
25 Zakon Respublikliki Uzbekistna, "O grazhdanstve Respubliki Uzbekistan" [The Law of the Republic of Uzbekistan "On Citizenship of the Republic of Uzbekistan"], https://regulation.gov.uz/uz/document/3460
26 Zakon Respublikliki Uzbekistna, "O grazhdanstve Respubliki Uzbekistan" [The Law of the Republic of Uzbekistan "On Citizenship of the Republic of Uzbekistan"], https://regulation.gov.uz/uz/document/3460
27 Postanovlenie Prezidenta Respubliki Uzbekistan, O shirokom prazdnovanii tridtsatiletiya prinyatiya zakona Respubliki Uzbekistan "O gosudarstvennom yazyke", http://uza.uz/ru/documents/o-shirokom-prazdnovanii-tridtsatiletiya-prinyatiya-zakona-re-04-10-2019

References

Abdulloev, J. (2019) Islam nasha religiya no on mozhet stat' nashei natsional'noi ideei. Asiaplus, 18 February. Available at: https://asiaplustj.info/ru/news/tajikistan/society/20190218/ibrohim-usmonov-islam-nasha-religiya-no-on-ne-mozhet-stat-nashei-natsionalnoi-ideei, accessed 24.11.2020.

Akbarzadeh, S. (1999) National Identity and Political Legitimacy in Turkmenistan. *Nationalities Papers* 27 (2): 271–290.

Bigozhin, U. and Schwab, W. (2016) Shrines and Neopatrimonialism in Southern Kazakhstan. In *Kazakhstan in The Making, Legitimacy, Symbols, and Social Changes*, edited by Marlène Laruelle, 89–111. Lanham, MD: Lexington Books.

Bohr, A. (2016) *Turkmenistan: Power, politics and petro-authoritarianism*. London: Chatham House, Royal Institute of International Affairs.

Brubaker, R. (1996) *Nationalism Reframed, Nationhood and the National Question in the New Europe*. New York: Cambridge University Press.

Burkhanov, A. (2017) Kazakhstan's National Identity-Building Policy: Soviet Legacy, State Efforts, and Societal Reactions. *Cornell International Law Journal* 50 (1): 1–15.

Burkhanov, A. and Sharipova, D. (2014) Kazakhstan's Civic-National Identity: Ambiguous Policies and Points of Resistance. In *Nationalisms and Identity Construction in Central Asia: Dimensions, Dynamics and Directions*, edited by Mariya Omelicheva, 21–35. Lanham, MD: Lexington Books.

Chong, J.O. (2006) Diaspora Nationalism: The Case of Ethnic Korean Minority in Kazakhstan and its Lessons from the Crimean Tatars in Turkey. *Nationalities Papers* 34 (2): 111–129.

Commercio, M. (2004) The "Pugachev Rebellion" in the Context of Post-Soviet Kazakh Nationalization. *Nationalities Papers* 32 (1): 87–113.

Commercio, M. (2010) *Russian Minority Politics in Post-Soviet Latvia and Kyrgyzstan: The Transformative Power of Informal Networks*. Philadelphia, PA: University of Pennsylvania Press.

Cummings, S. (2006) Legitimation and Identification in Kazakhstan. *Nationalism and Ethnic Politics* 12 (2): 177–204.

Dadabaev, T. (2013) Recollections of Emerging Hybrid Ethnic Identities in Soviet Central Asia: The Case of Uzbekistan. *Nationalities Papers* 41(6): 1026–1048.

Dave, B. (2004) Entitlement through Numbers: Nationality and Language Categories in the First Post-Soviet Census in Kazakhstan. *Nations and Nationalism* 10(4): 439–459.

Davenel, Y. (2012) Cultural Mobilization in Post-Soviet Kazakhstan: Views from the State and from Non-Titular Nationalities Compared. *Central Asian Survey* 31(1): 17–29.

Fierman, W. (2000) Changing Urban Demography and the Prospects of Nationalism in Kazakhstan. *Canadian Review of Studies in Nationalism* XXVII: 7–19.

Kasymov, S. (2013) Regional Fragmentation in Tajikistan: The Shift of Powers between Different Identity Groups. *Asian Geographer* 30(1): 1–20.

Kehl-Bodrodi, K. (2006) Islam Contested: Nation, Religions, and Tradition in Post-Soviet Turkmenistan. In: *The Post-Socialist Religious Question: Faith and Power in Central Asia and East Central Europe*, edited by Chris Hann and the Civil Religion Group. Berlin: LItVerlag.

Kesici, Ö. (2011) The Dilemma in the Nation-Building Process: The Kazakh or Kazakhstani Nation? *Ethnopolitics and Minority Issues in Eurasia* 31: 52–54.

Kiepenheuer-Drechsler, B. (2006) Trapped in Permanent Neutrality: Looking behind the Symbolic Production of the Turkmen Nation. *Central Asian Survey* 25 (1–2): 129–141.

Koch, N. (2016) The "Personality Cult" problematic: Personalism and mosques memorializing the "Father of the Nation" in Turkmenistan and the UAE. *Central Asian Affairs* 3 (4): 330–359.

Kolstø, P. (1999) Bipolar Socities? In *Nation-Building and Ethnic Integration in Post-Soviet Socities*, edited by Pål Kolstø, 15–43. Boulder: Westview Press.

Kuru, A. (2002) Between the State and Cultural Zones: Nation-Building in Turkmenistan. *Central Asian Survey* 21 (1): 71–90.

Laruelle, M. (2012) The Paradigm of Nationalism in Kyrgyzstan. Evolving Narrative, the Sovereignty Issue, and Political Agenda. *Communist and Post-Communist Studies* 45 (1–2): 39–49.

Laruelle, M. (2016) Which Future for National-Patriots? The Landscape of Kazakh Nationalism. In: *Kazakhstan in the Making: Legitimacy, Symbols, and Social Changes*, edited by Marlène Laruelle, 155–180. Lanham, MD: Lexington Books.

Lowe, R. (2003) Nation-building and Identity in the Kyrgyz Republic. In: *Central Asia: Aspects of Transition*, edited by Tom Everett-Heath, 113–131. London: Routledge.

Luong, P.J. (2002) *Institutional Change and Political Continuity in Post-Soviet Central Asia: Power, Perceptions, and Pacts*. Cambridge: Cambridge University Press.

Luong, P.J. and Weinthal, E. (2010) *Oil Is Not a Curse: Ownership Structure and Institutions in Soviet Successor State*. Cambridge: Cambridge University Press.

Marat, E. (2016) We Disputed Every Word': How Kyrgyzstan's Moderates Tame Ethnic Nationalism. *Nations and Nationalism* 22 (2): 305–324.

Ó Beacháin, D. and Kevlihan, R. (2011) State-building, Identity and Nationalism in Kazakhstan: Some Preliminary Thoughts. *Working Papers in International Studies* (Centre for International Studies, Dublin City University) 1: 1–18.

Oka, N. (2006) The "Triadic Nexus" in Kazakhstan: A Comparative Study of Russians, Uighurs, and Koreans. In: *Beyond Sovereignty: From Status Law to Transnational Citizenship?* edited by Osamu Ieda, 365–366. Sapporo: Slavic Research Center, Hokkaido University.

Peyrouse, S. (2008) The Imperial Minority: An Interpretive Framework of the Russians in Kazakhstan in the 1990s. *Nationalities Papers* 36 (1): 105–123.

Peyrouse, S. (2012) The Kazakh Neopatrimonial Regime: Balancing Uncertainties among The "Family," Oligarchs and Technocrats. *Demokratizatsiya* 20 (4): 345–370.

Polese, A. and Horák, S. (2015) A Tale of Two Presidents: Personality Cult and Symbolic Nation-Building in Turkmenistan. *Nationalities Papers* 43 (3): 457–478.

Rees, K. and Burkhanov, A. (2018) Constituting the Kazakhstani Nation: Rhetorical Transformation of National Belonging. *Nationalism and Ethnic Politics*, 24 (4): 433–455.

Rees, K. and Webb Williams, N. (2017) Explaining Kazakhstani Identity: Supraethnic Identity, Ethnicity, Language, and Citizenship. *Nationalities Papers* 45 (5): 815–839.

Schatz, E. (2000) The Politics of Multiple Identities: Lineage and Ethnicity in Kazakhstan. *Europe–Asia Studies* 52 (3): 489–506.

Sharipova, D., Burkhanov, A. and Alpeissov, A. (2017) The Determinants of Civic and Ethnic Nationalisms in Kazakhstan: Evidence from the Grass-Roots Level. *Nationalism and Ethnic Politics*, 23 (2): 203–226.

Statistics Agency of the Republic of Kazakhstan (2000) *Natsionalnyi sostav naseleniia Respubliki Kazakhstan. Itogi perepisi naseleniia 1999 goda v Respublike Kazakhstan*. Almaty: Statistics Agency of the Republic of Kazakhstan.

Statistics Agency of the Republic of Kazakhstan (2010) *Natsionalnyi sostav, veroispovedanie i vladenie iazykami v Respublike Kazakhstan. Itogi natsionalnoi perepisi naseleniia 2009 goda v Respublike Kazakhstan* Astana: Statistics Agency of the Republic of Kazakhstan.

Statistics Committee of the Kyrgyz Republic (2011) *2009 - Natsionalnii sostav naseleniia (na nachalo goda). Archived from the original (PDF).* http://www.stat.kg/stat.files/tematika/демограф/Кыргызстан_в_ци фрах/, accessed 22.11 2020.

Vesti.kg (2013) V respublike otmechaetsya 1170-letie Kyrgyyzkogo kaganata, 13 November. Available at: https://vesti.kg/politika/item/24047-v-respublike-otmechaetsya-1170-letie-kyirgyizskogo-kaganata.html, accessed 24.11.2020.

Vlast.kz (2019) Etnicheskaia karta Kazahstana: Kazahov bolshe, evropeitsev menshe, tretii mononatsionalnii region Vlast.kz, 30 April. Available at: https://vlast.kz/obsshestvo/32977-etniceskaa-karta-kazahstana-kazahov-bolse-evropejcev-mense-tretij-mononacionalnyj-region.html, accessed 04.04. 2020.

8
UNSETTLED SPACE
Unfinished histories of border delimitation in the Ferghana Valley

Madeleine Reeves

According to the rules of the UN and other global bodies, any self-respecting state *[polnokrovnoe gosudarstvo]* in today's world system must have clear, juridically determinate borders, established in accordance with international law. This is a historical and political demand. When we gained independence, it turned out that not a single metre of our border had been determined in accordance with such requirements. Not with China, with whom the Soviet Union had external borders that also turned out also to be merely provisional *[kotorie okazalis' tozhe uslovnymi]*, and not with our three Soviet neighbours.
Salamat Alamanov, head of the Department of Regional Problems under the President of the Kyrgyz Republic, speaking in 2007.
(Alamanov 2008)

If we don't have a border, what kind of independent state can we consider ourselves? *[kaisy egemendüü mamleketpiz?]*
(Isakov 2002)

Introduction: unsettled space

The collapse of the Soviet Union in 1991 brought unprecedented economic, political and security challenges to the newly independent states of Central Asia. Internal borders between former Soviet republics, often marked only by a river channel, an irrigation ditch, a line of trees or a roadside monument became the external boundaries of new sovereign states. One-time external borders of the Soviet Union became the responsibility of poorly-equipped national militaries to defend. Markets, roads, irrigation canals, reservoirs and bridges that had been constructed to integrate constituent Union republics into a shared socialist space became reconfigured as national patrimony.

These legal and institutional transformations gave a new urgency to questions of access to, use-rights regarding, and responsibility for the maintenance of ageing and often precarious transboundary infrastructures. New systems for regulating the movement of humans, animals, food and currencies had to be worked out in a context of political upheaval and economic devastation. As each of the Central Asian states sought to articulate a distinct national ideology

DOI: 10.4324/9780429057977-8

and vision of a secular, modern (etho-)national future, new concerns emerged over the illicit movement of religious ideas, the circulation of undesirable texts, the import of 'alien' values and political ideologies and the invisible movement of diseases into national space.

The challenge facing local and national governments in Central Asia was not one simply of reinforcing or reinstating controls on borders that were juridically, cartographically and physically determinate. It was also one of delimiting borders that were officially disputed (*spornye*) or 'undescribed' (*neopisanny*). With Central Asia's external neighbours the 'provisionality' of Soviet-era borders, as Alamanov put it in the quote above, created a host of administrative and political obstacles for new post-Soviet administrations, beginning with the simple fact that the state that had authorised many of those border adjudications no longer existed and that the documents that might have helped to ground a process of negotiation were now located far away in Moscow. For the newly independent states of Central Asia, negotiating previously internal Soviet borders was, if anything, even more challenging, given repeated adjustments to the location of those boundaries in the second half of the twentieth century as agricultural land, pastures, reservoirs and irrigation canals were leased from one Union republic to another, and parity committees repeatedly adjusted the line of the inter-republican boundary. New governments faced new dilemmas: should the decision of a parity committee that had been ratified by the Supreme Soviet of only one union republic be considered authoritative? Which map should be taken as definitive for determining the adjudication of claims? And what to do with the management and maintenance of infrastructure that had been constructed on land that was loaned for 'long-term use' (*na dolgosrochnoe polzovanie*) between neighbouring Soviet republics?

I argue in this chapter that for all of these institutional and administrative obstacles, the challenges posed by delimiting, demarcating, securing and managing these new borders should not be reduced simply to questions of administrative, legal or technical complexity. As Alamanov's reflections demonstrate, such adjudications were also occurring in a geopolitical and institutional context in which territorial integrity was framed as a 'historical and political demand' of nation-statehood, such that undelimited borders came to be seen as an intrinsic threat to the existential security and the physical and ideational integrity of the state. Like other postcolonial 'sensitive spaces' (Cons 2016), undelimited borders in Central Asia figured as sites where concerns about national survival have been mapped onto territory, with profound consequences for the populations whose livelihoods those borders now transect. In such a context, undelimited borders have come to crystallise concerns over 'creeping migration' – the incremental loss of territory through the undocumented sale or exchange of land between private citizens of neighbouring states – just as the presence of territorial enclaves has come to amplify anxieties about connectivity, coherence and territorial integrity. Such 'unsettled spaces', I suggest, are both empirically generative and analytically important. They reveal the fragility and instability at the heart of all territorial projects: projects that may be particularly salient and particularly fraught in new states, but which have resonances across the globe (Reeves 2014a).

To develop this argument I track the unfinished history of border delimitation in one region of Central Asia where Kyrgyzstan, Tajikistan and Uzbekistan meet at the southern edge of the Ferghana basin. I explore the reasons for the seeming intractability of certain boundary disputes in this region, and the consequences of territorial indeterminacy for borderland populations. I do so by taking a genealogical approach (Foucault 1978) to spatial transformation, recognising that the current territorial configurations are not shaped in any determinist fashion by past events, but rather are the product of contingent, shifting configurations at the intersection of domestic political struggles, local initiatives and the material intransigence of territory itself (Moore 2005, Reeves 2014b, Cons 2016).

I draw inspiration from analyses that emphasise the intrinsically *political* nature of contemporary boundary disputes in Central Asia, recognising the border to be, as Megoran (2004: 731) puts it, a 'material and discursive site where elites struggle for the power to inscribe conflicting gendered, nationalistic visions of geopolitical identity.' Drawing on ethnographic research between 2004 and 2015 in the Sokh, Isfara and Sumbula valleys, as well as archival and documentary research, I seek to build on elite-focused textual accounts in two ways. First, I aim to bring a historical sensibility to our understanding of contemporary boundary disputes in the Ferghana valley, by charting the contingent historical and geopolitical configurations in the Soviet period that have made certain stretches of new international border in Central Asia particularly sensitive: that is, particularly challenging to adjudicate, to delimit and to manage, and particularly salient in public culture as indices of national survivability.

Second, I draw on ethnography to consider the ways that the undelimited border becomes a site for economically and politically marginalised populations living at new international borders to make claims and to assert their political visibility vis-a-vis national capitals, political elites and international organisations. I follow Donald Moore (2005: 2) in arguing for ethnographic attention to 'micropractices': the way, that is, that 'the outcome of cultural struggles remains crucially dependent on the diverse ways land comes to be inhabited, laboured on, idiomatically expressed and suffered for in specific moments and milieus.' To portray current disputes as the inevitable outcome of a single moment of national–territorial delimitation, I argue, is to bracket out both the long history of territorial transformation that succeeded this moment of boundary-marking and to ignore the ways in which particular political and economic decisions in the post-Soviet period, including arbitrary border closures, the unequal privatisation of land, the disempowering of local institutions of conflict resolution, and the securitisation of daily life, have impacted upon the capacity for local disputes to be resolved peaceably or to escalate into much larger, inter-state disputes.

In developing this analysis, my aim is not to provide an encyclopaedic account of Central Asian border disputes: something that is in any case beyond the scope of a single chapter. Nor is it to over-determine Central Asian borders as sites of tension. Indeed, social life along disputed borders in the Ferghana valley could and should be studied as much for the salience of everyday practices of ordering and dispute resolution as they should as 'flashpoints of conflict'.[1] My concern, rather, is to illuminate the historical conjunctures that have made certain stretches of international border both unsettled and unsettling: *unsettled* in the sense that they are the locus of ongoing political and legal dispute and of periodic social conflict; *unsettling* in the sense that their indeterminacy and perceived 'porosity' troubles national imaginaries rooted in visions of contiguous, bounded territories.

Setting the scene

The Ferghana basin, my case study for this exploration, should be taken as illustrative rather than as representative of the wider Central Asian space: it illuminates with particular clarity the long legacies of what I called the 'unfinished delimitation' of Central Asia that began in the 1920s.

The side valleys at the southern perimeter of the much larger Ferghana basin share a common residential pattern of densely populated farming settlements located on either side of the river basin and deriving a living through irrigated agriculture. Watercourses beginning in the Alay mountain range are surrounded by summer pastures in the highlands, domestic plots and privately-owned strips of orchard and agricultural land along the river course, draining into the fertile and intensively farmed lowlands of the Ferghana basin. At different altitudes sheep-farming, apricot orchards, rice and cotton cultivation are the mainstays of domestic and state-farm production, with remittances from seasonal or long-term work in Russia now constituting a foundational source of income for family budgets throughout the region (Bichsel 2009, Murzakulova 2017, Reeves 2009, 2012).

Physical and political geography have historically generated complex inter-dependencies between ethno-linguistic and occupational communities, who are found on all sides of the Kyrgyz, Uzbek and Tajik borders in this region. To give one example: in late-Soviet Batken, a small town at the western end of the Kyrgyz SSR (and today the provincial capital of Batken oblast') men and women would travel to the town of Isfara in the Tajik SSR for hospital appointments. They would often visit Shorab, a mining town just inside the Tajik SSR on public holidays, to shop for fancy goods that were imported from Moscow, or to look at the creamy cakes in the window of the *gastronom*. They might travel to the pre-Soviet pilgrimage sites of Shahimardan, in the Uzbek SSR or the shrine-turned-Soviet health resort, Zumrad, in the Tajik SSR, to stay for a few days in a sanatorium if they had been given a holiday voucher (*putevka*) by the administration of their collective farm. Until cheap air transport arrived in the 1970s connecting Batken with the republican capital, Frunze, anyone wanting to travel from Batken to the capital of the Kyrgyz SSR had to travel through Tajik, Uzbek and Kazakh republics, since there was no land-route available between the north and south of the republic. Family photo albums, studio photographs taken at local landmarks, and dressers displaying family treasures attest to the significance and pleasure associated with these forms of late-Soviet mobility.

Economic life in the late-Soviet Ferghana valley was also premised on free movement across republican borders. Factories and mines – used here to extract coal, mercury and antimony – would employ young men from all three Ferghana valley republics. Weekly markets in provincial centres were considered common spaces, with traders typically using Uzbek as a regional lingua franca among Kyrgyz, Tajik and Uzbek traders and customers. Transboundary linkages were particularly intense for ethnic minorities in each of the Union republics, who have historically sustained close relations of marriage and ritual exchange with kin on the other side of the republican boundaries. During the late Soviet period it was common for Tajik-speaking minorities in the Uzbek and Kyrgyz SSRs to seek Tajik language higher education in Khujand or Dushanbe (in the Tajik SSR), for Uzbeks from Osh to study in Andijan (in the Uzbek SSR), and for marriages to be conducted with little regard to whether a *kelin* (bride) hailed from another Union republic.

These social and cultural links have been transformed (although not universally curtailed) after the end of the Soviet Union. It was and remains common for Kyrgyz shepherds to tend sheep belonging to lower-lying valley dwellers, for Uzbek traders in the valley basin to bring early summer fruits for sale in higher-altitude border markets in Kyrgyzstan, and for Tajik craftsmen to be hired to complete the decorative work on Kyrgyz homes. But the scale and density of such connections have been curtailed and transformed by new economic differentials that channel asymmetrical movement for day-labour and trade, as well as by the vagaries of visa regimes and travel permits, which have circumscribed permitted cross-border movement, particularly between Uzbekistan and Tajikistan.

As well as communities of kin and trade, international borders today transect roads, irrigation channels and private plots, creating what is locally referred to as a 'chessboard' border (in Kyrgyz: *shakhmat chek ara*). In certain places the international border runs through the middle of settlements, bisecting fields and pastures; in other places, the roadway itself comes to mark the border, with a row of petrol stations and currency exchange offices marking out the physical perimeter of the state. Populations in all three of the states that meet here rely upon fragile transboundary infrastructures for access to drinking and irrigation water, leading to the sequential rationing of water and creating seasonal tensions between upstream and downstream communities over cycles of distribution and maintenance.

The region contains two of the world's most densely populated full enclaves/exclaves, Vorukh (population c. 33,000) and Sokh (population c. 56,000), administratively subordinate to Tajikistan and Uzbekistan, respectively, but entirely enclosed within the territory of Kyrgyzstan. It also includes an indeterminate number of *de facto* micro-enclaves: single villages or stretches of agricultural land that are administratively subordinate to one state but surrounded by the territory of another.[2] In practice, this means that while not all borders are marked by customs and border posts or other state infrastructure, borders can often materialise at times of particular tension: in the form of a mobile border patrol, a line of stones blocking passage along shared roads, or a customs post mounted at the exit of a market. Borders in the region 'come and go', I was often told, indexing shifting inter-state relations and magnifying the impression, locally, that a trans-boundary movement was subject to the whim of politicians or 'big men' (*kattalar*) in distant national capitals.

Exceptional space?

Such zones have often been approached in policy and scholarly literature as exceptional or anomalous, and thus as intrinsically conflict-generating (Rus: *konfliktogennyi*): as territory 'out of place' because of the threat they present to visions of contiguous national territory. One recent book on the Ferghana Valley, for instance, begins by inviting its readers to picture a region 'so rife with tensions and intrigue' that 'in less than a decade it managed to produce two revolutions in the same country, murders straight out of a thriller, a massacre of unarmed civilians, a drug-smuggling superhighway, and corruption schemes so brazen and lucrative they would be hard to invent' (Shishkin 2013: 1). Even in scholarly analyses, the Ferghana borders often figure as illustrations of 'political oddities at the edge of the nation-state' (Diener and Hagen 2010), with the risk of conflict emanating from the 'gap' that exists between ethnic boundaries and 'artificially drawn' political borders (Slim 2002). Such accounts tend to over-determine and to naturalise conflict, which is seen to emerge from the malice of Stalin's cartography, from the apparent 'absurdity' of non-contiguous borders, or from the mismatch between the boundaries of ethnic groups and those of nation-states. They imply that a more 'rational' figuration of borders here – one in which ethnic and state boundaries correspond exactly – would obviate local tensions.

While it is certainly the case that there are a multitude of systemic pressures which have exacerbated inter-communal conflict at international borders in the region, including a series of deadly clashes along the Kyrgyzstan–Tajikistan border in April and May 2021, these should not be read in any deterministic way. There are specific political dynamics, including the progressive militarisation of borderland space, the lack of progress on juridical delimitation of boundaries and the suppression of the political opposition in Tajikistan, which have exacerbated and weaponised existing grievances over the allocation of agricultural land, access to pastures and the distribution of water. It is critical to recognise the very real conflict potentials in the Ferghana valley without naturalising these as 'inevitable' consequences of inter-ethnic tensions.

Instead, I draw attention in this chapter to two intersecting dynamics that have served to make Ferghana valley borders touchstones for a host of territorial anxieties about national viability and survivability. The first is the contingent configuration of political and economic logics, beginning in the early Soviet period, that has made border delimitation here an unfinished project. The second is the broader political and institutional post-Soviet context that has served to amplify border disputes, turning issues of territorial indeterminacy into touchstones for broader anxieties about sovereignty and existential viability in a world of nation-states.

Unfinished delimitation

This approximate contours of today's Central Asian states were first conceived in the early Soviet period but were readjusted at multiple points during the 70 years of the USSR's existence. Beginning in 1924, Soviet officials embarked on a process of so-called national-territorial delimitation (*natsional'no-territorialnoe razmezhevanie*): an exercise in geographical and ethnic mapping that was intended to transform the formerly multi-ethnic Turkestan, Bukharan and Khivan republics into notionally mono-national (*odnorodnye*) Soviet republics. This process of explicit national consolidation was guided by a Marxist teleology that saw the articulation of national consciousness as a necessary precondition for the emergence of real class-based antagonisms. As one of the architects of the delimitation, Juozas Vereikis put it to a meeting of the party faithful in Tashkent in 1924:

> We must foster in all ways possible the appearance of revolutionary, class consciousness among the peasants [*batraki*] and the poorest farmers. For that reason we must unravel as quickly as possible all those interethnic contradictions [*rasputat' vse mezhnatsional'nye protivorechiia*], which are obscuring class relations, preventing class conflict. The national delimitation, illuminating the clarity of national relations among the Uzbeks, Kirgiz, Turkmens, Kara-Kirgiz and Tajiks, will untangle the network of international contradictions and in that way will clear the stage for the social, class war.
>
> (Vareikis 1924, 61)

The process of national–territorial delimitation served to mobilise 'nation' as a category through which demands for rights to land and water could be mobilised (Hirsch 2000, Khalid 2015: 242). But it is also the first constitutive iteration of a conception of 'territory' as a finite, bounded landmass to which a particular national group, practicing a particular mode of livelihood (agricultural production, stockbreeding, transhumant herding) has a privileged claim.

While the process of national–territorial delimitation was officially heralded as complete by 1936, the process as it was carried out in the Ferghana basin created a host of enduring uncertainties. For one thing, the physical terrain in the Alay mountains was often not conducive to precise determination, which was conducted hastily, in a context of popular revolt from insurgents (pejoratively labelled the *basmachi* or 'rebels' in Russian sources at the time), and with limited input from ethnographic experts (Khalid: 2015: 270). It was also premised on a 'sedentarist metaphysic' (Malkki 1992) according to which distinct national groups occupied finite, non-overlapping and clearly distinguishable areas of land. The tendency to take *narodnost'* (nationality) as a proxy for determining where borders should lie was liable to generate contestation and confusion. Kyrgyz and Tajik communities living in southern Ferghana were as likely to define themselves by religion, lineage (*uruu/ avlod*) or valley as they were in exclusive national categories. Pastoral communities circulated between summer and winter pastures, meaning that their regular seasonal patterns of movement confounded sedentarist visions of national space (Bushkov 1995). And other registers of identity, in terms of religion or profession, were often more salient in daily life than those of nationality. The celebrated orientalist, Vasilii Bartol'd, warned in 1925 that 'the national principle, as it was brought to life during the delimitation of Middle Asia in 1924, is a product of West European history of the 19th century and is completely alien [*sovershenno chuzhd*] to local historical traditions' (Bartol'd, [1925] 1991).

Quite apart from the difficulties of establishing where ethnic boundaries lay, conceptually and spatially, the national imperative conflicted from the start with the economic one: the need to ensure that republics were economically coherent, that mountain populations were not cut off from the markets they used, and that the integrity of irrigation systems was preserved (Haugen 2003, 188–191). It is for this reason that the cluster of Tajik-majority mahallas in the Sokh and Isfara valleys were initially integrated into the Uzbek SSR, becoming full enclaves as opposed to territorial salients – that is, entirely surrounded by the neighbouring Kyrgyz SSR rather than connected through a thin strip of land – only following the determination of post-war boundary commissions (Bergne 2007: 52–53, Gorshenina 2012: 296–297; Reeves 2014: 29–31).

Cold war historiography often presented the delimitation that was initiated in 1924 as a cynical act of divide and rule, intended to stymie a nascent pan-Turkism by dividing Turkic peoples against themselves or cynically leaving a portion of one ethnic group 'stranded' inside another majority ethnic republic (e.g. Caroe 1967 [1953]). Such an approach, however, conflates effect with intention. For all the hubris and haste of the national-territorial delimitation, the archival record suggests that Bolshevik activists saw themselves as undertaking a thoroughly rational, modern and emancipatory project: one that would act as a corrective to the 'artificial [*iskusstvennye*] administrative boundaries' of the Tsarist era, which 'did not correspond either to the national nor the economic demands of the peoples' (Khodzhaev 1934, 3). Nor was it an exclusively top–down process. It was rather a fraught business of compromise – between Moscow, Tashkent and a host of competing regional elites; as well as between 'national' and 'economic' imperatives (Khalid 2015: 269–273). These competing priorities led to a proliferation of claims and counterclaims by those living in border districts that continued well into the 1930s (Bergne 2007; Koichiev 2001: 48–79). Indeed, by 1927 there were so many disagreements concerning the proper adjudication of lands lying in Sokh and Isfara valleys that on May 4, after a brief spate of land exchanges in southern Ferghana, the Central Executive Committee of the USSR issued a decree prohibiting any further changes to the existing borders for three years (Koichiev 2001: 79).

Delimitation deferred

In the southern fringes of the Ferghana basin subsequent socio-spatial transformation was inseparable from the long, violent history of collectivisation from the 1930s onwards; the transformation of previously unirrigated hillside (*adyr*) into regions of intense cultivation through the building of new irrigation canals, pumping stations and reservoirs; and the large-scale resettlement of mountain populations, who were considered too scattered to be productive, into grid-like 'planned villages' (*planovye sela*) in the lowlands.

This pattern of spatial transformation can be seen as a prototypical instance of 'seeing like a state': The high modernist Soviet government sought to transform land into territory and render populations legible – particularly nomadic, pastoral or transhumant populations whose seasonal movement frustrated local administrators (Scott 1998). But while this interpretation captures something of the impulse behind the national–territorial delimitation, such processes of territorial production were neither singular nor uncontested. Grand schemes of social transformation are often undermined by *métis* – everyday practices of 'muddling along' (Scott 1998: 313): in this case by administrators, water engineers and collective farm administrators who needed to meet production targets, to get their sheep to pastures, or simply to build new homes for rapidly expanding populations. This led to exchanges of land that were ratified in only one of the two constituent union republics, to informal land swaps between collective farms, and to systems of 'leasing' whereby infrastructure that lay inside one republic, such as a reservoir or pumping station, was administered by the neighbouring republic.

While the Soviet Union existed as a single economic space, the fact that such arrangements complicated and undermined earlier attempts at cartographic clarity had little bearing on daily life. After all, as the population grew and small collectives (*artely*) were consolidated into larger state farms (*sovkhozy*), the main priority for local administrators was to meet production targets by increasing the area of irrigated land under cultivation. The post-war population of the Ferghana valley expanded dramatically, leading to the creation of new settlements and the resettling of dispersed mountain populations in the valley basin (Bushkov 1990). The process of establishing new collective farm boundaries was thus always in practice catching up with a changing reality. When in 1949 a parity commission was established to determine the rightful boundaries between Kyrgyz and Tajik SSRs, for instance, it noted that maps from a decade earlier bore little correspondence to the actual current distribution of land. As the report of the 1949 commission noted:

> In order to prevent future potential land conflicts and misunderstandings in the use of unallocated [*neraspredelennykh*] lands, [we] ... consider it imperative in the near future to clarify the inter-republic boundaries between the Tajik SSR and the Kirgiz SSR, considering that the borders shown on the maps ... published in 1938–40 do not reflect the actual location of both republics [*fakiticheskogo raspolozheniia obeikh respublik*], as a result of which fourteen collective farms belonging to Batken district of the Kirgiz SSR have found themselves [having lands] within the borders of the Tajik SSR, including settlements belonging to eight of these collectives.
>
> (quoted in Alamanov 2010, 39–40)

Such commissions typically recommended adjusting the republican borders to fit current de facto land use (*fakticheskoe zemlepol'zovanie*) at the time of their work, rather than treating the original 1924–1927 delimitation as authoritative. Such an approach appears to have privileged more sedentary modes of life, because it is easier to tell that land is being 'used' productively when it is being cultivated rather than grazed (Bichsel 2009: 111). It also served to reinforce an assumed homology between ethnicity and territory: an assumption that land that is being cultivated by ethnic Kyrgyz members of a Kyrgyz collective farm belongs to the Kyrgyz SSR, and vice versa for ethnic Tajiks. In short, it fostered a particular conception of territory in which the ethnic affiliation of somebody living in a region of disputed territory was seen to determine not only that person's own administrative membership (in which republic they are registered), but the very identity of the land on which they lived.

The perils of *perestroika*

By the late Soviet period, population growth, the expansion of collective farms and leases of land and critical infrastructure between neighbouring republics meant that the new national borders of the post-Soviet Central Asian states were anything but settled. Social and economic life in Central Asia was densely integrated into systems of redistribution that originated far beyond the particular national republic. Collective farms and whole towns were often specialised towards the production of particular crops, the breeding of particular livestock, or the extraction of a single raw material that was manufactured in another republic. Remote and mountainous communities received subsidies (*dotatsiia*) or systems of targeted provisioning (*obespechenie*) directly from Moscow to sustain these mono-industries (Reeves 2014a: 111–119).

The Soviet authorities were not unaware of the challenges faced by dramatic population growth. Throughout the post-war period, the expansion of collective farms and the creation of new villages were accompanied by new parity commissions (*paritetnye kommissii*) that sought to determine the rightful location of inter-republican borders. In the Isfara valley, the most important of these were conducted in 1958, 1975 and 1989; the last two in response to violent escalations of conflict over the cultivation of land that local populations, Tajik and Kyrgyz, both saw as historically their own.[3]

The 1989 commission is particularly interesting because its work coincided with a high moment of perestroika-era debate over the legacies of Soviet environmental, agricultural and national policies. Whereas the previous commissions' work passed with little public commentary, Gorbachev's policy of *glasnost'* (openness) allowed journalists to draw attention to the fact that large sections of the inter-republican borders in Central Asia had yet to be formally determined, with the adjudications of parity committees concerning the *de jure* allocation of land still awaiting ratification by the Supreme Soviets of the respective republics. For the first time in Soviet history, commentators came to publicly decry the situation of 'extra-territoriality' that this produced:

> When the border has only a symbolic character, people carry on living according to their own established principles. The population of [ethnically] mixed villages would receive their documents and get registered in the nearest village administration, with Tajiks in the Tajik [administrative centre], and Kyrgyz in the Kyrgyz one. Alongside this practice of registration, people got used to an understanding of extraterritoriality [*voshlo poniatie ekstraterritorial'nosti*], that is, the right of representatives of the other republic, irrespective of their place of residence, to follow only their own laws. And the same is true of their land holdings.
>
> *(Popov 1989)*

The 1989 commission, which followed a period of extended inter-communal conflict over land and water use, prompted first fleeing, and then more sustained discussion of the legacies of the 'unfinished business' of the national territorial delimitation conducted sixty years earlier. Writing in the regional Tajik newspaper, *Leninabadskaya Pravda,* at the height of the 1989 conflict, journalists Kriuchkov and Morozov launched a searing attack on the failures of past parity committees. Drawing on a metaphor from a Russian fable they argued that past commissions had acted 'on the principle of Trishkin's kaftan', when in order to fix the torn elbows of the coat 'you cut out a part of the sleeve, and to mend the shortened sleeves you cut away at the coat-tails.' Repeated commissions had sought to remedy past failures in determining the location of inter-republican boundaries but in doing so, they 'hastily [*v pozharnom poriadke*] tried to put out the hot-spots without solving the problem in any global way'. Today, the authors concluded,

> We urgently need the borders of land use to be determined in a completely clear and legally rigorous way. We are not just talking about the redrawing [*perekroika*] of the borders between the two republics, but also about a clear determination of the right to appropriate empty lands. These need to be resolved at the very highest levels. All the preceding republican commissions didn't resolve anything.
>
> *(Kriuchkov and Morozov 1989)*

In these *glasnost'*-era articles, searing critique was often accompanied by dramatic headlines and scenes of physical destruction--something that would have been unimaginable in a provincial newspaper just a few years earlier. Writing in a June 1989 article under the heading, *Conflict Could have Been Avoided* [Konflikta moglo ne byt'], for instance, M. Popov launched one of the first sustained public critiques of the national–territorial delimitation of 1924–25, which made the map of Central Asia appear as though it had been 'cut with scissors'. In particular, he critiqued the last major round of territorial redrawing in the Isfara valley, which occurred in 1958:

> There was so much freedom at that time that in 1958 the leadership of the Kalinin kolkhoz on the Isfara district even considered it possible to gift (*peredat' v dar*) 144 hectares of land belonging to the Kalinin kolkhoz of Batken raion. That stretch of land lies right next to the territory of Oktiabr'. In Kyrgyzstan, ratification of that donation of land went through all the necessary levels, but in Tajikistan, not all the formalities were observed. The presidium of the Supreme Soviet of the republic did not issue a decree in regard to this exchange. But that did not stop the neighbours using the land that was given to them. Today, thirty years later, the short-sightedness (*neobdumannost'*) of that step is particularly stark. The population of Oktiabr' has grown rapidly and it is necessary to increase the number of domestic irrigated plots to ease problems with agricultural production. But there is no contiguous land left now next to the village.
>
> (Popov 1989)

To this day, the major obstacle slowing the delimitation of the Kyrgyz-Tajik border around the former Oktiabr kolkhoz (today's Khojai-A'lo) is disagreement over which maps and normative acts, ratified in one Union republic but not the other, should be taken as the authoritative basis for inter-governmental border negotiations.[4]

Unsettled politics, unsettled space

In the last three decades, this lack of juridical determination has progressively transformed new state borders into material and symbolic objects of concern for national publics, borderland residents and local governments alike. The qualifier 'progressively' here is significant: transformations in the degree to which new border regimes impacted on the lives of those living in their midst were neither immediate, consistent across different stretches of border, nor uniform in their effects for differently positioned populations. Over the last three decades, the degree and salience of border control along the Kyrgyzstan–Uzbekistan border in the Sokh valley, for instance, has reflected the changing temperature of inter-state relations: at certain times a 'corridor' linking Sokh to Rishton and Ferghana to the north has been open and the Uzbekistani Sokh enclave has been accessible to transiting cars passing west-to-east through Kyrgyzstan. At other times, these borders have been closed, necessitating significant and costly detours for enclave residents to reach their nearest administrative centre in the Uzbekistani mainland.[5] In addition to this temporal variation, there is also a complex geography of differential control. The 'border' that appears on the map as a singular, contiguous line belies a complex, punctuated geography of restriction and control, threat and possibility that in some cases extends deep into the territory of the three Ferghana valley states.

This geographical and temporal variation notwithstanding, the general shift has been towards greater securitisation and militarisation of the Ferghana valley borders, particularly since the early 2000s. While border and customs posts were established at key crossing points in the early 1990s, their presence had little immediate impact while physical movement was unrestricted. Systems of public transport remained integrated, border markets continued to function, and families continued to cross for lifecycle ceremonies and for study throughout the 1990s. Indeed, spaces of juridical indeterminacy often acted as *de facto* border markets, as sites for the buying and selling of day-labour (*mardikor*), as hubs for the sale of petrol, coal and oil, or as pick-up points for the informal share-taxis that took people to regional centres.

In the immediate post-Soviet period, there was also a degree of hope, at least among some Soviet-trained officials, that the legacies of Soviet solidarity and international 'friendship' would obviate the need for complex legal procedures to determine new international borders. Salamat Alamanov, the geographer who chaired negotiations on behalf of the Kyrgyz government, recalled meetings in the early 1990s between heads of the new national committees of delimitation and demarcation:

> We had no idea at the time [1992-3] what a challenge it would be to establish the borders between our former union republics…If you leaf through the documents from those early meetings of the heads of state, it's written there that we wouldn't have any borders, that we wouldn't bother with any of that business, that we would keep the same community [*obshchnost'*] that we had in the Soviet Union….We thought that would be enough to live in our community without any kind of border problems. Life turned out to be a lot more complex than we had imagined.
>
> (Alamanov 2008: 39)

In part this was a question of technical expertise being in short supply. Alamanov lamented the lack of historians, geographers and boundary specialists whose expertise would assist the boundary negotiations, not to mention unequal access to crucial archival documents. But delimitation was slow primarily for political rather than technical reasons. Tajikistan suffered a devastating civil war between 1992 and 1997 followed by an 'authoritarian peace' that stymied both the state's institutional and technical capacity to engage in extensive delimitation negotiation, let alone in significant border management. To this day, Tajikistan's 1357km border with Afghanistan is defended by troops from Russia's 201st Military Base.

From the mid-1990s, Uzbekistan embarked on an increasingly autarkic ideology of 'national independence', premised upon the physical protection of national space from a multiplicity of human and non-human threats, stretching from terrorist insurgents to rodents to counterfeit currency to the SARS epidemic in 2003. As Nick Megoran (2004) has demonstrated, the securitisation of the Kyrgyzstan–Uzbekistan boundary increased dramatically in 1999 and 2000, following bomb blasts in Tashkent and incursions into the territory of Tajikistan and Kyrgyzstan by militants from the Islamic Movement of Uzbekistan (IMU), an outlawed Islamist organisation seeking to overthrow the government of Islam Karimov. Following these threats, Uzbekistan unilaterally mined stretches of border with Tajikistan and Kyrgyzstan, dismantling border bridges, terminating trans-boundary public transport, and embarking on the construction of barbed wire border fences around the perimeter – and sometimes right through the middle of border villages.

In Kyrgyzstan, meanwhile, the 'border issue' was taken up in the early 2000s by the political opposition to challenge the authority of the first president of the state, Askar Akaev, particularly over accusations that the President had secretly ceded land to China in closed-door negotiations. Incursions by the IMU in 1999 and 2000 across Kyrgyzstan's southern borders exposed the ill-preparedness of the military against external threat. By the end of 2001, having suddenly been cast into a 'strategic ally' of a previously indifferent United States, Kyrgyzstan came to host a huge tent city of American servicemen flying sorties over Afghanistan as a key service base in the global 'war on terror'. The following year, Russia announced that it, too, would be opening an airbase on Kyrgyz soil – 30 kilometres from the US one, on the other side of the capital city. In this context, the inability of Kyrgyzstan to defend its borders served to condense a host of broader public anxieties concerning the sapping of state sovereignty.[6] A 2001 article in the opposition *Res Publica* newspaper, for instance, explicitly linked the arrival of US and Russian troops on Kyrgyz soil with the state's perceived inability to secure its territory. Noting ironically the great honour of 'being able to demonstrate our hospitality [*gostepriimstvo*] to the powerful air-forces of the USA,' the article discursively linked the new geopolitical realities with the indeterminacy of Kyrgyzstan's borders, which exposed Kyrgyzstan to the whim of her neighbours' territorial demands:

> At the same time [as we have welcomed the USA and Russia], inch by inch, all year round we have been giving away our land to neighbouring states. In February [2001] there was the scandal over Sokh, about connecting it to Uzbekistan, in April, there was the question of delimiting borders with China, and in December it suddenly emerged that we were 'using' a piece of Kazakh territory that we had to 'return'. And each time from somewhere there emerge ever older and older maps, which have even more corrections to the border of Kyrgyzstan. In which case, what kind of sovereignty for the statehood of Kyrgyzstan did we declare exactly twelve years ago, if today there is a real threat to her integrity?
>
> (Sydykova 2001)

Border-talk – and specifically anxiety over the risks of undelimited borders that could apparently be renegotiated on the whim of Kyrgyzstan's neighbours – came to act as a vehicle for the Kyrgyz political opposition to articulate political demands at a time of acute national anxiety over the state's sovereign identity. The opposition's critical political move, as Megoran (2004: 752) argues, was to channel such concerns 'into a coherent and comprehensive assault on President Akaev's claim to be an authentic defender of the body politic of the Kyrgyz nation and territory' – something that contributed to Akaev's dramatic removal from power in 2005.

Living in unsettled space

Such anxieties were not confined to the political elite. Or, more precisely, in 'narrating the nation,' through the border issue, the political opposition was also drawing upon, amplifying, and feeding back into a host of political and existential anxieties for border-dwellers surrounding access to life-sustaining resources, restrictions upon local movement, and the inability of states to adjudicate upon the status of disputed territory. The 'border issue' was a politically-charged symbol in national capitals, to be sure, but for those living at these indeterminate borders it was also an intensely material reality, in which disputed territory complicated the allocation of water between upstream and downstream users, politicised access to grazing lands, pastures, roads and waterways, and led to the increasing securitisation of everyday mobility (Bichsel 2009, Matveeva 2017, Murzakulova 2017, Reeves 2018).

In the Isfara valley, for instance, tensions over water allocation and the status of disputed land that had led to violent conflict in 1989 persisted after independence, now magnified through a nationalist press and stymied by inter-state commissions that first had to agree upon the parameters of their work, including particular maps, resolutions and legal texts that would constitute the foundation for future negotiations. Local officials whom I interviewed between 2004 and 2010 were frustrated that such negotiations were occurring too slowly, prioritising areas of border in mountainous areas that are sparsely inhabited rather than those of dense population and acute land shortage where the stakes of moratoriums on construction were far more severe. My fieldwork also revealed an often-voiced sentiment that boundary commissions making decisions in distant capitals took little note of local expertise and historical memory: the embodied, vernacular knowledge of place-through-cultivation that linked particular fields and pastures to particular groups of kin going back to the Tsarist era. Such lack of local involvement in the delimitation process magnified the sense, locally, that border adjudication was opaque and politicised, that decisions of parity commissions were arbitrary and that political leaders were not acting in good faith.

As Central Asian states have taken increasingly divergent political and economic paths, four factors have compounded the intractability of the 'border issue' locally. The first is the political economy of land itself. In a region of acute land shortage and rapidly growing populations, border negotiations have invariably taken place far more slowly than the material transformation of lived landscapes. As populations have continued to grow apace, new areas of land continue to be brought under cultivation and construction; lands that were (and are still, officially) 'disputed' are now home to well-established *mahalla* populations, complete with hundreds of homes and all the associated infrastructure of a small village settlement. Land that was once 'loaned' is now treated as 'owned', even as older residents lament the fact that 'that land over there was once *ours.*'

As populations have grown, so has the area under domestic cultivation, as collective farmland is privatised and domestic plots allocated to newly-formed families. In the absence of juridical determination of borders, this can intensify the *perception* that the 'border' itself is moving, as new homes are constructed, new orchards planted, or areas of formerly uninhabited and uncultivated land are allocated to newly-formed families (see also Murzakulova 2017:13–14 for maps outlining these physical shifts in land use in the Isfara valley since the 1970s). In the Kyrgyzstani border village of Ak-Sai, for instance, I was told that the presence of a new Tajik mahalla close to the entrance of the village constituted evidence of territorial encroachment ('creeping migration'), even when the land on which such construction occurred was not officially disputed and houses were simply being constructed on land earmarked for the purpose.

Second, infrastructure has increasingly been used to 'mark out' a border in the absence of definitive juridical determination. In the Sokh and Isfara valleys, for instance, Kyrgyzstani authorities, with significant international financial support, have embarked on projects of road construction premised upon bypassing the Sokh and Vorukh enclaves to enable Kyrgyzstani border villagers to access markets and pastures without needing to cross through the neighbouring state. Such infrastructure projects are premised upon the need to facilitate mobility and obviate costly customs checks (World Bank 2009). In practice, they have also come to figure as flashpoints of inter-communal dispute, as new roads facilitate the mobility of some, while significantly curtailing the mobility of others. A new bypass road around the Tajik settlements of Chorkhuh and Surh, for instance, has cut off these villagers' access to firewood and kindling, and has led to increase in military patrols around the perimeter of those villages (Reeves 2014b). As a 2009 World Bank 'Resettlement Action plan' noted, in the absence of formal adjudication, the new road would help to mark a *de facto* boundary between states and to shore up state presence in a region liable to informal cross-border land use: 'Although the proposed road does not run directly along the border at any point', the Action plan noted, 'it will serve to define the nearby border into the future and reduce the risk of encroachment' (World Bank 2009: 5).

Such explicitly 'national' infrastructures have served, third, to undermine spaces of everyday or 'banal' cross-border mixing between populations, particularly in markets, at bust-stops and on public transport. The effects of such 'unmixing' cannot be under-estimated, particularly given that an ever-increasing part of the population in all three states has no lived memory of the

Soviet era and limited, if any, fluency in the neighbouring village's primary language (Kyrgyz/ Tajik). Throughout the early 2000s, the continued existence of cross-border bus routes in the Isfara valley created spaces for the performance of everyday respect, particularly between village elders (*aksakals*) whose elaborate rituals of greeting, and of giving up/ accepting offers of a seat on overcrowded buses created an informal but enduring fabric of convivial relations that could be invoked and mobilised at times of conflict. Such spaces of mixing also created a context of visible familiarity among elders who recognised one another's authority: as a rule, elders from Kyrgyz-majority Ak-Sai *knew*, at least by sight, elders from Tajik Vorukh and Chorkuh. Key local actors, such as a Tajik doctor who worked in the Kyrgyz medical clinic just across the border from his home could be called upon to mediate in times of dispute. Teachers who taught children in nearby villages across the border were accorded significant respect, as were religious teachers and ethnomedical healers (*bakshy* and *tabip*) who worked across borders. It was common until the mid-2000s for Kyrgyz children to be sent to study the Koran and the Arabic language with religious educators in Tajik Chorkuh, locally recognised to be a centre of religious learning (and often correspondingly vilified in the Tajik press as a centre of support for the Islamic Party of Tajikistan). As infrastructures of connectivity have diminished, so have the opportunities for such informal, habitual, and non-antagonistic communication across borders. Such impacts have fallen unequally, across age groups and genders: at the time of my most recent visit to the Isfara valley, in 2015, unmarried women were explicitly warned not to take public transport belonging to the 'other' state, significantly restricting their mobility in the name of protecting their (and their fellow villagers') honour.

Finally, and perhaps most importantly, local tensions around unsettled space have been amplified over the last decade by the increasing securitisation of everyday life in the form of local border and customs checks, occasional troop movements, and sporadic exchanges of fire between military personnel (Reeves 2018). While the border itself remains in significant part indeterminate, the area on either side of the neutral 'indeterminate' territory has become increasingly militarised. My research suggests that far from increasing existential security, the presence of military personnel in border villages has led to the domestication and normalisation of military force, such that it was common during my fieldwork for otherwise mundane or localised inter-village disputes (such as a cow trampling crops, or an upstream water-user polluting an irrigation canal with dirty washing water), to quickly escalate into much larger conflicts, with village men quickly mobilised, and the head of the local border unit called upon to demonstrate that physical force could be met with a militarised response.

Conclusion

Independence elicited new debates in Central Asia about what 'civilised' international borders should look like and how they should function to regulate movement into and out of the state. It exposed the limits of state capacity to police the movement of people and things across boundaries that are criss-crossed by a multiplicity of roads, tracks and domestic courtyards. It revealed geopolitical hierarchies and inequalities as newly-independent states sought to negotiate complex claims over territorial limits with larger and more powerful neighbours. And it generated protracted disagreement over the very documents and associated maps that should be considered the authoritative basis on which inter-state discussion over boundary issues should proceed. To understand the contours of such contention, I have argued that we need to approach territory processually, treating it, as Cons (2016: 16) argues for another site of politically-contentious 'sensitive space', as the outcome of 'contingent events, strategic political projects, and long histories of struggle and place-making across multiple scales.' Viewed from this perspective we can see that the national–territorial delimitation of 1924–1927 should be seen, not as a single and conclusive moment of border-drawing, but as the first iteration of an ongoing story of twentieth-century border-moving in rural central Asia, which has continued well beyond the Soviet Union's demise, with profound and long-lasting consequences for those who have to make a living in the margins of these new states.

Notes

1 Murzakulova (2018: 22), for instance, has shown that along parts of the Kyrgyzstan–Tajikistan boundary, entrepreneurial networks that span national borders represent important agents of inter-ethnic cohesion, even as the role of other trans-boundary actors, such as teachers and medical personnel, has diminished.
2 There are conventionally eight recognised full enclaves in the Ferghana valley: four enclaves of Uzbekistan in Kyrgyzstan (Sokh, Shahimardan, Jani-Aiyl and Qalacha/Chongara), two Tajik enclaves in Kyrgyzstan (Western Qal'acha/Kairagach, and Vorukh), one Tajik enclave in Uzbekistan (Sarvan) and one Kyrgyz enclave in Uzbekistan (Barak). The number of de facto micro-enclaves, a few hectares in size, is indeterminate given the indeterminacy of the border line.
3 For a chronology of these events, see Bichsel 2009: 106–112; Reeves 2016.
4 In the context of worsening inter-state rhetoric in the weeks preceding the violent escalation of conflict along the Kyrgyzstan-Tajikistan border in the spring of 2021, Asia-Plus published an extended interview with the former mayor of Isfara town (Tajikistan) and participant in the 1989 parity committee, Mirzosharif Islomidinov (Nadirov 2021), where it is argued that, on the basis of incomplete ratification of parity committee protocols, Vorukh should not be considered an 'enclave' in juridical terms at all – a term that it couches in scare quotes. Needless to say, Kyrgyzstani officials and scholars have vigorously contested this interpretation of historical events.
5 The complex recent history of the Sokh-Rishton road openings and closures is summarised in *The Economist* (2019), though under a characteristically unhelpful header, 'Stalin's Splatter'.
6 A newspaper cartoon at the time portrayed American and Russian generals pouring over a giant map of Bishkek, on which were marked newly-renamed American and Russian streets and the city landmarks that would serve as suitable flag-posts for their respective flags. The cartoon portrayed the cigar-smoking generals having happily carved up the city, squabbling over which side would have 'sovereign access' to the Dostuk hotel, notorious locally as the hub of the city's red-light district.

References

Alamanov, S. (2008) "Protsess priniatiia reshenii v uregulirovanii prigranichnykh konfliktov v Kyrgyzstane. Stennogramma meropriiatiia." In *Bridging Mass Media and Public Policy Making in Kyrgyzstan*, 38–44. Bishkek: Institute of Public Policy.
Alamanov, S. (2010) "Ob istorii, sovremennom sostoianii i perspektivakh iuridicheskogo oformleniia Kyrgyzsko-Tadzhikskoi gosudarstvennoi granitsy." In *Kyrgyzstan-Tadzhikistan: kurs na ukreplenie partnerstva v kontekste regional'nykh sviazei*, edited by Nur Kerim, 38–42. Bishkek: Friedrich Ebert Stiftung.
Bartol'd, V. [1925] (1991) "Zapiska po voprosu ob. Istoricheskikh vzaimootnosheniiakh turetskikh i iranskikh narodnostei Srednei Azii." Unpublished document, reproduced with commentary in A.A. Prazukas, "O natsional'nom razmezhevanii v Srednei Azii." *Vostok* 5: 163.
Benjamin, W. [1928] (1978) *Reflections: Essays, Aphorisms, Autobiographical Writings*, edited by Peter Demetz, translated by Edmund Jephcott. New York: Schocken Books
Bergne, P. (2007) *The Birth of Tajikistan: National Identity and the Origins of the Republic*. London: I.B. Tauris.
Bichsel, C. (2009) *Conflict Transformation in Central Asia: Irrigation Disputes in the Ferghana Valley*. Abingdon: Routledge.
Bushkov, V. (1990) "O nekotorykh aspektakh mezhnatsional'nykh otnoshenii v Tadzhikskoi SSR." In *Issledovaniia po prikladnoi i neotlozhnoi etnologii Seriia A: Mezhnatsional'nye otnosheniia v SSSR No. 9*. Moscow: Institute of Ethnography of the Academy of Sciences of the USSR.

Bushkov, V. (1995) *Naselenie severnogo Tadzhikistana: formirovanie i rasselenie.* Moscow: Russian Academy of Sciences.

Caroe, O. [1953] (1967) *Soviet Empire: The Turks of Central Asia and Stalinism.* London: Macmillan.

Cons, J. (2016) *Sensitive Space: Fragmented Territory at the India-Bangladesh Border.* Seattle: University of Washington Press.

Diener, A. and J. Hagen (2010) *Borderlines and Borderlands: Political Oddities at the Edge of the Nation-State.* Lanham: Rowman and Littlefield.

Economist. (2019) "Stalin's Splatter: Convoluted Borders are Hampering Central Asian Integration." October 31. https://www.economist.com/asia/2019/10/31/convoluted-borders-are-hampering-central-asian-integration

Foucault, M. (1978). "Nietzsche, Genealogy, History." In *Language, Counter-Memory, Practice: Selected Essays and Interviews*, edited by D. Bouchard. Ithaca: Cornell Univeristy Press, 139–164.

Gorshenina, S. (2012). *Asie Centrale: L'Invention des frontières et l'héritage russo-soviétique.* Paris: CRNS Editions.

Haugen, A. (2003) *The Establishment of National Republics in Soviet Central Asia.* London: Palgrave Macmillan.

Hirsch, F. (2000) "Toward an Empire of Nations: Border-Making and the Formation of 'Soviet' National Identities." *Russian Review* 59 (2): 201–226.

Hirsch, F. (2005) *Empire of Nations: Ethnographic Knowledge and the Making of the Soviet Union.* Princeton: Princeton University Press.

Isakov, I. (2002) "K voprosu o kyrgyzsko-kitaiskoi gosudarstvennoi granitse – prodolzhenie." *Res Publica*, May 17.

Khalid, A. (2015) *Making Uzbekistan: Nation, Empire and Revolution in the Early USSR.* Ithaca: Cornell University Press.

Khodzhaev, F. (1934) "Doklad predsedateliia SNK Uzbekskoi SSR tov. Faizully Khodzhaeva." In *O natsional'nom razmezhevanii. Doklady na plenume Sredazbiuro TsK VKP(b) 1934 5 sentiabria 1934 g,* 1–16. Moscow: Ob"edinenie gosudarstvennykh izdatel'stv, Sredneaziatskoe otdelenie.

Koichiev, A. (2001) *Nasional'no-territorial'noe razmezhevanie v ferganskoi doline (1924–1927 gg.).* Bishkek: Kyrgyz State National University Press.

Kriuchkov, Iu. and V. Morozov. (1989) "Byt' liud'mi! Reportazh iz zony deistviia komendantskogo chasa." *Leninabadskaia Pravda,* July 21, pp. 1, 3.

Malkki, L. (1992) "National Geographic: The Rooting of Peoples and the Territorialization of National Identity among Scholars and Refugees." *Cultural Anthropology* 7(1), 24–44.

Matveeva, A. (2017) "Divided we Fall….Or Rise? Tajikistan-Kyrzstan Border Dilemma". *Cambridge Journal of Eurasian Studies* 1(2017): 1–20.

Megoran, N. (2004) "The Critical Geopolitics of the Uzbekistan–Kyrgyzstan Ferghana Valley Boundary Dispute, 1999–2000." *Political Geography* 23: 731–764.

Moore, D. (2005) *Suffering for Territory: Race, Place and Power in Zimbabwe.* Durham: Duke University Press.

Murzakulova, A. (2017) *Contextual Factors of Conflict in Border Communities in Batken Province, Kyrgyzstan.* Bishkek: University of Central Asia Mountain Societies Research Institute.

Murzakulova, A. (2018) *Challenges of Social Cohesion and Tensions in Communities on the Kyrgyz-Tajik Border.* Bishkek: University of Central Asia Mountain Societies Research Institute.

Nadirov, B. (2021) "Kak Vorukh stal 'anklavom'. Istoriia Tadzhiksko-Kyrgyzskogo konflikta." Asia-Plus, April 5. https://asiaplustj.info/ru/news/tajikistan/society/20210405/kak-voruh-stal-anklavom-istoriya-tadzhiksko-kirgizskogo-konflikta

Popov, M. (1989) "Konflika moglo ne byt'." *Kommunist Tadzhikistana*, 28 June, p. 1.

Reeves, M. (2009) "Materialising State Space: 'Creeping Migration' and Territorial Integrity in Southern Kyrgyzstan." *Europe–Asia Studies* 61 (7): 1277–1313.

Reeves, M. (2012) "Black Work, Green Money: Remittances, Ritual, and Domestic Economies in Southern Kyrgyzstan." *Slavic Review* 17 (1): 108–134.

Reeves, M. (2014a) *Border Work: Spatial Lives of the State in Rural Central Asia.* Ithaca: Cornell University Press.

Reeves, M. (2014b) "Roads of Hope and Dislocation: Infrastructure and the Remaking of Territory at a Central Asian Border." *Ab Imperio* 2: 235–257.

Reeves, M. (2016) "'And Our Words Must be Constructive': On the Discordances of Glasnost' in the Central Asian Press at a Time of Conflict." *Cahiers d'Asie Centrale* 26: 77–110.

Reeves, M. (2018) "Intimate Militarism: Domesticating the Border in Rural Central Asia." In *Routledge Handbook of Asian Borderlands*, edited by A. Horstmann, M. Saxer and A. Rippa, 42–55. Abingdon: Routledge.
Scott, J. (1998) *Seeing Like a State. How Certain Schemes to Improve the Human Condition Have Failed*. New Haven: Yale University Press.
Shishkin, P. (2013) *Restless Valley: Revolution, Murder and Intrigue in the Heart of Central Asia*. New Haven: Yale University Press.
Slim, R. (2002) "The Ferghana Valley: In the Midst of a Host of Crises." In *Searching for Peace in Central and South Asia: An Overview of Conflict Prevention and Peace-Building Activities*, edited by Monique Mekenkamp, Paul von Tongeren and Hans vn der Veen, 489–515. Boulder, CO: Lynne Reiner.
Sydykova, Z. (2001) "Vagonchik tronetsia, piron ostanetsia." *Res Publica*, 25 December.
Vareikis, I. [Juozas] (1924) "Novyi etap natsional'nogo stroitel'stva v Srednei Azii." In *Natsional'no-gosudarstvennoe razmezhevanie Srednei Azii*, edited by Iozas Vareikis and Isaak Zelenskii, 39–68. Tashkent: Sredne-Aziatskoe Gosudarstvennoe Izdatel'stvo.
World Bank (2009) *National Roads Rehabilitation Project: Osh Isfana Section. Updated Feasibility Study. Resettlement Action Plan*. Bishkek: World Bank.

PART III
Geography

9
BOUNDARIES, BORDERS AND IDENTITIES

Vincent Artman and Alexander C. Diener

Where – and what – is 'Central Asia?' At first glance, these questions seem slightly bizarre. After all, the existence of 'Central Asia' is not only axiomatic but, as this volume attests, is something that has attracted the attention of numerous scholars and policymakers. And yet *defining* 'Central Asia' turns out to be surprisingly elusive, since not only are there competing visions of the spatial extent of Central Asia, but those visions of regional boundary that have shifted substantially over time and circumstance. In this chapter, therefore, we will argue that Central Asia is best understood as a *geographical imaginary* whose boundaries and attendant meanings continue to evolve.

The concept of a geographical imaginary is closely connected with the notion of 'imaginative geographies,' a term borrowed from Edward Said (1979). Derek Gregory has pointed out the 'intimate connection between the spatialities of ... imaginative geographies and the precarious and partial formation of identity' (Gregory 1995: 475). As Edith Clowes writes, for example, 'geographical discourses dominant in current [Russian] discourse about identity convey the sense that *who* a Russian is depends on how one defines *where* Russia is. Overarching values attach to that place, however it is defined' (Clowes 2011: xii). Geographical imaginaries thus become irrevocably intertwined with the construction of identity, both at the individual and collective scales.

The concept of the geographical imaginary also implies some degree of *boundedness*,[1] 'sustain[ing] images of "home" as well as "abroad," "our space" as well as "their space"' (Gregory et al. 2009: 370). That is to say, in that geographical imaginaries, with their implicit ordering, are inscribed with any number of spatial and ideological divisions (between 'ours' and 'theirs,' for example, but also between 'Europe' and 'Asia' or 'metropole' and 'colony'). With this in mind, and in keeping with the focus of this volume, we return to the questions of where and what is 'Central Asia,' and what could it mean to be 'Central Asian.' The chapter begins with a consideration of the rather amorphous and ill-defined boundaries of 'Central Asia' as a world region. After all, as Morgan Liu suggests, 'Central Asia is a curiously overdetermined yet understudied region of the world ... a neglected hole in the map of Western academia' (Liu 2011: 116). And so, providing even a provisional definition of such a large-scale geographic imaginary is necessary to any understanding of the geopolitical, historical, economic and cultural factors out of which emerge different understandings of 'Central Asian' identity.

This chapter will therefore pay special attention to the complex landscapes of identity that emerge from the negotiations between different groups over geographies of power and belong-

DOI: 10.4324/9780429057977-9

ing at numerous scales. These contestations are linked, ultimately, with the legitimacy of states and their capacity to project power and impose normative conceptions of identity within their sovereign territories. Such issues are also connected with the question of mobility. This is to say that borders, in addition to functioning as a technology of control over sovereign territory, also regulate mobilities. Parsing these various forms of mobility (e.g. ideological, financial, corporeal, economic and resource) is one of the foremost challenges facing Central Asia (Diener 2015) – a challenge that is intimately connected with questions of identity.

'Central Asia' as a mutable regional imaginary

As others in this volume have suggested, the deceptively simple questions 'what is Central Asia?' and 'who are Central Asians?' have been the subject of much discussion and debate. For example, Owen Lattimore's notion of 'Inner Asia' emphasises the region's historical and economic proximity with China, and particularly what is now known as Xinjiang (1962, 1995), while the term 'Eurasia' today often connotes the region's connections with Russia and the Soviet Union. Others, meanwhile, have proposed the term 'Central Eurasia,' which includes Afghanistan, Iran and Mongolia, but excludes Eastern Europe (Schoeberlein 2002). Still others prefer the term 'Greater Middle East,' which emphasises the region's connections with both the Islamic hearth as well as its historical and cultural ties with Iran and the greater Indian subcontinent (Amineh 2007).[2] As the existence of all these competing definitions makes clear, even defining what constitutes 'Central Asia' as an object of analysis is a matter of some disagreement, and the kinds of research questions that might emerge from each context could differ substantially (Figure 9.1).

Figure 9.1 Map of Historical Regions of Central Asia. Source: Prepared by the University of Kansas Cartographic Laboratory, Modeled on Bregel 2003.

This definitional fluidity should not be surprising. While many consider the Ural Mountains to be the ostensible 'geographic' boundary between 'Europe' and 'Asia,' such a demarcation may be regarded as wholly arbitrary from a geographical perspective. Physically and ecologically speaking, similar assemblages of flora and fauna, landforms and climate are found on both sides of the Urals.[3] Human geographies also span the mountain range, with closely related linguistic families (Turkic, Altaic and Slavic) and religious communities (Islam, Eastern Orthodox Christianity, Buddhism and various indigenous faiths) transcending the putative divide. From the perspective of political geography, moreover, the Urals have rarely proved much of a barrier to state expansion. Bounding Central Asia is thus more conceptually problematic than it might seem at first glance. As Andre Gunder Frank (1992) has observed, the region is often depicted as a 'dark *tabula rasa*' populated by 'migrants or invaders who periodically emerge' to 'impinge' on the cultures and empires of China, Europe or the Middle East. But 'Central Asia,' however defined, has often been at the very center of truly global affairs.[4]

With the Russian expansion into Central Asia in the eighteenth and nineteenth centuries, new – and often competing – geopolitical imaginaries were projected onto the region. Incorporation into the Russian Empire rendered Central Eurasia legible, at least from a Eurocentric perspective. This was achieved by bounding the region and subjecting it to imperial administration; it was limited, reimagined, conceptually transformed, and reconfigured as a modern political territory, rather than as a wild, dangerous *terra incognita*. As Daniel Brower argues, the Russian leadership 'set out to reshape the imperial dominion to give it the unity and might of a modern (Western) state' (2003: 20) (Figure 9.2).

At the same time, however, while 19th-century Russian society saw Westernisers (*Zapadniki*) advocate following Western Europe's embrace of technology and liberal government, Slavophiles and later Eurasianists, interpreted the empire's conquest of Asia as imbuing

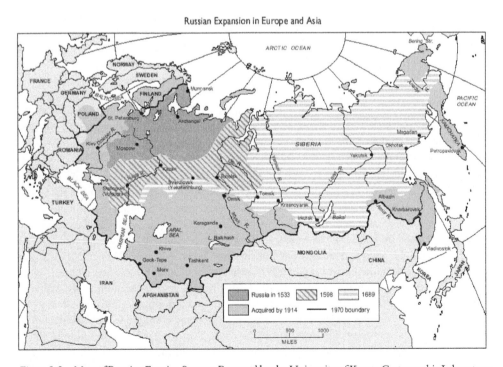

Figure 9.2 Map of Russian Empire. Source: Prepared by the University of Kansas Cartographic Laboratory.

Russia with its own unique identity (Bassin 2010; Laurelle 2009; Hauner 1992; Danilevskii 1895 and Lamanskii 1916). At its core, the so-called Eurasianist ideology imagined the Russian Empire as a continent-spanning cultural-geographic entity. Eurasianists regarded it as extending organically into Siberia, while Central Asia and the Far East were considered colonial possessions akin to those of other European powers of the time (see Kohn 1960: 190–210; Bassin 1991: 13–15).[5]

The late 19th-century rivalry with the British Empire, often referred to as 'the Great Game' or the 'Tournament of Shadows' (*Turniry Teney*), moreover, framed Central Asia for the first time as a zone of contestation between *European* powers (Myers and Brysac 1999; Hopkirk 1994). Central Asia's inhabitants, meanwhile, were increasingly viewed in terms of their loyalty, reliability and usefulness to the Russian Empire and its geopolitical ambitions. The Great Game only subsided with the signing of the Anglo-Russian Convention of 1907 and the subsequent demarcation of borders. The human geographical and geopolitical legacies of inter-imperial rivalry in Central Asia remains, however, in the precarious existence of the state of Afghanistan, which was established as a buffer between the British Raj and Russian Empire. Indeed, the 'cartographic anomaly' called the Wakhan Corridor, meant to ensure that the Russian and British Empires would not share a common border, even in the remote and inaccessible Pamir Mountains, is testament to the effects of European geopolitics on the contemporary map of Central Asia (Rowe 2010).

Ultimately, the bounding and reconstitution of Turkestan as *Russian* Turkestan also meant (re)constructing the identities of its peoples in new, and often humiliating, ways. Once-feared conquerors became abject imperial subjects; Muslim peoples found themselves ruled by an Orthodox Christian state that often dismissed them as 'fanatical' and disloyal (Crews 2006); modern commodity agriculture was introduced; and the European 'civilising mission' was brought, unbidden, to ancient cities like Samarkand and Bukhara. Few Europeans questioned the assumption that 'backward' peoples would … recognize the superiority and desirability of the civilization (and civic spirit) offered to them by the empire' (Brower 2003: 18).

The Bolshevik victory in the Russian Civil War (1917–22) likewise brought fundamental transformations to previous systems of social, economic and political organisation. Through a combination of repression, collectivisation, sedentarisation and industrialisation, the Soviet government eventually implemented new forms of agriculture, land-use, urbanisation and social organisation in Central Asia. At the same time, famines and large-scale migrations, not the least of which were the Stalin-era deportations in the 1930s and 1940s and the so-called 'Virgin Lands' campaign in the 1950s, brought millions of people into the region, effecting broad-ranging changes on the region's demographics.

Furthermore, long-standing trans-regional mobilities were truncated and the region's center of gravity was reoriented toward the political center in Moscow, essentially rendering Soviet Central Asia a geopolitical periphery. Centuries-old exchanges were limited, if not halted, as borders were fortified, and even mundane aspects of life became subject to the Kremlin's dictates. Once defined by its role as 'crossroads,' Central Asia was substantially disconnected from its historical geographies and increasingly dependent upon distant Moscow (Diener 2013). At the same time, supplanting the historical patterns of mobility in Central Eurasia was a Union-wide system of supply and exchange, as well as, the COMECON system that ultimately included Cuba, Eastern Europe, Vietnam, Venezuela, North Korea and, for a time, China, effectively 're-globalising' Central Asia, albeit within the context of socialist and communist states (Kaser 1967).

Arguably one of the most significant transformations that occurred was the imposition on Central Asia of a system of territorial organisation modeled on the nation-state. Lack of space prevents discussion of Soviet nationalities or policies in any depth, but it is worth noting that they were predicated on the assumption of a connection between territory and identity: certain populations were afforded higher degrees of territorial autonomy, which implied a higher level of cultural autonomy (Kaiser 1994; Hirsch 2005; Martin 2001). National delimitation (*razmezhivanie*) entailed the creation of modern territorial units in Central Asia, each with its own borders, capital cities, political structures, transportation systems, educational, cultural and material infrastructures, many of which represented novel developments in the region. These territorial divisions would in turn become the basis of the contemporary, state-centric Central Asian territorial imaginary.

In time, national identity came to be accepted as normative (Smith 1995). So too was the cosmopolitan 'Soviet' identity that transcended 'bourgeoise' notions of class, ethnicity, nationality and race (Kaiser 1994; Hirsch 2005). Other forms of identity persisted as well, though often in a far-more ambiguous relationship with the state. Religion, for example, never ceased being an important identity category in the Soviet Union, even though it was an atheist state (Ro'i 2000). While official anti-religious campaigns periodically broke out, and while the state never ceased trying to eradicate 'backwards' religious 'survivals' (DeWeese 2011), the Soviet government also created and supported official institutions that governed religious life. Mark Saroyan, for example, has pointed out that the Spiritual Administration of the Muslims of Central Asia and Kazakhstan (SADUM) made earnest efforts, grounded in Islamic theology, to 'establish both a new Soviet and a new Muslim identity—identities which [were] defined as mutually compatible and not contradictory' (Saroyan 1997: 65).

As the foregoing suggests, identity in the Soviet Union was multifaceted and multi-scalar: cosmopolitan Soviet identities overlapped with national or regional identities, while religious, tribal or local allegiances persisted in varying degrees of tension with normative forms of identity. In the wake of the Soviet collapse, however, the newly independent states faced the daunting task of managing multi-national, multi-linguistic, multi-religious societies with highly varied (and at times irrational) economic geographies (Hill and Gaddy 2003; Turganbayev and Diener 2018). While official atheism has disappeared in the post-Soviet era, various restrictions and controls on the free practice of religion remain. However, in the context of post-communist nation-building and religious revival, the interplay between religious identity, nationality and political geography has taken on new salience (Artman 2018; 2019).

Boundaries and borders of Central Asia today

Today, 'Central Asia' as a regional imaginary is most typically defined with reference to the nation-states that became independent after the Soviet collapse. Though indicative of the centrality of the nation-state in contemporary geopolitical thinking, as we have seen this was not always the case. Prior to the Soviet period, centers of power were buffered by shifting frontiers, rather than fixed borders. But the Soviet government imposed more static and formal boundaries, as well as strong external borders, and with that state's demise, formerly internal boundaries between republics became international borders. In accordance with their respective state-building ideologies, newly independent national governments established border policies to enable greater and lesser control over economy, identity, security and sustainability. In doing so, George Gavrilis (2008) contends that border security is revealed to be a product, not of state capacities or strength usually measured in per capita GDP and military spending but of institutional design. Consequently, various territorial markers (e.g. posts, signage, fences and guards) were rapidly and unevenly deployed, materialising borders that separated increasingly divergent economies, political systems and jurisdictions of authority.

Territorial complexities resulting from the rapid transformation of Soviet republics into sovereign nation-states is nowhere more apparent than in the problems associated with the numerous enclaves and exclaves (most famously in Kyrgyzstan and Azerbaijan – Bayan 2014), patterns of trans-boundary spatial activity (see Reeves 2014; Parham 2017; Megoran 2012, 2017), and the existence of awkward territorial protrusions (e.g. Fergana Valley and the Wakhan Corridor). Likewise, *internal* boundaries also assumed new significance: for example, provincial and municipal intra-state borders became sites of contestation in the evolving political geographies of emergent regimes of private and public property. Such disputes, moreover, were also frequently enmeshed in contestations between ethnic groups or patron–client networks (Ismailbekova 2017).

Each border, of course, is unique, contingent and varied in its local dynamics. But rather than being understood as static lines, both intra-state and international borders of Central Asia must be considered to be *processual*. Borders both divide *and* unite, manifesting both as sources of conflict and as mechanisms of cooperation and not infrequently both (see, for example, Reeves 2014; Megoran 2017). Contemporary Central Asia provides numerous examples of this interplay between borders, boundaries and identity. In the next section, we will briefly outline a few examples that help to convey the relevance of political geography and hopefully catalyse future research.

Borders, boundaries and identities in Contemporary Central Asia

Kazakhstan–Russia: Border as juncture

The Kazakhstan–Russia borderland has long been emblematic of Kazakhstan's place in the contemporary Central Asian imaginary, a place that by virtue of contiguity, history and long-standing patterns of spatial interaction, includes what is now the Russian Federation. In 1991, ethnic Kazakhs constituted 39.7 per cent of the population of their own state, while ethnic Russians constituted 37.8 per cent.[6] Significantly, Russians also were the majority population in *oblasts* along Kazakhstan's 3,485-kilometer border Russia (Table 9.1).

After considerable emigration during the 1990s, roughly 20 per cent of Kazakhstan's population today is ethnically Russian. Kazakhstan's government harbors some concerns about the degree to which its citizens embrace a civic 'Kazakhstani' identity, or even regard the country as their 'homeland' (Rees et al. 2020; Jašina-Schäfer 2018, Rees and Webb Williams 2017; Diener 2015; Laruelle 2018). Russians in Kazakhstan, however, demonstrate little opposition to the government and, given their disinterest in secession (Peyrouse 2007; Diener 2016), there is no real motive to benefit for their removal. Significantly, though, Kazakhstan's capital city was relocated in 1997 from Almaty, in the far south of the country, to Astana (now Nur-Sultan), in no small part, because the new capital's location is more central and less distant from the Russian borderlands (Koch 2018: 49).

Rather than becoming a site of tension and conflict, however, the Russian-Kazakh borderland has typically been a place of cultural encounter and regional integration (Issbayev et al. 2016). In many respects, this represents a continuation of long-standing patterns of social and economic interactions between the populations of northern Kazakhstan and adjacent Russian oblasts. Examples of such trans-border links include shared electrical grids, industrial infrastructure, 200 roads and 16 rail lines, some of which weave in and out of the other state's territory en route to their terminal stations. Furthermore, several of Russia's largest regional cities (e.g. Novosibirsk, Chelyabinsk, Samara, and Omsk) are closer, and offer more services, than many Kazakhstani provincial capitals, making them attractive destinations for citizens of Kazakhstan.[7]

Table 9.1 National Composition of Kazakhstan 1989, 1999 and 2009

Nationalities	1989		1999		2009	
	Count	%	Count	%	Count	%
Kazakhs	6534616	39.7	7985039	53.4	10096763	63.1
Russians	6227549	37.8	4479620	30.0	3793764	23.7
Ukrainians	896240	5.4	547054	3.7	333031	2.1
Germans	957518	5.8	353441	2.4	178409	1.1
Uzbeks	332017	2.0	370663	2.5	456997	2.9
Tatars	327982	2.0	248954	1.7	204229	1.3
Uighurs	185301	1.1	210365	1.4	224713	1.4
Belarusian's	182601	1.1	111927	0.7	66476	0.4
Koreans	103315	0.6	99665	0.7	100385	0.6
Others	717325	4.4	546398	3.7	544326	3.4
Total	16464464	100.0	14953126	100.0	16009597	100.0

Sources: 1989 USSR Population Census (CD Rom). 1996 East View Publications. Natsionalnoe Statisticheskoe Agentstvo Respubliki Kazakhstan, 1996. Demograficheskii Yezhegodnik Kazakhstana, pp. 56–58 Almaty. Agenstvo Respubliki Kazkahstana po Statistike, 2000. Natsionalnyi Sostab Naselenia Respubliki Kazakhstana: Itogi Perepisi Naselenia 1999 v Respublike Kazakhstana, vol.1 pp. 6–8. Natsionalnyi Sostab Naselenia Respubliki Kazakhstana: Itogi Perepisi Naselenia 2009 v Respublike Kazakhstana, vol.1 pp. 6–8.
Note: Changes in Kazakhstan's territorial administrative structure have altered some of the population data from 1989 to 1999.

From one perspective, Kazakhstan's economic and geopolitical autonomy are limited, in certain respects, due to its landlocked geography. This means that Kazakhstani exports, especially oil and natural gas, must pass through neighboring countries, chiefly Russia. Nevertheless, Kazakhstan has maintained control over its substantial resources and has concluded separate agreements with China and others for extraction and export, ensuring that it does not succumb to dependence on Russian goodwill. Furthermore, Kazakhstan is less dependent than many of its Central Asian neighbors on remittances from guest workers in Russia. Russia, for its part, has at times threatened to impose a visa regime that would limit movement of Central Asian peoples into its territory (Putin 2012). And in 2014 Vladimir Putin stoked anxiety in Kazakhstan when, in the wake of the annexation of Crimea, he argued that Kazakhstan is 'a state on territory where no state had ever existed … Kazakhs had never had statehood' (Trilling 2014). Overall, though, the two countries have enjoyed largely cordial relations since 1991.

While Kazakhstan's government has been successful in promoting its image abroad and forging ties with other states, and indeed has at times defied Russia's preferences (particularly vis-à-vis energy), it nevertheless remains a reliable partner to Moscow on most fronts (Laruelle 2015, 2018). As noted by Laruelle et al. (2019), 'Kazakhstan is far from a passive object of Russia's actions and should be considered a fully-fledged actor in the relationship in its own right, even if the relationship would in theory seem to be weighted toward Russia.' Pre-existing transnational economic interdependencies between Russia and Kazakhstan are augmented by daily, informal, cross-border connections amongst borderland dwellers. Both states, moreover, are founding members of the Eurasian Economic Union (EaEU), share memberships in a variety of other international organisations and are signatories to over 60 bilateral agreements.[8] The border between Russia and Kazakhstan is thus emblematic of the two countries' firm, but independent, relationship.

The Russian-Kazakh border is highly significant, then, not only in what it divides, but in how it has been negotiated into an ongoing functional juncture of political sovereignties, economic systems, cultural evolution and regional strategies. The sustainability of such functionality is nevertheless contingent on each state, both in terms of foreign and domestic policies as well as those of borderland dwellers whose lives are inscribed by the negotiation of spatial distinction and connection.

Uzbekistan–Kyrgyzstan: Border as disjuncture

Understanding the evolving political–territorial ideals of Kyrgyzstan and Uzbekistan requires consideration not only of the processes by which their 1,314-kilometer boundary was drawn during national delimitation, or the volatility associated with the international border between them since the late 1990s (e.g. the riots in 1990, the massacre of 2005, and the riots of 2010), but also the ongoing trans-border interactions that have continued in spite of ongoing securitisation after 1999 (Reeves 2014; Valine 2019; Dowell 2018). Such interactions, argues geographer Nick Megoran (2017) in his insightful 'biography' of the Kyrgyzstan/Uzbekistan border, include a complex interplay of domestic and international politics, culture, national identity, economics and scale, enacted through the practices of elites and ordinary citizens alike, even in times of crisis.

Scholars have proposed various explanations for the causes of Uzbekistan–Kyrgyzstan border tensions. Some suggest that they are the result of long-suppressed ethnic antagonisms rooted in the 'divide and rule' legacy of the Soviet nationalities policy, which subsequently exploded once Moscow's control over the region dissolved.[9] Others argue that conflict between these two states relates wholly to material factors, including control of territory, arable land, water and other natural resources, and that the tensions are the inevitable legacy of poorly conceived boundaries from the Soviet period (O'Hara 2000). Megoran, meanwhile, contends that, while such factors must be regarded as contributing to tensions along the border, too much focus on such explanations risks lapsing into historical determinism, ultimately obscuring the geopolitics driving the conflict.

Megoran argues, for example, that Kyrgyzstan and Uzbekistan are motivated by divergent nationalist imperatives – the former driven by poverty, state weakness, insecurity about national identity, and paranoia regarding the large Uzbek minority in the south, the latter obsessed with an 'all-pervading ideology of national independence' and defending against putative security threats emanating from abroad (Megoran 2017: 64). At the same time, elite geopolitical narratives about the border prove awkward fits when confronted with the lived experiences of borderlanders themselves, many of whom earn their livings in trans-border commerce, live in ethnic exclaves or cross the border to participate in familial and cultural affairs, including weddings and funerals, that are deeply connected with their religious beliefs, communal or cultural traditions, and, ultimately, their sense of self (Reeves 2014; Megoran 2017).

Megoran's ethnographic study of Chek, a village spanning the Uzbekistan–Kyrgyzstan border is amongst the most insightful studies on life as a borderlander. After outlining the historic interconnections of the border region, this case study offers a textured portrayal of the violence of border closure. Megoran depicts the effects of these closures on bodies, livelihoods, senses of well-being, community and identity. But he also reveals resistance by citizens and border guards to the imposition of difference and distance. The state is shown to be eminently present but not omnipotent, as activities ranging from smuggling to postal delivery subvert the imposed division of a village caught between two states.

Reflecting the innate correlation between the practice of boundary-making, the construction of geographic imaginaries, and the articulation of identity, the dynamics of the Kyrgyzstan–Uzbekistan border might be best understood as the product of the interaction of domestic power struggles in the two states, the discursive terrain of post-Soviet Central Asian geopolitical space, and the lived realities of border life (Reeves 2014). Border disputes have provided opportunities for states (and indeed rival factions within those states) to attempt to impose their geopolitical visions for post-Soviet Central Asia, and to assert control over national space through various textual, cartographic, security and governmental strategies, with often painful and confusing results for border dwellers (Gavrilis 2012).

China–Kyrgyzstan–Tajikistan: Borderland dynamics

The particular dynamics that characterise borderland regions can be observed in Steven Parham's study of the borderlands of Kyrgyzstan, Tajikistan and China (2017), wherein he argues that the imposition of borders fundamentally altered the identities of the peoples that they divided. Ethnographic research suggests that the meaning of 'Kyrgyz-ness,' for example, has been shaped in different ways by how different states interact with their respective Kyrgyz populations. A number of other recent studies, including work on the Dungan (Laruelle and Peyrouse 2009), Mongolian-Kazakhs (Barcus and Werner 2017), the Crimean diaspora (Charron 2016) and on China's Mongolian borderlands (Bulag 2002), have followed such lines of inquiry. In each of these cases, we find members of the same ethnic group living on different sides of a border that has fostered substantial differences between them. Parham's work is worthy of particular mention, since he succeeded in carrying out cross-border fieldwork in Xinjiang, as well as in Kyrgyzstan and Tajikistan.

Following the path blazed by Madeleine Reeves in her book *Border Work* (2014), Parham's study also analyses the complex negotiations of power, geopolitics, nation-building and economic livelihood that shape life among border dwellers and pose challenges for representatives of the state in the peripheral regions. Crucially, the very existence of such negotiations, which are not always acknowledged in the literature, forces us to reconsider 'the power of borderlanders ... in accepting, subverting, and/or renegotiating the borderline as the ultimate limit of the territorial state' (Parham 2017: x).

Borderland dynamics are perhaps nowhere better illustrated than in Parham's depiction of one ethnic Kyrgyz interlocutor from Tajikistan's Gorno-Badakhshan[10] region, whose livelihood requires him to buy and sell in markets in two different states. The survival of this man's family depends on his ability to negotiate three currencies (Tajik somoni, Kyrgyz som and US dollars), to communicate in three languages (Kyrgyz, Tajik and Russian), to juggle two passports, two SIM cards, two sets of car registration plates and indeed two wallets. Even this brief description of his predicament indicates the complexities – and challenges – inherent in borderland life.

Like Reeves border ethnography and Megoran's biography of the Uzbekistan/Kyrgyzstan border, moreover, Parham's study serves as a reminder that borders are mutually constituted: states on either side play roles in creating the conditions that prevails there. Borders are, ultimately, expressions of state control and official identity narratives; however, there is always 'slippage' between how the state envisions the border and how the border functions in practice. For example, illegal night crossings may occur regularly. Similarly, border guards might routinely demand bribes from those wishing to cross, while at the same time permitting others (the elderly, friends, relatives, etc.) to pass without incident, complicating the notion of the border as the most intensive manifestation of state power. Reeves, Parham and Megoran thus argue for research not only on borders and ordinary borderlanders, but also on those who patrol the border, those who transgress the border, those for whom the border is either resource or an impediment, as well as gender and other aspects of identity that are frequently crucial factors in life at and across the border.

Central Asia's maritime borders: In flux

Although landlocked, several Central Asian states do have maritime borders. And while the Black Sea region has recently attracted far more international attention due to Russia's annexation of Crimea and its ongoing war against Ukraine, the Caspian Sea remains a potential flashpoint (Dekmejian and Simonian 2003). Of the Caspian's five littoral states, only three – Azerbaijan, Kazakhstan and Russia – have agreed on principles according to which they will divide the Caspian and demarcate national maritime territories. Iran, meanwhile, has rejected the method favored by those states, which would allocate to each littoral country a percentage of the Caspian proportional to the length of their respective coastlines. This would render to Iran only 13 per cent of the Caspian. Tehran instead favors a scheme based on allocating equal proportions, which would afford 20 per cent of the sea. Turkmenistan, meanwhile, has refused to sign any agreements due to a dispute over an oil and gas field also claimed by Azerbaijan. There have been a number of near-clashes along the disputed portions of the Caspian Sea over the years, and increased naval investment by the littoral states draws the imminent fruition of demarcation into question (Greenwood 2018).

Further east, and in a somewhat unique development, the Aral Sea has lost its status as a maritime border between Kazakhstan and Uzbekistan: the almost total disappearance of the sea means that the border there is now a land border in the new 'Aralkum' desert. The almost total erasure of the Aral Sea provides an interesting case study in political geography's physical manifestations. The contrasts between the Kazakh and Uzbek governments' priorities vis-à-vis environmental preservation, as well as their capacities to implement conservation strategies are inscribed on the landscape itself. Although much of Kazakhstan's portion of the sea was beyond repair, and damming, conservation, and water revitalisation have been remarkably successful in saving the North Aral Sea, which became disconnected from the rest of the Aral Sea in the 1980s. In Uzbekistan, by contrast, virtually nothing has been done to stymie the total collapse of this ecosystem, and what remains of the South Aral Sea continues to salinise and evaporate (White 2016).

Apart from its environmental and political geographic implications, the Aral Sea crisis is also deeply implicated in the politics of identity in northwestern Uzbekistan. Afforded semi-autonomous (ASSR) territorial status within Uzbekistan during the Soviet period, the Karakalpak ethnic group has been disfavored by the Uzbek government since independence (Omirbek 2015). Not only have the Karakalpak people seen their autonomy profoundly attenuated by discriminatory state policies, but their health and livelihood have also been seriously damaged by the ecocide of the Aral Sea. Formerly dependent on the now-extinct fishing industry, they and other communities that reside on the Aral's shores also face poisoning from long-dormant chemical waste. Vozrozhdeniya Island, which once hosted biological weapons testing sites and Soviet anthrax stockpiles, is now little more than an undulating feature of in a desert landscape, the northern tip of which is bisected by the Uzbek–Kazakh border (White 2016). Additionally, the receding waters exposed to the winds substantial amounts of salt, fertilisers and other chemicals that had subsided on the bottom of the Aral Sea. According to one analysis, the long-term outcome of the desiccation of the Aral Sea will be that the region will become 'a region of continued wind erosion, acute health problems for residents dependent on the [Amu Darya and

Syr Darya] rivers for drinking water and irrigated agriculture, and likely farm abandonment ... and rural depopulation' (Brunn et al. 2012).

Concerns about environmental collapse, to say nothing of the health and wellbeing of disfavored ethnic minorities, however, have been of little consequence for the Uzbek government, which has expressed more interest in exploiting the rich natural gas fields that have been identified in the new Aralkum desert. Once again, the interplay between political geography and identity cannot be ignored.

Central Asia's 'other borders'

There are myriad other boundaries in Central Asia, each with its own unique spatial manifestation. Among the more obvious are information borders: power over information and media spaces is no less a function of borders than other forms of mobility, and the notion of cyber borders has become an increasingly urgent topic for scholars interested in the region (Warf 2009; Laruelle et al. 2019; Kaiser 2015). Unfortunately, all of the states of Central Asia, with the exception of Kyrgyzstan, are ranked among the world's worst in terms of journalistic freedom.

Broadcast media tends to be fairly tightly controlled. For example, the Kazakhstani government, aware that television can be an avenue for political and cultural influence, has limited Russian media containing political content, especially from outlets that are under Russian governmental control. Overall, though, Russian-origin media is regarded as largely benign throughout Central Asia, despite some interest in replacing it with more reliable domestic content. Social media too has become a contested space between the state and citizens. For example, Facebook postings determined to be demeaning to the leadership or promoting civil unrest have drawn arrests in Kazakhstan (Lillis 2018), while Facebook and YouTube have at different times been blocked in Uzbekistan.

Online content blocking, most associated with the so-called 'Great Chinese Fire Wall,' is also present in Central Asia. This often takes the form of 'event-based filtering' or 'internet blackouts,' which are orchestrated to prevent the spread of particular narratives or messages regarding specific events. Examples include the Kyrgyzstani government filtering internet traffic during the 2005 parliamentary elections and Kazakhstan shutting down internet access altogether in specific towns, ostensibly to prevent the spread of ethnic unrest (Reporters without Borders 2019). In hard-authoritarian states like Uzbekistan and Turkmenistan, internet service providers typically operate under tight governmental control, which regulates international connections and monitors all Internet traffic. Among other things, this enables these governments to shut down websites associated with opposition parties, or block access to those that are hosted in other countries (Privacy International 2003).

A perhaps less obvious and more informal border regime that exists throughout Central Asia is the limited accommodations available for people with disabilities. One need only traverse the crumbling sidewalks of most major cities (to say nothing of smaller, more remote communities) or inspect virtually any building to realise just how serious a problem accessibility actually is in most places. Many apartment buildings, for example, have neither wheelchair ramps nor elevators, and attempting to make use of public transportation, including the ubiquitous overpacked *marshrutka*, in a wheelchair presents an almost insurmountable obstacle for many people. Furthermore, profound differences in access to educational, healthcare and employment opportunities between rural and urban communities are further exacerbated for people with disabilities. Further research on this subject, which limits access to people with disabilities to all sorts of institutions, and indeed large segments of society, is sorely needed (Panier and Tahir 2019).

There are countless other social inequities that manifest in spatial exclusions in Central Asia as well. Among the more globally sensitive are pervasive forms of gender-based discrimination that persists in many places, as well as often severe restrictions on the LGBTQ+ community (Fershtey and Sharifzoda 2019). Although the plight of the LGBTQ+ community in the Caucasus (particularly in Chechnya) has received more international attention, Central Asian LGBTQ+ groups have faced intense pressure in the wake of many regional governments' decision to adopt, almost word-for-word, a 2013 Russian law prohibiting promotion of 'non-traditional sexual relationships' (Masci 2014). This legislation has not yet made it through the legislatures in Kyrgyzstan and Kazakhstan, but it nevertheless remains on the docket for future consideration. Labrys, an LGBTQ+ organisation that operates throughout Central Asia, especially in Kyrgyzstan,[11] reported a 300 per cent increase in violent attacks against Bishkek's gay community following the introduction of the proposed legislation in the Zhogorku Kenesh in 2016. In addition to the shuttering of gay clubs and a general uptick in reported beatings and sexual violence, there have been stories of police officers trolling internet sites and extorting users by threatening to reveal their identities unless paid (North 2016; Bratukhin 2014). Kazakhstan, meanwhile, nearly adopted a 'gay propaganda' law in 2015, but the Constitutional Council overruled it. But while the LGBTQ+ climate in Kazakhstan is better than in the rest of Central Asia, violence and discrimination still exist.

Without unduly feeding the 'discourse of danger' common to the region (Heathershaw and Megoran 2011), it is worth noting that road blockage, border closure or targeted mobility impediment, water divergence, animal theft, pasture intrusion and a number of other catalysts of violence have manifested with varying frequency and intensity in recent years. In September 2019, clashes between Tajikistani and Kyrgyzstani border authorities resulted in 4 dead and 18 wounded. The two states share a 971-kilometer border, of which 451 kilometers have been poorly delineated. Concerns over the construction of a barrier fence along the border in Tajikistan's Babojon Gafurov district compelled Kyrgyzstani residents to respond in kind. The situation escalated to a shooting match and loss of life. While both governments have made efforts to manage this particular situation, the fact that efforts at border delimitation can spark such ethnic unrest suggests that national territoriality is a reality in even the most remote and historically interdependent regions of these states. Efforts at border management are plentiful and often draw the support of international agencies, but have yet to assuage parochialisms from galvanising around land and resources (Gavrilis 2012).

Conclusion

We conclude this chapter with a brief commentary on the normative aspects of borders, their complex relationship with questions of identity, and the more practical aspects of their study.

The interplay of borders, boundaries and identities, broadly construed, is among the most difficult issue facing both scholars and policy makers. This is because borders are intimately connected with a wide range of basic human concerns, including standards of living, governance, the environment and security, to say nothing of tradition, social ties and family (Maier 2016: 4). At the risk of over-simplification, we suggest that there has been a normative debate among scholars relating to borders, boundaries and identity founded on two seemingly incompatible positions. On one side are those who view the spatial divisions that materialise at borders as sites of violence, extortion and pejorative exclusion, a mechanism for the accumulation and institutionalisation of advantage and privilege in select locales, thereby perpetuating inequity (Nevins 2002: 216).

Others, however, argue that borders frame the practical extent of social reciprocity, civil beneficence, and participatory democracy (Walzer 1983: 39–50). While certain elites may promote 'global citizenship' or 'cosmopolitanism,' the everyday experiences of most people are mediated by both individual and collective senses of territorial belonging. These memberships, ultimately, are bounded, de jure or de facto, at some scale (Williams 2003: 42).

This brings us to more practical considerations of border studies. While maps and physical infrastructure make borders appear immutable, even natural, they are never static, whether in policy, practice or even actual location. Scholars, therefore, have increasingly conceptualised borders as processes, performances, methods or technologies (Diener and Hagen 2018), moving beyond the simple binaries of nation, state, ethnicity or personal bias. Too often, border-related scholarship and policy has failed to comprehend borders' capacity to serve as spaces of opportunity *and* insecurity; zones of contact *and* conflict; sites of cooperation *and* competition; and places of ambivalent identities *and* aggressive assertions of difference, where an array of possibilities that transcend simple binaries are enabled.

The first part of this chapter traced the evolving imaginaries of Central Asia over time, demonstrating how the distinctions produced by boundaries, and indeed the nature of boundaries themselves, are subject to evolution and reconstruction. As we saw, 'regional' boundaries are social constructs that determine which states, territories, resources and populations are properly 'Central Asian.' Such boundaries, however, have been influenced by the frontiers of polities, the borders of states and the boundaries of identity that have formed and reformed within the region over many centuries, and as such are constantly in flux. The five former Soviet republics, which are today commonly referred to as 'Central Asia,' share borders with each other but also with neighboring states who have at different times or by different criteria also been included in the 'Central Asian' imaginary. Although the regional imaginary today conforms with state boundaries, this has not always been the case.

To better make sense of the role borders of Central Asia currently play and how they will function in the near future, it is essential to understand how the state insinuates itself into territorial peripheries. In this regard, normative assessments of borders as 'good' or 'bad' are problematic, since defining such categories occurs in relation to some policy or practice, rather than the border itself (Diener and Hagen 2019). While a fair amount of work exists from the perspective of the state, less has been done to trace the ways in which the state is experienced by ordinary people living in these locales. What, for example, are the means by which borderlanders negotiate their allegiances, and how might such allegiances blur? More research remains to be done on such questions.

Scholars, however, need to engage with not only the long-term 'autochthonous' residents of borderland regions, but also with the transitory travelers and temporarily assigned functionaries whose job it is to implement the will of the state at the border. Parham, for example, has suggested further inquiry into 'the relationship between such agents and borderlanders (who can be implicated as such agents themselves) in the production of power and reproductions of boundedness' (2017: 32). Ultimately, the boundedness of the state does not emerge in a sociopolitical vacuum; the project of border control is a 'peopled' project. The narratives and identities of border controllers must therefore be considered as vital in constituting, and being constituted by, narratives of the borderlanders themselves (Reeves 2014; Megoran 2017).

While far from unique in the world for the spatialised forms of social and political exclusions that we might identify as constituting boundaries, Central Asia is as rich a setting as any for research on such issues (Stephan-Emmrich and Schröder 2018). A new generation of scholars is confronted with a fertile field in which to explore how modes of governance shift at the spatial limits of authority but are also transgressed as part of quotidian encounters within and across boundaries, borders and identities. For the aspiring researcher, making sense of borders, identities and narratives requires a willingness to enter the lifeworld of the border. Though not without value, quantitative analysis alone cannot suffice in bringing to life the complex dynamics of borderland existence, in its social, political or institutional aspects. One must communicate in the various languages of the state and the borderlanders; such languages might include bureaucratic jargon, national literatures and traditions, historical narratives, or even the colloquial parlance specific to a particular border region.

As a final note, it should be emphasised that borders are not uncommonly sites of transgression and avoidance of legal norms. Understanding the border, and the identities that are intertwined with them, may require identifying and engaging segments of the population regarded as subversive or unreliable. Pitfalls of human-subjects protocols abound … but what alternative course could render legible truths so elusive and so tied to the margins?

Notes

1 A note on terminology: This chapter will employ the term *boundaries* to refer to abstract spatial delimitations, while the term *borders* will be used to denote the physical or de jure materializations of spatial boundaries.
2 Notably, the US State Department has embraced a version of this imaginary by designating Central Asia as being in the South Asian region, while Russia is classified as being in Eastern Europe.
3 For a detailed discussion of the Urals as a boundary between Europe and Asia, see Lewis and Wigen (1997, 27–72).
4 Lack of space prevents our addressing the connection between identity and geopolitical imaginaries across various historical eras with much specificity; we can nevertheless note, for example, that the Mongol Empire loosely united territories from China to modern-day Ukraine, and that the various successor polities emerging after the death of Chinggis Khan in 1227 were soon identified with their respective localities (e.g. the Golden Horde in the Russian steppe, the Ilkhanate in Iran, the Yuan state in China, etc.) So powerful was this ideology animating the Mongol rule that the ability to trace descent, however tenuous, from Chinggis Khan conferred substantial political and moral authority even into the early 20th century.
5 Ethno-centric discourses were prominent in the Slavophile movement (see Hauner 1992, 49–68), as evidenced by the 'Yellow Peril' narratives that were employed to promote a stronger Slavic presence in the Russian Far East. Anti-Islamic and anti-nomadic discourses were also deployed in order to rationalize Russian dominance in Central Asia and the Caucasus (see Schechla 1993; Bassin 1991, 13). One might also note that Classical Eurasianist geo-philosophy rejected the binary conception of a 'European Russia' west of the Urals counterpoised with an 'Asiatic Russia' to the east. Instead, they ideologically framed the empire through the historical and cultural legacy of Chinggis Khan (Bassin 1991, 15), thus making expansion into Central Asia an almost pre-ordained process of constructing 'a transcendental geo-historical, geo-political, geo-cultural, geo-ethnographical, and … geo-economic entity' (Bassin 1991, 16).
6 The large percentage of Russians within the population is a result of several factors. These include the famine of the early 1930s, which killed upwards of 30 per cent of the ethnic Kazakh population, migration of Slavic peoples following various reforms in the Tsarist and programs (e.g. Virgin Lands) during the Soviet period.
7 For example, the route from Orsk to Nikeltau along the South Ural railway crosses into Kazakhstan nine times, while the Trans-Siberian Railway between Kurgan and Omsk passes through 100 miles of Kazakhstan's territory.
8 Other organizations in which Kazakhstan and Russia share membership include the Commonwealth of Independent States, the Customs Union, the Collective Security Treaty Organization, the Euro Atlantic Partnership Council and the Shanghai Cooperation Organization.
9 For a detailed critique of these arguments, see Heathershaw and Megoran 2011.
10 The Gorno-Badakhshan Autonomous Oblast (GBAO) in Tajikistan is itself a unique case study in the Central Asia's borderland complexity. Over the last several years the oblast has become increasingly unstable, with the potential to threaten security both within and beyond the Tajikistan's bor-

ders. Functionally independent from the central government, authority in GBAO lies with local warlords linked to profitable drug-smuggling routes that pass through the remote and mountainous area (Panier 2018).
11 http://www.labrys.kg/en/info/.

Bibliography

Allsen, T. (2015) "Population Movements in Mongol Eurasia" in Amitai, R., Biran, M. eds. *Nomads as Agents of Cultural Change: The Mongols and Their Eurasian Predecessors*. Honolulu: University of Hawaii Press, pp. 119–151.

Amineh, M. Parvizi ed. (2007) *The Greater Middle East in Global Politics: Social Science Perspectives on the Changing Geography of the World Politics*. Brill: International Studies in Sociology and Social Anthropology Lieden.

Amitai, R. (2015) "The Impact of the Mongols on the History of Syria: Politics, Society, and Culture" in Amitai, R., Biran, M. *Nomads as Agents of Cultural Change: The Mongols and Their Eurasian Predecessors*. Honolulu: University of Hawaii Press, pp. 228–251.

Artman, V. (2018) "Nation, Religion, and Theology: What Do We Mean When We Say 'Being Kyrgyz Means Being Muslim?'" *Central Asian Affairs* 5(3), pp. 191–212.

Artman, V. (2019) "My Poor People, Where are We Going? Grounded Theologies and National Identity in Kyrgyzstan" *Europe–Asia Studies* 10(71), pp. 1734–1755.

Barcus, H.R., Werner, C. (2017) "Migration Decision Making and Immobility Among Rural Ethnic Minorities: The Case of the Mongolian-Kazakh Diaspora" *Globalizations* 14(2), pp. 32–50.

Bassin, M. (1991) "Russia between Europe and Asia: The Ideological Construction of Geographical Space" *Slavic Review* 50(1), pp.1–17.

Bassin, M. (2010) "Nationhood, Natural Regions, Mestorazvitie—Environmentalist Discourses in Classical Eurasianism" in Bassin, M., Ely, C., Stockdale, M.K. eds. *Space, Place, and Power in Modern Russia: Essays in the New Spatial History*. Dekalb, IL: Northern Illinois University Press, pp. 49–78.

Bayan. (2014) "The Post Imperial Chessboard" *The Economist* https://www.economist.com/banyan/2014/04/02/the-post-imperial-chessboard (accessed 05 October 2019).

Beckwith, C.I. (2011) *Empires of the Silk Road: A History of Central Eurasia from the Bronze Age to the Present*. Princeton: Princeton University Press.

Beckwith, C.I. (2012) *Warriors of the Cloisters: The Central Asian Origins of Science in the Medieval World*. Princeton: Princeton University Press.

Benson, L. (1997) *China's Last Nomads: History and Culture of China's Kazakhs*. New York: Routledge.

Blank, S. (2009) *Challenges and Opportunities for the Obama Administration in Central Asia*. Washington, DC: SSI.

Bratukhin, M. (2014) "Kyrgyzstan: Police Abuse, Extortion of Gay men" *Human Rights Watch*, 28 January https://www.hrw.org/news/2014/01/28/kyrgyzstan-police-abuse-extortion-gay-men (accessed 11 September 2019).

Bregel, Y. (2003) *An Historical Atlas of Central Asia*. London: Brill.

Brower, D. (2003) *Turkestan and the Fate of the Russian Empire*. London: RoutledgeCurzon.

Brunn, S., Toops, S., Gilbreath, R. (2012) *The Routledge Atlas of Central Eurasian Affairs* New York: Routledge.

Bulag, U. (2002) *The Mongols at China's Edge History and the Politics of National Unity* Lanham: Rowman and Littlefield.

Charron, A. (2016) "Whose is Crimea? Contested Sovereignty and Regional Identity" *Region* 5(2), pp. 225–256.

Clowes, E. (2011) *Russia on the Edge: Imagined Geographies and Post-Soviet Identity*. Ithaca: Cornell University Press.

Cooley, A. (2012) *Great Games, Local Rules*. New York: Oxford University Press.

Crews, R. (2006) *For Prophet and Tsar: Islam and Empire in Russia and Central Asia*. Cambridge: Harvard University Press.

Danilevski, N.Y. (1895) *Rossia o Evropa Vzgliad na kul'turniye I politiheskie ostnosheniiaslavranskogo mira k germane-Romanskomu (Russia and Europe. A Look at the Cultural and Political Relations of the Slavic World to the German-Roman)*. Moscow: Kniga.

Dekmejian, R., Simonian, H. (2003) *Troubled Waters: The Geopolitics of the Caspian Region*. London: I.B. Tauris.

DeWeese, D. (2011) "Survival Strategies: Reflections on the Notion of Religious 'Survivals' in Soviet Ethnographic Studies of Muslim Religious Life in Central Asia" in Mühlfried, F., Sokolovskiy, S. Eds. *Exploring the Edge of Empire: Soviet Era Anthropology in the Caucasus and Central Asia*. Berlin: Lit-Verlag, pp. 35–58.

Diener, A.C. (2013) "Russian Repositioning: Mobilities and the Eurasian Regional Concept" in Walcott, S., Johnson, C. eds. *Eurasian Corridors of Connection from the South China to the Caspian Sea*. London: Routledge, pp. 82–119.

Diener, A.C. (2015) "Parsing Mobilities in Central Eurasia: Border Management and New Silk Roads" *Eurasian Geography and Economics* 56(4), pp. 376–404.

Diener, Alexander (2016) *Kazakhstan or Kazakhstani-stan Negotiations of Homeland and Titular Nationality in* Laruelle, M. and Peyrouse, S. *Kazakhstan in the Making*. New York: Lexington Books.

Diener, A., Hagen, J. (2018) "The Political Sociology and Geography of Borders" in Outhwaite, W., Turner, S. eds. *Sage Handbook on Political Sociology*. Thousand Oaks: SAGE Publishing, pp. 330–346.

Diener, A., Hagen, J. (2019) "Border Control as a Technology of Social Control" in Deflem, M. ed. *The Handbook of Social Control*. Malden, MA: Wiley Blackwell, pp. 403–415.

Diener, A., Megoran, N. (forthcoming) "Central Asia as Geographic Imaginary" in Montgomery, D. ed. *Central Asia in Context: A Thematic Introduction to the Region*. Pittsburg: University of Pittsburg Press.

Dowell, A. (2018) "Uzbekistan's Pivot to Regional Engagement" *EraInstitute* https://erainstitute.org/uzbekistans-pivot-to-regional-engagement/ (accessed 05 October 2019).

Fershtey, A., Sharifzoda, K. (2019) "Life in the Closet: The LGBT Community in Central Asia" *The Diplomat*, January https://thediplomat.com/2019/01/life-in-the-closet-the-lgbt-community-in-central-asia/ 09 (accessed 14 May 2019).

Gavrilis, G. (2008) *The Dynamics of Interstate Boundaries*. New York: Cambridge University Press.

Gavrilis, G. (2012) "Central Asia's Border Woes & the Impact of International Assistance" *Central Eurasia Project, Occasional Paper #6*, New York: Open Society Foundation.

Golden, P. (2010) *Central Asia in World History*. New York: Oxford University Press.

Greenwood, P. (2018) "Landmark Caspian Deal Signed by Five Coastal Nations" *The Guardian* https://www.theguardian.com/world/2018/aug/12/landmark-caspian-sea-deal-signed-among-five-coastal-nations (accessed 05 October 2019).

Gregory, D. (1995) "Imaginative Geographies" *Progress in Human Geography* 19(4): pp. 447–485.

Gregory, D., Johnston, R., Pratt, G., Watts, M., Whatmore, S. (2009) *The Dictionary of Human Geography*, 5th Edition. Malden: Wiley-Blackwell.

Gunder Frank, A. (1992) "The Centrality of Central Asia" *Studies in History* 8(2), pp. 43–97.

Hauner, M. (1992) *What is Asia to us? Russia's Asian Heartland Yesterday and Today*. London: Routledge.

Hauner, M. (2013) "Russia's Asian Heartland Today and Tomorrow" in Megoran, N., Sharapova, S. eds. *Central Asia in International Relations: The Legacies of Halford Mackinder*. London: Hurst and Co. pp. 117–148.

Heathershaw, J., Megoran, N. (2011) "Contesting Danger: A New Agenda for Policy and Schoalrship on Central Asia" *Inernational Affairs* 87(3), pp. 589–612.

Hill, F., Gaddy, C. (2003) *The Siberian Curse: How Communist Planners Left Russia out in the Cold*. Washington, DC: Brookings Institution Press.

Hirsch, F. (2005) *Empire of Nations: Ethnographic Knowledge and the Making of the Soviet Union*. Ithaca, NY: Cornell University Press.

Hopkirk, P. (1994) *The Great Game: The Struggle for Empire in Central Asia*. New York: Kodasha.

Hormats, R. (2011) *The United States' New Silk Road Strategy: What is it? Where is it Headed?* September http://www.state.gov/e/rls/rmk/2011/174800.htm (accessed 02 January 2015).

Ismailbekova, A. (2017) *Blood Ties and the Native Son: Poetics of Patronage in Kyrgyzstan*. Bloomington: Indiana University Press.

Issabayev, N. Zh., Sadykov, Tlegen S., Seitkazina, Kuralay, O, Bekmaganbetov, Umyrbai Zh. (2016) "Kazakhstan and Russia: Experience and Prospects of Transfrontier Cooperation (1991-2015)" *International Journal of Environmental and Science Education* 11(17), pp. 9669–9677.

Jašina-Schäfer, A. (2019) "Where Do I Belong? Narratives of Rodina among Russian-speaking Youth in Kazakhstan" *Europe-Asia Studies* 71(1), pp. 97–116.

Kaiser, R. (1994) *The Geography of Nationalism in Russia and the USSR*. Princeton: Princeton University Press.

Kaiser, R. (2015) "The Birth of Cyber War" *Political Geography* 46, pp. 11–20.

Kaser, M. (1967) *Comecon: Integration Problems of the Planned Economies.* New York: Oxford University Press.
Kennedy, P. (1987) *The Rise and Fall of Great Powers.* New York: Vintage Book Company.
Khodarkovsky, M. (2002) *Russia's Steppe Frontier: The Making of a Colonial Empire 1500–1800.* Bloomington: Indiana University Press.
Koch, N. (2018) *The Geopolitics of Spectacle: Space, Synecdoche, and the New Capitals of Asia.* Ithaca: Cornell University Press.
Kohn, H. (1960) *Pan-Slavism: Its History and Ideology.* New York: Vintage.
Kotkin, S. (2007) "Mongol Commonwealth: Exchange and Governance Across the Post Mongol Space" *Kritka* 8(3), pp. 487–531.
Kuhrt, N. (2012) "The Russian Far East in Russia's Asia Policy: Dual Integration or Dual Periphery" *Europe–Asia Studies* 64(3), pp. 471–493.
Lamanskii, V. (1916) *Tri Mira Aziiskogo-Evropeiskogo Materika (Three Worlds of the Asian-European Continent).* Petrograd: Novoe Vremeia.
Lamb, A. (2018) "The Search for Prester John" *History Today* https://www.historytoday.com/miscellanies/search-prester-john (accessed 05 October 2019).
Laruelle, M. (2015) "Kazakhstan's Posture in the Eurasian Union: In Search of Serene Sovereignty" *Russian Analytical Digest* 165, pp. 7–10.
Laruelle, M. (2016a) "Which Future for National Patriots?" in Laruelle, M., Peyrouse, S. eds. *Kazakhstan in the Making.* New York: Lexington, pp. 155–180.
Laruelle, M. (2016b) *Russian Eurasianism: Theory and Ideology.* Baltimore: Johns Hopkins University Press.
Laruelle, M. (2018) "Why No Kazakh Novorossiya? Kazakhstan's Russian Minority in a Post-Crimea World" *Problems of Post-Communism* 65(1), pp. 65–78.
Laruelle, M., Peyrouse, S. (2009) "Cross-Border Minorities As Cultural And Economic Mediators Between China and Central Asia" *The China and Eurasia Forum Quarterly* 7(1), pp. 93–119.
Laruelle, M.D. Royce, Beyssembayev, S. (2019) "Untangling the Puzzle of Russia's Influence in Kazakhstan" *Eurasian Geography and Economics* 60(2), pp. 211–243.
Lattimore, O. (1962) *Studies in Frontier History: Collected Papers 1928-1958.* London: Oxford University Press.
Lattimore, O. (1995 [1929]) *The Desert Road to Turkestan.* London: Kodansha.
Levi, S. (2012) "Early Modern Central Asia in World History" *History Compass* 10(11), pp. 866–878.
Levi, S., Sela, R. (2010) *Islamic Central Asia: An Anthology of Historical Sources.* Bloomington: Indiana University Press.
Lewis, M., Wigen, K. (1997) *The Myth of Continents: A Critique of Metageography.* Berkeley: University of California Press.
Lillis, J. (2018) "Kazakhstan Political Facebook Posts Land Man 4-Year Prison Sentence" *Eurasianet* https://eurasianet.org/kazakhstan-political-facebook-posts-land-man-with-4-year-jail-term (accessed 16 June 2019).
Liu, M. (2011) "Central Asia in the Post-Cold War World" *Annual Review of Anthropology* 40, pp. 115–131.
Liu, X. (2010) *The Silk Road in World History.* New York: Oxford University Press.
Mackinder, H. (1904) "The Geographical Pivot of History" *Journal of Geography* 23(4), pp. 421–437.
Mahan, A. (1900) "The Problem of Asia" *Harper's New Monthly Magazine* DXCVII: (March), pp. 536–547; (April) pp. 747–759; (May) pp. 929–941.
Maier, C.S. (2016) *Once within Borders: Territories of Power, Wealth and Belonging since 1500.* Cambridge, MA: Belknapp.
Martin, T. (2001) *The Affirmative Action Empire: Nations and Nationalism in the Soviet Union 1923–1939.* Ithaca, NY: Cornell University Press.
Martin, L., Kären, W. (1997) *The Myth of Continents: A Critique of Metageography.* London: University of California Press.
Martin, V. (2001) *Law and Customs of the Steppe: The Kazakhs of the Middle Horde and Russian Colonialism of the Nineteenth Century.* London: Routledge.
Masci, D. (2014) "Gay Rights in Russia and the Former Soviet Republics" *Pew Research Center* https://www.pewresearch.org/fact-tank/2014/02/11/russia-is-not-the-only-former-soviet-state-to-restrict-lgbt-rights/.
McSmith, A., Reeves, P. (2003) "Afghanistan Regains its Title as World's Biggest Heroin Dealer" *The Independent*, 22 June http://www.globalresearch.ca/articles/MCS306A.html

Megoran, N. (2004) "Revisiting the 'pivot': The Influence of Halford Mackinder on Analysis of Uzbekistan's International Relations" *The Geographical Journal* 170(4), pp. 347–358.
Megoran, N. (2012) "Rethinking the Study of International Boundaries: A Biography of the Kyrgyzstan–Uzbekistan Boundary" *Annals of the Association of American Geographers* 102: pp. 464–481.
Megoran, N. (2017) *Nationalism in Central Asia: A Biography of the Uzbekistan-Kyrgyzstan Boundary*. Pittsburgh: University of Pittsburg Press.
Megoran, N., Sharapova, S. eds. (2013) *Central Asia in International Relations*. London: Hurst.
Myers, K.E., Brysac, S.B. (1999) *Tournament of Shadows: The Great Game and the Race for Empire in Central Asia*. Washington, DC: Counterpoint Press.
Nevins, Joseph (2002) *Operation Gatekeeper: The Rise of the Illegal Alien and the Making of the US–Mexico Boundary*. London: Routledge.
North, A. (2016) "We'll cut Yoru Head off Open Season for LGTBQ in Kyrgyzstan" *The Guardian*, 04 May https://www.theguardian.com/world/2016/may/04/kyrgyzstan-lgbt-community-fear-attacks-russia (accessed 11 September 2019).
O'Hara, S. (2000) "Lessons from the Past: Water Management in Central Asia" *Water Policy* 2(4–5), pp. 365–384.
Omribek (2015) "Uzbekistan's Separatist Movement Threatens Ancient Culture" *The Guardian* https://www.theguardian.com/world/2015/feb/05/uzbek-separatist-movement-threatens-ancient-culture (accessed 10 October 2019).
OSCE (2009) "The OSCE and Transnational Security Challenges Security and Human Rights" No. 3, 239, pp. 1–132.
Panier, B. (2018) "Tajikistan's Unconquerable Gorno-Badakhshan" *RFERL* https://www.rferl.org/a/tajikistan-unconquerable-gorno-badakhshan-region/29534057.html (accessed 14 October 2019).
Panier, B., Tahir, M. (2019) "Majlis Podcast: Challenges for Disabled People in Central Asia" *Radio Free Europe / Radio Liberty* https://www.rferl.org/a/majlis-podcast-the-challenges-for-disabled-people-in-central-asia/29774710.html (accessed 16 June 2019).
Parham, Steven (2017) *China's Borderlands the Faultline of Central Asia*. Taurus Press.
Peyrouse, S. (2007) "Nationhood and the Minority Question in Central Asia: The Russians in Kazakhstan" *Europe–Asia Studies* 59, pp. 482–501.
Poe, M. (2000) *A People Born to Slavery: Russia in Early Modern European Ethnography 1476–1784*. Ithaca, NY: Cornell University Press.
Putin, V. (2012) "Poslanie Prezidenta Federalnomu Sobraniio" *President of Russia Website* file:///Users/a189d877/Desktop/Президент%20России.webarchive (accessed 16 June 2019).
Privacy International (2009) *"Uzbekistan"* 2003 https://privacyinternational.org/report/837/private-interests-monitoring-central-asia (accessed 20 May 2019).
Rees, K.M., Webb Williams, N. (2017) "Explaining Kazakhstani Identity: Supraethnic Identity, Ethnicity, Language, and Citizenship" *Nationalities Papers* 45(5), pp. 815–839.
Rees, K., Williams, N., Diener, A. (2021) "Territorial Belonging and Homeland Disjuncture: Uneven Territorialisations in Kazakhstan" *Europe-Asia Studies*. https://doi.org/10.1080/09668136.2021.1891206
Reporters without Borders (2009) "Internet Enemies" http://www.rsf.org/en-ennemi26106-Turkmenistan.html (accessed 9 June 2019).
Reeves, M. (2014) *Border Work: Spatial Lives of the State in Rural Central Asia*. Ithaca: Cornell University Press.
Reporters without Borders (2019) "Heavy Internet Censorship in Kazakhstan" *Reporters Without Borders* https://rsf.org/en/news/heavy-internet-censorship-kazakhstan (accessed 16 June 2019).
Rezakhani, K. (2010) "The Road That Never Was: The Silk Road and Trans Eurasian Exchange" *Comparative Studies of South Asia, Africa and the Middle East* 30(3), pp. 420–433.
Rorlich, A. (1986) *The Volga Tatars: A Profile in National Resilience*. Stanford: Hoover Press.
Ro'i, Y. (2000) *Islam in the Soviet Union: From World War II to Perestroika*. New York: Columbia University Press.
Rossabi, M. (2012) *The Mongols and Global History*. New York: Norton.
Rossabi, M. (2015) "The Mongol Empire and Its Impact on the Arts of China" in Amitai, R., Biran, M. eds. *Nomads as Agents of Cultural Change:" The Mongols and Their Eurasian Predecessors*. Honolulu: University of Hawaii Press, pp. 214–227.
Rowe, W. (2010) "The Wakhan Corridor: Endgame of the Great Game" in Diener, A.C., Hagen, J. eds. *Borderlines and Borderlands: Political Oddities at the Edge of the Nation State*. Lanham: Rowman and Littlefield, pp. 53–68.
Said, E. (1979) *Orientalism*. New York: Vintage Books.

Saroyan, M. (1997) "The Reinterpretation and Adaptation of Soviet Islam" in Saroyan, M. ed. *Minorities, Mullahs, and Modernity: Reshaping Community in the Former Soviet Union*. Berkley: University of California Press, pp. 57–87.

Schechla, J. (1993) "The Ideological Roots of Population Transfer" *Third World Quarterly* 14(20), pp. 239–275.

Schoeberlein, J. (2002) "Setting the Stakes of a New Society" *Central Eurasian Studies Review* 1(1), pp. 4–8.

Sela, R. (2011) *The Legendary Biographies of Tamerlane: Islam and Heroic Apocrypha in Central Asia*. Cambridge: Cambridge University Press.

Smith, G. (1995) *The Nationalities Question in the Post-Soviet States*. Addison-Wesley Longman Ltd; 2 edition.

Spykman, N. (1944) *The Geography of the Peace*. Harcourt: Brace and Company.

Starr, S.F. (2004) *Xinjiang: China Muslim Borderland*. New York: Routledge.

Starr, S.F. (2007) "Introduction" in Starr, S. Frederick ed. *The New Silk Road: Transport and Trade in Greater Central Asia*. Washington, DC: Central Asia-Caucasus Institute & Silk Road Studies Program, pp. 5–32.

Starr, S.F. (2011) "Afghanistan beyond the Fog of Nation Building: Giving Economy Strategy a Chance" *Silk Road Paper* January, pp. 1–27.

Starr, S.F. (2013) *The Lost Enlightenment*. Princeton: University of Princeton Press.

Stephan-Emmrich, M., Schröder, P. eds. (2018) *Mobilities, Boundaries, and Travelling Ideas: Rethinking Translocality Beyond Central Asia and the Caucasus*. Cambridge: Open Book. http://www.jstor.org/stable/j.ctv8j3t2 (accessed 16 June 2019).

Trilling, D. (2014) "As Kazakhstan's Leader Asserts Independence, Did Putin Just Say, 'Not So Fast'?" *Eurasianet* https://eurasianet.org/as-kazakhstans-leader-asserts-independence-did-putin-just-say-not-so-fast (accessed 13 September 19).

Turganbayev, Y., Diener, A. (2018) "Kazakhstan's Evolving Regional Economic Policy: Assessing Strategies of Post-Socialist Development" *Eurasian Geography and Economics* 59: 5–6, pp. 657–684.

UNODC (2007) *Securing Central Asia's Borders with Afghanistan*. UNODC, p. 4.

Valine, D. (2019) "Uzbekistan Receives Ravens to Bolster Border Security" *U.S. Army Military Article* https://www.army.mil/article/218187/uzbekistan_receives_ravens_to_bolster_border_security

Vásáry, I. (2015) "The Tatar Factor in the Formation of Muscovy's Political Culture" in Amitai, R., Biran, M. eds. *Nomads as Agents of Cultural Change:" The Mongols and Their Eurasian Predecessors*. Honolulu: University of Hawaii Press, pp. 252–270.

Walzer, M. (1983) *Spheres of Justice*. New York: Basic Books.

Warf, B. (2009) "The Rapidly Evolving Geographies of the Eurasian Internet" *Eurasian Geography and Economics* 50(5), pp. 564–580.

White, Kristopher (2016) "Kazakhstan's Northern Aral Sea Today: Partial Ecosystem Restoration and Economic Recovery" in E. Freedman, M. Neuzil eds. *Environmental Crisis in Central Asia: From Steppes to Seas, from Deserts to Glaciers*, pp. 129–140.

Williams, John (2003) "Territorial Borders, International Ethics and Geography: Do Good Fences Still Make Good Neighbours?" *Geopolitics*, 8(2), pp. 25–46.

10
THE HISTORY OF WATER POLITICS IN CENTRAL ASIA

Christine Bichsel

Could there be a better starting point than the Aral Sea to discuss water politics in Central Asia? The Aral Sea is without doubt the best-known water body of Central Asia. Once the fourth largest inland lake in the world, its size and volume have been shrinking dramatically since the 1960s. This resulted from the development of large-scale irrigated agriculture in Central Asia fed by water of the lake's tributaries Syr Darya and Amu Darya. By the end of the 1980s, the lake had split into the North Aral Sea and the South Aral Sea, with the South Aral Sea later splitting again and forming an eastern and a western lobe (Micklin 2014a). These severed remnants fluctuate seasonally and annually in size, leaving the former lake floor exposed to form a new anthropogenic landscape: the Aral desert or *Aralkum* (Breckle et al. 2012). From space, satellite images have been tracing the waning of the blue and green colours of water amidst the desert over the last decades. However, the most famous images come from the ground: Moynak's former fishing ships stranded in desert sand and slowly rusting away became icons of environmental disaster.

The Aral Sea is in many ways the pivot of water politics in Central Asia. Its desiccation became a symbol for the hubris of modernist science with its unshakable belief in the possibility of controlling nature and of fixing any problems arising in the process. The shrinking Aral Sea stands also for the wastefulness and short-sightedness of the Soviet command economy for irrigated agriculture in Central Asia. At the same time, when its shrinking became apparent during the 1970s and 1980s, the lake became a hinge of the growing environmental awareness among scientists both within and outside the Soviet Union (Obertreis 2017). Drawing on clinical vocabulary, scholars coined the term 'Aral Sea Syndrome' to grasp the plethora of negative changes for the economy, ecology and human welfare for the region (Klötzli 1997). Alongside similar phenomena, the Aral Sea Syndrome came to represent a cluster of problems in Earth System theory to diagnose negative global change (Schellnhuber et al. 1997). Lastly, the Aral Sea became the arena for the collision and collusion of international development, post-Soviet bureaucracy and emerging nationalism in the context of the many aid programmes to restore the lake and its environment (Small and Bunce 2003).

The Aral Sea has a long history of alternating phases of regression and transgression, which scholars attribute variously to climatic, tectonic or anthropogenic causes, or a combination of these (Crétaux et al. 2013). First, there are high inter-annual variations for precipitation attributed to the influence of the El Nino Southern Oscillation in the region with an arid to semi-

DOI: 10.4324/9780429057977-10

arid climate. This results in a complex pattern of dryer and wetter years that is difficult to predict (Hu et al. 2017). Warmer and cooler years affect the storage and release of water from glaciers and snow in the high mountains, thereby decreasing or increasing the river flow of the Syr and the Amu Darya. Second, the two rivers repeatedly changed their courses throughout history due to tectonic shifts, at times emptying only partly or not at all in the Aral Sea (Breckle and Geldyeva 2012). And third, humans have withdrawn water from tributaries to the Aral Sea for around 6,000 years, thereby actively shaping the water landscape of Central Asia (Sala 2019: 96). The Aral Sea as a pivot is therefore not a stable reference, but rather an expression of the highly dynamic environment of the region throughout history.

It is with this perspective in mind that I take the Aral Sea as a starting point for discussing the history of water politics in Central Asia. My approach is best characterised as a political environmental history, as I focus on the historical trajectories of entanglements between politics and the physical environments of Central Asia (Kim and Pianciola 2019). I argue that a historical approach helps us understand the successive imperial and post-imperial political configurations that took shape in and shaped this landscape in motion, that is, Central Asia. In this chapter, I present a political environmental history of irrigation, which reflects my research expertise. Such a choice, however, entails a bias. It privileges the history of sedentary people and their relation to water in Central Asia, while giving insufficient attention to transhumant and nomadic forms of life, which to date remain little explored. This results partly from the lack of sources, but also from its frequent perception of being 'marginal and needy' (Frachetti and Maksudov 2014) – a characterisation symptomatic of evolutionary ideas about human development, regarding sedentary forms as more advanced than mobile ones. To counter this, I try to pay attention to the long-standing and complex interactions between irrigated agriculture and pastoralism in Central Asia. Geographically, I maintain a focus on Khorezm, a large oasis region in the lower reaches of the Amu Darya towards the Aral Sea today divided between Uzbekistan and Turkmenistan. For the remainder of this chapter, I trace the political environmental history of irrigation in Central Asia from the earliest irrigation practices dated back to the Stone Age to the present days, with periodisation being rather pragmatic than programmatic. At the end of the chapter, I offer a short conclusion on water politics in Central Asia.

The archaeology of irrigation

The oldest traces of small irrigation systems in Central Asia were found in the piedmont areas of the Kopet Dagh mountains in Turkmenistan, where early farmers abstracted and diverted water from the lower course of spring-fed mountain streams as early as 5000 BC (Lewis 1966). Irrigation began later in the lowland river deltas towards the Aral Sea and dates to around 2000 BC (Itina 1977). Initially, the scale of irrigation in the deltas remained small. But as time went on, the area south of the Aral Sea developed into one of the most extensive irrigation works in Central Asia: the large oasis region of Khorezm. The riparian environment of the Amu Darya offered favourable conditions for building irrigation systems with a perennial flow early on in history. However, the Amu Darya delta is also one of the most changeable deltas in the world, and natural re-channelling of streams occurs very frequently and often abruptly, thereby either flooding or cutting people off from water. The environmental setting is highly volatile, and Khorezm has been the site of recurrent collapse and re-emergence of its irrigation systems over millennia (Brite 2016). Scholars explain the repeated expansion and contraction of Khorezm with both human influence and natural causes (Boroffka 2010; Cretaux et al. 2013). In what follows, I will examine the relationship between politics and the physical environment in Khorezm.

Irrigation in Khorezm reached its first apex from the seventh century BC to the fifth century AD as part of the Persian Empire with a proliferation of human settlements and significant expansion of agriculture (Lewis 1966). Archaeological research found traces of a vast and complex irrigation system for this period with head works, long and wide trunk canals, feeder channels and drainage networks (Brite et al. 2017). Within the oasis, scholars noted two different forms of irrigation economies. In the Eastern part of Khorezm, irrigation likely served to cultivate cereals and to support vineyards, melon plantations, fruit orchards and possibly cotton fields. In the Western part, the canal network should provide water equally for livestock grazing, fodder production and some small-scale agriculture (Brite 2016). Semi-mobile and pastoral lifestyles were thus integrated into the settlement and subsistence systems, which also showed in art and architecture of this period (Kidd and Betts 2010). The irrigated area of Khorezm is estimated by scholars to have been around 5 million hectares (Andrianov 1969; Tolstov 1962), a figure close to the 6.5 million hectares officially under irrigation in the entire Soviet Union by 1991 (Boomer et al. 2000). However, the actually irrigated area was probably considerably lower and submitted to long fallow cycles (Sala 2019). This first high period of irrigation in Khorezm met a definitive and likely catastrophic end during the fourth century AD, when the sites and canals were almost completely abandoned (Brite 2016). This coincided with the invasion of the Huns to Central Asia, and the concomitant destruction of the irrigation settlements and facilities (Létolle and Mainguet 1996). The observed regression of the Aral Sea around the fourth century AD may be a first instance of significant anthropogenic change through intensive irrigation, but could also result from a dryer climate (Oberhänsli et al. 2007).

Soviet archaeology had a keen interest in researching the rise and fall of Khorezm. In 1937, the 'Khorezmian Archaeological-Ethnographic Expedition' under the auspices of the Soviet Academy of Sciences began its systematic research in the lower reaches of the Amu Darya with the aim of establishing the historical trajectory of Khorezm from earliest settlements to the present days. Research was multidisciplinary and included large archaeological excavations, field and air surveys, and ethnographic and environmental studies. The well-funded expedition lasted for 60 years – thereby outliving the Soviet Union – and provided a very rich account of the history of Khorezm (Tolstov 1948; Andrianov 1969; Itina 1977). The expedition's charismatic leader and patron Sergei P. Tolstov successfully negotiated the Soviet framework of ideology and rule to realise his ambition of archaeological research in Khorezm (Arzhantseva 2015; Arzantseva and Haerke 2019). At the same time, Soviet archaeology was part of an imperial project of knowing Central Asia that had already begun during the Tsarist period through the work of Russian officers and scholars (Gorshenina 2019). In addition, the establishment of an evolutionary account of Central Asian history, both being in line with and serving to strengthen the historical-materialist understanding of the past, was of key importance to the Soviet project.

The study of irrigation had a high priority in the Khorezm expedition. Rather than being merely an academic concern, scholars saw it as closely related to the contemporary efforts to 'revitalise' the lands of Central Asia through Soviet irrigation development. In classical colonial fashion, Khorezm should be restored to its past *grandesse*, of which only ruins seemed to exist at the moment of Russian conquest. Evidence from ancient irrigation systems could make available baseline data for this endeavour (Andrianov 1969: 232). The analysis of past socio-political forms of irrigation as successive modes of production should also provide the political and ideological background for Soviet policy. Soviet archaeology in Khorezm brought forward a theory about the relation between irrigation and the state. Scholars argued that these irrigation systems were, necessarily, built and maintained by a centralised state with the authority to compel its subjects to forced labour. They supported this argument with numbers of the amount of earth moved and labourers and days required to achieve this (Tolstov 1948; Andrianov 1969).

Past irrigation systems were thus represented as predicated upon despotic power – a reversal of Wittfogel's hydraulic society (Francfort and Lecompte 2002, Stride et al. 2009). The archaeology of irrigation was inseparably linked to the Soviet framing of irrigation campaigns in Central Asia.

The medieval period

After a transitional phase during which agro-pastoralism prevailed, irrigated agriculture in Khorezm slowly resumed and reached another apex during the medieval period. By the eleventh and twelfth centuries, most of the ancient irrigation systems in Khorezm had been reconstructed, and a big part of the fertile land was again cultivated (Andrianov 1969). Cultural change had already set in during the seventh and eights centuries, with a markedly different material culture and industries such as cotton farming and specialised sheep rearing (Brite et al. 2017). With the Arab conquest of Central Asia, new scientific and technological knowledge led to complex irrigation systems including protective dams along the Amu Darya, head works, main canals, large distributors, auxiliary irrigation ditches, water control and water-lifting devices. The latter made it possible to irrigate higher fields and to enlarge the actual area of irrigation (Andrianov 1995). The requirements of irrigation both inspired and profited from the fast-developing sciences including mathematics, chemistry and astronomy in Khorezm, which led to great advances in hydraulic engineering (Dukhovny and de Schutter 2011). A rapid development of towns and a general expansion of urban culture took place in Khorezm between the ninth and the twelfth centuries.

Urbanisation also began elsewhere in Central Asia during medieval times. This was a particularly prosperous period for the middle and lower reaches of the Syr Darya. From the sixth century on, many new towns emerged along the Syr Darya and in the Northern Tian Shan. By the tenth century, there were more than 400 occupied walled towns in the Syr Darya basin, forming together with large unfortified villages an urban area of 2,350ha. The Chach oasis – today's Tashkent – represented the biggest urban area in the basin. Of particular interest is the geographical development of the urban pattern. A comparison shows the increasing density of walled towns in the middle reaches of the Syr Darya towards the tenth century, and a decrease of urban sites in the river's lower reaches during the same time (Sala 2019). We might see here the first evidence of a large-scale upstream–downstream constellation in which upstream water users deprived downstream dwellers from sufficient water. In addition, the increased water consumption of a growing urban population and intensive agricultural activities to sustain an urban mode of life likely affected the lake level. Indeed, the medieval period coincided with a long regression of the Aral Sea, showing declining water level from the eighth to the thirteenth centuries. However, Central Asia also witnessed dryer climatic conditions between the tenth and the thirteenth century (Sala 2012).

Irrigated agriculture was not the only economic domain generating prosperity in the Syr Darya basin. Metallurgy and international trade equally played an important role in the economy of the region. Scholars noted the importance of mining, working and trading metals such as silver, iron and copper in the Tian Shan and Pamir mountains (Stark et al. 2010, Sala 2012). The privileged northern branches of the Silk Road for long-range international trade and the region's monopoly in silver production in Eurasia contributed to urban development and prosperity during this period (Sala 2011, 2012). Nomadic and semi-nomadic herders importantly shaped these mobility patterns (Frachetti et al. 2017). Scholars repeatedly pointed to the long-standing and complex interactions between sedentary farmers and mobile herders in Central Asia and contested their frequently bimodal representation (Stride et al. 2009; Frachetti and Maksudov

2014; Brite et al. 2017). A variety of social and economic systems in Central Asia have integrated agriculture and pastoralism for millennia (Frachetti and Maksudov 2014). The difficulty of imagining their integration rather than separation stems, as Sala (2003: 17–18) put it, '[…] from our tendency to think the settler as too settled and the shepherds as too nomadic. […] optimal environmental conditions can stabilize shepherds and unstable hydrological conditions can mobilize farmers […].' This flexibility created societal resilience to environmental change, which was of particular importance for people living in the dynamic river environments of Central Asia.

The prosperous medieval times rapidly declined with the invasion of the Mongols in Central Asia during the early thirteenth century. The invasion initiated a period of repeated war and destruction, which brought into view the fragility and vulnerability of irrigated agriculture. As the invaders recognised that populations, agricultural systems and even modes of production often depended on a single source of water, they turned the destruction of dams and irrigation infrastructure into a military strategy and technique (White 2013). Khorezm suffered almost complete destruction by the Mongol army under Genghis Khan in 1221. According to historical sources, the Mongols destroyed dams and weirs across the main tributaries of the delta, which led to a flooding of the capital Kunya Urgench and vast areas of western Khorezm. The destruction of Khorezm's irrigation infrastructure also caused a partial river course diversion of the Amu Darya into the Sarykamysh depression and further on via the Uzboy channel into the Caspian Sea. A preceding major earthquake in the region in 1208/1209 could have contributed to the weakening the dams (Boroffka 2010). This river course diversion resulted in a major regression of the Aral Sea. After further destruction of the rebuilt Khorezm during the Timurid wars at the end of the fourteenth century, the Amu Darya eventually returned, or was returned, to the Aral Sea, which regained its former level only by the mid-sixteenth century (Micklin 2016).

The time of the Khanates

The changes in the riparian environment of the Amu Darya delta during the sixteenth century led to a geographical shift of political power in Khorezm. As the Daryalyk, one of the most important branches of the river leading towards the Sarykamysh lake, dried out, the rebuilt former capital Kunya Urgench and other important urban settlements were deprived of water for irrigation. The capital of Khorezm was therefore transferred to Khiva, a settlement situated further south-east. This led to a replacement of the territorial name 'Khorezm' with 'Khiva' (Annanepesov and Bababekov 2003). Since the early sixteenth century, Uzbek tribes had governed the region and established what later became known as the 'Khanate of Khiva.' After much political turmoil and warfare, a first attempt at rebuilding the irrigation system and resettling the area was made during the seventeenth century. However, it was not until the Qongrat dynasty took power in the Khanate of Khiva in the eighteenth century that a more stable period emerged. In the eighteenth and nineteenth centuries, the expansion of irrigation in Khorezm became a state project led by the Qongrat khans and his ministers. The allocation of newly irrigated land was fundamental to their rule, as the success or failure of the dynasty hinged on it (Seitz 2013). Being of Uzbek tribal origin, the Qongrat khans were under pressure to legitimise their authority, no longer being descendants of Genghis Khan like their predecessors. The expansion of irrigation in the central area and western fringes of Khorezm were part of this effort, and enabled the Qongrat Khans to attest their ability to control the water of the Amu Darya (Shioya 2011, 2013).

Irrigation as a state project was part of a network of military strategy, agriculture and bureaucracy (Seitz 2013; Sartori and Abdurasulov 2017). The creation and allocation of new arable land increased the power of the khans, as they were able to generate more revenue through tax and to draft new populations into the military. As the Khanate of Khiva had a low population density in comparison to other Central Asian oases, the khans sought to attract, and, occasionally, to forcibly relocate new subjects to populate the land. For example, captives taken during a military campaign against the Emirate of Bukhara were relocated to several parts of Khorezm (Shioya 2011; Seitz 2013). The khans offered arable land to the Turkmen tribes living in the surroundings of Khiva in exchange for military service – an offer that mostly smaller and less powerful tribes took up. Rather than bounty, they were given irrigated land for settlement together with being exempted from corvee for building and maintaining canals (Seitz 2013). Thereby, the khans sedentarised these groups, but also integrated them into the state system by rendering them dependent on water supply (Abdurasulov 2016). In turn, the khans de-militarised the administration of the khanate and created a professional bureaucracy to record and update the allocation of water shares to communities, organise corvee and levy tax. The khans also introduced a standard irrigation unit called 'su' (lit: water) to measure and quantify water shares (Sartori and Abdurasulov 2017).

The practices of irrigated agriculture were not homogenous throughout Khorezm, but represented a continuum from intensive agriculture to agro-pastoralism. This continuum went along with an ethnic stratification, representing the settlement histories of the different groups. The Sart and Uzbek communities who had settled early lived closest to the main canals. They practiced intensive irrigated agriculture, cultivating mainly wheat as food crop, but also other food and cash crops including fruit. They lived in the areas that were also the heartland of the Khanate with its main cities. Animal husbandry played a negligible role in these areas, except for draft animals used for ploughing, milling and powering water-lifting devices. Nomadic or semi-nomadic agriculture was on the other end of the continuum, typically practiced in the peripheries with scarce and less reliable water supply (Seitz 2013). In these areas, communities focused on the production of millet as a food crop, melons as a cash crop and some fishing (Abdurasulov 2016). Animal husbandry played a key role in this form of agriculture. This form of agro-pastoralism was typically practiced by Turkmen and Qaraqalpaq tribes, which had settled in the Khanate more recently. As mentioned previously, changes in climate, water supply or political could lead to communities to shift these communities' agricultural practices along the outlined continuum. The general tendency of this period was, however, towards a more settled irrigated agriculture (Seitz 2013).

The relationship between users at the head and at the tail of canal systems is often tension-ridden. The Sart and Uzbek peasants in the upper reaches of the canals in the Khanate of Khiva were confronted with the challenge of silting and erosion. While silting carried valuable nutrition, it also blocked irrigation canals through clogging. In addition, a fast-flowing water led to increased erosion at the head of canals. To cope with these challenges, upstream communities tried to slow down the flow of water and to use multiple smaller intakes instead of one big intake. This was diametrically opposed to the needs of the Turkmen and Qaraqalpaq communities living downstream. The lower and slower flow not only meant that less water reached their fields, but also that it carried less silt to deposit and improve fertility. Lastly, the available water was not sufficient to flush the fields in order to avoid salinisation. Turkmens tried to cope with these challenges by practicing fallow and by keeping up a semi-nomadic way of life, but also by contesting upstream users' practices (Seitz 2013). Conflicts over water rights and distribution were thus frequent in the Khanate of Khiva, and if taken to court adjudicated according to Islamic law (Sartori and Abdurasulov 2017). Yet creating water shortage also became a political strategy of the leadership in the Khanate of Khiva. In the 1850s, the Qongrat khan ordered the construction of a dam to block water supply for the rebellious Yomut Turkmen with the aim of subduing them (Shioya 2011). The dam blocked the Daryalyk riverbed and the Lawsan canal built in the early nineteenth century to supply water to Western Khorezm (Shioya 2014: 233), along which the Turkmen had previously been allocated land in exchange for military services. Through withholding water, the khan exerted control over the Turkmen settlers, hazarding the consequences that the previous expansion of irrigated land was reversed and the area abandoned.

Russian colonial rule

After several attempts of conquest during the early eighteenth century, the Khanate of Khiva became a protectorate of the Russian Empire in 1873. The khan's loss of power ended the state-led projects of irrigation expansion. However, it did not mean that the expansion itself came to a halt. According to Russian records, the amount of irrigated land in the Khanate of Khiva almost doubled between 1903 and 1913 (Matley 1994). Moreover, the rapid increase in cotton production after the Russian conquest suggests that the expansion of irrigated land had already began prior to 1903. As no major irrigation campaign launched by the khan is recorded for this period, it seems that peasants themselves took initiative. Thus, they no longer relied on the direction of the khan as was customary in the Khanate of Khiva. They probably used two forms of expanding irrigated land. First, they might have simply expanded the minor irrigation canals to unirrigated land adjacent to their fields. This appears feasible, as historical sources report that Khorezm was no contiguous block of irrigated land, but rather an area interspersed with spaces of desert land. Second, farmers might have restored former, and at that moment unused, irrigation canals and land, as had happened many times in the history of Khorezm. A new force drove the resulting expansion of the irrigated area: Khorezm's integration into the market economy and, in particular, into the cotton market (Seitz 2013).

Peasants in Khorezm had been growing cotton since 300–500 AD (Brite and Marston 2013). However, the emerging cotton market during the late nineteenth century significantly changed the landscape in the region and brought about the integration of Khorezm into the capitalist world economy. Prior to Russian conquest, the Khanate of Khiva had already exported 1.8 million pounds of cotton on average per year to Russia. This amount rose by 11 times over the next 40 years. By 1850, Russia started to import more raw cotton than cotton yarn, as Britain had abolished the existing ban on cotton machinery, thereby enabling Russia to expand its ginning capacity. The increasing demand for cotton in Russia during the early stages of industrialisation and development of its textile industry led to the introduction of new varieties of cotton and to the expansion of cotton plantation in Khorezm. The building of the Central Asian Railroad in 1896 and later the Orenburg-Tashkent Railroad in 1905 facilitated export from Khiva, even if cotton still had to be transported by caravan to the railway stations (Seitz 2013). This may be one of the reasons why during Russian colonial rule, cotton plantation in this area never took the form of widespread monoculture as it did elsewhere in the Ferghana Valley (Thurman 1999). In Khorezm, cotton production was limited by a shortage of labour for the time-consuming process of cultivating and harvesting cotton, the absence of a fully cash-based local economy with a credit system and the presence of a market for alternative cash crops such as wheat, alfalfa and fruit (Seitz 2013).

In addition to a growing need for cotton, Russia also had an interest in shaping waterways in Khorezm. Stories circulated in Imperial Russia that the Amu Darya once connected to the Caspian Sea, and had been diverted artificially by the khans of Khiva to the Aral Sea. Consequently, it was assumed that the Amu Darya could be 'restored' to its original course, thereby realising a geopolitical vision of Russia by creating a navigable water route to India. The Russian press and scientific community took the flooding of the Amu Darya in Summer 1878, which breached the dams of the Lawsan and the Daryalyk and led water to the Sarykamysh depression, as a proof that it was possible to revert the river to its presumed former course (Shioya 2014). However, the Amu Darya has never entirely drained into the Caspian Sea (Létolle et al. 2007). The charismatic Grand Duke Nikolai Konstantinovich Romanov, fallen in disgrace at the Russian imperial court and exiled to Central Asia, developed a particular interest for this project (Pravilova 2009). He was also known for his engagement in irrigation projects elsewhere in Central Asia, notably on the Hungry Steppe (Peterson 2019). Fascinated by the idea of human control over the river, he tried, unsuccessfully though, to lobby for the diversion of the Amu Darya with the khan of Khiva and the Russian Government. Local legends of a formerly flourishing kingdom of Khorezm fell on fertile ground and served as a colonial narrative, aiming to restore the region to its supposed former splendour. Although disproving of the Grand Duke's activism, the Governor-Generals of Turkestan Kaufman and Chernayaev nevertheless emulated the khans in their attempts to gain authority. Both of them began their positions in Central Asia with the construction of canals, thereby acknowledging the relationship between water and power. It is noteworthy that they did not primarily establish new canals, but rather focused on restoring ancient irrigation systems in line with the colonial narrative (Pravilova 2009).

If the waters of the Amu Darya held geopolitical and economic potential for Russians during this period, the opposite was true for the Aral Sea. The lake was dispensable for contemporaries, as the water draining into it was seen as lost for irrigation. Desiccation of the Aral Sea was understood as inevitable and even desirable, offering the potential of developing the bottom of the lake for irrigated agriculture (Pravilova 2009). Whether or not the construction of the New Lawsan canal in 1984 represented an extension of the vision to divert the Amu Darya remains unclear. Russian administrators and planners aimed at partly restoring the main stream of the Lawsan – completely blocked by the khan in the 1850s – and thereby bringing water to the Daryalyk. The new canal should also revive irrigated agriculture in Western Khorezm. This intervention was justified on the grounds of restoring former Turkmen agriculture in this area. A large number of Khivan peasants ranging between 4,500 and 8,500 annually were mobilised to carry out to build the New Lawzan canal, and to dredge and expand the riverbed of the Daryalyk. Construction did not progress well, and was hampered by constant interruptions. Due to the low level of the Amu Darya from around 1893, the New Lawsan canal and the Daryalyk did not fill up with sufficient water. Eventually, the project of building the New Lawsan canal was not successful (Shioya 2014). Its failure provoked the Yomut Turkmen uprising in 1899, and represented the starting point of a prolonged series of conflict over water delivery and taxation in Khorezm (Shioya 2013). Ultimately, it contributed to the deterioration of the relationship between the Khivan Government and the Turkmen tribes.

The Soviet period

The Khanate of Khiva became the People's Soviet Republic of Khorezm in 1920. At this time, the republic covered the area from the south-western shores of the Aral Sea on the left bank of the Amu Darya. However, the process of national–territorial delimitation starting in 1924 completely reorganised Khorezm, dividing it up into three political entities (Karasar 2008: 1248). The starting point for this process was the reinterpretation of the continuous rebellion of the Turkmen tribes against the Khivan Government over issues of water and tax as an ethnic conflict (Shioya 2014). In the emerging ethno-territorial framework, the Soviet Government perceived of ethnic tensions as highly destabilising for the new state. The relationship between Uzbeks and Turkmens in multi-ethnic Khorezm was of particular concern. In turn, the Turkmens used the emerging platform of the Soviet Communist Party to present themselves as being economically and politically suppressed in the People's Republic of Khorezm. Eventually, they lobbied successfully for the inclusion of the north-western part of Khorezm into the newly created Turkmen SSR. This included also the city of Tashauz, which in spite of its Uzbeks population, became part of the Turkmen SSR. The latter had requested Tashauz with the argument that the Turkmens needed a city to undergo socialist development (Haugen 2003; Edgar 2004). The Qaraqalpaqs were granted titular territory in the northern part of the Republic of Khorezm, included into the Kazak ASSR and later Uzbek SSR (Hanks 2000). At the end of national–territorial delimitation, the irrigation system of Khorezm spanned three Soviet republics.

The revolution and Civil War of the early Soviet Union brought devastation to the irrigation systems in Central Asia (Thurman 1999), and the ensuing mass collectivisation in agriculture in 1929 and 1930 was met with resistance also in Khorezm (Edgar 2004). Plans to overhaul and rebuild the irrigation system were firstly developed in the 1930s, aiming at reducing the many smaller intakes with a big headwork and a main canal (Gulyamov 1957). The Tash Saka, a stone sluice gate of built by the Qongrat khan in 1928 to supply Khiva with water (Shioya 2011), was rebuilt as the main intake for the restored and expanded canal system built from 1938 to 1941. This should happen through 'people's construction', a term referring to the voluntary mobilisation of collective farm workers to undertake the building or repair of canals (Obertreis 2017; Peterson 2019). Gulyamov (1957) describes 'people's construction' in Khorezm as a happy event during which women worked alongside men, and each collective farm fulfilled its tasks. Other sources suggest that the construction used forced labour (Teichmann 2007). As elsewhere in Central Asia, workers used only simple tools rather than mechanisation to construct the new canals. While this might be counterintuitive for the strong focus on technological modernity of the Soviet Union, the 'people's construction' was aimed at demonstrating the sheer power of labour for building socialism through manual work (Peterson 2019). Ironically, the number of workers and the cubic meters of earth moved was central to the Bolshevik's notion of success (Obertreis 2017) – the same measures that later served Soviet archaeologists to claim that ancient irrigation works must necessarily have been built through coercion (Tolstov 1948; Andrianov 1969).

The main expansion of the irrigation system in Khorezm took place between the 1950s and the 1980s by linking, widening and extending existing canals, but also by building new ones. Construction happened by leaps and bounds, resulting in a dendritic irrigation network characterised by bricolage rather than an overarching hydraulic design (Mollinga and Veldwisch 2016). This expansion was supported by the building of the Tuyamuyun reservoir upstream of the main inlet of the Khorezm irrigation system (Zonn et al. 2009). The large reservoir and hydropower complex served to stabilise the seasonal variability of the Amu Darya flow, allowing to regulate almost the entire lower reaches of the Amu Darya. To cope with rising groundwater tables and salinisation, a collector and drainage system was built during the 1950s and 1960s, using the old riverbeds Daryalyk and Daudan to remove excessive water into the depression of the Sarykamysh lake (Awan et al. 2011). As it were, the former promised waterways to the Caspian Sea now became the corridors for excess water. The economy in Khorezm underwent a decisive shift, aiming to expand intensive, sedentary agriculture towards a maximum extent by focussing on the production of a limited range of economically viable but water-intensive crops such as cotton and, to a lesser degree, rice (Brite 2016). A further expansion of the system was planned already during the 1970s, but its realisation, it was argued, would have to wait for the additional water supply from the diversion of Siberian rivers (Irrigatsiya Uzbekistana 1979).

The Siberian Water Transfer Scheme was an attempt to enhance further the scope and productivity of agriculture in the lower reaches of the rivers, but also to mitigate the then already apparent negative influence of intensive irrigated agriculture with high-level water abstraction in Central Asia on the deltaic ecosystem and the lake itself (e.g. Rafikov and Tetyukhin 1981). It entailed a partial river transfer scheme via a canal from the Ob river to the lower reaches of the Syr and the Amu Darya (Zonn et al. 2009). Ideas for the scheme were already brought up during the Tsarist period, when engineer Demchenko proposed diverting water from the Ob river to the Aral and further on to the Caspian Sea. This plan was, however, well beyond the financial capacity and construction technology of the period. The idea of the transfer scheme resurfaced during the Stalin era, and finally became concrete during the 1970s and the early 1980s (Micklin 2014b). In Central Asia, the scheme received very wide support (Obertreis 2017). The plan was of particular interest to Khorezm, as the Siberian-Aral canal should connect to the Tuyamuyun reservoir, thereby directly providing additional water for irrigation (Zonn 1999). The politics and ideology of the Soviet Union were favourable to mega engineering projects, with economic determinism and mastery over nature for human improvement through science and technology being a fundamental tenet of Marxism-Leninism. On the verge of implementation, the project was, however, put on hold for an indeterminate period in the wake of the Chernobyl disaster and the political changes in the Soviet Union during 1985 and 1986 (Micklin 2014b).

After the Soviet Union

The water from the Siberian rivers never arrived in Khorezm. Nor were former ambitious plans to expand further its irrigated area realised. With the collapse of the Soviet Union, the overarching political and economic system, within which Khorezm's agricultural production was embedded, disappeared. Moreover, Khorezm was no longer divided into two separate Soviet republics, but part of two separate newly independent nation states: the Republics of Uzbekistan and Turkmenistan. With the political change in Central Asia, the Amu Darya as well as former inter-republican canals became transboundary and required international agreements about water distribution. Khorezm inherited an irrigation infrastructure designed to deliver water to large-scale collective and state farms with centrally organised irrigation water scheduling and delivery that had not seen any investments during the 1980s and was in need of repair (Thurman 2002). It also inherited an inflexible economic production system, geared towards maximising agricultural output irrespective of the required inputs, in particular water. Soviet social engineering projects had collectivised land and sedentarised nomadic groups, thereby obliterating older forms of mixed agro-pastoral production based on nomadic or semi-nomadic ways of life and removing the flexibility to adapt to changing political and environmental conditions (Brite 2016). Lastly, it bore the brunt of the negative consequences of industrial agriculture and the shrinking of the Aral Sea that threatened the environment and livelihoods in an ecological disaster zone.

Between 1995 and 2005, multilateral organisations, bilateral donnors and Central Asian groups provided a total of 825 million USD to mitigate the disaster affecting the Aral Sea region (Micklin 2014a). Despite this large sum and related efforts, the Aral Sea did not stop shrinking. Zooming into Khorezm sheds light on a part of this puzzle. Despite changes in water management and land ownership (Wegerich 2009; Djanibekov et al. 2012; Veldwisch et al. 2012), the disintegration of the Soviet Union did not lead to a fundamental transformation of Khorezm's agricultural system. Uzbekistan's leadership opted to continue cotton farming to generate national revenue based on the infrastructure and the production and market systems inherited from the Soviet Union. Under the guise of liberalisations, the agricultural sector remains strongly regulated in Khorezm with a state order on cotton and, more recently, wheat, being mandated at a fixed quota and price and with little monetary benefit for farmers. Complying with the state's cotton and wheat production requirements, in turn, gives farmers the opportunity to produce other kinds of cash crops on the remaining land. While they grow a wide range of grains, vegetables and fruit on household gardens for personal consumption and local markets, the remainder of commercial production focuses on wetland rice. Although rice consumes an exceptional amount of water and is thus a poor fit for an oasis like Khorezm, it can be grown on reclaimed land from desiccated desert lakes, which are too saline for cotton production. Farmers have robust markets to sell rice both locally and for export. While formerly eaten only by wealthy elites in Central Asia, it became a widely consumed grain during the era of prosperity in the Soviet Union after World War II in the form of the cultural rice dish *plov* (Brite 2016). In combination with very high amounts of withdrawal per area unit and high-water losses through seepage, evaporation and overflow into drainage systems, water withdrawal from the Amu Darya into Khorezm remains thus at a very high level (Tischbein et al. 2012).

Water politics: a conclusion

In this chapter, I focussed on the political environmental history of irrigation in Khorezm. I could have written this history for other irrigated areas in Central Asia – such as the Ferghana Valley for example. This would have resulted in a different narrative, but not a fundamentally different trajectory of the entanglements between politics and the physical environment. The case of Khorezm is particularly instructive for discussing water politics in Central Asia for two main reasons. First, the stark and volatile physical environment of Khorezm brings into view the history of irrigation very sharply. Agriculture, but also agro-pastoralism in Khorezm has always been dependent on the additional supply of water as precipitation in the area is extremely low with less than 100 mm per year. Moreover, the highly dynamic deltaic ecosystem with shifting river branches and low-fertility soils required mobility, but also flexibility and adaptation in societal arrangements. Second, the history of irrigation in Khorezm is very well researched, mainly thanks to the 'Khorezmian Archaeological-Ethnographic Expedition', but also to later research efforts after the disintegration of the Soviet Union. The available literature makes it possible to trace the long history of irrigation in Khorezm throughout almost 4,000 years. At the same time, this literature provides also an entry point for critically examining the historical narratives about water politics. It is a solid reminder that most of what we know about the history of irrigation in Central Asia is knowledge produced by Imperial Russian or Soviet science with their specific colonial and later Marxist-Leninist interpretations.

The case of Khorezm shows that water politics in Central Asia has a very long history. Khorezm's irrigation system has gone through repeated phases of expansion and collapse brought about by a range of factors including foreign invaders, internal strife, excessive water abstraction and environmental change, frequently in combination and exacerbating each other. The current state of Khorezm is characterised not by collapse, but by a post-imperial political configuration with much political and infrastructural obduracy and very high environmental cost. An important insight from this political environmental history of irrigation is that re-emergence of irrigation in Khorezm after a collapse is possible, but it takes a long time and much effort. The irrigation infrastructure attests to this long and changeful history, representing the outcome of successive attempts to water the lands of Khorezm. The history of Khorezm also shows that control over water has never been a purely technical affair or economic necessity, but also is an expression of political rule and ideologies. The vision of controlling the waters of the Amu Darya was as much a pragmatic concern as it was an orchestration of political power. The connections between political rule and technological innovation – for example the invention of lift through the water wheel *(chigir)* or other water-lifting devices, and later pumps – certainly requires further research. Through their histories of innovation and transmission, they also provide an excellent entry point to linking the history of water politics in Central Asia to a more international history of irrigating arid lands. The general trend during the last 200 years in Central Asia has been one towards the expansion of intensive irrigated agriculture that is practiced by sedentary populations. Governed both by policies and markets, this process has led to the present-day de-coupling of more integrated forms of productions and lifestyles (agricultural – pastoralist, sedentary – mobile). While agriculture's past in Central Asia is well researched, the political and environmental outcomes of sedentarisation as well the historical narratives in Central Asia that it engendered deserve much more research.

References

Abdurasulov, U. (2016) The Aral Region and Geopolitical Agenda of Early Qongrats. *Eurasian Studies* 14(1-2):3–36.

Andrianov, B.V. (1969) *Drevnie Orositel'nye Sistemy Priaral'ia (v svyazi s istoriei vozniknoveniya i razvitiya oroshaemogo zemledeliya)*. Moscow: Nauka.

Andrianov, B.V. (1995) The History of Economic Development in the Aral Region and Its Influence on the Environment. *GeoJournal* 35(1):11–16.

Annanepesov, M. and H.N. Bababekov. (2003) The Khanates of Khiva and Kokand and the Relations between the Khanates and Other Powers. In: Adle, C. and I. Habib (eds). *History of Civilizations in Central Asia. Volume V. Development in Contrast: From the Sixteenth to the Mid-Nineteenth Century*. Paris: UNESCO Publishing, pp. 63–88.

Arzhantseva, I. (2015) The Khorezmian Expedition: Imperial Archaeology and Faustian Bargains in Soviet Central Asia. *Public Archaeology* 14(1):5–26.

Arzhantseva, I. and H. Härke. (2019) 'The General and His Army.' Metropolitans and Locals on the Khorezmian Expedition. In: Gorshenina, S., P. Bornet, M.E. Fuchs and Claude Rapin (eds). *'Masters' and 'Natives.' Digging the Others' Past*. Berlin: Walter de Gruyter, pp. 137–173.

Awan, U.K., B. Tischbein, C. Conrad, M. Sultanov and J.P.A. Lamers. (2011) *Irrigation and Drainage Systems in Khorezm, Uzbekistan*. ZEF Working Paper for Sustainable Development in Central Asia. Bonn: Center for Development Research.

Boomer, I, N. Aladin, I. Plotnikov and R. Whatley. (2000) The Palaeolimnology of the Aral Sea: A Review. *Quaternary Science Reviews* 19(13):1259–1278.

Boroffka, N.G.O. (2010) Archaeology and its Relevance to Climate and Water Level Changes: A Review. In: Kostianoy, A.G. and A.N. Kosarev (eds). *The Aral Sea Environment*. Heidelberg: Springer, pp. 283–303.

Breckle, S.W. and G.V. Geldyeva. (2012) Dynamics of the Aral Sea in Geological and Historical Times. In: Breckle, S.-W., W. Wucherer, L.A. Dimeyeva and N.P. Ogar (eds). *Aralkum – a Man-Made Desert. The Dessicated Floor of the Aral Sea*. Heidelberg: Springer, pp. 13–35.

Breckle, S.-W., W. Wucherer, L.A. Dimeyeva, N.P. Ogar. (2012) *Aralkum – a Man-Made Desert. The Dessicated Floor of the Aral Sea*. Heidelberg: Springer.

Brite, E.B. (2016) Irrigation in the Khorezm Oasis, Past and Present: A Political Ecology Perspective. *Journal of Political Ecology* 23(1):1–25.

Brite E.B. and J.M. Marston. (2013) Environmental Change, Agricultural Innovation, and the Spread of Cotton Agriculture in the Old World. *Journal of Anthropological Archaeology* 32(1): 39–53.

Brite, E.B., G. Khozhaniyazov, J.M. Marston, M. Negus Cleary and F.J. Kidd. (2017) Kara-teppe, Karakalpakstan: Agropastoralism in a Central Eurasian Oasis in the 4th/5th Century AD Transition. *Journal of Field Archaeology* 42(6):514–529.

Cretaux, J.-F., R. Letolle and M. Bergé-Nguyen. (2013) History of Aral Sea Level Variability and Current Scientific Debates. *Global and Planetary Change* 110 (Part A):99–133.

Djanibekov, N., I. Bobjonov and J.P.A. Lamers. (2012) Farm Reform in Uzbekistan. In: Martius, C., I. Rudenko, J.P.A. Lamers and P.L.G. Vlek (eds). *Cotton, Water, Salts and Soums: Economic and Ecological Restructuring in Khorezm, Uzbekistan*. Dordrecht: Springer, pp. 95–112.

Dukhovny, V.A. and J. de Schutter. (2011) *Water in Central Asia: Past, Present, Future*. Leiden: CRC Press.

Edgar, A.L. (2004) *Tribal Nation. The Making of Soviet Turkmenistan*. Princeton: Princeton University Press.

Frachetti, M.D. and F. Maksudov. (2014) The Landscape of Ancient Mobile Pastoralism in the Highlands of Southeastern Uzbekistan, 2000 b.c.-a.d. 1400. *Journal of Field Archaeology* 39(3):195–212.

Fracheti, M.D., C. Evan Smith, C.M. Traub and T. Williams. (2017) Nomadic Ecology Shaped the Highland Geography of Asia's Silk Roads. *Nature* 543:193–198.

Francfort, H.-P. and O. Lecompte. (2002) Irrigation et société en Asie Centrale des origines à l'époque achéménide. *Annales. Histoire, Sciences Sociales* 57e année(3):625–663.

Gorshenina, S. (2019) Russian Archaeologists, Colonial Administrators, and the 'Natives' of Turkestan: Revisiting the History of Archaeology in Central Asia. In: Gorshenina, S., P. Bornet, M.E. Fuchs and Claude Rapin (eds). *'Masters' and 'Natives.' Digging the Others' Past*. Berlin: Walter de Gruyter, pp. 31–86.

Gulyamov, Y.G. (1957) *Istoriya orosheniya Khorezma s drevneishikh vremen do nashikh dnei*. Tashkent: Izdatel'stvo Akademii Nauk Uzbekskoi SSR.

Hanks, R. (2000) A Separate Space?: Karakalpak Nationalism and Devolution in Post-Soviet Uzbekistan. *Europe–Asia Studies* 52(5): 939–953.

Haugen, A. (2003) *The Establishment of National Republics in Soviet Central Asia*. Basingstoke: Palgrave Macmillan.

Hu, Z., Q. Zhou, X. Chen, C. Qian, S. Wang and J. Li. (2017) Variations and Changes of Annual Precipitation in Central Asia over the Last Century. *International Journal of Climatology* 37(Suppl.1): 157–170.

Irrigatsiya, Uzbekistana. (1979) *Tom III. Sovremennoe sostoyanie n perspektivy razvitiya irrigatsii v basseine r. Amudar'i*. Tashkent: Fan.

Itina, M.A. (1977) *Istoriya stepnykh plemen Yuzhnogo Priaral'ya*. Moscow: Nauka.

Karasar, H.A. (2008) The Partition of Khorezm and the Position of Turkestanis on *Razmezhevanie*. *Europe–Asia Studies* 60(7):1247–1260.

Kidd, F. and A.V.G. Betts. (2010) Entre le Fleuve et la Steppe: Nouvelles Perspectives sur le Khorezm Ancien. *Comptes Rendus des Seances de l'Académie des Inscriptions et Belles-Lettres* 154(2):637–686.

Kim, L. and N. Pianciola. (2019) Introduction: Watering the Land-Based Empires. *Journal of the Economic and Social History of the Orient* 62:525–559.

Klötzli, S. (1997) The 'Aral Sea Syndrome' and Regional Cooperation in Central Asia: Opportunity or Obstacle? In: Gleditsch, N.P (ed). *Conflict and the Environment*. Dordrecht: Springer, pp. 417–434.

Létolle, R. and M. Mainguet. (1996) *Der Aralsee. Eine ökologische Katastrophe*. Berlin: Springer.

Létolle, R., P. Micklin, N. Aladin and I. Plotnikov. (2007) Uzboy and the Aral Regressions: A Hydrological Approach. *Quaternary International* 173–174:125–136.

Lewis, R.A. (1966) Early Irrigation in West Turkestan. *Annals of the Association of American Geographers* 56(3):467–491.

Matley, I.M. (1994) Agricultural Development (1965–1963). In: Allworth, E. (ed). *Central Asia: 130 Years of Russian Dominance*. Durham: Duke University Press, pp. 266-308.

Micklin, P. (2014a) Introduction to the Aral Sea and Its Region. In: Micklin, P., N.V. Aladin and Igor Plotnikov (eds). *The Aral Sea. The Devastation and Partial Rehabilitation of a Great Lake*. Heidelberg: Springer, pp. 15–40.

Micklin, P. (2014b) The Siberian Water Transfer Schemes. In: Micklin, P. (ed). *The Aral Sea. The Devastation and Partial Rehabilitation of a Great Lake*. Heidelberg: Springer, pp. 381–404.

Micklin, P. (2016) The Future Aral Sea: Hope and Despair. *Environmental Earth Sciences* 75:844.

Mollinga, P.P. and G.J. Veldwisch. (2016) Ruling by Canal: Governance and System-Level Design Characteristics of Large-Scale Irrigation Infrastructure in India and Uzbekistan. *Water Alternatives* 9(2):222–249.

Oberhänsli, H., N. Boroffka, P. Sorrel and S. Krivonogov. (2007) Climate Variability During the Past 2,000 Years and Past Economic and Irrigation Activities in the Aral Sea Basin. *Irrigation and Drainage Systems* 21:167–183.

Obertreis, J. (2017) *Imperial Desert Dreams. Cotton Growing and Irrigation in Central Asia, 1860–1991*. Göttingen: V&R Unipress.

Peterson, M.K. (2019) *Pipe Dreams. Water and Empire in Central Asia's Aral Sea Basin*. Cambridge: Cambridge University Press.

Pravilova, E. (2009) River of Empire: Geopolitics, Irrigation, and the Amu Darya in the Late XIXth Century. *Cahiers d'Asie centrale* 17/18:225–287.

Rafikov, A.A. and Tetyukhin. (1981) *Snizhenie Urovnya Aral'skogo morya i izmenenie prirodnykh uslovii nizov'ev Amudar'i*. Tashkent: Fan.

Sala, R. (2003) *Historical Survey of Irrigation Practices in West Central Asia*. Available from: lgakz.org, accessed: March 2020.

Sala, R. (2011) *The Medieval Urbanization of Northern Central Asia and the International Monetary System*. Available from: http://www.lgakz.org/Texts/LiveTexts/Urb-Silver-2011.pdf, accessed June 2020.

Sala, R. (2012) Mediveal Urbanization of Mid-Lower Syr Darya and Northern Tienshan: Structure, Development and Environmental Impact. In Kubota, J. and M. Watanabe (eds). *Toward a Sustainable Society in Central Asia: An Historical Perspective on the Future*. Kyoto: RIHN, pp. 59–74.

Sala, R. (2019) Quantitative Evaluation of the Impact on Aral Sea Levels by Anthropogenic Water Withdrawal and Syr Darya Course Diversion During the Medieval Period (1.0–0.8 ka BP). In: Yang, L. E., H-R. Bork, X. Fang and S. Mischke (eds.). *Socio-Environmental Dynamics along the Historical Silk Road*. Cham: Springer, pp. 95–121.

Sartori, P. and U. Abdurasulov. (2017) Take me to Khiva: *Sharīʿa* as Governance in the Oasis of Khorezm (19th-Early 20th Centuries). *Islamic Law and Society* 24:20–60.

Schellnhuber, H.J., A. Block, M. Cassel-Gintz, J. Kropp, G. Lammel, W. Lass, R. Lienenkamp, C. Loose, M.K.B. Lüdecke, O. Moldenhauer, G. Pretschel-Held, M. Plöchl and Fritz Reusswig. (1997) Syndromes of Global Change. *GAIA – Ecological Perspectives on Science and Society* 6(1):19–34.

Seitz, J.B. (2013) *Irrigation and Agriculture in the Khanate of Khiva 1768–1914*. Master thesis. Department of Central Eurasian Studies, Indiana University.

Shioya, A. (2011) Irrigation Policy of the Khanate of Khiva Regarding the Lawsan Canal (1), 1830–1873. *Area Studies Tsukuba* 32:115–136.

Shioya, A. (2013) Who Should Manage the Water of the Amu Darya? Controversy over Irrigation Concessions between Russia and Khiva, 1913-1914. In: Sartori, P. (ed). *Explorations in the Social History of Modern Central Asia (19th-Early 20th Century)*. Leiden: Brill, pp. 111–136.

Shioya, A. (2014) *Povorot* and the Khanate of Khiva: A New Canal and the Birth of Ethnic Conflict in the Khorazm Oasis, 1870s-1890s. *Central Asian Survey* 33(2):232–245.

Small, I. and N. Bunce. (2003) The Aral Sea Disaster and the Disaster of International Assistance. *Journal of International Affairs* 56(2):59–73.

Stark, S., U. Eshokulov, M. Gütte and N. Rakhimov. (2010) Resource Exploitation and Settlement Dynamics in High Mountain Areas. The Case of Medieval Ustrūshana (Northern Tadzhikistan). *Archäologische Mitteilungen aus Iran und Turan* 42:67–85.

Stride, S., B. Rondelli and S. Mantellini. (2009) Canals Versus Horses: Political Power in the Oasis of Samarkand. *World Archaeology* 41(1):73–87.

Teichmann, C. (2007) Canals, Cotton, and the Limits of De-Colonization in Soviet Uzbekistan, 1924–1941. *Central Asian Survey* 26(4):499–519.

Thurman, J.M. (1999) *Modes of Organization in Central Asian Irrigation: The Ferghana Valley, 1876 to Present*. Doctoral thesis. Bloomington: Indiana University.

Thurman, M. (2002) *Irrigation and Poverty in Central Asia: A Field Assessment*. Washington, DC: World Bank.

Tischbein, B., U.K. Awan, I. Abdullaev, I. Bobojonov, C. Conrad, H. Jabborov, I. Forkutsa, M. Ibrakhimov and G. Poluasheva. (2012) Water Management in Khorezm: Current Situation and Options for Improvement (Hydrological Perspective). In: Martius, C., I. Rudenko, J.P.A. Lamers and P.L.G. Vlek (eds). *Cotton, Water, Salts and Soums: Economic and Ecological Restructuring in Khorezm, Uzbekistan*. Dordrecht: Springer, pp. 69–92.

Tolstov, S.P. (1948) *Drevnii Khorezm. Opyt istoriko-archeologicheskogo issledovaniya*. Moscow: MGU.

Tolstov, S.P. (1962) *Po Drevnim Del'tam Oksa i Yaksarta*. Moscow: Izdatel'stvo vostochnoi literatury.

Veldwisch, G.J., P. Mollinga, D. Hirsch and R. Yalcin. (2012) Politics of Agricultural Water Management in Khorezm, Uzbekistan. In: Martius, C., I. Rudenko, J.P.A. Lamers and P.L.G. Vlek (eds). *Cotton, Water, Salts and Soums: Economic and Ecological Restructuring in Khorezm, Uzbekistan*. Dordrecht: Springer, pp. 127–140.

Wegerich, K. (2009) Shifting to Hydrological Boundaries – The Politics of Implementation in the Lower Amu Darya Basin. *Physics and Chemistry of the Earth* 34(4–5):279–288.

White, K.D. (2013) Nature-Society Linkages in the Aral Sea Region. *Journal of Eurasian Studies* 4(1):18–33.

Zonn, I.S. (1999) The Impact of Political Ideology on Creeping Environmental Changes in the Aral Sea Basin. In: Glantz, M.H. (ed). *Creeping Environmental Problems and Sustainable Development in the Aral Sea Basin*. Cambridge: Cambridge University Press, pp. 157–190.

Zonn, I.S., M.H. Glantz, A.G. Kostianoy and A.N. Kosarev. (2009) *The Aral Sea Encyclopedia*. Heidelberg: Springer.

11
RETHINKING SPECTACULAR CITIES
Beyond authoritarianism and mastermind schemes

Mateusz Laszczkowski and Natalie Koch

On 20 March 2019, Kazakhstan's parliament passed a resolution changing the name of the country's capital city Astana to Nur-Sultan. In so doing, the parliament commemorated Nursultan Nazarbayev who had ruled Kazakhstan for 30 years, first as the country's last Soviet-era leader and subsequently as the first President of the independent post-Soviet Republic. Nazarbayev, aged 79, had unexpectedly abdicated the day before.

For the city, this was already a third name-change in less than three decades. Established in the 19th century as a tsarist colonial outpost called Akmolinsk, the city was renamed Tselinograd in 1961 under Nikita Khrushchev. Following the USSR's demise and Kazakhstan's independence, in 1992 it was called Aqmola. Finally, in 1998 Nazarbayev had the city renamed yet again: Astana, meaning 'Capital' in Kazakh. The seat of the country's government was moved here from the much larger city of Almaty (Alma-Ata) that had been the capital of the Kazakh Soviet Republic.

The construction boom that followed in Astana – fueled largely by revenues from Kazakhstan's oil and gas exports – captured the imaginations of journalists, political commentators and international scholars. Astana was reckoned to serve as Nazarbayev's 'personality cult by proxy' (Adams and Rustemova 2009). In Kazakhstan, the President was credited with planning the city, from the general idea of the capital relocation down to the designs of particular buildings – such as the prominent Bayterek monument, allegedly outlined by Nazarbayev's hand on a handkerchief. He was frequently depicted literally as Astana's architect, and a national holiday – Astana Day – was celebrated on his birthday (see also Isaacs 2010) (Figure 11.1).

From this perspective, the latest city name-change was easily seen as a logical further step on the way toward a full-blown personality cult, akin to the one established in Turkmenbashy's Turkmenistan (cf. Denison 2009; Šír 2008). Kazakhstan seemed to descend into a modern-day version of Oriental despotism.

In this chapter, we steer clear of such exoticising interpretations. We take this recent episode in the history of Kazakhstan's capital city as a starting point to reflect on the social complexities of spectacular city-building beyond orientalising imagination, as well as beyond a focus on elite schemes and 'ideology.' We draw on the case of Astana for two main reasons. First, this city stands

DOI: 10.4324/9780429057977-11

Figure 11.1 President Nursultan Nazarbaev as the architect of Astana (statue at the Presidential Cultural Center, Astana). Photo by Mateusz Laszczkowski.

out as the region's only new capital and the site of the most extensive architectural transformation, matched perhaps only by Azerbaijan's Baku (cf. Grant 2014). Second, quite simply, this is the city in Central Asia we both know the best (cf. Koch 2018; Laszczkowski 2016). Our respective ethnographic insights allow for a 'bottom-up' view of Astana. Anthropologist Mateusz Laszczkowski carried out a year of ethnographic fieldwork in Kazakhstan's capital in 2008–2009. He worked with primarily ethnically Russian Soviet-era residents as well as ethnically Kazakh post-capital relocation migrants to Astana, exploring these different groups' experiences of living in the rapidly transforming city through participant observation and countless informal conversations. Similarly, geographer Natalie Koch conducted repeated visits to Astana and other towns and cities throughout Kazakhstan's hinterlands from 2005 to 2015, primarily using interviews, participant observation and event ethnography. Later traveling to other capitals in Central Asia, the Caucasus, the Arabian Peninsula, and Southeast Asia, she aimed to put Astana in comparative perspective. Together, this analysis has implications for other 'spectacularly' re-built cities across the region, capitals and not, from Baku and Tbilisi to Almaty and Kazakhstan's regional centers like Aktau and Shymkent.

We argue that the rise of Astana is best understood as a complex socio-material process involving multiple heterogeneous agendas and aspirations of diversely situated actors. It is not just an expression of a singular political 'cult' or ideology. We contend that spectacular cities are *technologies of government* (Koch 2018) that work not as stand-alone showpieces but through specific relations to their particular social, geographic and historic contexts. The term 'technology of government' is meant to emphasise that 'spectacular cities' are not a particular category of cities defined by any set of essential characteristics. A technology is a set of practices that various actors may use to different ends, with different skills and degrees of control. Following Foucault's (1991) work on governmentality, technologies of government are such sets of practices that actors may use in attempts to shape the order of socio-material relations in which they partake.

Political elites may be able to control these technologies and use them more effectively than other actors. However, 'ordinary people', too, navigate the technologies as best they can to their advantage. Spectacular cities are thus not reducible to elite projects (better or worse implemented). Rather, they are shifting aggregate products of a multiplicity of diverse and diversely positioned actors. These actors' actions and aspirations to shape their own lives and the urban environment around them cohere as often as they collide or partly overlap (Laszczkowski 2016). By having Astana built, the Kazakhstani elite put forth a particular vision of the national future within a global context. Residents' individual practices and imaginings of self, place, time, sociality and politics have developed in creative relation to that vision and its material realisation in built forms.

Below, we begin with a brief overview of Astana's recent history and contextualise its transformations in the wake of the capital relocation as part of a broader phenomenon of spectacular capital city projects found across the world. Drawing on Mateusz Laszczkowski's anthropological fieldwork among Astana's residents (2008–2009), we show how the rise of the capital city represented a landscape of opportunities as well as challenges for 'ordinary people' in pursuit of more satisfying lives. The selection of individual life-stories we draw on is by no means representative of the enormous diversity of people's experience in any large city. It should, however, be suggestive of how the rise of Astana as a technology of government worked by attracting and channeling the agency of individual citizens struggling to realise their own, usually quite concrete and mundane, visions of personal betterment. In concluding, we outline the implications of our analysis of 'spectacular cities' for contemporary urban life in Asia, as well as the broader social science writing on political theory – in particular, questioning the boundaries between 'authoritarian' and 'democratic' regimes.

Astana beyond mastermind thinking

Large-scale capital city projects are found in places as diverse as Ankara, Beijing, Brasília, Islamabad, Paris, Rabat, Riyadh, Rome and St. Petersburg (e.g. Agnew 1998; Bozdoğan 2001; Harvey 2003; Holston 1989; Rabinow 1981; Vale 1992; Wagenaar 2000; Yakas 2001). These cities were all designed to be 'spectacular' – a visual and experiential effect largely achieved through intensive master-planning unprecedented for their contexts. Because of the exceptional role of centralised, often autocratic, planning that made these capitals so remarkable, scholars have logically given much attention to the relationship between state power and spectacle in grand planned city schemes. Yet these historical cases were spectacular in a specific historical moment and in a particular geopolitical context: few people would characterise these cities as 'spectacular' today. This simple fact underscores how spectacle is necessarily *relative* – and often quite fleeting (Koch 2018: 2–3).

The idea of spectacle also raises questions about spectators. Further, actors with the desire (and means) to transform their ideas into reality always have multiple audiences in mind: sometimes these audiences are primarily domestic and other times, they have a stronger international orientation. These actors and their constituencies are also always in flux: certain individuals move in and out of positions of power, while local, regional and global realities change both temporally and spatially (Koch 2018: 17). In short, there is always a multiplicity and dynamism to what is and isn't understood as spectacular, and by whom. Accounting for the spectacle of any city therefore requires a firm rooting in history that accounts for its multiple authors and audiences – and this is where we begin with the case of Astana.

Upon Kazakhstan's capital relocation in 1997, Aqmola (soon Astana), with a population of approximately 250,000, was a mid-size post-industrial city – one among hundreds of similar cities that dotted the former Soviet Union, from Eastern Europe to Kamchatka. The city had grown since the 1960s around the agricultural machinery-producer TselinSelMash as its 'city-forming enterprise' (*gradoobrazuyushchee predpriyate*; cf. Collier 2010). Following the collapse of the Soviet economic system and the breakup of TselinSelMash, the city's economy had sunk into stagnation.

The capital relocation became an unexpected and unprecedented stimulus for growth. Beginning in the early 2000s, an expansive area of gigantic government buildings, shiny office towers, hotels, residential estates, shopping centers, and symbolic monuments were built – mainly on previously undeveloped land across the river from the Soviet-era city. The pace and scope of the construction astonished local residents and international commentators alike (Koch 2012). The development covered at least around 80,000 acres in the so-called 'Left Bank' area (from the left – that is, southwestern – bank of the river Ishim). By 2007, the cost of the development had reached at least 15 billion USD (Dave 2007: 168). The architectural style of this emerging new capital was diverse and extravagant. Blue domes and neoclassicist colonnades shared space with the abstract geometrical forms of glass-and-steel skyscrapers, fake minarets and pagodas, and grandiose edifices designed to conjure an enchanting image of modernity and the future (Figure 11.2). The eclectic cityscape presented itself as an enthusiastic exercise in 'the art of being global' (Bissenova 2014).

The quickly expanding new quarter stood in sharp contrast to the generally grey box-shaped Soviet-era apartment blocks and the clusters of simple self-built mud-brick (*samannye*) dwellings of the urban poor that made up the bulk of the city's built environment.

Parallel to this architectural transformation, Astana also underwent sweeping demographic change. The city's population grew from about 250,000 in the mid-1990s to 600,000 or even 800,000, according to different estimates, by the late 2000s, and over 1 million in 2017. At the time of the USSR's collapse, the population was generally Russophone and largely ethnically Russian and Slav. Kazakhs were a local minority. Some of the ethnic Russians, Germans and other 'European' nationalities moved out to what were, supposedly, their 'historic homelands' (Kendirbaeva 1997: 747). The capital relocation brought a massive influx of Kazakhs from all parts of Kazakhstan, near and far. A first wave of migrants comprised government clerks relocated from Almaty along with their jobs. They were soon followed by people of all walks of life, hailing from urban as well as rural locations, and seeking employment in the booming construction business but also in trade and the service sector (Tatibekov 2005; Zabirova 2002a, 2002b). Only a few of these migrants could count on residence in the spectacular new areas. Commercially available housing in the Left Bank was unaffordable to most. State employees – low-ranking bureaucrats, but also school teachers, doctors, nurses and academics, among other groups – were offered access to government-subsidised housing. However, demand exceeded supply. There were eligibility criteria for hopeful tenants to meet in order to be enrolled in a housing program, and in the best-case scenario one should expect to spend several years on a waiting list. Still, as we discuss below, the rising forms of the new city inspired hopes and captured imaginations (see also Buchli 2007).

Official propaganda – including books authored by, or attributed to, President Nazarbayev – presented the capital relocation as a bold but rational technocratic development project.

Figure 11.2 Spectacular new architecture in Astana. Photo by Mateusz Laszczkowski.

The building of the new capital, it was argued, would stimulate national economic growth. Moreover, it was claimed, thanks to Astana's location near the geometric centre of Kazakhstan, the capital would become a natural hub for economic exchanges, and the benefits of growth would 'radiate out' across the national territory (e.g. Nazarbayev 2005; cf. Koch 2013). Images of Astana quickly became ubiquitous in the Kazakhstani 'visual sphere' (Nathanson and Zuev 2013). Representations of the most spectacular buildings appeared on television, in the news and in short videos played between shows; in propaganda visuals displayed along roads across the country; on souvenir knick-knacks; and on every Kazakhstani banknote. Through frequent use of aerial perspectives and broad angles, these visuals created a sensation of a panoptic view of a perfectly designed ideal city. They were usually views of monumental buildings and vast empty spaces with very few people ever present in the frame. The visuals created a selective collage of decontextualised sights that stood for the new capital – a hyper-reality, in Jean Baudrillard's (1983) sense of a representation that precedes and displaces what it supposedly represents.

Social science commentary on Astana, at least in English, was generally dominated by an elite-centric optic. Scholars focused on explaining the capital relocation as a nationalist strategy. One American political geographer, for instance, called Astana 'nothing less than a centerpiece of the official nation-building project in Kazakhstan' (Anacker 2004: 515; cf. Fauve 2015). Scholars in this vein suggested that Astana was built to mark ethnic Kazakh dominance upon the heavily Slav-populated north of Kazakhstan (e.g. Anacker 2004; Schatz 2004; Wolfel 2002; cf. Dave 2007) and to project a fusion of Soviet legacies with a manufactured Kazakh 'traditional' imagery (Bekus and Medeuova 2017). At the same time, the city was supposedly meant to convey a vague notion of openness to international markets, mainly addressed to foreign audiences (Bissenova 2014). Finally, according to some scholars, Nazarbayev's goal in relocating the capital was to undermine rival patronage networks *within* the ruling elite and bolster his own (Shatz 2004; cf. Cummings 2005). And, of course, there was the 'personality cult' hypothesis. According to this latter idea, Astana was a symbol of 'modernity' and development, and an object of admiration, closely identified but at the same time conveniently non-identical with the figure of the city's 'creator', the President. This sophisticated symbolism helped Nazarbayev bask in a cult of personality while avoiding the criticism such a cult might provoke (Adams and Rustemova 2009).

While each and all of these hypotheses may be true – in some sense and to some extent – here we propose a different way of thinking about spectacular city-building in relation to political power. As opposed to an old-fashioned view of power as something 'held' by elites or located within institutions, we prefer a relational notion of power. Following Foucault (1983, 1991), power is an aspect of relations among variously situated actors who influence – generally indirectly – each other's actual and potential conduct. Accordingly, we propose, when seeking to understand spectacular city-building as a technology of government, it might not be the most fruitful choice to assume that the city is simply a, more or less successful, implementation of a strategy conceived by one or more members of 'the elite.' Instead, a more complete perspective on spectacular cities results if scholars follow the manifold relations that give rise to the city as a dynamic aggregate effect (cf. Mitchell 1999).

Of course, it is never possible to draw a full map of all such relations, as their number is infinite. However, ethnographic focus on individuals and groups whose experience is evocative if not necessarily statistically representative can offer a sense of the processes whereby a seemingly coherent whole ('city', 'society' or 'state') emerges out of contingent articulations of heterogeneous actions and aspirations by a plurality of actors. And crucially, ethnography decenters a still-commonplace stereotype about citizens in illiberal settings as 'dupes' or 'cogs' in the wheel of a mastermind scheme of some authoritarian leader or city planner. Instead, by taking the agency of ordinary people seriously, we can locate the differential *kinds* of agency of political subjects, as well as their multiple, often contradictory, perspectives on structural violence and inequalities in their societies. More often than not, these individuals simply live 'normally,' without directly engaging in the public political sphere (Koch 2018: 156–157). This sort of active disengagement is an important form of agency, which is often overlooked by analysts who approach places like Kazakhstan with certain liberal assumptions intact. In contrast, we show how residents of Astana are neither dupes nor cogs, but active participants in urban life who are faced with chances to live, build, love, hope or even despair – just as in any city. To this end, we now turn to a few individual life-stories from Laszczkowski's ethnographic research in Astana.

'See the new ... and become contemporary'

The personal experience shared by participants in Laszczkowski's (2016) research testifies how the 'spectacle' of Astana worked through juxtaposition to other places and times. The narratives of migrants to Astana also reveal how the 'spectacle' depended on the personal involvement of individuals in pursuit of personal betterment. For those individuals, the spectacle translated into usually quite concrete, even mundane, material practices.

Sasha and Olga were a young couple, recently married and with a young child. They were ethnic Russians and lived in Temirtau, an industrial town located in north-central Kazakhstan, some 200 kilometers south-east of Astana. They were both construction engineers. By the end of the 1990s, when they completed their education and were about to enter their professional lives, Temirtau had fallen into the worst of post-Soviet decline (cf. Nazpary 2002). The town had depended on an enormous metallurgical complex that had collapsed. Unemployment was rampant. Those who still had jobs received meager and irregular wages, often paid not in cash but in coupons to exchange for cigarettes at the factory shop. The cigarettes could then be traded for food on the informal market. Crime and drug addiction rates skyrocketed. Blackouts and water shortages became endemic.

In 1998, Sasha received a temporary assignment as a technical supervisor at a housing development project in the nascent new capital. The following year, his performance was rewarded with a permanent position. Olga and their schoolboy son joined him in 2000. The early years were not easy. The couple had very little resources and no social networks to rely on in the new city. Olga worried about their child finding his way in a new school and new environment. She also suffered emotionally from having to stay at home, unemployed and – in her own eyes – idle. The family was nearly penniless. They had sold their apartment in Temirtau for 500 USD, but, as Olga put it, all that money could buy in Astana was a doormat – except they had no door to put it in front of in the first place. Eventually, they rented a small flat, but the rent consumed Sasha's entire monthly salary equivalent to 100 USD.

Olga and Sasha took walks in the newly developing areas. Watching the city 'grow as fast as mushrooms' was exciting. With dreamy eyes that were at the same time the knowing eyes of professionals, they watched foundations being laid for what would become skyscrapers, government palaces and monuments. Olga desired to be part of the process, to contribute her skills and hard work to the spectacle of mass construction. After some time that dream came true for her: Olga got a job on a housing project. The city 'grew in the blink of an eye,' she recalls, 'literally within a few years.' Soon, the couple were able to purchase a modest but comfortable two-bedroom apartment in one of the 1960s 'sleeper districts.' Soviet-era apartment blocks were sturdy and despite their age they remained desirable good-quality housing. Sasha and Olga could now afford new dreams: they began saving money to buy land and build themselves a suburban house.

For people like them, the spectacular development of Astana offered opportunities for a life that would be morally as well as materially satisfying. This was not a utopian vision, but rather a promise of material conditions that could allow those who managed to make it to live 'normally' (*normal'no*) – to live modestly but well, like one should (cf. Buchli 2007: 65). For Sasha and Olga, the move to Astana and the participation in the new capital's development meant breaking away from the post-Soviet condition of collapse and stagnation. As Sasha put it, back in Temirtau they had been stuck 'like frogs in the mud.' In Astana, by contrast, they regained a sense of agency and direction that let them feel truly human.

Similarly, for other migrants, with other backgrounds, the spectacle of the new capital became personally meaningful by being translated into material practices that marked a difference from where those migrants had previously lived. Oraz, a Kazakh and about 15 years younger than Sasha and Olga, was born and raised in an ex-kolkhoz village in an out-of-the-way corner of southeastern Kazakhstan. After finishing school, he moved to Astana. At the time of Laszczkowski's fieldwork, Oraz lived with his sister in a cheap rented flat. He worked as a technician at a lab and doubled as a night watchman at a car park. 'Where I used to live', he explained,

> life once used to be at least a bit civilized. There used to be kolkhozes and sovkhozes – back when there was the Soviet Union. ... But then, when the Union collapsed, everything fell apart. Nothing was left. ... Only when I moved to Astana did I understand what urban life was, not sooner. ... I don't want my children to grow up like I did, in a village.

Oraz emphasised the attraction of the architectural spectacle of the new capital and how that spectacle inspired aspirations of personal development:

I came to Astana, I saw high-rise buildings, new architecture, investments from foreign countries … I saw this new kind of life. This was attractive because … you can see new things here … your mind receives something new, and you see the new, and you become a contemporary person.

(adapted from Laszczkowski 2016: 46)

Oraz further specified that this exciting new urban lifestyle largely consisted in everyday bodily practices. One such practice was the habit of showering daily, which had not been possible back in his native village. Another was the freedom from coal dust, which had been so ubiquitous in the coal-heated rural houses that it went unnoticed unless one had experienced the contrast of living in a city home where heat came through pipes from a power plant. Cleanliness was one of the essential characteristics of city life for Oraz.

The exciting spectacular architectural forms (in Oraz's phrase, 'high-rise buildings, new architecture' and 'investments from foreign countries') evoked a sense of living in a place that was catching up with the cosmopolitan modern world 'out there' (cf. Ferguson 1999). This was a spatial as well as temporal phenomenon. Astana was a place that, owing to its emerging material forms, was becoming co-temporal, coeval (Fabian 1983), with that imagined world of cosmopolitan modernity. Crucially, through everyday material practices this coevalness became a personal experience: thanks to his modest flat, his job and newly developed quotidian bodily habits Oraz felt he was becoming a *contemporary person*.

Implicit in the narratives above is a potentially destabilising tension between the spectacular vision of Astana as 'the city of the future' and the quite drab realities of living with which aspiring migrants were often confronted. The contrast between expectations fed by televised images of Astana on the one hand, and the material experience of living in the city on the other, could easily lead to disenchantment. Maintaining the effect of the 'future in the present' (Laszczkowski 2016: 47) required from migrants hard everyday labor to make a living as well as stretching the imagination and suspending disillusion.

This was also expressed by Sultan – a young medical technician hailing from a rural area in the southern Shymkent region. Sultan recalled his feelings of shock and disappointment upon first arriving in Astana. Like most others, Sultan's arrival in the 'big city' was actually an encounter with the area surrounding Astana's Soviet-built train station: dilapidating Khrushchev-era's two-storey apartments mixed with rural-looking mud-brick dwellings, and a crowd of people – passengers, hawkers and long-distance bus-drivers – bustling among vehicles in the chaotic station plaza. 'When I first came to Astana – I couldn't see Astana!' Sultan concluded. 'Only on the TV', he went on, 'they show it as if everything was beautiful. They use the greatest megapixels and colors … And people think: "Oh, oh, oh! Astana is so great!"' (adapted from Laszczkowski 2016: 48).

As for Sasha and Olga and for Oraz – as well as virtually all other migrant participants in Laszczkowski's research – also for Sultan, housing was a measure of truly becoming a part of the Astana spectacle. 'If I had a house to myself, my own apartment, then I could say: I live in Astana', he declared (Laszczkowski 2016: 51). He lived with his wife and a baby in a rented room in an area of detached coal-heated houses with outside toilets and no running water, located on the semi-rural outskirts of Astana. He worked two full-time jobs at public polyclinics. In addition, with the money he had borrowed from friends and relatives, he bought a 19-year-old Volkswagen Golf to work the nights and weekends as an unlicensed taxi driver. Through one of his polyclinic jobs, he managed to enroll in a subsidised housing program (*gosprogramma*) for young families on public payroll. He had even been shown the site where the building would rise in which he would eventually receive an apartment. Although the construction was painfully slow and its completion repeatedly delayed, Sultan remained hopeful. He was certain the day would finally come when he could call himself truly an 'Astanaian' (*astanchanin*).

Meanwhile, as he scrambled to make ends meet, Sultan regularly sent money to his relatives back home. When his sister was getting married back in the village, he sent her the equivalent of a thousand U.S. dollars – triple his monthly salary. He also bought her a large TV set on which, ironically, she would doubtless watch the same spectacular visions of Astana in which Sultan was becoming disillusioned. Similarly, when friends visited, Sultan would always show them around the most spectacular areas of recent development, with spacious boulevards, grandiose monuments and shiny shopping centers – the same sights, he pointed out to Laszczkowski, that the TV always showed. Despite his disillusionment, Sultan upheld his material and emotional investment in the Astana spectacle.

The geopolitics of spectacle

Cities have always been privileged places for leaders to express political power and their nation's unity, promise and modernity (Vale 1992). In some places, elites take this to an extreme and pour resources into developing spectacular landscapes. Given how often these projects are used by elites to send a message to outside observers, it makes sense that so much scholarship has focused on the authors of such messages and spectacular visions. Yet a grounded, ethnographic perspective on spectacular city projects like Astana shows how elites govern through multiple logics that are experienced differently by their subjects. That is, the very same urban development scheme may simultaneously be deemed oppressive and unjust by some, and liberating and worthy by others (Koch 2018: 154). Approaching spectacle as a political technology that is differentially engaged by multiple authors and audiences thus shifts the analytical imperative to a question: What makes a city 'spectacular' and for whom?

As Laszczkowski's examples show, and as Koch (2018) also illustrates in her book on Astana, many people in Kazakhstan today perform their political subjectivity as one of real love, appreciation and respect for the homeland and the alleged benevolence of the country's 'founding father,' President Nazarbayev. The spectacle of the capital city project has figured centrally in allowing people to develop this self-understanding – but not because it has been imposed top–down by the leader. Rather, as a political technology, the spectacle provides opportunities for people to pin their hopes and aspirations onto something concrete, engaging in urban life and working with the diverse material and rhetoric opportunities the capital city project sets in motion. Of course, the city is built on strategic exclusions, structural violence and grossly unequal social relations. Yet the power of any spectacle is to divert attention from socially inconvenient facts: to make 'inequality enchant' (Geertz 1983: 123).

Indeed, the case of Astana demonstrates how Nazarbayev's government was largely successful in making inequality enchant through the spectacle of the centre, but the centre–periphery relationships that give it meaning are not unique. As Koch's (2018) comparative work on similar projects in Central Asia and the Caucasus (Ashgabat, Turkmenistan and Baku, Azerbaijan), the Arabian Peninsula (Doha, Qatar and Abu Dhabi, the United Arab Emirates) and Southeast Asia (Bandar Seri Begawan, Brunei and Naypyidaw, Myanmar) shows, the most important axis of similarity across other spectacular city projects in these cases is the idea of a benevolent state offering up the spectacular city as a space and symbol of progress and future development. Synecdochically imagined to represent the magnanimous paternalism of the state, this spatial metaphor is strategically designed to obscure the temporally elongated and unspectacular forms of structural violence that otherwise prevail (Koch 2018: 149).

Viewed as a political strategy, however, spectacle is in no way limited to authoritarian systems. This is important to emphasise because it is still something that observers in liberal democracies most often caricature as uniquely authoritarian – found only in 'nondemocratic,' 'illiberal,' or otherwise 'backward' places (Koch 2017, 2018). Rather, actors in diverse polities have found spectacle useful for buying and selling particular visions of modernity, cosmopolitanism, development, geopolitical alignments or even environmental progressiveness (cf. Holston 1989; Çınar and Bender 2007; Diener and Hagen 2019; Koch 2015; Murawski 2019; Roy and Ong 2011). Soviet authorities transformed Central Asian cities such as Tashkent to project a prescriptive image of socialist modernity (Crews 2003; Stronski 2010). More recently, the post-Soviet governments in the region have worked to transform their capitals to manifest the opposite: the integration of their respective nations as active players into the brave new world of capitalist global markets. This is evident in both Kazakhstan's capital (Koch 2012) and in peripheral cities. For example, Trevisani's (2014) research on Uzbekistan's regional city of Namangan, where planners have tried to foster a new 'middle class' of local entrepreneurs, suggests that city-planning spectacle may also operate at smaller scales and be primarily directed at domestic audiences and particular class constituencies. The real question at hand, then, is: *Who* is buying and selling visions in the city? Laszczkowski's ethnographic work offers a vivid, if partial, view of who is buying and selling these visions within Kazakhstan. In closing, then, we want to consider the international community of observers and actors involved in this transactional politics, and shift the attention back to our own roles as scholars of Central Asian studies.

Academics and nonacademics alike often dismiss ostensibly 'peripheral' regions like Central Asia as irrelevant to the 'core' concerns of international affairs and urban studies. Our work shows how geographers, anthropologists, and other social scientists can use critical ethnography in a place like Kazakhstan to challenge the 'metrocentricity' (Bunnell and Maringanti 2010) of mainstream accounts of cities in the non-West. A grounded perspective that centres human beings in their full emotional and cognitive range strips away the normative baggage that is still so prevalent in Anglophone writing on Central Asia, which fixates on questions about whether spectacle is 'uniquely' authoritarian, if people are 'true' believers, or how elites manage to impose 'mastermind' schemes, as if by fiat. Moving beyond metrocentricity means moving beyond such clichéd questions that imply a liberal normative framework without naming it. Not only is this move an academic imperative, but it is also of political significance because it raises questions about how power relations are produced through scholarly analyses.

William Mazzarella (2015) underscores this point in discussing liberal commentaries about the North Korean masses shown crying in public after Kim Jong-il's passing in 2011. Fixated on the question 'Do they really mean it?', these commentaries reify the idea of a mastermind dictator – less to pose a serious inquiry and more to reaffirm a superior liberal narrative of the self:

> What could be more titillating to liberal publics than a spectacle of thwarted enlightenment in which the forced retardation of these childish citizens fed a monstrous swelling of the leader, whose overstuffed, singular subjectivity was directly proportionate to the massification of the people? In this picture, the North Korean tears might well be sincere, but they also had to be pathological.
>
> *(Mazzarella 2015: 97)*

Critical scholars of Central Asian studies are familiar with the pernicious effects of such Orientalist language, but it is a relentless thread in liberal reporting on the region – and indeed, on 'nondemocratic' places around the world (Koch 2019). The constant self-reflection demanded by ethnographic research, we suggest, is essential to overcome the challenges of this kind of commentary about spectacular cities and their 'masterminds.' It may not be an exotic morality play that irresistibly affirms liberal values, but there are no masterminds in Central Asia; only real people living complex, loving, painful, beautiful and normal lives.

References

Adams, L.L., and A. Rustemova (2009) Mass Spectacle and Styles of Governmentality in Kazakhstan and Uzbekistan. *Europe–Asia Studies* 61(7): 1249–1276.

Agnew, J. (1998) The Impossible Capital: Monumental Rome under Liberal and Fascist Regimes, 1870–1943. *Geografiska Annaler,: Series B, Human Geography* 80(4): 229–240.

Anacker, S. (2004) Geographies of Power in Nazarbayev's Astana. *Eurasian Geography and Economics* 45(7): 515–533.

Baudrillard, J. (1983) *Simulacra and Simulation*. Translator S.F. Glaser. Ann Arbor: University of Michigan Press.

Bekus, N., and K. Medeuova (2017) Re-Interpreting National Ideology in the Contemporary Urban Space of Astana. *Urbanities: Journal of Urban Ethnography* 7(2): 10–21.

Bissenova, A. (2014) The Master Plan of Astana: Between the 'Art of Government' and the 'Art of Being Global.' In: Madeleine Reeves, Johan Rasanayagam, and Judith Beyer (eds), *Ethnographies of the State in Central Asia: Performing Politics*. Bloomington: Indiana University Press, 127–148.

Bozdoğan, S. (2001) *Modernism and Nation Building: Turkish Architectural Culture in the Early Republic*. Cambridge, MA: The MIT Press.

Buchli, V. (2007) Astana: Materiality and the City. In: Catherine Alexander, Victor Buchli, and Caroline Humphrey (eds), *Urban Life in Post-Soviet Asia*. London: University College Press, 4069.

Bunnell, T., and A. Maringanti (2010) Practising Urban and Regional Research Beyond Metrocentricity. *International Journal of Urban and Regional Research* 34(2): 415–420.

Çınar, A., and T. Bender (2007) *Urban Imaginaries: Locating the Modern City*. Minneapolis: University of Minnesota Press.

Collier, S. (2010) *Post-Soviet Social: Neoliberalism, Social Modernity, Biopolitics*. Princeton: Princeton University Press.

Crews, R. (2003) Civilization in the City: Architecture, Urbanism, and the Colonization of Tashkent. In: James Cracraft and Daniel Rowland (eds), *Architectures of Russian Identity: 1500 to the Present*. Ithaca: Cornell University Press, 117–132.

Cummings, S.N. (2005) *Kazakhstan: Power and the Elite*. London: I.B. Tauris.

Dave, B. (2007) *Kazakhstan: Ethnicity, Language and Power*. London: Routledge.

Denison, M. (2009) The Art of the Impossible: Political Symbolism, and the Creation of National Identity and Collective Memory in Post-Soviet Turkmenistan. *Europe–Asia Studies* 61(7): 1167–1187.

Diener, A., and J. Hagen (eds) (2019) *The City as Power: Urban Space, Place, and National Identity*. Lanham: Rowman & Littlefield.

Fabian, J. (1983) *Time and the Other: How Anthropology Makes Its Object*. New York: Columbia University Press.

Fauve, A. (2015) A Tale of Two Statues in Astana: The Fuzzy Process of Nationalistic City Making. *Nationalities Papers*.

Ferguson, J. (1999) *Expectations of Modernity: Myths and Meanings of Urban Life on the Zambian Copperbelt*. Berkeley: University of California Press.

Foucault, M. (1983) Afterword: The Subject and Power. In: H.L. Dreyfus and Paul Rabinow (eds), *Michel Foucault: Beyond Structuralism and Hermeneutics*, 2nd ed. Chicago: The University of Chicago Press, 206226.

Foucault, M. (1991) Governmentality. In: Graham Burchell, Collin Gordon, and Peter Miller (eds), *The Foucault Effect: Studies in Governmentality*. Chicago: The Chicago University Press, 87104.

Geertz, C. (1983) Centers, Kings, and Charisma: Reflections on the Symbolics of Power. In: C. Geertz (eds) *Local Knowledge: Further Essays in Interpretive Anthropology*. New York: Basic Books, 121–146.

Grant, Bruce (2014) The Edifice Complex: Architecture and the Political Life of Surplus in the New Baku. *Public Culture* 26(3): 501–528.

Harvey, D. (2003) *Paris, Capital of Modernity*. New York: Routledge.

Holston, J. (1989) *The Modernist City: An Anthropological Critique of Brasilia*. Chicago: Chicago University Press.

Isaacs, R. (2010) 'Papa' – Nursultan Nazarbayev and the Discourse of Charismatic Leadership and Nation-Building in Post-Soviet Kazakhstan. *Studies in Ethnicity and Nationalism* 10(3): 435–452.

Kendirbaeva, G. (1997) Migrations in Kazakhstan: Past and Present. *Nationalities Papers* 25(4): 741–751.

Koch, N. (2012) Urban 'Utopias': The Disney Stigma and Discourses of 'False Modernity'. *Environment and Planning A: Economy and Space* 44(10): 2445–2462.

Koch, N. (2013) The 'Heart' of Eurasia? Kazakhstan's Centrally Located Capital City. *Central Asian Survey* 32(2): 134–147.

Koch, N. (2015) The Violence of Spectacle: Statist Schemes to Green the Desert and Constructing Astana and Ashgabat as Urban Oases. *Social and Cultural Geography* 16(6): 675–697.

Koch, N. (2017) Orientalizing Authoritarianism: Narrating US Exceptionalism in Popular Reactions to the Trump Election and Presidency. *Political Geography* 58: 145–147.

Koch, N. (2018) *The Geopolitics of Spectacle: Space, Synecdoche, and the New Capitals of Asia*. Ithaca: Cornell University Press.

Koch, N. (2019) Post-Triumphalist Geopolitics: Liberal Selves, Authoritarian Others. *ACME: An International E-Journal for Critical Geographies* 18(4): 909–924.

Laszczkowski, M. (2016) *'City of the Future': Built Space, Modernity and Urban Change in Astana*. New York: Berghahn.

Mazzarella, W. (2015) Totalitarian Tears: Does the Crowd Really Mean It? *Cultural Anthropology* 30(1): 91–112.

Mitchell, T. (1999) Society, Economy, and the State Effect. In: George Steinmetz (ed), *State/Culture: State Formation after the Cultural Turn*. Ithaca: Cornell University Press, 7697.

Murawski, M. (2019) *The Palace Complex: A Stalinist Skyscraper, Capitalist Warsaw, and a City Transfixed*. Bloomington: Indiana University Press.

Nathanson, R., and D. Zuev (eds) (2013) *Sociology of the Visual Sphere*. New York: Routledge.

Nazarbayev, N.A. (2005) *V Serdtse Evrazii*. Astana: Atamura.

Nazpary, J. (2002) *Post-Soviet Chaos: Violence and Dispossession in Kazakhstan*. London: Pluto Press.

Rabinow, P. (1989) *French Modern: Norms and Forms of the Social Environment*. Cambridge: MIT Press.

Roy, A., and A. Ong (eds) (2011) *Worlding Cities: Asian Experiments and the Art of Being Global*. Malden: Wiley-Blackwell.

Schatz, E. (2004) What Capital Cities Say About State and Nation Building. *Nationalism and Ethnic Politics* 9(4): 111–140.

Šír, J. (2008) Cult of Personality in Monumental Art and Architecture: The Case of Post-Soviet Turkmenistan. *Acta Slavica Iaponica* 25: 203–220.

Stronski, P. (2010) *Tashkent: Forging a Soviet City*. Pittsburgh: University of Pittsburgh Press.

Tatibekov, B.L. (2005) *Migranty v Novoy Stolitse Kazakhstana*. Astana: International Organization for Migration.

Trevisani, T. (2014) The Reshaping of Cities and Citizens in Uzbekistan: The Case of Namangan's 'New Uzbeks'. In: Madeleine Reeves, Johan Rasanayagam, and Judith Beyer (eds), *Ethnographies of the State in Central Asia: Performing Politics*. Bloomington: Indiana University Press, 243260.

Vale, L. (1992) *Architecture, Power, and National Identity*. New Haven: Yale University Press.

Wagenaar, M. (2000) Townscapes of Power. *GeoJournal* 51(1–2): 3–13.

Wolfel, R.L. (2002) North to Astana: Nationalistic Motives for the Movement of the Kazakh(Stani) Capital. *Nationalities Papers* 30(3): 495–506.

Yakas, O. (2001) *Islamabad, the Birth of a Capital*. Karachi: Oxford University Press.

Zabirova, A.T. (2002a) Astana: A City Like Others or a Catalyst of Changes? *Central Asia and the Caucasus* 5(17): 169–174.

Zabirova, A.T. (2002b) *Migratsiya, Urbanizatsiya i Identichnost' u Kazakhov: Case Study Astana*. Almaty: NITs 'Ghylym'.

12
POLITICS OF GREEN DEVELOPMENT
Trees vs. roads

Emil Nasritdinov

In the fall of 2017, a major social urban drama took place in Bishkek, the capital city of Kyrgyzstan. The Chinese government offered a grant to renovate several streets in the city. The Mayor's office was responsible for coordinating the work. One of the most controversial components of the plan was renovation and widening of Toktonalieva Street (informally known as Dushanbinka) located in the southern part of the city. The widening included cutting down trees along the road. The street's residents wished to preserve their trees and attempted to negotiate with the Mayor's office. But when their pleas were ignored, they rallied in protest against Mayor Albek Ibraimov. Urban activists joined the residents in their struggle. However, the mayor still ordered for the trees to be cut and sent police to aid the cutters. When residents and activists tried to stop the cutters, several of them were arrested. The Mayor's plan was implemented the way it was intended – decade-old trees towering the street were demolished. Toktonalieva was not the only street that lost trees. Similar developments took place in other parts of the city where streets were renovated. The city of Bishkek lost a significant amount of greenery that year.

This chapter demonstrates how Mayors like Ibraimov can transform cities according to individual visions and preferences of a person in power. Even when a city's residents disagree with the higher-level decisions, the judicial system serves as support to officials. Court appeals by the residents of Dushanbinskaya street against the Mayor's office were lost by them despite evidence of Irbaimov's illegal actions in the realisation of road expansion. The judge ruled in favour of the city, even though the city failed to present a single proper document justifying their project. Kyrgyzstan is a country that lacks a strong institutional and legal framework that would keep the activities of city governors and officials in check. Ibraimov was only stopped from cutting down more trees after his falling out of favour with the new President Sooronbai Jeenbekov, which led not just to his removal from the Mayor's position but also eventually to his arrest and sentence of imprisonment for 15 years for corruption.[1]

Dushanbinka

Some 30–60 years ago, the city of Frunze (now Bishkek) was divided among informal youth gangs called "rayons" (regions). One of the most famous rayons was called Botanika in the mid-upper part of the town. The name Botanika was born from the name of its main street – Botanicheskaya

DOI: 10.4324/9780429057977-12

(Botanical) that ran North–South and connected the community to the Botanical garden and one of the largest city parks – Park Druzhby (Park of Friendship). The street itself was lavishly green; it had large oak and elm trees planted more than half a century early when the neighbourhood was just created, and many four-storey apartments were built. Later, in the 1980s, the street was renamed into Dushanbinskaya, perhaps as a gesture of friendship with another Central Asian republic – Tadjikskaya SSR and its capital Dushanbe. When the Soviet Union collapsed, the street was renamed again, this time into Toktonalieva Street after Aliaskar Toktonaliyev, who was the Kyrgyz Finance Minister for 26 years. But among city residents the street is still widely known as 'Dushanbinka.'

Dushanbinka runs parallel (two blocks to the East) to Prospect Mira – one of the main streets that connects the city centre with the president's residency located in the southern edge of Bishkek, near the mountains. In the best traditions of many post-Soviet leaders, when the president travels to work in the morning and home in the evening, the street is completely emptied: police block all streets coming onto the Prospect Mira. City residents in their cars wait for the president to pass. President Almazbek Atambayev (2011–2017) regularly publicly apologised for road closures, including those caused by renovation efforts financed by Chinese grants. He proposed to turn Dushanbinka into an alternative thoroughfare that would allow people to continue traveling when Prospect Mira is closed. The problem was that Dushanbinka was narrow – only nine meters wide. So, Atambayev charged Mayor Ibraimov with the task of finding the solution and widening the street. That's when Ibraimov embarked on a massive demolition of trees.

Residents of Dushanbinka didn't want to see their small street turn into a highway with heavy traffic and the trees cut. They protested. They came to the Mayor's office demanding public discussion and their participation in the decision making, which was their right. When the Mayor declined to consider citizens' demands on Thursday, June 1, 2017, they went to the City Council and tried to convince the city deputies. The latter were slightly more inclined to listen since residents were their main constituents and they promised to meet with the residents on a site in the morning of Saturday. Satisfied, Dushanbinka residents went home hoping that the situation can be resolved and happy that they secured a meeting. But the Mayor outmanoeuvred both the residents and city deputies. In the morning on Friday, June 2, residents woke up to the sound of heavy machinery. Puzzled, frightened and desperate, residents came out to the streets. One of them was a young man under the name of Dima Vetoshkin.

Dima Vetoshkin and the apocalypses

Dima Vetoshkin was a true 'botanik' both literally and figuratively.[2] *Botanik* is a Russian slang term for a nerd, a bookworm, a good student with eyeglasses in thick frames. Dima was all of that, but he also was a botanist by profession (*botanik* in Russian). From his childhood he was fascinated by the flora and fauna around him and his fascination took him through all kinds of interests in school and brought into the university, where he studied botany and biology. Like Albek Ibraimov, Dima was born and raised in Bishkek. But unlike the Mayor, Dima loved trees. He studied them, knew their varieties and learned how to care for them. He also devoted his life to their protection. The trees on Dushanbinka were particularly dear to him because these were the trees of his childhood. Dima was an active member of the residents' group that tried to protect the street and went to negotiate to the City Council.

On that Friday morning, Dima had breakfast, packed his bag and left for work. He cancelled everything to have the Saturday morning free for the meeting with the deputies. As he was exiting his apartment complex, he was thinking of all those arguments he and his neighbours could use to convince the city to keep the trees. Once on the street, he didn't understand right away what was happening outside with all the machinery and police occupying the street. When the realisation finally hit him, it came with a shiver down his spine. He panicked, he started running around trying to make sense of what was happening. As he ran along the street, he saw other residents gathering near their houses with worried looks, anger and agitation against the city authorities. He saw elderly people and kids crying in the anticipation of what was going to happen.

Tension escalated as the woodcutters ignored the residents' pleas and arguments and began their work. According to Dima, four sows were operating in different parts of the street on that day. Their sound was reaching deep into the souls of community members bringing out their most terrible fears. Dushanbinka residents felt powerless in the face of that brutal force brought onto them by the Mayor. There was no space for negotiation and the desperation had completely enveloped the street: in the last attempt to save trees, residents were trying to hug them to defend from the sows, but police were there to pull people off the trees. For Dima and many others, this was their worst nightmare: falling trees, screeching sound of saws, crying children and the faces of policemen obstructing any attempts to save the trees. This was the day Dima was never to forget.

When nothing worked, Dima and other residents, now joined by activists from across the city, sat in front of the machinery to stop it from moving up and down the street. Ten people formed a sitting circle in front of one of the machines and refused to stand up when Zelenhoz[3] workers and police demanded it. In response, the police pulled the sitting protesters from the street into a police van and drove them to the main police precinct in the city centre. Dima along with nine other activists and residents spent the rest of the day behind bars.

Toward the end of the day, a small court session took place in the Pervomaiskii Court. The protesters were accused of disobeying authorities and obstructing the flow of traffic. After hearing all sides, the judge let everyone free, but first issued official warnings to them against any other forms of protest. Dima returned home when it was already dark. The home he returned to was no longer his, the street was completely transformed. Dushanbinka laid barren in front of his eyes with stumps instead of trees and with foliage and branches covering the asphalt. Tears were flowing down Dima's exhausted face as he was strolling along Dushanbinka in the surreal unbelief of what happened to him and to the street of his childhood in just one day.

Chinese grant and local politics

The demolition of trees on Dushanbika was indirectly facilitated by two grants from the Chinese government. There was only one requirement on the Chinese side – the projects had to be carried out by the Chinese road construction company. The Kyrgyz side announces a bid among the Chinese companies and selects the China Road. The first grant titled 'The development of street network of Bishkek' amounted to 1 billion yuan ($150 million). This grant is broken into two phases. The first phase during 2016–2020 included the reconstruction of 49 segments of different streets in Bishkek with an overall length of 95 km. The second phase was scheduled to begin in 2020 and include the reconstruction of 60 more segments of streets with an overall length of 74 km. The second grant is called "Rehabilitation of city streets" and it includes the reconstruction of 23 segments of streets 38 km long. The amount of this grant is 160 million yuan ($23 million).[4]

The physical condition of roads in Bishkek after independence was always poor. Over the last three years, the city was able to renovate only two streets using its own budget. In addition, the quality of road construction by the local companies is very substandard. China's help was widely appreciated. The city roads did become significantly better in the last three years since the project started and it is expected that they are going to further improve. In addition to road construction, Chinese companies are building several bridges, which help create a better-connected road network and reduce traffic pressure on the existing bridges. According to the agreement with the Chinese company, if the road performs poorly within a period of warranty (five years for new and reconstructed roads and three years for renovated roads) and there are defects, the construction company is expected to fix the defects at no additional cost.

Many city drivers truly appreciate the improved quality of roads. Even cyclists compliment the better quality that makes cycling easier and safer. Considering that reconstruction involved not only the road, but also irrigation channels and sidewalks along the roads, the project also benefited the pedestrians.

Yet the reconstruction of city streets also meant a loss of nearly 3,000 trees in Bishkek. It is unlikely that the demolition of trees was inbuilt in the conditions of the Chinese grants. Rather, the decision of reconstruction at the expense of the city's vegetation was made by different mayors. For instance, Mayor Isa Omurkulov (2010–2013) was much more considerate. Under his watch, the reconstruction of Suyorkulova street avoided demolition of trees. Initially he, too, planned to cut trees down. He even deployed heavy machinery onto the street on a Friday to begin demolition the next day. But the street's residents became alarmed and they contacted him late on Friday night and asked him to come to the street immediately. He was not in town, but he promised not to cut trees during the weekend and to come on Monday. He kept both of his promises and on Monday he had a meeting with residents and activists, who were able to convince him not to cut the trees. As a result, the street was renovated without cutting down trees and today the sidewalks on Suyorkulova are extremely popular. There are always pedestrians and one could easily see that these are not just regular commuters, but there are also many leisure walkers.

His successor Mayor Kubanychbek Kulmatov (2014–2016) didn't renovate many roads but was the first one to begin cutting trees in the city centre. One of the main central streets, Toktogul, was reconstructed under his watch. A number of new high-rise buildings were constructed, the street was widened and trees were cut.

The period of Albek Ibraimov (2016–2018) was the worst. The Chinese grants were received, and trees were cut in the city centre and in micro districts.

Since the current Mayor Aziz Surakhmatov replaced Ibraimov in August 2018, the mass destruction of trees was stopped. His approach to road reconstruction is more considerate of trees. He also inherited the ecological crisis from its predecessors with the levels of air pollution reaching its highest points ever. That forced him to be more cautious with urban ecology and green spaces.

Lessons learned

Dushanbinka is now a naked four-lane road without a single tree. The whole endeavour to expanding the street was a complete waste of resources, because the extra two lanes on the side of the road are now used to park cars and traffic happens only in two opposite lanes in the middle. So effectively, it is still a two-lane road with more space for parking. Then there is a new bridge at the end of the road across the Ala-Archa river connecting Dushnabinka with Mederova Street. The road towards the bridge starts ascending long before it reaches it and, as a result, houses on the side of the road lost their car access, but residents were not given any compensation for that loss.

Mayor Ibraimov promised to plant more trees than Dushanbinka originally had, but that was unrealisable because there was no space left to plant trees between the sidewalk and the road. The old trees used to protect the residents of apartment buildings that face Dushanbinka from the sun in the hot season. Now, the windows on all floors have a direct exposure to the sun and it is impossible to open windows for ventilation because the air on Dushanbinka is both very hot and polluted from the continuous traffic. Electricity poles were moved over to the middle of sidewalks. People who had smaller houses on the Western side of the road had to rebuild their gates because the sidewalk now runs right next to them and they cannot open the gates outside.

However, the most significant impact was on people's feelings.[5] Many felt depressed for a long time because they lost a lavishly green street. Some residents lost the trees they themselves or their parents planted many decades ago. The residents felt cheated and violently abused by the city administration that used the brutal force of police to complete their tasks. Years after that fateful day, the pain has not gone away due to the realisation that the damage cannot be undone and Dushnabinka has changed forever.

The tragedy moved some residents to become committed green activists. They continued to fight for other streets and green spaces in the city, for example for Bishkek's Botanical garden. As activists and residents were trying to comprehend what happened, they were able to learn some lessons.

Dushanbika residents realised that protests are not always a helpful tactic and if they are organised, they are to be taken seriously by the organisers. When residents organised a protest in front of the Mayor's office, only 20 people showed up and once the Mayor saw how little public support this group has, he moved on with his plan.

After the destruction of trees, residents started writing petitions to the President and to the Parliament; they also launched a complaint with the Prosecutor's Office on the illegal actions of police and on the Mayor's Office. They demanded transparency in the Mayor's office work, to stop all projects, to publish all urban design plans, and they started talking not only about Dushanbinka, but about all streets of Bishkek, which were subject to renovation. At the same time, they knew that the Botanical Garden was also under threat and they included this into the petition as well.

Residents referred to several legal articles in their court appeal: the violation of residents' right to a safe and healthy environment, violation of their right to participate in decisions concerning their neighbourhood and the right to self-governance. They identified the construction of bridge over the river as a 'gradostroitelnyi' (urban design) act, which as such required public discussion and presentation at the Gradostroitelnyi Soviet (Urban Design Council). Nothing of that took place and thus the road was built with the violation of major legal procedures.

They also claimed that Bishkek's Master Plan had a status of law and according to the Master Plan, Dushanbinka was marked as a two-lane road. Thus, creating a four-lane road was also against the law. Moreover, apparently, the original contract between Kyrgyzstan and China did not include the renovation of Dushanbinka. Finally, no assessment was done on the effect of road renovation on the environment. The Mayor's office ignored all of residents' requests and ignored all alternative solutions to traffic. Residents submitted their petitions to the Inter-regional Court and demanded two things: for the Mayor's office to prove that they followed the procedures and for them to stop all current work. The Mayor's office failed to present a single document to the Court, which was proof of the illegality of their actions. Nonetheless, after the four Meetings of the Court, the Judge ruled out against residents' petition.

As a result, residents came to the realisation that there are no effective mechanisms of holding city officials accountable over their actions and it is impossible to prevent any illegal actions. The Mayor's Office is disinterested in providing transparency to their decisions: officials do not provide public and even the court with official records of their activity. This creates fertile ground for corruption. In addition, the Mayor's Office lacks transparency in how it spends its budget; this destroys any possibility of public control.

The Mayor's Office is not interested in building a dialogue with the citizens. The city's police will defend the city officials by resorting to arrests and violence.

There is no inter-departmental work between different city agencies: one agency introduces changes, which other agencies are unaware of. The Mayor's Office is unaccountable not only to city residents, but even to the City Council that elects the Mayor.

There are also legal reasons why trees and other green spaces in the city are not protected. Specifically, there is a legal loophole created as a result of administrative reform carried out in the mid-2000s: all legal acts can only be introduced and approved by the government, while agencies like the Mayor's office must reregister all legal acts previously ascertained by the government. But the Mayor's office failed to reregister legal acts on sanitary norms and therefore was able to essentially ignore them while reducing the number of trees in the city. Another problem is that the norms for building and construction are standard and as such, according to the Law on Technical Regulation, they have a voluntary character. Different ministries interpret the voluntary aspect differently: The Ministry of Economics suggests that it means that the builder can voluntarily choose between different standards to follow, while the Ministry of Justice argues that it means that the builder can choose whether to follow these standards or not. Thus, the norms do not have to be followed.

When construction norms were compared with sanitary norms, there were many contradictions. For example, sanitary norms require 50 per cent of school territories to be green, while the construction norms require only 30 per cent. So, the legal basis is quite a mess and this has an effect on how the city develops.

Finally, the residents learned not to trust the promises of city officials. They also learned that the courts always take the side of officials. To successfully oppose such developments, there is a need to consolidate resources across neighbourhoods. Strategic intellectual effort must replace spontaneous protests. Residents and activists need to use the expert knowledge to advance their cause. The most important lesson though is that residents of different communities must help each other. They cannot fight this battle individually.

New activist strategies

Dima Vitoshkin's experience with Dushanbinka became a turning point in his life. He always was an activist, already in his student years, he joined the BIOM movement.[6] The group comprised of biology students and thus they had more of a scientific approach to ecology. They later created their own foundation 'Archa,' the main purpose of which was to protect and develop Bishkek's Botanical Garden, which by the mid-2010s was in a poor condition and under the continuous threat from various developers. But they also understood that it was impossible to engage in the protection of the Botanical Garden in isolation from other ecological concerns and without appropriate knowledge about greenery in the city. So, they decided to concentrate on efforts on protecting green spaces in Bishkek in general. In 2016, Dima describes his activism as a pleasant initiative: they wrote papers for newspapers and websites and created a new resource centre and even a course on landscape design. This was until 2017. The events of Dushanbinka changed Dima's life completely.

The apocalyptic scene of Friday, June 2, 2017, is still imprinted in his memory: falling trees and destroyed electric poles, exploding electricity lines, crying grandmothers and children, police violently pulling people away from the trees. He couldn't sleep for a month after the event because he was hearing electric saws. He was left with a terrible sense of despair and pessimism, which stayed with him for another year.

Yet, Dima did not give up and he sent the rest of that summer running from court to court along with other residents and activists trying to fight the city and stop the project realisation. It was in this condition of despair, that they wrote a book and started organising courses for citizens.[7] They tried to turn the Botanical garden into a centre of knowledge and over one year they were able to compile a strong citizen lobbying group. Dima himself became a spokesperson for different communities that tried to protect their trees. During this period, more city residents became concerned about green spaces. When Dima and his colleagues tried to bring people for a round table discussion in 2016, slightly more than 10 people showed up. Two years later, in 2018, when they announced the meeting of a green forum, nearly 250 people expressed their interest. They had to look for a large space to accommodate all participants. The workshop lasted for three days with no money even for coffee-breaks. Then came a period of more quiet work. They started working on developing instructions for the inventory of greenery, developing the legal framework, they studied and then taught workers of Zelenhoz how to cut the tree branches properly.

Dima argues that it is impossible to live in Bishkek without greenery. All favourable conditions are created by trees. For example, the research they conducted depicts how temperatures are significantly lower in summer in the areas with trees. They also measured the PM 10 particles and noise pollution and there is a clear negative correlation of both with the amount of greenery. Trees can help save energy. Finally, trees are good for restaurant business. For example, 7 trees create space for 5 tables with 20 sitting places. Many popular cafes in Bishkek today portray themselves as green spaces.

The Archa Foundation decided to conduct research using GIS (Geographic Information Systems) mapping. They saw the need to record how green spaces are changing. Special methodology of working with satellite imagery afforded them the review of how green spaces have been changing in the city since 2013. The analysis shows how over the years, the city centre and micro-districts were steadily losing the trees. Dima refers to Emil Shukurov, an ecologist and a long-term Bishkek resident, who described how it was possible to go from his home in the micro districts to the city centre while it was raining and not get wet, because there were long and thick corridors of trees over sidewalks that protected people from the rain and sun. Today, the trees, which are planted by the Mayor's Office are called facade trees. They are used for the decoration of building facades; they cannot generate large crowns capable of creating good shade. Instead, the city installs benches covered with roof. In the summer, temperature under such covers reaches 54 degrees Celsius. So, the technical decisions do not work.

Finally, they work on convincing the Mayor's office of the need to do a proper inventory of trees. By that they mean not just counting trees, but incorporating much more extensive information on each tree. The current data provided by the Mayor's office about how many trees they cut and how many they planted, doesn't say much. In fact, it is misleading. There is a huge difference in the value of old and new trees. Dima argues that the real ratio is 1:210, so to replace 1 adult elm tree, the city needs to plant 210 new seedlings.

Together with the Organisation for Security and Cooperation in Europe Centre in Bishkek and request from the Mayor's office, Archa developed a special software for conducting a proper inventory. This software allows creating a database with the GIS platform. Now, if a tree is to be cut, it has to be marked three weeks in advance with the following information recorded in the database: location, code, photo, trunk diameter, crown diameter, height of the tree, year of planting, age, physical condition, irrigation condition.

What will such inventory give the city? First, it will help the city to plan its budget for maintaining green spaces. Currently, the city gives 243 som ($3.5) a year per tree for maintenance, but this is not sufficient. To cut the trees properly would cost approximately 5,000 som ($70). It is seemingly high, but it is only half of what the city pays for one new seedling. This inventory methodology will allow the city to see the real amount of change – in terms of the physical biomass of greenery, not the quantity of trees. Dima believes that science is important. It allows the city to operate with more powerful instruments and more precise data and it allows activists to be more influential in the decision-making process.

This is what Dima and his colleagues from the Archa Foundation do. Since the events of Dushanbinka, fighting for green spaces became their full-time job. They describe how the city perceives them as crazy townies, who are always there and who are just never happy. However, as time goes by, it is not just Archa, but more and more people are unhappy about how Bishkek turns from one of the greenest cities in the former Soviet Union to one of the most polluted cities in the world. Dima and his colleagues are not alone in this struggle. There are several other ecology groups that join them in this struggle or fight for the same cause individually.

Environmental activists

The community of activists in Bishkek is a heterogeneous group, but the nature of connections is more vertical (e.g. from donors to NGOs and to beneficiaries of various projects) than horizontal (between NGOs). There are more connections across different types of communities than within specific sectors (e.g. business communities, NGOs, local territorial communities and artist groups). Even among activists, the degree of collaboration was quite low, many activist groups, particularly with different ideological platforms, were quite critical of each other.[8]

Interestingly, one of the few exceptions, was the sector of environmentalist and ecological groups. The level of collaboration among these groups was significantly higher compared to other activist communities. Activists and analysts from different communities worked together on joint projects, participated in each other's conferences, produced joint publications and often protested together. The list of groups with environmental focus is quite high. Besides Dima Vetoshkin's Archa, it includes such groups as the Ecological Movement BIOM, ECOIS (Ecological Information Services), Yrystan Foundation, CAMP Ala-Too Foundation, youth ecological movement MoveGreen, CSR Central Asia, Independent Ecological Expertise, CAVEN (Central Asian Youth Environmental Network), Ecological Movement of Kyrgyzstan 'Aleine,' and such networking groups as Unison and Climatic Network of Kyrgyzstan. Kyrgyzstan even has the Green Party – a political group with an environmental focus. These local groups have a large list of international partners and donors (e.g. Soros Foundation, WWF, European Commission, various UN agencies, JICA, and many others) that aid them in many of their projects. Kyrgyz environmentalists also collaborate with several state institutions and universities, and also with activist groups, such as Urban Initiatives, that do not have ecology as their primary agenda. In fact, 2 (out of 10) people who were arrested by the police on that tragic day in Dushanbinka, were members of Urban Initiatives.

The Green Mobilisations conference that took place in November 2019 in Bishkek and Tbilisi revealed that the level of environmental concern and participation was significantly higher in Bishkek. The conference became one of many platforms, where representatives of similar groups meet to raise issues and seek solutions. The interaction was not without some degree of rivalry between these groups, but that does not stand against the strong sense of unity and a joint cause.

The winter of 2019 became a period when air pollution in Bishkek reached one of its highest levels and city residents were shocked by the widespread news of Bishkek becoming the most polluted city in the world, worse than Beijing. The video went viral of a person filming Bishkek from the nearby mountain to depict a thick cloud of smog enveloping the city completely, so much so that no single building could be seen, but a lonely pipe of Bishkek's power plant raising above the grey cloud and producing its own strip of smoke. Parts of the city, which are closer to the mountains, have a slightly fresher air, but as the city descends down the plane to the centre and swamps in the North, the smog is so thick, one could almost touch it.

There are several main sources of air pollution in Bishkek. First, it is the residents of the private sector, who use coal to heat their houses in winter.[9] The number of *novostroikas* (new settlements on the city periphery) and their residents has been steadily increasing and coal for them is the cheapest way to keep their families warm. A solution could be switching to natural gas, but that would require mass-scale projects on bringing gas pipes. In the places, where gas is available, the installation of new equipment can cost around $300–400 and not many novostroika residents can afford that. In addition, the cost of gas itself is more expensive than the cost of coal. The second source of air pollution is cars. Their number has been increasing very steadily too as Kyrgyzstan was joining the Eurasian Economic Union and there were multiple speculations about the increasing tariffs on imported cars. Most cars imported to Kyrgyzstan are second-hand and quite old. They do not have proper emission-filtering technologies. The solution to cars would be a proper public transport, but that is in crisis too in Bishkek. The city has a very small stock of buses and trolley-buses. Instead, the majority of residents ride in *marshrutkas* (mini-buses), which themselves pollute the air more than any other vehicles, but they are also often very inconvenient and crowded to ride. So, for many who can afford, cars are a preferred option. Finally, the power plant that supplies the city with hot water is also one of the main sources of pollution.

Yet, if we take into consideration that all three sources are nothing new and that novostroikas, cars and the big pipe were polluting the city for many years now. The cutting of thousands of old trees, which used to clean Bishkek's air and contribute to better air circulation, is likely one of the main reasons why the pollution in the last two years has reached unprecedented levels. Thus, besides the aesthetics and shade during summer times, Albek Ibraimov's vision and his obsession with cutting the trees cost Bishkek residents their health and well-being in cold months as well. Now, not only common citizens, but Parliament deputies are concerned too. Lawmakers can live in fancier houses and ride in expensive cars, but they have to breathe the same air. The introduction of a new law was recently initiated[10] for the protection of green plants and spaces. The proposal was not officially launched yet, but there is a hope that if it passes, it can be of a significant legal aid for green activists.

Dushanbinka through theory

To make sense of Bishkek's story it's useful to reference literature on urban conflict, activism and right to the city. According to Harvey (2003), today, the right to the city is confined in the hands of small political and economic elite, who shape the city after their own desires. The actions of Mayor Ibraimov fit into what Harvey describes as predatory practices and daylight robbery fuelled by the spirit of capitalism. Ibraimov is corrupt, immoral and interested only in the immediate gain, without any long-term perspectives or concerns. The struggle over Dushanbinka then becomes what Mitchel (1995) calls the struggle of ideologies.

The city becomes an instrument and device to produce homogeneity, monotony, geometric isotopy, mental and social misery (Lefebvre 1991) and all this happens due to primitive economic rationality of people in power. Ibraimov represents the violent masculine approach to city based on the brutal force and uncompromising position. Such dominant, politically, economically and even culturally justified ways of thinking must be challenged (Massey 1994).

It is also important that the power of Ibraimov does not originate locally. Massey stresses the need to place cities in the context of economic globalisation, where powerful external sources create new hierarchies of power and influence. Ibraimov by himself has nothing. His actions were empowered by the grant from the Chinese government, by the money, which is the product of global geopolitical struggles. We can see how cities are shaped by the political and economic logic and reinforced using violent power (Lefebvre 1991). Neoliberalism leads to embedding the city into transnational elite networks driven by the principles of economic growth (Swyngedouw 2010).

What is happening in Bishkek is a global trend. Suyungedouw (2010) describes how cities all around the world as sites for political encounter and democratic negotiation are retreating as they are colonised by techno-managerial policies. The new city is post-political post-democratic; it is managed by Foucauldian governmentality based on control and policing.

Finally, one must understand that violence from above is also reinforced by structural violence (Wacquant 2008). In the context of Bishkek, that means unemployment, poverty, inequality and poor infrastructure. When the majority of residents are entrapped in the circle of day-to-day matters of survival and providing for their families, ecological concerns and trees become less relevant to them. The corrupted elites know that they emphasise the economic and/or infrastructural aspects of their projects and they are not worried about the opposing reaction.

To challenge the hegemony of wild global capitalism and its local agents, the right to the city must be reclaimed. This is what Dima Vetoshkin and his friends are engaged in. The crisis of Dushanbinka created a new momentum in the field of local environmental activism and activists employ all kinds of techniques available to them: protests, negotiations, collaboration with other activists, research, dissemination of knowledge, providing expertise, etc.

Activists understand that the right to the city requires a transfer of decision-making from the state to citizens (Purcell 2003). It also demands handling multiple forms of knowledge, knowledge that belongs to the array of actors and demands a collaborative approach to problem solving (Perrone 2011). At the same time, for activists today, it is impossible to reach their goals without an open conflict. The violent power of Ibraimov backed by the money from the Chinese government cannot be opposed with simple technical solutions and negotiation. According to Suyungedouw, true politics includes conflict and is based on inherent antagonism.

The story of Dushanbinka also taught us that online space is unreliable and that revolutions take place in real spaces (Mitchel 1995). Albek Ibraimov's actions on cutting trees generated hundreds of angry posts and critical memes in social media. People express all their anger online and feel as if they have fulfilled their duty. But when the real protest took place in front of the Mayor's office, only 20 people showed up and that convinced the Mayor that there was not going to be much opposition on the ground, so he moved on with his plan on cutting trees.

We also realise that individual human rights cannot challenge the hegemony of neoliberalism. According to Harvey (2003), only collective rights – rights over urban spaces – can bring important results. Specifically, the right for participation in decision making and for appropriation of space can challenge the logic of capitalism. Mitchel shows how this struggle over rights produces space, place and location and how the struggle over a specific place obtains symbolic capital. Dushanbinka became a symbol of state violence and public resistance and as such it mobilised many city residents into different forms of activism.

Conclusions

This story of Dushanbinka includes three main characters: the king inconsiderate of its subjects' demands (President Atambaev), the corrupt governor who pursued his own interests while following the king's orders (Mayor Ibraimov) and the struggling poet who devoted his life to saving trees (green activist Dima Vetoshkin). The story is about the struggle between good and evil. It is a drama that has love, friendship, betrayal, violence, death, despair and rebirth. All within a city scape. Does this drama have a good ending? Justice did take place and now both President Atamabayev and Mayor Ibraimov are in prison, while the poet Dima Vetoshkin and his good friends have recently succeeded in building a broad coalition with local and international activists to revive the Botanical Garden.[11] But the end is still sad: Dushanbinka is not likely to be green again. Its lavishly green character is to remain only in the memories of city residents and in old photographs.

Notes

1 *Current Time*. (2018). 'Goskomitet po natsional'noi bezopasnosti zadershal mera Bishkeka. Ego podozrevayut v koruptsii,' 19 July.
2 I've observed his work since 2017 and last interviewed in November 2019.
3 Department within the Mayor's office responsible for vegetation in Bishkek.
4 Abduvaitova, A. (2018). 'Remont ulic v Bishkeke. Glavnoe o kachestve i kolichestve,' *Kaktus Media*,' 1 May.
5 Skolysheva, M. (2017). 'Graficheskie zametki "Sudbografiya: Dushanbinka,' *Kaktus Media*, 15 December; as well as interviews with urban activists Raushana Sarkeyeva and Gulnar Djurabaeva.
6 Environmental Movement "BIOM" is a public non-profit organisation created in 1993, uniting on a voluntary basis young professionals, scientists and leaders involved in solving environmental problems of the Kyrgyz Republic and Central Asia. http://www.biom.kg/.
7 These are mostly courses for city residents on how to plant trees and other forms of vegetation. Courses take place in the office space of Bishkek Botanical Garden on a weekly or bi-weekly basis.
8 Based on my study of activist communities in 2017.
9 Sabyrbekov, R. (2018). 'Istochniki zagryaznniya vozduha v gorodah Kyrgyzstana,' Center for Environment and Development, AUCA. http://ced.auca.kg/wp-content/uploads/2019/10/Воздух-РС-для-сайта.pdf, accessed on 26 December 2020.
10 The law was initiated by the parliament members Iskender Gaipkulov and Aisuluu Mamasheva in the fall of 2019. It included several main rules for protecting green spaces in the cities: registration of all trees, financial compensation for every cut tree, 20 per cent green space requirement for all new construction projects, and others. The Archa Foundation played an important role in helping to draft the law.
11 Dmitry Vetoshkin's presentation 'Case Study: "Asia's Mountain Garden". A Story of the Botanical Garden's Regeneration in Bishkek' at the Creative Central Asia 2019, 18 February 2019. https://www.youtube.com/watch?v=TuwP7MnsjZE

Bibliography

Harvey, D. (2003) The right to the city. *International Journal of Urban and Regional Research*, 27(4), 939–941.
Lefebvre, H. (1991) *The production of space*. Oxford: Blackwell.
Massey, D. (1994) *Space, place and gender*. University of Minnesota Press, Minneapolis.
Mitchell, D. (1995) There's no such thing as culture: towards a reconceptualization of the idea of culture in geography. *Transactions of the Institute of British Geographers*, 20(1), 102–116.
Perrone, C. (2011) What would a 'DiverCity' be like? Speciation on difference-sensitive planning and living practices, in Perrone, Manella & Tripodi (eds) *Everyday life in the segmented city*, Emerald Group Publishing.
Purcell, M. (2003) Citizenship and the right to the global city: reimagining the capitalist world order. *International Journal of Urban and Regional Research*, 27(3), 564–590.
Swyngedouw, E. (2010) Apocalypse forever? *Theory, Culture & Society*, 27(2–3), 213–232.
Wacquant, L. (2008) *Urban outcasts: A comparative sociology of advanced marginality*. Polity, Cambridge.

PART IV

International Relations

13
RUSSIA AND CENTRAL ASIA
Evolving mutual perceptions and the rise of postcolonial perspectives

Marlene Laruelle

A rise in Russia's presence has been visible in many regions of the world in the past decade, but Central Asia has not really been one of them. There, not only had Russia already accomplished an early 'return' in the previous decade, but its presence has also been partly overshadowed by China's growing power. Nonetheless, the Russia–Central Asia relationship is anything but static: though it may appear stable in many obvious respects, other less visible ones are on the move.

To capture these dynamics, it is necessary to dissociate what is contingent on actors' political will, on one hand, from historical and geographical determinants that will continue to shape decision-making, on the other. Territorial contiguity, for instance, is a geographical given that pushes Russia and Kazakhstan to avoid conflict and remain strategically close no matter which elites are in power. For the four other states, Kazakhstan and then Russia are seen as the pathway to Europe – either symbolically (in cultural terms) or physically (in terms of infrastructure); the prospect of a connection to Europe via the Caspian, South Caucasus and then Turkey, which was devoutly desired by Western observers in the 1990s, thus far seems destined to remain a very minor part of the international landscape. In terms of historical legacy, Russia and Central Asia's shared past of 100–150 years is also a given, even if the passage of years has seen the emergence of new realities that have transformed, reframed and sometimes erased that legacy. The status of the Russian language as a regional *lingua franca* is probably the most enduring feature of that shared past, while the presence of the Russian minority in Kazakhstan is a declining one that will lose its political acuity in the coming decades – among the cohort under the age of 15, Russians represent only 13 per cent of the Kazakhstani population (Laruelle, Royce and Beyssembayev 2019). On the contrary, the status of the Russian language looks likely to survive the ethnic decline of the Russian minority through reappropriation by Central Asians themselves as part of their identity.

Some other features of the relationship are known in the medium term, if not the *long durée*. Such is the case of the migration wave that pushes millions of Central Asians to work in Russia – between three and five million at any given time, depending on how the numbers are calculated and the state of the Russian economy (Schenk 2018). The need for the Central Asian workforce, especially Tajiks and Uzbeks, to go abroad in order to find work will not diminish before 2040–2050; however, the dynamics of the Russian economy could push them to seek out

DOI: 10.4324/9780429057977-13

employment opportunities further from home. New horizons are already identifiable: the Gulf countries, South Korea, Turkey, Europe, etc.

Another medium-term feature relates to Russia's status as a regional hegemon. While Moscow will not cease to be a nuclear power with international ambitions, there are many different ways in which Moscow might express this status in the coming decades, both coercive – forcing the Central Asian states to remain under its geopolitical influence – and cooperative – carried out in agreement with the local authorities, in a way adapted to each country and not exclusive of other alliances. One could also imagine a Russia for whom Central Asian states have become critical partners – a consolidated Eurasian vision of Russia – or, on the contrary, a Russia almost totally disinterested in Central Asia and turned towards its relationship to Europe – a plausible scenario if the rise of xenophobia in Russia impacts decision-making and perceptions of the country's place in Eurasia. Already, a majority of Russians support introducing a visa regime for Central Asia in order to slow down migration – this support peaked at 81 per cent in 2013, then hit its lowest point (54 per cent) in 2017 before rebounding to 64 per cent in 2018 (*The Moscow Times* 2018).

All the other components of the relationship can be described as 'unknowns': the evolution of political regimes in both Russia and Central Asia that may one day reshape the 'authoritarian consensus' (Kneuer and Demmelhuber 2016; Koesel and Bunce 2013; Cameron and Orenstein 2012) that underpins the current friendly relationship; the arrival in power of new generations that have not been socialised in the same Soviet and then post-Soviet framework; cultural transformations of the social fabric that push Russians away from Central Asians (xenophobia, identification with a 'Christian Europe') and Central Asians away from Russians (Islamic identity); and a rising sense among Central Asians that they do not want to be the subordinate partner in a colonial relationship, a perception that could affect relations not only with Russia but also with China and the United States.

Russia's perceptions of Central Asia

Russia considers Central Asia to be one of its most 'secured' regions of influence. Indeed, Moscow has to manage situations that are challenging for its status as a regional power in its western neighbourhood–Ukraine and potentially Belarus–resulting in major tensions with the European Union and the United States. It has also gradually reinvested in more remote spaces of influence, such as the Middle East and Africa, in which its aspirations to great-power status are more rewarded. Central Asia thus did not serve as a test zone for Moscow to try out new forms of hybrid power: Russia tested its portfolio in the Baltic countries and in Ukraine, then in Syria and in Europe, before setting out to conquer more distant regions.

That said, Central Asia remains a key region for Moscow: Russia cannot claim to be a Eurasian power without demonstrating its capacity to exert influence over the region, as symbolised by institutions such as the Eurasian Economic Union (EAEU) and the Collective Security Treaty Organization (CSTO) (see Sakwa and Dutkiewicz 2014; European Politics and Society 2016). As relations with Ukraine have deteriorated for the long term and those with Belarus and the countries of the South Caucasus are shaky, Russia's status as a regional hegemon depends on Central Asia, especially close relations with Kazakhstan. The fact that Turkmenistan and, to a lesser extent, Uzbekistan are averse to Russian regional projects (EAEU, CSTO) does not disturb Russian policy in the region: Moscow can accept the autonomy claimed by Ashgabat and Tashkent as long as they maintain cordial bilateral relations and do not look to draw too close to NATO, a balance that has been maintained thus far.

The stakes confronting Russia in Central Asia have changed little in recent years and can be schematically grouped into three major categories (Skalamera 2017):

- The preservation of Russian oversight of the region, which plays out in different ways depending on the country;
- The securitisation of Russian strategic interests, in particular along the southern borders with Afghanistan via the maintenance of a strong military presence in the two weakest states (Tajikistan and Kyrgyzstan), as well as the strengthening of military ties with Kazakhstan, which reduces Nur-Sultan's strategic autonomy from its northern neighbour;
- The advancement of Russian global interests in the region, but on the condition that the cost–benefit ratio is judged not to be excessive. Moscow invests far more energy in its relations with its western neighbours than it does in Central Asia, and systematically refuses Central Asian demands when they do not directly serve its economic or political interests.

If the fundamental issues with which Russia has been dealing in Central Asia have remained stable, Russian strategic thinking has adapted to reflect the reduction of its capacity to influence and changes in the local geopolitical context:

- Moscow has duly noted Chinese economic domination, which it can counter with institutional tools for regional cooperation (such as the EAEU) but not bilateral trade and investments, given that Russia, too, is in pursuit of Chinese financial support to develop its Far East and Far North. The equilibrium between Moscow and Beijing can be regularly renegotiated in specific sectors (a priori in favour of China) as long as their mutual priority – the exclusion of the United States from the equation and respect for Russia's symbolic supremacy – are guaranteed.
- Moscow has in part turned away from Central Asian energy resources: it no longer needs Turkmen gas since implementing its major Arctic projects around the Yamal peninsula; it is willing to accept that some Kazakh oil will be exported to China or via the Caspian Sea so long as it maintains control over the core of oil exports to Europe; and major Russian companies are gradually upskilling themselves to provide products with greater added value (refineries, power stations) while leaving to China the market of investment in infrastructure.
- Moscow has been able to adjust its regional policy to the bilateralism of the Central Asian states: it deals with Kazakhstan as an ally (albeit of lesser standing); it treats Tajikistan and Kyrgyzstan as clients without much leeway; it is happy with Turkmenistan's autonomy; and it draws closer to post-Karimov Uzbekistan when Tashkent asks for it, but without coercing Uzbekistan to join the regional institutions.
- Lastly, Moscow has adjusted its cultural domination over the region: it cannot fight against demographic evolutions such as the ageing of the Russian minority and the emergence of new generations that speak national languages more than Russian and that are sometimes oriented towards countries other than Russia. However, to slow down the cultural distancing of the Central Asian region, it has boosted its tools of influence, in particular through the media (developing media in Russian and in local languages, making Sputnik in particular one of the most visited websites in the region) and the establishment of large-scale scholarship programmes for young Central Asians.

Central Asia's perceptions of Russia

Unlike Russia's vision of Central Asia, Central Asia's perceptions of Russia have been fairly understudied thus far. The Gallup annual survey of approval of world leaders, conducted throughout the region (with the exception of Turkmenistan), gives us some insights into local public opinion trends over the past decade. Approval of Russia has remained at a very high level (see Figure 13.1), with ebbs and flows depending on the year and the country but nevertheless far above approval of China, which has stood between 40 per cent and 60 per cent approval, and still higher than approval of the United States and Europe, which have ranged from a low of 20 per cent to a high of 50 per cent.

These numbers make Central Asia the most Russophile region of the post-Soviet space. Globally, Tajikistan and Kyrgyzstan position themselves as the main supporters of Russia, followed by Kazakhstan and then Uzbekistan (see Table 13.1). It is worth noting that although the disapproval figures are quite low, this may be offset by the relatively high percentage of 'don't know' responses in Uzbekistan and Kazakhstan, which can be interpreted in different manners, including as unwillingness to answer a politically sensitive question.

These data are useful for constructing a 'big picture' but say little about what approval of Russia looks like and whether certain constituencies have different perspectives on their neighbour. By conducting statistical regression analysis on the Gallup survey data for Kazakhstan, Laruelle and Royce (2019) found, for example, that Kazakhstanis are not defined by an exclusive pro-US/pro-Russian dichotomy but by a divide between those who are more favourable towards external engagement with *all* actors and those who are more isolationist. Moreover, eth-

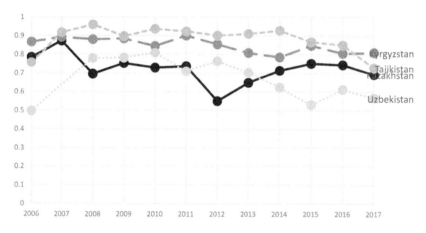

Figure 13.1 Kazakhstan, Kyrgyzstan, Tajikistan and Uzbekistan's approval of the Russian leadership, 2006–2017. Source: Gallup Worldwide Research Data.

Table 13.1 Average Percentage Approval of Russian Leadership, Including 'Do Not Know' Responses, Gallup World Poll Surveys, 2006–2018*

	Approve (%)	Disapprove (%)	Do Not Know (%)	Refused (%)
Kazakhstan	71.29	6.59	19.51	2.62
Kyrgyzstan	85.16	5.58	8.79	0.47
Tajikistan	87.62	4.51	7.17	0.70
Uzbekistan	66.62	7.03	25.99	0.35

Source: Gallup Worldwide Research Data
*Tajikistan World Poll data for 2018 is not available. Tajikistan percentage approval is calculated using the 2006–2017 Gallup World Polls.

nicity *does* affect some of the attitudes under consideration, but its effects are not large enough to produce markedly different opinions among ethnic Kazakhs (supposedly more anti-Russian) and ethnic Russians (supposedly more pro-Russian) on aggregate.

In another study based on perceptions of Russia conducted with ten focus groups (a total of 100 participants) in Kazakhstan – in both Russian and Kazakh and in both Russian-dominated and Kazakh-dominated cities – Laruelle and Royce (2020) found that perceptions of Russia were largely positive yet nuanced, showing that Kazakhstanis are able to both enjoy proximity to Russia and maintain a critical distance from it.

When participants were asked to identify two or three images that they spontaneously associated with Russia, none of them were negative: they evoked spatial or cultural features (wilderness, taiga, bears, Hermitage, Leningrad, Moscow, music, literature, etc.), as well as Russian leaders – with Putin obviously leading, but also Sergey Lavrov and Sergey Shoigu, and all with positive connotations. When asked if they considered Russia a more advanced country than Kazakhstan, around two-thirds answered in the affirmative: Russia was said to have a better economy, technology, science, military and space conquest programmes, as well as more advanced culture, sport and welfare (pensions and maternal capital were among the most frequently mentioned benefits), more freedom of speech, more civility, etc. The other third of the answers were divided between those who indicated that it was impossible to compare the two cultures because they were different and those who said that Kazakhstan, while 'backward' in some respects, had better cultural features than Russia: respect for family and elders, solidarity, hospitality and less alcohol consumption.

When asked about the process by which the Kazakh steppes 'joined' the Russian empire in the nineteenth century, the majority reproduced the standard interpretation of the Kazakh hordes needing the protection of Russia, yet all agreed that colonisation had had ambivalent results: loss of national language, religion and independence, but improved access to education and techniques. When asked about the Soviet era, the majority of participants likewise reproduced the narrative that all Soviet nations were brothers and sisters under Russia's leadership, with only a few denouncing the planned destruction of the Kazakh nation, collectivisation, the exploitation of natural resources, the Semipalatinsk nuclear polygon, etc. When asked about the Soviet Union in general, positive qualifiers dominated (the Soviet Union offered order, discipline, ideology, humanity, spirituality, free education and medicine, high-quality products, etc.); however, almost all participants were explicitly opposed to the idea of recreating the Soviet Union and very happy with independent Kazakhstan.

Moving to contemporary relations, about three quarters of participants declared that they saw Russia as a partner, ally and brother nation (*bratskii narod*) with whom relations were excellent. Some mentioned that Russia acted like a leader or older brother, sometimes not treating Kazakhstan as an equal, but this was never a very sharp critique and several participants even showed understanding. As one explained, 'Yes, they have their imperial wishes … that said, it's understandable and there is no threat in that' (Kazakh-speaking FG, Astana). None saw the Russian minority as a fifth column. Military partnership with Russia was particularly celebrated, while economic dependency was less consensual: participants were divided between those who saw dependency as positive and those who felt that it limited Kazakhstan's prosperity. On questions related to international affairs, almost all participants expressed total support for Russia: an overwhelming majority defended Moscow against the United States, evoking Russia's right to preserve its great-power status and its legitimacy in annexing Crimea; they also often expressed admiration for the way in which the country and its leader have been able to recover and stand up.

Although limited, this research nevertheless offers us some insights into the nuances of Central Asians' perceptions of Russia. Obviously, it would need to be complemented by more in-depth research and large-scale surveys and to be broken out by country. It is, for instance, likely that Uzbek public opinion would be more critical than its Kazakhstani counterpart, while the Kyrgyz audience might be more polarised, with more vocal anti-Russian groups.

Across the region, the constituencies openly critical of Russia are easier to identify than the Russophile majority. These include: (1) the very tiny liberal groups, mostly among urban elites and middle classes in the capitals, that believe that Russia reinforces the authoritarian nature of the local political regimes; (2) the broader nationalist circles, to be found among the middle classes in the capitals *and* in provincial cities, who denounce Russia as a colonial power; and (3) the wider groups animated by different Islamic beliefs – traditionalist Sunnis, Tablighi Jamaat, Muslim Brotherhood, Quranism or Salafism – for which Russia is an atheist and/or Christian country whose culture is incompatible with Islam.

The rise of postcolonial perspectives in Central Asia

One of the most interesting features of the cultural distancing between Russia and Central Asia in recent years has been the rise of a postcolonial perspective on the relationship. During the perestroika years, local nationalist groups were already denouncing the Soviet experience as a colonial one, but this trend was limited to intellectual circles, mostly working on linguistics and literature (on Uzbekistan, see, for instance, Fierman 1985; Critchlow 1991). The majority of these circles expressed pan-Turkic (and sometimes pro-Turkey) solidarity, and occasionally an Islamic sensibility that could not be accommodated by the young Central Asian states after 1991, all of which insisted on their national sovereignty, uniqueness and secularism. This nationalist dissidence was shut down by the Central Asian independent regimes by the mid-1990s not because of the dissidents' statements on Russia but because they were accusing local authorities of representing continuity with Soviet domination and its bureaucratic structures, such as local Communist parties (Kudaibergenova 2016).

Almost three decades later, the broader context has evolved dramatically. While Central Asian governments remain strong proponents of bilateralism, it is now 'good taste' to express at least symbolic support for regional cooperation, especially since the 2016 Uzbek political thaw initiated by Shavkat Mirzyoyev. Secularism remains the official discursive line, but the reality has become much more complex: with the rise of Islamic identity and piety among Central Asians (Jones 2017; Laruelle 2018), and especially the younger generations, the regimes know they have to acknowledge these cultural evolutions and would prefer to embrace them rather than confront them. Moreover, a new generation of nationalist-minded public intellectuals has emerged whose use of social media allows them to reach a broader audience than the literary circles of the perestroika years. They defend ethnonationalist views that have a strong Turkic component – celebrating the greatness of Turkic civilisation and the unique role of their own nation within it – without being pan-Turkic in the sense of calling for a political unity of Turkic peoples and taking even less interest in Erdogan's Turkey as a model to follow (see, on the Kazakh case, Laruelle 2016).

Contrary to their predecessors of the early independence years, these public intellectuals have been able to find a median way in their relationship with the authorities. They position themselves as a kind of 'constructive opposition,' just as Russian nationalists position themselves towards the Putin regime: depending on the situation, they may support the regime as the protector of the nation or be critical and then face administrative troubles or even arrest, but even when they come into conflict with the regime they usually receive gentler treatment by the authorities than pro-Western human rights defenders. They all benefit from some patrons inside the system that share their nationalist vision, and this median position allows them to exist in a quite restrictive political environment. One of these difficult equilibrium moments happened in 2016, when the centenary anniversary of the 1916 Steppe Revolt activated the nationalist groups and all those who wanted to discuss the event in an open and frank environment, whereas the Kazakh and Kyrgyz authorities hesitated between supporting the trend in order to satisfy this segment of their constituencies – as well, in the case of Kazakhstan, to show autonomy from Moscow – and repressing it as a threat to their good relationship with Russia.

These nationalist public intellectuals have also succeeded in blending old-fashioned, perestroika-era claims about the destruction of the national language and the 'genocidal' policies of the Soviet regime with more updated debates on a sovereignty threatened by globalisation, the hidden hands manipulating world affairs – a narrative usually underpinned by anti-Semitism – the murder of the nation's "gene pool" by Western pro-LGBTQI+ policies, etc. These narratives target not only Russia, as the former imperial centre, but also China and the West, whose presence in the region is interpreted as new forms of imperialism (on the Kyrgyz case, see Gullette and Heathershaw 2015). They are perfectly adapted to the new way in which the average citizen consumes news and accesses broader debates in a social media environment that promotes *confrontainment* – focusing on conflict rather than compromise; relying on emotions, polarisation and stereotyping for storytelling; and deploying negative content, incivility, conspiratorial explanations and character attacks.

In academic circles, one may also note the rising interest in postcolonial studies (Kudaibergenova 2016). Whereas 30 years ago it was difficult for local scholars to accept any comparison of Central Asia with the developing world, new generations are more inclined to look towards other postcolonial situations – such as India's relationship with the UK or those of Francophone African countries with France – and to accept comparison with the 'Global South' without feeling humiliated. A new generation of Central Asian experts has been socialised in international organisations working on development aid or financial assistance and has discovered that Asian and African countries are much more advanced in debating these questions. The ability to integrate Central Asia's situation into the wider discussion on postcolonial situations and to engage for the first time in comparative case studies will help to structure a higher-quality debate that will be rooted more in the social sciences and less in emotional reactions – see, for instance, the Esimde project in Bishkek that is devoted to studying the 'blank pages' of national history through memory studies (http://esimde.org/), as well as the research of Alima Bissenova (2016) and Mokhira Suyarkulova (2011).

It is usually agreed that Russia's colonisation of Central Asia in the nineteenth century was part of the broader European colonisation trend in that century, albeit with some unique characteristics, such as territorial contiguity and the earlier case of the conquest of Siberia, which was closer to the US experience of the 'frontier.' Perceptions of the Soviet Union as a colonial experience appear more complex and spark vivid discussions, with elements that support the interpretation that it was classic colonialism (raw material exploitation and mass acculturation patterns, for instance) and others that make it look like a unique experiment (uniform mechanisms of power that also applied to Russia, mass literacy and the indigenisation of elites). One aspect of the discussion that has so far remained overlooked relates to the nature of Russia's 'empire': whether it was a colonial empire, like the French or British ones, or a Habsburg- or Ottoman-style empire, which would presuppose the existence of some shared 'civilisational' features. While this discussion has long raged in Russia between proponents and opponents of Eurasianism, Central Asians' position on whether they do or do not share certain 'civilisational' features with Russia that are not solely the product of colonial domination remains underdiscussed by local public opinions.

Conclusions

Central Asia remains the post-Soviet region most integrated into Russia-led regional economic and strategic institutions and still has very dense bilateral relations with the former center. Although stable in the short term, this relationship is likely to face many unpredictable evolutions in the medium and long terms, related either to the actions of other external actors or to the evolutions of domestic scenes and decision-making.

Paradoxically overlooked because considered obvious, the relationship still remains to be studied in depth. Such an exploration might allow for comparison between Central Asia and the rest of the post-Soviet space – to date, the only comparative studies we have focus on language policy and citizenship issues in Kazakhstan and the Baltic states (see, for instance, Kudaibergenova 2020). It would also open up the huge world of postcolonial studies, which would help us renew our vision of the current relationship – for example, comparing migration from Central Asia to Russia and from Algeria to France as a postcolonial phenomenon (Malakhov 2019). Domestic cultural changes among Russian and Central Asian public opinions likewise merit in-depth studies on the transformations of a shared historical background and its adjustments to new self-perceptions of collective identities.

Bibliography

Bissenova, A., and Medeuova, K. (2016). Davlenie metropolii i tikhii natsionalizm akademicheskikh praktik. *Ab Imperio*. 4: 207–255.

Cameron, D.R., and Orenstein, M.A. (2012). Post-Soviet Authoritarianism: The Influence of Russia in Its 'Near Abroad'. *Post-Soviet Affairs*. 28(1): 1–44.

Critchlow, J. (1991). *Nationalism in Uzbekistan*. Boulder, CO: Westview Press.

Dudoignon, S.A. (1993). Changements politiques et historiographie en Asie Centrale (Tadjikistan et Ouzbékistan, 1987–1993). *Cahiers d'Études sur la Méditerranée orientale et le monde turco-iranien*. 16: 84–135.

Eurasian Politics and Society. (2016). The Eurasian Project in Global Perspectives (special issue). *European Politics and Society*, 17(1).

Féaux de la Croix, J., and Suyarkulova, M. (2015). The Rogun Complex: Public Roles and Historic Experiences of Dam-Building in Tajikistan and Kyrgyzstan. *Cahiers d'Asie centrale*. 25: 103–132.

Fierman, W. (1985). Cultural Nationalism in Soviet Uzbekistan. *Soviet Union*. 12(1): 1–41.

Gullette, D., and Heathershaw, J. (2015). The Affective Politics of Sovereignty: Reflecting on the 2010 Conflict in Kyrgyzstan. *Nationalities Papers*. 43(1): 122–139.

Jones, P. (2017). *Islam, Society, and Politics in Central Asia*. Pittsburgh: University of Pittsburgh Press.

Kneuer, M., and Demmelhuber, T. (2016). Gravity Centres of Authoritarian Rule: A Conceptual Approach. *Democratization*. 23(5): 775–796.

Koesel, K.J., and Bunce, V.J. (2013). Diffusion Proofing: Russian and Chinese Responses to Waves of Popular Mobilizations Against Authoritarian Rulers. *Perspectives on Politics*. 11(3): 753–768.

Kudaibergenova, D.T. (2020). *Toward Nationalizing Regimes: Conceptualizing Power and Identity in the Post-Soviet Realm*. Pittsburgh: Pittsburgh University Press.

Kudaibergenova, D.T. (2016). The Use and Abuse of Postcolonial Discourses in Post-Independent Kazakhstan. *Europe–Asia Studies*. 68(5): 917–935.

Laruelle, M. (2016). Which Future for National-Patriots? The Landscape of Kazakh Nationalism. In: Laruelle, M., ed., *Kazakhstan in the Making: Legitimacy, Symbols and Social Changes*. Lanham, MD: Lexington: 155–180.

Laruelle, M. (2018). *Being Muslim in Central Asia*. Leiden: Brill.

Laruelle, M., and Royce, D. (2019). Kazakhstani Public Opinion of the United States and Russia: Testing Variables of (Un)favorability. *Central Asian Survey*. 38(2): 197–216.

Laruelle, M., Royce, D., and Beyssembayev, S. (2019). Untangling the Puzzle of 'Russia's Influence' in Kazakhstan. *Eurasian Geography and Economics*. 60(2): 211–243.

Laruelle, M., Royce, D. (2020). Love with Nuances: Kazakhstani Views on Russia. *PONARS Eurasia Policy Memo* no. 658 (June) https://www.ponarseurasia.org/love-with-nuances-kazakhstani-views-on-russia/.

Malakhov, V. (2019). Why Tajiks Are (Not) Like Arabs: Central Asian Migration into Russia Against the Background of Maghreb Migration into France. *Nationalities Papers*. 47(2): 310–324.

Mokhira, Suyarkulova. (2011). Becoming Sovereign in Post-Soviet Central Asia: "Discursive Encounters" between Tajikistan and Uzbekistan'. PhD diss. University of St. Andrews.

The Moscow Times. (2018). Xenophobia on the Rise in Russia, Poll Says. *Moscow Times*. Available at: https://www.themoscowtimes.com/2018/08/27/xenophobia-on-rise-in-russia-poll-says-a62681 [Accessed 13 August 2019].

Sakwa, R., and Dutkiewicz, P., eds. (2014). *Eurasian Integration: The View from Within*. London: Routledge.

Schenk, C. (2018). *Why Control Immigration? Strategic Uses of Migration Management in Russia*. Toronto: University of Toronto Press.

Skalamera, M. (2017). Russia's Lasting Influence in Central Asia. *Survival*. 59(6): 123–142.

14
CHINA–CENTRAL ASIA RELATIONS
Re-learning to live next to the giant

Nargis Kassenova

China's relations with Central Asian states – Kazakhstan, Kyrgyzstan, Tajikistan, Turkmenistan and Uzbekistan – have undergone an impressive evolution since 1991. From a limited interaction and trade across the militarised border, they bloomed into strategic partnerships and a myriad of political, economic and cultural ties. This chapter does not aim to give a comprehensive overview of these rich, complex and dynamic relations. Instead, it focuses on four clusters of factors that define them: the continuing salience of the historical experiences of the interaction between China and Central Asia, including the division of the region between the Russian and Chinese empires; the challenge and importance of controlling Xinjiang for consecutive Chinese governments, and the extent to which this influences Beijing's policy towards Central Asian states; the imbalance of power between China and the countries of the region, softened by synergies of their interests and China's way of managing relations with small neighbours; and the changing regional and global orders, with China shaping them, and Central Asian states adapting.

Such a frame helps to reconstruct the logic of China–Central Asia relations and understand drivers and constraints of policies. Historical legacies, informing current attitudes and policies, are considered, and the notion of statecraft is treated as important. The choice of factors allows us to consider relations at different levels of analysis – national, regional and global, and note how developments at these levels feed into each other.

The cast of the past: Between two empires

China recognised the independence of Central Asian states on 27 December 1991, and signed a communiqué establishing diplomatic relations with them in January 1992. On the one hand, it was a fresh start, with new connections to foster and new sets of agreements to sign. On the other, these relations were not developed from scratch but built both on the recent normalisation of Sino-Soviet relations and growing connectivity between China and the Soviet Central Asian republics, as well as on centuries of shared history and interaction. The sides had little familiarity with each other due to decades of estrangement but had inherited memories, perceptions, fears and unresolved territorial disputes.

The shared history that is most relevant for our discussion can be dated back to the eighteenth century, when the Russian and Chinese empires had begun to expand into the region and

DOI: 10.4324/9780429057977-14

the Central Asian khanates chose to manoeuvre in between them. The Kazakh Khanates and the Kokand Khanate had the most intense relations with the Qing Empire.

The Kazakh Khanates sent missions and rendered homage both to the Russian Empire in the west and to the Qing Empire in the east, creating a complex triadic relationship and competing jurisdictions over their lands. The episode that is often referred to is Ablai Khan's bilateral diplomacy which allowed him to build his power drawing on the competition between the two empires (Noda 2016: 70). This is seen as a prototype of Kazakhstan's current multi-vector foreign policy, which includes a special emphasis on maintaining strategic partnerships with Russia and China.

The Kokand city-state became the intermediary of trade between China and Russia after the defeat of the Zungars by the Qing. Using the volatile situation in the region, Kokand khans managed to gain major concessions from Chinese authorities and have their merchants in Xinjiang trade tax-free (Millward 2007: 113). They developed a system of khanate representatives – Aqsakals – in Xinjiang trade posts who collected revenues for the Kokand coffers. Formally, however, the khanate was a vassal of the Qing emperor and part of the Chinese tributary system (Clarke 2011: 25). Unlike the case with the Kazakh Khanates, this historical experience does not seem to inform discussions of Uzbekistan's current foreign policy.

By the end of the nineteenth century, Russia completed its conquest of Central Asia, incorporating both nomadic and settled areas, including the khanates of Khiva and Kokand and the emirate of Bukhara, into the empire. While Russia was on the rise, China was mired in rebellions and external interventions. The former used this circumstance to solidify its territorial gains at the expense of its less fortunate neighbour. They signed several treaties (1860 Treaty of Beijing, 1879 Treaty of Livadia and 1881 Treaty of St. Petersburg) and subtreaties (1884 Protocol of Chuguchak/Tarbagatai being the most important) that defined the borders between the two empires. The two sides made joint surveys and set down new border posts in line with modern nineteenth-century linear borders: 500,000 square kilometres of land.[1]

The border continued to be contested in the twentieth century, but this time by the Soviet Union and the People's Republic of China. The worsening of relations between the two socialist countries and the breakdown of border delimitation negotiations in 1964 led to its militarisation and transformation into a *cordon sanitaire* (Fravel 2005: 70). The tensions reached their peak in 1969 with clashes between Soviet and Chinese troops on the border between Kazakh SSR and XUAR.

The conflict was diffused, but the issue remained unaddressed until the new leader of the USSR Mikhail Gorbachev initiated reopening of negotiations in 1987. Deng Xiaoping's China, increasingly concerned with domestic security challenges, moderated its demands, and the parties signed the 1991 Sino-Soviet border agreement that settled the eastern sector (Siberia), leaving the western (Central Asia-Xinjiang) one for later. Thus, when three Soviet Asian republics – Kazakhstan, Kyrgyzstan and Tajikistan – acquired independence in December 1991, they inherited both the territorial dispute and the negotiation process. Not surprisingly, the border issue became the predominant question in their relations with China (Laruelle and Peyrouse 2012).

Despite the strong initial fears of the newly independent Central Asian states, China assumed a benign stance and continued negotiations in a friendly and accommodating manner. As a result, in 1996, China, Kazakhstan, Kyrgyzstan, Russia and Tajikistan concluded a five-nation 'Agreement on Confidence-Building in the Military Sphere in the Border Areas' in Shanghai. The document emphasised the need to maintain the multilateral nature of inter-state military and security dialogue, ruled out conducting military exercises and stipulated that the concerned sides would invite each other to observe their military exercises.

The demilitarisation and normalisation of the border occurred in parallel with the bilateral border delimitation negotiations. Kazakhstan and Kyrgyzstan signed their treaties with China in 1994 and 1996, respectively, with the last disputed sections settled in 1999. Negotiations with Tajikistan were concluded in 1999, having initially been stalled by the Tajik civil war, which concluded in 1997.

The Kazakh, Kyrgyz and Tajik governments expressed satisfaction with the results and took pride in being able to keep substantial portions of disputed territory. According to Kazakhstan's first president, Nursultan Nazarbayev, and Kyrgyzstan's first president, Askar Akayev, their warm relations with China's president Jiang Zemin helped them secure 50 per cent and 70 per cent of the contested land, respectively (Tokayev 2019: 112).[2] According to Tajik foreign minister Hamrokhon Zarifi, China received about 5 per cent of the disputed land (Gleason 2013: 283).

Notwithstanding good personal relations, Beijing's readiness to compromise with the Central Asian states seems to be part of the general trend of its territorial dispute settlement with neighbours in the 1990s. According to M. Taylor Fravel, it tended to moderate its demands and usually received less than 50 per cent. Somewhat surprisingly, China did not use its power advantage to bargain hard over contested land, especially with weaker neighbours (Fravel 2005: 46). Further, he argues that this is best explained by regime insecurity in frontier regions. In times of ethnic unrest near its international boundaries, China's leaders were much more willing to offer concessions in exchange for cooperation that strengthened their control of these areas, such as denying external support to separatists or affirming recognition of Chinese sovereignty over these regions (Fravel 2005: 50). This explanation fits well with the circumstances under which border negotiations took place, since starting from the late 1980s and throughout the 1990s, Beijing was challenged by outbreaks of unrest in Xinjiang.

However, the public in all three Central Asian states, poorly informed throughout the process, was less happy with the result. In Kyrgyzstan, the demarcation of the border in 2001 triggered protests from parliamentary deputies (claiming that they had not ratified the agreement, and had not even seen it).[3] The arrest of Parliament Deputy Azimbek Beknazarov, one of the most vocal critics, sparked country-wide protests, culminating in bloody clashes in Aksy in March 2002. These events were partially responsible for the fall of the government in the first Tulip Revolution of 2005. In 2010 in the aftermath of the second Tulip Revolution, former president Askar Akayev was stripped of immunity for several crimes, including transfer to China of 'originally Kyrgyz lands.'[4]

In all three countries this remains a sensitive topic, combining the anger about the lost land with the fear of China and its intentions. Protests broke out in cities in Kazakhstan in spring 2016 in reaction to new legislation that allowed for the extension of land leased to foreign companies from ten to 25 years.[5] People were afraid that the change would allow Chinese companies to capture more land. In April 2020, social media networks in the country spread the translation of an article 'Why Kazakhstan Is Trying to Return to China,' published on Chinese online platform *Sohu.com*, that was claiming that Kazakh Khanates and their territories had been part of China. Kazakhstan's Ministry of Foreign Affairs (MFA) issued a note of protest and summoned the Chinese ambassador in the country.[6] Around the same time a similar article titled 'Kyrgyzstan Used to Be China's Land' appeared on Toutiao.com. However, it did not cause a similar reaction from the Kyrgyz government, which might be explained by the fact that it was in the process of asking Beijing for debt relief.[7]

These developments show that despite the resolved territorial disputes, there remain deep insecurities in Central Asian societies with regard to China's possible future intentions. This is not surprising, given that Central Asian states had agency in defining their borders only at the last stage of the centuries-long process of the division of the region between the Russian and

Chinese empires. The timing for negotiations was fortunate for Kazakhstan, Kyrgyzstan and Tajikistan. There is a suspicion, however, that the fortune might change with time.

Xinjiang as a pivot of China–Central Asia relations

Central Asia for Chinese authorities is first and foremost the neighbourhood of Xinjiang, and Beijing's policies towards the region are largely an extension of its governing of this restive province. The main goal is to retain control over Xinjiang and ensure that all the 'stans' surrounding it fully cooperate with Beijing in this endeavour.

The political and social dimensions

Since the second half of the eighteenth century, with some interruptions, the main strategy of Chinese policy makers towards Xinjiang has been its integration with China's interior. The Qing dynasty aimed to create political, economic, cultural and ideological links by establishing Han officialdom, promotion of Han migration and assimilation of local population through Confucius education (Clarke 2011: 27). In the middle of the nineteenth century they established military agricultural colonies that became a unique mechanism of Chinese colonisation. Local rebellions were harshly suppressed and local elites were co-opted, such co-optation being a more generic mechanism. The People's Republic of China used a similar playbook, with Confucianism substituted by communist ideology, and military agricultural colonies reinvented in the form of People's Liberation Army's offshoots – Xinjiang Production and Construction Corps.

The Soviet Union, with its active engagement in Xinjiang before the Sino-Soviet split and limited but unfriendly interest after, had been the biggest external challenge by Chinese leadership. Once the USSR collapsed, the threat of intervention or subversion by the superpower disappeared; however, in its place, there appeared another set of worries. The sudden independence of Central Asians could inspire dreams of self-determination among Muslim minorities of Xinjiang. In 1990, the population of Xinjiang included 1.1 million Kazakhs and 140,000 Kyrgyz, along with 7.2 million Uighurs and 5.7 million Han (Toops 2000: 159). The danger seemed particularly acute, given the outbreaks of unrest in the late 1980s and early 1990s.

Chinese policy makers were worried that new solidarity networks would be formed and that Uighur 'separatists' would find safe haven and support across the border. Fravel quotes a leaked document from the CCP's Central Committee on China's Xinjiang policy instructing the government to secure the border and use diplomacy 'to urge these countries to limit and weaken the activities of separatist forces inside their borders' (Fravel 2005: 79).

Such fears, however, proved to be wrong. Central Asian governments were highly responsive to China's sensitivities. They suppressed Uighur activism in their countries, and from the mid-1990s started extraditing Uighurs fleeing from repression back to China. In 1996 Beijing initiated its first 'Strike Hard' campaign targeting 'splittism' and illegal religious activities and arrested hundreds of Uighurs. Since then such campaigns were carried out with renewed vigour in 2009, 2014 and 2016.

In 2001 Kazakhstan, Kyrgyzstan, Tajikistan and Uzbekistan, together with China and Russia, established a regional security organisation – the Shanghai Cooperation Organization (SCO) – to combat the 'three evils' of terrorism, extremism and separatism. In 2002 they jointly set up the Regional Anti-terrorist Structure (RATS) in Tashkent, in line with the global 'war on terror' triggered by the September 11 attacks on the United States. Starting from 2002 China, with its Central Asian partners, started conducting military exercises emphasising border security and attacks on mock terrorist training camps (Hastings 2011: 909).

While in the 1990s Beijing was worried about insecurity spillovers from Central Asia to Xinjiang, in the 2000s, instead, Central Asia found itself on the receiving side of spillovers of tensions in Xinjiang. In September 2000, Kazakh security services made an armed assault on a group of 'Uighur extremists-separatists-terrorists' in the centre of Almaty, killing four.[8] In August 2016, a suicide bomber rammed the gates of the Chinese embassy in Bishkek, injuring three embassy staff. The authorities blamed the attack on Uighur militants.

Tensions in Xinjiang gradually started affecting domestic politics in Kazakhstan and Kyrgyzstan. Following the 2009 'Strike Hard' crackdown, Uighur activists organised protest rallies in Almaty and Bishkek.[9] Kyrgyz police detained two Uyghur community leaders after they accused China of 'state terrorism' at a rally and called for an independent investigation.[10]

These were unpleasant but manageable outbursts for the governments of Kazakhstan and Kyrgyzstan. The situation worsened with the change of leadership in Xinjiang in 2016. The new Communist Party secretary, Chen Quanguo, transferred to this position from Tibet, stepped up the already harsh security measures aimed at the 'de-extremification' of Muslim minorities, including a massive increase of police forces and the introduction of high-tech surveillance methods (Roberts 2018; Zenz 2019). Hundreds of thousands of people, Kazakhs and Kyrgyz included, were sent to the so-called 're-education centres,' where they were required to 'recite Chinese and Xinjiang laws and policies,' compelled to watch pro-government propaganda videos and renounce their ethnic and religious identities, reciting slogans such as 'religion is harmful' and 'learning Chinese is part of patriotism.'[11]

That 'Strike Hard' policy of the Chinese government previously focused on Uighurs now spread to ethnic Kazakhs and Kyrgyz came as a shock. The public opinion in Kazakhstan and Kyrgyzstan that had been largely indifferent to the travails of Uighurs in neighbouring Xinjiang began to put pressure on the authorities to react to the mistreatment of Kazakh and Kyrgyz minorities in the camps.

The issue was raised both in Kazakh and Kyrgyz parliaments, and the governments promised to monitor the situation. Representatives of the Kazakh MFA held talks with their Chinese counterparts both in Beijing and Astana regarding 'frequent complaints by ethnic Kazakhs about [the] problems they face in the People's Republic of China.' In January 2019, the authorities announced that 2,000 ethnic Kazakhs received permission to leave Xinjiang and move to Kazakhstan.[12]

The mistreatment of co-ethnics in Xinjiang became an important issue for the nationalist movements across the spectrum: from the respectable *Halyk kurulayi* (People's Assembly) in Kazakhstan to the marginal *Kyrk Choro* (Forty kolpaks) group in Kyrgyzstan. The former, on the eve of the presidential elections in 2019, made a statement that included a call for the resolution of the situation with ethnic Kazakhs in Xinjiang.[13] The latter organised protests in front of the Chinese embassy in December 2018, calling on the Chinese government to explain why it had arrested ethnic Kyrgyz and put them in internment camps, and also demanding that the Kyrgyz government expel any Chinese found to be staying in the country illegally.[14]

The economic dimension

Another important facet of Beijing's Xinjiang policy influencing its relations with Central Asian states has been economic development. Since Deng Xiaoping's reforms, Chinese policy makers have seen the latter as the main road to gaining legitimacy and fostering security. In the 1980s, following the example of successful eastern provinces, the authorities in Beijing and Urumqi (XUAR's capital) wanted to embed the development of the province in the broader regional growth, connecting it to Central Asia and South Asia. They tried to encourage foreign investment and cross-border travel.

The warming up of relations with the Soviet Union allowed for resumption of cross-border trade and annual trade fairs alternating between Urumqi and Soviet Central Asia (Clarke 2011: 87). The Kazakh SSR was at the forefront of this process and its head, Nursultan Nazarbayev, visited Xinjiang in July 1991 to explore the potential for further expansion of trade relations. In December 1991, immediately in the aftermath of the collapse of the USSR, China's Minister for Foreign Economic Relations and Foreign Trade Li Lanqing and deputy foreign minister led a government delegation to all Central Asian states and signed trade agreements and accords on establishing diplomatic relations, promising to quickly set up trade representations (Nichol 1995: 157).

China and the Central Asian states started projects to build and upgrade transport infrastructure and took measures to improve border-crossing procedures. In 1992 China and Kazakhstan completed the Urumqi–Almaty rail line and opened the Dostyk–Alatau (Alashankou) border post that rapidly became a busy port handling trade with Xinjiang. Kyrgyzstan opened two border crossings with China – Irkeshtam and Torugart – and by the end of the 1990s became an *entrepôt* for trade in Chinese goods in the region (Pomfret 2019: 242).

Central Asian countries exported coal, iron, steel, cotton, leather and other primary products, and imported manufactured goods from China. Most of these goods were of poor quality, but they helped millions of Central Asians muddle through the difficult times by engaging in trans-border shuttle trade.

The first strategic economic link between China and Central Asia was the acquisition by the Chinese National Petroleum Company of more than 60 per cent of the AktobeMunaiGas Company and the production licence for a number of oil fields in Kazakhstan. Kazakhstan and China agreed to build a 3,000-kilometre pipeline from western Kazakhstan to Xinjiang that would be financed mainly by China. The first section of the pipeline, completed in 2006, started bringing crude oil from western Kazakhstan to the Dushanzi oil refinery. Interestingly, the refinery was first built in 1939 with the help of Soviet financing and technicians, when the goal of Moscow was to make Xinjiang a resource-base for the Soviet economy (Kinzley 2018: 58).

In 2000 Beijing launched the 'Open Up the West' programme to boost the economic development of its western provinces, including Xinjiang, driven by the interlinked goals of 'common prosperity' and 'strengthening of national unity, safeguarding of social stability, and consolidation of border defence' (Goodman 2004: 319). These provinces were allocated more than US$100 billion over the next ten years in support of major infrastructure projects, including regional highway construction, telecommunications, water conservancy, environmental rehabilitation, agricultural expansion, and exploration, extraction, processing and delivery of energy resources (Becqueline 2004: 364). Such massive investments in Xinjiang resulted in the change of image of Xinjiang in the eyes of Central Asians – a previously sleepy backyard province now featured sleek modern city landscapes, good-quality roads and an upgraded international airport in Urumqi, dwarfing capital airports in Central Asian states.

One of the biggest projects envisioned in the programme was the construction of the West–East Gas Pipeline to connect the eastern markets of China with the western resources to allow mutual and sustainable development. The works on the first pipeline started in 2002 and completed in 2004. China engaged in negotiations with Kazakhstan, Uzbekistan and Turkmenistan, and over the period of 2007–2014 they built Central Asia–China Gas Pipeline Lines A, B and C that linked Turkmen gas fields and Khorgos, from where the second and third West–East Gas Pipelines were built in 2008–2012 and 2012–2018, respectively, which accordingly could bring

Central Asian gas across 8,000 kilometres to Shanghai, Hong Kong and Fuzhou.[15] This megaproject integrated Central Asian gas reserves with China's gas market.

The China–Central Asia transport and energy connectivity plans have been overall successful; however, some projects stalled. The 'Open up the West' program envisioned the construction of a railway link from Kashgar to Kyrgyzstan. As of 2020, this project still has not materialised. Line D of the Central Asia–China Gas Pipeline that is planned to pass through Kyrgyzstan and Tajikistan has also experienced a series of delays and remains under construction.[16]

Beijing's efforts to integrate Xinjiang better with China's interior and make it a prosperous link with neighbouring regions, including Central Asia, received a boost with the launch of the Silk Road Economic Belt initiative (SREB) by Xi Jinping on his tour of Central Asia in 2013 which was later transformed into the global Belt and Road Initiative (BRI). This mega-project is discussed in more detail below.

Over the past three decades Beijing's efforts aimed at making Central Asia a benign environment for its Xinjiang policies have been largely successful. Central Asian states are complicit in suppressing Uighur activism. China carried out ambitious and well-funded plans to integrate Central Asia with Xinjiang and core China, with major breakthroughs in the oil and gas sectors, and more projects in the pipeline. However, Beijing's current harsh policies towards Xinjiang Muslim minorities have created negative public opinion,[17] increasingly affecting domestic politics in Kazakhstan and Kyrgyzstan, and causing tensions in the bilateral relations that are likely to last.

The imbalance of power

The imbalance of power between China and the Central Asian states is apparent. If we compare them taking any component of the Comprehensive Power Index, such as territory, population size, natural resources, military might, economic wealth, political power and science and technology, China dwarfs its Central Asian neighbours.[18] Such inequality could translate into boorish and/or arrogant treatment of the weak by the strong.

However, the described earlier border dispute resolution demonstrated the benign approach adopted by China. Instead of threatening weak Central Asian states, it made efforts to ameliorate their fears. Beijing agreed to demilitarise borders. In 1995 it provided security guarantees to Kazakhstan to support its decision to get rid of the substantial nuclear arsenal located on its territory (Xing 2001: 155).

As already discussed, the benign approach to border negotiations with Central Asian states is explained by its insecurities during that particular period. They, however, cannot explain China's consistent treatment of Central Asian states and leaders with a good amount of respect and sensitivity to their insecurities and aspirations. Chinese presidents and other top officials frequently visit the region and receive Central Asian leaders and officials in Beijing. President Xi on his tour to Central Asia in 2013 visited all five capitals. It can be argued that such an approach is a product of Chinese statecraft of managing relations with small countries.

Stating equality, while managing inequality

Chinese official rhetoric emphasises equality and mutual benefit in bilateral relations with other states. This is one of the 'Five Principles of Peaceful Coexistence' officially guiding the People's Republic of China's foreign policy since 1954.[19] In this narrative, China treats other developing states in the spirit of non-imperialist South–South cooperation. Even if this rhetoric does not represent genuine thinking, the country's foreign policy to a considerable extent is bound and framed by it.

Over the past decades, the narrative acquired a new layer drawing on pre-revolutionary periods. According to Feng Zhang, reform-era Chinese leaders from Jiang Zemin onwards have occasionally invoked Confucian concepts in foreign policy statements. President Xi, in particular, made use of ancient Chinese classics, including Confucian texts, one of the hallmarks of his political discourse (Zhang 2015).

In the Confucian world, the Chinese emperor, as the patriarch and ultimate authority of the world, should treat his subjects, including vassals, with moral excellence expressed with humaneness and grace, cherishing the loyal with moral excellence and punishing the disobedient by withholding humaneness and grace and, in the extreme, applying military force. Humaneness or benevolence (*ren*) in treating subjects, including tributary states and peoples, is a key feature. This hierarchical approach seems to fit better China's rise, providing guidance for developing its relations with small countries.

Xi Jinping in his 2014 speech stated that the pursuit of peace, amity and harmony is an integral part of Chinese character, running deep in the blood of the Chinese people, and quoted several ancient Chinese axioms, including 'Seek harmony without uniformity' and 'Replace weapons of war with gifts of jade and silk.'[20] 'Harmony without uniformity' is interchangeable with non-interference in domestic affairs, one of the five principles of China's foreign policy. It features prominently in key bilateral documents signed by China and Central Asian states. The 'gifts of jade and silk' co-optation mechanisms can also be noted in China's relations with Central Asian states. The former provides the latter with concessional loans and grants with a strong political expediency element.

Central Asian states have largely adapted to the reality of powerful and ambitious China. From the early days of independence they adopted 'multi-vector' foreign policies (with Turkmenistan opting for a more extraordinary neutrality), aimed at balancing the interests and influences of three main external powers, Russia, China and the United States. Such an approach is reminiscent of the Central Asian khanates trying to balance their big neighbours in the eighteenth and nineteenth centuries. The twenty-first-century game has a different structure and actors. Central Asian states, no matter how weak, are not afraid of being conquered by China. Although, as mentioned earlier, we see indications that people in Kazakhstan and Kyrgyzstan have concerns about potential loss of territory. The most clear and present danger, however, is excessive economic dependence on China and its translation into political influence.

Economic imbalance

China has become one of their top three trade partners. It is a major investor in several sectors, and the biggest provider of loans to Kyrgyzstan, Tajikistan and Turkmenistan. The increase in the volume, spectrum and intensity of economic cooperation is an overall positive development. Challenges can arise when the dependence of a small country on access to markets and finances of a bigger one allows the latter to impose policies and decisions that it wouldn't have made otherwise. The fear that economic dependence can have significant political implications is more acute, given the fact that Chinese business is not separated from the state.

The five Central Asian countries have different sets of dependencies and vulnerabilities regarding China (Reeves 2016). Kazakhstan is the biggest economy and China's biggest economic partner in the region. From pre-independence times, it has always been eager to tap into opportunities of cooperation with its eastern neighbour. At the same time Kazakhstan's policy makers have been eager to maintain the diversity of trade partners and investors in line with the multi-vector foreign policy. In the most strategic and lucrative oil and gas sector, Western, Chinese and Russian companies have significant shares, and none of them dominates the field. Chinese companies produce about a quarter of Kazakh oil and Kazakhstan exported 14 per cent of its crude oil to China in 2019.[21]

China is an important partner in developing the transport and industrial capacity of the country. Kazakhstan prides itself on investing its own money in transport infrastructure. Out of the 16 highways started in 2017, nine are financed by the government of Kazakhstan, five are financed in cooperation with international financial institutions and two are funded by China's EXIM Bank. Kazakhstan's national railway company, Kazakhstan Temir Zholy (KTZ), owns 51 per cent of the stakes in the Khorgos dry port, planned as a major hub of Eurasian transport network. Kazakhstan's external debt to China is modest, and in December 2019 it stood at $10.5 billion, or around 7 per cent of its overall debt.

A similar dynamic can be seen in China–Uzbekistan relations. Uzbekistan has a diversified pool of foreign investors, with Chinese, South Korean, Russian and Western companies well represented. However, its export of gas is less balanced. In 2018 China accounted for 48 per cent of its total export of 'blue fuel' (Pirani 2019: 15). China is also the biggest lender to Uzbekistan, accounting for $2.8 billion (or 20.6 per cent of total external public debt) in 2019 (Ministry of Finance of Uzbekistan 2019: 24).[22]

The negative implications of the economic imbalance are more pronounced in cases of Kyrgyzstan, Tajikistan and Turkmenistan. Kyrgyzstan and Tajikistan took major loans from China's EXIM Bank for various infrastructure projects, such as road construction and rehabilitation, modernisation and construction of transmission lines, renovation of thermal plants and others. In 2019, Bishkek's public debt to China stood at $1.7 billion (or 46 per cent of the total public debt), and Dushanbe's – at 1.5 billion (or 52 per cent of the total public debt).[23]

As for Turkmenistan, it strongly depends on Chinese investments and China's demand for gas. Chinese companies – CNPC and Petronas – are responsible for more than a quarter of its gas output. In 2018 gas exports to China accounted for 93 per cent of total export (Pirani 2019: 2). Turkmenistan's external debt situation is not clear, but reportedly Ashgabat borrowed around $9 billion from China to finance the development of the country's gas deposits and build a gas pipeline.[24]

While governments seem to be rather confident in their own ability to manage power imbalances with China, the public is more nervous, particularly in Kazakhstan and Kyrgyzstan. As already mentioned, fears of China's territorial claims are widespread in these two Central Asian countries. Interestingly, in Tajikistan, where Chinese farmers are leasing 18,000 hectares, such fears seem to be absent or weak.[25] The danger of debt dependence on China is another popular topic throughout the region.[26] Even in Kazakhstan, despite the low level of official public debt to China, there is concern about the implications of Chinese loans. The already mentioned *Halyk kurultayi* movement in their statement on the eve of the 2019 presidential elections demanded to stop taking loans from China.

China and Central Asian states operate in conditions of normative equality, regularly emphasised in China's official rhetoric, but structural de facto inequality. So far, the governments of the region accepted the situation and benefited from China's superiority-based generosity, while also trying to partially hedge it through their multi-vector foreign political and economic policies. However, there are constraints on this type of relationship, and one of them is the public fear of the implications of such massive imbalance of power. Such views are present throughout the region but are particularly apparent in Kazakhstan and Kyrgyzstan.

Changing regional and global order

China's relations with Central Asian states are also shaped by how the former conceives and shapes the regional and global order, and the ways the latter adapt and manoeuvre. In case of the regional order, Chinese policy makers can draw on historical experiences and accumulated statecraft of managing relations with peripheral states. In the case of global order, there is no such background and they have to chart their path as they go or, using Deng Xiaoping's expression used to describe China's economic reform course, 'cross the river by feeling the stones.'

Regional order: Competition with Russia

For centuries, the destiny of Central Asians was shaped by a competition, sometimes pronounced, sometimes latent, between Russia and China. They have been the main actors and shapers of the regional order for Central Asian states. Changes in their policies and capacities to implement them define the features of the region.

From the time of the collapse of the USSR, China has been respectful of Russia's interests in Central Asia, despite the weakness of the northern neighbour in the 1990s and the growing gap in their fortunes and capacities (Zhao 2007: 180; Kerr 2010: 131). In his 2013 speech in Astana Xi Jinping stated that China stands 'ready to enhance communication and coordination with Russia and all Central Asian countries to strive to build a region of harmony.'

The SCO became an arrangement convenient for all parties to manage security cooperation in the region, and less so for economic cooperation. Beijing and Moscow led the SCO Peace Mission exercises, first conducted in 2005. China started training Central Asian officials and military personnel. According to Rafaello Pantucci, these mechanisms helped 'socialize Chinese security norms and build links with Central Asia' (2019: 63).

The Eurasian 'colour revolutions' (Georgia in 2003, Ukraine in 2004, and Kyrgyzstan in 2005) first threatened Beijing and Moscow, but in the end strengthened their positions in Central Asia because local authoritarian regimes got scared too. In 2005, SCO countries issued a statement calling for the United States to set a timetable for the withdrawal of military forces from the region.[27] The 'Arab spring' reinforced that dynamic. Tellingly, at the 2012 SCO summit, the Chinese then deputy foreign minister, Cheng Guoping, stated that China would 'absolutely not allow the unrest that happened in West Asia and North Africa to happen in Central Asia' (Mariani 2013: 9).

The informal 'division of labor,' with Russia responsible for security and China in charge of economic development, was gradually challenged. At the 2012 SCO summit, a rule was adopted providing for a collective response to events 'threatening the peace, stability and security of a member state or of an entire region' (Mariani 2013: 14). In 2016 China, together with Afghanistan, Pakistan and Tajikistan, created the Quadrilateral Coordination and Cooperation Mechanism to discuss border security and counterterrorism, and the same year there appeared media reports about the deployment of Chinese People's Armed Police troops on the Afghan–Tajik border (van der Kley 2019: 73).

China also used the SCO frame for its economic expansion into the region. Some of the proposals it put forward, such as establishing a free-trade zone, joint SCO fund and development bank, were not successful. Beijing's direct offers of concessionary loans to Central Asian states at SCO summits were gratefully accepted. In 2004 President Hu Jingtao announced China's readiness to lend $900 million. In 2009, during the global economic crisis, at another SCO summit he offered $10 billion.

Beijing's initiatives to set up special SCO development funds have not been supported by Moscow, guarding its own economic integration project. In 2010, Russia, together with Belarus and Kazakhstan, launched the Customs Union with unified tariffs for imports from third countries. In 2015 it transformed into the Eurasian Economic Union, aiming for freedom of movement of goods, people, capital and services, and included Kyrgyzstan and Armenia as members. The creation of the Customs Union was watched with concern by Chinese policy makers and businesses trading with Kazakhstan and Kyrgyzstan. However, ultimately it did not hinder China–Central Asia economic cooperation.

As already mentioned, in 2013 Chinese president Xi Jinping, on his tour of Central Asia and visiting Kazakhstan's capital Astana (renamed Nur-Sultan in 2019), announced Beijing's new international initiative – the Silk Road Economic Belt (SREB). He outlined the five priorities of the SREB: advancing regional cooperation through policy communication and coordination; improving road connectivity (cross-border transportation infrastructure) between East Asia, West Asia and South Asia; promoting unimpeded trade through trade and investment facilitation, removing trade barriers, reducing trade and investment cost, and increasing the speed and quality of regional economic flows; enhancing monetary circulation through realising local currency convertibility and settlement under current and capital accounts; and people-to-people exchanges.[28]

The initiative was received with much enthusiasm by Central Asian governments since it promised more resources coming their way for infrastructure development and integration into international production value chains and trade flows. Kazakhstan, Kyrgyzstan, Tajikistan and Uzbekistan linked their national development strategies to the BRI. In 2015 the Kazakh and Chinese prime ministers announced that their countries would develop a plan for linking the SREB and Kazakhstan's 'Nurly Zhol' economic development plan, featuring three priorities: transport infrastructure, energy and manufacturing (Kassenova 2017: 110). The main goals of the 'National Development Strategy of the Republic of Tajikistan for the Period up to 2030' (adopted in 2016), such as energy security, becoming a transit country and food security, fully aligned with already well-developed areas of China–Tajikistan cooperation.[29] Under President Shavkat Mirziyoyev, Uzbekistan was also eager to align its 'Strategy of Actions in Five Priority Directions of Development of Uzbekistan for 2017–21.' In a joint statement made by President Xi and President Mirziyoyev in May 2017, the two sides promised to strengthen cooperation in the context of BRI in trade, investment, finance, transport and communication, agriculture, industrial parks and others.[30]

Given the triumphant launch of the BRI, Moscow had to find an accommodation with it. In 2015, President Putin and President Xi made a joint declaration on cooperation in aligning the Eurasian Economic Union with the Silk Road Economic Belt, stating support for each other's megaprojects.[31] Unsurprisingly, this cooperation proved to be modest and slow.[32]

Global order: Certain rise, uncertain implications

Over the past decade, China has emerged as a global superpower. Beijing takes preparation for the world leadership role seriously and increasingly preoccupies itself with matters of global governance, trying to decide what role China should play, what needs to be maintained and what needs to be changed. It positions itself as a provider of public goods, with the SCO being its first laboratory for multilateral cooperation. Since 2013 it has been promoting the BRI, to provide transcontinental connectivity, as China's major contribution to regional and global development and security. The role for Central Asian states in this transforming global order is to participate in China-created international organisations and support China's positions in the incumbent global order, most importantly in the United Nations Organization.

As already discussed, Central Asian states have been fully onboard with the BRI, and it is not by accident that the initiative was announced in the region. All five governments send representatives to the high-profile BRI fora hosted by the Chinese government and are members of the Asian Infrastructure Investment Bank (AIIB).

In the United Nations, they share with China the normative agenda of non-interference in domestic affairs and state-centric narratives and norms.[33] Central Asian states, together with China and Russia, and other members of the SCO, co-sponsored a 'Code of Conduct for Information Security' submitted to the UN General Assembly in 2015. The code underlined the states' 'right to independent control of information and communications technologies,' and the role of the state in 'encouraging a deeper understanding by all elements in society, including the private sector and civil-society institutions, or their responsibility to ensure information security.'[34]

While they are on the same page with China in the area of human rights, it is more difficult for some Central Asian states to endorse Beijing's recent policies in Xinjiang because it involves their co-ethnic groups. In January 2019 Kazakhstan, Kyrgyzstan and Uzbekistan abstained from signing either of the two letters prepared by different coalitions of countries and sent to the UN Human Rights Council, one denouncing China's policies in Xinjiang, the other supporting them. The letter of support, however, was signed by Tajikistan and Turkmenistan.[35]

The forceful approach to the inter-ethnic issues in Xinjiang can be considered as representative of Xi Jinping's governance philosophy. Deng Xiaoping's 24-character strategy, 'Observe calmly; secure our position; cope with affairs calmly; hide our capacities and bide our time; be good at maintaining a low profile; and never claim leadership,' guided China's foreign policy under the second, third and fourth generations of Chinese leaders. However, with the ascent to power of Xi Jinping, Beijing adopted a more assertive approach, claiming a global leadership position that would fulfil the 'Chinese dream' of national rejuvenation. The implications of this change for China, the world and Central Asian neighbours are not clear.

Conclusion

Relations between China and Central Asian states were not developed from scratch. They could and had to draw on pre-Soviet and Soviet history of interaction, including its most dramatic moments. Territorial and peoples' divisions in broader Central Asia still create insecurities and tensions in the region.

Beijing's policy towards Central Asia is to a great extent defined by the interests of security and developing Xinjiang. While security and development are perceived as interlinked by Chinese policy makers, each of them pushes for different approaches: stricter control for strengthening the former, and liberalisation and opening up for the latter. This contradiction has resulted in oscillations between opening and closing of Xinjiang over the past several decades, with an extreme swing to harsh policies since 2016 till today. The mass internment of Muslim minorities, who happen to share ethnic and cultural affinity with peoples of Central Asia, has created tensions likely to have serious and long-term implications for bilateral relations, particularly with Kazakhstan and Kyrgyzstan.

Another source of tension is the power imbalance between China and Central Asian states. While they are equal nation-states from the international law perspective, and Chinese official rhetoric regularly stresses the principle of equality, there is full realisation of unequal stature and capacities. This power imbalance informs the policies of all the parties. China is drawing on the millennia-long statecraft of managing relations with small neighbours through a benign attitude and co-optation mechanisms.

Central Asian states try to hedge China's growing influence through their multi-vector foreign policies. States with more capacity – Kazakhstan and Uzbekistan – can do it more successfully, while less endowed states, like Kyrgyzstan and Tajikistan, find themselves more vulnerable and dependent. The case of Turkmenistan is a special one, with the poverty of statecraft largely responsible for its strong dependence on China.

China–Central Asia relations are imbedded in the regional and global contexts.

They entered the twenty-first century with the tide turned in favour of China. This shift is the biggest structural factor of current China–Central Asia relations. Latent competition between Russia and China defines the regional order development. China's rise and determination to play the role of a global leader gives Central Asian states additional cards as constituents of the global order. However, the growing multipolarity also ironically challenges their multi-vector foreign policies. It will require a lot of statecraft for the Central Asians to benefit from opportunities and successfully deal with challenges in their relations with China.

Notes

1 National Palace Museum. The lost frontier – treaty maps that changed Qing's northwestern boundaries [Viewed 10 December 2019]. Available: http://www.npm.gov.tw/exh98/frontier/en2.html
2 Gezitter.org. Connection bridge. Askar Akayev, ex-president of Kyrgyz Republic: 'I made mistakes in selecting cadre' (in Russian), 12 February 2015 [Viewed 15 January 2020]. Available: https://www.gezitter.org/interviews/37298_most_svyazi_askar_akaev_eks-prezident_kr_ya_dopustil_nedostatki_v_otbore_kadrov/
3 Pannier, B. Kyrgyzstan: Parliament angry over demarcation of Sino-Kyrgyz border. RFE/RL, 29 June 2001 [Viewed 15 January 2020]. Available: https://www.rferl.org/a/1096823.html
4 Glushkova, S. Tajikistan transferred part of the land to China (in Russian). Radio Azattyq, 6 October 2011 [Viewed 15 January 2020]. Available: https://rus.azattyq.org/a/china_tajikistan_kazakhstan_kyrgyzstan_land/24350707.html
5 BBC News. Kazakhstan's land reform protests explained. 28 April 2016 [Viewed 15 October 2019]. Available: https://www.bbc.com/news/world-asia-36163103
6 Radio Azattyq. Publication on Kazakhstan's 'belonging to China' led to a note of protest (in Russian). 14 April 2020 [Viewed 14 April 2020]. Available: https://rus.azattyq.org/a/kazakstan-and-china-note-of-protest/30553220.html
7 RFE.RL. Kyrgyzstan asks China for debt relief amid economic strain of pandemic. 15 April 2020 [Viewed 15 April 2020]. Available: https://www.rferl.org/a/kyrgyzstan-jeenbekov-china-debt-xi-coronavirus/30555118.html
8 IAC Eurasia. Night military operation in the centre of Almaty (in Russian). Khabar, 28 September 2000 [Viewed 10 January 2020]. Available: https://www.neweurasia.info/archive/2000/ka_press/09_28_khabar-28.html
9 Golovnina, M. Uighurs in Kazakhstan rally against China crackdown. Reuters [Viewed 15 January 2020]. Available: https://www.reuters.com/article/us-uighurs-kazakhstan-sb/uighurs-in-kazakhstan-rally-against-china-crackdown-idUSTRE56I0SE20090719
10 RFE/RL. Kyrgyzstan Uyghur leaders detained after protest. 10 August 2009 [Viewed 20 October 2019. Available: https://www.rferl.org/a/Kyrgyzstan_Uyghur_Leaders_Detained_After_Protest/1796440.html
11 Human Rights Watch. China: Free Xinjiang 'Political Education' Detainees, 10 September 2017 [Viewed 15 October 2019]. Available: https://www.hrw.org/news/2017/09/10/china-free-xinjiang-political-education-detainees
12 Radio Azattyk. Astana: Two thousand ethnic Kazakhstan are allowed to leave Xinjiang (in Russian). 10 January 2019 [Viewed 10 January 2019]. Available: https://rus.azattyk.org/a/29700839.html
13 Toiken, S. Nazarbayev, election boycott, land issue. What was discussed at the 'kurultai'? (in Russian). 1 June 2019 [Viewed 2 June 2019]. Available: https://rus.azattyq.org/a/kazakhstan-nur-sultan-kurultay/29976007.html
14 Wood, C. Why did Kyrgyz stage a protest outside the Chinese embassy? The Diplomat. 29 December 2018 [Viewed 15 January 2020]. Available: https://thediplomat.com/2018/12/why-did-kyrgyz-stage-a-protest-outside-the-chinese-embassy/

15 CNPC. West – East Gas Pipeline project (2002–2013). Special report on social responsibility. 2014 [Viewed 13 December 2019]. Available: http://www.cnpc.com.cn/en/cs2012en/201407/7572081fc158451cbbf5a835f6428b2d/files/ea40888641b5423ba32206cdb15441fc.pdf
16 Pannier, B. Tajik claim of pipeline progress is welcome news in Turkmenistan. RFE.RL, 31 January 2020 [Viewed 1 February 2020]. Available: https://www.rferl.org/a/tajik-claim-of-pipeline-progress-is-welcome-news-in-turkmenistan/30410670.html
17 For a sample of negative public opinion see Radio Azattyk *Serikzhan Bilash na svobode. Chto proiskhodilo v sude I vokrug nego? Radio Azattyk*, 16 August 2019 [viewed 11 August 2020]. Available: https://rus.azattyq.org/a/kazakhstan-bilash-court/30113833.html
18 The concept of Comprehensive National Power, first developed by American scholars, was adopted by the Chinese foreign policy community during the Deng Xiaoping period and developed with rigour since then.
19 Other principles are respect for territorial integrity and sovereignty; non-aggression; non-interference in each other's internal affairs; and peaceful coexistence.
20 Varrall, M. Chinese worldviews and China's foreign policy. Lowy Institute. 26 November 2015 [Viewed 27 February 2020]. Available: https://www.lowyinstitute.org/publications/chinese-worldviews-and-china-s-foreign-policy
21 Trading economics. Kazakhstan exports by country [Viewed 15 January 2020]. Available: https://tradingeconomics.com/kazakhstan/exports-by-country
22 Ministry of Finance of the Republic of Uzbekistan. Overview of the state and dynamic of state debt of the Republic of Uzbekistan. Third quarter of 2019 [Viewed 1 March 2020]. Available: https://www.mf.uz/media/file/euro/2019.pdf
23 Chorshanbiyev, P. The size of Tajikistan's debt to China exceeded $1.5 billion. This is more than half of the external state debt of the country (in Russian). Asia-plus, 28 October 2019 [Viewed 16 December 2019. Available: https://asiaplustj.info/ru/news/tajikistan/economic/20191028/razmer-dolga-tadzhikistana-pered-kitaem-previsil-15-mlrd-eto-bolee-polovini-vneshnego-gosdolga-strani
24 Jakoboswski, J. and Marszewski, M., (2018). Crisis in Turkmenistan: A Test for China's Policy in the Region, OSW Commentary, 31 August 2018 [Viewed 1 September 2019]. Available from: https://www.osw.waw.pl/en/publikacje/osw-commentary/2018-08-31/crisis-turkmenistan-a-test-chinas-policy-region-0
25 Aminjonov, R. and Kholmatov, M. The Belt and Road Initiative in Central Asia: A view from Tajikistan. The Impact of the Belt and Road Initiative in Central Asia and the South Caucasus: the 'inside-out' perspectives of experts from the region. The Emerging Markets Forum. 27–29 January 2019 [Viewed 14 March 2019]. Available: http://www.emergingmarketsforum.org/wp-content/uploads/2019/02/Inside-Out-Compilation-2018-12-21-FOR-WEB-WITH-HYPERLINKS.pdf
26 Asanov, B. Kyrgyzstan and Chinese credits: worse things ahead? (in Russian). Radio Azattyk, 29 August 2018 [Viewed 30 August 2018]. Available: https://rus.azattyk.org/a/kyrgyzstan_kitay_kredity_dolg/29459979.html
27 Parsons, R. Central Asia: China-Russia block challenges U.S. in the region. RFE/RL, 25 October 2005 [Viewed 20 March 2020]. Available: https://www.rferl.org/a/1062378.html
28 Ministry of Foreign Affairs of the People's Republic of China. Speech by H.E. Xi Jinping, President of the People's Republic of China at Nazarbayev University. Astana, 7 September 2013 [Viewed 15 December 2019]. Available: https://www.fmprc.gov.cn/mfa_eng/wjdt_665385/zyjh_665391/t1078088.shtml
29 Agency of Social Insurance and Pension under the Government of the Republic of Tajikistan. National development strategy of the Republic of Tajikistan for the period up to 2030. Dushanbe, 2016 [Viewed 14 March 2019]. Available: https://nafaka.tj/images/zakoni/new/strategiya_2030_en.pdf
30 Uza.uz. Joint statement of the Republic of Uzbekistan and the People's Republic of China on further deepening of relations of the comprehensive strategic partnership (in Russian). 18 May 2017 [Viewed 13 February 2019]. Available: http://uza.uz/ru/politics/sovmestnoe-zayavlenie-18-05-2017?m=y&ELEMENT_CODE=sovmestnoe-zayavlenie-18-05-2017&SECTION_CODE=politics
31 Site of the President of Russia. Press statements following Russian-Chinese talks, 8 May 2015 [Viewed 15 May 2015]. Available: http://en.kremlin.ru/events/president/transcripts/49433
32 Kassenova, N. More politics than substance: Three years of Russian and Chinese economic cooperation in Central Asia. Foreign Policy Research Institute. 24 October 2018 [Viewed 24 October 2018]. Available: https://www.fpri.org/article/2018/10/more-politics-than-substance-thee-years-of-russian-and-chinese-economic-cooperation-in-central-asia/

33 Hart, M. and Johnson, B. Mapping China's Global Governance Ambitions. Center for American Progress. 28 February 2019 [Viewed 15 November 2019]. Available: https://www.americanprogress.org/issues/security/reports/2019/02/28/466768/mapping-chinas-global-governance-ambitions/
34 United Nations Digital Library. Letter dated 9 January 2015 from the Permanent Representatives of China, Kazakhstan, Kyrgyzstan, the Russian Federation, Tajikistan and Uzbekistan addressed to the Secretary-General, United National General Assembly [Viewed 24 April 2019]. Available: https://digitallibrary.un.org/record/786846?ln=en
35 Putz, C. Which countries are for or against China's Xinjiang policies? The Diplomat, 15 July 2019 [Viewed 15 July 2019]. Available: https://thediplomat.com/2019/07/which-countries-are-for-or-against-chinas-xinjiang-policies/

References

Bechquelin, N. (2004) 'China's Campaign to 'Open Up the West': National, Provincial and Local Perspectives'. *The China Quarterly*, 178: 358–78.
Clarke, M. (2011) *Xinjiang and China's Rise in Central Asia – A History*. London and New York: Routledge.
Fravel, M. (2005) 'Regime Insecurity and International Cooperation. Explaining China's Compromises in Territorial Disputes'. *International Security*, 30 (2): 46–83.
Gleason, G. (2013) 'Tajikistan-China Border Normalization'. In B. Elleman, S. Kotkin, and C. Schofield, eds. *Beijing's Power and China's Borders. Twenty Neighbors in Asia*. Armonk: M.E. Sharpe.
Goodman, D. (2004) 'The Campaign to "Open Up the West."' *The China Quarterly*, 178: 317–34.
Hastings, J. (2011) 'Charting the Course of Uyghur Unrest'. *The China Quarterly*, 208: 893–912.
Kassenova, N. (2017) 'China's Silk Road and Kazakhstan's Bright Path: Linking Dreams of Prosperity'. *Asia Policy*, 24: 110–16.
Kerr, D. (2010) 'Central Asian and Russian Perspectives on China's Strategic Emergence'. *International Affairs*, 86 (1): 127–52.
Kinzley, J. (2018) *Natural Resources and the New Frontier. Constructing Modern China's Borderlands*. Chicago, IL: University of Chicago Press.
Kley, van der D. (2019) 'China's Security Activities in Tajikistan and Afghanistan's Wakhan Corridor'. In: N. Rolland, ed. *Securing the Belt and Road Initiative. China's Evolving Military Engagements along the Silk Roads*. The National Bureau of Asian Research. NBR Special Report No. 80.
Laruelle, M. and Peyrouse, S. (2012) *The Chinese Question in Central Asia. Domestic Order, Social Change and the Chinese Factor*. London: Hurst & Company.
Mariani, B. (2013) *China's Role and Interests in Central Asia*. London: Saferworld.
Millward, J. (2007) *Eurasian Crossroads. A History of Xinjiang*. London: Hurst & Company.
Nichol, J. (1995) *Diplomacy in the Former Soviet Republics*. Westport, CT: Greenwood Publishing Group.
Noda, J. (2016) *The Kazakh Khanates between the Russian and Qing Empires*. Leiden: Brill.
Pantucci, R. (2019) 'The Dragon's Cuddle: China's Security Power Projection into Central Asia and Lessons for the Belt and Road Initiative'. In N. Rolland, ed. *Securing the Belt and Road Initiative. China's Evolving Military Engagements along the Silk Roads*. The National Bureau of Asian Research. NBR Special Report No. 80.
Pirani, S. (2019) *Central Asian Gas: Prospects for the 2020s*. Oxford Institute for Energy Studies, OIES Papers: NG 155. https://www.oxfordenergy.org/wpcms/wp-content/uploads/2019/12/Central-Asian-Gas-NG-155.pdf
Pomfret, R. (2019) *The Central Asian Economies in the Twenty-First Century: Paving a New Silk Road*. Princeton: Princeton University Press.
Reeves, J. (2016) *Chinese Foreign Relations with Weak Peripheral States. Asymmetrical Economic Power and Insecurity*. London: Routledge.
Roberts, S. (2018) 'The Biopolitics of China's 'War on Terror' and the Exclusion of the Uyghurs'. *Critical Asian Studies*, 50 (2): 232–58.
Tokayev, K. (2019) *Light and Shadow* (in Russian). Almaty: Meloman Publishing.
Toops, S. (2000) 'The Population Landscape of Xinjiang/East Turkestan.' *Inner Asia*, 2 (2): 155–70.
Xing, G. (2001) 'China and Central Asia'. In R. Allison and L. Jonson, eds. *Central Asian Security: The New International Context*. London: Royal Institute of International Affairs.

Zenz, A. (2019) "'Thoroughly Reforming Them towards a Healthy Heart Attitude': China's Political Re-education Campaign in Xinjiang'. *Central Asian Survey*, 38 (1): 102–28.

Zhang, F. (2015) 'Confucian Foreign Policy Traditions in Chinese History.' *The Chinese Journal of International Politics*, 8 (2): 197–218.

Zhao, H. (2007) 'Central Asia in China's Diplomacy.' In E. Rumer, D. Trenin, and H. Zhao, eds. *Central Asia. Views from Washington, Moscow, and Beijing.* Armonk, NY: M. E. Sharpe.

15
U.S. POLICY AND CENTRAL ASIA

Charles E. Ziegler

American foreign policy towards Central Asia has been largely derivative of its relations with Russia and China, linked to U.S. anti-terrorist operations in Afghanistan, and connected to American interests in energy and democracy promotion. The emphasis placed on each of these interests has varied over the past three decades, and U.S. policy has often reflected contradictory impulses. However, the location of Central Asia at the nexus of great power competition, energy and the threat of terrorism has elevated this remote region to a relatively outsized position in U.S. foreign policy. In other words, geopolitical strategic considerations, together with skillful diplomacy on the part of Central Asian leaders, have enabled these small, landlocked countries to punch well above their weight in global politics, and to command Washington's attention.

There have been at least three distinct phases in U.S. policy towards Central Asia. In the first decade (1991–2001) Washington sought to establish sovereignty and independence for these new states, secure nuclear weapons and materials located in the former Soviet republics, assist in the transition towards more democratic and market-oriented systems, and promote opportunities for American businesses. In the second phase (2001–2014) security concerns dominated as Central Asia became a key staging point for America's campaign in Afghanistan following the 9/11 terrorist attacks. U.S. bases in Uzbekistan and Kyrgyzstan, together with overflight rights and vital transportation networks, were instrumental in the initial phase of the war under George W. Bush, and during the surge implemented by the Obama administration. In the third phase (2014–present) fatigue with the conflicts in Afghanistan and the Middle East, and reduced interest in democracy promotion, have led to a gradual disengagement from the region, though Central Asia is still needed to assist U.S. efforts in Afghanistan and reforms in Uzbekistan present modest new economic opportunities.

Phase I: Transitioning from communism

When the Soviet Union fragmented at the end of 1991 the United States was faced with the task of establishing relations with 14 newly independent countries, including the five Central Asian states. The George H.W. Bush administration quickly set up embassies in each of the five. Washington's initial goals were securing nuclear weapons, supporting American oil companies that had begun developing the region's hydrocarbon resources, establishing trade links, and promoting

DOI: 10.4324/9780429057977-15

political reform and market economies to forestall the possibility of a regression towards communism or authoritarianism (Talbott 1994). Washington supported the sovereignty and independence of these new states, to prevent Russia or any other power from exercising undue influence.

The Bush administration and members of Congress viewed the Soviet collapse as an historic opportunity to integrate the former republics into a stable, democratic international order. The Freedom Support Act passed by Congress in 1992 was designed to pre-empt a new Cold War and to bury communism by supporting reformers in the new states in their efforts to create democratic political institutions and develop economies based on private enterprise (Freedom Support Act). The act included demilitarisation and nuclear non-proliferation provisions and provided technical assistance to the new countries to develop previously untapped markets that would create opportunities for American firms (Armitage 1992). The Clinton administration stressed the importance of conflict resolution so that firms could exploit the region's massive reserves of hydrocarbons (Talbott 1997).

The United States also moved quickly to counter a perceived threat from Iran, which was seeking to gain influence among the five newly independent Muslim states. Washington recognised the potential for Islamic radicalism in the region, and sought Turkey's help as a secular role model and NATO member to promote moderate Islam and ensure the Central Asians would forgo nuclear weapons (Friedman 1992). However, the threat from Iran was exaggerated, as was the expectation that Ankara could play the role of regional leader and exemplar to Central Asia. Outside the great powers, it was Saudi Arabia, with its huge oil revenues, that established a foothold in the region by funding mosques and Islamic education (Goldstein 2004: 191–2).

Kazakhstan quickly became a key partner for the United States, in part because it was the one Central Asian state that had nuclear weapons, and in part because U.S. oil giant Chevron was negotiating a contract for the huge fields near the Caspian Sea. In May 1992 presidents George H.W. Bush and Nursultan Nazarbayev met in Washington, D.C. Nazarbayev pledged Kazakhstan would join the Non-Proliferation Treaty (NPT) as a non-nuclear state and would eliminate all nuclear weapons within the seven-year frame provided for by the START I Treaty (US–Kazakhstan Relations 1992). Over 1,000 nuclear warheads mounted on SS-18 missiles had been based in Kazakhstan, a central element of the Soviet nuclear force. The United States provided substantial aid for dismantling these weapons through the Nunn-Lugar Threat Reduction Program, together with assistance for securing weapons-grade nuclear materials located at the Semipalatinsk testing site in northeastern Kazakhstan.

George H.W. Bush's successor as president, Bill Clinton, praised Nazarbayev for his role in nuclear non-proliferation at their first meeting in February 1994, in Washington D.C., while remarking on the trade and business potential between the United States and Kazakhstan, and the two countries' commitment to democratic partnership ('The U.S. and Kazakhstan' 1994). In December 1993 Kazakhstan ratified the Nuclear Non-Proliferation Treaty (NPT), and this early cooperation served as the basis for an enduring partnership between the United States and Kazakhstan.

As the largest of the Central Asian states, Kazakhstan and Uzbekistan commanded the bulk of Washington's attention. Some experts, such as S. Frederick Starr (1996), argued that Uzbekistan was the most important country in Central Asia, and could serve as an anchor for regional stability. Moreover, a fully independent Tashkent could curtail Russia's imperial nostalgia. Uzbekistan under President Islam Karimov was resistant to Russian influence in Central Asia and used ties with the United States – most notably access to the Karshi-Khanabad military base – to balance off Moscow (Cooley 2012). But following the 2005 Andijan massacre Karimov demanded U.S. forces leave Karshi-Khanabad, and ties with Tashkent deteriorated as domestic repression intensified.

Aside from Kazakhstan's nuclear weapons, and the potential for Islamic radicalism and Iranian influence, U.S. security interests in Central Asia were limited during the 1990s. Washington did seek to engage these states through NATO's Partnership for Peace initiative, and provided military assistance to Uzbekistan in 1999 to counter threats from the Islamic Movement of Uzbekistan (IMU). The United States also sponsored the creation of a Central Asian Battalion (CENTRASBAT) for training and equipping Central Asian forces under the Partnership for Peace programme. However, CENTRASBAT, a combined peacekeeping unit with companies drawn from Kazakhstan, Uzbekistan and Kyrgyzstan, was a modest operation. Washington's objective was to provide an alternative to Russia in managing regional crises, enhance Central Asian independence from Russia, encourage regional cooperation and promote stability. However, Western experts disparaged skill levels among Central Asian participants, and by 2000 CENTRASBAT was largely defunct (McCarthy 2007: 44–8). Still, the contacts established during this period provided the United States with connections that would prove useful after the terrorist attacks in 2001. Multinational Steppe Eagle military exercises, for example, are held annually with the goal of strengthening Central Asian military forces, improving peacekeeping and emergency response capabilities, and making units fully interoperable with those of NATO.

Another key interest of the United States was assisting in the development of oil and natural gas production in Central Asia and ensuring that Russia did not monopolise the pipeline export routes. American oil majors Chevron and ExxonMobil were keen to tap new fields, and U.S. energy policy has long supported diversification of supply. Towards that end Washington promoted multiple pipelines to work around the Soviet-era infrastructure dominated by Russia. By 1999 the Clinton administration listed as its accomplishments technical and legal support for the Baku-Tbilisi-Ceyhan pipeline, and (through the Gore-Chernomyrdin Commission) agreement with Russia on the Caspian Pipeline Consortium that facilitated opportunities for U.S. companies in the region. Signalling the importance it attached to regional energy development, the government created a Special Advisor for Caspian Basin Energy Diplomacy (U.S.-Caspian Energy Policy 1999).

Democracy promotion was a major component of American strategy towards Central Asia in the 1990s and 2000s. Under the Freedom Support Act the United States provided $561 million in democracy assistance to the five Central Asian states from 1992 to 2006 (Omelicheva 2015: 36). As part of its War on Terror the George W. Bush administration promoted the idea of democracy as a universal value and emphasised the importance of elections in an attempt to transform and stabilise Central Asia. By Bush's second term, however, the administration's interventionist policies and the colour revolutions in Georgia, Ukraine and Kyrgyzstan led to a backlash against democracy promotion in the form of restrictive laws on NGOs and resistance to international electoral monitoring (Carothers 2006).

Keen to maintain links to the United States, Central Asian rulers promised democratic progress while pursuing authoritarian forms of governance. Kyrgyzstan's president Askar Akayev raised expectations by suggesting his country would become the Switzerland of Central Asia, a model of democracy and tolerance. As the decade progressed, however, the Akayev regime became increasingly corrupt, a process that only intensified when the United States began using the air transit hub at Manas (Toktomushev 2015). Under Nursultan Nazarbayev Kazakhstan declared it was committed to building democracy, albeit gradually, and with concessions to Kazakh cultural traditions. In an effort to preserve close ties to the United States and Europe, Kazakhstan promoted religious tolerance and pluralism, welcomed U.S. democracy building programmes funded by the State Department and US AID, and hosted American democracy promotion organisations like the International Republican Institute, National Democratic Institute and Freedom House.[1] Uzbekistan's Islam Karimov touted his country's democratic credentials while imposing increasingly harsh repressive measures; in Turkmenistan, Saparmurat Niyazov constructed a totalitarian system replete with a bizarre personality cult. Tajikistan emerged from its five-year civil war riven with tribal factions, poor and far from democratic. In short, American democracy promotion efforts had little effect, with the possible exception of Kyrgyzstan.

In addition to sovereignty, security and energy development, U.S. policy promoted the transition to market economies among the five Central Asian states and provided modest assistance. The U.S. Agency for International Development led these efforts, focusing primarily on promoting the transition to market economies, political transitions towards democracy, and improvements in the health and education sectors. The agency provided over $2 billion in assistance from 1993 through 2013, with about 30 per cent allocated to each Kazakhstan and Kyrgyzstan, 20 per cent to Uzbekistan, 10 per cent to Tajikistan and 5 per cent to Turkmenistan (US AID 2019). Beyond energy, however, the United States had minimal interest in the Central Asian economies.

To summarise, the first phase of U.S. policy after the Soviet collapse focused on helping Central Asian states maintain their sovereignty and independence, promoting democratic and free market reforms, securing nuclear materials and weapons of mass destruction, and encouraging measures towards greater regional integration.

Phase II: Security dominates U.S. policy

The terrorist attacks of September 11, 2001, had a major impact on U.S. foreign and national security policy. In place of a reactive policy of deterring states, the 2002 National Security Strategy called for pre-emptive measures against terrorists and states that harbour them. Other great powers – Russia and China – were viewed as partners against a common threat, with middle and smaller powers in Central and South Asia and the Middle East as vital members of the anti-terrorism coalition. The Central Asian countries would provide critical support as a logistics hub for the campaign in Afghanistan. The Strategy's emphasis on promoting free and open societies as a bulwark against extremism, however, contradicted the authoritarian perspectives of many coalition partners, which became a continuing source of tension (Daalder, Lindsey and Steinberg 2002).

Initially, Russia and China did not oppose America's military presence in Central Asia. The American War on Terror affirmed Putin's agenda – he could use the argument of a terrorist threat from Muslim extremists and terrorists in the Caucasus to legitimise the regime's brutal operation in Chechnya. Putin resisted pressure from Minister of Defense Sergei Ivanov and others who opposed cooperation with Washington and an American military presence in Central Asia (McFaul 2001). President Jiang Zemin, cognisant of the links between al-Qaeda and Muslim Uighurs in Xinjiang province, condemned the attacks and expressed support for the United States, but urged that any military action be in accord with international law and conducted through the United Nations (Malik 2002).

Sensing opportunities, the Central Asian states readily cooperated with Washington. U.S. and NATO operations in Afghanistan relied heavily on the Karshi-Khanabad (K2) base in Uzbekistan near the Afghan border, and the Manas transit centre in Kyrgyzstan, just outside Bishkek. Defense Secretary Donald Rumsfeld negotiated the K2 base agreement with Karimov shortly after the 9/11 attacks, and in 2002 the United States and Uzbekistan signed a strategic partnership agreement. Manas operated from 2001 to 2014 and was critical to supplying fuel and transiting cargo and troops for U.S. operations in Afghanistan. However, DOD's single-minded focus on logistics facilitated corruption associated with fuel contracts awarded to Mina and Red Star Enterprises, secretive companies owned by Kyrgyz and American nationals.

A congressional investigation found that the Department's Defense Logistics Agency-Energy failed to conduct due diligence in mitigating corruption, while the U.S. embassy in Bishkek claimed to know little about the fuel contracts and asserted the sole responsibility rested with DOD (*Mystery at Manas* 2010). Ultimately, the scandal tarnished America's moral authority and damaged U.S.–Kyrgyzstan relations.

Putin's initial support for the U.S. position in Central Asia evaporated after the invasion of Iraq in 2003. Manas quickly became a source of contention between Moscow – which occupied a nearby base at Kant – and Washington, and by 2005 Putin was encouraging the Central Asians to close down American facilities. At the 2005 meeting of the Shanghai Cooperation Organization members claimed the situation in Central Asia had changed and urged the United States to set dates for withdrawal from Uzbekistan, Kyrgyzstan and Tajikistan. This declaration convinced American conservatives that Russia and China were scheming through the SCO to thwart Washington's goals in Iraq and Afghanistan (Ziegler 2013).

Certainly, much had changed by 2005. The U.S. campaigns in Iraq and Afghanistan had bogged down and it was increasingly clear that Washington had no real exit strategy. Russia was experiencing rapid economic growth under President Vladimir Putin and was seeking to re-establish itself as a great power with privileges in neighbouring states. China was still biding its time internationally, as Deng Xiao-ping had recommended, but the country's economic and military modernisation together with a more active foreign policy positioned the country as a potential challenger to the United States, at least along its periphery (*Military Power* 2005).

Perhaps more importantly, the Central Asian states and their great power partners in the SCO feared U.S. support for human rights, democracy and 'color revolutions,' especially after the Andijan events and Kyrgyzstan's Tulip Revolution, both of which occurred in 2005 (Cooley 2012: 37–8). The Bush administration's Freedom Agenda was premised on spreading democracy throughout the broader Middle East on the assumption that democracies provided less fertile ground for nurturing terrorism and extremism. Political reform was viewed as crucial in eroding support for such extremist groups as Hizb-ut Tahrir and the IMU. While the U.S. government played a minimal role in the Kyrgyzstan uprising, the administration welcomed the demonstrations against Askar Akayev's increasingly authoritarian regime as an example of popular empowerment.

Washington's policy towards Uzbekistan reflected the rather fragmented and at times contradictory priorities of the Bush administration and the foreign policy bureaucracy (Levine 2016: 179). The State Department under Condoleezza Rice, and most other sectors of the American government, engaged in vocal criticism of Uzbekistan after the Andijan violence (Stent 2014: 119–22). By contrast, the Pentagon under Secretary of Defense Donald Rumsfeld needed the K2 base for the Afghanistan campaign and preferred to overlook Tashkent's human rights abuses. Congress was also critical of the Karimov regime. Arizona senator John McCain led an investigation and fact-finding tour of Uzbekistan in May 2005, contributing to a rise in tensions with the United States.

By contrast, Moscow and Beijing voiced unequivocal support for Tashkent (Cooley 2012: 38–40). China honoured President Karimov with a summit meeting in Beijing in May, immediately after the events in Andijan. Premier Hu Jintao referred to Karimov as an 'old friend' and declared the two countries were united in the face of terrorism ('China welcomes Uzbek president' 2005). Although Uzbekistan since independence has sought to balance among the great powers, distancing itself from Russia in an effort to protect its sovereignty, in the wake of human rights criticism over Andijan, Tashkent asked the United States to vacate the K2 base, and rejoined the Russian-dominated Collective Security Treaty Organization in November 2005 (see Fumagalli 2007).

Andijan highlighted a tension in U.S. policy between security needs and interests in promoting human rights and democracy. While the terrorist attacks in September 2001 generated considerable sympathy for the United States, the Bush administration's 'war of choice' in Iraq significantly eroded America's soft power as an exemplar and exporter of democratic values and human rights. Central Asia's authoritarian leaders feared religious extremism, but democratic accountability was hardly less threatening to regime survival. Faced with these conflicting pressures, the United States made concessions on human rights, civil society and democracy, recognising the strategic need to cooperate with authoritarian and corrupt Central Asian states. In the Central Asian context, the United States learnt it had to play by the local rules to maintain access to vital facilities, and to compete with Russia and China for influence (Cooley 2012).

While the United States and Russia briefly cooperated on security issues after 9/11, energy continued to be an arena of competition, but one in which the United States realised far fewer gains than initially predicted. Moscow sought to maintain its monopoly on pipeline export routes to benefit state companies Gazprom and Transneft; Washington by contrast promoted private investment and development and opposed monopolistic energy practices (Jaffe and Soligo 2004). Washington supported American energy companies and consistently promoted multiple pipelines from the Central Asia–Caspian region to avoid excessive Russian influence and to bypass routes through Iran. After a decade of negotiations and planning, the Caspian Pipeline Consortium began transporting oil in late 2001; the Baku-Tbilisi-Ceyhan pipeline was completed and went into operation in 2006. American companies Chevron and ExxonMobil are partners in both operations, but neither has close to a majority stake, and Russian firms hold a majority share in the CPC.[2]

By the end of the second phase in U.S. relations with Central Asia most major energy projects had been completed, and the demand for Caspian oil peaked. In addition, the development of the fracking industry in the United States and the dramatic increase in the production of oil and gas, together with new hydrocarbon discoveries worldwide, made Central Asia's hydrocarbons less important in the global energy market.

The early years of Barack Obama's administration reflected continuity with Bush administration's policy towards Central Asia. Faced with repeated attacks on NATO supply lines through Pakistan, the United States secured cooperation among Central Asian states and Russia to use the Northern Distribution Network (NDN), a complex of rail and road links vital in providing non-lethal materiel for Operation Enduring Freedom in Afghanistan (2009–2015). Security assistance to Central Asia peaked with the Obama administration's 2011–2012 surge in Afghanistan, and then declined after 2015 (Omelicheva 2017).

The U.S. military needed the NDN routes during the surge as an alternative to highly vulnerable transit routes through Pakistan: troop levels in Afghanistan increased from about 30,000 when Obama first took office to 100,000 in 2011. The Obama administration planned eventually to utilise the NDN network as a framework for the civilian New Silk Road, integrating Central Asia and Afghanistan to enhance trade and energy cooperation, coordinate border operations, and improve prospects for peace and stability. In a 2011 speech in Chennai, India, Secretary of State Hillary Clinton had outlined America's vision for a complex of electrical projects, trade networks and pipelines that would enhance commerce among the Central Asian states, Afghanistan, India and Pakistan, while undermining support for violent extremism in the region.

By 2014 the United States began drawing down its forces in Afghanistan and, following the Ukraine crisis, Prime Minister Medvedev announced the official end of the Northern Distribution Network (Trilling 2011; Daly 2015). While the NDN had largely served its function by 2015, Washington's plans for a New Silk Road foundered on regional tensions, U.S.

budgetary constraints and competition from China's Belt and Road Initiative. The U.S. government was unwilling to allocate significant funding for infrastructure, preferring instead that the Afghan government and neighbouring countries 'take ownership' of the project (Kucera 2011). By 2013 Xi Jinping had rolled out China's far more ambitious Belt and Road Initiative, which dwarfed Washington' proposal.

On democracy promotion, the Obama administration did not reverse Bush's agenda, maintaining roughly the same programmes and level of expenditures. Obama's approach, however, toned down the strident rhetoric employed by Bush administration officials, deemphasised the practice of introducing American-style democracy forcibly through military power and stressed rebuilding America's reputation as a democratic exemplar. Obama also continued the longstanding realist U.S. practice of advocating democracy and human rights while maintaining good relations with autocratic governments for security or economic reasons. In Central Asia, this meant lifting a ban on military aid and ramping up security assistance to Uzbekistan in 2012, to facilitate the surge in Afghanistan. That year Uzbekistan quit the CSTO, and three years later the U.S. government provided Karimov's regime with a range of military equipment, ostensibly for defensive purposes in countering terrorism and narcotics smuggling (Michel 2015).

Kyrgyzstan, in contrast, was disappointed with the United States for focusing too much on democracy promotion and civil society, and not allocating more assistance to business and industry, which comprised only 20 per cent of the total assistance in 2012. A CSIS report found that Kyrgyzstan's elites wished the United States would expand trade, take more Kyrgyz exports and show more interest in broadening or deepening the relationship (Kuchins, Mankoff, Backes 2015: 21–3). Relations worsened when Azimjan Askarov, an Uzbek activist jailed after the 2010 ethnic violence, was awarded the State Department's Human Rights Defender Award. The Kyrgyz government subsequently pulled out of the 1993 bilateral assistance treaty with Washington.

Phase 3: Fatigue and disillusionment?

The Obama administration's C5+1 dialogue format, launched in November 2015, marked a new phase in U.S. policy towards Central Asia. With the Northern Distribution Network closed, American troops withdrawn from the Manas base, and the gradual pullout of U.S. troops from Afghanistan, Central Asia was no longer perceived as critical to American security. Economic cooperation now constituted the main focus of U.S. engagement. In late 2015 Secretary of State John Kerry toured all five Central Asian states to reaffirm U.S. interest in the region, express his support for economic integration and encourage their leaders to develop closer trade relations with the United States (Pannier 2015; 2016). The C5+1 mechanism, formalised in Kerry's November 2015 Samarkand meeting with foreign ministers, was an attempt to institutionalise consultations among all six countries that would help preserve an American foothold in Central Asia.

The Trump administration's approach to Central Asia has differed only marginally from the later Obama years. The new president's security team continued to view Central Asia as a derivative of the broader regional security order. The 2018 National Defense Strategy, strongly influenced by Secretary of Defense Jim Mattis, refers to China's use of predatory economics and military modernisation to intimidate its neighbours, with Russia seeking veto authority over neighbouring states in politics, economics and diplomacy. In this environment U.S. objectives include maintaining favourable balances of power in vital regions of the world (National Defense Strategy 2018).

Trump, however, was less interested in security considerations or great power competition than in commercial opportunities, and his administration embraced the C5+1 format. Secretary of State Rex Tillerson hosted the third C5+1 meeting in New York in September 2017, discussing possibilities for greater cooperation to promote Afghanistan's economic development (Sanchez 2018). In September 2019 Secretary of State Mike Pompeo met with the foreign ministers of the Central Asian states on the sidelines of the UN General Assembly. Pompeo praised the Central Asian states for their efforts to reintegrate families of terrorists linked to ISIS, urged them not to repatriate ethnic Uyghurs back to China, warned his counterparts about the pitfalls of China's Belt and Road investment strategy, and promised them better and more transparent deals if they did business with the United States ('Pompeo' 2019).

Washington acknowledges that as the region's major economy, Kazakhstan is playing an increasing role in supporting Afghanistan's development and integration into broader Central Asia, a key U.S. goal. According to Kazakhstan's Special Representative for Afghanistan Stanislav Vassilenko, his country is committed to stabilising Afghanistan by constructing schools and hospitals, developing transportation infrastructure, working with the European Union to empower women through scholarships and educational programmes, and providing humanitarian food aid (Akhmetova 2019). U.S. firms continue to pursue business opportunities in Kazakhstan, with the focus largely on oil and gas. American energy companies Chevron and ExxonMobil have significant holdings in Kazakhstan – by early 2019 U.S. foreign direct investment totalled $36 billion, of which nearly $34 billion was in the mining sector. Kazakhstan was also the largest U.S. trading partner in Central Asia, although total bilateral trade in 2018 was just $1.59 billion (Gadimova 2019).[3]

President Trump initially met Nazarbayev on the sidelines of the Arab Islamic American summit in Riyadh, and the Kazakhstan president was the first Central Asian head of state to visit the White House, in January 2018. At the Washington meeting, Trump praised Kazakhstan for purchasing goods from the United States, acknowledged the country was a 'valued partner' in U.S. efforts to denuclearise the Korean peninsula, and noted that Kazakhstan played a role in the administration's South Asia/Afghanistan strategy (Remarks 2018). Shortly after the Trump–Nazarbayev summit Kazakhstan agreed to allow the United States to use two Caspian ports (Aktau and Kuryk) to provide non-lethal supplies to NATO forces in Afghanistan ('Kazakhstan Grants' 2018). In addition, Kazakhstan has supported American security interests in calling for Iran and North Korea to give up their nuclear weapons ambitions. Kazakhstan's government supported the peace process in Syria and has been an exemplar of moderate Islam in the region. However, Kazakhstan's staged leadership transition and slowing economic growth contrasts sharply with the dynamic reform process underway in Uzbekistan. An increasingly open, liberal Uzbekistan under Shavkat Mirziyoyev may prove more attractive to the U.S. administration than a Kazakhstan that appears to be marking time under Kassym-Jomart Tokayev, Nazarbayev's designated successor.

The United States had been pressuring Uzbekistan to enact political and economic reforms for years, but there was virtually no progress while Islam Karimov was president. A large component of Mirziyoyev's reform strategy has been to reengage with the outside world, especially the West, in an effort to restore Tashkent's international position after more than a decade of isolation (Sullivan 2019a). The United States and Uzbekistan have common interests in stabilising Afghanistan. Tashkent wants to forestall a disorderly American retreat that might worsen the regional security situation, while the Trump administration is seeking some form of viable exit strategy. On trade and investment, Uzbekistan has adopted a multi-vector diplomatic strategy similar to Kazakhstan's, balancing relations among the great powers. The United States, however, opposes Chinese state-influenced economic dominance over Central

Asia through the Belt and Road Initiative, though Washington has failed to propose a credible alternative to the BRI.[4]

Mirziyoyev clearly envisions Uzbekistan playing a larger role in stabilising Afghanistan, and he is encouraging higher levels of foreign investment and trade from the West. American officials believe Uzbekistan's reforms create new opportunities for intraregional cooperation, improved business ties, a better foreign investment climate and a more stable, sovereign and secure Central Asia (Imamova 2018). The United States has praised Uzbekistan's release of political prisoners, its moves to relax censorship and greater tolerance for religion. In June 2019 the U.S. State Department removed Uzbekistan from its list of countries with the worst records for religious tolerance, and its 2018 Report on International Religious Freedom noted Uzbekistan's substantial progress in this area, though Uzbek officials continue to harass believers and impose some restrictions on religious freedom (Prince 2019a; 2018 Report).

In May 2018 Trump invited the Uzbek president to the White House. The U.S. president praised Uzbekistan for purchasing U.S. military equipment and noted that in the week prior to the summit 20 major business deals worth $4.8 billion were signed (Davis 2018). Trump did not press his visitor on human rights or democracy, although the president's advisors saw the meeting as an opportunity to encourage Tashkent's cautious liberalisation on human rights, freedom of the press and freedom of religion. A Security Council official responsible for Central Asia praised the 'great strides' made under Mirziyoyev and suggested the United States would seek Uzbekistan's help in brokering peace in Afghanistan (Eckel 2018).[5]

Military cooperation also figures prominently in current U.S.–Central Asian relations. During Mirziyoyev's visit the two sides signed a five-year military plan, and General Joseph Votel, head of Central Command, made several visits to Uzbekistan in 2018. There were modest military-to-military contacts following the summit, though Tashkent also increased military cooperation with Russia, China and Turkey (Omelicheva 2019). Central Command regards Uzbekistan as a constructive partner in the Afghanistan peace process and a contributor to regional stability. Votel claimed improving relations with Tashkent would increase border security, enhance counter-terrorism and counter-narcotics operations, and address the issue of domestic extremist fighters returning from Syria, Iraq and Afghanistan. The general explained that the United States will continue to build its security relationship with Tajikistan, though 'Kazakhstan remains the most significant Central Asian contributor to Afghan stability.' However, strained bilateral relations with Kyrgyzstan, Bishkek's turn towards Russia and China, and the lack of a Status of Forces Agreement impede security cooperation between the United States and Kyrgyzstan. In sum, Votel observed, U.S. security assistance makes it possible for the Central Asian states to balance between Russian and Chinese influence (Votel 2019).

Discussion

President Trump's abrupt withdrawal of American troops from Syria calls into question the U.S. commitment to a continued presence in the Middle East and South/Central Asia. In his August 2017 speech on Afghanistan Trump acknowledged the American people's frustration with the country's longest war but cited the 2011 withdrawal from Iraq as a strategic mistake, implying he would not repeat the error in Afghanistan. The president rejected previous nation-building strategies and declared the United States would no longer use military might to construct democracies (Trump 2017). Washington's political dysfunction makes it difficult to predict whether Central Asia will retain its position in Washington's strategic calculations, but by late 2019 administration had yet to have a confirmed assistant secretary for South and Central Asian affairs. More than two years into her tenure, Alice Wells, a career diplomat and former ambassador to Jordan, was still acting assistant secretary.[6]

A new official U.S. strategy for Central Asia was released in February 2020 that spelled out the Trump administration's goals. The core policy objectives of the strategy were to support the sovereignty and independence of Central Asian states, reduce terrorist threats in the region, expand support for stability in Afghanistan and encourage closer ties with that country, promote human rights and the rule of law, and support U.S. investment in Central Asia ('United States Strategy'). As a high-level State Department official explained, the United States sought to limit Russian and Chinese influence in the region, contain China's Belt and Road Initiative, encourage Uzbekistan's reform process and expanded participation in global politics, and enlist the Central Asian states in fighting terrorism (37Prince 2019b). A key objective is to stabilise and integrate Afghanistan into the broader region as the United States undertakes a phased withdrawal of its military forces. And by deepening political, economic and military engagement through the C5+1 mechanism Washington can provide Central Asia's rulers with a useful counterweight to Russian and Chinese influence.

That said, the Trump administration does not seem inclined to invest heavily in Central Asia, and the government's strategy towards Afghanistan remains unclear. Negotiations with the Taliban led by Zalmay Khalilzad collapsed in September 2019 when the president abruptly cancelled a secret Camp David meeting with Taliban delegates (Baker, Mashal and Crowley 2019). In February 2020 the Trump administration concluded an agreement with the Taliban that called for pulling out American troops by May 2021, but President Biden resisted an abrupt withdrawal. Should the United States withdraw completely from Afghanistan much of the rationale for remaining engaged with Central Asian states would evaporate. The Biden administration will likely retain the C5+1 dialogue format. However, coordination among the main executive branch agencies that have responsibility for Central Asia – State, DOD, Commerce and US AID – is haphazard, making coherent policy difficult. Officials and analysts who view Central Asia largely through the security lens are likely to accept disengagement with the region following U.S. withdrawal from Afghanistan. Those who want to remain engaged point to business opportunities and the confluence of neighbouring great powers – four of which possess nuclear weapons, and one of which is an aspiring nuclear power (Starr 2017).

U.S. efforts to counter China's Belt and Road Initiative may keep Washington engaged with Central Asia, though American programmes such as the International Development Finance Corporation are modest proposals at best. Especially designed to help transition countries to utilising market-oriented rather than state-centred approaches, the IFDC is ideally suited to address Central Asian investment needs (Runde and Bandura 2018). A more transparent investment process may partially erode China's predatory policies, which are becoming increasingly apparent to vulnerable lower and middle-income countries (Mendis and Wang 2019).

Beyond Afghanistan, the United States faces a choice of either competing with China, Russia and Iran in Central Asia, or retreating from the region and conceding influence. While no major changes in Central Asian policy were apparent during the first months of the Biden administration, the new president's willingness to confront Beijing and Moscow over human rights issues and democracy could increase regional tensions. Moscow appears determined to preserve and expand its regional presence through the Eurasian Economic Union, the Collective Security Treaty Organization and the Shanghai Cooperation Organization, and will likely continue to resist an American presence barring a radical improvement in U.S.–Russian relations. Beijing shares leadership of the SCO with Moscow, and like Russia seeks to reduce American influence along its Western border, but their relationship in Central Asia is competitive. Russia has a military advantage in the region but cannot match the financial resources China is committing through the BRI nor can the United States. In this environment the United States could become an 'offshore balancer,' relying on Kazakhstan, Uzbekistan and India to assume more responsibility for regional stability (see Rumer, Sokolsky and Stronski 2016).

To summarise, the prospects for extending or even preserving American influence in Central Asia are not favourable. Deep partisan divisions in the United States carry over to international relations, making consistent policy towards Central Asia – or to any other region for that matter – increasingly difficult. Promoting human rights and democracy is part of the Biden administration's agenda, but this approach, though different in tone from Trump's, is not likely to yield major policy changes. There are some economic opportunities for American business, most notably in energy and in a reforming Uzbekistan, but major oil and gas fields are already under production. Unlike certain other nationalities, the Central Asians have a miniscule demographic presence and no influential lobbies in the United States. Moreover, Russia's actions in Ukraine have induced Central Asia's rulers to lean more towards Russia in an effort to avoid antagonising Moscow (Sullivan 2019b).

Conclusion

U.S. policy towards Central Asian has progressed through three discernable stages. In the first decade following the Soviet collapse, Washington advocated the sovereignty and independence of the new states, provided funding and technical assistance for decommissioning nuclear weapons, supported Western firms eager to develop the region's energy sector, and promoted market economies and democratisation. The first three objectives could be considered a success. Only one country – Kyrgyzstan – made any real progress towards developing a more pluralistic political system. Three of the five Central Asian states remained in the lower-middle-income category, with only Kazakhstan and Turkmenistan achieving upper-middle-income status according to the World Bank.[7]

In the second phase of relations the George W. Bush administration prioritised the War on Terror in its foreign policy, with bases in Kyrgyzstan and Uzbekistan serving as vital staging grounds for the campaign in Afghanistan. However, American military needs frequently clashed with the administration's democracy promotion agenda, leading to bureaucratic infighting and inconsistent policy. The Obama administration's surge in Afghanistan renewed attention to the logistical importance of Central Asia, while the emphasis on building American-style electoral democracy was toned down.

The third phase of U.S. policy has been marked by a growing fatigue with and the search for an exit strategy from Afghanistan. As U.S.-Russian relations deteriorated sharply in the wake of the Ukraine crisis, Moscow became increasingly antagonistic towards U.S. presence in the Central Asian region. In addition, China's massive Belt and Road Initiative overshadowed more modest American development and investment proposals. The Trump administration has recognised and sought to promote economic opportunities for American business in Kazakhstan and Uzbekistan, but even with U.S. government support American firms are not likely to erode Beijing's dominant position. The U.S. policy towards Central Asia under Biden will display greater professionalism and nuance, reflecting a return to traditional statecraft, but the basic contours of Washington's approach to the region are likely to remain unchanged.

Notes

1 Full disclosure – the author conducted a civil society building programme in Kazakhstan from 2006 to 2011 with the financial support of the Bureau of Democracy, Human Rights and Labor (DRL) in the U.S. State Department.

2 Chevron is a 15 per cent shareholder in the CPC; Mobil Caspian holds a 7.5 per cent stake. Chevron has an 8.9 per cent share in BTC; ExxonMobil holds 2.5 per cent equity. Together, Transneft, LukArco and Rosneft-Shell control 51 per cent of the CPC.
3 According to the U.S. Department of State, as of 1 January 2018, the United States had a total of $27.28 billion in FDI in Kazakhstan. State Department website, https://www.state.gov/reports/2018-investment-climate-statements/kazakhstan/, accessed 11 August 2019.
4 In July 2018 Secretary of State Mike Pompeo announced a $113 million infrastructure initiative for the entire Indo-Pacific, a tiny fraction of the supposed $1 trillion that China plans to invest in its BRI (Wroughton and Brunnstrom 2018). No comparable plans have been announced for Central Asia. Formation of the U.S. International Development Finance Corporation (a revamped and expanded OPIC) through the 2018 BUILD Act is Washington's attempt to provide private investment for lower and lower-middle-income countries, in large part to counter the BRI.
5 Trump reportedly resisted staff recommendations that he raise human rights concerns, preferring to focus on the potential benefits of trade deals (Davis 2018).
6 The State Department website indicated Ambassador Wells' term ended on 1 June 2020, apparently without her ever having been confirmed.
7 Data for Turkmenistan are limited, and there are widespread reports of poverty in the countryside. The country's status as upper-middle income is largely the result of large revenues from natural gas exports.

Bibliography

Akhmetova, Z. (2019). 'Kazakhstan's Assistance to Afghanistan Helps Strengthen Regional and Global Security, Diplomat Says.' *Astana Times*, 25 September, https://astanatimes.com/2018/09/kazakhstans-assistance-to-afghanistan-helps-strengthen-regional-and-global-security-diplomat-says/, accessed 14 October 2019.

Armitage, R. (1992). 'Achieving National Consensus on the Freedom Support Act.' *U.S. Department of State Dispatch* 3(9): 1051–7693. 11 May.

Baker, P., M. Mashal, and M. Crowley. (2019). 'How Trump's Plan to Secretly Meet with the Taliban Came Together, and Fell Apart.' *New York Times*, 8 September.

Blake, R.O. (2009). 'Remarks on the Occasion of the Launch of the Congressional Caucus on Central Asia,' U.S. Department of State, 18 November, https://2009-2017.state.gov/p/sca/rls/rmks/2009/132127.htm, accessed 24 June 2019.

Blank, S. (2008). 'The Strategic Importance of Central Asia: An American View.' *Parameters* 38 (1): 73–87.

Carothers, T. (2006). 'The Backlash against Democracy Promotion.' *Foreign Affairs* 85 (2): 55–68.

Cooley, A. (2012). *Great Games, Local Rules*. Oxford: Oxford University Press.

Daalder, I.H., J.M. Lindsay, and J.B. Steinberg. (2002). 'The Bush National Security Strategy: An Evaluation.' Brookings Institution, 1 October, https://www.brookings.edu/research/the-bush-national-security-strategy-an-evaluation/, accessed 25 October 2019.

Daly, J.C.K. (2015). 'Russia Shutters Northern Distribution Network.' *Eurasia Daily Monitor* 12 (111), 15 June.

Davis, J.H. (2018). 'Trump Meets Uzbek President, Making No Mention of Human Rights.' *New York Times*, 16 May.

Eckel, M. (2018). 'White House Says It Will Push Uzbek Leader on Rights, Economic Reform.' *Radio Free Europe/Radio Liberty*, 15 May.

Eurasianet. (2015). 'Kyrgyzstan Ditches Key Treaty with U.S.' 21 July.

Eurasianet. (2019). 'Kazakhstan Grants U.S. Access to Ports for Afghan-Bound Goods.' 7 March.

Friedman, T.L. (1992). 'U.S. to Counter Iran in Central Asia.' *New York Times*, 6 February.

Fumagalli, M. (2007). 'Alignments and Realignments in Central Asia: The Rationale and Implications of Uzbekistan's Rapprochement with Russia.' *International Political Science Review* 28 (3): 253–71.

Gadimova, N. (2019). 'The US Looks to Strengthen Ties with Kazakhstan's Markets.' *Caspian News*, 8 November.

Goldstein, L.J. (2004). 'Beyond the Steppe: Projecting Power into the New Central Asia.' *Journal of Slavic Military Studies* 17: 183–213.

Imamova, N. (2018). 'What's New in U.S. Policy toward Central Asia?' *Amerika Ovozi*, 26 February.

Jaffe, A.M. and R. Soligo. (2004). 'Re-evaluating US Strategic Priorities in the Caspian Region: Balancing Energy Resource Initiatives with Terrorism Containment.' *Cambridge Review of International Affairs* 17 (2): 255–68.

Kleveman, L. (2004). *The New Great Game: Blood and Oil in Central Asia*. New York: Grove Press.
Kucera, J. (2011). 'The New Silk Road?' *The Diplomat*, 11 November.
Kuchins, A.C., J. Mankoff, and O. Backes. (2015). *Central Asia in a Reconnecting Eurasia: Kyrgyzstan's Evolving Foreign Economic and Security Interests*. Lanham: Rowman & Littlefield.
Levine, I. (2016). *US Policies in Central Asia: Democracy, Energy, and the War on Terror*. London: Routledge.
Malashenko, A. (2013). *The Fight for Influence: Russia in Central Asia*. Washington, DC: Carnegie Endowment for International Peace.
Malik, J.M. (2002). 'Dragon on Terrorism: Assessing China's Tactical Gains and Strategic Losses after 11 September.' *Contemporary Southeast Asia* 24 (2): 252–93.
McCarthy, M.J. (2007). *The Limits of Friendship: US Security Cooperation in Central Asia*. Walker Paper No. 9, October. Montgomery: Air University Press.
McFaul, M. (2001). 'U.S.-Russian Relations after September 11, 2001.' *Carnegie Endowment*, 24 October.
Mendis, P. and J. Wang. (2019). 'China's Era of Debt-Trap Diplomacy May Pave the Way for Something Sinister.' *National Interest*, 3 February.
Michel, C. (2015). 'The Obama Administration Is Gifting War Machines to a Murderous Dictator.' *New Republic*, 3 February.
National Defense Strategy (Summary). (2018). https://dod.defense.gov/Portals/1/Documents/pubs/2018-National-Defense-Strategy-Summary.pdf, accessed 1 January 2020.
Office of the U.S. Secretary of Defense. (2005). *Military Power of the People's Republic of China*. https://archive.defense.gov/news/Jul2005/d20050719china.pdf, accessed 21 October 2019.
Omelicheva, M.Y. (2015). *Democracy in Central Asia: Competing perspectives and alternative strategies*. Lexington: University Press of Kentucky.
Omelicheva, M. (2017). 'U.S. Security Assistance to Central Asia: Examining Limits, Exploring Opportunities.' *PONARS Eurasia*, October, http://www.ponarseurasia.org/memo/us-security-assistance-central-asia, accessed 7 October 2019.
Omelicheva, M. (2019). 'The United States and Uzbekistan: Military-to-Military Relations in a New Era of Strategic Partnership.' *PONARS Policy Memo* 604, July, http://www.ponarseurasia.org/memo/united-states-and-uzbekistan-military-to-military-relations, accessed 12 October 2019.
Pannier, B. (2015). 'A New Relationship between the United States and Central Asia?' *RFE/RL*, 31 October.
Pannier, B. (2016). 'With Kerry Meeting, Washington Seeks New Path in Central Asia.' *RFE/RL*, 3 August.
Prince, T. (2019a). 'U.S. Removes Uzbekistan from Nations with Worst Religious Tolerance.' *RFE/RL*, 21 June.
Prince, T. (2019b). 'U.S. to Publish New Central Asia Strategy Amid Russian, Chinese Competition, Afghan Threat.' *RFE/RL*, 14 December.
RFE/RL. (2018). 'Uzbekistan's Mirziyoev Meets Trump in "Historic" White House Visit.' 16 May.
RFE/RL. (2019). 'Pompeo: Reject Beijing's Demand to Send Ethnic Uyghurs Back to China.' 22 September.
Rumer, E., R. Sokolsky, and P. Stronski. (2016). 'U.S. Policy toward Central Asia 3.0.' Carnegie Endowment for International Peace, 25 January, https://carnegieendowment.org/2016/01/25/u.s.-policy-toward-central-asia-3.0-pub-62556, accessed 8 June 2019.
Runde, D.F. and R. Bandura. (2018). 'The BUILD Act Has Passed: What's Next?' CSIS, 12 October, https://www.csis.org/analysis/build-act-has-passed-whats-next, accessed 24 June 2019.
Sanchez, W.A. (2018). 'Central Asia in 2018: What's the Future of the C5+1?' *Geopolitical Monitor*, 11 July.
Semler, P.K. (2019). 'Trump Takes Aim at China's Belt and Road Lending.' *Asia Times*, 22 October.
Starr, S.F. (1996). 'Making Eurasia Stable.' *Foreign Affairs* 75 (1): 80–92.
Starr, S.F. (2017). 'The New Central Asia Nexus.' *American Interest* (July/August): 63–9.
Starr, S.F. and S.E. Wimbush. (2019). 'U.S. Strategy towards Afghanistan and (the Rest) of Central Asia.' *American Interest*, 24 January.
Stent, A.E. (2014). *The Limits of Partnership: U.S.-Russian Relations in the Twenty-First Century*. Princeton, NJ: Princeton University Press.
Sullivan, C. (2019b). 'The Superpower and the "Stans": Why Central Asia is not "Central" to the United States.' *SAIS Review of International Affairs*, 27 March.
Sullivan, C.J. (2019a). 'Uzbekistan and the United States: Interests and Avenues for cooperation.' *Asian Affairs* 50 (1), 102–11.
Talbott, S. (1994). 'Promoting Democracy and Prosperity in Central Asia.' *US Department of State Dispatch*, 3 May, 10517693, 5 (19), 9 May.

Talbott, S. (1997). 'Farewell to Flashman: American Policy in the Caucasus and Central Asia.' *U.S. Department of State Dispatch* 10517693, 8 (5), 21 July.

The Guardian. (2005). 'China Welcomes Uzbek President.' 26 May, https://www.theguardian.com/world/2005/may/26/china, accessed 21 October 2019.

The U.S. Department of State. (2019). 'Background Briefing on U.S.-Central Asian Relations.' 13 December, https://www.state.gov/background-briefing-on-u-s-central-asian-relations/, accessed 15 January 2020.

Toktomushev, K. (2015). 'Regime Security, Base Politics and Rent-Seeking: The Local and Global Political Economies of the American Air Base in Kyrgyzstan, 2001–2010.' *Central Asian Survey* 34 (1): 57–77.

Trilling, D. (2011). 'Northern Distribution Nightmare.' *Foreign Policy*, 6 December.

Trump, D. (2017). 'Remarks by President Trump on the Strategy in Afghanistan and Central Asia,' 21 August, White House website, https://www.whitehouse.gov/briefings-statements/remarks-president-trump-strategy-afghanistan-south-asia/, accessed 11 August 2019.

U.S. Department of State. (2019). '2018 Report on International Religious Freedom: Uzbekistan.' 29 May, https://preview.state.gov/reports/2018-report-on-international-religious-freedom/uzbekistan/, accessed 24 June 2019.

U.S. Department of State Dispatch. (1992). 'US-Kazakhstan Relations.' 25 May, 10517693, 3 (21).

U.S. Department of State Dispatch. (1994). 'The U.S. and Kazakhstan: A Strategic Economic and Political Relationship.' 14 February, 10517693, 5(8).

U.S. House of Representatives. (2010). *Mystery at Manas: Strategic Blind Spots in the Department of Defense's Fuel Contracts in Kyrgyzstan*. 2010. Report of the Majority Staff, Subcommittee on National Security and Foreign Affairs, December, https://www.washingtonpost.com/wp-srv/politics/documents/subcommittee_report_12222010.pdf, accessed 2 January 2020.

US AID Central Asia. (2019). 'Regional Development Cooperation Strategy 2015–2019.' https://pdf.usaid.gov/pdf_docs/pbaab464.pdf, accessed 23 October 2019.

Votel, J.L. (2019). 'Statement before the Senate Armed Services Committee.' 5 February, https://www.centcom.mil/ABOUT-US/POSTURE-STATEMENT/

White House. (1999). 'U.S.-Caspian Energy Policy.' 15 April, https://clintonwhitehouse5.archives.gov/textonly/WH/EOP/NSC/html/nsc-14.html, accessed 23 October 2019.

White House. (2018). 'Remarks by President Trump and President Nursultan Nazarbayev of Kazakhstan in Joint Press Statements.' 16 January, https://www.whitehouse.gov/briefings-statements/remarks-president-trump-president-nursultan-nazarbayev-kazakhstan-joint-press-statements/, accessed 18 November 2019.

Wroughton, L. and D. Brunnstrom. (2018). 'Wary of China's rise, Pompeo announces U.S. initiatives in emerging Asia.' *Reuters*, 20 July.

Ziegler, C.E. (2013). 'Central Asia, the Shanghai Cooperation, and American Foreign Policy: From Indifference to Engagement.' *Asian Survey* 55 (3): 484–505.

16
DOMESTIC SOURCES OF FOREIGN POLICY IN CENTRAL ASIA

Shairbek Dzhuraev

As the five former Soviet republics approach 30 years of their independence, discussing their foreign policies in a single chapter is an increasingly difficult task. First, as hopes for Central Asian regionalism gradually faded (e.g. Krapohl and Vasileva-Dienes 2020; Patnaik 2019), it also became difficult to maintain a 'regional' focus in academic writing. As Laruelle (2013: 6) put it, 'Ashgabat and Bishkek or Astana and Tashkent see the world differently.' Reflecting the above observation, the country-specific research has been on the rise, as the following sections demonstrate. Second, regional scholarship is also increasingly diverse theoretically. Knowledge about Central Asia's international engagements comes from scholars working in different disciplines, including international relations, foreign policy analysis (FPA) and comparative politics. For some, the shadows of the Soviet past or the great game loom large while others place foreign policy within the context of domestic institutions or political processes. In this context, doing justice to Central Asian countries' foreign policies in a single chapter becomes a difficult task both practically and theoretically.

The purpose of this chapter, therefore, is not to inform readers about foreign policymaking in Central Asia but review and appraise the regional literature on this subject. What are the most dominant theoretical frameworks employed, and explanations found, in the analyses of foreign policy in Central Asia? What are the 'gaps' in the field, or 'niches' emerging for new research? How could we reimagine a framework for analysis to address the above? These are the central questions that this chapter will address.

The chapter makes three arguments. First, there are two distinct strands of literature that have emerged as sources of knowledge on Central Asia's international relations. One strand has intellectual, if not theoretical, roots in the systemic theories of International Relations. Another strand is closer to FPA perspective, unpacking the state and focusing on domestic sources of international relations. Second, despite this growing volume and theoretical diversity, the literature has still struggled to move beyond monocausal and structural explanations for foreign policy. This is especially interesting in the case of domestically oriented literature. It emerged out of disillusionment with theoretical poverty of geopolitics-leaning arguments but rarely moved beyond its own 'straitjacket' of political ruling regimes. Finally, the chapter concludes with a call for greater analytical eclecticism in studying foreign policies of Central Asian states. A framework of 'ideas, interests and institutions' (the 3-i's for shorthand), is proposed as an example of

DOI: 10.4324/9780429057977-16

an approach to better reflect the multicausal and dynamic nature of foreign policymaking and help integrate area studies of Central Asia with foreign policy analysis.

The chapter is organised into three parts. The first section reviews IR-centric approaches to Central Asia's international relations. While it is legitimate to view Central Asia as part of the broader web of interstate relations, such an approach carries significant implications for what does and does not get discussed in the region's international relations. The second section reviews work that 'unpacks' the state to understand foreign policymaking in Central Asia. It consists of three sections addressing different dimensions of domestic-level explanations of foreign policy. The third section appraises some theoretical implications and limitations of the focus on political regimes and discusses ways in which a greater analytical eclecticism might help address them.

Learning Central Asia's international relations: A collateral benefit of geopolitics?

One of the sources of knowledge about international relations in Central Asia is research devoted to the interaction of the region with non-regional players. Two clusters of literature can be distinguished. The first includes works that are primarily interested in explaining the foreign policy of other countries, such as the United States, Russia or China, or the interaction between them. In this case, Central Asia acts as a site of interaction between these actors. Brzezinski's book *The Great Chessboard* (1998), which depicts the Eurasian region as a battleground for geopolitical competition, is an early and influential example. The heyday of Central Asia as the focus of the 'great games' of the great powers came after the events of September 11, with the arrival of American airbases in Central Asia, Putin's ascent to power in Russia and China's rise in the region (e.g. Menon 2003; Trenin 2003; Allison 2004; Swanström 2005; Kazantsev 2008).

A related but separate literature is work that focus on explaining the international relations of the Central Asian states through the study of their relations with selected foreign policy partners (e.g. Fumagalli 2007; Spechler and Spechler 2009; Huskey 2008). Like the first group, these publications often cover Central Asia's relations with the same set of 'great powers,' such as the United States, Russia or China. However, this literature comes mostly from country specialists, with the central interest in respective Central Asian states rather than their external partners. Thus, Fumagalli (2007) and Huskey (2008) demonstrate a deep understanding of the tangle of internal and external problems facing Uzbekistan and Kyrgyzstan, although Russia and the United States figure prominently in both works. That said, both groups of literature portray the agency of Central Asian states in international relations to be limited.

So, what do we learn from the above literature about Central Asia's international relations? At the risk of a crude generalisation, two propositions can be made. First, Central Asian states are small and weak international actors. Thus, Allison (2004) argued that in determining the post-9/11 geopolitical outcome in Central Asia, the 'evolution of Russian policy under President Putin [would] be a defining influence.' Other works contend, suggesting 'power asymmetry' in the region's engagement with the European Union (Kluczewska and Juraev 2020: 231) or 'power imbalance' in Central Asia's relations with China (Kassenova in this volume). Some political leaders shared this view: the former Kyrgyz president Akaev's repeatedly stressed that 'small states needed big friends' (Akaev 2003; 2004).

The second takeaway from the above literature is that Central Asian states' biggest foreign policy problem is to decide on friends and foes. The countries of the region are not only small and weak but also find themselves confronted with difficult geopolitical choices (e.g. Fumagalli 2007; Huskey 2008; Krasnopolsky 2013). The problem of 'taking a side' has become acute in the early 2000s, correlating with the tension between Washington and Moscow. The colour revolutions, the Andijan events, the Georgian-Russian war in 2008 were some of the milestones of the trend, and Crimea and the subsequent war in Ukraine marked its climax (e.g. Dzhuraev 2015; Tolipov 2015).

Although the Central Asian states are small and weak international actors, they are not necessarily pawns on the board. In fact, as Cooley (2012) argued, if there was a great game in Central Asia, then the local leaders set at least some of the rules. Likewise, Lewis (2015) argues that 'significant popular support in Kyrgyzstan for closer ties with Moscow' was important to understand Russian dominance in this country. However, none of these arguments contradicts the proposition that the countries of the region remained on the 'recipient' side, even if occasionally able to juggle between competing partners.

Overall, the IR-centric literature makes compelling arguments but at significant theoretical costs. First, these works adopt, even if without articulating it, the neorealist 'billiard ball' concept of the states. In other words, Central Asian states are unitary and rational actors whose foreign policies constitute predictable responses to the environment within which they find themselves. The smallness of Central Asian states only helps cement this proposition. Small states in IR, as Neumann and Gstohl (2006: 18) underline, are seen 'as objects, not subjects of international relations' (see also Hey 2003; Thorhallsson and Steinsson 2017). Such an approach does not leave space for a discussion of how exactly different actors within Central Asian states may interpret the external environment, and thus, reduces agency to the singular concept of a 'state.'

Second, and related, the adoption of an IR-centric approach limits the scope of phenomena deemed interesting for research. If Central Asian states are a group of small and weak states, their foreign policy agendas are mostly reduced to the questions of international alignment. Most interesting research questions, in this case, end up around discerning the critical interests *of* other actors in Central Asia or the strategies of Central Asian states to balance great powers and survive. Thus, we see international orientation, alignment and different forms of multivectorism emerge as prominent foreign policy analysis topics (e.g. Tolipov 2007; Hanks 2009; Indeo 2010; Dzhuraev 2019; Kurc 2018). Such limitation, however, should not be necessary. As Carlsnaes (2007: 12) framed it, the smallness of states is 'an empirical not a conceptual attribute,' and hence, it should not foreclose inquiries into domestic-level sources of foreign policies.

To sum up, the study of Central Asia from the perspective of systemic International Relations theories reveals as much about the region's foreign policymaking as it conceals. What are the dimensions of Central Asia's international relations that the above approaches overlook and how have they been addressed? The next section addresses the question by reviewing works devoted to the domestic sources of foreign policy in Central Asia.

Domestic matters: Foreign policy as an extension of regime survival?

Approaches examining the domestic sources of Central Asian international relations represent a more recent strand of the region's scholarship. Its emergence demonstrated a growing unease with the geopolitical straitjacket in the literature (e.g. Laruelle 2013). Few of these would reject the countries' smallness or difficulties posed by relations with greater powers. However, collectively, domestically oriented writings address the problems identified with the literature in the preceding section. They do so, mainly, through (a) focusing on Central Asian states as primary research objects and (b) unpacking the 'state' as a unit of analysis by examining the roles of domestic-level actors or processes in shaping foreign policies.

The research on domestic sources of foreign policy is increasingly diverse. This is not a surprising phenomenon since foreign policy analysis is inherently an interdisciplinary domain.

As Rosenau (2007: xv.) wrote, 'the student of a country's foreign policy ... must be a student of sociology and psychology, as well as political science, history, and economics.' Indeed, most Central Asian foreign policy analysis writing discussed below shed light on different dimensions of domestic politics. Ruling regimes' self-serving interests, matters of nation-building and national identity, the personal legacies of particular country leaders are some of the prominent themes found in the region's foreign policy-related research. These topics do not merely demonstrate the range of possible explanations for foreign policy but also speak about different levels of analysis applied in the works.

The discussion follows in three subsections. Each of them examines foreign policy studies of Central Asia as found to belong to one of 'ideas,' 'interests' or 'institutions.' The trio will not reflect the entirety of research done in the field. However, as Hay (2004: 204) put it, ideas, interests and institutions reflect the 'conventional three-fold classification of independent variables,' and thus, shall be helpful to structure the discussion. Since ideas, interests and institutions feature centrally in different parts of FPA literature, the sections below start with conceptual propositions relating to each of the 'i's before looking at regional scholarship on the subject.

Ideas in the foreign policy of Central Asian states

The scope of phenomena that 'ideational' sources of foreign policy may include is vast. One may list national culture, political ideologies, public opinion or individual beliefs as ideas attributed to different types of social actors. The list exposes not only the vagueness of the notion but also points to the multiplicity of methodological approaches within which ideas may operate as a critical concept. Studies of ideational dimensions of foreign policy, therefore, will need to articulate what and whose 'ideas' matter, what type of actors 'own' ideas and how to theorise the linkage between ideas, interests and policy outcomes.

Despite being a broad church of research traditions, idea-based foreign policy explanations have a shared predisposition to avoid, if not reject, 'materialist' explanations. First, ideational approaches counter the assumption of foreign policy actors being rational units. For the latter, the state behaviour in the context of anarchy and survival is, to crudely simplify, as predictable as the trajectories of billiard balls on the board. Such 'timeless wisdom' will not hold when ideas develop that are not assumed but are constructed and reconstructed. Second, ideational approaches challenge the assumption of the state as a unitary actor of international relations. States are not units that can have ideas unless one accepts a Wendtian version of constructivism in international relations (e.g. Hudson 2014). Instead, we have ruling parties' ideologies, powerful leaders' beliefs or the culture and identity of communities as the underpinning forces shaping the ideational in international relations. Finally, idea-based explanations allow an understanding of change in foreign policy, a challenge that rationality-based approaches are less well equipped to address (e.g. Welch 2005). Beliefs are not fixed in time, which contrasts with the 'utility-maximizer' logic of rational actor approaches.

There is no single way to theorise ideas in foreign policy analysis. The relationship between the ideational and the material is open for interpretations and debate. First, since ideas are constructed, there may always be an 'interest' behind such construction. As Herman and Chomsky (2002) powerfully and popularly argued, public opinion, one form of 'idea' that can influence foreign policy, can be *manufactured* by powerful actors. Second, the very notion of juxtaposing ideas and interests can be problematic. Interests are nothing but ideas, and thus, the two are constitutive rather than competing notions (e.g. Laffey and Weldes 1997; Goldstein and Keohane 1993). Thus, 'ideas' is an essential but not readily employable concept for foreign policy.

What ideas came to replace the communist ideology as a foundation of foreign policy in post-communist countries? This is the question Fawn's edited volume (2003b) poses, with chapters covering post-communist countries of Europe and former Soviet republics, including Kazakhstan and Kyrgyzstan. While all cases ascertain the death of state ideology, the answers to the posed question differs across countries. In place of official Marxism, ideational underpinning in foreign policies now could be located at different levels, from leaders' beliefs (as Havel in Fawn 2003a) to views and concepts of the competing elite groupings (as in Light 2003), to the relevance of deep-seated cultural paradigms (Jones 2003). What would be the answer to the above question for Central Asia?

Two chapters on Central Asian states in Fawn's volume extend a common argument: Central Asian states had a weak sense of national identity, allowing greater freedom for state leaders to craft one 'from scratch' (Cummings 2003; Huskey 2003; see also Hanova 2019; Mullojanov 2019). Two factors routinely figure as the premise of this argument. First, Central Asian states lacked pre-Soviet statehood, and thus, were effectively new states rather than just newly independent states (e.g. Huskey 2003). Second, the countries of the region became independent not as a result of a national struggle for independence but simply because there was no alternative following Soviet disintegration in 1991. Thus came a dream moment for constructivist scholars: Central Asian leaders suddenly found themselves in charge of nation-building.

The primary implication of the 'dearth of usable national history,' as Huskey (2003) put it, was a substantial autonomy of state leaders, and government bureaucracy in general, in devising grand ideas (e.g. Mullojanov 2019). This autonomy, in turn, had two implications on the development of foreign policy ideas. First, the ruling elites proposed and promoted ideas that directly served their political legitimation and regime survival. Thus, Kazakhstan's much-publicised Eurasian/neo-Eurasianism foreign policy was, as Anceschi (2014: 733) argued, a case of 'subjugation of foreign policy rhetoric to the logic of regime-building.' Similarly, Laruelle (2013: 6) suggests the foreign policy rhetoric of Central Asian states remained primarily oriented to the domestic audience aimed at 'legitimizing new states, with the countries leaders framing themselves as 'fathers of the nation,' while promoting national 'values' the population are supposed to share in common.'

The second implication of Central Asian leaders' autonomy in constructing national identity was a high degree of flexibility in crafting international identities. Without a history of independent statehood, the new Central Asian states had no historic enemies or binding alliances that would tie their hands. As Cummings (2003: 146) suggests, a weak national identity 'facilitate[d] the practice of flexible relations with all states.' A most prominent name for such a policy came to be 'multi-vectorism' (Hanks 2009; Dzhuraev 2019). In a practical sense, one could call it a 'policy of noncontradiction in foreign policy and friendly relations with all' (Kuchins et al., 2015: 4) or, even more bluntly, an ability to 'adopt the image that is expected [by external partners] of them' (Laruelle 2013: 9).

The final note concerns the glaring lack of the bottom-up dimension of foreign policy ideas. The above discussions outline the context: weak bottom-up nationalism combined with authoritarian regimes left little chance for the public, and its ideas and beliefs, to matter. Noteworthy, in a recent piece, Laruelle and Royse (2020) confirm that Russia is by far the most popular foreign partner among Central Asian residents. This confirms Lewis's (2015) observation that Moscow's hegemony for Kyrgyzstan sits well with Russia's genuine popularity in this country. Questions remain open, however, of whether the surveys point to the concurrence of foreign policy and public opinion, a case of 'manufactured' public opinion or merely the existence of data that may or may not carry relevance to governments' actions.

Interests in the foreign policy of Central Asian states

'No nation has friends, only interests,' the popular saying goes. But what are interests? Do nations have a property of 'having' interests? Furthermore, what interests have driven Central Asian foreign policies? One starting point for IR students is Morgenthau's (1954) concept of 'interest defined as power,' one of the premises of classical realism. For neorealists, the interests of the states are tied to ensuring survival in an anarchic world. Interests, thus, are theorised to be given and fixed, a highly debated question. The underlying assumption, however, is shared attribution of interest to states, leading to the ubiquitous notion of 'national interest.'

In contrast to IR theories, approaches in FPA do not assume the existence of some known interests of the nation. This view does not reject the notion of 'national interests' but defines it, borrowing from Hagan (1989: 146), as 'the ruling group's core beliefs about their nation's international situation.' In other words, national interest as a concept is better treated as an 'idea,' allowing contestation on what interests are/should be and the possibility of their change over time.

Thus, moving beyond the notion of 'national interests,' FPA-oriented works focus on the political interests of foreign policymakers as crucial to understanding foreign policy actions. Achieving power and retaining office once they reach power is their primary interest political actors (Siverson and Bueno de Mesquita 2017: 2; Schultz 2013: 480–1). Foreign policy is not unrelated to these interests. Thus, Volgy and Schwarz (1991: 618) proposed significant foreign policy changes are most likely to happen when they serve the interests of (elected, in their case) politicians to survive in office. Factors such as 'prospects of electoral defeat' or 'threat to regime survival' or 'intra-party rivalry' gain primary importance for leaders in their assessment of foreign policy actions (Mintz 2004: 9; also Goldmann 1989; Kneuer 2017).

Central Asian foreign policy studies demonstrate a strong focus on domestic political interests as an explanation for foreign policy. The argument found across the literature is that the ruling regime interests drive foreign policy. The underlying proposition of the regimes–foreign policy linkage is that the ruling regimes of Central Asia have effectively hijacked the state. This is not something surprising for former Soviet citizens; simply put, presidents replaced the Communist Party as the embodiment of the regime and the state. The post-communist transition literature describes the above in terms of sultanism, neopatrimonialism, clanism informal type networks (e.g. Ilkhamov 2007; Lewis 2012; Kunysz 2012). While the analytical value of this form of conceptualisation has been challenged (e.g. Isaacs 2014), the common contention is that the state as an institution, in Central Asia, was put at the service of ruling elites' narrow interests. Such a circumstance underpins two related arguments in the Central Asian literature on domestic political sources of foreign policy.

The first is a classic regime security argument. Cooley (2012: 21) put succinctly that: 'regime survival is state security' in Central Asia. Writing on Uzbekistan, Allison (2008: 185) argues that 'the reinforcement of regime security and legitimacy' as opposed to 'security, economic or trade goals' was the key to understanding Tashkent's seemingly contradictory stance on various regional initiatives. His article covers the post-2005 period, when in the aftermath of 2005 Andijan events, Uzbekistan severed its ties with the West and re-joined regional initiatives in the CIS area. Just a few years later, the same ruling regimes' interest explained Uzbekistan's openness to the United States (McGlinchey 2012). The underlying concept is straightforward: Central Asian regimes' foreign policy decisions reflect their interests in retaining power.

The second form of regime interest – foreign policy linkage lies in the economic dimension. Foreign policy in Central Asia, the argument goes, is used to extract material benefits for the ruling regimes. Corruption at high levels, just as at any other level, of government, is no news in Central Asia (e.g. Marat 2006; Engvall 2014). Foreign policy was not left untouched. Kyrgyz government's decisions on the fate of the US airbase at the Manas airport directly reflected illegal material benefits ripped by the inner circles of presidents Akaev and Bakiev (McGlinchey 2011; Cooley 2012; Toktomushev 2015). Cooley and Heathershaw (2017) demonstrate the scale and depth of this business, with Central Asian dictators proven skilful in using Western banks, offshore zones and other offerings of the globalised world to store the hard-earned resources.

Institutions in the foreign policy of Central Asian states

While individuals are primary actors carrying ideas, interpreting the signals from outside and making decisions, they do not operate as 'free agents' but are embedded within particular institutional contexts (Checkel 1993: 277). Foreign policy decision-making, one of the major strands of FPA, examines, among others, the effects of such institutional contexts on decision-making processes. FPA literature is vast and diverse on the topic, but a shared assumption is that it matters 'who and how' make foreign policy decisions. There is no unitary and rational actor such as the state that takes a decision. Instead, the latter comes as a result of a complex and often opaque deliberation process as Allison's (1971) bureaucratic politics model demonstrated. This leads us to another dimension of a domestic source of foreign policy – policymaking institutions.

In assessing an institution's impact on foreign policy, two approaches stand out. The first approach takes a broad look at political institutions and their relationship. In democracies, for instance, decision-makers face robust institutional constraints, and thus, are less likely to demonstrate foreign policy changes than non-democratic regimes (Mattes et al. 2015: 289; see also Bueno de Mesquita et al. 1999). Relatedly, stronger parliaments, Reiter and Tillman (2002: 824) contend, impose stronger constraints on the executive's freedom to use force internationally. The second approach focuses on the ultimate decision-unit (Hermann 2001), i.e. actors immediately involved in making decisions. Thus, the extremely cohesive small group will likely lead to poor decisions due to self-censorship, a situation known as groupthink (Janis 1982; Mintz and Sofrin 2017). In contrast, if the group includes veto players, i.e. individuals 'whose agreement is required for a policy decision,' that would reduce the likelihood of foreign policy change (Tsebelis 1995; Oppermann and Brummer 2017).

The dimension of 'institutions' is relatively underpopulated in Central Asian foreign policy studies. The most prominent theme is that of the president's dominant role in shaping foreign policies (e.g. Abazov 1999; Ayazbekov 2013). Thus, Sari (2012: 136) argues that Kyrgyz presidents made the decisions, and the government agencies implemented them, reflecting 'overwhelming political superiority of leaders who control the state mechanism.' In an earlier piece, Abazov (1999: 62) writes of 'the strong personal influence of the leaders on the formation of the Central Asian republics' foreign policy.' Wood (2005: 347) provides a rare challenge, arguing that 'the Kyrgyz bureaucratic elites were central to foreign policy formation and thinking.'

The relative paucity of research on foreign policymaking institutions can partly relate to the nature of political systems that emerged in Central Asia after 1991. Political and policymaking institutions work differently in 'neo-patrimonial,' 'clientelistic' systems (Radnitz 2012; Collins 2004, Engvall 2011). Presidents emerged as chief patrons, combining the formal hierarchy with informal influence (e.g. Hale 2014). In addition to making most policymaking institutions irrelevant, such types of regimes also pose significant problems with access to data. In other words, what goes on within the corridors of power is rarely accessible to the broader public.

To sum up the above, what do we learn about the domestic sources of foreign policy in Central Asia? The single biggest argument reveals itself in the ideas, interests and institutions sections: foreign policy in Central Asia is at the service of corrupt and authoritarian regimes.

Ruling regimes' political survival in troubled times and enrichment in better times are found to be the driving forces behind foreign policy decisions. Political ideologies, public opinion or national culture remain marginally interesting for scholars. Instead, foreign policy ideas are designed at the top level, again, with regime legitimation featuring centrally as the motive. Examining the nature of decision-making groups in Central Asian capital cities appears to be an irrelevant research task for the unchallenged dominance of the regime leaders, i.e. presidents.

The above arguments are familiar and understandable to those who closely follow Central Asian politics. However, they also raise several important questions for prospective scholars of Central Asian foreign policies. First, are Central Asian political systems so unique to warrant such a preponderance of political regimes in foreign policy research? Second, what are the ways to move beyond and beneath the notion of 'regimes' to expose foreign policymaking at a more subtle level? Put differently, what are the ways to learn and study foreign policy in Central Asia through the theories and concepts of foreign policy analysis without losing a critical eye on the kind of politics we face? These are the questions that the final section will address.

Beyond rogue regimes: A case for analytical eclecticism

There are good reasons for the dominance of 'regimes' in studies of Central Asian politics. Thirty years after becoming independent, these countries have not yet experienced peaceful power succession through elections. Sitting presidents have never lost elections, including in Kyrgyzstan, where national voting carries greater meaning than in the rest of the region. Power changes hands when the leader dies (as it happened in Turkmenistan and Uzbekistan), is thrown out of power through uprising (as happened twice in Kyrgyzstan) or gracefully steps aside, having put a trusted 'successor' (as in Kazakhstan and Kyrgyzstan). Central Asian states are routinely found in the top of rankings of corrupt and non-democratic countries (e.g. Freedom House 2018). With the 'transition paradigm' mostly dead (e.g. Carothers 2002; Ambrosio 2014), scholars' attention has understandably turned to the new regimes and their implications.

Importantly, Central Asian regimes, though willing and skilful in employing foreign policy to advance their parochial political interests, are not unique in this business. Nor does this argument apply to authoritarian and/or corrupt regimes only. The relationship between domestic political standing of leaders and foreign policy is a common point within various FPA approaches (e.g. Mintz 2004; Hagan 1995). One prominent, if extreme, approach is the diversionary war theory, also referred to as elite survival or scapegoat theory (e.g. Levy 1988; Hagan 1994; Morgan and Bickers 1992). In a basic version, the theory contends that when a 'government, democratic or not, is under domestic pressure, it enacts an adventurous, diversionary foreign policy' (Smith 1996: 133). Thus, the findings on regime interests and foreign policy in Central Asia are in line with and contribute to particular strands of FPA.

That said, there are at least three ways in which an exclusive focus on regime interests may limit understanding of Central Asian foreign policies. First, the acceptance of 'regimes' as a unit of analysis portrays them as a form of unitary and rational actors, reproducing rather than challenging the premises of structural approaches. Second, regime security literature has thus far mostly kept domestic politics 'bracketed,' limiting readers' attention to external threats to the regimes. Finally, limiting the explanatory variables to ruling regimes' interests reveals predominantly monocausal views of Central Asian foreign policies.

The first reservation about limiting the unit of analysis to regimes is theoretical. The interests of ruling regimes are often brought up as evidence of 'agency' of Central Asian states, contrary to IR-oriented approaches that view these countries as pawns in the great game (e.g. Laruelle 2013; Cooley 2012). However, the result is only a replacement of one presumably unitary and rational actor such as a state with another one, which is a regime. But do the ruling regimes have qualities justifying the assumptions of their solid and unitary nature and rational (thus, predictable) behaviour? Does it matter who exactly constitutes the 'ruling regime' at any given time? While autocrats and dictators are called so for a reason, do they and their inner circles, rather than 'a regime' remain ultimate actors? The focus on regime interests is a welcome step away from IR-centric bracketing of states. However, if left unpacked, regimes risk becoming the endpoint of 'domestic-level' inquiries into foreign policies of Central Asian states.

Second, the shift of research from IR-centric views of states to domestic ruling regimes is meant to introduce domestic politics to the picture but often does not. The logic of the ruling regime's political survival is primarily a function of domestic politics. In Central Asia, however, the primary threat to the regimes appears to be outside the countries. Thus, Allison (2008) argues that Uzbekistan's regionalism policy reflected Tashkent's reaction to the threat to the regime which emanated from the US rather than from domestic political actors and processes. Such approaches may stem from a plausible assumption that opposition posed no credible threat to the ruling elites. However, such assumption, while very accurate, does not make domestic politics analytically irrelevant. Moreover, the assumption of 'no domestic threat to the regime' is more accurate for some Central Asian states and less for others. Thus, the notion of 'ruling regime' should help shed light on domestic politics, not exclude it.

Third, the prominence of regime interests as explanations for Central Asian foreign policies indicate the primacy of monocausal approaches to foreign policy analysis. Put simply, the logic of regime interests exhausts the scope of phenomena considered relevant to the subject. There is nothing wrong with such an approach when the research's interest is primarily with understanding the implications of a selected 'variable' (such as the domestic political regime) as an explanation for foreign policy. Some better-known FPA theories belong to this literature, such as the bureaucratic politics and foreign policy (Allison 1971; Halperin 1974) or leaders' operational codes (George 1969). However, the monocausal approach becomes a limitation when a researcher seeks to appraise the complexity of the environment within which foreign policy is made. Focusing on a single aspect of foreign policy would be akin to, as Hudson (2014: 186) put it, 'figuring out a chemical reaction taking place in a vacuum.' Would our understanding of Central Asian foreign policies benefit if the explanations included, but were not limited to, wise presidents, power-hungry regimes or kleptocratic ruling families? If so, what analytical framework might allow that?

Before addressing the above questions, it is worthwhile to acknowledge the main reasons for the prominence of monocausal explanations. One is the sheer volume of information relevant to the subject. Foreign policy action is an outcome of different factors at different levels of analysis, as FPA textbooks state (e.g. Smith et al. 2008). Moreover, as Hudson writes, foreign policy is 'dynamic and full of contingencies' and can also be opaque, posing a challenge for the use of integrative approach (2014: 187). Accounting for multiple sources of foreign policy, therefore, can be both an analytical and practical challenge. A related reason for monocausal approaches may lie in the difficulties of transcending the 'metatheoretical principles' underpinning particular research traditions (Katzenstein and Sil 2008: 2). In words of Hirschman, social scientists may get 'happy enough when they have gotten hold of *one* paradigm or line of causation' (1970: 341).

So, how do we move beyond monocausal explanations in foreign policy? One of the answers to this question, proposed in this chapter, is the recognition of analytical eclecticism as a legitimate way to design social research. FPA is itself a broad church, with theoretical eclecticism being its essential characteristic (e.g. Alden and Aran 2017). More specifically, however, analytical eclecticism is an approach that would bring together, as Katzenstein and Sil wrote (2008: 2-3), the 'features of analyses in theories initially embedded in separate research traditions' to address research questions in 'original, creative ways.' The above does not imply a random selection of concepts. Instead, it is the overarching research purpose or research question more specifically that informs and guides the selection of theories and concepts into one analytical framework (e.g. Katzenstein and Sil 2008; Blavoukos and Bourantonis 2014).

There is a limited number of works on Central Asian foreign policies that move beyond a monocausal approach. Fumagalli's (2007) assessment of Uzbekistan's realignment after 2005 acknowledges the interplay of domestic and external factors. Thus, while the regime's insecurity explains Uzbekistan's 'falling-out' with the United States, the event could not have occurred 'without a sudden availability of Russia's energy revenues' (Fumagalli 2007: 266). Cummings reviews foreign security relations of Central Asian states within Carlsnaes's 'synthetic approach.' The latter suggests viewing a foreign policy as a reflection of the simultaneous interplay of three dimensions, intentional, dispositional and structural (Carlsnaes 2007; 2013). Wood (2005) in his analysis of Kyrgyzstan's foreign policy brings together different explanations together, including the country's smallness, Soviet and post-Soviet politics of nationalism as well as the influence of specific individuals in charge of formulating foreign policy. However, such studies in Central Asia scholarship are not only a few in number but also mostly limited to domestic–external dichotomy, with the domestic part solidly locked under either national or regime interests.

An alternative analytically eclectic framework to study Central Asian foreign policy could be drawn from the very selection of variables discussed in the previous section: ideas, interests and institutions. Bringing the three 'i's as part of a single model is found in various parts of social science. It was employed, for instance, in the analyses of protectionism in international political economy (Bhagwati 1989), global economic governance (Schirm 2016) or welfare policies (Hudson et al. 2008). A textbook in comparative politics proposes ideas, interests and institutions as a framework to understand the influence of global development on domestic politics (Kopstein and Lichbach 2005: 22). In a rare case of the model referenced in a foreign policy study, Checkel (1993: 276) studies the role of ideas in Soviet foreign policy 'by examining the institutional and political contexts that have shaped and filtered these ideas.'

The 3-i's framework carries a simple message: each of ideas, interests and institutions is central to understanding foreign policy actions of any country. Within foreign policy analysis, each of 'i's feature at the core of different theoretical strands. Actual foreign policy events, however, are 'too complicated to vindicate a single theory' to adapt from Evans (in Kohli et al. 1995: 4). For an analytically eclectic framework, therefore, ideas, interests and institutions are not three alternative or competing 'variables' but constitutive components of foreign policy action. Borrowing from Kopstein and Lichbach (2005: 28), institutions can 'influence the formation of interests and identities,' but themselves can be changed by different groups seeking to 'gain the political power needed to satisfy their own interests and identities.'

The application of the 3-i's framework will enrich the existing approaches to foreign policy studies in Central Asia in three ways. First, it will offer a more nuanced notion of a foreign policy actor. While Central Asian leaders may be authoritarian and corrupt, the 3-i's framework would also treat them as bearers of ideas *and* as units of specific (and changeable) decision-making institutions. One example could be Kyrgyzstan's decisions on Manas airbase, argued to be tightly linked to corrupt interests of the ruling regimes (Cooley 2012; Toktomushev 2015). The 3-i's scheme would shed additional light on how President Bakiev's declared 'pragmatism' in foreign policy and the rise of his family members as insulated decision-making group were part of the broader political context in which Kyrgyzstan's infamous U-turn on the airbase came about in 2009.

Second, the 3-i's model will open-up an opportunity to trace and assess changes in the foreign policy of a country over time. When a powerful president is replaced, either through revolution or managed succession, the new leader may end up being more of a 'crusader,' a type of leader more prone to extreme policies (Hermann et al. 2001: 87–8). A regime change could similarly alter established decision-making institutions, replacing not only influential personalities but also the mode of deliberating and making decisions among them. The nature of the political regime in Uzbekistan could not have changed with the death of the long-time president Islam Karimov. His successor, however, has demonstrated a visibly greater inclination towards more openness in foreign policy (Tolipov 2020). In his turn, Kazakh president Kassym-Jomart Tokayev sits over a very different foreign policy decision-making institution to that enjoyed by his predecessor, Nursultan Nazarbayev (Bohr et al. 2019). Such details may prove interesting to scholars in the context of FPA literature on particular decision-making institutions being more prone to taking extreme foreign policy decisions (e.g. Hermann and Hermann 1989; Mintz and Sofrin 2017).

Third, the 3-i's framework will allow researchers to focus on individuals as foreign policy actors. First, 'only human beings can have ideas' as Hudson (2014: 12) powerfully argues. Whether we speak of Akaev's Silk Road diplomacy, Nazarbaev's Eurasianism or Karimov's 'self-sufficiency' doctrine, individual humans are actors to author, promote or dismiss such ideas. Second, taking Hudson's quote further, we may suggest that only human beings can interpret, rationalise or reflect on the kind of political environment they find themselves in. Regime insecurity, thus, is not a condition to be assumed to occur under certain conditions but a specific situation defined to be such by specific individuals. Finally, individual level is key to make sense of institutions. Knowing the type of political regime or system will not help with identifying key decision-making actors. As if with Central Asia in mind, Hermann and Hagan (1998: 131) remind that 'understanding a government's formal structure is less important than understanding whose positions actually count at a particular point in time.' Thus, the focus on an individual will unlock the benefits of the 3-i's approach to foreign policy.

Conclusion

The volume and variety of foreign policy research in Central Asia has grown in the past decades. This change signalled a move away from geopolitics as the paradigm of international relations of the region. The increased attention to domestic sources of foreign policy has revealed an intricate relationship between the type of political regimes emerging in the region and their foreign policy ideas and actions. Central Asian states, the regional scholarship maintains, have to be seen as more than mere pawns on the chessboard of geopolitics.

The diversity of approaches to understanding Central Asian foreign policies, however, has not addressed some important imbalances in the scholarship. In particular, intellectual inquiries into foreign policymaking in the region retained the prominence of structural and monocausal approaches. If no more pawns in the hands of chess grandmasters, Central Asian states still retained the qualities of billiard balls. The latter came in the form of a focus on ruling regimes, a unit of analysis often ascribed the properties of a unitary and rational actor, akin to the state in traditional IR theories. Furthermore, the overwhelming attention to ruling regimes' parochial political interests only underscored, and perhaps also explained, the paucity of research on other sources of foreign policy.

The suggestion of imbalance in the literature is not a rebuke against excellent works on foreign policy in Central Asia. Instead, it points to more avenues for research on Central Asian politics and foreign policies that lie ahead for researchers of the future. As the chapter suggested, one way forward might be a greater openness of scholars to analytically eclectic approaches. Frameworks such as the '3-i's: ideas, interests and institutions' could draw on the wealth of theoretical propositions in FPA and growing empirical observations in the region to offer novel ways to interpret the foreign policies of Central Asian states.

Bibliography

Abazov, R. (1999). *The Formation of Post-Soviet International Politics in Kazakhstan, Kyrgyzstan, and Uzbekistan.* 21. University of Washington: The Henry M. Jackson School of International Studies.

Akaev, A. (2003). 'Speech at the United Nations,' 2 October, https://www.un.org/webcast/ga/58/statements/kyrgeng031002.htm (Accessed 17 August 2020).

Akaev, A. (2004). *Dumaya o buduschem s Optimizmom: Razmyshleniya o vneshnei politike i miroutroistve (Thinking of the future with optimism: Reflections on foreign policy and the world order).* Moscow: Mezhdunarodnye otnosheniya.

Alden, C. and A. Aran. (2017). *Foreign Policy Analysis: New Approaches.* Second edition. London: Routledge, Taylor & Francis Group.

Allison, G.T. (1971). *Essence of Decision: Explaining the Cuban Missile Crisis.* Boston: Little, Brown.

Allison, R. (2004). 'Strategic Reassertion in Russia's Central Asia Policy,' *International Affairs* 80(2), pp. 277–93.

Allison, R. (2008). 'Virtual Regionalism, Regional Structures and Regime Security in Central Asia,' *Central Asian Survey* 27(2), pp. 185–202.

Ambrosio, T. (2014). 'Beyond the Transition Paradigm: A Research Agenda for Authoritarian Consolidation,' *Demokratizatsiya: The Journal of Post-Soviet Democratization* 22(3), pp. 471–94.

Anceschi, L. (2008). *Turkmenistan's Foreign Policy: Positive Neutrality and the Consolidation of the Turkmen Regime.* London: Routledge.

Anceschi, L. (2010). 'Integrating Domestic Politics and Foreign Policy Making: The Cases of Turkmenistan and Uzbekistan,' *Central Asian Survey* 29(2), pp. 143–158.

Anceschi, L. (2014). 'Regime-building, Identity-making and Foreign Policy: Neo-Eurasianist Rhetoric in Post-Soviet Kazakhstan,' *Nationalities Papers* 42(5), pp. 733–49.

Ayazbekov, A. (2013). *Independent Kazakhstan and the 'black box' of Decision-making: Understanding Kazakhstan's Foreign Policy in the Early Independence Period (1991–4).* PhD Thesis. University of St Andrews. http://research-repository.st-andrews.ac.uk/handle/10023/4895.

Bhagwati, J.N. (1989). *Protectionism.* Cambridge: MIT Press.

Blavoukos, S. and D. Bourantonis. (2014). 'Identifying Parameters of Foreign Policy Change: An Eclectic Approach,' *Cooperation and Conflict* 49(4), pp. 483–500.

Bohr, A., B. Brauer, N. Gould-Davies, N. Kassenova, J. Lillis, K. Mallinson, J. Nixey and D. Satpayev. (2019). *Kazakhstan: Tested by Transition.* Chatham House Report, November.

Brzezinski, Z. (1998). *The Grand Chessboard: American Primacy and Its Geostrategic Imperatives.* New York: Basic Books.

Carlsnaes, W. (2007). 'How Should We Study the Foreign Policies of Small European States?,' *Nação e Defesa* 118(3), pp. 7–20.

Carlsnaes, W. (2013). 'Foreign Policy,' in Carlsnaes, W., Risse-Kappen, T. and Simmons, B.A. (eds.) *Handbook of International Relations.* 2nd edition. Los Angeles: SAGE, pp. 298–325.

Carothers, T. (2002). 'The End of the Transition Paradigm,' *Journal of Democracy* 13(1), pp. 5–21.

Checkel, J. (1993). 'Ideas, Institutions, and the Gorbachev Foreign Policy Revolution,' *World Politics* 45(2), pp. 271–300.

Collins, K. (2004). 'The Logic of Clan Politics: Evidence From the Central Asian Trajectories,' *World Politics* 56(2), pp. 224–61.

Cooley, A. (2012). *Great Games, Local Rules: The New Great Power Contest in Central Asia.* Oxford: Oxford University Press.

Cooley, A. and J. Heathershaw (2017). *Dictators Without Borders: Power and Money in Central Asia.* 1st edition. New Haven: Yale University Press.

Cummings, S.N. (2003). 'Eurasian Bridge or Murky Waters Between East and West? Ideas, Identity and Output in Kazakhstan's Foreign Policy,' *Journal of Communist Studies and Transition Politics* 19(3), pp. 139–55.

Cummings, S.N. (2014). 'A Synthetic Approach to Foreign Security Relations and Policies in Central Asia,' in Pekkanen, S., Ravenhill, J., and Foot, R. (eds.) *The Oxford Handbook of the International Relations of Asia.* New York: Oxford University Press, pp. 481–502.

De Mesquita, B.B., J.D. Morrow, R.M. Siverson and A. Smith (1999). 'An Institutional Explanation of the Democratic Peace,' *American Political Science Review* 93(4), pp. 791–807.

Dzhuraev, E. (2015). 'Central Asian Stances on the Ukraine Crisis: Treading a Fine Line?,' *Connections* 14(4), pp. 1–10.

Dzhuraev, E. (2019). '"Multi-vectoral" Central Asia: On the Other Side of Major Power Agendas,' in Frappi, C. and Indeo, F. (eds.) *Monitoring Central Asia and the Caspian Area: Development Policies, Regional Trends, and Italian Interests.* Venice: Edizioni Ca' Foscari (Eurasiatica), pp. 15–33.

Engvall, J. (2011). *The State as Investment Market: An Analytical Framework for Interpreting Politics and Bureaucracy in Kyrgyzstan*. PhD Thesis. Uppsala University, http://www.diva-portal.org/smash/record.jsf?pid=diva2:445254 (Accessed 5 October 2015).

Engvall, J. (2014). 'Why Are Public Offices Sold in Kyrgyzstan?,' *Post-Soviet Affairs* 30(1), pp. 67–85.

Fawn, R. (2003a). 'Reconstituting a National Identity: Ideologies in Czech Foreign Policy After the Split,' in Fawn, R. (ed.) *Ideology and National Identity in Post-communist Foreign Policies*. London: Frank Cass Publishers, pp. 201–224.

Fawn, R. (2003b). *Ideology and National Identity in Post-communist Foreign Policies*. London: Frank Cass Publishers.

Freedom House. (2018). *Nations in Transit 2018: Kyrgyzstan*.

Fumagalli, M. (2007). 'Alignments and Realignments in Central Asia: The Rationale and Implications of Uzbekistan's Rapprochement With Russia,' *International Political Science Review* 28(3), pp. 253–71.

George, A.L. (1969). ''The' Operational Code': A Neglected Approach to the Study of Political Leaders and Decision-making,' *International Studies Quarterly* 13(2), pp. 190–222.

Goldmann, K. (1989). 'The Line in Water: International and Domestic Politics,' *Cooperation and Conflict* 24(3), pp. 103–16.

Goldstein, J. and R.O. Keohane. (1993). 'Ideas and Foreign Policy: An Analytical Framework,' in Goldstein, J. and Keohane, R.O. (eds.) *Ideas and Foreign Policy: Beliefs, Institutions, and Political Change*. Ithaca: Cornell University Press, pp. 3–30.

Hagan, J.D. (1989). 'Domestic Political Regime Changes and Foreign Policy Restructuring in Western Europe: A Conceptual Framework and Initial Empirical Analysis,' *Cooperation and Conflict* 24(3), pp. 141–62.

Hagan, J.D. (1994). 'Domestic Political Systems and War Proneness,' *Mershon International Studies Review* 38(2), pp. 183–207.

Hagan, J.D. (1995). 'Domestic Political Explanations in the Analysis of Foreign Policy,' in Neack, L., Hey, J.A.K. and Haney, P.J. (eds.) *Foreign Policy Analysis: Continuity and Change in Its Second Generation*. Englewood Cliffs, NJ: Prentice Hall, pp. 117–44.

Hale, H.E. (2014). *Patronal Politics: Eurasian Regime Dynamics in Comparative Perspective*. Cambridge: Cambridge University Press.

Halperin, M.H. (1974). *Bureaucratic Politics and Foreign Policy*. Washington, DC: Brookings Institution Press.

Hanks, R.R. (2009). "Multi-vector Politics' and Kazakhstan's Emerging Role as a geo-strategic Player in Central Asia,' *Journal of Balkan and Near Eastern Studies* 11(3), pp. 257–67.

Hanova, S. (2019). 'State Identities in Post-Soviet Foreign Policy: Theories and Cases in Central Asia,' in Isaacs, R. and Frigerio, A. (eds.) *Theorizing Central Asian Politics*. Cham: Springer International Publishing, pp. 213–36.

Hay, C. (2004). 'Review: Ideas, Interests and Institutions in the Comparative Political Economy of Great Transformations,' *Review of International Political Economy* 11(1), pp. 204–26.

Herman, E.S. and N. Chomsky (2002). *Manufacturing Consent: The Political Economy of the Mass Media*. Reprint edition. New York: Pantheon.

Hermann, M.G. (2001). 'How Decision Units Shape Foreign Policy: A Theoretical Framework,' *International Studies Review* 3(2), pp. 47–81.

Hermann, M.G. and J.D. Hagan (1998). 'International Decision Making: Leadership Matters,' *Foreign Policy* 110, pp. 124–37.

Hermann, M.G. and C.F. Hermann (1989). 'Who Makes Foreign Policy Decisions and How: An Empirical Inquiry,' *International Studies Quarterly* 33(4), pp. 361–87.

Hermann, M.G., T. Preston, B. Korany and T.M. Shaw (2001). 'Who Leads Matters: The Effects of Powerful Individuals,' *International Studies Review* 3(2), pp. 83–131.

Hey, J.A.K. (2003). *Small States in World Politics: Explaining Foreign Policy Behavior*. Boulder: Lynne Rienner Publishers.

Hirschman, A.O. (1970). 'The Search for Paradigms as a Hindrance to Understanding,' *World Politics* 22(3), pp. 329–43.

Hudson, J., G.-J. Hwang and S. Kühner. (2008). 'Between Ideas, Institutions and Interests: Analysing Third Way Welfare Reform Programmes in Germany and the United Kingdom,' *Journal of Social Policy* 37(2), pp. 207–30.

Hudson, V.M. (2014). *Foreign Policy Analysis: Classic and Contemporary Theory*. 2nd edition. Lanham: Rowman & Littlefield.

Huskey, E. (2003). 'National Identity From Scratch: Defining Kyrgyzstan's Role in World Affairs,' *Journal of Communist Studies and Transition Politics* 19(3), pp. 111–38.

Huskey, E. (2008). 'Foreign Policy in a Vulnerable State: Kyrgyzstan as Military Entrepot Between the Great Powers,' *China and Eurasia Forum Quarterly* 6(4), pp. 5–18.

Ilkhamov, A. (2007). 'Neopatrimonialism, Interest Groups and Patronage Networks: The Impasses of the Governance System in Uzbekistan,' *Central Asian Survey* 26(1), pp. 65–84.

Indeo, F. (2010). 'The Geopolitical Consequences of the US-Russian 'Military Airbase Race' in Central Asia,' *China and Eurasia Forum Quarterly* 8(3), pp. 149–72.

Isaacs, R. (2014). 'Neopatrimonialism and Beyond: Reassessing the Formal and Informal in the Study of Central Asian Politics,' *Contemporary Politics* 20(2), pp. 229–45.

Janis, I.L. (1982). *Groupthink: Psychological Studies of Policy Decisions and Fiascoes*. 2nd edition. Boston: Cengage Learning.

Jones, S. (2003). 'The Role of Cultural Paradigms in Georgian Foreign Policy,' in Fawn, R. (ed.) *Ideology and National Identity in Post-communist Foreign Policies*. London: Frank Cass Publishers, pp. 81–108.

Katzenstein, P. and R. Sil (2008). 'Eclectic Theorizing in the Study and Practice of International Relations,' *The Oxford Handbook of International Relations*, August.

Kazantsev, A. (2008). *Bol'shaya Igra» s Neizvestnymi Pravilami: Mirovaya Politika i Tsentral'naya Aziya*. Moscow: Nasledie Evrazii.

Kluczewska, K. and Juraev, S. (2020). 'The EU and Central Asia: Nuances of an Aided Partnership,' in Fawn, R. (ed.) *Managing Security Threats along the EU's Eastern Flanks*. Cham: Springer International Publishing, pp. 225–252.

Kneuer, M. (2017). 'Autocratic Regimes and Foreign Policy,' *Oxford Research Encyclopedia of Politics*, https://oxfordre.com/politics/view/10.1093/acrefore/9780190228637.001.0001/acrefore-9780190228637-e-392.

Kohli, A., Evans, P., Katzenstein, P.J., Przeworski, A., Rudolph, S.H., Scott, J.C. and Skocpol, T. (1995). 'The Role of Theory in Comparative Politics: A Symposium,' *World Politics* 48(1), pp. 1–49.

Kopstein, J. and M. Lichbach (2005). 'The Framework of Analysis,' in Kopstein, J. and Lichbach, M. (eds.) *Comparative Politics: Interests, Identities, and Institutions in a Changing Global Order*. 2nd edition. Cambridge: Cambridge University Press, pp. 16–38.

Krapohl, S. and A. Vasileva-Dienes. (2020). 'The Region That Isn't': China, Russia and the Failure of Regional Integration in Central Asia,' *Asia Europe Journal* 18(3), pp. 347–66.

Krasnopolsky, P. (2013). 'Major Powers and Regionalism in Central Asia,' http://web.isanet.org/Web/Conferences/GSCIS%20Singapore%202015/Archive/8e26ebb3-f4a3-4a13-ac59-adb0ee445aa5.pdf.

Kuchins, A.C., J. Mankoff and O. Backes. (2015). *Central Asia in a Reconnecting Eurasia: Kyrgyzstan's Evolving Foreign Economic and Security Interests*. Lanham: Rowman & Littlefield.

Kunysz, N. (2012). 'From Sultanism to Neopatrimonialism? Regionalism Within Turkmenistan,' *Central Asian Survey* 31(1), pp. 1–16.

Kurç, Ç. (2018). 'The Puzzle: Multi-vector Foreign Policy and Defense Industrialization in Central Asia,' *Comparative Strategy* 37(4), pp. 316–30.

Laffey, M. and J. Weldes. (1997). 'Beyond Belief: Ideas and Symbolic Technologies in the Study of International Relations,' *European Journal of International Relations* 3(2), pp. 193–237.

Laruelle, M. (2013). 'Vneshnyaya Politika i Identichnost' v Tsentral'noy Azii (Foreign Policy and Identity in Central Asia),' *Pro et Contra* 58, pp. 6–20.

Laruelle, M. and D. Royce. (2020). 'No Great Game: Central Asia's Public Opinions on Russia, China, and the US,' *Kennan Cable* 56.

Levy, J.S. (1988). 'Domestic Politics and war,' *Journal of Interdisciplinary History* 18(4), 653–73.

Lewis, D. (2012). 'Understanding the Authoritarian State: Neopatrimonialism in Central Asia,' *Brown Journal of World Affairs* 19(1), pp. 115–26.

Lewis, D. (2015). 'Reasserting Hegemony in Central Asia: Russian Policy in Post-2010 Kyrgyzstan,' *Comillas Journal of International Relations* 3, pp. 58–81.

Light, M. (2003). 'In Search of an Identity: Russian Foreign Policy and the end of Ideology,' in Fawn, R. (ed.) *Ideology and National Identity in Post-communist Foreign Policies*. London: Frank Cass Publishers, pp. 41–57.

Marat, E. (2006). *The State-crime Nexus in Central Asia State Weakness, Organized Crime, and Corruption in Kyrgyzstan and Tajikistan*. Washington, DC: Central Asia-Caucasus Institute & Silk Road Studies Program.

Mattes, M., B.A. Leeds and R. Carroll (2015). 'Leadership Turnover and Foreign Policy Change: Societal Interests, Domestic Institutions, and Voting in the United Nations,' *International Studies Quarterly* 59(2), pp. 280–90.

McGlinchey, E. (2011). *Chaos, Violence, Dynasty: Politics and Islam in Central Asia*. Pittsburgh, PA: University of Pittsburgh Press.

McGlinchey, E. (2012). 'Foreign Policy and Aging Central Asian Autocrats,' *Demokratizatsiya* 20(3), pp. 262–7.

Menon, R. (2003). 'The New Great Game in Central Asia,' *Survival* 45(2), pp. 187–204.

Mintz, A. (2004). 'How Do Leaders Make Decisions?: A Poliheuristic Perspective,' *Journal of Conflict Resolution* 48(1), pp. 3–13.

Mintz, A. and A. Sofrin. (2017). 'Decision Making Theories in Foreign Policy Analysis,' *Oxford Research Encyclopedia of Politics*, https://oxfordre.com/politics/view/10.1093/acrefore/9780190228637.001.0001/acrefore-9780190228637-e-405.

Morgan, T.C. and K.N. Bickers. (1992). 'Domestic Discontent and the External Use of Force,' *Journal of Conflict Resolution* 36(1), pp. 25–52.

Morgenthau, H.J. (1954). *Politics Among Nations; the Struggle for Power and Peace*. New York: Knopf.

Mullojanov, P. (2019). 'In Search of 'National Purpose': In Theory and Practice. Formation and Main Features of National Ideologies in Post-Soviet Central Asia,' in Isaacs, R. and Frigerio, A. (eds.) *Theorizing Central Asian Politics*. Cham: Springer International Publishing, pp. 121–44.

Neumann, I.B. and S. Gstohl. (2006). 'Lilliputians in Gulliver's World?,' in Beyer, J. et al. (eds.) *Small States in International Relations*. Seattle: University of Washington Press, pp. 3–36.

Oppermann, K. and K. Brummer. (2017). 'Veto Player Approaches in Foreign Policy Analysis,' *Oxford Research Encyclopedia of Politics*, https://oxfordre.com/politics/view/10.1093/acrefore/9780190228637.001.0001/acrefore-9780190228637-e-386.

Patnaik, A. (2019). 'Regionalism and Regional Cooperation in Central Asia,' *International Studies* 56(2–3), pp. 147–62.

Putnam, R.D. (1988). 'Diplomacy and Domestic Politics: The Logic of Two-Level Games,' *International Organization* 42(3), pp. 427–60.

Radnitz, S. (2012). *Weapons of the Wealthy: Predatory Regimes and Elite-Led Protests in Central Asia*. Ithaca: Cornell University Press.

Reiter, D. and E.R. Tillman. (2002). 'Public, Legislative, and Executive Constraints on the Democratic Initiation of Conflict,' *The Journal of Politics* 64(3), pp. 810–26.

Rosenau, J.N. (2007). 'Foreword,' in Smith, S., Hadfield, A. and Dunne, T. (eds.) *Foreign Policy: Theories, Actors, Cases*. Oxford: Oxford University Press.

Schirm, S.A. (2016). 'Domestic Ideas, Institutions or Interests? Explaining Governmental Preferences Towards Global Economic Governance,' *International Political Science Review* 37(1), pp. 66–80.

Schultz, K. (2013). 'Domestic Politics and International Relations,' in Carlsnaes, W., Risse-Kappen, T. and Simmons, B.A. (eds.) *Handbook of International Relations*. Second edition. Los Angeles: SAGE, pp. 478–502.

Siverson, R.M. and B. Bueno de Mesquita. (2017). 'The Selectorate Theory and International Politics,' *Oxford Research Encyclopedia of Politics*, https://oxfordre.com/politics/view/10.1093/acrefore/9780190228637.001.0001/acrefore-9780190228637-e-293.

Smith, A. (1996). 'Diversionary Foreign Policy in Democratic Systems,' *International Studies Quarterly* 40(1), pp. 133–53.

Smith, S., A. Hadfield and T. Dunne. (eds.) (2008). *Foreign Policy: Theories, Actors, Cases*. Oxford: Oxford University Press.

Spechler, D.R. and M.C. Spechler. (2009). 'Uzbekistan Among the Great Powers,' *Communist and Post-Communist Studies* 42(3), pp. 353–73.

Swanström, N. (2005). 'China and Central Asia: A New Great Game or Traditional Vassal Relations?,' *Journal of Contemporary China* 14(45), pp. 569–84.

Thorhallsson, B. and S. Steinsson. (2017). 'Small State Foreign Policy,' *Oxford Research Encyclopedia of Politics*, https://oxfordre.com/politics/view/10.1093/acrefore/9780190228637.001.0001/acrefore-9780190228637-e-484.

Toktomushev, K. (2015). 'Regime Security, Base Politics and Rent-Seeking: The Local and Global Political Economies of the American Air Base in Kyrgyzstan, 2001–2010,' *Central Asian Survey* 34(1), pp. 57–77.

Tolipov, F. (2007). 'The Foreign Policy Orientations of Central Asian States: Positive and Negative Diversification', in Iwashita, A. (ed.) *Eager Eyes Fixed on Eurasia*. Sapporo: Slavic Research Center, pp. 23–40.

Tolipov, F. (2015). 'Strategic Implications of the War in Ukraine for the Post-Soviet Space: A View From Central Asia,' *Connections. Partnership for Peace Consortium of Defense Academies and Security Studies Institutes* 14(4), pp. 11–20.

Tolipov, F. (2020). *Thirty Years of Uzbekistan's International Relations: Quo Vadis?* Bishkek: Crossroads Central Asia, https://www.crossroads-ca.org/ccapb4/.

Trenin, D. (2003). 'Southern Watch: Russia's Policy in Central Asia,' *Journal of International Affairs* 56(2), pp. 119–31.

Tsebelis, G. (1995). 'Decision Making in Political Systems: Veto Players in Presidentialism, Parliamentarism, Multicameralism and Multipartyism,' *British Journal of Political Science* 25(3), pp. 289–325.

Volgy, T.J. and J.E. Schwarz. (1991). 'Does Politics Stop at the Water's Edge? Domestic Political Factors and Foreign Policy Restructuring in the Cases of Great Britain, France, and West Germany,' *The Journal of Politics* 53(3), pp. 615–43.

Welch, D.A. (2005). *Painful Choices: A Theory of Foreign Policy Change*. Princeton, NJ: Princeton University Press.

Wood, T.J. (2005). *The Formation of Kyrgyz Foreign Policy 1991–2004*. PhD Thesis. Tufts University.

Yaşar, S. (2012). 'Foreign Policy of Kyrgyzstan Under Askar Akayev and Kurmanbek Bakiyev,' *Perceptions: Journal of International Affairs* 17(3), pp. 131–50.

17
MILITARY POWER AND CAPACITY

Erica Marat

Three decades ago, the five Central Asian states inherited asymmetric military capabilities that reflected the Soviet military projection in the world, not the individual needs of republics. Since then, the new countries have tried to reorient their militaries and security structures to serve national interests, while also seeking new opportunities for cooperation with Russia, China and the West. Disparities in civilian control, combat readiness and international ties soon emerged and widened over time. The political courses chosen by the five Central Asian leaders influenced their emerging national security sectors, with authoritarian Turkmenistan and Uzbekistan using security institutions to coerce political opponents and society. Meanwhile, Kazakhstan has participated in international peacekeeping operations and maintained balanced relations with all international partners. Kyrgyzstan and Tajikistan lagged behind the other three in fortifying their armed forces with new weapons and skills. Despite known weaknesses, leaders throughout the region learned to rely on the security sector to prop up their regimes. They appointed loyalists to key positions, but the Soviet military tradition of non-interference in national politics continues to this day.

While Central Asian militaries have seldom been deployed, they nevertheless serve as an important venue for international political engagement. They link to countries (especially the United States, Russia and China), as well as to regional security organisations, including NATO, the Shanghai Cooperation Organization (SCO) and the Collective Security Treaty Organization (CSTO). Central Asian regime incumbents were able to play regional powers against each other, indirectly reinforcing their own hold on power at home (Cooley 2012). Both Russian and U.S. influence on the armed forces brought mixed results, mostly pursuing own national security agendas rather than building partnership capacity of the Central Asian states. Chinese influence in the security sector, in the meantime, has been rapidly rising since the mid-2000s and may one day rival that of Russia. Military institutions have had the potential to develop international connections, but these opportunities seldom address the real security needs of the Central Asian societies. This chapter begins with a brief overview of the Central Asian armed forces and then shifts to examine the changing geopolitical environment in the region.

The Soviet legacy

In the first decade of Soviet rule, Moscow used military conscription to penetrate Central Asia. When the Red Army first arrived in Turkistan in the late 1910s, it was overwhelmed by

DOI: 10.4324/9780429057977-17

perceived local tribal divisions and cultural peculiarities. Leaders decried the lack of knowledge about the indigenous populations and called for ethnographic studies to improve the military's ability to persuade the local male population to join the communist armed forces (Bubnov et al. 1930; Marat 2009). While forming the first battalions, the army had to rely mostly on studies produced by Russian Imperial Orientalists in the late nineteenth and early twentieth centuries. At first, the Red Army strategy viewed the local Muslim conscripts as a religious community, tailoring their social engineering strategies accordingly. Aspects of Turkistani culture were incorporated into uniform design and daily food rations:

> In the work with Muslim soldiers their everyday habits and customs were considered. In this way, in connection with religious holidays *kurban bairams,* all Red Army Muslim conscripts and workers – were given rice, meat, sultana grapes, tobacco and 100 Rubles for three days of celebration.
>
> *(Klimov 1987)*

Along with food handouts, the cultural influence of Russian agitators on the local population was widespread. Bolshevik efforts to increase their knowledge of local culture eventually led to the formation of distinct ethnic nations within the Soviet Union.

Following the Bolshevik victory in the Russian civil war in 1920, the Red Army quickly turned into a producer and promoter of ethnographic knowledge. The army became the Communist Party's instrument to establish class and national consciousness among the indigenous populations, as well as to divide Central Asia into Soviet ethno-republics (Hirsh 2014; Adelman 1980; Movchin 1926). In forming Turkistan military units, the Bolsheviks first determined the ethnicity of the local conscripts, then put them on horseback and equipped them with sabres, machine guns or shovels – depending on their perceived cultural differences (Klimov 1987). The army conducted the first regional census among potential conscripts and fired the first metaphorical shots in Moscow's assault on religious identity. The Central Asian conscripts were forced to suppress the *basmachi* rebellion and to facilitate collectivisation (Chokayev 2001).

Soviet Central Asian troops fought on almost all major fronts of World War II, including the defence of Leningrad and Moscow in 1941, Crimea and Donbas in 1942, Stalingrad in 1942 and the siege of Leningrad in 1941–1943. Russians commanded almost all units, even those entirely comprised of Central Asian draftees. After the war's end, local soldiers, including many women, were honoured by the regime. The war produced a group of national heroes from the region's population, helping boost the popularity of military service. More than 120,000 natives of Uzbekistan were awarded decorations for service, 69 received the country's highest honour, the Hero of the Soviet Union. Another 50,000 from Tajikistan were decorated, including 14 Heroes of the Soviet Union; 100,000 from Kyrgyzstan were decorated, including a dozen Heroes of the Soviet Union; and 19,000 from Turkmenistan were decorated, with 18 Hero of the Soviet Union honours (Khudoiberdiyev 1984). These revered veterans became role models for the post-war generation, including the reluctant conscripts sent to Afghanistan four decades later.

The Afghan campaign (December 1979–February 1989) was the largest Soviet military undertaking in Central Asia since 1922. Almost all divisions of the Soviet armed forces participated in the campaign; roughly 500,000 soldiers, mostly from the Fortieth Army, were mobilised. In addition, some 130,000–150,000 civilians and over 50,000 Central Asian civilians provided support services to Soviet troops in Afghanistan, and billions of dollars were spent to sustain the Fortieth Army (Volkov 2003). The Turkistan Military District (MD) served a significant component in the Soviet security complex. The MD's major cities – Ashgabat, Tashkent, Dushanbe and Termez –

became military procurement bases for Soviet troops in Afghanistan. Most of the officers and soldiers deployed to Afghanistan were drafted, trained or temporarily stationed at the Turkistan MD.

For the Central Asian republics the collapse of the Soviet regime in 1991 meant both the end of an integrated Soviet military and the need to contend with rapidly changing world politics. With the demise of the Soviet Army, successor states lost their long-term international policy contacts. Central Asian military institutions, like other Soviet state structures, had to reorient their loyalty from the Soviet Central Command to the newly established national governments. Except in Tajikistan, which collapsed into civil war, this process was fairly smooth because Soviet officers had also functioned as bureaucrats and implemented Party decisions. Most non-Russian officers were promoted after their Russian colleagues immigrated to the Russian Federation. New ruling regimes rapidly nationalised military institutions, and new legislatures and national symbols were adopted. All Central Asian states unanimously enacted a new legal framework for the armed forces and began to nationalise the Soviet military property located on their territories.

Acquiring materiel and financial support for the military institutions, however, was more challenging. Not only were all Soviet successor states left without a coherent army, but they also had Russian troops present on their territories. Military officials proposed several models for restructuring the Soviet military under the auspices of the Commonwealth of Independent States (CIS). The CIS armed forces could be combined or unified either by Colonel General Konstantin Kobet or by USSR Minister of Defense Marshal Yevgeny Shaposhnikov, respectively. Both models granted various degrees of autonomy at the republic level (Odom 2000). Kobet's model gave the heads of successor republics more autonomy in military planning and command, while Shaposhnikov favoured multiple layers of control over unified armed forces at the CIS level. At that time Kobet's plan seemed more feasible as a number of republics had already begun nationalising their militaries. The military operational base, economy and personnel had been so interconnected that keeping it under the CIS command would be much easier than dividing it (Odom 2000).

Kazakhstan and Uzbekistan inherited large military installations, with a greater degree of independent military production and available equipment. Kazakhstan inherited 196 large and small military industrial sites, including army corps centres, armour and motor rifle divisions, military educational complexes, brigade ordinance, an air-assault division and other military formations (Kozyulin 2014). Similarly, Uzbekistan gained control over a substantial number of armoured vehicles and military aircrafts, as well as respected regional military academies. Turkmenistan's late president Saparmurat Niyazov inherited naval forces as part of the border guard forces, and his successor, Gurbanguly Berdymuhammedov, transformed it into a separate Naval Force. The country also inherited the region's best equipped and manned Air Force, operating from an airbase in Mary. By contrast, almost all of the post-Soviet military equipment in Tajikistan was placed under Russian control and assigned to the Russian 201st Motor Rifle Division, which had been stationed in the country since 1943. Tajikistan was the rare post-colonial state without state monopoly over the armed forces. Kyrgyzstan received several types of ammunition but lacked any significant military industry. The asymmetric distribution of Soviet military infrastructure allowed leaders to assess their potential capabilities vis-à-vis different neighbours.

Early independence

During the 1990s, the world showed little interest in Central Asian military sectors. Kazakhstan was briefly an exception, until it – along with Ukraine and Belarus – relinquished 1,410 nuclear warheads deployed on its territory to Russia in the mid-1990s. This cooperative dynamic changed after Vladimir Putin became Russia's president in 2000 and several regional and international developments convinced him to reinstate traditional security and military ties with Central Asia. First, the China-led 'Shanghai Five' border arrangement transformed into the Shanghai Cooperation Organization in June 2001, revealing Beijing's ability to organise Central Asian leaders in security alliances. Second, the United States suddenly became interested in strategic partnerships in Central Asian as part of the War on Terror following the 9/11 attacks. After the United States established air force bases in Bishkek, Kyrgyzstan and Kharshi-Khanabad, Uzbekistan, in late 2001, Putin upgraded the Collective Security Treaty into a formal Collective Security Treaty Organization.

The Central Asian countries handled these geopolitical shifts differently. In Kazakhstan, President Nursultan Nazarbayev expanded his signature multi-vector approach to economics and politics to the security and military domains. Nazarbayev was also determined to play a more active role on the international scene and established a dedicated peacekeeping brigade, KAZBRIG. Following domestic criticism for deploying a token contingent of troops to Afghanistan in late 2001, Kazakhstan has avoided further deployment to foreign combat zones. But Nazarbayev has continuously shown interest in sending more officers to the U.S.-led International Military Education and Training (IMET) programme. The government also openly supported the Northern Distribution Network supply chains to Afghanistan as part of the International Security Assistance Force. Kazakhstan is the only country in the region that has deployed peacekeepers to the UN Interim Force in Western Sahara and Lebanon (Snachez 2019). As part of its focus on multi-national interoperability, Kazakhstan has begun to emphasise the procurement of Western weapons and equipment as well (Golovnina 2008; Gorenburg 2014). Nur-Sultan (formerly Astana) tries to mimic Western command-and-control systems in military planning. In 2018, the regime in Nur-Sultan granted the United States access to its Caspian ports, angering Russia (Eurasianet 2018).

But most of Kazakhstan's military industries are Russia-centric and have been expanding in recent years. The key enterprises have been combined into a single state-owned holding company, Kazakhstan Engineering (KE). These include: the Zenit plant in Uralsk, which builds ships, including minesweepers and patrol boats; the Ziksto plant in Petropavlovsk, which makes anti-ship missiles; the Metalist plant in Petropavlovsk, which manufactures high calibre machine guns; the Granit plant in Almaty, which builds air defence systems; and the Kirov machine-building plant in Petropavlovsk, which makes torpedoes. Kazakhstan coproduces Il-103M aircraft with Russia.

President Islam Karimov in Uzbekistan avoided alignment with any one regional organisation, instead preferring to retain a unilateral approach to national security. The internal structure of the Uzbek military did not change until 1998 and remained nearly identical to that in the Soviet era. Similar to other Central Asian and former Soviet states, Uzbekistan broadened the definition of armed forces to include any force that possesses weapons. Internal armed forces were redistributed among the National Security Service (NSS). Throughout his nearly three decades in power the late president Karimov was the ultimate decision-maker in the security domain. He identified national threats and configured his armed forces accordingly. In effect, a security threat only gained 'legitimacy' when Karimov announced it publicly. However, the vague threat of terrorism proved to be a poor strategy to maintain Karimov's popularity in Uzbekistan, instead providing grounds for the consolidation of national military forces.

Karimov's successor Shavkat Mirziyoyev updated the country's defence doctrine[1] and introduced new elements such as information and psychological warfare, precision weapons and unmanned vehicles and robotics (Ibragimov 2019). These innovations aim at responding to the irregular threats of terrorism, drug-trafficking and criminal groups. Mirziyoyev signed a new law regulating the functions of its security services. Critics posit that this law gives security officials de facto immunity: 'Article 12 of the new law forbids state bodies, other organisations or officials from interfering in the operations of the [National Security Service] SGB. And Article 37 grants SGB servicemen immunity for actions committed during service.'[2]

In Tajikistan, the 1992–1997 civil war between the United Tajik Opposition forces and a rapidly formed pro-government Popular Front left the country with oversized military structures rich in war experience and subject to both government and opposition loyalty. After the peace agreement was reached with the help of Russian and Uzbek mediators, the Tajik government faced the difficult challenges of finding jobs for pro-government veterans and integrating opposition troops into the national army. By the mid-2000s, President Imomali Rakhmon had centralised the government, secured stability and overseen modest economic growth. The international community largely praised his accomplishments. Yet, the stability was short-lived as Rakhmon purged his political opponents from government jobs and the parliament. He installed loyalists in the security structures, such as Defense Minister Sherali Khairulloyev from his native Kulyab oblast. Once he had complete control over all military institutions, Rakhmon issued his first military doctrine in 2005, almost a decade later than his neighbours. Although some improvement in the armed forces' professionalism has been achieved in the 2000s, conscripts and reservists in Tajikistan remain poorly trained. International military exercises with CSTO and SCO are often the only opportunity for conscripts to get acquainted with modern weapons, technology and mountain-warfare techniques.

When Islamic Movement of Uzbekistan (IMU) militants entered Kyrgyzstan from Tajikistan in 1999–2000, all Central Asian countries announced some type of security sector reform, but not in the sense of democratic control over the armed forces. Instead, activities aimed at bolstering national security based on the narrow views of the incumbent regimes were considered to be reforms (Boonstra, Marat and Axyonova 2013). The countries tried to reorient their armies from fighting traditional wars to responding to insurgencies and terrorism. This would require a transition to contract-based service to retain highly professional special forces. But two decades since the IMU incursions, a higher paid military service continues to be constrained by a lack of resources. Kazakhstan is the only Central Asian country to enlist over 70 per cent of officers based on contracts. For other states, compulsory service offers opportunities for bribery to avoid serving, essentially converting the military draft into a 'poverty tax.' But even in Kazakhstan military service can be a political tool. At least five men of draft age were conscripted into military service after they joined political action to reform Kazakhstan's political system, a move widely seen as a way of punishing them (Toiken 2019).

Although Central Asian armed forces continue the Soviet practice of conscripting from different ethnicities, in part due to compulsory service, they are by far dominated by the majority ethnic groups. Police forces have greater ethnic and gender diversity, but are also represented by one ethnic group. This dynamic further reflects other government agencies that tend to have fewer ethnic minorities than the private sector.

Civil-military relations

Without effective state mechanisms for peaceful transfers of power, Central Asian ruling regimes try to secure the loyalty of military officials. Central Asian militaries generally have continued the Soviet tradition of not taking sides in political affairs. Thanks to this Soviet legacy of civilian control of the armed forces, incumbent political leaders can rely on the armed forces, intelligence and police to remain in power for decades without facing the risk of military coups. However, the Soviet system of military and police ranks has been overshadowed by patrimonial relations. At times, Karimov and Mirziyoyev, Rakhmon and former president of Kyrgyzstan

Kurmanbek Bakiyev blurred the line between presidential rule (by an individual) and presidential rule (by an institution) over the armed forces.

In Uzbekistan, Karimov used his two decades in power to centralise his personal power to such a degree that the Ministry of the Interior and the Ministry of Defense would crumble should Karimov's regime collapse. The Interior Ministry and the National Security Service together fortified his regime. Both agencies violently suppressed the Andijan uprising on 13 May 2005, which began as a protest about economic grievances. Tashkent claimed that over 150 Islamist terrorists were killed in the subsequent fighting, but reports by international human rights groups suggest a much higher number of civilian casualties (HRW 2008). The president's efforts to strengthen the armed forces and support security leaders inserted greater uncertainty into the succession of his power as well.

Following Karimov's death in 2016, the transition to Mirziyoyev was smooth, perhaps thanks to a behind-the-scenes inter-elite consensus on his candidacy. He quickly moved to reorganise personnel cadres across all security structures. Mirziyoyev sacked or jailed top security officials who served under Karimov, including Rustam Innoyatov, the long serving (nearly 23 years) and powerful head of the National Security Service; Interior Minister Adham Ahmadboyev; Prosecutor General Rashid Qodirov, members of his family and dozens of former colleagues; and Tashkent Deputy Prosecutor Miraghlam Mirzoyev, along with his wife and son, who both worked in law enforcement.[3] Dozens of other regional security chiefs were sent to prison on corruption charges as well. Mirziyoyev then installed his eldest son-in-law, Oybek Tursunov, as head of the Uzbekistan presidential administration and his younger son-in-law Otabek Shahanov as deputy head of the president's security service. Arrests of Karimov loyalists continued in 2019, with Ikhtiyor Abdullayev (head of NSS for just a year) supposedly fired for 'health purposes' and subsequently jailed for bribery and abuse of office stemming from allegedly tapping the president's telephone and tailing his family.[4] General Prosecutor Otabek Murodov was soon fired as well and was charged with corruption/bribery.[5] In effect, like Karimov, Mirziyoyev is rebuilding patrimonial control over the security sector.

Like Mirziyoyev, President Gurbanguly Berdymuhammedov also sacked and jailed his predecessor's officials with KGB connections. His erratic cadre politics typically include promotions and demotions of the same individuals on a whim. For example, Turkmenistan's defense minister, Major General Begench Gundogdyev, has served in various key security positions since 2009. During that time, he has been both promoted and demoted in rank.

In Kyrgyzstan, Bakiyev (2005–2010) installed family members and cronies into state security posts, thus guarantying their loyalty should the opposition organise mass protests against him. Minister of Interior Moldomusa Kongantiyev, Minister of Defense Bakytbek Kalyev and the head of the Security Council, Adakhan Modumarov, worked closely with Bakiyev to strengthen his power and that of the pro-regime Ak Zhol party. As the presidential elections in 2010 neared, the Interior Ministry and Defense Ministry worked to quieten the opposition forces, exposing their obedience to the ruling regime. Relying on the loyalty of the security apparatus, Bakiyev responded with deadly violence when crowds against his regime convened on 7 April 2010. Special forces shot and killed 86 people and wounded dozens more within a few hours. Seeing the historic levels of bloodshed, Bakiyev first fled to his native village in the south and later escaped the country.

The violent removal of Bakiyev undermined the historic separation of the civil and military sectors in Kyrgyzstan. Following the April 2010 regime change and the ensuing political instability, high-ranking military officials informally discussed stepping into power.[6] This alarming potential scenario was never voiced publicly, nor is there any indication that a serious attempt was made. This option may have been suppressed because of the biased police and military response to ethnic violence in Osh on 10–14 June 2010. They reportedly failed to prevent seizure of weapons and ammunition by crowds and unopposed attacks against the Uzbek minority (KIC 2014). Interim President Roza Otunbayeva was forced to call up reserve officers to sustain a 24-hour curfew in Osh. The police were ordered to shoot-to-kill on the morning of 13 June, although the police had already been randomly using loaded weapons against the population (Marat 2018). Roughly 500 people, predominantly ethnic Uzbeks, died during the four days of violence, and hundreds of thousands of ethnic Uzbek residents temporarily fled to Uzbekistan.

International ties after 9/11

The international anti-terrorism campaign conducted in Afghanistan following the 9/11 attacks renewed Western and especially U.S. interest in Central Asia. Beginning in late 2001, security cooperation overshadowed humanitarian and democracy-building programmes in the region, and local military institutions greatly benefitted from external aid. U.S. security assistance programmes peaked during the combat surge of 2008–2012 and subsequently returned to pre-2001 levels.[7] The decline coincided with the U.S. drawdown from Afghanistan. Both Kyrgyzstan and Tajikistan received the greatest assistance for border management programmes, including counter-drug and counterterrorism operations. Thanks to Kyrgyzstan's hosting a U.S. military base at Manas airport during 2001–2014, the country received roughly $300,000 in rent payments (see Figure 17.1). Uzbekistan was the largest recipient of overall U.S. military assistance in the early 2000s, but trailed behind its neighbours after the U.S. airbase in Karshi-Khanabad closed in 2005. Since then Kazakhstan has been the largest financial recipient of U.S. military assistance, but mostly related to nuclear threat reduction.

Programmes in Tajikistan trained military units who were assigned to directly protect the ruling regime. In Tajikistan, U.S. diplomatic cables reveal how the U.S. Special Operations Command Central training of the National Guard benefitted President Rakhmon personally (Kucera 2011). The country's National Guard is an elite unit informally subject to the president's personal control. Despite these reservations, Washington continued to train hundreds of National Guard personnel in the late 2010s, making the National Guard the largest U.S.-trained force in Tajikistan (Kucera 2018). In Kyrgyzstan, U.S. rent payments for the Manas airport and purchase of jet fuel eventually made their way to the Bakiyev regime (Cooley & Heathershaw 2017).

The SCO and CSTO answered the increased U.S. presence with joint military drills. China and Russia, the founders of these organisations, declared joint principles of cooperation and became important agents of military change in Central Asia. Both the CSTO and SCO are notorious for designing their military exercises to counter threats to ruling regimes. SCO training focused mostly on counterterrorism activities. Western donors, too, have been vague about the purpose of military-to-military collaboration. The United States, for instance, has rarely made clear whether security sector reform is part of bilateral cooperation for the needs of the Central Asian countries or part of the Western-led anti-terrorism coalition that corresponded with the interests of Western nations. Simultaneously, both the CSTO and SCO have created their own rapid reaction forces. But they also mostly served the political interests of Russia and China in the region.

The CSTO's main principle mimics NATO's Article 5 (an attack against one state is an attack against all member states), while the SCO seeks to fight the three evils of 'terrorism, extremism, and separatism.' Neither the CSTO nor the SCO is able to match NATO's considerable military infrastructure, and neither requires member states to spend a particular percentage of their gross domestic product on defence. But except for the restive Xingjian province in Western China, which drove Beijing to establish cooperative relations with bordering states, neither Russia's ongoing crises in the North Caucasus nor China's troublesome control over Tibet has ever figured in the CSTO and SCO agendas. Likewise, the CSTO has never taken collective action regarding any of the conflicts on its members' territory, including Nagorno-Karabakh, Osh or Russia's invasions of Georgia and Ukraine. Annual activities have been limited to multilateral and bilateral drills by both organisations.

Although both organisations contextualise security among their member states in different ways, the CSTO and SCO have also mutually reinforced each other's existence. The CSTO expanded the scope of its activities after China established economic, political, security and cultural ties with the Central Asian states, while the SCO has reduced Russia's role in the region and downgraded terrorism as a primary security concern. These new cooperation regimes in the region, in turn, influenced the national security decisions of the individual governments in different ways: Central Asian leaders built their security strategies on the premise of entrenched collaboration with Russia and China and insecurity as defined by the CSTO and SCO. The countries' military doctrines reflected threat perception defined by both organisations.

In the late 2000s the divide between the Russian and Chinese approaches in Central Asia widened. CSTO summits devolved into meetings of like-minded Russophiles nostalgic for the mighty Red Army, while SCO summits were constrained by a lack of translation capacity from Chinese to Russian and the Central Asian languages, with some defence officials unable to pick up on the Beijing ways of communication that avoid discussion of contentious issues in public. The cultural gap between China and its Central Asian partners has been bridged thanks to Beijing's effort to woo partners through military and security diplomacy. Educational exchange programmes and invitations for high-ranking officials to visit state-of-the-art facilities in China have attracted more military partners from across the world, including Western countries (Stevis-Gridneff 2019).

International military education

Central Asian military leaders continue to be educated at Russian military academies. High-ranking defence officials across the region all studied the same Soviet-style curriculum. Kazakhstan defense minister Nurlan Ermekbayev graduated from the Red Banner Military Institute of the USSR Ministry of Defense (Военный Краснознамённый институт Министерства обороны СССР) shortly before the Soviet regime collapsed. His colleagues from Kyrgyzstan, Erlis Terdikbayev, and Tajikistan, Sherali Mirzo, received their military education from the prestigious Military Academy of the General Staff of the Armed Forces of Russia in the 2000s. The same common threads connect most top-ranking security officials across Central Asia.

More recently, China extended its military education programmes to more foreign students as well. PLA National Defense University (PLA NDU) accepted students from more than 100 partner nations (Jiansheng and Jinmu 2018). Beijing puts a priority on strong relations across the entire Asian region, but the Central Asian countries account for only a fraction of all military interactions (Allen, Saunders and Chen 2017). According to one student from Central Asia who had studied in both U.S. military academies and PLA NDU, the chief difference is the imagined wall separating the Chinese and international students and they rarely interact. In contrast, Western institutions emphasise collaboration between U.S. and international officers.[8] Graduates of Chinese and Western military academies also stress that although each host country openly seeks to advance its own strategies and operations, Western schools encourage more debate, critique and critical thinking in the process. But no student – Chinese or international – is allowed to criticise China's military operations or treatment of Muslim minorities.

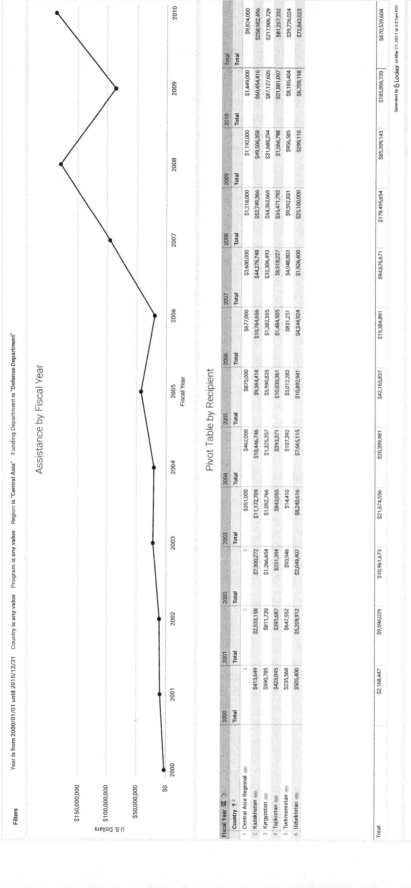

Figure 17.1 U.S. security aid to Central Asia. Source: Security Assistance Monitor (https://securityassistance.org/).

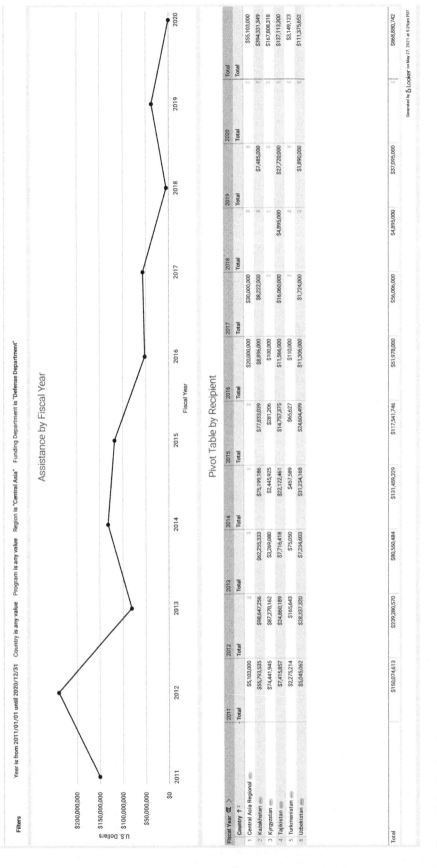

Figure 17.1 Continued

Chinese military education is especially attractive for Turkmenistan and Uzbekistan, who historically have had limited access to Western academies but wish to move away from the Russian influence (Marat 2021). In 2014 Beijing established the China National Institute for SCO International Exchange and Judicial Cooperation in Shanghai, which had trained 300 officials from the SCO countries by 2018 (van der Kley 2019).

To date, Western professionals military education (PME) institutions hosted over 13,000 Central Asian military and civilian officers as part of the IMET programme, as well as the Marshall European Center for Security Studies in Germany, Foreign Military Financing (FMF), the Combating Terrorism Fellowship Program (CTFP), International Narcotics Control and Law Enforcement, and Section 1004 Counter-Drug Assistance (Omelichieva 2017). IMET programmes offer short certificate-level courses and graduate programmes across U.S. senior service institutions and focus on partnership building, decision-making, strategic and critical thinking, and interoperability. As part of PME, Washington also increased the frequency of special-forces training with the Central Asian states. Hundreds of troops are trained annually in each country, adding up to over 1,000 troops across the region. U.S. Central Command (CENTCOM) and NATO forces hold annual Steppe Eagle exercises with Kazakhstan to enhance interoperability and peace support operations. In 2019, CENTCOM conducted joint military exercises in Tajikistan with Tajikistan, Mongolia and Uzbekistan. Joint special-forces trainings expanded under the Obama administration and continued at the same level under Trump.

Compared to other U.S. ally countries in the former Soviet spaces or in South Asia and Middle East, however, these gains are modest. In the post-Soviet space, the U.S. Department of Defense prioritised the countries in direct confrontation with Russia – Georgia and Ukraine – followed by countries in conflict with each other – Armenia and Azerbaijan. Central Asian countries are mentioned in discussions of irregular warfare, but the region is otherwise a very low priority. As discussed in Ziegler's chapter in this volume, U.S. interest in Central Asia is limited to existing stabilisation campaigns for Afghanistan.

The 2010s: The changing dynamics

The closure of the U.S. air base at the Manas airport in Bishkek in mid-2014 ended Washington's military presence in Central Asia, but relations with Uzbekistan improved. The base closure coincided with the winding down of the military campaign in Afghanistan and the drawdown of U.S. troops. The United States transferred over 300 armoured vehicles to Uzbekistan in 2015 under the U.S. Excess Defense Articles (EDA) programme. Smaller transfers included 'patrol ships to Kazakhstan and Turkmenistan and utility helicopters to Kazakhstan' (Kucera 2015). The generous military support of Uzbekistan despite its poor human rights record indicates how the United States separates security interests from democratic values. Mirziyoyev, in turn, has sought to strengthen ties with both NATO and the United States, paving the way for increased ties with CENTCOM to improve tactical communication and further broaden military-to-military cooperation (CENTCOM 2020). As part of an effort to modernise Uzbekistan's military performance, Uzbekistan's special forces participated in trainings in the United States with the U.S. National Guard in Mississippi and U.S. Central Command in Florida (Omelicheva 2019). Uzbekistan plans to further increase the number of officers enrolled in professional military schools in both the United States and EU countries as part of NATO programmes.

Amid the reduced U.S. presence in Afghanistan, Russia has continued to be the main supplier of arms to Central Asian militaries and still enjoys interoperability thanks to the momentum from the Soviet period. Kazakhstan's military cooperation with Russia is the most expansive in the region, reaching $18 billion to date since independence and expected to further increase (Khrolenko 2019). Tashkent has also renewed military cooperation with Moscow. Uzbekistan is slated to increase annual military spending in the next few years to $7 billion, with the bulk of the costs paying for Russian weapons, including new Su-30SM fighters, Mi-35M attack helicopters and radar systems. Other purchases may include Yak-130 training aircraft, equipment to modernise about 30 MiG-29 fighters, and other military technologies (Khrolenko 2019). In December 2019, Russian president Vladimir Putin introduced a bill in the State Duma to allow the use of drones from the Kant airbase in Kyrgyzstan. The Kant base currently hosts 500 Russian officers, Su-25 attack aircraft and Mi-8 helicopters. It is also used for airborne training related to the Tu-95MS and Tu-160 aircraft stationed at Russia's Engels airbase in Saratov oblast.

However, China's rapidly expanding levels of military training and military equipment provision threatens to surpass that of Russia and the United States (Rolland 2019). Culturally, Central Asian political elites are closer to Russia and are predominantly native speakers of the Russian language. Russian media and, hence, Moscow's worldview, is popular in Central Asian cities. But Russia's cultural capital may not be able to trump China's military and economic influence in the region. China has already emerged as a more dominant supplier of surveillance technologies across the region, despite competition from state-backed Russian companies. Likewise, to secure its Belt and Road Initiative investments, China has expanded the presence of its private security companies in Central Asia and globally. China's economic power paves the way for Beijing's influence in the Central Asian military complex.

In 2015, China amended its counterterrorism law to allow Beijing's participation in international campaigns. As part of this strategy, Chinese Peoples' Liberation Army Navy stationed the country's first foreign military base in Djibouti in 2017. But in Central Asia, the effect of China's expanding global influence was felt as early as 2016 when China organised its first Quadrilateral Cooperation and Coordination Mechanism (QCCM), a framework combining Afghanistan, China, Pakistan and Tajikistan and based in Urumqi, China (Duchâtel 2019). The new regional initiative intends to foster military-to-military ties, yet details of any completed agreements, including an Agreement on the Coordination Mechanism in Counterterrorism by Afghanistan-China-Pakistan-Tajikistan Armed Forces and a Protocol on Counterterrorism Information Coordination Center, have not been made public. QCCM may be designed to facilitate future deployment of Chinese troops in Tajikistan and Afghanistan.

Since 2016 Chinese troops have reportedly been monitoring the Tajikistan–Afghanistan border in the Wakhan Corridor (Shih 2019). Neither Tajikistan nor China acknowledges having such a military outpost, but it suggests that Beijing's military involvement in Central Asia may fill the void left after the United States completely withdraws from Afghanistan. Yet some pundits claim that China's troops in Tajikistan are stationed at a de facto military base expected to significantly expand in the coming years. China's suppression of Uighurs and other Turkic ethnic groups in its western provinces colour Beijing's attitude towards the Central Asian countries as a security priority. Beijing has considerable leverage over the countries thanks to the large debts incurred through Chinese investment and physical infrastructure grants. China may already be in talks to 'refurbish or rebuild' 30–40 border outposts in Tajikistan (Nelson and Grove 2019).

China is also emerging as a military arms supplier in Central Asia, offering products that are compatible with Russian weapons. In 2018 Kazakhstan purchased a Chinese Y-8 military plane, and Turkmenistan purchased the QW-2 Vanguard 2 (Yan 2019). Since 2002, China has also participated in more than 20 bilateral or multilateral military exercises with the Central Asian republics. In 2014, China agreed to provide $6.5 million in military assistance to Kyrgyzstan and promised hundreds of millions of dollars to Tajikistan for uniforms and training. China also donated equipment to the police forces of Kyrgyzstan and Tajikistan. Between 2003 and 2009, China hosted 65 Kazakh officers, in addition to 30 Kyrgyz and Tajik officers in 2008 (Stratfor 2016). The major spheres of cooperation between China and Central Asia are financial investment, high tech, transportation, infrastructure, energy and agriculture (Odgaard 2017).

Some tensions with Russia may have emerged as a result of China's military presence in the region. But even if that does make Moscow nervous about China's military presence, on top of its economic dominance, these concerns have not surfaced officially. In December 2019, China and Russia agreed to conduct a joint air defence drill in the Asia Pacific region. Russian influence continues to be strong, at least in part thanks to the CSTO and military academies. Like Russia, the Trump administration saw China's rising influence in Central Asia as justification for increasing Washington's ties with the region. The U.S. National Defense Strategy adopted in 2018 focuses on Russia and Chinese near-peer competition across the world and calls for increasing the U.S. global military presence in response. Yet although both Moscow and Beijing have long been the dominant security and military partners in Central Asia, the United States prioritises other parts of Eurasia and is unlikely to compete in any contest for Central Asia.

Conclusions

Three decades after the collapse of the Soviet Union, the Central Asian militaries remain under the civilian control of incumbent political regimes, but corruption is palpable across the region. Merit-based promotions rooted in the Soviet tradition of military service have been gradually replaced with family and neopatrimonial ties, especially following the murky regime changes in Kyrgyzstan, Uzbekistan and Turkmenistan. This may further delay or complicate political democratisation, since Central Asian presidents rely on armies and special forces to suppress political opponents. Uzbekistan and Kazakhstan will remain the region's military leaders thanks to the vast military infrastructure inherited from the Soviet era and new acquisitions made from Russia, the United States and now increasingly from China as well.

The national armed forces offer one pathway for building international ties with regional powers and the West. Kazakhstan is ahead of its neighbours in terms of its connections to the United Nations, NATO, United States, Russia and China. It is the region's most innovative reformer, striving to contribute to international peacekeeping efforts. Uzbekistan, on the other hand, still has the largest army and clearly intends to remain that way. Under Mriziyeev's leadership, Tashkent has been more amenable to establishing military ties with Russia, the United States and likely China as well. Russia and China pursue political dominance and a cohesive understanding of regional power by building regular military-to-military contacts. Since the U.S. drawdown from Afghanistan, the United States and NATO have prioritised border security and stabilisation operations in the region.

In the 1990s, Russia was the only regional player to foster collective security ties, but Moscow was then largely oriented towards ties with the West and disinterested in Central Asia. The post-9/11 dynamic, the installation of U.S. military bases in the region and the rise of Putin's regime have increased the influence of the CSTO in the region. The organisation, although practically useless in responding to or preventing conflicts in the region, has increased its political activity in Central Asia. Simultaneously, an economically rising China could engage Central Asian states in helping control Turkic minorities in Xinjiang by forming the SCO. Since the late 2010s, however, China has been emerging as a new dominant military and security actor in Central Asia, potentially able to overshadow Russia.

Notes

1. About the 'Defensive Doctrine of the Republic of Uzbekistan,' Law of the Republic of Uzbekistan ZRU-458, CIS [Commonwealth of Independent States] Legislation, 9 January 2018, accessed 23 December 2019, https://cis-legislation.com/document.fwx?rgn=102814
2. Eurasianet.org, 'Uzbekistan security service agents' immunity worries experts,' 11 April 2018.
3. RFE/RL, 'Former Uzbek Deputy Security Service Chief Reportedly Detained In Purge,' 3 April 2018.
4. Eurasianet.org, 'Uzbekistan: Head of security services gets chop amid talk of surveillance,' 12 February 2019, Eurasianet.org 'Uzbekistan: Former security service chief goes on trial,' 18 July 2019.
5. Eurasianet.org, 'Uzbekistan: President thunders as another General Prosecutor faces probe,' 21 July 2019.
6. Interview with a high-ranking Defense Ministry official, September 2011.
7. Source: Security Assistance Monitor, https://securityassistance.org/central-eurasia.
8. Interview, Washington, DC, February 2019.

Bibliography

Adelman, J.R. (1980). *The Revolutionary Armies: The Historical Development of the Soviet and Chinese People's Liberation Armies.* Westport, CT: Greenwood Publishing Group.

Allen, K., P.C. Saunders and J. Chen. (2017). *Chinese Military Diplomacy, 2003–2016: Trends and Implications.* Washington, DC: National Defense University Press.

Boonstra, J., E. Marat and V. Axyonova. (2013). *Security Sector Reform in Kazakhstan, Kyrgyzstan and Tajikistan: What Role for Europe,* Vol. 14. EUCAM working paper.

Bubnov, A.S. ed. (1930). *'Kampaniya v Bukhare v 1920 g. i kratkii ocherk pohodov 1921 i 1922 gg.' Grazhdanskaya voina: 1918–1921,* Vol. III. Moscow: Otdel Voennoi Literatury.

CENTCOM. (2020). 'US, Uzbek Soldiers Build New Lines of Communication,' https://www.centcom.mil/MEDIA/igphoto/2001767292/, accessed 10 January.

Chokayev, M. (2001). *Otryvki iz vospominanii o 1917.* Tokyo: Islamic Area Studies Project, Central Asian Research Series 1.

Cooley, A. (2012). *Great Games, Local Rules: The New Power Contest in Central Asia.* Oxford and New York: Oxford University Press.

Cooley, A. and J. Heathershaw. (2017). *Dictators without Borders: Power and Money in Central Asia.* New Haven, CT: Yale University Press.

Duchâtel, M. (2019). 'Overseas Military Operations in Belt and Road Countries: The Normative Constraints and Legal Framework,' in N. Rolland ed. *Securing the Belt and Road Initiative: China's Evolving Military Engagement Along the Silk Roads.* National Bureau of Asian Research.

Eurasianet.org. (2018). Report: Russia Chides Kazakhstan on US Cooperation. 12 June.

Eurasianet.org. (2019). Uzbekistan: Head of Security Services Gets Chop Amid Talk of Surveillance. 12 February.

Golovnina, M. (2008). 'U.S. and Kazakhstan Snub Russia with New Military Deal', *Reuters,* 1 February.

Gorenburg, D. (2014). 'External Support for Central Asian Military and Security Forces,' *SIPRI and Open Society Foundation,* January.

Hirsch, F. (2005). *Empire of Nations: Ethnographic Knowledge and the Making of the Soviet Union.* Ithaca: Cornell University Press.

Human Rights Watch. (2008). Uzbekistan: Repression Linked to 2005 Massacre Rife. 11 May.

Ibragimov, M.M. (2019). 'Priorities of the Construction of the Armed Forces of the Republic of Uzbekistan in the Conditions of Development of Forms and Methods of Contemporary Armed Struggle,' *Military Review,* January-February.

Jiansheng, Z. and L. Jinmu. (2018). 'China's National Defense University Builds Ties with Military Academies in above 100 Countries,' *China Military Online,* August. http://eng.mod.gov.cn/news/2018-08/02/content_4821607.htm

Khrolenko, A. (2019). 'Postavki Voennoy Tehniki is RF v Uzbekistan Ukrepiyat Bezopasnost' v Regione', *Uz.sputnik.ru,* 7 November.

Khudoiberdiyev, O. (1984). *Boyevaya druzhba, pozhdennay Oktyabrem. Iz istorii voennogo stroitel'stva i likvidatsii kontrrevolutsii v srednei Azii.* Moscow: Nauka.

Klimov, S. (1987). *Voenno-organizatorskaya rabota kommunisticheskoi partii v Srednei Azii v 1917–1924 gg.* Tashkent: Uzbekistan.

Kozyulin, V. (2014). *Voenno-tehicheskoe Sotrudnichestvo Rossii: Vmeste, No Porozn.* Kazahstan i Mir: Oboronnaya Politika, May.

Kucera, J. (2011). 'Central Asia: US Special Forces Help Train Praetorian Guards,' *Eurasianet.org*, 11 December.

Kucera, J. (2015). 'No Longer Under Sanctions, Uzbekistan Gets 300 Armored Vehicles from U.S.,' *Eurasianet.org*, 22 January.

Kucera, J. (2018). 'US Planned Big Boost in Military Aid to Tajikistan,' *Eurasianet.org*, 11 January.

Kyrgyzstan Inquiry Commission. (2014). *Report of the Independent International Commission of Inquiry into the Events in Southern Kyrgyzstan in June 2010.* Osh: KIC, May. http://www.k-ic.org/images/stories/kic_report_english_final.pdf.

Marat, E. (2009). *The Military and the State in Central Asia: From Red Army to Independence.* New York: Routledge.

Marat, E. (2018). *The Politics of Police Reform: Society Against the State in Post-Soviet Countries.* New York: Oxford University Press.

Marat, E. (2021). 'China's Expanding Military Education Diplomacy in Central Asia,' *PONARS Eurasia Policy Memo 687.* Washington, DC: George Washington University.

Movchin, N.N.(1926). 'Komplektovanie Krasnoj Armii: (Istorich. ocherk),' *Upr. po issled. i ispol'zovaniju opyta vojn.* Voen. tip. Upr. delami Narkomvoenmor. i RVS SSSR.

Nelson, C. and T. Grove. (2019). 'Russia, China Vie for Influence in Central Asia as U.S. Plans Afghan Exit,' *The Wall Street Journal*, 18 June.

Odgaard, L. (2017). 'Beijing's Quest for Stability in its Neighborhood: China's Relations with Russia in Central Asia,' *Asian Security* 13(1): 41–58.

Odom, W.E. (2000). *The Collapse of the Soviet Military.* New Haven, CT: Yale University Press.

Omelicheva, M. (2019). 'The United States and Uzbekistan: Military-to-Military Relations in a New Era of Strategic Partnership', *PONARS Policy Memo 604*, July.

Omelicheva, M. (2017). 'U.S. Security Assistance to Central Asia: Examining Limits, Exploring Opportunities,' *PONARS Policy Memo 487*, October.

Price, T. (2019). 'U.S. To Publish New Central Asia Strategy Amid Russian, Chinese Competition, Afghan Threat,' *RFE/RL*, 14 December.

Rolland, N. (2019). 'Securing the Belt and Road: Prospects for Chinese Military Engagement Along the Silk Roads', in N. Rolland ed. *Securing the Belt and Road Initiative: China's Evolving Military Engagement Along the Silk Roads.* National Bureau of Asian Research.

Sanchez, W.A. (2019). 'The Significance of Kazakhstan's Growing Role in Peacekeeping Operations,' *The Diplomat*, 1 March.

Shih, G. (2019). 'In Central Asia's Forbidding Highlands, a Quiet Newcomer: Chinese Troops,' *The Washington Post*, 18 February.

Stevis-Gridneff, M. (2019). 'Blocked in U.S., Huawei Touts 'Shared Values' to Compete in Europe,' *The New York Times*, 27 December.

Stratfor. (2016). China's Long March into Central Asia. 27 April.

Toiken, S. (2019). 'Uncle Toqaev Wants You! Kazakh Conscriptions, Jailings Greet Wave of Preelection Protests,' *RFE/RL*, 7 June.

van der Kley, D. (2019). 'China's Security Activities in Tajikistan and Afghanistan's Wakhan Corridor,' in N. Rolland ed. *The Dragon's Cuddle: China's Security Power Projection into Central Asia and Lessons for the Belt and Road Initiative.* The National Bureau of Asian Research, September.

Volkov, A. (2003). '40ya armya: Istroirya sozdaniya, sostav, izmenenie struktury,' *Voennyi Kommentator: Voenno-istorichesky Almanakh* 1(5).

Yan, Y.T. (2019). 'What Drives Chinese Arms Sales in Central Asia?,' *The Diplomat*, 11 September.

18
GLOBALISATION AND MIGRATION IN CENTRAL ASIA

Caress Schenk

Central Asia has historically been a region of mobility and connection to global power. The construction and reconstruction of borders, and the people flows across those variously conceived borders are of enduring interest to scholars (Reeves 2014, Diener 2015, Grant 2020, Megoran 2017). The fall of the Soviet Union complicated sometimes fuzzy notions of borders by creating newly independent countries with presumably concretised boundaries. People movements that were once domestic became international. Ethnic movements of people to their historical homelands became a priority for policymakers. Economic disintegration and ensuing poverty acted as an additional push factor for workers of all ethnic backgrounds in search of employment (Abashin 2014).

Central Asian countries became independent in a time of intense globalisation, forcing them to confront issues of internal stateness and external sovereignty simultaneously. A perennial question of globalisation even for more established polities concerns the degree to which the state remains relevant amid countless forces that seem outside its control. Migration in the Central Asian region displays many of the tensions demonstrating transnational and globalising forces amid resilient state activities to maintain sovereignty. Entrenched people movements and transnational networks, an active bilateral and multilateral policy environment, financial interdependencies, international threat environments, and a geostrategic location pressed between China, Russia and the Islamic world place pressures on the states of Central Asia from every side.

This chapter looks at four migration-related issues that affect the countries of Central Asia as a way to demonstrate the complex nature of globalisation in the region. Migration touches on a number of issues that are politically salient and rise to the forefront of analysis of Central Asian states. In each of these areas, the states of Kazakhstan, Kyrgyzstan, Tajikistan and Uzbekistan struggle for decision-making capacity vis-à-vis their regional and geopolitical interdependencies, yet also retain important leverages. Looking at the financial interdependencies between states created by labour migration and remittances, political and economic efforts to integrate through the Eurasian Economic Union, transnational social relations, and the international nature of security threats offers a way to analyse a breadth of factors affecting migration patterns, policies and outcomes in the region.

DOI: 10.4324/9780429057977-18

Labour migration and remittances: Flows across borders

Transnational labour migration demonstrates the global nature of labour markets in the modern era. For Central Asian citizens, labour migration has become an important strategy for economic survival. Most of these migrants go north towards Russia, some stopping in Kazakhstan, while there are also lesser flows going to Turkey, South Korea and the Middle East. Assessing the scale of this migration is an important starting point to establish the degree of dependence the region has on labour migration. This dependence is in many ways beyond state control, though each of the Central Asian countries has made various efforts to control the exit of migrants (Turaeva 2015), establish migration services to coordinate between home and abroad, and/or scrutinise migrants upon their return for potential integration problems (Lemon and Thibault 2018).

Without a doubt, the migration flows that receive the most attention in the Eurasian region are those from Kyrgyzstan, Tajikistan and Uzbekistan to Russia. Notwithstanding data problems that tend to underestimate the flows, figures on labour migration in Russia are more systematically collected than flows to Central Asian countries, showing millions of Central Asian migrants working in Russia each year. Kazakhstan is also a migration destination, though few migrant workers are employed with the required documentation. Data is available on the number of migrant workers to Kazakhstan only for some years. From 2010 to 2017, anywhere from 20,000 to 30,000 foreign workers have been recorded in Kazakhstan each year, and of these 2,000–3,000 come from the Commonwealth of Independent States (CIS) countries. The reality is quite different, however, with many migrant workers from Uzbekistan, Kyrgyzstan, and increasingly from Tajikistan, filling jobs in construction, bazaar and shuttle trade, agriculture, renovation and janitorial services.

Migration flows in the Eurasian region are difficult to assess because of how data is collected not only in different countries but also across agencies within any given country. Typically, border control agencies issue statistics on the number of foreigners crossing the border, whereas labour or migration agencies issue figures on the number of foreigners working. These figures may differ still from census or registration figures on the number of foreigners residing in the country. Multilateral organisations such as CIS or Eurasian Economic Union (EAEU) rely on national data for their statistics, and have not given any particular attention to the harmonisation of methodologies of data collection. Migration statistics are most developed in Russia, but efforts to develop cohesive methodologies for categories such as estimates of undocumented migrants remain diffuse, among expert and academic institutions, and are not supported by the state statistical agencies. Migration statistics in Central Asian countries, by comparison, are woefully underdeveloped and their development is receiving almost no official attention.

In the absence of data on migration flows, remittance data can help to build a picture of the interconnectedness of people across borders. Table 18.1 shows the large financial flows from Russia to Kyrgyzstan, Tajikistan and Uzbekistan, which can be seen as traditional remittances of labour migrants to their families at home. Considering remittances as a percentage of GDP, Tajikistan (29.7 per cent) and Kyrgyzstan (29.6 per cent) are particularly dependent on wages earned abroad.[1] In dollar terms, remittance flows dipped significantly after the 2014 ruble crisis in Russia, showing how the livelihood of migrants can be affected by global crises (Marat 2009). However, predictions that there would be dramatically fewer migrants in Russia as a result of the crisis have proved unfounded. Instead, wages have remained depressed, sending ripple effects of the crisis throughout Central Asia. Kyrgyzstan's remittance level recovered more quickly than those to Tajikistan, and by 2017 had reached pre-crisis levels, perhaps due to their freer access to the labour market through the terms of the Eurasian Economic Union. Tajikistan and Uzbekistan have yet to fully recover.

Table 18.1 Remittance flows 2017,[1] millions of US dollars

To / From	Kazakhstan	Kyrgyzstan	Tajikistan	Uzbekistan	China	Russia	Turkey
Kazakhstan	–	20.66	141.07	–	30.74	1,713.13	26.60
Kyrgyzstan	1.31	–	6.25	–	1.72	89.46	0.36
Tajikistan	0.06	25.10	–	–	–	174.26	0.20
Uzbekistan	8.34	37.14	45.66	–	11.99	422.54	2.32
China	0.43	2.98	1.86	–	–	–	–
Russia	225.59	1,904.33	1,687.57	2,838.69	–	–	–
Turkey	1.10	13.54	1.50	–	–	–	–

Source: World Bank Migration and Remittance Data
[1] Latest available data from the World Bank.

The data in Table 18.1 shows some surprising flows that are rarely mentioned in discussions on cross-border financial flows. Remittances sent from Kazakhstan to Russia far outstrip those sent the other direction. Flows from the other Central Asian countries also should not be dismissed as they are far larger than flows between Kyrgyzstan, Tajikistan and Uzbekistan. This suggests that while labour migrants are supporting their families back home, those families are also providing support to those working in Russia as needed.

Financial support extends to family and local networks from home offering support to migrants in their destination place, sharing money as needed among migrants while in Russia (Urinboyev 2018). These figures of course do not show up in the remittance data, or elsewhere in terms of measurable financial flows. However, they are an important part of the informal transfers that occur between migrants abroad and between families at home, who share financial burdens across groups within a locality (Djabarova, Perez-Studer and Aminmadani 2017, Urinboyev and Polese 2016, Rubinov 2014). Therefore, remittance data is only suggestive of the wider patterns of financial interdependence among migrants and their families across borders. It also does not capture the intangible gains of social remittances, such as skills improvement, that migrants bring home after their time in migration (Zotova and Cohen 2016, Tynaliev and McLean 2011).

As we will see in the following two sections, policies (established through the Eurasian Economic Union) and practices of migrants at the everyday level show that the reach of the state in the process of labour migration is limited. Despite ongoing efforts to shape migrant flows by sending and receiving states, flows in the Eurasian region, as throughout the world, are resistant to policy change (Schenk 2018). Global economic dynamics, transnational networks and other geopolitical factors combine to impact migration flows in complex and interlocking ways.

Institutional integration through the Eurasian Economic Union

The Eurasian Economic Union was established in 2015 as a free trade and labour zone between member countries of Armenia, Belarus, Kazakhstan, Russia and (later) Kyrgyzstan. In terms of labour migration, the EAEU agreement allows citizens of member countries to work in other member countries with only a labour contract (other migration work documents are not required). On the surface, the agreement gives states little leverage to protect their labour markets from incoming migrants. In reality, there are many areas in which states and employers demonstrate their preferences even within the free labour zone. Comparing migrants' access to the labour market, bilateral negotiations over terms that should be settled in the EAEU agreement, and continued work at the institutional level towards integration, demonstrates the limits of the union, and therefore opportunities for states to assert their interests.

Citizens of EAEU member states can be hired without the labour permit or work visa required of other foreign workers. For Kyrgyzstani citizens, this offers a seeming advantage over workers from Tajikistan and Uzbekistan, both in Russia and in Kazakhstan. In Russia, Kyrgyzstanis can work legally as long as they have a work contract that is filed with the migration services and their employer pays income tax on their earnings. However, many employers prefer to hire workers informally to save these tax expenditures.[2] As a result, many EAEU workers have dropped out of the labour migration statistics. The EAEU itself does not provide figures on the labour flows between countries, nor does Kazakhstan or Russia as the main recipients issue these data. Kazakhstan does not publish these statistics at all, and in Russia the figures can only be found scattered among regional-level reports of the migration services.

In Kazakhstan, Kyrgyzstani migrants were slow to be afforded the advantages of their membership in the EAEU (Schenk 2017). Kazakhstan failed to make necessary changes to their procedures until February 2016, finally extending the period for registration for Kyrgyz citizens coming to work from 5 to 30 days (Russian citizens were already allowed 30 days to register, according to a bilateral treaty). However, only migrants planning to work, and not their families, were given this extension. Around this time, the Kyrgyz consulate in Kazakhstan indicated the two governments were still negotiating over giving family members access to an extended period for registration. However, when I talked to a representative of the foreign ministry of Kyrgyzstan in summer 2016, he indicated there was no ongoing negotiation and that Kyrgyzstan was simply waiting for Kazakhstan to implement the provisions of the EAEU treaty. Only in October 2016 was it announced that all Kyrgyz citizens would enjoy the extended period for registration, but the new procedure would come into effect only 'after internal procedures of the two countries' (Lymar 2016). According to the Eurasian Economic Commission's migration department, 'changing the length of stay without registration [for] Kyrgyz citizens in Kazakhstan belongs to the sphere of bilateral agreements' (Bnews .kz 2016). Some claim that the introduction in 2016 of registration procedures in Kyrgyzstan (requiring registration within five days) were partly in retaliation for Kazakhstan's slow adoption of EAEU provisions on the same issue, though the measures were repealed within a few months (Abduvali 2016). Tit for tat actions continued into 2017, when the border was closed between Kazakhstan and Kyrgyzstan over contention that Kazakhstan was meddling in Kyrgyzstan's presidential elections, leaving trade stymied until negotiations could go forward (Pannier 2017).

Bilateral negotiations in some cases have allowed Central Asian states to assert their interests vis a vis stronger neighbours. When Kyrgyzstan was negotiating its entry into the EAEU, it was able to convince Russia to remove a number of its citizens from re-entry ban lists (Sagynbekova 2017). This demonstrates how in the context of Russia's great need for low-skilled labour, sending states are able to make demands that benefit the state and its citizens. However, bilateral negotiations made in the context of the larger institutional structure of the Eurasian Economic Union suggest a lack of overarching authority of the organisation. A closer look at the work at the level of the EAEU further demonstrates this dynamic.

At the upper institutional levels, in the Eurasian Commission (the executive body of the EAEU), the negotiations over pension transferability hint at the difficulty in coming to decisions that will require harmonisation of institutions beyond the simple dictates of the treaty to open up labour markets. It took nearly five years for the Eurasian Commission to conclude a pension agreement, which was expected to go into force January 2020 but was delayed to January 2021. The agreement was long in coming because the pension systems in each member country are organised differently and do not offer uniform benefits to foreign workers (Sharifzoda 2019). The eventual agreement demonstrates that little progress was made to harmonise pension systems; rather, many references are made to individual state systems and even the vocabulary of each national scheme (Pension Agreement 2019). In the end, the agreement confers a commitment to pay pensions to workers even once they have returned to their home countries, and little else.

Migrant workers' eventual ability to access pension fund depends on their ability to find documented work (i.e. work with a labour contract) in the host country. For workers at the high-skilled end of the labour market, there are few problems with these obligations. For low-skilled workers, all of the previous problems associated with labour migration still apply. However, as we will see in the following section, labour migrants find ways to manage their life and work abroad regardless of their legal status.

Transnational life and work

Many of the migration patterns Central Asians find themselves in an international, cross-border space, without being altogether different than historical movements. What was domestic became international with the fall of the Soviet Union, and the process of disentangling political, economic and social identities began. Certainly, historical patterns and experiences (Bahovadinova and Scarborough 2018, Sahadeo 2019) have contributed to the mobility we see today. Yet, where migrants once travelled under the auspices of the friendship of the peoples (Sahadeo 2007), now they are variously framed as the post-colonial or racialised other, though at times they are also seen as compatriots (Woodard 2019).

Not only migrants who leave Central Asia to work abroad but also the families they leave at home are increasingly located in transnational spaces. Many migrants live across different spaces that could be termed translocal or multi-local (Thieme 2011), being rooted in the ecosystems of multiple places (Schröder and Stephan-Emmrich 2016). The literature conceives of the transnational lives of migrants in several different frames, with focus on the various economic and social aspects of connections that are increasingly less bounded by borders. These studies come primarily from sociology and anthropology and do not always explicitly engage the concept of the state (with several important exceptions), but lay an important foundation for how social groups interact and behave in a globalised space.

Economic aspects of transnationalism often look at the livelihoods that are available to mobile people. The literature on shuttle trading as a type of transnational economic activity, focusing primarily on the transport of Chinese goods to bazaars throughout the region, is an early and ongoing exploration of how traders leverage their mobility and ability to operate in several socio-political contexts (Shamatov and Niyozov 2006, Mukhina 2009, Kaminski and Raballand 2009, Cieslewska 2013, Karrar 2019, Fehlings 2018). Turaeva's (2014) work on cross-border entrepreneurship offers a look into a different type of economic activity, analysing the activities of intermediaries who broker the labour relations who operate in the nebulous space between the formal and the informal economies. This and other studies on the leveraging of social relationships in managing migrant labour demonstrate the crucial importance of origins and the ongoing interaction with those at home for finding jobs and securing livelihood in migration (Urinboyev and Polese 2016, Djabarova, Perez-Studer and Aminmadani 2017, Rubinov 2014, Urinboyev 2018, Urinboyev 2017b).

Often the economic relations migrants have between each other while in migration extend beyond work activities. Social ties with compatriots have a major impact on the ability to navigate the migration context and may help migrants adapt and integrate into their host society and economy (Agadjanian, Gorina and Menjívar 2014, Virkkunen 2017). In some ways they also reproduce social and moral norms from home within the migrant community (Rocheva and Varshaver 2017). These social relations are often transnational in nature, relying on connections not only between migrant compatriots but including regular communications with those who remain at home. Several scholars have shown how mahallas are recreated in migration among those from the same villages (Urinboyev 2017a, Boboyorov 2018). Migrants are in daily contact and assist each other with navigating life and with any difficulties that may arise. Social relationships, accountability and discipline are reinforced by regular communications and information sharing between migrants and their families at home.

Often decisions to migrate in the first place are family decisions, representing a wider economic strategy that takes place in a family lifecycle. At various periods when migration to Russia has been difficult, for example, as a result of increased deportation and re-entry bans, families send another person to take their place in Russia, extending beyond the typical pool of young men to include female members of the family. In Tajikistan and elsewhere, this has led to increasingly feminised flows of migrants (Kholmatova 2018). However, with increasing numbers of women going abroad, families become more transnational. Migrants continue to contribute to and participate in households at home, often leaving children with extended family, travelling home as they are able and communicating frequently while they are abroad. Though migrants often maintain minimal households abroad, conserving funds to support those at home, their horizons are altered by their social networks, experiences and skills gained abroad.

Communications between families across borders are facilitated by technologies such as smart phones (Stephan-Emmrich 2018, Ruget and Usmanalieva 2019, Urinboyev 2017a). These technologies become particularly important when we consider how migration in the Eurasian region not only separates working-age adults from their extended family, but how the children of migrants are often left behind to be raised by grandparents (Isabaeva 2011, Thieme 2014). The transnational parenting practices that arise as a result are greatly facilitated by mobile technologies allowing parents in migration to retain relationships with their children at home (Borisova 2016, Djabarova, Perez-Studer and Aminmadani 2017).

Research finds mixed effects on the health and welfare of the children left behind (Kroeger and Anderson 2014, Dietz, Gatskova and Ivlevs 2015). Many of these look at education outcomes as a way to measure the impact of transnational family structures on children (Cebotari 2018), though research on transnational parenting beyond the region also includes important developments in assessing the level of contact between parents and children and the psychological impact of migration on families (Wu and Cebotari 2018, Mazzucato and Cebotari 2017). Ethnographic research on the impact of migration on families has uncovered the emotional costs of migration on children (Nazridod, Pereira and Guerreiro 2021) created a more complex picture of the consequences and effects of migration for those left behind (Reeves 2011, Kikuta 2016, Isabaeva 2011, Thieme 2008). These studies document pressures on traditional marriage and gender roles such as the prevalence of dual families where migrants add a second wife in their work destination (Turaeva 2014) and the phenomenon of SMS-divorces (Thibault 2018b).

Migration brings positive effects as well. In most cases remittances are used to meet basic needs, compensating for economic difficulties of unemployment and poverty (Schmidt and Sagynbekova 2008). However, a great deal of the money earned abroad is also used to finance social celebrations and rituals such as weddings and funerals, to build houses, and sometimes invest in new businesses at home, all of which have important social and economic functions

(Rahmonova-Schwarz 2012, Rubinov 2014, Marat 2009, Ilkhamov 2013). As a result, migrants often return home to increased prestige both for their cosmopolitan experiences abroad and the value of their earnings (Kikuta 2016), and increasingly migration is seen as an initiation rite marking the transition from youth to adulthood (Jaborov 2017, Massot 2013). These effects have further implications for the development of the state, society and economy. However, as we will see in the next section, migrants are not always seen in terms of the benefits they bring to the home or host country. Rather, they are securitised in various ways depending on the goals of the state.

Globalised threat perception

The literature on crises and crisis decision-making shows how modern crises often have a transboundary nature that makes them difficult to contain not only within state borders but even within other categories, such as time or issue-area (Boin 2009). Whether an event or set of events poses an actual security threat, or whether it is rhetorically constructed as a crisis, is sometimes difficult to disentangle, and policy responses are not always proportionate to risks. An analysis of transnational threats, or perceived threats, could be discussed using any number of examples in Central Asia. Even focusing on those aspects that could be directly related to migration would give us ample material. Border security, secessionist threats or territorial disputes (Jaxylykov 2017, Gabdulhakov 2017, Reeves 2005), the potential diffusion of instabilities across borders (Koch 2018), human trafficking (Kelly 2013) and geopolitical balancing, including the occasional bilateral spat over migrants (Ryazantsev and Korneev 2013), could all be developed as examples of how migration and globalisation can be framed as security threats that potentially pose a threat to the state. Here, I will develop two contrasting examples that demonstrate the ways in which states choose to focus on certain threats over others, focusing first on Central Asian migrants who travel to Russia and become seen as potential religious radicals both at home and abroad, and then turning to the case of Chinese migrants in Central Asia. Framing migrants as potential radicals and extremists has become a discourse that aligns well with international rhetoric and the policy agendas of Western governments, lending legitimacy to Central Asian governments' efforts to fight radicalisation. On the other hand, despite widespread Sinophobia that might predict a securitised approach towards Chinese migrants, we see Central Asian governments choosing to prioritise geopolitical ties with China.

Radicalisation and terrorism: From domestic fears to international justifications

A startling degree of attention has been giving to the migration–radicalisation nexus in the Central Asian context, especially given the lack of empirical evidence studies have revealed to substantiate claims of a relationship between migration and extremism. The fear of radicalisation and fundamentalism more generally (not linked to migration) has been a long-established theme in the politics of Central Asian countries. It has led to the banning of religious political parties and movements and tightening of religious laws in most of the countries (Thibault 2019). Typically, responses by states to Islam have mixed securitisation of Islam with a fear of any political opposition to the regimes that define themselves on a secular basis (McGlinchey 2005a, Omelicheva 2016, Khalid 2007), and elided increased religiosity with radicalism (Thibault 2018a). Often these states have legitimised their actions by linking their efforts to global counterterrorism programmes (Omelicheva 2011, Rasayanagam 2017); nevertheless scholarship has repeatedly demonstrated that the links between religion and radicalisation are dubious (Heathershaw and Montgomery 2014, Montgomery and Heathershaw 2016).

Discourse on the links between religion and radicalism took on new vigour with the rise of the Islamic State and war in Syria. Reports of an estimated several thousand citizens of Central Asian states joining the Islamic State to fight in Syria and Iraq, many of them having been recruited while working in Russia, created a link between migration and radicalisation. Reports of Central Asian fighters in Syria began as early as 2013 from international organisations, media and private security firms (Paraszczuk 2014, Basit 2014, Soliyev 2013), and many were quick to make a link between those who had gone to fight and migrant workers in Russia (Qosimzoda, et al. 2014, Tucker 2015, E. J. Lemon 2015).

As a migration issue, the topic of radicalisation illustrates the transnational nature of religious activity. However, the link between migration and radicalisation came to the attention of governments and international agencies alike (US House of Representatives 2015, International Crisis Group 2015). Many agencies soon began to frame migration as a potential risk factor for radicalisation and to fund large-scale projects investigating the link between migration and radicalisation. The International Organization for Migration (funded by USAID), Search for a Common Ground, and Organization for Security and Cooperation in Europe have merged existing counter-extremism agendas with the migration–radicalisation link, often framing the results of studies in terms of risk and threat assessments. The emerging studies have uncovered little proof of migration creating risk of radicalisation, though the idea is persistent in certain circles.

As Edward Lemon (2018b) has pointed out, even though thousands of Central Asians have counted themselves among militants in Syria, this amounts to only 0.0001 per cent of the region's population. This reality feels very different than reports that 'Today, the biggest number of IS group recruits in Iraq and Syria come from Central Asia' (Nordstrom 2017). Similarly, claims that most or all of the Central Asian militants in Syria were either recruited in Russia or had at some point been in Russia as a labour migrant becomes a numbers game. While the number of legal migrants in Russia has never risen above 3.7 million in 2014, the scale of undocumented work is immense, producing estimates as high as 5–10 million migrants in Russia at any given time. We do not have any credible estimates of the number of migrants who have migrated to Russia even for just one trip in the past decade, though that would likely produce a figure well above 10 million. Even if we use the upper estimates of 4,000 Central Asians in Syria and Iraq alongside the upper estimates of 5–10 million migrants in Russia, this indicates around 0.04–0.08 per cent of the migrant population in Russia radicalises. In other words, 99.92–99.96 per cent of migrants in Russia do not radicalise.

Migration is a way of life for many Central Asians. In migration, citizens of Central Asia experience various forms of precarity and vulnerability, and many also experience increased religiosity (Turaeva 2019, Eraliev 2018). These should not be elided with propensities to radicalise. Scholars suggest that Central Asians radicalise owing to various types of grievances and reactions to the political conditions of authoritarianism and to mobilisation through personal networks, and not particularly for religious or ideological reasons (McGlinchey 2005b, Tucker 2019). Political grievances are likely to be activated prior to migration, and may be the very same factors pushing migrants to Russia.

The mentalities and rhetoric connecting migration and radicalisation continue to be repeated by think tanks and the media and, along with events linking Central Asians to terrorist activities while they are in migration (in Russia and the United States), have served to further securitise migration with little evidence or justification of the root causes of radicalisation (Lynch, et al. 2016, Sanderson 2018, Sonmez 2017). In this way the migration–radicalism link is manipulated in much the same way as the Islam–radicalism link, to produce crack-downs and harsh policies that are likely to have their own negative effects that are disproportionally leveraged on non-radicals (Montgomery and Heathershaw 2016, E. Lemon 2018a). Some of this activity may be the unwitting result of pressure from international organisations and foreign governments who are quick to fund research on the migration extremism link as a part of their ongoing efforts to combat extremism (Gavrilis 2017).

The China factor

The relationship between China and Central Asian states shows a contrasting thrust, where governments are reluctant to mobilise public opinion around migration-related issues, as it might be counterproductive to geopolitical goals. States on the one hand covet Chinese investment and on the other hand must balance against significant fears among the population about China's creeping influence. Sinophobia has long had roots in Central Asia due to historical territorial disputes and Soviet-era propaganda (Owen 2017, Peyrouse 2016, Grant 2020) but has been renewed since the initiation of China's One Belt One Road (OBOR) or Belt and Road Initiative (BRI) in 2013. These dynamics are most relevant for those states that border China: Kazakhstan, Kyrgyzstan and Tajikistan.

Scholars disagree on whether the BRI project, or Chinese relations in general, leaves Central Asian countries without agency. Some argue Chinese activity in the region is unilateral, leaving certain Central Asian states with little ability to direct the agenda (Bitabarova 2018). Others maintain that Central Asian states retain the ability to assert their desires (Owen 2017), in much the same way as in their relationship with Russia (Ortmann 2018). However public opinion is critical and suspicious of their governments' interactions with China (Peyrouse 2016, Jochec and Kyzy 2018), though perhaps less-so among the younger generation (Chen and Jiménez-Tovar 2017).

The migration issue again demonstrates larger political and geopolitical factors at play in how Central Asian countries navigate their place in a globalised world. Contrasting the increased securitisation aimed at radicals discussed in the previous section, with rhetoric on Chinese migrants alongside policies inviting Chinese investment provides a sharp contrast. The case of Kazakhstan aptly illustrates this contrast. For instance, in 2016, the Kazakhstani government proposed a constitutional amendment that would have extended the maximum period for foreigners to lease land from 10 to 25 years, which was an opening to foreign workers and investors. This quickly became framed as a measure that would allow China to take over Kazakhstan's territory and tap into the fear of an invasion by Chinese migrants (S. Peyrouse 2012). The proposal produced a series of protests before then-President Nazarbayev announced a delay in adopting the measure. These events occurred just prior to terrorist attacks in Aktobe in June 2016 that became associated with foreign influence and resultant calls to increase migration control pulled in a closed and securitised direction. Even prior to the Aktobe events and protests, representatives of the Kazakhstani Security Council discussed the need to regulate migration in a way that would stimulate economic growth while still maximally controlling the entry of terrorist or criminal elements or illegal migrants (23 February 2016 meeting of the Security Council, akorda.kz).

Legal changes that were quickly enacted in direct response to the Aktobe events had an important impact on migration. A new law on terrorism was rapidly developed that had implications for registration (*propiska*) policies for international migrants and citizens.[3] The biggest migration-related policy change that comes out of the new law on terrorism is the changes to registration procedures, which affect both international and internal migrants. The amendments included new fines for violating the terms of registration, including being registered in a place one does not physically reside. While the fines were not substantial, fears of being caught, or potentially informed on for living in an apartment where they are not registered, were actively stoked by the government and in social media. As a result, there was a rush of citizens to register, as Kazakhstan's quite mobile urban population is often not registered where they live. Though advertised as an effort to be able to more easily identify and find potential terrorists, procedures have a dubious link to any counterterrorism effect, since those involved in terrorist or other criminal activities are the least likely to comply with the law. The procedures further placed an unnecessary burden on the law-abiding portion of the population, especially since a lack of any further enforcement efforts following the initial push allowed citizens to lapse back into their previous practices of not maintaining accurate registration records.

This resolute action (even if not systematically enforced in the long run) of security-oriented rhetoric and policy change contrasts with the Kazakhstani government's activities vis a vis Chinese migration. In spring and summer 2016, public fears about migration from China were mobilised as a result of the land-lease legislation proposal. Social media lit up with discussion and very vocal criticism of the government's plans. Months after the initial unrest, the Kazakhstani ambassador to China was keen to dispel the 'myth' of Chinese migration, saying that of the nearly 120,000 visas issued to Chinese citizens in 2015, 70 per cent were given to ethnic Kazakhs. The remaining included 19,000 business and 10,000 work visas.[4] These numbers do not include any Chinese workers in Kazakhstan for priority projects, allowing them to work outside the standard foreign labour quotas. There are many such exemptions, though no comprehensive list of priority projects is available, nor is data issued on the number of foreign workers involved. Therefore, claiming a partial picture of Chinese migration as a strategy to counter public moods can be seen as, at best, dismissive of societal fears. There seems to be a greater willingness on the part of Kazakhstani elites to alienate the public (through securitising policies that are targeted at citizens and not shifting the blame to the potential threat of international migrants) than sacrifice policy goals that depend on increasing openness to migration from China that comes with BRI projects.

Inaction on the part of Kazakhstan in accepting refugees from China in the wake of widespread re-education efforts of Xinjang's Muslim population further demonstrates how migration policies and practices reflect larger geopolitical balancing. As of this writing, the Kazakhstani government plans to deport two ethnic Kazakhs who had crossed illegally into Kazakhstan back to China. As with a similar case, where an ethnic Kazakh woman was not allowed to stay in Kazakhstan but was eventually given asylum in Sweden, the Kazakhstani government's pattern has been to favour its geopolitical ties with China by avoiding the politically sensitive issue of the re-education camps, even at the expense of its ethnic compatriots abroad (RFE/RL 2019).

Conclusion

The four migration-related issues in this chapter – labour migration and remittances, institutional integration, transnational life and work, and globalised threat perception – demonstrate different aspects of the state's leverage over the processes of globalisation. The emerging picture is one where the policy efforts of the state are not always its most powerful tool in asserting its agenda. Often rhetoric, whether directed at the public or in the course of bilateral negotiations, is a more effective way of pursuing interests in light of migration flows that are socially driven and not contained within normal legal channels and suprainstitutional mechanisms purporting to regulate these flows.

Labour migrant movements, tracked imperfectly through remittance data, begins to uncover how dependent the countries of Kyrgyzstan, Tajikistan and Uzbekistan are on the wages of its citizens earned abroad. The financial inputs are important for economic development and additional skills gained in migration contribute to the future growth and sustainability of the countries. However, since development is dependent, it is vulnerable to global economic shocks. Many of these processes take place outside the scope of state policy. The transnational nature of these migration networks also operate largely outside the reach of the state, and together represent the bottom-up power and development potential of migration in the region.

The examples of the Eurasian Economic Union and geopolitical threats offer a contrast to the bottom-up factors pressuring Central Asian states. These forces pressure states from outside and above. It is in these examples that we see the efforts of the state through formal institutions such as the EAEU contrasted with the often informal nature of diplomatic relations visible in how the state chooses to focus on certain threats but not others. In these ways, the state is able to leverage its interests in a way sometimes not possible through formal institutions. The strategic enforcement and non-enforcement of policy on the books, such as that through the EAEU, is a further way that the state often asserts itself informally (Schenk 2018).

In the brief discussion in this chapter, we've barely touched on the variation of migration within Central Asia, of which there is much. This a crucial need for future research, as in the analysis of migration many studies look at each of the Central Asian countries either as an undifferentiated mass or as individual case studies. This set of cases is a valuable ground for more systematic comparative analysis in terms of how each state actualises its capacity in search of policy interests in a complex context of globalised pressures.

Notes

1 World Bank figures as of October 2019 https://www.worldbank.org/en/topic/migrationremittances diasporaissues/brief/migration-remittances-data.
2 Interview with migration expert, Russia, June 2018.
3 The law 'О внесении изменений и дополнений в некоторые законодательные акты Республики Казахстан по вопросам противодействия экстремизму и терроризму' was passed on 22 December. It amends the Criminal Code, the Criminal Procedural Code, the Criminal Enforcement Code, the Code of Administrative Offenses, the Entrepreneurial Code, the laws *On Citizenship, On Operational Search Activities, On the Legal Status of Foreign Citizens, On the Organs of National Security, On Housing Relations, On the Special Status of the City of Almaty, On State Control of the Circulation of Certain Types of Weapons, On Countering Terrorism, On Mass Media, On Security Activities, On Local Government Management and Self-Management, On Tourist Activities, On State Legal Statistics and Special Accounts, On Communications, On the Status of the Capital, On Counteracting the Legalization (Laundering) of Criminally Obtained Incomes and the Financing of Terrorism, On Migration, On Religious Activities and Religious Associations, On the National Guard, On introducing amendments and additions to some legislative acts of the Republic of Kazakhstan on migration and employment issues.*
4 https://tengrinews.kz/kazakhstan_news/posol-razveyal-mif-o-migratsii-kitaytsev-v-kazahstan-305268/

Bibliography

Abashin, Sergei. 2014. 'Migration from Central Asia to Russia in the new Model of World Order.' *Russian Politics & Law* 52 (6): 8–23.

Abduvali, Gulnaz. 2016. Казахстан упростил порядок пребывания гражданам Кыргызстана [Kazakhstan simplified the procedures for stay for citizens of Kyrgyzstan]. *Nur.kz*, June 1. Accessed December 2, 2016. https://www.nur.kz/1145956-kazakhstan-uprostil-poryadok-prebyvan.html.

Agadjanian, Victor, Evgenia Gorina, and Cecilia Menjívar. 2014. 'Economic Incorporation, Civil Inclusion, and Social Ties: Plans to Return Home Among Central Asian Migrant Women in Moscow, Russia.' *International Migration Review* 48 (3): 577–603.

Bahovadinova, Malika, and Isaac Scarborough. 2018. 'Capitalism Fulfills the Final Five-Year Plan: How Soviet-Era Migration Programs Came to Fruition in Post-Soviet Eurasia.' In *Eurasia on the Move:*

Interdisciplinary Approaches to a Dynamic Migration Region, edited by Marlene Laruelle and Caress Schenk, 1–12. Washington, DC: Central Asia Program.

Barcus, Holly, and Cynthia Werner. 2010. 'The Kazakhs of Western Mongolia: Transnational Migration from 1990–2008.' *Asian Ethnicity* 11 (2): 209–28.

Basit, Abdul. 2014. 'Foreign Fighters in Iraq and Syria – Why So Many?' *Counter Terrorist Trends and Analyses* 6 (9): 4–8.

Bitabarova, Assel G. 2018. 'Unpacking Sino-Central Asian Engagement Along the New Silk Road: A Case Study of Kazakhstan.' *Journal of Contemporary East Asia Studies* 7 (2): 149–73.

Bloch, Alexia. 2011. 'Intimate Circuits: Modernity, Migration and Marriage Among Post Soviet Women in Turkey.' *Global Networks* 11 (4): 502–21.

Boboyorov, Hafiz. 2018. 'Translocal Securityscapes of Tajik Labor Migrants and the Families and Communities They Leave Behind.' In *Tajikistan on the Move: Statebuilding and Societal Transformations*, edited by Marlene Laruelle, 223–46. London: Lexington Books.

Boin, Arjen. 2009. 'The new World of Crises and Crisis Management: Implications for Policymaking and Research.' *Review of Policy Research* 26 (4): 367–77.

Borisova, Elena. 2016. 'Parenting at a Distance: Transnational Practices in Migrant Families from Tajikistan.' *Forum for Anthropology and Culture* 12: 125–38.

Cebotari, Victor. 2018. 'Transnational Migration, Gender and Educational Development of Children in Tajikistan.' *Global Networks* 18 (4): 564–88.

Chen, Julie Yu-Wen, and Soledad Jiménez-Tovar. 2017. 'China in Central Asia: Local Perceptions from Future Elites.' *China Quarterly of International Strategic Studies* 3 (3): 429–45.

Cieslewska, Anna. 2013. 'From Shuttle Trader to Businesswomen: The Informal Bazaar Economy in Kyrgyzstan.' In *The Informal Post-Socialist Economy: Embedded Practices and Livelihoods*, edited by Abel Polese Jeremy Morris, 141–54. London: Routledge.

Darieva, Tsypylma. 2005. 'Recruiting for the Nation: Post-Soviet Transnational Migrants in Germany and Kazakhstan.' In *Rebuilding Identities: Pathways to Reform in Post-Soviet Siberia*, edited by Erich Kasten, 153–72. Berlin: Dietrich Reimer Verlag.

Diener, Alexander C. 2015. 'Parsing Mobilities in Central Eurasia: Border Management and new Silk Roads.' *Eurasian Geography and Economics* 56 (4): 376–404.

Dietz, Barbara, Kseniia Gatskova, and Artjoms Ivlevs. 2015. 'Emigration, Remittances and the Education of Children Staying Behind: Evidence from Tajikistan.' *IZA Discussion Papers No. 9515*. November. Accessed November 6, 2019. https://www.econstor.eu/bitstream/10419/125032/1/dp9515.pdf.

Djabarova, Zamira, Rut Perez-Studer, and Sheila Aminmadani. 2017. 'Together on the Move. Tajik Migrants in Olympic Sochi.' In *Tajikistan: Islam, Migration, and Economic Challenges*, edited by Marlene Laruelle, 61–7. Washington DC: George Washington University, Central Asia Program.

Eraliev, Sherzod. 2018. 'Growing Religiosity Among Central Asian Migrants in Russia.' *Journal of International and Advanced Japanese Studies* 10: 137–50.

Fehlings, Susanne. 2018. 'Informal Trade and Globalization in the Caucasus and Post-Soviet Eurasia.' In *Mobilities, Boundaries, and Travelling Ideas: Central Asia and the Caucasus*, edited by Manja Stephan-Emmrich and Philipp Schröder, 229–62. Cambridge: Open Book Publishers.

Gabdulhakov, Rashid. 2017. 'The Highly Securitized Insecurities of State Borders in the Fergana Valley.' In *New Voices from Central Asia: Political, Economic, and Societal Challenges and Opportunities, Volume 1*, edited by Marlene Laruelle, 169–174. Washington, DC: George Washington University, Central Asia Program.

Gavrilis, George. 2017. 'Central Asia's Uncertain Radicalization and the Opportunities for the Russia-U.S. Cooperation.' *Pathways to Peace and Security* 1 (52): 251–61.

Grant, Andrew. 2020. 'Crossing Khorgos: Soft Power, Security, and Suspect Loyalties at the Sino-Kazakh Boundary.' *Political Geography* 76. https://doi.org/10.1016/j.polgeo.2019.102070

Heathershaw, John, and David W. Montgomery. 2014. *The Myth of Post-Soviet Muslim Radicalization in the Central Asian Republics*. London: Chatham House, The Royal Institute of International Affairs.

Ilkhamov, Alisher. 2013. 'Labour Migration and the Ritual Economy of the Uzbek Extended Family.' *Zeitschrift für Ethnologie* 138: 259–84.

International Crisis Group. 2015. 'Syria Calling: Radicalisation in Central Asia.' *BRIEFING No. 72*. Accessed October 30, 2019. https://www.crisisgroup.org/europe-central-asia/central-asia/syria-calling-radicalisation-central-asia.

Isabaeva, Eliza. 2011. 'Leaving to Enable Others to Remain: Remittances and new Moral Economies of Migration in Southern Kyrgyzstan.' *Central Asian Survey* 30 (3–4): 541–54.

Ismailbekova, Aksana, and Emil Nasritdinov. 2012. 'Transnational Religious Networks in Central Asia: Structure, Travel, and Culture of Kyrgyz Tablighi Jama'at.' *Transnational Social Review* 2 (2): 177–95.

Jaborov, Safovudin. 2017. 'Youth Radicalization in Tajikistan: Causes, Consequences, and Challenges to Address.' In *Tajikistan: Islam, Migration, and Economic Challenges*, edited by Marlene Laruelle, 72–80. Washington, DC: George Washington University, Central Asia Program.

Jaxylykov, Serik. 2017. *The Northern Region and the Southern People: Migration Policies and Patterns in Kazakhstan*. CAP Papers 184. Washington, DC: Central Asia Fellowship Series.

Jochec, Marek, and Jenny Jenish Kyzy. 2018. 'China's BRI Investments, Risks, and Opportunities in Kazakhstan and Kyrgyzstan.' In *China's Belt and Road Initiative and its Impact in Central Asia*, edited by Marlene Laruelle, 67–76. Washington, DC: George Washington University, Central Asia Program.

Kaminski, Bartłomiej, and Gaël Raballand. 2009. 'Entrepôt for Chinese Consumer Goods in Central Asia: The Puzzle of Re-exports Through Kyrgyz Bazaars.' *Eurasian Geography and Economics* 50 (5): 581–90.

Karrar, Hasan H. 2019. 'Between Border and Bazaar: Central Asia's Informal Economy.' *Journal of Contemporary Asia* 49 (2): 272–93.

Kelly, Liz. 2013. 'A Conducive Context: Trafficking of Persons in Central Asia.' In *Human Trafficking*, edited by Maggie Lee, 85–103. Portland: Willan.

Khalid, Adeeb. 2007. *Islam After Communism: Religion and Politics in Central Asia*. Berkeley: University of California Press.

Kholmatova, Nodira. 2018. 'Changing the Face of Labor Migration? The Feminization of Migration from Tajikistan to Russia.' In *Eurasia on the Move: Interdisciplinary Approaches to a Dynamic Migration Region*, edited by Marlene Laruelle and Caress Schenk, 42–54. Washington, DC: George Washington University, Central Asia Program.

Kikuta, Haruka. 2016. 'Remittances, Rituals and Reconsidering Women's Norms in Mahalla s: Emigrant Labour and its Social Effects in Ferghana Valley.' *Central Asian Survey* 35 (1): 91–104.

Koch, Natalie. 2018. 'Disorder Over the Border: Spinning the Spectre of Instability Through Time and Space in Central Asia.' *Central Asian Survey* 37 (1): 13–30.

Kroeger, Antje, and Kathryn H. Anderson. 2014. 'Remittances and the Human Capital of Children: New Evidence from Kyrgyzstan During Revolution and Financial Crisis, 2005–2009.' *Journal of Comparative Economics* 42 (3): 770–85.

Lemon, Edward. 2015. 'Daesh and Tajikistan: The Regime's (In)Security Policy.' *The RUSI Journal* 160 (5): 68–76.

Lemon, Edward. 2018a. 'Kennan Cable No. 38: Talking Up Terrorism in Central Asia.' *Wilson Center, Kennan Institute*. December 18. Accessed October 30, 2019. https://www.wilsoncenter.org/publication/kennan-cable-no-38-talking-terrorism-central-asia.

Lemon, Edward. 2018b. 'Assessing the Terrorist Threat in and from Central Asia.' *Voices on Central Asia*. October 18. Accessed October 30, 2019. https://voicesoncentralasia.org/assessing-the-terrorist-threat-in-and-from-central-asia/.

Lemon, Edward, and Hélène Thibault. 2018. 'Counter-extremism, Power and Authoritarian Governance in Tajikistan.' *Central Asian Survey* 37 (1): 137–59.

Liebert, Saltanat. 2010. 'The Role of Informal Institutions in U.S. Immigration Policy: The Case of Illegal Labor Migration from Kyrgyzstan.' *Public Administration Review* 70(3): 390–400.

Lymar, Anton. 2016. Kyrgyz Citizens to Have Right to Stay in Kazakhstan 30 Days without Registration. *24.kg*, October 17. Accessed December 2, 2016. http://www.eng.24.kg/news-stall/182432-news24.html.

Lynch, Thomas F., Michael Bouffard, Kelsey King, and Graham Vickowski. 2016. *The Return of Foreign Fighters to Central Asia: Implications for U.S. Counterterrorism Policy*. Institute for National Strategic Studies Strategic Perspectives, No. 21, Washington, DC: National Defense University Press.

Marat, Erica. 2009. *Labor Migration in Central Asia: Implications of the Global Economic Crisis*. Stockholm: Silk Road Studies Program, Institute for Security and Development Policy.

Massot, Sophie. 2013. 'Economic Migrations from Uzbekistan to Moscow, Seoul, and New York: Sacrifice or Rite of Passage?' In *Migration and Social Upheaval as the Face of Globalization in Central Asia*, edited by Marlene Laruelle, 283–302. Boston: Brill.

Mazzucato, Valentina, and Victor Cebotari. 2017. 'Psychological Wellbeing of Ghanaian Children in Transnational Families.' *Population, Space and Place* 23 (3). https://doi.org/10.1002/psp.2004

McGlinchey, Eric. 2005a. 'Autocrats, Islamists, and the Rise of Radicalism in Central Asia.' *Current History* 104 (684): 336–42.

McGlinchey, Eric. 2005b. 'The Making of Militants: The State and Islam in Central Asia.' *Comparative Studies of South Asia, Africa and the Middle East* 25 (3): 554–66.

Megoran, Nick. 2017. *Nationalism in Central Asia: A Biography of the Uzbekistan-Kyrgyzstan Boundary.* Pittsburgh: University of Pittsburg Press.

Montgomery, David W., and John Heathershaw. 2016. 'Islam, Secularism and Danger: A Reconsideration of the Link Between Religiosity, Radicalism and Rebellion in Central Asia.' *Religion, State & Society* 44 (3): 192–218.

Mukhina, Irina. 2009. 'New Losses, new Opportunities:(Soviet) Women in the Shuttle Trade, 1987–1998.' *Journal of Social History* 43 (2): 341–59.

Nazridod, Shukriya, Cláudia Patrícia da Cruz Pereira, and Maria das Dores Horta Guerreiro. 2021. 'Adolescents who Stay, Parents who Migrate: Gender Inequalities, Resilience and Coping Strategies in Tajikistan.' *Journal of Ethnic and Migration Studies* 47 (7): 1613–1630.

Nordstrom, Louise. 2017. 'Why Uzbeks Became a key Fighting Force for IS Group.' *France24.* November 1. Accessed October 30, 2019. https://www.france24.com/en/20171101-islamic-state-group-jihad-why-uzbekistan-central-asia-key-fighting-force-radicalisation.

Omelicheva, Mariya Y. 2011. 'Islam in Kazakhstan: A Survey of Contemporary Trends and Sources of Securitization.' *Central Asian Survey* 30 (2): 243–56.

Omelicheva, Mariya Y. 2016. 'Islam and Power Legitimation: Instrumentalisation of Religion in Central Asian States.' *Contemporary Politics* 22 (2): 144–63.

Ortmann, Stefanie. 2018. 'Beyond Spheres of Influence: The Myth of the State and Russia's Seductive Power in Kyrgyzstan.' *Geopolitics* 23 (2): 404–35.

Owen, Catherine. 2017. '"The Sleeping Dragon Is Gathering Strength": Causes of Sinophobia in Central Asia.' *China Quarterly of International Strategic Studies* 3 (1): 101–19.

Pannier, Bruce. 2017. 'Kazakhstan-Kyrgyzstan Row: A Spat Between Friends Or A Parting Of Ways?' *RFE/RL,* October 25. Accessed November 10, 2019. https://www.rferl.org/a/kyrgyz-kazakh-row-spat-between-friends-parting-ways/28815387.html.

Paraszczuk, Joanna. 2014. 'Central Asian Militants In Syria Pledge Allegiance To IS.' *Radio Free Europe/Radio Liberty,* October 30: online. Accessed October 30, 2019. https://www.rferl.org/a/under-black-flag-central-asia-militants-allegiance/26666098.html.

Peyrouse, Sébastien. 2007. 'Islam in Central Asia: National Specificities and Postsoviet Globalisation.' *Religion, State & Society* 35 (3): 245–60.

Peyrouse, Sebasien. 2012. 'Power Differential and Security Issues in Central Asia: Threat Perceptions of China.' In *Eurasia's Ascent in Energy and Geopolitics: Rivalry or Partnership for China, Russia, and Central Asia?,* edited by Robert Bedeski and Niklas Swanström. London: Routledge, 92–107.

Peyrouse, Sébastien. 2016. 'Discussing China: Sinophilia and Sinophobia in Central Asia.' *Journal of Eurasian Studies* 7 (1): 14–23.

Qosimzoda, Siyovush, Saule Mukhametrakhimova, Inga Sikorskaya, and Timur Toktonaliev. 2014. 'Central Asian Migrants in Russia Find Religion.' *Institute for War & Peace Reporting,* June 13: online. Accessed October 30, 2019. https://iwpr.net/global-voices/central-asian-migrants-russia-find-religion.

Rahmonova-Schwarz, Delia. 2012. *Family and Transnational Mobility in Post-Soviet Central Asia.* Baden-Baden: Nomos.

Rasayanagam, Johan. 2017. 'Counter-extremism, Secularism, and the Category of Religion in the United Kingdom and Uzbekistan.' In *Constructing the Uzbek State: Narratives of Post-Soviet Years,* edited by Marlene Laruelle, 151–68. London: Lexington Books.

Reeves, Madeleine. 2005. 'Locating Danger: Konfliktologiia and the Search for Fixity in the Ferghana Valley Borderlands.' *Central Asian Survey* 24 (1): 67–81.

Reeves, Madeleine. 2011. 'Staying put? Towards a Relational Politics of Mobility at a Time of Migration.' *Central Asian Survey* 30 (3–4): 555–76.

Reeves, Madeleine. 2014. *Border Work: Spatial Lives of the State in Rural Central Asia.* Ithaca: Cornell University Press.

Rocheva, Anna, and Evgeni Varshaver. 2017. 'Gender Dimension of Migration from Central Asia to the Russian Federation.' *Asia-Pacific Population Journal* 32 (2): 87–135.

Rubinov, Igor. 2014. 'Migrant Assemblages: Building Postsocialist Households with Kyrgyz Remittances.' *Anthropological Quarterly* 87 (1): 183–215.

Ruget, Vanessa, and Burul Usmanalieva. 2019. 'Can Smartphones Empower Labour Migrants? The Case of Kyrgyzstani Migrants in Russia.' *Central Asian Survey* 38 (2): 165–180.

Ryazantsev, Sergey, and Oleg Korneev. 2013. *Russia and Kazakhstan in Eurasian Migration System: Development Trends, Socio-Economic Consequences of Migration and Approaches to Regulation.* CARIM-East Research

Report 2013/44. CARIM East: Consortium for Applied Research on International Migration. Accessed June 18, 2014. http://www.carim-east.eu/media/CARIM-East_RR-2013-44.pdf.

Sagynbekova, Lira. 2017. *International Labour Migration in the Context of the Eurasian Economic Union: Issues and Challenges of Kyrgyz Migrants in Russia*. WORKING PAPER No. 39, University of Central Asia.

Sahadeo, Jeff. 2007. 'Druzhba Narodov or Second-class Citizenship? Soviet Asian Migrants in a Post-colonial World.' *Central Asian Survey* 26 (4): 559–79.

Sahadeo, Jeff. 2019. *Voices from the Soviet Edge: Southern Migrants in Leningrad and Moscow*. Ithaca: Cornell University Press.

Sanderson, Thomas M. 2018. 'From the Ferghana Valley to Syria and Beyond: A Brief History of Central Asian Foreign Fighters.' *Center for Strategic & International Studies*. January 5. Accessed October 30, 2019. https://www.csis.org/analysis/ferghana-valley-syria-and-beyond-brief-history-central-asian-foreign-fighters.

Schenk, Caress. 2017. 'Labour Migration in the Eurasian Economic Union.' In *Migration and the Ukraine Crisis: A Two Country Perspective*, edited by Abnieszka Pikulicka-Wilczewska and Greta Uehling, 164–77. Bristol: E-International Relations.

Schenk, Caress. 2018. *Why Control Immigration: Strategic Uses of Migration Management in Russia*. Toronto: University of Toronto Press.

Schmidt, Matthias, and Lira Sagynbekova. 2008. 'Migration Past and Present: Changing Patterns in Kyrgyzstan.' *Central Asian Survey* 27 (2): 111–27.

Schröder, Philipp, and Manja Stephan-Emmrich. 2016. 'The Institutionalization of Mobility: Well-being and Social Hierarchies in Central Asian Translocal Livelihoods.' *Mobilities* 11 (3): 420–43.

Sgibnev, Wladimir, and Andrey Vozyanov. 2016. 'Assemblages of Mobility: The Marshrutkas of Central Asia.' *Central Asian Survey* 35 (2): 276–91.

Shamatov, Duishon, and Sarfaroz Niyozov. 2006. 'Trading or Teaching: Dilemmas of Everyday Life Economy in Central Asia.' *Inner Asia* 8 (2): 229–62.

Sharifzoda, Khamza. 2019. *The Eurasian Economic Union's Pension Problem*. June 20. Accessed October 21, 2019. https://thediplomat.com/2019/06/the-eurasian-economic-unions-pension-problem/.

Sodatsayrova, Nazira. 2018. 'Domestic and International Mobility: Being Present and Living in the Present Moment Through Educational Mobility.' In *Eurasia on the Move: Interdisciplinary Approaches to a Dynamic Migration Region*, edited by Marlene Laruelle and Caress Schenk, 55–68. Washington, DC: George Washington University, Central Asia Program.

Soliyev, Nodirbek. 2013. 'Caucasian and Central Asian Fighters in Syria: A Security Concern for the SCO.' *Counter Terrorist Trends and Analyses* 5 (11): 21–3.

Sonmez, Goktug. 2017. 'Violent Extremism Among Central Asians: The Istanbul, St. Petersburg, Stockholm, and New York City Attacks.' *CTC Sentinal* 10 (11). December. Accessed October 30, 2019. https://ctc.usma.edu/violent-extremism-among-central-asians-the-istanbul-st-petersburg-stockholm-and-new-york-city-attacks/.

Stephan-Emmrich, Manja. 2018. 'iPhones, Emotions, Mediations: Tracing Translocality in the Pious Endeavours of Tajik Migrants in the United Arab Emirates.' In *Mobilities, Boundaries, and Travelling Ideas: Rethinking Translocality Beyond Central Asia and the Caucasus*, edited by Manja Stephan-Emmrich and Philipp Schröder, 291–318. Cambridge: Lightning Source for Open Book Publishers.

Tazmini, Ghoncheh. 2001. 'The Islamic Revival in Central Asia: A Potent Force or a Misconception?' *Central Asian Survey* 20 (1): 63–83.

Thibault, Hélène. 2018a. *Transforming Tajikistan: State-building and Islam in Post-Soviet Central Asia*. London: IB Tauris.

Thibault, Hélène. 2018b. 'Labour Migration, sex, and Polygyny: Negotiating Patriarchy in Tajikistan.' *Ethnic and Racial Studies* 41 (15): 2809–26.

Thibault, Hélène. 2019. 'Political Islam in Central Asia.' In *Handbook of Political Islam*, edited by Shahram Akbarzadeh. London: Routledge.

Thieme, Susan. 2008. 'Sustaining Livelihoods in Multilocal Settings: Possible Theoretical Linkages Between Transnational Migration and Livelihood Studies.' *Mobilities* 3 (1): 51–71.

Thieme, Susan. 2011. 'Sustaining a Multi-local Life: Possible Theoretical Foundations for Livelihood and Transnational Migration Studies.' In *Wiesmann, Urs; Hurni, Hans*, edited by Experiences, and Perspectives. Research for Sustainable Development: Foundations, 331–41. Bern: Universität Bern.

Thieme, Susan. 2014. 'Coming Home? Patterns and Characteristics of Return Migration in Kyrgyzstan.' *International Migration* 52 (5): 127–43.

Tucker, Noah. 2015. *Central Asian Involvement in the Conflict in Syria and Iraq: Drivers and Responses*. Arlington, VA: USAID.

Tucker, Noah. 2019. *Terrorism Without a God: Reconsidering Radicalization and Counter-Radicalization Models in Central Asia*. Central Asia Program Paper #225, Washington, DC: Central Asia Program, George Washington University.

Turaeva, Rano. 2014. 'Mobile Entrepreneurs in Post-Soviet Central Asia.' *Communist and Post-Communist Studies* 47 (1): 105–14.

Turaeva, Rano. 2015. *Migration and Identity in Central Asia: The Uzbek Experience*. New York: Routledge.

Turaeva, Rano. 2019. 'Imagined Mosque Communities in Russia: Central Asian Migrants in Moscow.' *Asian Ethnicity* 20 (2): 131–47.

Tynaliev, Urmat M., and Gary N. McLean. 2011. 'Labour Migration and National Human Resource Development in the Context of Post-Soviet Kyrgyzstan.' *Human Resource Development International* 14 (2): 199–215.

Urinboyev, Rustam. 2017a. 'Establishing an "Uzbek Mahalla" via Smartphones and Social Media: Everyday Transnational Lives of Uzbek Labor Migrants in Russia.' In *Constructing the Uzbek State*, edited by Marlene Laruelle, 119–50. Lexington: Lexington Books.

Urinboyev, Rustamjon. 2017b. 'Migration and Transnational Informality in Post-Soviet Societies: Ethnographic Study of po Rukam ('handshake') Experiences of Uzbek Migrant Workers in Moscow.' In *Migrant Workers in Russia: Global Challenges of the Shadow Economy in Societal Transformation*, edited by Anna-Liisa Heusala and Kaarina Aitamurto, 70–93. Abingdon: Routledge.

Urinboyev, Rustamjon. 2018. 'Migration, Transnationalism, and Social Change in Central Asia: Everyday Transnational Lives of Uzbek Migrants in Russia.' In *Eurasia on the Move: Interdisciplinary Approaches to a Dynamic Migration Region*, edited by Marlene Laruelle and Caress Schenk. Washington, DC: George Washington University, Central Asia Program.

Urinboyev, Rustamjon, and Abel Polese. 2016. 'Informality Currencies: A Tale of Misha, his Brigada and Informal Practices Among Uzbek Labour Migrants in Russia.' *Journal of Contemporary Central and Eastern Europe* 24 (3): 191–206.

US House of Representatives. 2015. *Wanted: Foreign Fighters – The Escalating Threat of ISIL in Central Asia*. Hearing: Commission on Security and Cooperation in Europe, Washington, DC: U.S. Government publishing office.

Virkkunen, Joni. 2017. 'Economic Aspects of Migration from Central Asia in Russia.' *Вестник Российского университета дружбы народов. Серия: Экономика* 25 (1).

Werner, Cynthia, and Holly Barcus. 2015. 'The Unequal Burdens of Repatriation: A Gendered View of the Transnational Migration of Mongolia's Kazakh Population.' *American Anthropologist* 117 (2): 257–71.

Woodard, Lauren. 2019. 'The Politics of Return: Migration, Race, and Belonging in the Russian Far East.' *Doctoral Dissertations*. Amhurst, MA, May. Accessed November 7, 2019. https://scholarworks.umass.edu/dissertations_2/1630.

Wu, Qiaobing, and Victor Cebotari. 2018. 'Experiences of Migration, Parent–child Interaction, and the Life Satisfaction of Children in Ghana and China.' *Population, Space and Place* 24 (7): 1–11. https://doi.org/10.1002/psp.2160

Zotova, Natalia, and Jeffrey H. Cohen. 2016. 'Remittances and Their Social Meaning in Tajikistan.' *Remittances Review* 1 (1): 5–16.

PART V
Political Economy

19
ECONOMIC REFORM AND DEVELOPMENT IN CENTRAL ASIA

Richard Pomfret

This chapter analyses the economic record of the five Central Asian countries since they became independent in 1991. Three periods are identified. The 1990s were dominated by nation-building and the transition from central planning to market-based economies; during this decade the five countries created distinctive varieties of market-based economies. From the turn of the century until 2014 the global resource boom brought large windfall gains to oil and gas exporters, as well as some mineral producers, and the poorer countries received substantial remittances from migrant workers in energy-rich countries, notably Russia; during this period economic performance was generally good and economic management improved, but reform was negligible. Finally, the years since 2014 have seen the end of the resource boom and, to varying degrees, efforts to diversify the five countries' economies away from resource or remittance dependence and to increase economic efficiency. The most recent period has also seen improved intra-regional relations and cooperation. The final sections assess the prospects for renewed economic reforms; all five countries now have a younger generation of post-Soviet presidents who have spent most of their adult lives in market-based economies, although the commitment to change varies considerably.[1]

The Central Asian republics were among the poorest and most culturally distinct in the Union of Soviet Socialist Republics (USSR), although for their income levels they had high social indicators (Table 19.1). In the final Soviet census in 1989, the Kyrgyz, Tajik, Turkmen and Uzbek republics had, with Azerbaijan, the lowest average incomes and the highest proportion of under-provisioned households. Nevertheless, there was little pressure to leave the USSR in the 1980s and early 1990s, in contrast to the Baltic, Caucasus and Ukrainian republics. The disintegration of the USSR in the second half of 1991 was unanticipated and not particularly welcome in Central Asia, although the First Secretaries appointed by Mikhail Gorbachev quickly reacted by transforming themselves into national presidents.

DOI: 10.4324/9780429057977-19

Table 19.1 Initial Conditions: Republics of the USSR 1989/1990

	Population (million) mid-1990	Per capita GNP[a] (1990)	Gini coefficient (1989)	Poverty (% of population)[b] (1989)	Terms of trade	Life expectancy (years)	Adult Literacy (percentage)
USSR	289.3	2870	0.289	11.1			
Kazakh	16.8	2600	0.289	15.5	+19	69	98
Kyrgyz	4.4	1570	0.287	32.9	+1	66	97
Tajik	5.3	1130	0.308	51.2	−7	69	97
Turkmen	3.7	1690	0.307	35.0	+50	66	98
Uzbek	20.5	1340	0.304	43.6	−3	69	99
Armenia	3.3	2380	0.259	14.3	−24	72	99
Azerbaijan	7.2	1640	0.328	33.6	−7	71	96
Georgia	5.5	2120	0.292	14.3	−21	73	95
Belarus	10.3	3110	0.238	3.3	−20	71	98
Moldova	4.4	2390	0.258	11.8	−38	69	99
Russia	148.3	3430	0.278	5.0	+79	69	99
Ukraine	51.9	2500	0.235	6.0	−18	70	99
Estonia	1.6	4170	0.299	1.9	−32	70	99
Latvia	2.7	3590	0.274	2.4	−24	69	99
Lithuania	3.7	3110	0.278	2.3	−31	71	98

Sources: Pomfret (2006, 4) – columns 1–2, World Bank; columns 3–4, Atkinson and Micklewright (1992, Table U13) – based on Goskomstat household survey data; column 5, Tarr (1994); columns 6–7 UNDP *Human Development Report 1992*.

Notes. (a) GNP per capita in US dollars computed by the World Bank's synthetic *Atlas* method; (b) poverty = individuals in households with gross per capita monthly income less than 75 rubles; (c) impact on terms of trade of moving to world prices, calculated at 105-sector level of aggregation using 1990 weights.

Transition from central planning

With the collapse of central control and rapid price liberalisation in Russia in January 1992, the Central Asian republics had no option other than to replace the centrally planned economy with some form of market-based economy. In Tajikistan the planned economy collapsed into an unregulated economy during civil war. The other four countries enjoyed a peaceful transition to market-based economies.[2] They created a striking variety of economic systems from the most regulated post-Soviet economy in Turkmenistan to the most liberal reforms in the Kyrgyz Republic.

The newly independent countries faced three major economic shocks in 1992. Central planning had been weakening in the late Soviet era, but there had been no experiments with market mechanisms in Central Asia. When the Union collapsed suddenly and Russia liberalised prices, the countries were forced into transition to market-based economies with few officials experienced in foreign trade, macroeconomic policy or competition policy and with little general understanding of how markets worked. The second shock was the rapid descent into hyperinflation as countries had neither adequate domestic tax systems nor access to capital markets in order to pay for public expenditures; the temptation to monetise public deficits was exacerbated by the continued use of the rouble as a common currency through 1992 and much of 1993.[3] The early 1990s were characterised by hyperinflation and the whole decade by a difficult transition from central planning to market-based economies amidst macroeconomic instability. Thirdly, Central Asian republics had been highly integrated into Soviet supply chains, often for processing their raw materials, and these chains quickly broke down amidst monetary confusion and the introduction of transport costs.[4]

The five countries adopted diverse transition strategies. All five countries during the 1990s made the fastest progress on price liberalisation and small-scale privatisation and their economies were least reformed with respect to large-scale privatisation and enterprise restructuring, competition policy to constrain abuse of monopoly power and creating an efficient financial sector (Table 19.2). However, by the EBRD Transition Indicators there was by 1999 a clear ranking from the most reformed to the least reformed country. On almost every indicator, the Kyrgyz Republic and Kazakhstan had reformed more extensively than Uzbekistan or Turkmenistan; the last two, together with Belarus, were consistently viewed as the most reluctant reformers among former Soviet republics, while Kyrgyz Republic was the poster boy for the 'Washington Consensus' rapid reforms advocated by the IMF and World Bank.

In Kyrgyzstan, rapid reforms in the early 1990s were accompanied by a deep transitional recession as unprofitable activities closed down. In May 1993 Kyrgyzstan became the first Central Asian country to adopt a national currency and in 1996 was the first to bring annual inflation below 50 per cent. Trade was liberalised and Kyrgyzstan became the first former Soviet republic to join the World Trade Organization. Low inflation is a prerequisite for an effective market economy as relative price signals are hard to distinguish among rapid general price increases, but expectations of economic prosperity after the 'shock therapy' were not borne out. By the late 1990s the economy was heavily dependent on a single project (the Kumtor goldmine). To maintain public expenditures, the government ran up external debts that exceeded 100 per cent of GDP by the turn of the century, leading to a debt crisis. The principal lesson was that rapid reform alone was insufficient without the institutional structure to support an efficient market economy (e.g. rule of law and ending impunity for corrupt practices).

Table 19.2 EBRD Transition Indicators, 1999 and 2009

		Large-scale privatization	Small-scale privatization	Enterprise restructuring	Price liberalization	Trade & forex system	Competition Policy	Banking & interest rates	Securities markets & NBFIs	Overall Infrastructure reform
Kazakhstan	1999	3	4	2	4	3+	2	2+	2	2
	2009	3	4	2	4	4–	2	3–	3–	3–
Kyrgyz Republic	1999	3	4	2	4+	4+	2	2	2	1+
	2009	4–	4	2	4+	4+	2	2+	2	2–
Tajikistan	1999	2+	3	2–	4–	3–	2	1	1	1
	2008	2+	4	2–	4–	3+	2–	2+	1	1+
Turkmenistan	1999	2–	2	2–	3–	1	1	1	1	1
	2009	1	2+	1	3–	2	1	1	1	1
Uzbekistan	1999	3–	3	2	3–	1	2	2–	2	1+
	2009	3–	3+	2–	3–	2	2–	2–	2	2–

Source: European Bank for Reconstruction and Development Transition Report 2000 and 2010.
Notes. 1 indicates no change from the centrally planned economy and 4+ indicates the standards of an advanced market economy.

Kazakhstan had the most promising initial conditions among the Central Asian countries, with an expectation that it would benefit from the opportunity to sell its minerals at world prices and from relatively high human capital endowment, although emigration of over a million people with German, Russian or other Slavic heritage eroded the second advantage. Kazakhstan, like Russia, started along the path of rapid reform but became mired in rent-seeking as valuable enterprises were privatised and foreign investors sought oil contracts.[5] President Nazarbayev, his family (especially his two older daughters and their husbands) and a handful of oligarchs became extremely wealthy. The Kazakh economy remained closely tied to that of Russia and, just after recovery began in 1997–1998, Kazakhstan suffered contagion effects from the 1998 Russian financial crisis. Both Kyrgyzstan and Kazakhstan ended the 1990s with lower real output than at the beginning of the decade (Table 19.3).[6]

At the other extreme, Turkmenistan's president introduced minimal economic reform. The Turkmen economy was dominated by cotton and natural gas, the revenues from both of which could be easily controlled by the president. Initially, President Niyazov adopted populist policies, providing free electricity, gas and water to the population. As those services deteriorated, he ruled increasingly by repression.[7] The revenues from cotton and gas went into off-budget accounts and funded expenditures on a presidential palace and many statues of the president, who adopted the title 'Turkmenbashi' (Father of the Turkmen) and established an extreme personality cult (Garcia 2006). The strategy led to a milder transitional recession over 1991–1995 than in Kazakhstan or the Kyrgyz Republic, but dependence on gas led to a sharp decline in the GDP in 1997 when exports to Ukraine and Azerbaijan were cut due to conflicts over payment; dependence on a pipeline through Russia left Turkmenistan with no alternative markets.

Uzbekistan was also a gradual reformer but more proactive in introducing market mechanisms in the mid-1990s. Briefly in 1996 Uzbekistan appeared as more reformist than Kazakhstan in the EBRD Transition Indicators. However, in October 1996, after falling world cotton prices cut export earnings, the government introduced draconian foreign-exchange controls. Once taken, that decision proved difficult to reverse (because some people benefited from their favoured access to foreign currency) and disastrous for the economy, because it distorted incentives for traders and foreign investors and against non-favoured producers. The government resisted reform of its major export, cotton, which continued to be heavily controlled and a source of international opprobrium due to use of child labour, and tightened controls over small-scale enterprises and bazaars.

Tajikistan was a special case insofar as the collapse of the central government led to rapid transition to a market economy but without the public institutions required to support an efficient economy. Although the civil war finished in 1997, until 2001 the government exerted limited control over large parts of the country

The types of market-based economies had been established by 1999, when the transition from central planning to market-based economies was essentially over. Although areas ripe for reform could be identified in all five countries' economies, the EBRD Indicators changed little after the turn of the century (Table 19.2).

All data and casual observation point to a steep transitional recession with 1989 living standards only achieved after the turn of century (Table 19.3). Falling GDP per capita plus increasing inequality led to massive increases in poverty in the two poorest countries, the Kyrgyz Republic and Tajikistan (Anderson and Pomfret 2003). Higher initial incomes and valuable oil and gas exports helped to alleviate the situation in Kazakhstan and Turkmenistan, although evidence for the latter is opaque. Uzbekistan, by contrast, had the shallowest transitional recession of any former Soviet republic.

Table 19.3 Growth in Real GDP, 1989–1999 (per cent)

	1989	1990	1991	1992	1993	1994	1995	1996	1997	1998	1999	1999; 1989 =100
Kazakhstan	0	0	-13	-3	-9	-13	-8	1	2	-2	2	**63**
Kyrgyz Republic	8	3	-5	-19	-16	-20	-5	7	10	2	4	**63**
Tajikistan	-3	-2	-7	-29	-11	-19	-13	-4	2	5	4	**44**
Turkmenistan	-7	2	-5	-5	-10	-17	-7	-7	-11	5	16	**64**
Uzbekistan	4	2	-1	-11	-2	-4	-1	2	3	4	4	**94**

Source: European Bank for Reconstruction and Development *Transition Report Update*, 15 April 2001.

The resource boom

Between 1999 and 2014, the Central Asian countries enjoyed continuous economic growth (Table 19.4).[8] In part, this was because the impacts of transition were asynchronous, with uncompetitive state enterprises going out of business during the 1990s and new activities being slower to start. Recovery from a deep transitional trough inevitably involved faster economic growth, and the deepest trough, in war-torn Tajikistan, gave the greatest scope for high percentage-change recovery in output after 2000. Differences in economic performance after 2000 were surely influenced by the type of market economy that each country had created in the 1990s, but that effect was outweighed by other determinants of growth, especially the resource boom. Oil and gas exporters Kazakhstan and Turkmenistan enjoyed huge windfall gains, while resource-poor Kyrgyz Republic and Tajikistan became labour exporters dependent on remittances from Russia.[9] Uzbekistan, more or less self-sufficient in gas and with valuable minerals such as gold and copper, lay somewhere in between. These outcomes had little to do with the choice of transition strategies, and economic growth reduced pressures for further economic reform.

The resource boom favoured several important Central Asian exports, including gold, copper and other minerals, but oil and gas saw the most dramatic boom. Oil prices soared from under $20 a barrel in 1999 to over $130 in 2008; after a sharp but brief dip in 2008, oil prices recovered to over $100 until 2014, when a more sustained decline to lower prices signalled the end of the boom. Gold prices rose from $260 per ounce in April 2001 to a peak of $1,770 in September 2011; after a trough of $1,100 in January 2016, the gold price returned to over $1,700 in April 2020. The price of copper (grade A cathode) was more volatile, rising from under $1,500 per metric ton in October 2002 to $8,680 in April 2008, before plummeting to $3,000 in December 2008 and recovering to a peak of $9,870 in February 2011; it then slid to $5,730 in February 2015. Other metals exported from Central Asia, such as zinc, lead, iron ore and uranium, experienced price booms between 2000 and 2014, albeit with specific time patterns. Meanwhile, the other major Central Asian export commodity, cotton, experienced more stable world prices; the Cotlook A price index was $1.41 per kilogram in January 2001 and $1.50 in March 2015, with much milder cycles than for the minerals and at best a slight upward trend.

For Kazakhstan the boom created a perfect storm. The Tengiz oilfield was coming into full production, so that oil exports soared in quantity just as their price was increasing. Discovery in 2000 of the Kashagan offshore oilfield, the largest new discovery in the world for several decades, was followed by an investment boom. Construction of new pipelines reduced previous dependence on the Russian oil pipeline monopoly and as world prices rose it became feasible to build longer, more expensive pipelines to the Mediterranean in 2003 and to China, increasing the choice of routes and reducing transport costs.

By size of GDP, Kazakhstan pulled ahead of its southern neighbours. President Nazarbayev used the windfall to pursue the *Kazakhstan 2030 Strategy* for long-term development. Rising incomes and improved public sector management eroded the petty corruption that had been prevalent in the 1990s; as police, teachers, health workers and others received higher wages that were promptly paid, they were less inclined to seek unofficial extra payments, especially as monitoring improved. The National Fund of the Republic of Kazakhstan (NFRK), created in 2000 to manage oil revenues, ensured that part of the windfall would be saved for future generations, and proved a useful source of emergency funding when Kazakhstan experienced a banking crisis in 2007. Attempts to diversify the economy away from resource-dependence had only limited success. Agriculture was targeted for particularly generous support, but policy success was constrained by physical obstacles to creating efficient supply chains and by corruption in the Ministry of Agriculture and in regional offices implementing agricultural support programmes.[10]

Table 19.4 Growth in Real GDP, 1999–2014 (per cent)

	1999	2000	2001	2002	2003	2004	2005	2006	2007
Kazakhstan	2.7	9.8	13.5	9.8	9.3	9.6	9.7	10.7	8.9
Kyrgyz Rep	3.7	5.4	5.3	0.0	7.0	7.0	-0.2	3.1	8.5
Tajikistan	3.7	8.3	9.6	10.8	10.9	10.4	6.6	7.0	7.8
Turkmenistan	16.5	5.5	4.3	0.3	3.3	5.0	13.0	11.0	11.1
Uzbekistan	4.3	3.8	4.2	4.0	4.2	7.4	7.0	7.5	9.5

	2008	2009	2010	2011	2012	2013	2014		
Kazakhstan	3.3	1.2	7.3	7.4	4.8	6	4.2		
Kyrgyz Rep	8.4	2.9	-0.5	6.0	-0.2	10.9	4.0		
Tajikistan	7.9	3.9	6.5	7.4	7.5	7.4	6.7		
Turkmenistan	14.7	6.1	9.2	14.7	11.1	10.2	10.3		
Uzbekistan	9.0	8.1	7.6	7.8	7.4	7.6	7.2		

Source: World Bank *World Development Indicators* (accessed 14 April 2020).

President Nazarbayev sought to increase the state's dominant position by resource nationalism, using the Samruk-Kasyna holding company to consolidate and manage key enterprises, including the state energy company Kazmunaigas, and ensuring that key institutions were managed by people close to the president (Kennedy and Nurmakov 2010; Kalyuzhnova and Nygaard 2011). In stark contrast to the limited conspicuous consumption by Soviet leaders before 1992, the presence of people who had become super-rich in the 1990s was evident. Two groups had benefited especially from the privatisation of mining companies. Vladimir Ni, who had shared offices with Nazarbayev in the Soviet era, was the original beneficiary of privatisation of the mining conglomerate Kazakhmys (Kazakh Copper) and his protégé Vladimir Kim became the chairman of Kazakhmys (Global Witness, 2010). Vladimir Kim has consistently headed the Forbes rich list for Kazakhstan (Table 5.1).[11] The 'Trio' – Alijan Ibragimov, Patokh Chodiev and Alexander Mashkevich – benefited from privatisation of chromium, alumina and gas in the 1990s, and controlled the mining company Eurasian National Resources Corporation (ENRC) that was listed on the London Stock Exchange in 2007 but delisted and privatised as the Eurasian Resources Group in 2013. Details of how wealth was acquired and used leaked out from court cases in Belgium, the Netherlands, Switzerland, the UK and the United States, although few cases ended with serious punishment (Olcott, 2002).

Although any assessment based on household surveys would have been biased by non-inclusion of the very rich, Anderson and Pomfret (2003) show that inequality in Central Asia increased during the transition and that those who did best during the 1990s lived in the capital cities were better educated and had fewer children. Household incomes in Kazakhstan's oil-producing regions did not do well even after the oil boom had started; Najman et al. (2008, 125–6) conclude their analysis of household survey data with, 'The oil boom has not resulted in higher average living standards in the oil-producing regions, but has been associated with higher living standards in the metropolitan centres where the country's elite lives.' In 2011 poor conditions for oilfield workers generated serious industrial unrest when demonstrations by oil workers in Zhanaozen were violently repressed with some 17 deaths and over a hundred injured (Kourmanova in Laruelle 2017: 15–20).

President Nazarbayev strengthened his grip on power between 2001 and 2007. In 2001, he broke the challenge of Democratic Choice of Kazakhstan (QDT).[12] In 2007, he clamped down on opposition parties, including one headed by his daughter Dariga (Isaacs, forthcoming). To forestall rivals with serious political experience, President Nazarbayev rotated his prime ministers, with ten men holding the position during his 27 years as national president.

As a natural gas exporter Turkmenistan also benefited from the resource boom, but the impact was delayed by dependence on Russian pipelines. After 1999, Turkmenistan no longer had problems receiving payment from customers, but the opaque arrangements often involved barter and prices far below what Russia was receiving for its gas exports to Europe. Eventually, in 2006 President Niyazov, who rarely travelled, went to Beijing to negotiate an agreement with China and a gas pipeline built between 2006 and 2009 ended dependence on Russia.

President Niyazov died in December 2006 and was succeeded by Gurbanguly Berdimuhamedow, who soon reversed three of his predecessor's most egregious policy errors: education reforms – reduction in the number of years of compulsory schooling needed for a university degree, non-recognition of foreign qualifications and emphasis on *rukhnama* (the thoughts of Turkmenbashi) – were discarded, cuts in pensions were reversed and reform of the exchange-rate system was initiated. However, it soon became clear that these and some initial cosmetic changes were turning back the clock to around 2000 rather than being the start of a serious reform programme. Turkmenistan's economic system would continue as before. With the completion of the gas pipeline to China, Turkmenistan no longer faced a single buyer for its natural gas and received substantially higher gas prices for the remainder of the energy boom. Berdimuhamedow established his own personality cult, taking the title 'Arkadag' (patron or protector of the nation), erecting gold statues and suppressing any opposition.

The main energy resource of the Kyrgyz Republic and Tajikistan, hydroelectricity, was difficult to develop due to conflicts with downstream countries dependent on water for irrigation.[13] For these countries, the main impact of the resource boom was through demand for manual labour in Russia. In 2013, Tajikistan received over $4 billion in remittances and the remittances to GDP ratio of over 40 per cent was the highest in the world; the Kyrgyz Republic had the world's third-highest remittances to GDP ratio. Even more migrant workers went from Uzbekistan, although as a proportion of the population, and remittances as a share of GDP, the percentages were lower than for the smaller Kyrgyz and Tajik economies.

The Kyrgyz Republic remained the most open economy and has since 2010 the least autocratic presidency. Living standards improved in the twenty-first century but economic performance was disappointing. The large markets outside Bishkek and Osh flourished (Kaminski and Mitra 2012) and agriculture responded to market-oriented reforms (Mogilevskii et al. 2015), but the Kumtor goldmine remained the sole dominant enterprise in mining and manufacturing. Despite the curtailing of presidential power since 2010, corruption remains a major problem and parliamentary conflicts centre on rent-seeking.

Tajikistan's good growth performance (Table 19.4) reflected the re-establishment of political and economic stability under President Rahmon. The economy remains based on indirect export of water through irrigated agriculture (primarily cotton) and hydro power for the aluminium smelter that dominates the industrial sector and direct and indirect export of labour via migrant workers and labour-intensive agriculture. The presidential family maintains control over the rents from aluminium and cotton exports. The migrant workers going to Russia were overwhelmingly males from rural areas, and a consequence has been the feminisation of Tajik agriculture; the proportion of women in the agricultural labour force increased from 54 per cent in 1999 to over 75 per cent in 2015 (Mukhamedova and Wegerich 2018).

Uzbekistan's twenty-first-century economic growth was clearly driven by the commodity boom. Uzbekistan became self-sufficient in gas and benefited from increased minerals prices. The intended diversification out of agriculture, supported by import-substituting industrial projects, did not promote much manufacturing growth. Between 2000 and 2010, as agriculture declined in importance, the rapid growth was in services, construction and mining, and not in manufacturing; agriculture's share of value-added fell from 34.4 per cent in 2000 to 19.5 per cent in 2010 and the share of manufacturing declined from 9.4 per cent in 2000 and 9.0 per cent in 2010, while the share of public and private services increased from 42.5 per cent to 45.1 per cent and that of mining, utilities and construction increased from 13.7 per cent to 26.4 per cent (Pomfret, 2019a, Table 5.1).

Uzbekistan succeeded in becoming energy-self-sufficient and an exporter of natural gas. The other major growth drivers were copper and gold exports, responding to soaring world prices. These were capital-intensive activities that failed to produce jobs for the growing population. The changing composition of exports was associated with shifts in the direction of trade as gas, cars and fruit and vegetables were primarily sold in Russia, whose share of Uzbekistan's exports increased from 17 per cent in 2000 to 33 per cent in 2010 (displacing the EU as Uzbekistan's major export market), although this would leave Uzbekistan exposed to changes in Russian market access, especially after the establishment of the Eurasian Economic Union in 2015.[14] After 2009, access to the Turkmenistan–China gas pipeline facilitated substantial gas exports to China.

The absence of diversification was connected to Uzbekistan's multiple exchange-rate regime, that favoured producing for the home market or, due to increased uncertainty about future returns, discouraged investment and enterprise altogether. Despite its illegality, dollarisation increased, reducing the effectiveness of monetary policy. Administrative restrictions on the amounts of cash that could be withdrawn from bank accounts and limits on foreign-exchange transactions explained Uzbekistan's low level of financial sector development and the limited access to credit in the country.

The desire for control stunted the growth of the initially flourishing retail sector as regulations became more onerous. Fearing the bazaars as hotbeds of potential discontent, the government imposed heavy crackdowns in the late 1990s and early 2000s, driving small-scale trading 'offshore,' largely to the Kyrgyz Republic's huge bazaars outside Bishkek (Dordoi) and Osh (Karasuu). Uzbek customers at these bazaars organised onward transport of goods back to Uzbekistan, including paying off customs officers and others.

Control of Uzbekistan's borders for security reasons as well as to support import-competing industries added to the obstacles facing would-be producers of new exports. Quality inputs were difficult to source from abroad and, if exports were produced, the exchange controls limited the legal revenue accruing to the exporter. Controls also damaged Uzbekistan's opportunities for hosting transit trade. In 1991 Tashkent was the transport hub of Central Asia whether by air, rail or road. A mix of regulations on transit (e.g. requirements for trucks to form convoys, and lengthy border delays), customs regulations and charges, and poor relations with neighbours (especially Turkmenistan and Tajikistan) exacerbated economic isolation.

Uzbekistan's social policies that had been a source of pride in the 1990s – or at least less dismay than in other post-Soviet states – were deteriorating by the 2010s. Education and health services remained universal but were increasingly perceived as low prestige employment riddled with corruption, as school grades and access to medical services were openly traded; higher education did particularly badly as its share of the education budget fell.[15] Widespread use of patronage to fill public offices was associated with the declining quality of public officials, and public services were being maintained (or not maintained) by continuous increases in the number of officials.[16]

The relative equality of the 1990s was replaced by the recognition that members of the elite were amassing large fortunes. The high-level corruption was especially associated with access to new economic sectors, such as the media, finance and mobile phones. Its face was the president's daughter Gulnara Karimova, described by the US ambassador in a *Wikileaks* cable as 'the most hated person in Uzbekistan.'[17] For the rest of the population, living standards surely improved, but the debate over whether performance could have been better is complicated by a lack of an agreed upon benchmark. Popov (2013) and Cornia (2014) laud the Uzbek model, highlighting the good performance in terms of economic growth while following 'heterodox' policies; critics question the accuracy of Uzbekistan's GDP data and sustainability of the Karimov model (Ruziev, Ghosh and Dow 2007; Olcott 2007) and Bogolov (2016) argues that the large number of Uzbeks migrating to Russia for work showed the miracle to be a mirage.

The positive economic performance in Central Asia after 2000 was not matched by political change. The presidents of Kazakhstan, Tajikistan and Uzbekistan tightened their grip, as did Turkmenistan's new president. The Kyrgyz president tried to do the same, but President Akayev was overthrown by a popular uprising in 2005 and his successor shared the same fate in 2010. Central Asia's first, and so far only, female president, Roza Otunbayeva, then guided the Kyrgyz Republic to a more balanced relationship between parliament and president before stepping down.

Foreign interest in Central Asia became more pronounced with the energy boom and following the US invasion of Afghanistan in 2001. The United States used Central Asia as a transit route for supplies shipped through Baltic ports, especially after the Pakistan route became less reliable, and used airbases first in Uzbekistan and then in the Kyrgyz Republic to transport troops to and from Afghanistan.[18] President Putin was more interested in Russia's Near Abroad than Yeltsin had been, and he gradually started to differentiate between friends and enemies, culminating in the creation of the Eurasian Economic Union (EAEU) between Russia, Belarus and Kazakhstan, which the Kyrgyz Republic joined in 2015. China's economic presence became stronger with the bazaars full of Chinese manufactures, with major infrastructure projects like the pipeline from Turkmenistan and many smaller projects such as road-building in Tajikistan and the Kyrgyz Republic, and with increasing investments in natural resource projects. Despite popular worries about being swamped by China, the Central Asian governments were generally successful in maintaining a balance between external powers, often claiming to be successfully pursuing multi-vector diplomacy.

The governments were less successful in promoting intra-regional cooperation. Attempts at regional cooperation and integration floundered and by 2005 the main regional bodies were all based outside Central Asia.[19] The 2006–2009 Turkmenistan-Uzbekistan-Kazakhstan-China gas pipeline was a rare example of regional cooperation and was a win-win outcome as Turkmenistan exported gas and the other two countries received transit fees (and the option to export gas through the pipeline in future). The fact that the five countries had competing rather than complementary economies partially explained the non-cooperation, but the prevalence of autocratic rulers also mattered as personal relations, especially between the presidents of Uzbekistan and Tajikistan and of Uzbekistan and Turkmenistan, were often dire.

Overall, the resource boom underpinned a period of rising incomes. Apart from in the Kyrgyz Republic, the autocratic leaders were able to stay in power while making little change to their economic or political strategies. Increased external interest in the region turned out to be non-threatening, largely because Central Asia was far from central to the major powers' foreign policies and Central Asian leaders were not desperate for any power's favours.

Responding to the end of the boom

The end of the oil boom in 2014 was a catalyst for a change in economic policy thinking in Central Asia. The break was highlighted by the sudden and large depreciation of the Russian rouble which overnight reduced the value of remittances to the Kyrgyz Republic, Tajikistan and Uzbekistan. Kazakhstan saw its oil revenues fall and Turkmenistan saw orders for its natural gas cut by Russia and by Iran. Although the five countries recorded continuing growth in real output (Table 19.5), GDP and GDP per capita in US dollars fell sharply in all but the Kyrgyz Republic (Table 19.6), i.e. the countries were producing more but due to the collapse of commodity prices and the dominance of primary exports their output was worth less.[20] All five governments appeared to recognise the need for economic diversification away from a handful of primary products or from dependence on remittances. Given the small size of domestic markets, diversification implied a fresh look at opening up to the global economy.

The challenges of diversification are internal and external. Domestic economies must become sufficiently efficient that producers can increase output or develop new goods and services that are competitive in export markets. At the same time, the hard and soft infrastructure of international trade must also be improved. For traditional exports (e.g. cotton, gold, minerals, oil and gas) comparative advantage was sufficiently strong that high trade costs did not prevent trade, but export competitiveness of other goods depends on reducing the costs of international trade.

Table 19.5 Macroeconomic Indicators 2015–2019

	GDP growth	Inflation	Budget deficit/GDP	Current account balance/GDP	Net FDI/GDP*	External debt/GDP
Kazakhstan						
2015	1.2	6.7	-6.3	-3.3	-3.6	83.0
2016	1.1	14.6	-4.5	-5.9	-12.6	118.9
2017	4.1	7.4	-4.4	-3.1	-2.9	100.3
2018	4.1	6.0	2.7	0	-0.1	88.5
2019	3.9	5.2	0.5	-1.5	-2.5	89.0
Kyrgyz Rep						
2015	3.9	6.5	-2.7	-15.9	-17.1	99.9
2016	4.3	0.4	-6.4	-11.6	-9.0	100.2
2017	4.7	3.2	-4.6	-6.2	1.4	91.0
2018	3.5	1.5	-1.3	-8.7	-0.6	84.0
2019	4.3	1.2	-3.0	-10.0	-2.0	n.a.
Tajikistan						
2015	6.0	5.8	-2.0	-6.1	-5.8	51.3
2016	6.9	5.9	-9.0	-4.2	-3.5	61.2
2017	7.1	7.3	-6.0	2.2	-2.6	71.2
2018	7.3	3.8	-2.8	-5.0	-2.9	69.8
2019	7.0	7.9	-4.5	-6.0	-2.5	n.a.
Turkmenistan						
2015	6.5	7.4	-0.7	-15.6	-8.5	21.8
2016	6.2	3.6	-2.4	-20.2	-6.2	23.1
2017	6.5	8.0	-2.8	-10.3	-5.5	25.1
2018	6.2	13.2	-0.2	-5.7	-4.9	25.4
2019	6.3	13.5	-0.1	-0.1	-5.0	n.a.

(Continued)

Table 19.5 Continued

	GDP growth	Inflation	Budget deficit/GDP	Current account balance/GDP	Net FDI/GDP*	External debt/GDP
Uzbekistan						
2015	7.4	8.5	1.1	0.6	-0.1	16.1
2016	6.1	8.8	1.6	0.4	-2.0	18.6
2017	4.5	13.9	1.8	2.5	-3.0	34.1
2018	5.1	17.5	2.2	-7.1	-1.2	34.5
2019	5.5	14.6	0.5	-6.0	-3.5	n.a.

Source: EBRD Transition Report 2019/20 at https://www.ebrd.com/transition-report-2019-20 (accessed 12 April 2020).
Notes. * negative sign = inflow of foreign direct investment; 2019 figures are projections.; n.a. not available. The source notes that 'Reliable economic data are hard to find in Turkmenistan.'

Table 19.6 Economic and Social Indicators, 2018

	Population	Life expectancy at birth	GDP	GDP per capita	External Debt	Internet users
	2018	2018	2018[a]	2018[a]	2018	2018
	WDI	HDR	WDI	WDI	WDI	WDI
	millions	years	$ billion	$	$ million	per 100 people
Kazakhstan	18.3	73.2	179.3 (221.4)	9,812 (12,602)	156,920	78.9
Kyrgyz Republic	6.3	71.3	8.1 (7.5)	1,281 (1,280)	8,119	38.0[b]
Tajikistan	9.1	70.9	7.5 (9.1)	827 (1,114)	5,977	22.0[b]
Turkmenistan	5.9	68.1	40.8 (43.5)	6,967 (7,962)	907	21.3[b]
Uzbekistan	33.0	71.6	50.5 (76.7)	1,532 (2,492)	17,630	55.2

Sources: UNDP Human Development Report 2019; World Bank World Development Indicators (accessed 12 April 2020).
Notes. (a) 2014 in parentheses; (b) 2017.

Central Asia is facing a window of opportunity for non-traditional exports. The Eurasian rail Landbridge began in 2011 by connecting regional value chains in East Asia and Europe, primarily transporting car components from Germany to factories in China and electronics goods from China to Europe, but more services have gradually been offered and the composition of freight diversified (Pomfret 2019b).[21] Regular services are offered between Chongqing and Duisburg (daily since 2016) and on other routes from China to Europe or to Iran. The Landbridge passes through Central Asia, bringing abundant transit revenues to Kazakhstan, but the trains do not stop. China has embraced the Landbridge as part of the Silk Road Economic Belt announced in Kazakhstan in September 2013, and formally launched in Beijing in May 2017 as the Belt and Road Initiative (BRI). The BRI promises funding for infrastructure, including a rail link from Kashi to Andijan that would shorten the China–Iran rail journey and provide an alternative China-EU Landbridge to routes through Kazakhstan and Russia.[22] China may be seeking to avoid dependence on a single route on which there could be hold-up possibilities for transit countries to raise rates, or China may be seeking access to markets in Iran, the Middle East and North Africa; irrespective of Chinese motives a second Central Asian route clearly offers potential benefits to the southern Central Asian countries.

Improved infrastructure of a modern rail network offers a window of opportunity, especially if China follows up on proposals to upgrade to high-speed lines. Whether Central Asian producers can take advantage of the window will depend on their governments improving domestic conditions for doing business and on facilitating trade though better soft infrastructure, e.g. removing bureaucratic and border regulations that inhibit firms and delay transport.

Trade facilitation should be win-win. The experience of the Turkmenistan-Uzbekistan-Kazakhstan-China pipeline built between 2006 and 2009 illustrated the benefits of cooperation. The prospects for regional cooperation to reduce regional trade costs are more positive than in earlier decades when Central Asian presidents were focussed on nation-building or accumulating revenues from resource exports. Moreover, within the government and the wider population, Central Asian countries have far greater global awareness than in 1991.

Low-hanging fruits include, literally, fruit and vegetable exports from Central Asia to Russia, China and Iran and the Middle East. Centuries ago melons from Bukhara were prized in Damascus, and more recently until the 1990s Uzbekistan and Kyrgyzstan had flourishing fruit and vegetable sales in Russia; the trade collapsed because of the high trade costs of transiting Kazakhstan and entering Russia, but in 2019 trucks were much less likely to face ad hoc stops and fees. The Kyrgyz Republic had already shown that new exports can be developed in agriculture (beans), manufacturing (garments) and services (entrepôt bazaars). With more cordial upstream-downstream relations the Kyrgyz Republic and Tajikistan should be able to develop their hydroelectric resources without risking armed conflict with Uzbekistan, and Afghanistan and South Asia offer huge potential markets.[23] Of course, the infrastructure of transmission lines needs to be built, and that in turn depends on security in Afghanistan and Pakistan.

Prospects for regional cooperation seem brighter since Mirziyoyev became Uzbekistan's president. Before 2016 transiting Uzbekistan was costly and time-consuming. Regional integration in Central Asia has also been disappointing despite many declarations of intent. The most successful regional organisation has been the customs union between Russia, Belarus and Kazakhstan which became the Eurasian Economic Union in 2015 and was joined by Armenia and the Kyrgyz Republic in 2015. However, the Russian annexation of Crimea and the ongoing military activities in eastern Ukraine have dampened the enthusiasm of some of the EAEU partners.

The political economy of economic reform

A striking feature of the transition in Central Asia was the creation of different varieties of market-based economies by 2000. Fifteen years later there was an added layer of differentiation resulting from the resource boom. In the 2010s, there was a shift to more outward-oriented policies in what had been the more closed economies. Turkmenistan agreed to construction of a rail link from Kazakhstan to Iran, and the Turkmen, Kazakh and Iranian presidents celebrated completion of the new line with a highly publicised ceremony to hammer in the final spike in December 2014. After the September 2016 death of Uzbekistan's president Karimov, his successor removed the exchange controls that hampered international transactions and quickly began bridge-building with neighbours. This paved the way for Uzbekistan, which is the most populous Central Asian country and has common borders with all four other Central Asian countries and Afghanistan, to resume its position as the cross-roads of Asia. In 2019 Uzbekistan followed the Kyrgyz Republic and Kazakhstan in removing visa requirements for many countries' citizens visiting the country.

Prospects for the domestic reforms that would improve the economies' prospects are less clear. In Central Asia, the replacement of the Soviet Union by independent states was followed by the creation of super-presidential political regimes; the First Secretaries who became presidents found they had far more power because they were no longer subject to checks and balances within the Communist Party. The opportunities to privatise state enterprises, to control cotton gins, to sign contracts to exploit oilfields or mineral deposits, to award licenses to financial institutions or to mobile phone operators provided avenues for accumulating huge wealth, typically in a small circle around the president. Having acquired wealth, the elite was suspicious of further change.

Is reform possible? A change in president could be a catalyst for resuming the reform process,[24] but the smaller economies have been characterised by economic policy continuity after change of president. The Kyrgyz Republic has been the reform leader and has had four presidents since the first president was driven out in 2005. While it remains palpably the most open society and the closest to a parliamentary democracy, the president remains powerful and the country is plagued by corruption. And further reforms since the 1990s have been limited. The other smaller countries (Tajikistan and Turkmenistan) show no sign of abandoning the super-presidential model with rulers who assume close to monarchical status with personality cults and ruling families.

The two most populous countries, Uzbekistan and Kazakhstan, offer the most interesting prospects for reform as their long-serving presidents' rule ended with Karimov's death in 2016 and Nazarbayev's resignation in 2019. Both were replaced by experienced political leaders. Although it is still early to assess whether President Mirziyoyev's proposals will be converted into a serious reform package, it is clear that he feels no constraint in overturning specific policies identified with Karimov, e.g. foreign-exchange liberalisation or elimination of forced labour in cotton-harvesting. By contrast, President Tokayev is heavily constrained by the continuing political influence of ex-President Nazarbayev, whose pride in his legacy and concerns for his entourage's freedom from punishment will limit Tokayev's flexibility; reform will require a bold step at least as long as Nazarbayev is alive.

A striking feature of the Nazarbayev era, in contrast to neighbouring Uzbekistan, was the commitment to improved human capital, efficient governance and international acceptance. Since 1993, Bolashak International Scholarships supported over 11,000 Kazakh students in 33 countries, most of whom returned to Kazakhstan to work and stay.[25] More recently, domestic universities have been upgraded with Nazarbayev University as the lead institution. A similar process of creating elite schools and then scaling up other schools to that standard has been implemented at the high school level. Del Sordi (2018) argues that the programme has twin goals of development and regime stability; after returning to Kazakhstan to use their new knowledge, the students have to adapt to the old patronage-dominated system if they want to progress in their careers. However, the cohorts of Kazakhs educated in foreign universities have contributed to the creation of a substantial educated middle class, especially in the main cities, that is likely to be a source of pressure for political reform. As long as he is alive, Nazarbayev will try to control policy to ensure his legacy and to protect his daughters and close associates. Should he fail, it will be because Kazakhstani society was transformed during his presidency. That would indeed be a positive legacy.

Conclusions

The five Central Asian countries faced unanticipated challenges and major shocks after December 1991. During the difficult transition decade of the 1990s, the governments established nations with different market-based economies and similar super-presidential regimes. During the 1999–2014 resource boom, the five countries' experiences diverged in a different dimension, with Kazakhstan and Turkmenistan benefiting from large oil and gas windfall gains, Uzbekistan benefitting to a lesser extent from mineral exports, and the Kyrgyz Republic, Tajikistan and, to a lesser extent, Uzbekistan becoming sources of migrant labour to the booming Russian economy. During these two periods, the five countries made little effort to integrate into the global economy beyond exporting raw materials and unskilled labour.

Since 2014 there has been a general recognition in the region that the resource boom is over and economic diversification is necessary. Fortuitously, this new perspective coincides with changes that create a potential window of opportunity as overland transport links across Eurasia are becoming more important and efficient. Whether individual countries can seize the opportunity to trade to the east and the west will depend on domestic conditions and on regional cooperation, given the importance of transit arrangements for most Central Asian trade.

The prospects for improved regional cooperation look good but whether meaningful economic reforms will be implemented is less certain. In the two largest countries, new presidents may be auguries of reform. President Mirziyoyev opened up Uzbekistan's forex markets in his first year and moved quickly to improve international relations, but whether these initial steps will be followed by deeper economic reforms and positive economic developments will only be seen in the 2020s. The position of President Tokayev in Kazakhstan is more difficult due to the ongoing policy involvement of the former president, which may be an obstacle to reform. However, Kazakhstan is the Central Asian country with the highest living standards and strongest civil society, which may be a deeper driver of reform.

Notes

1 In December 1991, the presidents were Nabiyev (Tajikistan, b.1930), Karimov (Uzbekistan, b.1938), Niyazov (Turkmenistan, b.1940), Nazarbayev (Kazakhstan b.1940) and Akayev (Kyrgyzstan, b.1944). All of the presidents in 2020 had been in their thirties when central planning ended: Rakhmon (Tajikistan, b.1952), Tokayev (Kazakhstan b.1953), Berdimukhamedov (Turkmenistan, b.1957), Mirziyoyev (Uzbekistan, b. 1957) and Jeenbekov (Kyrgyz Republic, b. 1958).
2 There have been tensions and some border violence, particularly associated with enclaves in the densely populated Ferghana Valley, but the only full-scale war has been the 1992–1997 Tajik civil war.

Central Asia has seen no inter-state wars and has no frozen conflicts comparable to those in Azerbaijan, Moldova, Georgia and Ukraine.
3 Within the ruble zone, each republic could issue ruble credits to pay for public spending, but no institution had control over the money supply. This created a free-rider problem as the credit-issuer gained all the benefits from money creation but only contributed marginally to national inflation (Pomfret 2016).
4 A striking example of disruption was a sugar refinery, the largest industrial enterprise in the Kyrgyz republic accounting for 3 per cent of the GDP, that processed Cuban cane sugar and was immediately unprofitable once transport costs had to be paid.
5 The 1990 agreement with Chevron to develop the Tengiz oil field was the largest foreign investment project signed by the USSR. Exploitation was delayed after the dissolution of the USSR by renegotiations of the contract. Levine (2007) provides an account of the corruption trials in the United States that saw a Mobil Oil senior executive sentenced to 46 months in jail; two Kazakhstanis identified as KO1 and KO2 were widely believed to be the president and prime minister.
6 These, and similar numbers from international agencies, are generally accepted indicators of the time-path of real output, but should be treated with caution, especially for the early 1990s when the output mix was changing dramatically, creation of effective statistical offices was not high on the nation-building agenda and the widespread informal economy was poorly measured. Pomfret (2006: 107-22) discusses the conceptual problems associated with measuring GDP during the transition from central planning to a market-based economy. Some national practices were non-transparent (e.g. Uzbekistan did not report output of gold, its second-largest export) or misleading (e.g. when Turkmenistan was not paid for its gas exports it still recorded the sales as exports and the IOUs were treated as foreign assets, although they would eventually only be paid at deep discounts).
7 The social transfers remained, in principle, until formally terminated in January 2019.
8 The Kyrgyz exceptions were due to disruption of production in the Kumtor goldmine in 2002 and to insurrections that led to the overthrow of the presidents in 2005 and 2010.
9 Natural gas prices were governed by long-term agreements and pipeline routes. Turkmenistan's GDP increased in 1999 due to the resumption of supplies to Ukraine and Azerbaijan. Gas revenues grew slowly during 2000–2004 due to the Russian pipeline monopoly. The terms offered by Ukraine and Russia only improved after Ukraine's 2004 orange revolution was followed by more transparent gas prices and, especially, after completion of the China pipeline in 2009 gave Turkmenistan access to alternative markets.
10 Petrick and Pomfret (2019) assess agricultural policies and performance. Satpayev (2014) claims that the Ministry of Agriculture was the most corrupt part of the administration.
11 Ni died in September 2010. Kim keeps a low profile and is reported living in Almaty and London, where he owns an apartment in One Hyde Park, 'which its developers insist is the world's most exclusive address and the most expensive residential development ever built anywhere on earth' (Shaxon 2013).
12 QDT was an opposition political movement that called for the decentralisation of political power, a strong legislature, and an independent judiciary to balance the power concentrated in the executive branch. The QDT's leader, Mukhtar Ablyazov, was convicted of 'abusing official powers as a minister' and sentenced to six years in prison and his fellow would-be reformers Galymzhan Zhakiyanov and Altynbek Sarsenbaev were also imprisoned.
13 Even when hydroelectricity is generated there is a need for investment in transmission lines before the electricity can be traded, unlike oil which can be shipped by rail or barge before pipelines are built.
14 The car exports, from the factory established by Daewoo in the 1990s and taken over by GM after Daewoo's bankruptcy, entered Russia under preferential CIS tariffs before 2015, but fell after 2015 as Russia introduced non-tariff barriers. Fruit and vegetable exports from Uzbekistan to Russia had been important in the early 1990s but collapsed in the face of the high costs of transiting Kazakhstan; as Kazakh governments reined in the levying of unofficial taxes along its main roads, Uzbek fruit and vegetable exports were restored
15 Uzbekistan is the only post-Soviet economy in which the share of school leavers going on to tertiary education has fallen since independence (Huisman et al. 2018). According to the World Bank's World Development Indicators the share of the relevant age group in tertiary education fell from 13 per cent in 1999 to 9 perr cent in 2017, while in the Europe and Central Asia region as a whole the share increased from 36 per cent to 68 per cent.

16 Perceptions of corruption were increasing; Uzbekistan ranked 153rd out of 167 in Transparency International's 2015 Corruption Perceptions Index, which is worse than 79th out of 90 in 2000 if we assume that the additional coverage tends to bring in poorer and more corrupt countries. According to Said (2014: 7), 'a dramatic increase of the government bureaucracy in the past two decades has coincided with a steep decline in its capacity to effectively implement policies.'

17 Gulnara Karimova was an especially high-profile figure due to an ostentatious lifestyle, and with a $600 million fortune in Swiss bank accounts (according to Said 2014: 5), until she was placed under house arrest in 2013. Cooley and Heathershaw (2017) provide more information about the wealth of the elite.

18 The Manas Transit Center in Bishkek airport faced domestic opposition and Russian pressure to close it, but it remained open and a source of revenue for the Kyrgyz Republic until US withdrawal in 2014. Fuel contracts to the Center were a major source of corruption, as sons of presidents monopolized the contracts from the early 2000s until 2010, stoking the popular discontent that led to the overturn of presidents in 2005 and 2010.

19 The secretariat of the Commonwealth of Independent States and that of the Union of Five (predecessor of the EAEU) were in Moscow, the Shanghai Cooperation Organization in Beijing, the Economic Cooperation Organization in Tehran, the Special Program for the Economies of Central Asia (SPECA) in the UN regional offices in Geneva and Bangkok, and Central Asian Regional Economic Cooperation (CAREC) at the Asian Development Bank in Manila.

20 This is fairly clearly related to energy and mineral prices (including aluminum for Tajikistan). The negative impact on remittances from workers in Russia was also important for Tajikistan and Uzbekistan, but was mitigated for the Kyrgyz Republic whose workers received preferential treatment as an inducement from Russia to join the EAEU in 2015.

21 The Landbridge is often dated from the first Chongqing-Duisburg service in 2011, but the service did not become daily until 2016. Other important rail infrastructure dates were the opening of a second China–Kazakhstan line in 2013 and completion of a north–south line between Kazakhstan and Turkmenistan in 2014 which became part of China–Iran routes after UN sanctions on Iran were eased in 2016.

22 If the Kyrgyz Republic were to finance construction of the line by Chinese loans, it would incur a debt roughly equal to GDP and with limited prospects of benefits beyond transit fees; Hurley, et al. (2018) highlight the possibility of debt dependence. See Pomfret (2020: Appendix) for more discussion of the project.

23 Completion of Tajikistan's Rogun Dam, begun in the Soviet era and potentially one of the world's highest, was effectively halted by Uzbekistan until President Karimov's death in 2016. His successor, President Mirziyoyev, signaled a more cooperative relationship with Tajikistan and Rogun began to generate power in 2019.

24 This was a frequently stated idea in the early twenty-first century, e.g. Sean Roberts in his online Roberts Report on Central Asia and Kazakhstan (http://roberts-report.blogspot.com/2007/10/conversation-with-steve-levine-author.html, posted 29 October 2007) said 'the next generations of all the Central Asian and Caucasus republics will be much different from today.'

25 The program, established in November 1993, allowed Kazakhs to study at designated foreign universities with expenses paid on condition that they returned to Kazakhstan for five years (Nessipbayeva 2015).

Bibliography

Anderson, K., and R. Pomfret. (2003). *Consequences of Creating a Market Economy: Evidence from Household Surveys in Central Asia*. Cheltenham: Edward Elgar.

Atkinson, A., and J. Micklewright. (1992). *Economic Transformation in Eastern Europe and the Distribution of Income*. Cambridge: Cambridge University Press.

Bogolov, P. (2016). *An Exodus Amid Tripled GDP: The Mirage of Uzbekistan's Economic Miracle*. Carnegie Moscow Center. Available at http://carnegie.ru/commentary/63771

Cooley, A., and J. Heathershaw. (2017). *Dictators without Borders Power and Money in Central Asia*. New Haven, CT: Yale University Press.

Cornia, G.A. (2014). *Uzbekistan's Development Strategies: Past Record and Long-term Options*. DISEI Working Paper No.26/2014. Florence: Università degli Studi di Firenze.

Del Sordi, A. (2018). Sponsoring Student Mobility for Development and Authoritarian Stability: Kazakhstan's Bolashak Programme. *Globalizations* 15(2), 215–31.

Garcia, D. (2006). *Le Pays où Bouygues est Roi*. Paris: Éditions Danger Public.

Global Witness. (2010). *Risky Business: Kazakhstan, Kazakhmys PLC and the London Stock Exchange*. London: Global Witness.

Huisman, J., A. Smolentseva, and I. Froumin. (2018). *25 Years of Transformations of Higher Education Systems in Post-Soviet Countries: Reform and Continuity*. London: Palgrave Macmillan.

Hurley, J., S. Morris, and G. Portelance. (2018). *Examining the Debt Implications of the Belt and Road Initiative from a Policy Perspective*. CGD Policy Paper No. 121. Washington, DC: Center for Global Development.

Isaacs, R. (2020). The Role of Party Interest Articulation in the Personalist-Authoritarian Regimes of the Central Asian Republics of Kazakhstan, Turkmenistan, and Tajikistan. *Problems of Post-Communism* 67(4–5), 375–387.

Kalyuzhnova, Y., and C. Nygaard. (2011). Special Vehicles of State Intervention in Russia and Kazakhstan. *Comparative Economic Studies* 53(1), 57–77.

Kaminski, B., and S. Mitra. (2012). *Borderless Bazaars and Regional Integration in Central Asia: Emerging Patterns of Trade and Cross-Border Cooperation*. Washington, DC: World Bank.

Kennedy, R., and A. Nurmakov. (2010). *Resource Nationalism Trends in Kazakhstan, 2004–2009*. Working Paper of RUSSCASP – Russian and Caspian Energy Developments and Their Implications for Norway and Norwegian Actors. Lysaker: The Fridtjof Nansen Institute, the Norwegian Institute of International Affairs and Econ Pöyry.

Laruelle, M., ed. (2017). *Kazakhstan: Nation-Branding, Economic Trials, and Cultural Changes*. Washington, DC: George Washington University Central Asia Program.

LeVine, S. (2007). *Oil and the Glory: The Pursuit of Empire and Fortune on the Caspian Sea*. New York: Random House.

Mogilevskii, R., N. Abdrazakova, A. Bolotbekova, S. Chalbasova, S. Dzhumaeva, and K. Tikeleyev. (2015). *The Outcomes of 25 Years of Agricultural Reforms in Kyrgyzstan*. IAMO Discussion Paper No.162. Halle: Leibniz Institute of Agricultural Development in Central and Eastern Europe.

Mukhamedova, N., and K. Wegerich. (2018). The Feminization of Agriculture in Post-Soviet Tajikistan. *Journal of Rural Studies* 57(1), 128–39.

Najman, B., R. Pomfret, G. Raballand, and P. Sourdin. (2008). Redistribution of Oil Revenue in Kazakhstan. In Boris Najman, Richard Pomfret and Gaël Raballand (eds.), *The Economics and Politics of Oil in the Caspian Basin: The Redistribution of Oil Revenues in Azerbaijan and Central Asia*. London: Routledge.

Nessipbayeva, O. (2015). The Bolashak Program in Building a Democratic and Prosperous Society. *Procedia – Social and Behavioral Sciences* 191, 2275–9.

Olcott, M. B. (2002). *Kazakhstan: Unfulfilled Promise*. Washington, DC: Carnegie Endowment for International Peace.

Olcott, M. B. (2007). Uzbekistan: A Decaying Dictatorship withdrawn from the West. In Robert Rotberg (ed.), *Worst of the Worst: Dealing with Repressive and Rogue Nations*. Washington, DC: Brookings Institution.

Petrick, M., and R. Pomfret. (2019). Agricultural and Rural Policies in Kazakhstan. In T. Johnson and W. Meyers (eds.), *Handbook on International Food and Agricultural Policy Volume I: Policies for Agricultural Markets and Rural Economic Activity*. Singapore: World Scientific Publishing.

Pomfret, R. (1995). *The Economies of Central Asia*. Princeton, NJ: Princeton University Press.

Pomfret, R. (2006). *The Central Asian Economies since Independence*. Princeton, NJ: Princeton University Press.

Pomfret, R. (2016). Currency Union and Disunion in Europe and the Former Soviet Union. *CESifo Forum* 17(4), 43–7.

Pomfret, R. (2019a). *The Central Asian Economies in the Twenty-First Century: Paving a New Silk Road*. Princeton, NJ: Princeton University Press.

Pomfret, R. (2019b). The Eurasian Landbridge and China's Belt and Road Initiative: Demand, Supply of Services, and Public Policy. *The World Economy* 42(6), 1642–53.

Pomfret, R. (2020). The Central Asian Countries' Economies in the Twenty-First Century. In Alexandr Akimov and Gennadi Kazakevitch (eds.), *30 Years since the Fall of the Berlin Wall: Turns and Twists in Economies, Politics, and Societies in the Post-Communist Countries*. London: Palgrave Macmillan.

Popov, V. (2013). *Economic Miracle of Post-Soviet Space: Why Uzbekistan Managed to Achieve What no Other Post-Soviet State Achieved*. MPRA Paper No.48723. Available at http://mpra.ub.uni-muenchen.de/48723/

Ruziev, K., D. Ghosh, and S. Dow. (2007). The Uzbek Puzzle Revisited: An Analysis of Economic Performance in Uzbekistan since 1991. *Central Asian Survey* 26(1), 7–30.

Said, A. (2014). *Uzbekistan at a Crossroads: Main Developments, Business Climate, and Political Risks.* Uzbekistan Initiative Papers No.10. Washington, DC: George Washington University.

Satpayev, D. (2014). *Corruption in Kazakhstan and the Quality of Governance.* IDE Discussion Paper No.475. Chiba: Institute of Developing Economies.

Shaxson, N. (2013). A Tale of Two Londons. *Vanity Fair*, April. Available at https://www.vanityfair.com/style/society/2013/04/mysterious-residents-one-hyde-park-london

Tarr, D. (1994). The Terms-of-Trade Effects of Moving to World Prices on Countries of the Former Soviet Union. *Journal of Comparative Economics* 18(1), 1–24.

20
OIL, CAPITAL AND LABOUR AROUND THE CASPIAN

Maurizio Totaro and Paolo Sorbello

A 'new energy frontier,' the 'new Gulf' and 'Oildorado.' Such were the monikers attached to the Caspian region in the 1990s, as transnational oil and gas companies (TNCs) rushed in for concessions and acquisitions on favourable terms, whilst newly independent governments rested their prospects for recovery from socio-economic collapse on the development of still largely untapped hydrocarbon resources. In particular for Turkmenistan and Kazakhstan, since independence oil and gas have been paramount for their incorporation within the global capitalist economy. In his 2008 book, *The Kazakhstan Way*, President Nursultan Nazarbayev succinctly expressed the material role that oil and gas have come to play as propellers for the country's socio-economic and political renewal. After describing oil as the country's 'foundation of economic independence' (*fundament ekonomicheskoy nezavisimosti*), he added:

> Given the way things have taken shape, the global economy has already, strictly speaking, decided upon Kazakhstan's membership dues to participate in the integrated economy: access for leading international companies to our natural resources [...] No wonder, then, that from the very first years of our independence we have devoted very serious attention to the development of the oil and gas sector of our economy in particular. You see, for us oil and gas are not only a fuel energy and strategic resource. They are the fundamental principle [*fundament*] that will enable us to deal more quickly with the complexities of the transitional period and make up for the damage caused by the disintegration of the united and integrated Soviet Union.
>
> (Nazarbayev 2008: 112)

Accordingly, scholarly production has devoted much attention to the role that oil and gas have come to play in shaping the socio-economic trajectories as well as the political relations in the region. Variously influenced by strands of the 'resource curse' hypothesis – such as the 'Dutch disease' and 'rentier state' – studies concentrated on the distribution of revenues accruing from the sale of hydrocarbons (Najman et al. 2008; Sakal 2015) and the way these are mediated by institutions, fiscal regimes and policies (Kalyuzhnova 2011; Luong and Weinthal 2010; Azhgaliyeva 2014); the security implications and concerns arising from the exploitation of the Caspian natural resources (Cummings 2003; Akiner 2004; Ebel and Menon 2000); as well as the role played by elites in capturing oil rents (Heinrich and Pleines 2012; Ostrowski 2010). Overall,

DOI: 10.4324/9780429057977-20

this selection of studies on resources and revenues in Central Asia has tended to concentrate on what happens *after* the sale of hydrocarbons, whilst overlooking the constitutive processes and regimes enabling oil and gas extraction in the first place. Moreover, they have tended to reduce 'the complexities' to which Nazarbayev alludes to the internal functioning of states, and their fallacies or successes in managing oil revenues. In sum, as noted by Appel et al. (2015), in such studies, 'oil' is often reduced to little more than a metonym for 'money.'

Reviewing the literature concerned with the effects of oil and gas in the Caspian region, anthropologist Morgan Liu (2018) has argued that an overwhelming emphasis on 'the state' has neglected the role other actors, such as corporations and NGOs, play in shaping developmental outcomes. As he aptly notes, the opening up of the Central Asian and Caspian region to flows of global capital, knowledge and organisational practices and techniques has not only shaped the socio-economic trajectories of these countries but it has reconfigured 'the state' itself. To paraphrase Nazarbayev, addressing post-Soviet complexities through the exploitation of hydrocarbons has thus been itself a complex endeavour, involving a multitude of actors enacted and constituted through relational practices and operational logics.

Whilst we share Liu's invitation to attend to the networked nature of this heterogeneous ensemble, we find it wanting of an engagement with how networks and forms – legal, infrastructural, organisational – enable the extraction, circulation and accumulation of value. Whilst this can be traced to Liu's main interest in the developmental outcomes of oil and gas, and how these emerge out of 'novel conjunctures of state, NGO, and corporate activity' (Liu 2018: 194), with this chapter we intend to complement his analysis by inserting additional actors to the picture – such as international financial institutions, banks and oil workers – legal forms such as oil contracts and reserves, as well as spatial ones – such as tax havens, extraction enclaves and oil towns. Our focus is on how these actors, forms and spaces are enmeshed in 'the processes by which a wider world obtains the energy that drives its material and technical life,' to quote Timothy Mitchell (2011: 2). For instance, we look at how oil contracts have secured access to hydrocarbons for corporations whilst consolidating authoritarian state-building; how inflated reserves and oil future markets maintain afloat hugely expensive extractive projects; and how tax havens act as nodes for the accumulation and circulation of profits. In other words, we focus on how oil production is inextricably linked to the creation, extraction and accumulation of value by capital.

Although financialisation has tended to increasingly detach the creation of value from material production, the accumulation of capital nevertheless necessitates its extraction from those who create it, i.e. workers. And yet, besides few exceptions (Atabaki et al. 2018; Yessenova 2012; Appel 2012; Labban 2014), labour and its governance have been largely ignored when analysing how political, economic and social relations are 'engineered out of the flows of energy' (Mitchell 2011: 5). In the second part of this chapter, we thus look at how labour in the oil industry is governed through discourses, practices, regulations and logics aimed at extracting value whilst maintaining stability in the production process. In particular, we look at how capital–labour relations are differently articulated through, and mediated by, infrastructural forms such as the 'oil enclave' and the 'oil town.' By looking at labour protests in Kazakhstan (Tengiz and Zhanaozen) we offer two variations on modes of labour governance and value extraction, but also two different modes of sociality, activism and protest. Before proceeding further, in the next section we overview the existing literature on the 'resource curse,' its shortcomings and biases, such as its pronounced 'state-centrism' and ahistorical leanings. This will offer the reader a critical introduction to the state of the art concerning the political economy of oil around the Caspian Sea. The following central parts of the chapter, on the other hand, are intended to provide examples of how the socio-economic and political dynamics related to oil and gas can be addressed with analytical tools and theoretical frameworks other than those provided by the resource curse approach.

Beyond curses and rents

As encapsulated in Nazarbayev's quote above, the development of oil and gas deposits around the Caspian became paramount for the newly independent states' transition to market economies. However, if on the one hand the endowment of hydrocarbon resources engendered the possibility of a steady economic recovery, it was also simultaneously problematised as a potential source of social, political and economic 'pathologies' such as ethnic and civil conflict (Ebel and Menon 2000), corruption and rent-seeking (Karl 1997), resource nationalism (Kennedy and Nurmakov 2010), and excessive public spending and debt. Such a thesis on the 'blessing' of natural resource endowment turning paradoxically into a host of negative socio-economic and political effects – known as the 'resource curse' –has had wide resonance in informing international financial institutions' (IFIs) recommendations and conditionalities, governments' reform programmes, as well as academic and policy debates about Central Asia throughout the 1990s and 2000s. The thesis is rather straightforward: the abrupt and steady inflow of revenues following the discovery of oil and gas deposits into the state coffers of developing countries hinders democracy inasmuch as rents provide governments with the fiscal tools to avoid accountability by their constituencies and elites with the economic resources necessary to co-opt popular demands through patronage and large public spending, whilst states utilise oil revenues to enlarge their repressive apparatuses (Ross 2001).

In a nutshell, this type of rentier dynamic makes a government 'completely autonomous from its society, winning popular acquiescence through distribution rather than support through taxation and representation' (Anderson 1987: 10). Moreover, the thesis goes, large grounded rents hamper economic growth – rather than stimulate it – as governments that are less likely to treat windfalls as temporary tend to spend them too quickly, and in so doing distort the economy by redirecting capital investments from other sectors (Auty 2004). The first 'resource curse' studies represented groundbreaking tests on the validity of an understudied aspect of macroeconomics. While originally an exercise rooted around the analysis of large datasets encompassing several countries and variables (Auty 1989; Ross 2001), the theory was quickly adopted as a normative policy instrument.

Officially endorsed by IFIs such as the World Bank and the International Monetary Fund (IMF), the rise and prominence of the resource curse thesis – as well as its applications to the Central Asian context – has to be collocated within the wider politico-economic and ideological shifts towards neoliberal modes of governance. In fact, by identifying the origin of the 'curse' with the establishment of OPEC and the nationalisation of oil industries from Venezuela to Saudi Arabia following the oil crisis of 1973–1974 (Ross 2012), the main criticism of this body of literature has centred on state ownership of natural resources and the revenues accruing to governments as a result. Conversely, when the management of oil operations is conducted along commercial lines alone, with resource ownership in the hands of corporations, resource curse scholars have shown 'little appetite for similar criticism' (Ehsani 2018: 24).

With its overarching emphasis on the liberalisation of markets, privatisation of assets and the creation of a favourable institutional environment for incoming capital, this body of literature can be criticised on a number of fronts. As recently noted by Morgan Liu in the case of the Caspian littoral states, such approaches assume and deliberately overemphasise the role played by the state in dominating 'the course and outcomes of development within national borders' (Liu 2018: 170). Concentrating largely on analysing 'the failures and inefficiencies of economic planning and state institutions in the Global South' (Logan and McNeish 2012: 9), oil curse theories have caused a considerable shift, away from critical inquiries of the intricate webs of social, economic and political relations constituting the global oil complex and its effects. Moreover, by overlooking the ongoing histories of colonialism, imperialism and dependency constituting the current politico-economic trajectories of 'petro-states,' resource curse scholars have tended to reify the state as 'the ultimate geopolitical fetish' (Huber 2011: 35), whilst their inherent economic determinism fetishises oil as a 'thing' endowed with 'causal powers' (Watts 2009: 6–7), detached from its global production network as well as the reproduction of the very lives whose fabrication it sustains or endangers.

Since the late 1980s, the resource curse thesis has turned into the main academic and policy infrastructure shaping statecraft in many oil- and gas-rich countries in the Global South. In the 1990s, as the Central Asian republics turned into independent states, the resource curse informed policies in Equatorial Guinea (Appel et al. 2015: 17), Chad (Leonard 2016), Bolivia and Kazakhstan (IBRD and World Bank 2015), to name but a few. The conjuncture in which the Central Asian states found themselves at independence was, however, radically different from the 1970s, pointing to how much the nationalisations which have been generalised by scholars formulating the curse thesis are in fact contingent (Luong and Weinthal 2010).

Indeed, since the mid-1980s, the relative power of oil-importing countries and resource-seeking firms increased considerably at the expense of resource-holding states (Bridge and LeBillon 2013: 58), with highly indebted governments in the Global South opening up again to TNCs. In Venezuela, after the collapse of the banking system in 1994 and the rampant rise of speculative financial capitalism, the government embarked on the *apertura petrolera*, a process of opening up access for foreign companies to carry out exploration and development activity (Coronil, 1997). In Nigeria, during the same years, Shell moved into deepwater drilling through a production sharing contract that gave the company 100 per cent equity participation (Bridge and LeBillon 2013: 60), with deregulation in the Niger Delta spiralling in a vortex of violence, insurgency and ecological catastrophe (Watts 2011). Shaped by what anthropologist James Ferguson has aptly named 'neoliberal extractivism' (Ferguson 2006; Shever 2012), 'the state' has been thoroughly reconfigured in its engagement with corporations and IFIs.

However, the resource curse literature has had remarkably little to say on the role of IFIs and corporations (but also of workers, NGOs and communities affected by extraction practices), as well as on the processes of neoliberalisation and financialisation they engender. In a similar vein, these actors and processes have been overlooked in the case of Central Asian hydrocarbon-rich countries. Phenomena such as corruption, patronage and authoritarianism have been explained away as though following from a 'double curse' (Franke et al. 2009), fully determined by the conjunction of resource endowment and the availability of large rents on the one hand, and the legacy of an illiberal, autocratic political culture rooted in Soviet authoritarian modes of governance on the other (see also Gel'man and Marganiya 2010). More generally, such approaches, as also underlined by Liu, have tended to present oil and other natural resources in the Caspian region as instrumental either to 'state strategies of alliance and rule' amidst geopolitical struggles (Liu 2018: 173), such as the so-called 'New Great Game' (Cooley 2012; Collins and Bekenova 2017; Kleveman 2003), or to regime maintenance and elite politics (Heinrich and Pleines 2012; Ostrowski 2010).

Although post-Soviet contexts have been used as case studies in order to confute the curse's deterministic assumptions which 'names a beast apparently capable of stalking any nation and any continent' (Logan and McNeish 2012: 7) – but then haunting only developing countries (Ross 2012) – the focus has remained on governments and their 'choices' on how they construct institutions, property rights and fiscal regimes in order to shed away the curse. A case in point is Pauline Jones Luong and Erika Weinthal's *Oil Is Not a Curse*, where the authors compare five post-Soviet cases (Azerbaijan, Kazakhstan, Russia, Turkmenistan and Uzbekistan) in order to dismantle the crudest determinism of resource curse theory by looking at how property and ownership regimes mediate and shape socio-economic and political outcomes. Nevertheless, although their analysis adds layers and nuances to the resource curse argument, it remains ultimately anchored to its core assumptions that strong fiscal regimes combined with light state control and resource ownership are (as in Kazakhstan and Russia) a measure of success against the curse.

Strategies of capital accumulation: Contracts, reserves and tax havens

During the 1990s, programmes of liberalisation and privatisation of the oil industries in Kazakhstan, Turkmenistan and Uzbekistan followed different trajectories. Uzbekistan held comparatively smaller hydrocarbon reserves and, despite a spike in oil production and successful gas explorations in the first decade since independence, it opted for retaining control of its underground resources whilst gradually expanding extraction in order to achieve energy self-sufficiency. Moreover, differently from its two neighbouring countries, Uzbekistan had less urgency to exploit oil and gas reserves for hard currency, relying primarily on cotton and gold exports in order to provide for the bulk of its revenue (Luong and Weinthal 2010: 79–80). Until the late 2000s, 'only an estimated 5% of Uzbekistan's total gas output was produced with participation of foreign capital' (Zhukov 2009: 373). Despite signing new production agreements with CNPC in 2006 (Wang 2006) and Petronas in 2008,[1] the bulk of Uzbekistan's total output remained firmly in the hands of state-owned Uzbekneftegaz.

On the contrary, by the end of the first decade since independence, Kazakhstan had largely privatised its oil fields, starting with the giant Tengiz to Chevron in 1993, revising an earlier agreement which had brought the US corporation in western Kazakhstan during the late Soviet years, and continuing with smaller and more mature fields in 1996–1997. Although Turkmenistan followed an economic policy less open than Kazakhstan's, several concessions were granted by its government to foreign companies until the end of the decade (Canzi 2004; Dankov 2013). Such measures have had a long-lasting influence over the economic policies and political practices of the latter two countries well *before* the large influx of oil money (Yessenova 2015: 293), and are thus paradigmatic cases in showing how indigenous capitalist classes and authoritarian modes of governance developed together with a large-scale privatisation (Kazakhstan) or 'make-believe liberalisation' (Turkmenistan) of their respective oil sectors.

Rather than a consequence of rent mismanagement, it was oil contracts and extraction prospects – articulated in private negotiations, adopted with speedy and authoritative measures, motivated by the anticipation of large profits – which enabled certain actors to 'perform the state' (Heathershaw 2014) and accumulate political power, whilst legitimising non-participatory decision-making practices. Indeed, as Saulesh Yessenova (2015) has argued, authoritarian statecraft in post-Soviet Kazakhstan has been largely shaped by oil privatisation, rather than by Soviet legacies and oil revenues. A crucial shift occurred in fact with the adoption of a new constitution in 1995 centralising power around the president in order to shed oil contracts with TNCs away from public scrutiny, with corporations framing the deals as 'private (corporate) matters to be negotiated in secrecy and in a speedy manner with the executive branch' (Yessenova 2015). Following IFIs recommendations, Nazarbayev instituted the State Investment Committee which, by enacting the state, helped consolidate his power by filtering incoming financial flows, whilst acting as the investment gateway for TNCs' 'one-stop' deals (Luong and Weinthal 2010: 264–5).

In the case of Turkmenistan too the consolidation of authoritarianism cannot be seen in isolation from its engagement with the global oil complex. Indeed, until the late 1990s, transnational companies obtained a large number of concessions which, in turn, played a crucial role for upbeat assessments by credit rating agencies, paving the way for the government's access to loans from multilateral and development banks in order to extract hydrocarbons (Canzi 2004: 165–6).[2] By the early 2000s, as the price for oil and gas increased substantially, the Turkmen government communicated to the IMF it required no further assistance, provided that the latter 'revives neighbouring economies so that their demand for natural gas increases' (Auty 2004: 107). Thus, in both cases, oil fostered authoritarianism well before the inflow of revenues, contradicting one of the main tenets of the resource curse.

If oil contracts make states, they also make companies, as it has been noted in the case of Tengiz. After acquiring the right to exploit the field, Chevron's market value skyrocketed as it certified the doubling of its standing oil reserves overnight (LeVine 2007: 100). Indeed, together with contracts, reserves are another example of how strategies of economic and political accumulation produce oil effects prior to the inflow of rents – and the material flows of oil. Speculations and rumours about the Caspian bed cloaking fortunes – a 'second Persian Gulf' – were deployed by the governments of Azerbaijan, Turkmenistan and Kazakhstan in order to attract more investments, as well as by corporations in order to increase their shareholder value by booking them as assets on their balance sheets, often without distinguishing between 'proven' and 'probable' reserves (Roberts 2003).

In this regard, the inflation of reserves epitomises how capital accumulation around the Caspian has been partially driven by the rampant financialisation of the oil complex and its 'economy of appearances' (Tsing 2005). The 'unattainable' Kashagan,[3] described as the largest field discovered since the 1970s and, successively, dismissively mocked by *The Economist* as 'Cash-All-Gone'[4] in 2014, is a quintessential example of how, by maximising *shareholder value*, the TNCs involved in the project capitalised on future returns based on inflated reserves and the forecasting of upward price fluctuations.[5] In this way 'oil companies earned good profits from Kashagan even without developing the field' (Crude Accountability 2017: 37). The start of production has in fact been regularly delayed for more than ten years – causing soaring costs and fines – alternatively attributed to the shallow frozen waters, the high content of hydrogen sulphide, corruption, organisational fallacies and disputes between the members of NCOC (North Caspian Operating Company). During all these years, however, the IMF had been channelling finances from over 30 of the world's top banks into the Kashagan project, whilst facilitating the negotiations postponing and refinancing it, as well as supervising talks to prolong its production sharing agreement for an additional 20 years (Crude Accountability 2017: 38).

Whereas IFIs and banks provided access to capital for TNCs' projects, tax havens have been the preferred sites for capital accumulation and reinvestment. As Logan and McNeish note, the proliferation of tax havens under financial capitalism 'was built into the complex tax avoidance strategies pioneered by oil companies like Standard Oil/Exxon' (Logan and McNeish 2012: 18). In Kazakhstan, the consortia operating at Karachaganak (KPO) and Kashagan (NCOC) are registered in the Netherlands. While the consortium members of KPO and NCOC are among the largest TNCs globally, in Kazakhstan they operate through subsidiary companies also registered offshore; similarly, the branches of ExxonMobil for exploration and production in Kazakhstan, Turkmenistan and Uzbekistan are also registered offshore, in the Bahamas.[6] The constellation of companies used for specific projects across the globe coalesces into the TNC's annual report, where the breakdown of operations serves the purpose of demonstrating the flexibility of operations and capital transfers to shareholders.

Similar to employees working at the headquarters of an oil and gas TNC, in fact, its shareholders – asset management companies, trust funds and a myriad of individual investors – are geographically and cognitively removed from the oil fields. By listing their shares in globally renowned stock exchanges, such as London and New York, TNCs feign being subjected to corporate accountability towards their shareholders. Yet, the web of companies registered offshore that they own are not bound to disclose any details of their deals. Shareholders are therefore content with the overall health of these companies and the dividends they receive, without demanding full accountability for the profits TNCs hide in tax havens. The progressive removal from the public eye of taxable profits and local deals goes hand in hand with the shortening of the distance between Central Asian elites and the centres of capital accumulation.

Increasingly cosmopolitan elites have also been utilising offshore domains in order to conceal profits, taxes, properties and bribes (Cooley and Heathershaw 2017).[7] The recent Panama and Paradise Papers, published by the International Consortium of Investigative Journalists (ICIJ), have revealed how Turkmenistani and Uzbekistani elites with links to the state have been trading hydrocarbons by means of companies registered in secretive tax havens such as the Bahamas and the British Virgin Islands. Whilst this 'marriage between entrepreneurs seeking to link up with the state and public officials seeking to intervene further in the market' has been considered causing a rentier effect distorting market rationality (Karl, 1997: 57), evidence suggests that these Central Asian 'entrepretchiki' (Verdery 2004) – half entrepreneurs and half apparatchiks – are driven by profit generation much more than by rent capture; their activities, in line with the general imperatives of capital accumulation, are constituting, rather than distorting, markets. The case of Sauat Mynbayev – then-chief executive of Kazakhstan's state-owned KazMunayGas oil and gas company (2013–2018) and former oil and gas minister (2010–2013) – is quite exemplary in this regard.

In late 2017, leaked documents obtained by the ICIJ revealed Mynbayev as one of the co-founders of Meridian, a multi-billion-dollar transnational holding based in the tropical tax haven of Bermuda, 'investing in everything from real estate to natural resources to banking to aviation, transportation, and dairy,' making it an empire stretching 'from the United States to Europe, Africa, Asia, and even Australia.'[8] The publication of the report spurred President Nazarbayev to address the issue of capital flight and tax dodging in a televised intervention, where he named a handful of companies part of the oil sector: 'Tengizchevroil has $4.5 billion abroad … KazMunayGaz has $3 billion abroad, KazMunayGaz Exploration and Production – $2 billion, Asian Gas Pipeline – more than $1 billion, the Beyneu-Shymkent Gas Pipeline – $100 million and so on' (Putz 2017). All in all, leaks and scandals opened a window on practices of capital accumulation, showing how national elites and state-owned companies, rather than idly sitting on accruing rents, use schemes akin to the ones used by TNCs to shield and reproduce their profits. In addition to the extraction of value from labour in the oil field, described in depth in the next section, the reproduction-by-diversion of financial capital – which moves both geographically and across industrial sectors – has come to be an additional strategy for those who own and exploit resources. It is by figuratively pulling the levers on the management of the labour force that corporations and elites can fulfil their goal.

Modular labour, local (dis)content, and the 'ghost class'

If financialisation and the maximisation of shareholder value have increasingly become privileged vectors through which value is produced, extracted and accumulated, these have nevertheless 'proceeded alongside the [material] expansion of production and the intensification of labour' (Labban 2014: 479). However, oil scholarship only sporadically considered the role and agency of workers in oil-producing countries, as well as the technologies and discourses through which their labour is governed. This tendency, far from being isolated to Central Asia, is widespread in the literature, both in its mainstream, resource curse strands and in more critically oriented scholarship. Several explanations are often deployed to justify such invisibility: the capital intensive nature of production processes and the implementation of labour-saving technologies, the increasing flexibilisation of labour markets and the spatial isolation of extraction points. Moreover, as Kaveh Ehsani argues, the erasure of the role of oil workers is also related to discursive shifts within the academic field, as well as to 'a number of interconnected maneuvers that include the repression of independent trade unions and political parties, and the drastic shifts in state policies from populist redistribution to market rationality.' By taking post-revolution Iran as a case study, Ehsani concludes that 'rather than becoming insignificant, oil workers have lost the ability to make their presence felt, because they are actively made invisible' (Ehsani 2018: 21).

Commenting on the repression of a hunger strike by oil workers in January 2017 in Aqtau, Kazakhstan, journalist Gul'nara Bazhkenova (2017) made a similar argument, noting how the outlawing of the country's Federation of Independent Trade Unions which workers were protesting, as well as the arrest of the strike leaders and the firing of several other activists in its aftermath, amounted to a further disarm of the labour movement, as part of a wider post-Soviet process in which 'workers have become a ghost class' (*rabochie stali klassom-fantom*). Indeed, the promulgation of a new Law on Trade Unions in 2014 severely restricted workers' ability to organise, whilst a new Labour Code the following year further atomised workers' solidarity by shifting from collective to individual agreements the cornerstone of employment relations.

Further, across Central Asia, the invisibility of oil workers has been influenced by the governments' own success in providing a modicum of progress and comfort for its citizenry. Until 2018,[9] the population of Turkmenistan was granted free access to a range of uncommodified public goods, such as electricity, gas and water (Bohr 2016: 92; Anceschi 2019: 37). In Kazakhstan, the price of petrol and other basic goods is capped by the government. Whilst these measures have tied the social reproduction of populations to the continued extraction of hydrocarbons, at the same time they have contributed to the social alienation of oil workers, who generally operate in remote areas near the oilfields, far from the sight of the vast majority of the population. In 2011, for example, the burgeoning middle class in Kazakhstan's two larger cities, Almaty and Nur-Sultan (formerly Astana), trivialised workers' demands in the aftermath of a bloody repression of a workers' strike in the western oil city of Zhanaozen as jeopardising their own ability to 'live normally' after the chaos and instability of the 1990s (Koch 2013). In doing so, they expressed a pervasive sentiment among the country's citizens, who 'failed to see … their work, their leisure and consumption, and their overall prosperity … to be connected with the processes of resource extraction and power relations in the state's "hinterlands"' (Koch 2013: A2).

Working in extraction enclaves, highly securitised and territorially secluded from political, economic and cultural centres – as well as from their proximate social milieus – workers have been cognitively and affectively severed from national publics. As James Ferguson has argued with regard to Angola, whilst extraction enclaves are 'tightly integrated with the head offices of multinational corporations and metropolitan centres' – as well as tax havens – they are simultaneously 'walled off from their own national societies' (Ferguson 2005). Labour, in its extremely modular form (Appel 2012), follows the movement of capital: rather than flowing from London or Amsterdam to Aqtau and Atyrau, it 'hops' (Ferguson 2005), connecting discrete points of the oil complex, 'thinning out' the socio-economic impact of oil production in extracting regions as well as the capacity of workers to establish solidarity out of enduring social ties in the workplace.

Besides continuously lobbying for governments to adopt less stringent labour legislation, TNCs also established employment machines that serve to atomise their workforce. If senior management and engineering teams are replete with men from the West, Middle East and East Asia, TNCs and the production consortia they form outsource most of the hiring to manpower agencies, originally intended as an intermediary body for the headhunting of specific skillsets and increasingly used as informal human resources departments that hire workers through temporary contracts. Progressively, precarious contract labourers sourced from manpower agencies started substituting full-time cadres of the principal companies that required their services (Trevisani 2018). Far from being a novelty, much like offshore havens, the use of manpower agencies has been championed in the oil complex for about a century across the globe, with the specific goal to exonerate the companies from any responsibility or accountability towards the workers (Tijerina 2018).

Secluded from the rest of society, workers with varying degrees of job security and pay grade coexist, working on the same project in shifts, generally of two or four weeks, during which they find themselves living in the same camp near the oilfield. Although such spaces are intended to insulate extraction operations from potentially unstable situations, paradoxically they also 'promote the very social tensions and insurgencies against which they were initially intended,' as Yessenova (2012: 96) has noted in the case of the Tengiz enclave.

In this 'industrial colony' – as Yessenova calls it – the concentrated work schedule forces not only foreign specialists but also local workers to be isolated from home, whilst the corporation controls their sociality in the living quarters of the rotation camp. Whilst at the time of the ownership transfer in 1993, Tengiz was 'populated by an experienced and well-organised labour force,' the strength of the labour movement has progressively been crushed by the tight control practised by the company over workers' lives and organisation: increasing security on site, switching non-core services – from drilling to catering – to contract labour, creating an employer-sponsored organisation which allowed the administration to cease interacting with 'the old union, which was delegalised and its leaders denied access to company premises' (Yessenova 2012: 102–3). As the exploitation of autochthonous labour stripped of 'paid time off, room and board, transportation to the worksite, and even accident insurance' (Yessenova 2012: 106)[10] grew alongside state regulations on the mandatory 'local content' of the project's employees, so did tensions between this increasingly precarious labour force and foreign workers enjoying substantial employment benefits and salaries up to ten times higher for comparable responsibilities. Episodes of violence – often pitting Kazakh workers against expats – have erupted several times, with peaks in 2004–2006, and as recently as 2019, when the posting of a picture by a Libyan worker beside a Kazakh young female colleague led to the hospitalisation and repatriation of over 40, largely Middle Eastern workers (Sorbello 2019) .

Media assessments of such events (Lillis 2006; Abishev 2010) often tend to dismiss them as crude expressions of ethnic-based xenophobia and bigotry. Such a narrative obscures, however, the regimes of labour governance which, by precarising workers' lives, disciplining them through the threat of layoffs (Labban 2014), repressing their autonomous organising, and adopting practices of labour discrimination filled with ethnic and racial overtones,[11] amount already to a state of existence moulded by structural, latent violence. Whilst this structural violence is also evident in how state security apparatuses subject labour activists to surveillance and harassment, it transmutes into full-fledged repression during workers' strikes, as for instance when Turkmen special security forces arrested 60 workers at the Burun field, developed by Italy's ENI, quashing the strikers' request to increase wages after a series of currency devaluations in 2008 (Sariyev 2008). Or as in the case of a hunger strike in Aqtau in 2017 (Toiken 2017; Leonard and Toleukhanova 2017). Or, more tragically, as in the case of Zhanaozen in 2011. Although the latter would certainly require a separate paper to be addressed, we can still make here a couple considerations on why this oil town has arguably afforded workers a sustained capacity to organise qualitatively different from the one afforded by how extraction is articulated in enclaves such as Tengiz.

In discerning the causes of the 2011 protests in Zhanaozen, conventional analyses have focused on conflicting 'clan' interests, the manipulation of workers' grievances by elites in their power struggles, corruption and the doubling of the city's population in the 2000s due to the inflow of ethnic Kazakhs attracted by the oil boom from neighbouring Turkmenistan and Uzbekistan (Satpayev and Umbetaliyeva 2015; Lillis 2019). Adding to the mix the fact that OzenMunayGas – the company exploiting the field – is state controlled, the 2011 protests have been reduced to the effects of the rentier Kazakhstani state, where 'a high level of corruption' combined 'with a weak system of state management' finally 'culminates in the opaque management of natural resources by a narrow circle of government officials.' In turn, corruption and opaqueness, these studies conclude, breed discontent among the population, particularly in oil-producing regions (Satpayev and Umbetaliyeva 2015: 122).

However, such analyses fall short of taking into account the broader socio-economic transformation which has reconfigured the relationship between the company, its workers and Zhanaozen's population at large. Such a transformation is connected to the restructuring of the city-forming enterprise and the rehabilitation of the Uzen' field between 1997 and 2007, financed by a World Bank loan once government efforts to privatise the company to the Chinese National Petroleum Corporation failed.

By 2007, OzenMunayGas had become the industrial and financial backbone of the newly formed, state-controlled KazMunayGas Exploration and Production (KMG EP). As the World Bank reported, instead of reaching its objective of slowing down or at least contain the field's sharp decline in production and thus 'save the city' (World Bank 2007: 1), the project had caused a progressive, unexpected increase in output: 'the target of the project was to raise [production] to 3.54 million tons in 2000 and then [it would decrease to] 2.96 million tons in 2006. In fact it was 4.1 million tons in 2000 and *then continued rising* to 6.73 million tons in 2006' (World Bank 2007: 5, emphasis added). Accordingly, net cash flow increased from $13.4 million in 1996 to $1.5 billion in 2005 (World Bank 2007: 5), providing KMG EP with the financial resources necessary to fund part of its costs in developing new fields – largely offshore – as well as to partially re-nationalise some of the enterprises sold during the previous decade.

Such an increase in production was achieved by different means: applying new recovery technology whilst substantially reducing the company's social role supporting the city of Zhanaozen in public works, infrastructure and budgets, and privatising construction and drilling operations whilst training a labour force consisting of low-paid ethnic Kazakhs – a substantial part of which were repatriates from Turkmenistan and Uzbekistan – which had been relieving the labour shortage due to the en masse outward migration of Russian and Caucasian workers in the 1990s. Together, these factors amounted to a huge transfer of value from citizens and workers to the company's shareholders on the London and Almaty Stock Exchanges, as well as to executives of KMG EP and the new owners of private service companies. It is at this time that workers' activism started to become louder, and strikes more frequent, forcing both OMG and some of the service companies – such as the drilling company Burgylau – to increase salaries six times between 2008 and 2011[12] (Satpayev and Umbetaliyeva 2015: 126). Thus, rather than corruption or state mismanagement, the rising dissatisfaction among citizens and workers seems to be rooted within the dynamics of accumulation, that is, the intensified extraction of value after the restructuring.

The second consideration has to do with the socio-spatial dimension of extraction. Differently from Tengiz, the town of Zhanaozen stands in proximity to the Uzen' oilfield and, rather than living in an isolated enclave, workers return to the city after their twelve-hour shifts, where they are enmeshed in a 'thick' web of social relations. During the long strike, workers in fact benefitted from extended support networks – family, friends and co-workers – to make up for their lost wages and, after the strike was ruled illegal and many workers returned to work, the remaining ones relied on the same networks for food and clothes whilst occupying the city's central square for months. Moreover, the proximity to the field meant that, instead of being confined to a labour dispute, workers were able to articulate their demands with larger social concerns affecting the city as a whole, such as shortages in drinking water, pollution and health problems, dilapidated housing stock, insufficient cultural and recreational facilities, as well as unemployment, gathering support and sympathy from large parts of the city's population whose direct experience of such issues was part and parcel of an everyday life shaped by oil extraction, whether they worked in the oil sector or not.

Conclusion

Drawing from insights mainly generated by the anthropology of oil and critical geography, this chapter highlighted the networked nature of the actors enabling hydrocarbon extraction in Central Asia, beyond the widespread arguments of the resource curse. Spatially, this emergent global production network reaches well beyond national boundaries, linking oil extraction hot spots to tax havens, stock exchanges and TNCs headquarters, to name a few. Moreover, rather than in the inherent properties of oil – as the 'resource curse' has it – or in Soviet path-dependent legacies, this chapter reviewed literature that helps focus on the analysis of a contemporary Central Asian oil and gas complex within the processes of capitalist transformation observable in the region since the breakup of the USSR.

As the brief example of Zhanaozen encapsulates, processes of capitalist restructuring have been reconfiguring previous Soviet modes of extraction in novel ways. Although the maximisation of shareholder value has come to take precedence over social provisioning after the restructuring of OMG, the former city-forming enterprise could not completely shake off the expectations of the population regarding its social role in the city's life. This has meant that the company has been constrained in its effort to operate along commercial lines alone. Rather than making clear-cut, simplistic distinctions between state-owned and privately owned companies, the case of OMG alerts us to be attentive to the ways in which labour-capital relations – as well as state-corporation-population ones – are shaped in a non-deterministic way and give rise to emergent arrangements. The increasing number of foreign, particularly Chinese, NOCs operating in Central Asia in the last 20 years necessitates a similar analysis rather than a normative separation between well-governed, 'transparent,' global/Western companies on the one hand, and corrupt, violent state-owned ones on the other.

Rather, this chapter showed how states and corporations come to be enacted in their engagement with one another, as well as with financial institutions, workers and citizens. Highlighting the role of artefacts such as contracts and reserves as co-constitutive of companies and states, we have critically reviewed the existing literature in an effort to go beyond the ordinary consideration of oil as just a traded commodity. Instead, in this chapter oil and its extraction are shown as vectors through which social, economic and political relations are constituted and engineered. In this regard, more research needs to be done on how TNCs perform many of the functions generally considered to be the prerogative of states, such as the 'quasi-sovereignty' they enjoy in oil extraction enclaves, or the formulation of projects for the retraining of the unemployed enlisted in state job offices.

Inverting a common trend in studies concerned with oil – whether in political economy, anthropology or geography – we have devoted considerable space to labour, pointing to how strategies of capital accumulation in the oil complex are inextricable from efforts to control and govern workers, the increasing relevance of financial capital notwithstanding. A heterogeneous apparatus has emerged in order to intensify the extraction of value from workers: stigmatising discourses, isolating infrastructural forms, atomising employment regulations and ethnic-based wage differentials have been deployed by capital – whether embodied in TNCs or NOCs – in order to maximise profit while reducing the capacity of workers to resist the increasing precarisation of their lives which, as Trevisani (2018) has noticed in the case of steel workers in Temirtau, tend to transform workers' very understanding of one's labour from 'work-as-resistance' into 'work-for-subsistence.' Future research might thus want to look more closely at how capitalist restructuring in the oil industry affects processes of subject formation and their transformation, in particular among oil workers and populations directly affected by oil and gas extraction (e.g. Yessenova 2018).

Last but not least, more attention needs to be devoted to how nature is 'put to work' (Moore 2016) in the oil complex through discourses and technologies aimed at its control, appropriation and management. In fact, if on the one hand oil and gas operations refashion natural environments – from the displacement of villagers living in proximity of extraction hotspots (Watters 2009), to the recurrent deaths of Caspian seals, to water contamination – on the other hand, they insert 'nature' in their strategies of capital accumulation in order to minimise risk and capital losses by commissioning 'independent' studies on the environment, controlling data on monitoring activities, sponsoring and co-opting local environmental organisations. However, besides reports by international NGOs such as Crude Accountability (2009) and Friends of the Earth Europe (2007), there has been remarkably little research on the environmental impact of oil and gas extraction in Central Asia. More specifically, no research to date has engaged with how local environmental activists and NGOs, together or in opposition to corporations and states, constitute apparatuses of environmental control embodied in corporate social responsibility and 'sustainability' projects through various mechanisms of public engagement. These apparatuses are themselves important components of the oil complex, since debating and managing environmental risk and hazard have become inherent to oil operations in Central Asia, as elsewhere.

Notes

1 Reuters, 'UPDATE 2-Malaysia's Petronas in Uzbekistan Oil-Production Deal,' 14 May 2008.
2 After the London-based credit rating agency Fitch Ibca gave Turkmenistan a B credit rating for hard currency loans, the government received funds from IMF, EBRD, the Japan Overseas Economic Co-operation Fund and the US Export-Import Bank (Canzi 2004).
3 'The field is named after the 19th century Kazakh poet Kashagan Kurzhimanuly. "Kashagan" can also be translated from Kazakh as "unreachable, unattainable," which accurately reflects the field's characteristics due to a unique combination of technical and natural challenges' (Crude Accountability 2017).
4 'Cash All Gone: One of the World's Biggest Oil Projects Has Become a Fiasco,' *The Economist*, 11 October 2014.
5 Taking ExxonMobil as an example, Tim Di Muzio (2015: 38) reflects on how 'as an owner of ExxonMobil's shares, one of your key considerations would be its proven oil and gas reserves, which are booked as assets on the company's balance sheets. Increasing reserves means ExxonMobil has the ability to sell more in the future, and declining reserves means ExxonMobil has less to sell in the future. The former is a good indicator for owners/investors, whereas the latter is not a strong signal of future earning's success – particularly if the company's reserves dip below its rivals.'
6 See the 'Offshore Leaks Database' by the International Consortium of Investigative Journalists [Online]. Available at: https://offshoreleaks.icij.org/.
7 See also the special issue of *Central Asian Survey* (2015, Vol. 34, Issue 1) edited by Heathershaw and Cooley on the subject of 'offshore Central Asia.'
8 Patrucic, Mi., V. Lavrov and I. Lozovsky, 'Kazakhstan's Secret Billionaires,' Organised Crime and Corruption Reporting Project, 5 November 2017.

9 Associated Press, 'Turkmenistan ends free utilities after a quarter century' 26 September 2018.
10 On the flexibilisation of labour markets and precarious work trajectories in the oil sector in Kazakhstan's Aktobe *oblast*,' see Jäger (2014).
11 For a pioneering historical study of the racial differentiations of labour in oil enclaves, see the work of Robert Vitalis (2007; 2002).
12 It is also important to note that a managed devaluation of the tenge currency against the US dollar in 2009 had cut the purchasing power and made imported goods more expensive for local residents.

Bibliography

Abishev, G. (2010). 'Abishev Analytics,' 29 June.
Akiner, S. (2004). 'Caspian Intersections: Contextual Introduction,' in S. Akiner (ed.) *The Caspian: Politics, Energy, and Security*, London and New York: RoutledgeCurzon, pp. 2–12.
Anceschi, L. (2019). 'A Tale of Four Pipelines: The International Politics of Turkmen Natural Gas,' *Spotlight on Turkmenistan, The Foreign Policy Center*, 12 July, 34–41.
Anderson, L. (1987). 'The State in the Middle East and North Africa,' *Comparative Politics*, 20(1): 1–18.
Appel, H. (2012). 'Offshore Work: Oil, Modularity, and the How of Capitalism in Equatorial Guinea,' *American Ethnologist*, 39(4): 692–709.
Appel, H., A. Mason, and M. Watts. (2015). 'Oil Talk,' in H. Appel, A. Mason, and M. Watts (eds.) *Subterranean Estates: Life Worlds of Oil and Gas*, Ithaca and London: Cornell University Press, pp. 1–26.
Associated Press. (2018). 'Turkmenistan Ends Free Utilities after a Quarter Century,' 26 September.
Atabaki, T., E. Bini, and K. Ehsani (eds.) (2018). *Working for Oil: Comparative Social Histories of Labor in the Global Oil Industry*, Basingstoke: Palgrave Macmillan, 11–34.
Auty, R. (1989). 'The Internal Determinants of Eight Oil-Exporting Countries' Resource-Based Industry Performance,' *The Journal of Development Studies*, 25(3): 354–372.
Auty, R. (2004). 'Natural Resources, Governance and Transition in Azerbaijan, Kazakhstan and Turkmenistan,' in S. Akiner (ed.) *The Caspian: Politics, Energy and Security*, London and New York: RoutledgeCurzon, pp. 96–112.
Azhgaliyeva, D. (2014). 'The Effect of Fiscal Policy on Oil Revenue Fund: The Case of Kazakhstan,' *Journal of Eurasian Studies*, 5: 157–183.
Bazhkenova, G. (2017). 'Bezoruzhnyi proletariat,' *Radio Azattyk*, 11 April.
Bohr, A. (2016). 'Turkmenistan: Power, Politics and Petro-Authoritarianism,' Chatham House, Research Paper. https://www.chathamhouse.org/sites/default/files/publications/research/2016-03-08-turkmenistan-bohr.pdf.
Bridge, G. and P. LeBillon. (2013). *Oil*, Cambridge and Malden: Polity Press.
Canzi, G. (2004). 'Turkmenistan's Caspian Resources and Its International Political Economy,' in S. Akiner (ed.) *The Caspian: Politics, Energy and Security*, London and New York: RoutledgeCurzon, pp. 162–79.
Collins, N. and K. Bekenova. (2017). 'Fuelling the New Great Game: Kazakhstan, Energy Policy and the EU,' *Asia Europe Journal*, 15(1): 1–20.
Cooley, A. (2012). *Great Games, Local Rules: The New Great Power Contest in Central Asia*, New York and Oxford: Oxford University Press.
Cooley, A. and J. Heathershaw. (2017). *Dictators without Borders: Power and Money in Central Asia*, New Haven: Yale University Press.
Coronil, F. (1997). *The Magical State: Nature, Money and Modernity in Venezuela*, Chicago: Chicago University Press.
Crude Accountability. (2009). *Turkmenistan's Crude Awakening: Oil, Gas and Environment in the South Caspian*. https://crudeaccountability.org/wp-content/uploads/2012/10/20090116-ReportTurkmenistansCrudeAwakening.pdf, accessed on 29 November 2019.
Crude Accountability. (2017). *The Kashagan Oil Bubble: The Case of an Offshore Field Development in Kazakhstan*. https://crudeaccountability.org/wp-content/uploads/ENG_Kashagan_report_Final1-1.pdf, accessed on 29 November 2019.
Cummings, S. (2003). *Oil, Transition and Security in Central Asia*, London and New York: Routledge.
Dankov, A. (2013). 'Razvitiye ekonomiki Turkmenistana v pervye gody nezavisimosti (1992–1998 gg.),' *Vestnik Tomskogo gosudarstvennogo universiteta*, n. 374. http://journals.tsu.ru/uploads/import/920/files/374-088.pdf, accessed 29 October 2019.
Di Muzio, T. (2015). *Carbon Capitalism: Energy, Social Reproduction and World Order*, London and New York: Rowman and Littlefield.

Ebel, R. and R. Menon (eds.). (2000). *Energy and Conflict in Central Asia and the Caucasus*, Lanham, Boulder, New York, and Oxford: Rowman and Littlefield.

Ehsani, K. (2018). 'Disappearing the Workers: How Labor in the Oil Complex Has Been Made Invisible,' in T. Atabaki, E. Bini, and K. Ehsani (eds.) *Working for Oil: Comparative Social Histories of Labor in the Global Oil Industry*, Basingstoke: Palgrave Macmillan, pp. 11–34.

Ferguson, J. (2006). *Global Shadows: Africa in the Neoliberal World Order*, Durham: Duke University Press.

Ferguson, J. (2005). 'Seeing Like an Oil Company: Space, Security, and Global Capital in Neoliberal Africa,' *American Anthropologist*, 107(3): 377–82.

Franke, A., A. Gawrich, and G. Alakbarov. (2009). 'Kazakhstan and Azerbaijan as Post-Soviet Rentier States: Resource Incomes and Autocracy as a Double 'Curse' in Post-Soviet Regimes,' *Europe-Asia Studies*, 61(1): 109–40.

Friends of the Earth Europe. (2007). *Kashagan Oil Field Development*. http://www.foeeurope.org/sites/default/files/publications/foee_kashagan_oil_field_development_1207.pdf, accessed on 29 November 2019.

Gel'man, V. and D. Marganiya. (2010). *Resource Curse and Post-Soviet Eurasia: Oil, Gas and Modernization*, Lanham and Boulder: Lexington Book.

Heathershaw, J. (2014). 'The Global Performance State: A Reconsideration of the Central Asian 'Weak State,'' in M. Reeves, J. Rasanayagam, and J. Beyer (eds.) *Ethnographies of the State in Central Asia*, Bloomington and Indianapolis: Indiana University Press, pp. 29–54.

Heinrich, A. and H. Pleines. (2012). *Challenges of the Caspian Resource Boom: Domestic Elites and Policy Making*, Houndmills and Basingstoke: Palgrave Macmillan.

Huber, M. (2011). 'Oil, Life, and the Fetishism of Geopolitics,' *Capitalism, Nature, Socialism*, 22(3): 32–48.

IBRD and World Bank. (2015). *World Bank Engagement in Resource-Rich Developing Countries: The Cases of the Plurinational State of Bolivia, Kazakhstan, Mongolia, and Zambia*, Clustered Country Program Evaluation Synthesis Report. http://ieg.worldbankgroup.org/evaluations/wbg-res-rich-dev-countries, accessed on 29 November 2019.

Jäger, P.F. (2014). 'Flows of Oil, Flows of People: Resource Extraction Industry, Labour Markets and Migration in Western Kazakhstan,' *Central Asian Survey*, 33(4): 500–16.

Kalyuzhnova, Y. (2011). 'The National Fund of the Republic of Kazakhstan (NFRK): From Accumulation to Stress-Test to Global Future,' *Energy Policy*, 29: 6650–7.

Kalyuzhnova, Y. and C. Nygaard. (2008). 'State Governance Evolution in Resource-Rich Transition Economies: An Application to Russia and Kazakhstan,' *Energy Policy*, 36(6): 1829–1842.

Karl, T.L. (1997). *The Paradox of Plenty: Oil Booms and Petro-States*, Berkeley: University of California Press.

Kennedy, R. and A. Nurmakov. (March 2010). 'Resource Nationalism Trends in Kazakhstan 2004–2009,' Oslo: Norwegian Institute of International Affairs – RussCasp Working Paper.

Kleveman, L. (2003). *The New Great Game: Blood and Oil in Central Asia*, New York: Grove Press.

Koch, N. (2013). 'Technologizing Complacency: Spectacle, Structural Violence, and 'Living Normally' in a Resource-Rich State,' *Political Geography*, 37: A1–A2.

Labban, M. (2014). 'Against Shareholder Value: Accumulation in the Oil Industry and the Biopolitics of Labour Under Finance,' *Antipode*, 46(2): 477–96.

Leonard, L. (2016). *Life in the Time of Oil: A Pipeline and Poverty in Chad*, Bloomington: Indiana University Press.

Leonard, P. and A. Toleukhanova. (2017). 'Kazakhstan: Authorities Using Intimidation to Quell Labor Unrest,' *Eurasianet*, 2 February.

LeVine, S. (2007). *The Oil and the Glory: The Pursuit of Empire and Fortune on the Caspian Sea*, New York: Random House.

Lillis, J. (2006). 'Oilfield Riot Dents Kazakhstan's Image,' *Eurasianet*, 24 November.

Lillis, J. (2019). *Dark Shadows: Inside the Secret World of Kazakhstan*, London and New York: I.B. Tauris.

Liu, M. (2018). 'Governance and Accumulation around the Caspian: A New Analytic Approach to Petroleum-Fueled Postsocialist Development,' *Ab Imperio*, 2: 169–98.

Logan, O. and J. McNeish. (2012). 'Rethinking Responsibility and Governance in Resource Extraction,' in J. McNeish and O. Logan (eds.) *Flammable Societies: Studies in the Socio-Economics of Oil and Gas*, London: Pluto Press, pp. 1–44.

Luong, P.J. and E. Weinthal. (2010). *Oil is not a Curse: Ownership Structure and Institutions in Soviet Successor States*, New York: Cambridge University Press.

Mitchell, T. (2011). *Carbon Democracy: Political Power in the Age of Oil*, London: Verso.

Moore, J.W. (2016). 'The Rise of Cheap Nature,' in J.W. Moore (ed.) *Anthropocene or Capitalocene? Nature, History, and the Crisis of Capitalism*, Oakland, CA: PM Press, pp. 78–115.

Najman, B., R. Pomfret, and G. Raballand. (2008). *The Economics and Politics of Oil in the Caspian Basin*, London and New York: Routledge.

Nazarbayev, N. (2008). *The Kazakhstan Way*, London: Stacey International.

Ostrowski, W. (2010). *Politics and Oil in Kazakhstan*, London and New York: Routledge.

Patrucic, M., V. Lavrov, and I. Lozovsky. (2017). 'Kazakhstan's Secret Billionaires,' *Organized Crime and Corruption Reporting Project*, 5 November.

Putz, C. (2017). 'Nazarbayev Rants against Offshore Holdings,' *The Diplomat*, 7 December.

Reuters. (2008). 'UPDATE 2-Malaysia's Petronas in Uzbekistan Oil-Production Deal,' 14 May.

Roberts, J. (2003). 'Caspian Oil and Gas: How Far Have We Come and Where Are We Going?,' in S. Cummings (ed.) *Oil, Transition and Security in Central Asia*, London and New York: Routledge, pp. 143–160.

Ross, M. (2001). 'Does Oil Hinder Democracy?,' *World Politics*, 53: 325–61.

Ross, M. (2012). *The Oil Curse: How Petroleum Shapes the Wealth of Nations*, Princeton: Princeton University Press.

Sakal, H.B. (2015). 'Natural Resource Policies and Standard of Living in Kazakhstan,' *Central Asian Survey*, 34(2): 237–54.

Sariyev, O. (2008). 'Zabastovku v Turkmenistane perektratil OMON,' *Deutsche Welle*, 10 June.

Satpayev, D. and T. Umbetaliyeva. (2015). 'The Protests in Zhanaozen and the Kazakh Oil Sector: Conflicting Interests in a Rentier State,' *Journal of Eurasian Studies*, 6: 122–9.

Sauarbek, Z. (2008). 'Kazakh-Chinese Energy Relations: Economic Pragmatism or Political Cooperation?,' *China and Eurasia Forum Quarterly*, 6(1): 79–93.

Shever, E. (2012). *Resources for Reform: Oil and Neoliberalism in Argentina*, Stanford: Stanford University Press.

Sorbello, P. (2019). 'Mass Brawl at Kazakh Oil Field Unveils Labor Dissatisfaction,' *The Diplomat*, 2 July.

Tijerina, S. (2018). 'The Zero-Sum Game of Early Oil Extraction Relations in Colombia: Workers, Tropical Oil and the Police State, 1918–1938,' in T. Atabaki, E. Bini, and K. Ehsani (eds.) *Working for Oil: Comparative Social Histories of Labor in the Global Oil Industry*, Basingstoke: Palgrave Macmillan, pp. 37–67.

Toiken, S. (2017). 'Kak razognali aktsiyu golodovki v Aktau,' *Radio Azattyk*, 22 January.

Trevisani, T. (2018). 'Work, Precarity, and Resistance: Company and Contract Labor in Kazakhstan's Former Soviet Steel Town,' in Chris Hann and Jonathan Parry (eds.) *Industrial Labor on the Margins of Capitalism: Precarity, Class, and the Neoliberal Subject*, New York: Berghahn Books, pp. 85–110.

Tsing, A.L. (2005). *Friction: An Ethnography of Global Connections*, Princeton: Princeton University Press.

Verdery, K. (2004). 'After Socialism,' in T. Nugent and J. Vincent (eds.) *A Companion to the Anthropology of Politics*, Malden: Blackwell, pp. 21–36.

Vitalis, R. (2002). 'Black Gold, White Crude: An Essay on American Exceptionalism, Hierarchy, and Hegemony in the Gulf,' *Diplomatic History*, 26(2): 185–213.

Vitalis, R. (2007). *America's Kingdom: Mythmaking on the Saudi Oil Frontier*, Stanford: Stanford University Press.

Wang, Y. (2006). 'CNPC Signs Second Oil Exploration Deal in Uzbekistan,' *China Daily*, 5 September.

Watters, K. (2009). 'The Fight for Community Justice against Big Oil in the Caspian Region: The Case of Berezovka, Kazakhstan,' in J. Agyeman and Y. Ogneva-Himmelberger (eds.) *Environmental Justice and Sustainability in the Former Soviet Union*, Cambridge, MA and London: MIT Press, pp. 153–88.

Watts, M. (2004). 'Resource Curse? Governmentality, Oil and Power in the Niger Delta,' *Geopolitics*, 9(1): 50–80.

Watts, M. (2009). 'Crude Politics: Life and Death on the Nigerian Oil Fields,' *Economies of Violence Working Papers*, No. 25.

Watts, M. (2011). 'Blood Oil: The Anatomy of a Petro-Insurgency in the Niger Delta, Nigeria,' in A. Behrends, S.P. Reyna, and G. Schlee (eds.) *Crude Domination: An Anthropology of Oil*, New York: Berghahn Books pp. 49–80.

World Bank. (2007). *Kazakhstan – Uzen Oil Field Rehabilitation Project*, Washington, DC: World Bank. http://documents.worldbank.org/curated/en/7417114680%2038646168/Kazakhstan-Uzen-Oil-Field-Rehabilitation-Project, accessed on 29 November 2019.

Yessenova, S. (2012). 'The Tengiz Oil Enclave: Labor, Business, and the State,' *PoLAR: Political and Legal Anthropology Review*, 35(1): 94–114.

Yessenova, S. (2015). 'The Political Economy of Oil Privatization in Post-Soviet Kazakhstan,' in H. Appel, A. Mason, and M. Watts (eds.) *Subterranean Estates: Life Worlds of Oil and Gas*, Ithaca and London: Cornell University Press, pp. 291–306.

Yessenova, S. (2018). "Oil is Our Wet Nurse': Oil Production and *Munayshilar* (Oil Workers) in Soviet Kazakhstan,' in N.T. Atabaki, E. Bini, and K. Ehsani (eds.) *Working for Oil: Comparative Social Histories of Labor in the Global Oil Industry*, Basingstoke: Palgrave Macmillan, pp. 369–98.

Zhukov, S. (2009). 'Uzbekistan: A Domestically Oriented Gas Producer,' in S. Pirani (ed.) *Russian and CIS Gas Markets and Their Impact on Europe*, Oxford: Oxford University Press, pp. 355–94.

21
CORRUPTION

Johan Engvall

Mukhtar Ablyazov is a Kazakh billionaire banker. Once an ally of Kazakhstan's first president Nursultan Nazarbayev and a former minister for energy and trade, he broke ranks with Nazarbayev in 2001 and cofounded the opposition party, the Democratic Choice of Kazakhstan. The leadership retaliated by sending him to jail for abuse of government office in 2002. He was released a year later on the condition of promising to stay out of politics. He eventually became chairman and main shareholder of BTA Bank – a financial institution he had acquired together with a consortium of investors in the 1990s. BTA quickly became the largest retail bank in Kazakhstan, but following a crash in value of many of the bank's holdings and derivatives during the international financial crisis, an audit of the bank discovered a $10 billion shortfall on the bank's books. Ablyazov was accused of masterminding the embezzlement of $6 billion from the bank through a complex array of offshore legal schemes. The bank had approved loans to mailbox entities based in tax havens in which Ablyazov allegedly held significant ownership interest. After the bank was effectively nationalised in 2009, Kazakhstan's prosecutor office launched legal proceedings against Ablyazov, who by that time had fled to London where he was granted political asylum in 2011. Since then, amidst a dozen international court cases, the government of Kazakhstan has pursued a, thus far unsuccessful, worldwide manhunt for Ablyazov's extradition to Kazakhstan. The fugitive banker now resides in France, having run away from a prison sentence in the United Kingdom for acting in contempt of court in attempting to conceal properties acquired in the United Kingdom (Bland 2018).

The story of Ablyazov can be contrasted with the following random example, also originating in Kazakhstan:

A resident in a suburb of Almaty who was required to submit as many as eight official documents to buy a house chose to 'speed up' the process by paying between KZT 1000 and KZT 10,000 for each of document obtained from the respective departments of the local administration instead of waiting for months (Oka 2015).

Ablyazov's alleged funnelling of bank loans to offshore shell companies under his secret control as well as the Kazakh citizen's payments under-the-table to get the permit to buy a house are typical variations on the same theme of corruption. A debated concept subject to multiple definitions, the most common definition of corruption, used by the World Bank and others, is 'the abuse of public office for private gain'. However, as noted by David Lewis, in the neo-patrimonial

DOI: 10.4324/9780429057977-21

political systems in Central Asia, the distinction between the public and private sectors is usually difficult to maintain, as demonstrated in the case of Ablyazov, and individuals with no direct public positions can wield substantial influence over the state. Consequently, he argues that the less specific definition 'the abuse of power for private gain' is preferable (Lewis 2016: 8).

Corruption, thus, encompasses everything from the small sums of money demanded by civil servants in return for legalising documents to the huge amounts that are in circulation in relation to, for example, the procurement of mining contracts or gigantic infrastructure projects. Conventionally, the literature on corruption draws a sharp line between the former, petty corruption, and the latter grand schemes of elite corruption. Petty corruption, on the one hand, is typically seen as a survival strategy among underpaid bribe-taking bureaucrats and ordinary people lacking other means than giving a bribe to access public goods and services (Ergashev 2006; McMann 2014). There are also studies arguing that everyday corruption in Central Asia is sustained by certain social and cultural practices (Urinboyev and Svensson 2013). Grand corruption, on the other hand, is predominantly seen as an entirely different beast, motivated by the insatiable greed of unaccountable political elites. This chapter argues that the inclination to separate between high-level political corruption and low-level administrative corruption, and see them as unrelated, is flawed and does not reflect the reality of the pyramid systems of corruption existing in Central Asia.

In analysing the role of corruption in the political economy of contemporary Central Asia, this chapter first examines the roots and evolution of corruption in the region. Then, it presents the character and structure of systemic corruption and its impact on political, social and economic development in Central Asia. Finally, the chapter turns to the question of why corruption has proved so resilient in the region despite numerous declared initiatives to fight it, both by domestic leaders and by international organisations.

Corruption in Central Asia – roots and evolution

Every so often, journalists and experts report on the widespread nature of corruption in Central Asia, with spectacular examples of greedy politicians and oligarchs channelling funds from corrupt practices to offshore accounts or investments in luxurious properties abroad. Various surveys of public perceptions and global indexes confirm the picture. In Transparency International's global Corruption Perception Index 2018 of 180 states, the average score for the five Central Asian states was 26 on a scale of 0–100 where higher figures means less corruption. This means that the 'average' state in the region would rank in 150th place, in-between Cameroon and Uganda (Transparency International Corruption Perceptions Index 2019). Other indexes and surveys, such as the joint European Bank for Reconstruction and Development (EBRD)-World Bank Business Environment and Enterprise Performance Survey (BEEPS), the World Bank's Worldwide Governance Indicators (WGI) and the University of Gothenburg's Quality of Government (QoG) expert survey on public administration around the world, further corroborate the perception of widespread corruption in the region.

Corruption in post-Soviet Central Asia did not emerge out of nowhere. It has long been recognised to have roots in the Soviet past (Sandholtz and Taagepera 2005). Officially, corruption did not have a place in the Soviet socialist system, but was a phenomenon reserved for capitalist and feudal economic systems. In practice, the situation was markedly different, not least in Soviet Central Asia. Under the tenures of Nikita Khrushchev and, especially, Leonid Brezhnev, Kremlin handed the local Communist Party leaderships in the union republics in Central Asia rather free rein as long as they maintained the degree of social control demanded by the Communist Party in Moscow. In Soviet Uzbekistan, for example, this leeway enabled local actors on all levels in the cotton sector– from the republican leadership to cotton farmers to participate in an elaborate system of fictitious production reports and private pocketing of surpluses (Critchlow 1988: 142–162). This practice of accounting fraud, known in Russian as *pripiski*, stemmed directly from the nature of the planned Soviet economy, in which performance was evaluated by the degree to which a plan was fulfilled. By overstating production, managers could obtain gains in the form of bonuses or reduced oversight, which then were shared with others in the state-owned enterprise (Harrison 2011). In Uzbekistan, this local system ran in parallel to the formal system in Moscow (Rumer 1989).

In the political economy of scarcity that came to characterise the planned Soviet economy, the informal sector increasingly worked in symbiosis with state enterprises and the formal economy (Millar 1985: 700). Informal networks provided access to a variety of resources unobtainable through other channels in the supply-driven socialist bureaucratic system (Ledeneva 1998; Schatz 2004). Moreover, those enterprise directors and bureaucrats charged with fulfilling the five-year plans' often unrealistic output targets had to turn to the growing informal economy to meet the goals as well as provide goods in demand from citizens. In short, the shadow economy developed as an 'alternative system' in response to failures of the command economy (Plekhanov 2004: 77).

That said, corruption in Central Asia emerged on a different level following independence and the transition from the planned economy. The major changing factor in the new states was the unprecedented influx of money, and the effect this had in transforming informal networks to a more market-based logic. At first, the problem was nonetheless poorly understood. The predominant assumption regarding corruption in the Central Asian states, as in other post-Soviet states, was that its burgeoning was a temporary phenomenon and that it would eventually wither away with the consolidation of new political and economic institutions (Cokgezen 2004). During the fumbling attempts to adapt political and economic institutions to the realities of independence, politicians, top bureaucrats and new businessmen acquired control over ministries, state agencies and formerly state-controlled enterprises, essentially turning them into private fiefdoms (Åslund 2007). These processes played out more or less chaotically in Central Asia. In Turkmenistan and Uzbekistan strong authoritarian rule and continued firm state control over the economy made the process less chaotic than in Kyrgyzstan, which introduced both political and economic liberalisation from the outset, or in Tajikistan where fighting over the state's political and economic assets resulted in complete breakdown and civil war. Kazakhstan's government, in turn, liberalised its economic system while resisting political liberalisation (see Freedom House rankings on political freedom and the European Bank for Reconstruction and Development (EBRD) indicators for economic reform, for example EBRD Transition Report 2003).

Since the consolidation of independent statehood in the early 2000s, corruption has not only become more entrenched, but has also become more standardised, centralised and institutionalised. The money involved grew exponentially and the methods applied turned ever more sophisticated. The neo-patrimonial systems in the region provide fertile ground for corruption and undue influence. Instead of formal political groupings, such as ideologically based political parties, informal patron–client networks are the primary competitors for control over political and economic resources in Central Asian states (Ilkhamov 2007; Marat 2012; Peyrouse 2012). These power networks can be divided into three broad categories (Hale 2015).

First, are the regional networks that exist in every country. These can be based on kinship ties or regional affiliation. In Uzbekistan, it is common to talk of local elites from the two largest cities, Samarkand and Tashkent, as the two dominant power groupings. In Tajikistan, the civil war led the northern elite of Khujand, which had run the state in Soviet times, to lose out on power to leaders from the southern region of Kulob; in Kyrgyzstan political power has oscillated between lineage groups from the north and south of the country.

Second, are networks that developed out of economic interests, and often with close ties to the political power. Often referred to as oligarchs, they hold substantial influence over whole sectors of the economy, whether cotton, energy, mineral extraction, real estate, bazaars, or banking. Some of them have roots in the Soviet economic production structures. Others, resembling the famed Russian oligarchs, emerged out of economic liberalisation with interests typically in banking, extraction and trade. In Kazakhstan – the region's wealthiest country – the most powerful oligarchical groupings include first president Nazarbayev's son-in-law Timur Kulibayev, a dominant player in the oil and gas sector. A trio of individuals at the helm of the Eurasian Natural Resources Corporation, with interests in sectors such as metallurgy, coal, mines and finances constitute another particularly strong influence group. Then, there are also Vladimir Kim in the mineral sector, Bulat Utemuratov, principal shareholder of Verny Capital with extensive interests in mining, and Nurzhan Subkhanberdin, chairman of Kazakhstan's largest bank Kazkommertsbank (Peyrouse 2012; Eurasian Center for Political Research & Agency for Social Technology 'Epicenter' 2005). In comparison with Russia's erstwhile oligarchs, Kazakhstan's economic barons have manifested a strong staying power.

Third, are powerful networks within state agencies, particularly those assigned the legal authority to use force and provide revenues to the state. The police, the security services and the customs and tax services have long run what can be described as state protection rackets. Holding top posts in these vital 'cash cows' "open up" for building private fortunes and exerting political influence. In Kyrgyzstan, influential customs officials have been known as *koshelki* (purses) of the presidential families (Engvall 2016). They stretch from Askar Akaev's infamous *koshelek* Muratbek Malabayev to the current president Sooronbai Jeenbekov's highly debated relationship with the former deputy chief of the customs service Rayimbek Matraimov, known in the country under the nickname 'Rayim Million' alluding to his alleged financial appetite (Djanibekova 2019). Matraimov was among those implicated in an award-winning series of investigative articles exposing staggering levels of corruption in Kyrgyzstan's customs service (Radio Azattyk, OCCRP and Kloop 2019).

In all Central Asian states, corruption is about more than greed. It functions as a way to secure the regimes' support among political and economic elites, as well as the vast bureaucracy. Elites provide assets and offices to allies in return for loyalty and cut of the spoils. In this distinct political-economic order, where corruption is institutionalised in the state apparatus, corruption itself is not the problem for leaders. The source of contention is rather when individuals or groups defy the unwritten rules of the game, for example by extracting money from the wrong people or neglecting to share the loot. Thus, it makes sense to distinguish between authorised and non-authorised corruption. In any given Central Asian state, the ultimate arbiter on the matter tends to be the presidential family and its closest circle. In this game of influence, the president is both the player and the ultimate arbiter making sure informal rules are followed and preventing any of the influence groups from becoming too powerful and a potential threat to power. The durability of the system is contingent on the leaders' ability to stand as the guarantor of a stable order. Although these systems may be perceived as stable from the outside, it nevertheless produces frequent conflicts within the elites, which demand constant attention. Occasional anti-corruption purges from the top emerges in this context.

When corruption and rent seeking is systemic, these features are intrinsically linked to political power configurations. Specific resource endowments lead to certain types of rents, the extraction of which raises demand for the creation of certain political institutions and organisation (Markowitz 2013). But formal political institutions also impact the way informal politics, including corruption, is played out. As Henry Hale has documented, in Eurasian states with constitutions stipulating a strong executive power, the dominant informal exchange gravitates toward a single pyramid of informal relations, while centralisation is more difficult to accomplish in countries where power is shared between the president's office and the cabinet (Hale 2015). Thus, practices related to systemic corruption are flexible and quick to adapt to different formal political systems (Engvall 2018).

The political economy of corruption as a mode of governance

Scholarship on corruption often departs from two basic assumptions: first, the state is distinguished from the private market and, second, high-level corruption is separated from low-level corruption. However, at the very least, these distinctions must be qualified in order to capture the realities of contemporary Central Asia.

The linchpin of the systems is the fusion of political and economic capital. Like in most other post-Soviet states, corruption is integral to a system of political and economic power that encompasses both the private and public sectors. The distinction between state and market, or public and private sectors, that is standard occurrence in the research on industrial democracies in the West is difficult to maintain in Central Asia and therefore not always analytically helpful. Even if it is tempting to draw a sharp distinction between countries that undertook significant privatisation, like Kyrgyzstan, and those that did not, notably Uzbekistan, the real situation is more complicated. In these types of systems, even state-owned corporations can have significant informal discretion in how they dispose of their resources. Similarly, the state can exert a strong degree of informal control over private enterprises through various means, including legislative and regulative (Hale 2015).

Approaching the grand schemes of elite corruption and the petty bribes people resort to giving to civil servants in order to speed things up or receive better services, as unrelated misses out fundamental aspects of the character, organisation and consequences of systemic corruption. Those at the bottom of the hierarchy are not purely extracting bribes out of personal greed; they are locked into a system that requires them to pay off their superiors. In this pyramid, corrupt payments are passed upwards in the organisational hierarchy. It is virtually impossible to conceive of the political systems in Central Asia without considering this relationship between clients and patrons. Corruption is the glue that binds the system together, gives it a structure and keeps it from falling apart (Engvall 2016; for a similar view on Afghanistan, see Chayes 2015, and for an early critique of the separation of high and low corruption, see Wade 1982).

The nature of access to public offices lies at the heart of forming this distinct system of governance. The typical recruitment to the notorious traffic police serves as one among several illustrative cases. In Kyrgyzstan, under Kurmanbek Bakiyev's presidency, a job candidate would typically pay approximately $3–5,000 to an intermediary. This broker, who functions as gatekeeper, kept a 10-per cent 'fee' for his services before passing the rest of the money to the head of department of the ministry of internal affairs. While this superior kept about half the sum, the rest was shared among other high-ranking officials in the organisational hierarchy. Similar arrangements regulated decisions on promotions (*Slovo Kyrgyzstana* 2013).

To a considerable extent, the state functions as a kind of corporation that concludes a franchise agreement. Holding certain lucrative jobs, known in Russian as *khlebnye mesta* (literally, bread places), in the state service essentially allows a person to claim the authority, mandate, resources and brand name of the state to collect rents from the position (Engvall 2017). In order for the license not to be discontinued, officials – similar to private franchisees – have to provide a regular supply of payments to their bosses. This dynamic gives the informal market a reciprocal character. Strong informal sanctions punish those who violate the tacit rules. In contrast to legally binding contracts, corrupt agreements cannot be enforced in courts. Instead, various self-regulating mechanisms circumscribe corrupt arrangements. One way to ensure compliance is to keep them within a circle of trusted partners. This helps to secure the longevity of the relations. If both parties trust the exchange to continue in the future, they have a mutual interest in protecting one another (Lambsdorff 2007: 212–215).

Four principal types of rents connected to certain *khlebnye mesta* stand out – economic, protection, territorial and legislative (Engvall 2018). *Economic rents* are extracted from control over economic resource flows. Crucial state structures include financial organs such as the ministry of finance, the national bank and bodies handling state properties, but also natural monopolies in mining, energy, transport, communications, etc. Among the highly priced assets are further private banks and profitable companies. The principles of *otkat* (kickbacks) and *rastrat* (embezzlement) are particularly common in this form of rent. *Otkat* is particularly widely used in public procurement, where officials accept an overpriced bid from a company in order to pocket the difference between the actual price and the stated price. *Rastrat*, in turn, pertains to outright embezzlement of public funds by a bureaucrat from a public project.

Protection rents are extorted from controlling coercion and the state's monopoly on the use of violence. The tax and customs services as well as policing and judiciary bodies are particularly active in dealing with extracting these types of rents. The impunity of law enforcement agencies forces private firms to seek state protection. The common description of this dynamic is to find *krysha*, i.e. a 'roof' under which to protect its business activities. Customs officials typically provide *krysha* for firms dealing with export and import while firms in the domestic service sector tend to stand under the 'protection' of tax officials. Thus, it is the government *krysha* rather than the criminal *krysha* that is the most powerful source of protection, or extortion (on the criminal *krysha* in Russia during the 1990s, see Volkov 2002).

Territorial rents emanate from the administration of territorial authority, both at the provincial (*oblast*) level and at the district (*raion*) level of administration. Local authorities, most notably governors, are delegated control over political and administrative resources at the territorial-administrative level. In some territorial parts where the central state power is weak, regional networks have, at times, been able to create what essentially resemble states within the state with vast influence over appointments and to extract resources and control the provision of goods within their turfs (Radnitz 2017).

Legislative rents, finally, pertain to a number of practices associated with direct access to the parliament. The role of the parliament in rent seeking includes its formal task of passing of legislation, but also a host of other informal functions, such as networking and vote trading, and information gathering and the use of immunity from prosecution as shield for private gains (Spector 2008).

What unites these rents is that they are typically accessed from state offices.

Global connections and domestic consequences

Since academics and policymakers traditionally have treated corruption as a national and law enforcement issue that is especially problematic in developing and ex-communist countries, rather than as an international and security problem, there is a much weaker understanding of the nature of corrupt practices across transnational borders (Kaufmann 2004; Rotberg 2009). In their book *Dictators without Borders*, Alexander Cooley and John Heathershaw have taken important steps to rectify this neglect with regard to Central Asia. With the help of legal cases, investigative reporting, data leaks or international audits, they reveal the extent to which Central

Asian political and economic elites have learned to master the use of global financial institutions and offshore tax havens to conceal their wealth. In 2011, the estimated capital flight in Tajikistan stood at 60 per cent of its GDP (Cooley and Heathershaw 2017).

Notable cases include the so-called *Kazakhgate* scandal. In 2003, New York police arrested American citizen James Giffen and charged him with paying 78 million dollars in bribes to high-level Kazakh officials on behalf of American oil giants in return for lucrative oil contracts in the 1990s. After lengthy criminal proceedings, Giffen, who had been an adviser to president Nazarbayev, pleaded guilty to a specific tax offense. The court dismissed all other prosecutions (LeVine 2007).

In Kyrgyzstan, the Bishkek power plant collapsed in January 2018 depriving thousands of residents in the capital of heating as temperatures plummeted. The failure occurred just months after the completion of major modernisation work on the plant. Subsequently, former Kyrgyz Prime Minister Sapar Isakov and other top officials were arrested and faced charges of corruption regarding the faulty renovation, awarded to a Chinese company for $386 million. Allegedly, this sum exceeded the actual costs of modernisation by more than $100 million, thereby enabling contracted Chinese and Kyrgyz firms' embezzlement on a grand scale (Kapushenko 2018).

In Uzbekistan, according to the Swedish television programme *Uppdrag granskning*, the Swedish-Finnish telecommunications company TeliaSonera had paid a total of $320 million in bribes to an Uzbek company connected to Gulnara Karimova, daughter of then-president Islam Karimov. The payments were made for licenses and access to the Uzbek market and largely went to Takliant, a company with no collateral registered in Gibraltar (*Svenska Dagbladet* 2014).

Corruption in Central Asia is thus not an isolated national or regional problem. The international financial system and its major hubs in the West enable it by providing many opportunities for elites to conceal assets and evade taxes. This dimension must be incorporated in efforts to comprehensively address the problem of corruption.

On the domestic level, the long list of negative political, social and economic impacts of widespread corruption include:

- *Political instability*. Conflict among rival groups over the distribution of resources and rent-seeking opportunities can lead to political instability. Especially in times of political uncertainty, corrupt practices may fuel instability, as was notably the case in Kyrgyzstan in relation to the two revolutions in 2005 and 2010, respectively (McGlinchey 2011). In Tajikistan, the presidential family's aggressive monopolisation of rents has marginalised other elites and supported the evolution of an ever more repressive regime.
- *Tax evasion and shadow economy*. Widespread tax evasion signifies that official statistics only partially reveal the truth about the Central Asian economies. Far more money circulates than officially documented. Entrepreneurs paying the full amount of taxes risk being run out of business since they are at a competitive disadvantage to firms with political connections and favourable tax terms. Throughout the region, representatives of the financial police or the tax service regularly conduct raids on behalf of powerful political and economic individuals or groups against successful private companies in order to gain control over the business activities. Weak private property rights create an insecure business environment and undermine foreign and domestic investment. The absence of rule of law means that cases rarely can be resolved on merit in fair court proceedings. In this context, the formal state institutions provide scant incentives for people to move from informal entrepreneurship, particularly in the bazaar sector, to formal entrepreneurship.
- *Welfare*. Corruption erodes the fiscal basis of the Central Asian states and thereby have a negative impact on welfare. Ordinary Central Asians have had to adjust to low levels of

public goods. In practice, many public services, including healthcare, education, electricity and property protection are of a private nature – available in exchange for payments under-the-table. Under conditions of uncertainty, costliness and inequality in access to state-provided goods, informal networks maintain a significant role in helping ordinary people to secure access to various essential goods, whether through kinship-based practices referred to as *uruuchuluk* in Kyrgyzstan or community-based welfare systems like *mahallas* in Uzbekistan (Ismailbekova 2017; Urinboyev 2013).

Anti-corruption efforts

International donors, such as international financial institutions, United Nations agencies and the European Union (EU) have made programmes on good governance, typically a euphemism for anti-corruption, a key pillar in their development strategies. On the general level, donors' idea of corruption in the region is relatively straightforward: the countries have pursued the wrong policies and enacted wrong pieces of legislation. If the countries adopt new policies, on the basis of best international practice, i.e. policies that have proven successful in developed countries, the situation will improve. Thus, highly corrupt countries should learn from countries with low levels of corruption. Nonetheless, the outcomes of the anti-corruption efforts remain disappointing. When the EU released its new Central Asia strategy in 2019, it included a brief evaluation of the preceding 2007 Central Asia strategy, which noted that the support to anti-corruption efforts had yielded little progress over 12 years (European Parliament 2019: 10).

Most of the programs in Central Asia focus primarily on technical aspects of anticorruption programs while failing to account for the complex systemic dynamics of corruption (Lewis 2016). However, when activities normally qualified as corrupt lie at the heart of political organisation, the system cannot be corrected with a technical fix or by increasing the costs of corrupt behaviour within the existing system (Diamond 2007). Indeed, overall, progress has been very limited in Central Asia. The only partial successes seem to stem from the introduction of electronic payment systems in some sectors and some cities, which led to some reduction in the corrupt exchanges between firms and citizens on the one hand and state officials on the other.

While it is true that Central Asian leaders' launch anti-corruption campaigns with varying degrees of regularity, these have not had any tangible impact on the level of corruption. In Kyrgyzstan, the presidential tenures of Akayev (1990–2005), Bakiyev (2005–10), Atambayev (2011–2017) and Jeenbekov (2018–2020) have all been characterised by the arrest and prosecution of political opponents on corruption charges. Still, with a judiciary subservient to the presidency, anti-corruption campaigns have not represented sincere efforts to eradicate the misuse of public power in the political system. Instead, these measures are applied selectively, fill symbolic purposes and are related to internal strife and the redistribution of power and assets among competing elites (Engvall 2019).

As noted by Lewis, the establishment of special anti-corruption agencies, as long advocated by international donors, are unlikely to achieve any success in present-day Central Asia. 'Any such body will simply become another mechanism for intra-elite struggles over property and rents' (Lewis 2016: 45). In the most blatant example, Tajikistan's president in 2015 appointed his son Rustam Emomali as head of the anti-corruption agency (Trilling 2015). Another drawback with this approach is that it tends to focus on treating the symptoms of corruption but not actually getting rid of the cause of corruption.

When corruption is the mode of governance, reforms must be fundamental and target both the political and economic foundations of corruption. For Central Asian states to curb corruption will require breaking with the current systems in several ways. First, the courts are highly politicised and corrupt. Therefore, save judicial reforms, purging business and political elites will not produce any actual change to the way the overall system works. Second, a clear line must be drawn between political appointments and civil service jobs. Research indicates a strong positive effect on the level of corruption when the interests of politicians and civil servants are clearly separated. Rather than coordinating corruption with bureaucrats appointed by a politician, the separation of politicians' and bureaucrats' careers through meritocratic recruitment gives a professional body of civil servants incentives to check politicians (Dahlström et al. 2012: 656-68). Finally, corruption can hardly be fought in isolation from measures to break up the fusion of political power and economic wealth, i.e. to address the issue of money being the path to political power and political power the source of wealth. In Central Asian corruption, the state serves as the centre of gravity, therefore it is necessary to strengthen the position of the private sector as an alternative path to prosperity and wealth.

Conclusion

Systemic corruption holds several consequences for how to understand the logic of political and administrative organisation in Central Asia. Theoretically, it represents an alternative to the weak state narrative prevalent in scholarship on the region. Rather than seeing the looting of public resources and the under-provision of public goods as symptoms of state dysfunctionality, they represent core mechanisms of the state. In this context, the concept of corruption is largely a misnomer for what is going on. The various types of activities associated with corruption do not infringe upon the formal rules of the state; they are the rules of the game and decisively shape how government officials interact within the state hierarchy and how state officials and citizens interact.

Corruption also functions as political control strategy. The political leadership actively uses corrupt activities for blackmail and control (Darden 2001). A cycle of corruption and informal rule tends to be self-sustaining since no participant has incentives to change behaviour. Partly because they profit from the system, and partly because defection is associated with selective repression on behalf of the power. Corruption in Central Asia is not used only for self-enrichment of elites, it is also a means of maintaining vertical political control; it is initiated from the top, but corrupt money flows from the bottom to the top through a system of patron–client networks sustained by reciprocal pecuniary exchanges. As a mechanism that binds together politics and business, corruption is an integral part of political and economic development in Central Asia. Breaking out of this order will require a strong political push.

References

Åslund, A. (2007) *How Capitalism Was Built: The Transformation of Central and Eastern Europe, Russia, and Central Asia*. Cambridge: Cambridge University Press.

Bland, S.M. (2018) 'The Ablyazov Affair: 'Fraud on an Epic Scale', *The Diplomat*, 23 February. https://thediplomat.com/2018/02/the-ablyazov-affair-fraud-on-an-epic-scale/ (accessed 29 October 2019).

Chayes, S. (2015) *Thieves of State: Why Corruption Threatens Global Security*. New York: Norton.

Cokgezen, M. (2004) 'Corruption in Kyrgyzstan: The Facts, Causes and Consequences', *Central Asian Survey* 23 (1): 79–94.

Cooley, A. and Heathershaw, J. (2017) *Dictators without Borders: Power and Money in Central Asia*. New Haven: Yale University Press.

Critchlow, J. (1988) 'Corruption, Nationalism and the Native Elites in Soviet Central Asia', *Journal of Communist Studies* 4: 142–61.

Dahlström, C., Lapuente, V. and Teorell, J. (2012) 'The Merit of Meritocratization: Politics, Bureaucracy, and the Institutional Deterrents of Corruption', *Political Research Quarterly* 65 (3): 656–68.

Darden, K. (2001) 'Blackmail as a Tool of State Domination: Ukraine under Kuchma', *East European Constitutional Review* 10: 67–71.

Diamond, L. (2007) 'A Quarter–Century of Promoting Democracy', *Journal of Democracy*, 18 (4): 118–20.

Djanibekova, N. (2019) 'Kyrgyzstan Activists Use Satire to Fight Powerful Kingmaker', *Eurasianet*, 14 August. https://eurasianet.org/kyrgyzstan-activists-use-satire-to-fight-powerful-kingmaker (accessed 29 October 2019).

Engvall, J. (2016) *The State as Investment Market: Kyrgyzstan in Comparative Perspective*. Pittsburgh: Pittsburgh University Press.

Engvall, J. (2017) 'License to Seek Rents: 'Corruption' as a Method of Post-Soviet Governance', in J. Heathershaw and E. Schatz (eds.), *Paradox of Power: The Logics of State Weakness in Eurasia*, pp. 73–87. Pittsburgh: University of Pittsburgh Press.

Engvall, J. (2018) 'From Monopoly to Competition: Constitutions and Rent Seeking in Kyrgyzstan', *Problems of Post-Communism* 65 (4): 271–83.

Engvall, J. (2019) 'The Capture of Atambayev and What it Means for Kyrgyz Politics', *Central Asia-Caucasus Analyst*, 10 September. https://www.cacianalyst.org/publications/analytical-articles/item/13585-the-capture-of-atambayev-and-what-it-means-for-kyrgyz-politics.html (accessed 29 October 2019).

Ergashev, B. (2006) 'Public Administration Reform in Uzbekistan', *Problems of Economic Transition*, 48 (12): 32–82.

Eurasian Center for Political Research & Agency for Social Technology 'Epicenter'. (2005) 'Gruppy vliyaniya vo vlastno-politicheskoi sisteme Respubliki Kazakhstan', 29 November.

European Bank for Reconstruction and Development (EBRD). (2003) *Transition Report 2003*. London: EBRD.

European Parliament. (2019) The EU's New Central Asia Strategy. *Briefing*. http://www.europarl.europa.eu/RegData/etudes/BRIE/2019/633162/EPRS_BRI(2019)633162_EN.pdf (accessed 29 October 2019).

Freedom House. (2003) *Nations in Transit 2003*. New York: Freedom House.

Hale, H.E. (2015) *Patronal Politics: Eurasian Regime Dynamics in Comparative Perspective*. New York: Cambridge University Press.

Harrison, M. (2011) 'Forging Success: Soviet Managers and Accounting Fraud, 1943–62', *Journal of Comparative Economics* 39 (1): 43–64.

Ilkhamov, A. (2007) 'Neopatrimonialism in Uzbekistan: Interest Groups, Patronage Networks and Impasses of the Governance System', *Central Asian Survey* 26 (1): 65–84.

Ismailbekova, A. (2017) *The Native Son and Blood Ties: Kinship and Poetics of Patronage in Rural Kyrgyzstan*. Bloomington: Indiana University Press.

Kapushenko, A. (2018) 'Modernizatsiya TETs Bishkeka: kak tratil $386 mln kredita, i chto seichas izvestno', *Kloop.kg*, 19 March. https://kloop.kg/blog/2018/03/19/modernizatsiya-tets-bishkeka-kak-tratili-386-mln-kredita-i-chto-sejchas-izvestno/ (accessed 29 October 2019).

Kaufmann, D. (2004) 'Corruption, Governance and Security: Challenges for the Rich Countries and the World'. October. http://unpan1.un.org/intradoc/groups/public/documents/un-dpadm/unpan044780.pdf (accessed 29 October 2019).

Lambsdorff, J.G. (2007) *The Institutional Economics of Corruption and Reform: Theory, Evidence, and Policy*. Cambridge: Cambridge University Press.

Ledeneva, A.V. (1998) *Russia's Economy of Favours: Blat, Networking and Informal Exchange*. Cambridge: Cambridge University Press.

LeVine, S. (2007) *The Oil and the Glory: The Pursuit of Empire and Fortune on the Caspian Sea*. New York: Random House.

Lewis, D. (2016) 'Tackling Corruption in Uzbekistan: A White Paper', *Policy Report, Open Society Eurasia Program*, June. https://www.opensocietyfoundations.org/uploads/ff271daf-1f43-449d-a6a2-d95031e1247a/tackling-corruption-uzbekistan-20160524.pdf (accessed 29 October 2019).

Marat, E. (2012) 'Kyrgyzstan: A Parliamentary System Based on Inter-Elite Consensus?' *Demokratizatsiya* 20 (4): 325–44.

Markowitz, L.P. (2013) *State Erosion: Unlootable Resources and Unruly Elites in Central Asia*. Ithaca: Cornell University Press.

McGlinchey, E. (2011) *Chaos, Violence, and Dynasty: Politics and Islam in Central Asia*. Pittsburgh: Pittsburgh University Press.

McMann, K.M. (2014) *Corruption as a Last Resort: Adapting to the Market in Central Asia*. Ithaca: Cornell University Press.

Millar, J.R. (1985) 'The Little Deal: Brezhnev's Contribution to Acquisitive Socialism', *Slavic Review*, 44: 694–706.

Oka, N. (2015) 'Informal Payments and Connections in Post-Soviet Kazakhstan', *Central Asian Survey*, 34 (3): 330–40.

Peyrouse, S. (2012) 'The Kazakh Neopatrimonial Regime and Its Actors: Balancing Uncertainties among the 'Family,' Oligarchs and Technocrats', *Demokratizatsiya*, 20 (4): 345–70.

Plekhanov, S. (2004) 'Organized Crime, Business and the State in Post-Communist Russia'. In F. Allum and R. Siebert (eds.), *Organized Crime and the Challenge to Democracy*, pp. 65–82. London: Routledge.

Radio Azattyk, OCCRP and Kloop. (2019) 'Power and Patronage in the Heart of Central Asia', 21 November. https://www.occrp.org/en/plunder-and-patronage/ (accessed 22 June 2020).

Radnitz, S. (2017) 'Power, Peripheries, and Pyramids in Post-Soviet Kyrgyzstan and Georgia', in J. Heathershaw and E. Schatz (eds.), *Paradox of Power: The Logics of State Weakness in Eurasia*, pp. 44–59. Pittsburgh: University of Pittsburgh Press.

Rotberg, R.I. (2009) *Corruption, Global Security, and World Order*. Washington, DC: Brookings Institution Press.

Rumer, B. (1989) *Soviet Central Asia: 'A Tragic Experiment'*. Boston: Unwin Hyman.

Sandholtz, W. and Taagepera, R. (2005) 'Corruption, Culture, and Communism', *International Review of Sociology*, 15 (1): 109–131.

Schatz, E. (2004) *Modern Clan Politics: The Power of 'Blood' in Kazakhstan and Beyond*. Seattle: University of Washington Press.

Slovo Kyrgyzstana. (2013) 'Prichiny i skhemi koruptsii v sisteme DPS', 25 December. http://slovo.kg/?p=28754 (accessed 29 October 2019).

Spector, R.A. (2008) 'Securing Property in Contemporary Kyrgyzstan', *Post-Soviet Affairs* 24 (2): 149–76.

Svenska Dagbladet. (2014) 'Telia riskerar miljardböter', 24 March. https://www.svd.se/telia-riskerar-miljardboter (accessed 29 October 2019).

Transparency International. (2019) 'Corruption Perceptions Index 2018'. https://www.transparency.org/cpi2018 (accessed 29 October 2019).

Trilling, D. (2015) 'Tajikistan's Strongman Appoints Son to Lead Corruption Fight', *Eurasianet*, 16 March. https://eurasianet.org/tajikistans-strongman-appoints-son-to-lead-corruption-fight (accessed 29 October 2019).

Urinboyev, R. (2013) *Living Law and Political Stability in Post-Soviet Central Asia: A Case Study of the Ferghana Valley in Uzbekistan*. PhD dissertation. Lund University.

Urinboyev, R. and Svensson, M. (2013) 'Corruption in a Culture of Money: Understanding Social Norms in Post-Soviet Uzbekistan', in Baier, M. (ed.), *Social and Legal Norms: Towards a Socio-Legal Understanding of Normativity*, pp. 267–284. Farnham: Ashgate.

Volkov, V. (2002) *Violent Entrepreneurs: The Use of Force in the Making of Russian Capitalism*. Ithaca: Cornell University Press.

Wade, R. (1982) 'The System of Administrative and Political Corruption: Canal Irrigation in South India', *Journal of Development Studies* 18 (3): 287–328.

22
MODERNISATION AND DEVELOPMENT IN CENTRAL ASIA

Liga Rudzite and Karolina Kluczewska

When international donors arrived in the Central Asian region in the 1990s, they saw it as a fertile terrain for their activities. With the Soviet collapse in 1991, the region suddenly became 'post-Soviet.' The prefix 'post-' left room for imagination of what it might become after almost seven decades under communist ideology. Donors believed Central Asia could be redesigned in accordance with the Western democratic and capitalist 'standards.' And yet, as Eric Sievers (2003: 1) pointed out, a few years before the donors' arrival, people in Central Asia 'overwhelmingly identified themselves as superpower citizens, as comparatively wealthy, and as distinct from their southern neighbours.' In such a case, could the Soviet past be effectively erased and a prosperous, Western-like future built?

After almost three decades of development initiatives, it appears that donors' expectations have not materialised as planned. As several authors have shown referring to different fields of international intervention – spanning from border management (Czerniecka and Heathershaw 2010) to monetary reform (Broome 2010), business (Ozcan 2010) and healthcare (Ackner and Rechel 2015) – many donor-funded initiatives in Central Asia were highly self-referential. They reflected the funders' priorities and *their* reading of local needs. This, however, does not mean that such interventions did not produce durable results, even if these were often different than anticipated (Kluczewska 2019). It is important to recognise that the outcomes of development projects have to do with complex implementation practices on the ground. Projects inevitably depend on everyday interactions between international and local actors, and involve negotiations of often divergent imaginaries of development. Soviet legacies should also not be overlooked. Thirty years after the Soviet collapse, policy-making in all Central Asian countries continues to be a domain of Soviet-trained cadres, and often the most active civil society leaders are still the former Komsomol members (Kluczewska and Foroughi, forthcoming). Furthermore, as Philipp Lottholz (2018a) argued, the 'old slogans [are] ringing hollow.' Soviet-inspired notions of development, achievable through industrial development and social engineering, are re-emerging across Central Asia – wrapped in banners of new national ideologies.

Given the persistence of Soviet legacies in development thinking in the region today, we start this chapter by briefly outlining the Soviet-era development model (which we refer to as 'Soviet modernisation'). We then provide an overview of three decades of donor-funded development initiatives in Central Asia after 1991 (which we describe interchangeably as 'international devel-

DOI: 10.4324/9780429057977-22

opment' and 'development cooperation'). In our analysis, we pay attention to the multiplicity of actors and heterogenous imaginaries of development on the ground, as well as an interplay between international projects and local state and nation-building processes. We also provide two case studies that explore the most recent trends in two countries in the region, Tajikistan and Kyrgyzstan. For nearly 30 years, both countries have been top-aid recipients in the region. However, as we explain below, their interactions with international donors have always differed significantly between the two cases. Finally, the conclusion outlines possible areas for future research on international development in the region.

Soviet modernisation and its legacies

The roots of Soviet modernisation go back to the October Revolution in 1917 and a rupture with the ideological and structural foundations of the Russian Empire. The Bolsheviks wanted the Soviet Union to become a strong, industrialised and socialist state, and, with regard to its peripheral zones such as Central Asia, anti-imperial and anti-colonial. The 1920s and 1930s in this region were thus characterised by Moscow-led rapid industrialisation, sedentarisation, and collectivisation. Ambitious infrastructure projects followed. They included the building of the Turksib, a railway connecting Central Asia with Siberia, the so-called Pamiri Highway (Mostovlansky 2017) and the Vakhsh River Valley which allowed irrigation and expanded farmland in Soviet Tajikistan (Reid 2017). After Stalin's death, Central Asia again received more attention from Moscow. Nikita Khrushchev's intensified engagement in the cold war has subsequently led to a rapprochement with the Third World countries in the 1950s and 1960s. As Artemy Kalinovsky (2018: 20) argued, 'the wave of decolonization occurring beyond the USSR's borders provided the impetus to complete the "decolonization" of the Central Asian republics within a Soviet framework.'

This framework included further industrialisation through five-year plans by giving more ownership to Central Asian Soviet republics and fostering local expert knowledge. It also involved a promotion of what Malika Bahovadinova (2018: 278) described as 'mutual constitution of the Soviet state and Soviet citizens.' Undoubtedly, people's labour allowed for extraordinary economic growth across the Soviet Union. Simultaneously, it served as a tool of Soviet socialisation. This was visible, for example, during the Virgin Lands campaign, launched in the mid-1950s in Soviet Kazakhstan with the aim of turning the steppe into fertile land, or during construction of massive man-made dams in Toktogul in Kyrgyzstan and Nurak in Tajikistan in the 1960s and 1970s (Féaux de la Croix and Suyarkulova 2015; Kalinovsky 2018). Development of mass-scale infrastructure was accompanied by the Soviet state's commitment to social welfare and provision of infrastructure facilitating everyday life – schools, kindergartens and playgrounds. Physical modernisation served societal advancement and aimed at improving the livelihoods of Soviet citizens (see Kalinovsky's chapter in this edited volume).

The formation of social life was another important component of the Soviet development project. This occurred by encouraging people's participation in state-led civil society – which in theory was voluntary, although in practice it was often mandatory. Such civil society included a broad range of institutions, starting from trade unions and cooperatives, the youth organisation *Komsomol* and educational circles (knows as *kruzhki*), and, particularly in the case of Muslim Central Asia, women's councils (*zhensovety*) (see Karimov 2008: 143). These institutions, operating on all administrative levels across the vast Soviet space, promoted a vision of citizenship based upon notions of solidarity, social justice and an equalised consumption of goods. Notably, until now the English-language history of civil society excludes the Soviet model, presumably because it was state-led. The dominant, Western model of civil society, on the contrary, implies that civic activism should not only be independent from the state, but also provide a counter-balance to the latter (see Putnam 1993).

Like Soviet civil society, while Soviet development efforts were glorified in Soviet historiography, particularly referring to industrialisation (Lelchuk 1984), they were downplayed or omitted in the history of international development written by scholars affiliated with Western research institutions, both in its mainstream (Lancaster 2008) and critical versions (Rist 2014; Kothari 2016). Soviet modernisation advanced economic growth and established and improved public service delivery in many parts of Central Asia. Nevertheless, on many occasions it missed its objectives, *de facto* reinforcing hardships and institutional, cultural and linguistic power hierarchies between the Soviet centre and peripheries (Bahovadinova 2018: 291; Abashin 2015). Importantly, however, the Soviet development model continues shaping local imaginaries of 'proper' development in contemporary Central Asia.

International development in Central Asia

The 1990s: One-size-fits-all support for democratisation and the free market

The establishment of an international development regime in Central Asia was greatly facilitated by a race of newly independent Central Asian states to join regional and international organisations, which started in the early 1990s. Becoming members of the international community brought international recognition to newly independent states and subscribing to international human-rights-related treaties made them eligible for development aid. The first phase of international development in Central Asia can be thus described as a set of programmes and projects fostering transition from socialism and centralised economy to democracy and free market, with humanitarian assistance serving as a carrot. Bearing in mind a relative transitional success of Central and Eastern European states, which after 1989 started enthusiastically moving beyond their socialist experience and actively embraced both the liberal norms and the market economy, international donors believed that a similar liberal socialisation process could be replicated in Central Asia (Lewis 2012: 1222). This approach assumed that democratisation can be 'aided' from abroad (Carothers 2011) and that democracy and the free market can be installed locally by external actors.

In the 1990s, internationally funded development included a broad range of interventions, which, however, often followed a one-size-fits-all logic. To start with, multilateral lenders, led by the International Monetary Fund (IMF) and the World Bank, began providing grants and concessional loans to foster capitalist market formation through privatisation of former state assets, tax reforms and stabilisation of state budgets (Broome 2010). From the donors' perspective, as Alexander Cooley (2000: 37) put it, 'both conditional assistance and technical assistance [were] supposed to promote institutional change and help consolidate newly introduced market mechanisms.' Democratisation interventions followed. In this field, the United States Agency for International Development (USAID) aspired to play a pivotal role by supporting political pluralism by fostering fair and free elections, formation of a party system, and drafting of liberal laws which would guarantee, among others, an independent judiciary (Omelicheva 2015: 36). As part of these democratisation efforts, donors started funding a new model of civil society in the region. So-called non-governmental organisations (NGOs) were supposed to provide a counter-balance to state institutions (Buxton 2011). These first development interventions were characterised by an underlying anti-Soviet approach (Sievers 2003). They aimed to create neoliberal subjects, as opposed to *New Soviet People*, that Soviet modernisation had fostered.

Table 22.1 Net ODA and Official Aid Received by Central Asian Countries (in million USD)

	1992	1995	2000	2005	2010	2015	2018
Tajikistan	11.8	65.1	124.1	252.4	433.1	527.1	397.5
Kyrgyzstan	21.1	284.7	214.7	267.5	383.9	770.0	465.0
Uzbekistan	1.5	83.7	186.4	169.1	234.4	447.8	556.0
Kazakhstan	12.1	64.8	189.2	225.3	211.8	82.5	75.6
Turkmenistan	6.6	30.7	35.5	29.1	43.8	23.6	17.9

Compiled based on the World Bank's data https://data.worldbank.org/indicator/DT.ODA.ALLD.CD

Table 22.1 shows the net official development assistance (ODA) to Central Asia, consisting of grants and disbursements of loans made on concessional terms by the members of the Development Assistance Committee (DAC) of the Organisation for Economic Co-operation and Development (OECD). In the 1990s, ODA has been steadily growing throughout the region.

While statistical data can show us tendencies with regard to disbursements, some additional explanation is needed to understand the differentiations in the volume of aid to various countries in the region. Besides donors' overall ideological, transition-oriented approach, in the 1990s international assistance to the region largely reflected specific donors' geopolitical and economic interests. For example, from the beginning of the European Union's (EU) engagement with Central Asia, this organisation maintained pro-active, lively relations with oil-endowed Kazakhstan and gas-rich Turkmenistan, and less dynamic interactions with resource-poor Kyrgyzstan and Tajikistan (Omelicheva 2015: 35; Kluczewska and Dzhuraev 2020: 227-228). As a result of trade-related agreements which the EU signed with Kazakhstan and Turkmenistan, European companies were able to invest in extraction-related infrastructure and access new markets in both countries (Paramonov et al 2017: 26, 83).

International development has never been a one-sided enterprise and the role played by Central Asian aid recipients should not be neglected. Both internal developments in individual countries of the region and political elites' extractive attitudes towards donors greatly influenced the outcomes of development projects. Table 22.1 shows that Kyrgyzstan, which under president Askar Akayev actively entered the path of economic liberalisation and market reforms, received the biggest share of international assistance to the region in the first decade after independence, with a peak of 284,7 million USD in 1995. In this context. complying with donors' visions should be viewed as a deliberate strategy, rather than as a submissive attitude or weak agency in international affairs. On the opposite side of the spectrum, as a result of a growing self-isolation of Turkmenistan under Saparmurat Niyazov aid allocated to this country was 10 times lower than in Kyrgyzstan. As for Tajikistan, against a common misconception, despite an ongoing civil war (1992–1997) and associated peacebuilding and humanitarian assistance (Heathershaw 2009: 30–32), the volumes of aid in this country did not differ much from assistance received by Kazakhstan and Uzbekistan.

The 2000s: Turn to security, growing scrutiny and differentiating donor-recipient relations in the region

As the transitional focus of development cooperation in Central Asia became increasingly challenged in the 2000s, the emphasis shifted from democratisation to 'development.' With a significant increase in volumes (see Table 22.1), scaling up and diversification of international development across Central Asia, the aid architecture in that period moved towards favouring transborder, regional and sector-wide approaches. Technically, besides (declining) humanitarian assistance, it incorporated project and programme aid, as well as budget support measures. While traditional development sectors, such as health and education, remained important, peace-building, conflict prevention and security-related reforms dominated the development efforts from the late 1990s well into the 2000s.

The Ferghana Valley had been on security radars since the late 1980s as a territory of potentially violent conflicts. It, however, received particular attention from development agencies only in the late 1990s. The military incursions of the Islamic Movement of Uzbekistan (IMU) to Kyrgyzstan and Uzbekistan in 1999 and 2000, as well as the ending of Tajikistan's civil war contributed to donors' interests in setting up various security-oriented programmes in the region. Luigi De Martino's (2001) inventory on early conflict prevention and resolution programmes identifies a broad variety of donors' intervention tools in Central Asia, from early warning systems to civil society and democracy-building activities.

The frequent, although small-scale, border clashes in the Ferghana Valley were seen as proof of the necessity of such interventions (Kim 2014). However, they often had less to do with (in) security experienced by people in Central Asia and more to do with development actors' failure to understand the region, resulting in potentially damaging aid practices (Heathershaw and Megoran 2011). For example, donor-funded conflict mitigation in the porous and contested borders of Ferghana relied on technical and military solutions to political issues. This led to diminishing interactions between neighbouring cross-border communities and further exacerbated insecurity (Reeves 2014).

Another major shift was caused by the events of 9/11 and launching of the 'global war on terror,' starting from the military campaign Enduring Freedom in Afghanistan. Given Central Asia's new strategic relevance for the USA (Cooley 2012), these events resulted in a boom of regional anti-trafficking, counter-narcotics and border control programmes (Czerniecka and Heathershaw 2010; De Danieli 2011). Table 22.1 shows that nearly all countries in the region, including self-isolating Turkmenistan, benefited from the newly gained international attention. For example, between 2001 and 2006 aid received by Kyrgyzstan and Tajikistan increased by 65% and 46% respectively. Military aid, which in the early 2000s was declared as foreign military financing by the USA (USAID Foreign Aid Explorer 2020), in the second part of the decade started to be seen locally as controversial, as, under the aegis of fighting international terrorism, it contributed to the strengthening of security services across the region.

Across the development sector, donors' tools and aims were increasingly scrutinised by both beneficiaries and the academic community. Development agencies were criticised for 'seeing like a project' and addressing social issues as a series of easily manageable activities (Bichsel 2009), thus overlooking complex local contexts and power dynamics (see Megoran et al. 2005; Heathershaw 2009a). Development actors' approach was seen as homogenising beneficiaries into static and ahistorical groups, limiting chances for the most vulnerable to benefit from projects (Simpson 2006; Kim et al. 2018). Donors' competition for local partners contributed to a stereotype of local civil society organisations as subordinated and dependent on foreign aid (Simpson 2006).

While the EU started dealing with broader issues of development and established itself cumulatively as one of the largest donors in Central Asia, albeit a rather invisible one (Bossuyt 2018), a significant share of criticism was directed at its good governance, human rights and democracy promotion efforts (Matveeva 2006; Sharshenova 2018). Academic research showed that the EU continued prioritising geopolitical and economic self-interest rather than the declared noble principles at the core of its assistance (Crawford 2008; Warkotsch 2008; Hoffmann 2010). The EU was not the only donor criticised for putting economic benefits first. Also, South Korea's approach of development through democratisation (Hwang 2012) was seen as reflecting donor's own interests and pursuing neoliberalism, at the same time providing entry points for the country's chaebols into new markets (Schwak 2020).

Public disappointment with socio-economic hardships continued despite many donor-funded projects aiming at alleviating such difficulties. Moreover, internal political struggles and processes of power consolidation made Central Asian governments reconsider their engagement with the 'traditional' aid donors.[1] As a result, some big projects were not completed in accordance with the initial plan. For example, the UN Ferghana Valley Development Programme, developed in 1999, was never fully implemented due to its boycott by the Uzbek government. Following the so-called colour revolutions in the post-Soviet space, the governments curtailed access of non-state sanctioned NGOs to international funding in Uzbekistan and Turkmenistan, and increased scrutiny of civil society organisations in Kazakhstan and Tajikistan (Buxton 2011: 26). Channelling aid through NGOs, as local implementors of donors' projects, remained relatively free in Kyrgyzstan. But even there, due to a lack of understanding of the nature of the local civil society on part of donors, international funding often failed to reach targeted communities (Axyonova and Bossuyt 2016).

In parallel with gradual reconsidering of their relations with Western donors, the governments in the region started to turn to non-Western, emerging donors offering economic, infrastructural, and humanitarian assistance with seemingly no strings attached. Several of such donors had been present in the region since independence and relied on historical, linguistic or religious commonalities with the Central Asian region. Against the backdrop of their increasing importance globally, development support from Turkey, as well as *zakat* flows[2] and loans from the Gulf States (see for example Li (2019) on Saudi Arabia and Koch (2017) on Qatar) increased significantly. The institutional frameworks for Islamic finance for development also expanded (Sharipov and Yuldashev 2019). Russia, however, remained the most anticipated and trusted donor in Central Asia.

When Moscow announced becoming a development donor during the G8 Summit in Saint Petersburg in 2006, Central Asia was high on its agenda. While comparatively low in volume, Russia's development assistance was implemented primarily through multi-donor trust funds and supported education and food programs, especially in Tajikistan and Kyrgyzstan. Russia also channelled a large part of its humanitarian aid to Central Asia (Brezhneva and Ukhova 2013; De Cordier 2016). The largest share of development finance related to Russia, however, were the remittances sent home by Central Asian labour migrants working in that country, which grew considerably, especially in the mid-2000s. The significance of remittances and the share of new donors in the Central Asian aid architecture continued to increase in the 2010s. These developments were accompanied by further discussions about the aims and means of 'proper' development interventions on the part of local elites and beneficiaries alike.

The 2010s: Multiple ideas of development, new donors and changing aid landscapes

The opportunity to receive foreign funding for NGOs remained under strain in most Central Asian countries throughout the last decade (Gussarova and Andzans 2018). Project-based aid began to increase again in the mid-2010s, in particular in Kyrgyzstan and Tajikistan (see Table 22.1). The largest part of the 'traditional' development assistance was composed of technical assistance, budget support, and ever-larger scale, sector-wide, multi-donor, and transnational programmes and projects. It is worth mentioning, for example, projects aiming to improve water and land management with the focus on the Aral Sea (Kim 2018), extension of the EU's Border Management Programme in Central Asia (BOMCA) and Central Asia Drug Action Programme (CADAP). However, with a significant increase of the so-called South–South cooperation in the region, the concessional loans and infrastructural development projects became the most common type of foreign assistance in the region.

These changes in the development landscape in the 2010s were largely spearheaded by Central Asia's eastern neighbour, China. Since launching its 'going out' strategy in 2000, China has been increasing its investments, grants, and loans for infrastructure and extraction projects abroad. These amounts surged after the announcement of the Belt and Road Initiative (BRI) in 2013, when China promised development investment amounting to tens of billions USD (Yakobashvili 2013), impressing Central Asian leaders. With their eager acquiescence, China became the largest investor in Central Asia and asserted itself as one of the biggest donors to Central Asia, even though the exact amounts of development aid were never revealed. China's focus on technical assistance and transportation connectivity as a key to economic growth blurred lines between development loans (as understood within ODA) and foreign investment. Nevertheless, the self-proclaimed lack of political conditionality of China's development cooperation, favoured by Central Asian governments, has met with the general public's growing fears of loss of state sovereignty under the weight of growing state debts.

Irrespective of which vision of development and implementation modalities are more beneficial for the region, the Western donors' or Chinese ones, China's arrival has shown that the assistance provided by emerging donors can be more aligned with the needs expressed by the recipient countries (Dunford 2020), less costly operationally and faster in reaching its target. These features make Chinese aid more effective and efficient (Kim and Lightfoot 2011). At the same time, despite the rhetoric suggesting the opposite, China's aid is inherently conditional and self-referential (Tian 2018). It involves exporting its development model to other parts of the world, monopolising new markets and gaining access to resources (Jaborov 2018). Rather than being a new project, BRI consolidated previously established, sparse initiatives of the Chinese government (Odgaard 2017).

As in other parts of the world, the spread of Chinese high-tech surveillance technologies across Central Asia has also caused concern among analysts and scholars. Claiming to assist the enforcement of rule of law which prioritises public order, these technologies simultaneously threaten the West-driven, values-based approach to law enforcement (Marat 2018). The fast expansion of Chinese aid, along with a lack of transparency and accompanying corruption, has fuelled significant distrust in Chinese donors among Central Asian societies (Bossuyt 2018).

Importantly, China should not be seen as a homogenous development agent. As Irna Hofman's (2016) work on Chinese farm enterprises in Tajikistan demonstrated, there is much to learn about the complexity of Chinese development landscape and diversity of actors engaging in it. More attention should also be paid to China's assistance in the people-to-people realm through, for instance, Confucius Institutes established in the region (Nursha 2018). China is also playing a significant role in supporting the health sector in Central Asia.

The growing influence of China encountered Russia's expanding development work in Central Asia, including bilateral assistance and focus on development finance (Dobrolyubova 2019). In 2013, Russia expanded the mandate of its national development agency, the Federal Agency for the Commonwealth of Independent States, Compatriots Living Abroad and International Humanitarian Cooperation (commonly known as *Rossotrudnichestvo*), to include international development assistance, and in 2014 established the first of the kind Russian-Kyrgyz Development Fund (RKDF). Against the backdrop of the global financial crisis of

2007–2008, Russia's confidence in what it could deliver in terms of development cooperation grew. At the Astana Economic Forum in 2013 one of the panels discussed the creation of a non-Western-centric financial system where development would be conceived as *Razvitie* (the Russian word for it, anglicised). This was perceived as a challenge to the Western monopoly of development (Sharshevnova 2018: 132), but it did not result in much action, as Russia's aid disbursements declined in the late 2010s.[3]

Among concessional loans, development finance, investment in infrastructure, as well as all-encompassing transnational projects that dominate the development landscape in Central Asia, Japan's development cooperation's turn has been an exception. Given the declining interest of Japanese companies in Central Asia (Dadabaev 2016), resources have been refocused to support local communities. Examples of these are One Village, a one-product programme in Kyrgyzstan, and the Water Users Association support programme in Uzbekistan. This illustrates another trend emerging within international development, when donors resort to less risky projects with measurable indicators that can showcase their successes. These initiatives, however, are less visible because attention is usually paid to big industrial and infrastructural development projects.

Current development landscapes
Tajikistan: Changing development architecture and power relations

Almost 30 years since the donors' arrival in Tajikistan, internationally-funded development interventions in the country to a large extent remain donor-driven. Rigid project frameworks ease reporting, but rarely allow donors and local implementers to address complex social processes. What has changed over time, however, are local perceptions of international development. This has to do with three trends: consolidation of a distinctive social class of local development workers; arrival of new donors and, consequently, an increasing heterogeneity of available development visions; as well as the emergence of the state's vision of what development (Tajik: *peshraft*) entails.

In development literature, local aid workers are often described as brokers (Lewis and Mosse 2006), given that they represent the so-called 'international community' on the ground (Heathershaw 2016). After three decades of international development, a new social group composed of local development workers established itself in Tajikistan. While working at local offices of donor agencies, international organisations (IOs) and international NGOs, these individuals implement projects and simultaneously appropriate their goals to avoid potential disagreements with the Tajik government. Currently, there are about 30 international and regional organisations, 9 UN agencies and 46 international NGOs present in the country,[4] in addition to hundreds of subcontractors, consultants and various implementing partners. This new social class consists of a few thousand professionals who grew up in Tajikistan, but at the same time are fluent English speakers and increasingly Western-educated. It is crucial to recognise the relevance of brokers to understand why Western-funded international development in Tajikistan has operated for years without major contentions between liberal norms promoted from outside and local re-traditionalising trends. Brokers' intersectional positionality and mastery over 'development buzzwords and fuzzwords' (Cornwall 2007), as well as their ability to maintain good relations both with donors and state actors, allow them to effectively create bridges between the two sides (Kluczewska 2018: 225–229).

As for new development architects, starting from the early 2010s an increasing number of non-Western donors have been working in Tajikistan. New donors, often states rather than multilateral organisations, frequently conflate development goals with foreign investment and loans. In 2006, China launched its projects in Tajikistan – seven years before Xi Jinping officially announced the Chinese global development strategy One Belt One Road, later renamed as BRI. Although only 5 per cent of Tajikistan's territory is arable, Chinese enterprises have been particularly interested in the agro-industrial and food market in the country. While multiple Western-funded rural development projects implemented over the years failed because of, for example, established patronage networks, China proved to be more effective in pursuing its land investment – despite negative societal perceptions of this country in Tajikistan (Hofman 2016). One reason behind China's success on the ground is considerable investment accompanying Chinese projects, which many Western projects, focusing on capacity-building and skill transfer, lack. Undoubtedly, financial incentives without visible normative conditionality have also allowed China to gradually gain support from the Tajik government. Researching Chinese investment and development initiatives, however, poses a challenge because neither China nor Tajikistan provide aggregated data on the scope and volume of this cooperation.

Other new, although significantly smaller development and investment partners of Tajikistan are Japan, South Korea, Turkey and India (Dadabaev 2018). Unlike China, all of them enjoy a predominantly positive image among the local population. As for fields of assistance, Japan has been providing grants for infrastructure development in the country –schools, hospitals and roads (Rakhimov 2014). In contrast with 'traditional' donors, the new donors tend to focus on technical assistance and transportation connectivity, without explicitly promoting liberal norms. Furthermore, the multiplicity of development donors and a subsequent diversity of available development imaginaries offer Tajik policy-makers a leverage to choose partners and allow them to negotiate their own priorities more effectively.

While until recently Tajik policy-makers could choose between different donors' development imaginaries but lacked their own vision of development, this is no more the case. The Tajik government's development model draws on several sources which at first glance might seem contradictory. As mentioned in the introduction, Soviet legacies are becoming increasingly visible in a longing for a strong welfare state which controls economic and social developments. Tajik policy-makers are thus increasing social spending (Asia Plus 2019a), while at the same time struggling with a limited state budget at their disposal. Such initiatives are regularly criticised by Western development agencies who argue that they are both too expensive and counter-productive, and instead advocate for a neoliberal development model with limited interference of the state in the market (Asia Plus 2019b).

The 'Tajikisation' of the public space is another manifestation of the state development model. Administrative buildings, hospitals, schools and construction sites across the country are covered with slogans fostering development in the realm of state and nation-building priorities. They incentivise pride in a glorious, ancient history of the Tajik nation and glorify the country's independence (Tajik: *istiqloliyat*) after the Soviet collapse, at the same time avoiding giving any account of the Soviet past. There is also a specific heteronormative dimension of this development discourse which concerns promoting the family unit as a basis of social unity. From a decolonial perspective, this can be seen as the government's attempt to provide a local alternative to the neoliberal development model and seemingly Western values – such as individualism and self-reliance, even if this alternative is largely nationalist and patriarchal (Kluczewska 2018: 236-238).

Finally, the Tajik government's development vision is characterised by an attachment to physical infrastructure, seen as an indicator of progress. On the one hand, this recalls the bases of Soviet-era modernisation. A case in point is an ongoing construction of the gigantic Roghun dam and hydropower plant, which, as Filippo Menga (2015) argued, aims to promote a sense of national unity and simultaneously bolster the government's legitimacy. On the other hand, this insistence on building recalls the trajectories of new, hyper-neoliberal market economies, where infrastructure deepens inequalities and principally serves the rich. The Dubai-inspired urban reconstruction of Tajikistan's capital city, Dushanbe, exemplifies this trend. In this development model, there is no space for low Soviet-era architecture, which is gradually replaced with multi-floor luxury buildings that are unaffordable for the majority of people. By erasing social memory, the state-led development model shapes both the space and the nation.

Kyrgyz Republic: Multiple donors and consolidation of development approaches

Similarly crowded with donors and implementers like Tajikistan, Kyrgyzstan continues to maintain what Abazov (1999) described as consistent and flexible engagement with donors. Tools and approaches that the government has used to navigate conflicting interests and ideologies of different donors, and to ensure donor coordination, have contributed to a sense of what could be called a saturated absence of donors. There are simultaneously many and visible donors, but they are also perceived as not achieving any change by local communities (Rudzite 2019). Crucially, though, while Kyrgyzstan's vision of development has seemed as eclectic and patchy as the donor map, the increasing diversity of donors and changing conditionality regimes have consolidated development ideas around the economic sector and strengthened the existing power relations within beneficiary communities.

In the 1990s, Kyrgyzstan was quick to actively embrace neoliberal capitalist reforms by liberalising prices, reducing government regulations, encouraging competition, enhancing trade and shifting to private ownership. International donors offered resources to support such reforms and assist the macroeconomic stabilisation (Abazov 1999). Yet, deteriorating living conditions and a stark rise of poverty rates in Kyrgyzstan[5] throughout the decade illustrated the complexity of livelihoods. Reforms proved difficult to enact (Keneshbaeva 2017). Rapid de-industrialisation, the removal of the state safety net, mass unemployment and the destruction of ties between the centre and the periphery, that those living in Kyrgyzstan's remote regions had relied on through forms of 'Moscow provisioning' (Pelkmans 2017; Reeves 2014), left a vacuum the post-independence government could not fill. While over time people's income became supported by labour migrants' remittances, dependent on favourable migrant labour regimes in Russia and elsewhere, public services became significantly reliant on aid. Not only has aid been a significant source of state budget of the Kyrgyz Republic,[6] various donors have also become the principal agents for public social welfare delivery. However, the notions of what development cooperation should aim to achieve and actually deliver continued to change.

Aid Data (2020) database alone retrieves 8,223 projects funded by 61 donors, ranging from country development agencies to multilateral organisations and private philanthropic funds, bringing over 8 billion USD between 1992 and 2013. Up to that point the prominent sectors of aid were education, health care, social protection, governance and agriculture.[7] However, the overall picture has since changed. According to Kyrgyzstan's Aid Management Platform (2000) data for 2010–2018, in the last decade China became the main funding source. Transportation and energy sectors received over 50 per cent of overall donor funding, followed by governance, infrastructure, agriculture and all other fields combined. It is no surprise that loans are the main funding type. They were actively used in the mid-1990s and again since 2009, peaking in 2013 when China announced BRI investments. However, the turn to sectors that can boost Kyrgyzstan's trade and economy has been facilitated not only by China's increased presence.

A significant contribution to Kyrgyzstan's changing donor landscape concerned Russia's reappearance as a partner and a donor with its own vision of development. The aforementioned

RKDF was established as a promise and a mechanism to integrate the Kyrgyz Republic into the Eurasian Economic Union (EAEU) that the country joined in 2015. RKDF provides loans to small enterprises (up to 1 million USD) through a network of banks, or large enterprises (over 1 million USD) directly through the fund. However, in practice RKDF works rather as a financial institution than a development actor, avoiding investment in higher-risk sectors, such as education and healthcare. This echoes China's vision of development through trickle-down economic growth and inclusive market access without the liberal load and implicit normative conditionality of 'traditional' development initiatives.

Even more than in Tajikistan, the expanding development landscape has increased Kyrgyzstan's ability to ascertain its agency in favour of particular donor approaches, while still treading carefully to retain funding from other donors. The Development Partners' Coordination Council was established in 2002 to coordinate both development partners and Kyrgyz counterparts, and now serves as a space for donors to compete over development visions and prestigious sectors of donor involvement. Along with a growing role of the private sector in global development cooperation, the development of business-related infrastructure, access to microcredit, private sector development and private–public partnerships are all becoming increasingly important development directions also for the 'traditional' donors in Kyrgyzstan.

One of the possible drivers of the shifting to economic development is the perceived potential to avoid the politicisation of aid, which has been criticised by beneficiaries and counterparts alike, making implementation of projects more difficult. Examples of these are peace-building projects. Through interfering in border delimitation processes and altering social action and material space on the Ferghana valley borders (Bichsel 2013; Reeves 2014) donors' projects contributed to national nation-building projects in Central Asia, which had not been their intentions. At the same time, when 1.1 billion USD was channelled to Kyrgyzstan in the 30 months after the 2010 April events and violence in South Kyrgyzstan to support the rebuilding and aid the revival of the economy (Sinitsina 2012), the government had little interest or means to engage with the peace-building efforts. As Lottholz (2018b) showed, it was the local-level administrative bodies and grass-roots activists who were tasked with problem-solving and preventive measures to maintain peace, while policy-makers, particularly on regional and national levels, did not contribute with policies that would support these efforts.

No approach to aid is devoid of power relations. As Mathijs Pelkmans (2017) noted, international donors and foreign employees of international and local organisations have been looked upon as both an opportunity for the usually excluded groups to access resources, and also as a threat because those in power could manipulate them to gain more resources for themselves. This applies equally to all donors and sectors of assistance.

The increased focus on Kyrgyzstan's economic development and market access is a case in point. The normative conditionality here is related to economic gains by donors and those in power positions in the recipient countries able to access funding and benefit from it. As the inequalities within Kyrgyzstan continue to persist, the hope for trickle-down effects seems misplaced. Importantly, though, these projects are not only elite-focused, but also reveal gendered elements of aid, when funding is channelled to largely male-dominated sectors such as construction, transport and logistics, and entrepreneurship. Particularly with the relatively small amounts of aid being disbursed through local (and gender issues-focused) organisations, there is a limited opportunity for the funding to be used to alleviate gendered aspects of poverty, social care work etc. Women's activism is being depoliticised through criticisms of civil society professionalisation (Pares Hoare 2016), but the market-focused development envisions the empowerment of women (particularly in rural areas) mainly through precarious reliance on microcredit and entrepreneurial training. Through the process of delivery and loan repayments women end up being further subjugated to those with resources.

It is very unlikely that the state or any of the development agents will be able to replace Moscow provisioning that had made life possible particularly in sedentarised, rural Kyrgyzstan. As the government continues to balance its position among the many donors, the coordinated efforts seem to aim at development which relies on state retrieve, promotion of moralities where individual welfare is to be ensured by entrepreneurial individuals and their links to family members abroad sending home remittances, assisted through minimal public goods provisions supplied by ever-present international donors.

Conclusion

As this chapter has shown, various development visions have raced through Central Asia in the Soviet and post-Soviet periods, capturing and reflecting global development debates. Meghan Simpson (2009: 37) has succinctly observed that regardless of the depiction of Central Asia that has been at the core of the interventions from various donors, each of them has been too simplistic to capture the 'more complicated – perpetual state of flux, uncertainty and instability for the people in these countries.'

A big part of internationally-funded development work in Central Asia has aimed at guaranteeing stability of the region, and in this way countering potential threats, such as radicalisation, terrorism and drug trafficking, which might have a negative impact on the Western world. While some donors were open about this stability imperative, others presented their projects as supporting democratisation. In both cases, from donors' perspective, the notions of economic and social development were crucial to secure the region. Importantly, this goal has been reflective of imaginaries held by donor agencies, rather than the situation in the region. As such, many interventions have been highly political, and many have only but contributed to reproduction of local power asymmetries – the ones which were traditionally present in Central Asian societies (for example related to age and gender) and the ones produced by globalising post-Soviet political and economic regimes. It is important to point out that not only the 'traditional,' Western donors engaged in such security and normative suasions. While the new donors ascertained themselves as providers of alternative development visions and practice, it is yet to be seen to what extent they will manage to tackle the complex and context-specific nature of poverty and inequalities in Central Asia. International development is also a complex field in itself. It can at once empower some, while disempowering others.

As a final remark, there are many areas of international development cooperation in Central Asia that need to be explored further. While the work of major donors has been covered in literature, little is known about the role of smaller philanthropic organisations or even missionary groups involved in development. There is also disproportionately little research on dispossession, donor-funded microfinance and private sector involvement in development in the region. Furthermore, more work needs to be done to bring together environmental and social issues in international development cooperation. There are also relatively few insights on interventions related to healthcare and education, even if these have for a long time been overwhelmingly the top spending sectors for the major donors in Central Asia, well ahead of fields like security and governance which are widely covered in academic literature. The current academic architecture and funding of research projects, which make researchers focus on certain development fields while neglecting others, also deserves analysis. It is safe to say that there is still much for development scholars to explore in Central Asia.

Funding

This work was supported by the following projects: 'Around the Caspian' (European Commission, grant number SEP-210161673); 'Tomsk State University Competitiveness Improvement Programme' (Tomsk State University, Mendeleev Fund, grant number 8.1.27.2018); Collaborative Research Centre SFB/TRR 138 'Dynamics of Security' (Deutsche Forschungsgemeinschaft, grant number 227068724).

Notes

1. We refer to 'traditional' donors as those who are members of OECD's DAC committee. They mostly overlap with Western states and donor organisations.
2. *Zakat* is considered a faith-based aid and is not included within ODA reported to OECD.
3. Russia's disbursements have declined from over 405 million USD across all Central Asian countries at its peak in 2015 to just over 76 million USD in 2018 (OECD.Stat 2020)
4. *Tadzhikistan i mirovoe obshchestvo*. President.tj. Retrieved from http://www.president.tj/ru/taxonomy/term/5/166
5. According to the National Statistics Committee, around 70 per cent of the population lived below the declared poverty line (UNDP 1996).
6. Kyrgyzstan's income from net ODA ranged from 17 per cent of GNI in 1999 to 5 per cent in 2018 (OECD.Stat 2020).
7. Omuraliev (2020) identified governance, civil society, education and health as the main ODA sectors (when loans are excluded). Also the EU Aid Explorer on EU's assistance shows that since 2007 its ODA has overwhelmingly gone to education management, social protection, health, formal sector financial intermediaries, and rural development, followed by energy and business-related sectors (European Commission 2020).

References

Abashin, S. (2015). *Sovetskiy kishlak. Mezhdu kolonializmom i modernizatsiyey [Soviet kishlak. Between colonialism and modernization]*. Moscow: Novoye literaturnoye obozreniye.
Abazov, R. (1999). Policy of economic transition in Kyrgyzstan. *Central Asian Survey* 18(2): 197–223.
AidData. (2020). *Analytic aid data* [data set]. Williamsburg, VA: AidData at William & Mary. http://dashboard.aiddata.org/#/advanced/analytic-dashboard, accessed on 12 December 2019.
Aid Management Platform. (2020). *Aid management platform for the Kyrgyz Republic* [data set]. http://www.amp.gov.kg/TEMPLATE/ampTemplate/dashboard/build/index.html, accessed on 20 April 2020.
Ancker, S. and Rechel, B. (2015). 'Donors are not interested in reality': the interplay between international donors and local NGOs in Kyrgyzstan's HIV/AIDS sector. *Central Asian Survey* 34(4): 516–530.
Asia Plus. (2019a). *Pochti polovina sredstv gosbyudzheta Tadzhikistana na budushiy god budet napravlena na sotsektor*, 5 September.
Asia Plus. (2019b). *VB: Tadzhikistanu nuzhno otkazatsya ot nyneshney modeli rosta*, 5 September.
Axyonova, V. and Bossuyt, F. (2016). Mapping the substance of the EU's civil society support in Central Asia: from neo-liberal to state-led civil society. *Community and Post-Communist Studies* 49(3): 207–217.
Bahovadinova, M. (2018). The 'mobile proletariat': the production of proletariat labor on a Soviet construction site. *Labor History* 59(3): 277–294.
Bichsel, C. (2009). *Conflict transformation in Central Asia. Irrigation disputes in the Ferghana Valley*. London: Routledge.
Bichsel, C. (2013). Dangerous divisions: peace-building in the borderlands of Post-Soviet Central Asia. In B. Korf and T. Raeymaekers, eds. *Violence on the margins. States, conflict, and borderlands*. Basingstoke: Palgrave Macmillan, pp. 145–165.
Bossuyt, F. (2018). The EU's and China's development assistance towards Central Asia: low versus contested impact. *Eurasian Geography and Economics* 59(5–6): 606–631.
Brezhneva, A. and Ukhova, D. (2013). Russia as a humanitarian aid donor. *Oxfam International Discussion Paper*. Oxford: Oxfam International.
Broome, A. (2010). *The currency of power: the IMF and monetary reform in Central Asia*. Basingstoke: Palgrave Macmillan.

Buxton, C. (2011). *The struggle for civil society in Central Asia: crisis and transformation.* Sterling, VA: Kumarian Press.
Carothers, T. (2011). *Aiding democracy abroad: the learning curve.* Washington, DC: Carnegie Endowment.
Cooley, A. (2000). International aid to the former Soviet states: agent of change or guardian of the status quo? *Problems of Post-Communism* 47(4): 34–44.
Cooley, A. (2012). *Gxreat games, local rules: the new power contest in Central Asia.* Oxford: Oxford University Press.
Cornwall, A. (2007). Buzzwords and fuzzwords: deconstructing development discourse. *Development in Practice* 17(4–5): 471–484.
Crawford, G. (2008). EU human rights and democracy promotion in Central Asia: from lofty principles to lowly self-interests. *Perspectives on European Politics and Society* 9(2): 172–191.
Czerniecka, K. and Heathershaw, J. (2010). Security assistance and border management. In A. Warkotsch, ed. *The European Union and Central Asia.* London and New York: Routledge, pp. 77–101.
Dadabaev, T. (2016). Japan's ODA assistance scheme and Central Asian engagement: Determinants, trends, expectations. *Journal of Eurasian Studies* 7: 24–38.
Dadabaev, T. (2018). "Silk Road" as foreign policy discourse: the construction of Chinese, Japanese and Korean engagement strategies in Central Asia. *Journal of Eurasian studies* 9(1): 30–41.
De Cordier, B. (2016). Russia's international aid donorship: from diplomatic status symbol to "frontline aid"? *Global Affairs* 2(1): 21–34.
De Danieli, F. (2011). Counter-narcotics policies in Tajikistan and their impact on state building. *Central Asian Survey* 30(1): 129–145.
De Martino, L. (2001). Peace initiatives in Central Asia. An inventory. *Situation report.* Geneva: Cimera.
Dobrolyubova, E. (2019). Russia's contribution to international development assistance. In Y. Jing, A. Mendez, and Y. Zheng, eds. *New development assistance. Emerging economies and the new landscape of development assistance.* Singapore: Palgrave Macmillan.
Dunford, M. (2020). Chinese and development assistance committee (DAC) development cooperation and development finance: implications for the BRI and international governance. *Eurasian Geography and Economics* 61(2): 125–136.
European Commission. (2020). *EU aid explorer* [data set]. https://euaidexplorer.ec.europa.eu/, accessed 28 April 2020.
Féaux de la Croix, J. and Suyarkulova, M. (2015). The Rogun complex: public roles and historic experiences of dam-building in Tajikistan and Kyrgyzstan. *Cahiers d'Asie centrale* 25: 103–132.
Gussarova, A. and Andzans, M. eds. (2018). Cultural and other relations. Mapping EU-Central Asia relations. *SEnECA Policy Paper.*
Heathershaw, J. (2009). *Post-conflict Tajikistan: the politics of peacebuilding and the emergence of legitimate order.* London: Routledge.
Heathershaw, J. (2009a). Tajikistan's virtual politics of peace. *Europe–Asia Studies* 61(7): 1315–1336.
Heathershaw, J. (2016). Who are the 'international community'? Development professionals and liminal subjectivity. *Journal of Intervention and Statebuilding* 10(1): 77–96.
Heathershaw, J. and Megoran, N. (2011). Contesting danger: a new agenda for policy and scholarship on Central Asia. *International Affairs* 87(3): 589–612.
Hoffmann, K. (2010). The EU in Central Asia: successful good governance promotion? *Third World Quarterly* 31(1): 87–103.
Hofman, I. (2016). Politics or profits along the "Silk Road": what drives Chinese farms in Tajikistan and helps them thrive? *Eurasian Geography and Economics* 57(3): 457–481.
Hwang, B. (2012). *The new horizon in South Korea-Central Asia relations: the ROK joins the 'Great Game.'* KoreaCompass. Washington, DC: Korea Economic Institute.
Jaborov, S. (2018). Chinese loans in Central Asia: development assistance or 'predatory lending'? In M. Laruelle, ed. *China's belt and road initiative and its impact in Central Asia.* Washington, DC: George Washington University, pp. 33–40.
Kalinovsky, A.M. (2018). *Laboratory of socialist development: Cold War politics and decolonization in Soviet Tajikistan.* Ithaca: Cornell University Press.
Karimov, S. (2008). *Rol' NPO v formirovanii grazhdanskogo obshchestva v Tadzhikistane. Istoriko-politologicheskoe issledovanie [The role of NGOs in formation of the civil society in Tajikistan. A historico-political research].* Dushanbe: Ofset Imperia.
Keneshbaeva, Z.M. (2017). Kyrgyzstan's economy in terms of the EEMA and the role of the Russian-Kyrgyz Development Fund as a support institution. *Contemporary Problems of Social Work* 3(2): 24–31.

Kim, E. (2014). *International development and research in Central Asia. Exploring the knowledge-based social organization of gender*. PhD thesis, University of Bonn.

Kim, E. (2018). Sustainability of irrigation in Uzbekistan: implications for women farmers. In P. Thanjavur Chandrasekaran, ed. *Water and sustainability*. https://www.intechopen.com/books/water-and-sustainability/sustainability-of-irrigation-in-uzbekistan-implications-for-women-farmers#B26, accessed on 5 November 2019.

Kim, E., Myrzabekova, A., Molchanova, E. and Yarova, O. (2018). Making the 'empowered woman': exploring contradictions in gender and development programming in Kyrgyzstan. *Central Asian Survey* 37(2): 228–246.

Kim, S. and Lightfoot, S. (2011). Does 'DAC-ability' really matter? The emergence of non-DAC donors: Introduction to policy arena. *Journal of International Development* 23: 711–721.

Kluczewska, K. (2018). *Development aid in Tajikistan: six global paradigms and practice on the ground*. PhD thesis, University of St Andrews.

Kluczewska, K. (2019). How to translate 'good governance' into Tajik? An American good governance fund and norm localisation in Tajikistan. *Journal of Intervention and Statebuilding* 13(3): 357–376.

Kluczewska, K. and Dzhuraev, S. (2020). The EU and Central Asia: nuances of an 'aided' partnership. In R. Fawn, ed. *Managing security threats along the EU's eastern flanks*. Cham: Palgrave Macmillan, pp. 225–252.

Kluczewska, K. and Foroughi, P. The soft power of neoliberal civil society: the case of post-communist Tajikistan. In S. Peyrouse and K. Nourzhanov, eds. *Soft power in Central Asia: the politics of influence and seduction*. Lexington Books. Forthcoming.

Koch, N. (2017). Qatar and Central Asia. What's at stake in Tajikistan, Turkmenistan, and Kazakhstan? *PONARS Eurasia Policy Memo* 484: 1–5.

Kothari, U., ed. (2016). *A radical history of development studies: individuals, institutions and ideologies*. London: Zed Books Ltd.

Lancaster, C. (2008). *Foreign aid: diplomacy, development, domestic politics*. Chicago: University of Chicago Press.

Lelchuk, V.S. (1984). *Industrializatsiya SSSR: istoriya, opyt, problemy* [Instustralisation in the USSR: history, experience, problems]. Moscow: Izdatelstvo Politicheskoy Literatury.

Lewis, D. (2012). Who's socialising whom? Regional organisations and contested norms in Central Asia. *Europe–Asia Studies* 64(7): 1219–1237.

Lewis, D. and Mosse, D., eds. (2006). *Development brokers and translators: the ethnography of aid and agencies*. Bloomfield: Kumarian Press.

Li, Y. (2019). Saudi Arabia's economic diplomacy through foreign aid: dynamics, objectives and mode. *Asian Journal of Middle Eastern and Islamic Studies* 13(1): 110–122.

Lottholz, P. (2018a). Old slogans ringing hollow? The legacy of social engineering, statebuilding and the 'dilemma of difference' in (post-) Soviet Kyrgyzstan. *Journal of Intervention and Statebuilding* 12(3): 405–424.

Lottholz, P. (2018b). *Post-liberal statebuilding in Central Asia: a decolonial perspective on community security practices and imaginaries of social order in Kyrgyzstan*. PhD thesis, University of Birmingham.

Marat, E. (2018). Chinese artificial intelligence projects expand in Eurasian cities. *PONARS Policy Memo* 540.

Matveeva, A. (2006). EU stakes in Central Asia. *Chaillot Paper* 91: 1–125.

Megoran, N., Raballand, G. and Bouyjou, J. (2005). Performance, representation, and the economics of border control in Uzbekistan. *Geopolitics* 10(4): 712–742.

Menga, F. (2015). Building a nation through a dam: the case of Rogun in Tajikistan. *Nationalities Papers* 43(3): 479–494.

Mostowlansky, T. (2017). *Azan on the moon: entangling modernity along Tajikistan's Pamir highway*. Pittsburgh: University of Pittsburgh Press.

Nursha, G. (2018). Chinese soft power in Kazakhstan and Kyrgyzstan: a Confucius Institutes case study. In M. Laruelle, ed. *China's belt and road initiative and its impact in Central Asia*. Washington, DC: George Washington University, pp. 135–143.

Odgaard, L. (2017). Beijing's quest for stability in its neighborhood: China's relations with Russia in Central Asia. *Asian Security* 13(1): 41–58.

OECD.Stat. (2020). *Development data* [data set]. Paris: OECD. https://stats.oecd.org/, accessed on 28 April 2020.

Omelicheva, M.Y. (2015). *Democracy in Central Asia: competing perspectives and alternative strategies*. Kentucky: University Press of Kentucky.

Omuraliev, A. (2020). Donor activity in Central Asian Countries since 1991. Central Asian Bureau for Analytical Reporting. https://cabar.asia/en/donor-activity-in-central-asian-countries-since-1991/#_ftn21, accessed on 4 May 2020.

Ozcan, G.B. (2010). *Building states and markets. Enterprise development in Central Asia.* Basingstoke: Palgrave Macmillan.

Paramanov, V., Aleksey, S. and Abduganieva, Z. (2017). *Vliyanie Evropeiskogo soyuza na Tsentral'nuyu Aziu: obzor, analiz i prognoz.* Almaty: Friedrich Ebert Stiftung.

Pares Hoare, J. (2016). Doing gender activism in a donor-organized framework: constraints and opportunities in Kyrgyzstan. *Nationalities Papers* 44(2): 281–198.

Pelkmans, M. (2017). *Fragile convictions. Changing ideological landscapes in urban Kyrgyzstan.* Ithaca, NY: Cornell University Press.

Putnam, R.D. (1993). *Making democracy work: civic traditions in modern Italy.* Princeton, NJ: Princeton University Press.

Rakhimov, M. (2014). Central Asia and Japan: bilateral and multilateral relations. *Journal of Eurasian studies* 5(1): 77–87.

Reeves, M. (2014). *Border work: spatial lives of the state in rural Central Asia.* Ithaca, NY: Cornell University Press.

Reid, P. (2017). 'Tajikistan's Turksib': infrastructure and improvisation in economic growth of the Vakhsh River valley. *Central Asian Survey* 36(1): 19–36.

Rist, G. (2014). *The history of development: from western origins to global faith.* London: Zed Books Ltd.

Rudzite, L. (2019). Theorizing the managerialism-neoliberalism-development nexus: changing donor landscapes and persistence of outcomes of practices in Kyrgyzstan. In R. Isaacs and A. Frigerio, eds. *Theorizing Central Asian politics: the state, ideology, and power.* London: Palgrave Macmillan, pp. 65–95.

Schwak, J. (2020). Nothing new under the sun: South Korea's developmental promises and neoliberal illusions. *Third World Quarterly* 41(2): 302–320.

Sharipov, A. and Yuldashev, N. (2019). Islamic finance and markets in Uzbekistan. *Lexology.* https://www.lexology.com/library/detail.aspx?g=9aaf1dd8-417e-408c-ba8f-79e069edf65c, accessed on 12 December 2019.

Sharshenova, A. (2018). *The European Union's democracy promotion in Central Asia. A study of political interests, influence, and development in Kazakhstan and Kyrgyzstan in 2007–2013.* Stuttgart: Ibidem-Verlag.

Sievers, E.W. (2003). *The post-Soviet decline of Central Asia: sustainable development and comprehensive capital.* London: Routledge.

Simpson, M. (2006). Local strategies in globalizing gender politics: women's organizing in Kyrgyzstan and Tajikistan. *Journal of Muslim Minority Affairs* 26(1): 9–31.

Simpson, M. (2009). *Local strategies in globalizing gender politics: a study of women's organizing and aid in contemporary Kyrgyzstan.* PhD thesis, Central European University.

Sinitsina, I. (2012). Economic cooperation between Russia and Central Asian countries: trends and outlooks. *Working paper no. 5.* Bishkek: University of Central Asia.

Tian, H. (2018). China's conditional aid and its impact in Central Asia. In M. Laruelle, ed. *China's belt and road initiative and its impact in Central Asia.* Washington, DC: George Washington University, pp. 21–33.

UNDP. (1996). *Kyrgyz Republic. National human development report.* New York: UNDP.

USAID Foreign Aid Explorer. (2020). *Foreign aid explorer* [data set]. https://explorer.usaid.gov/, accessed on 22 January 2020.

Warkotsch, A. (2008). Normative suasion and political change in Central Asia. *Caucasian Review of International Affairs* 2(4): 240–249.

Yakobashvili, T. (2013). A Chinese Marshall Plan for Central Asia? *Central Asia-Caucasus Analyst*, 16 October.

PART VI

Society and Culture

23
THE NATIONALISATION OF TRADITIONS

Svetlana Jacquesson

Traditions have been and still are a matter of never-ending debates between scholars who are defining and redefining tradition as a concept,[1] cultural elites who claim custody of traditions, politicians and policy makers who attempt to harness them, and the folks who carry them on. Long gone are the times when anyone could comfortably claim an authority over traditions. Any claim today – whether scholarly, political or folk – is open to debate.

Tradition stands for both the process of handing down and what is being handed down. Any skill, knowledge, belief or practice can be handed down and can thus be considered traditional. But if there is any agreement on tradition and traditional, it stops here. For some, the process of handing down has to do with face-to-face interactions and oral transmission. For others, neither face-to-face nor oral should define the process of transmission: written traditions are plentiful in Central Asia as elsewhere, not to mention the eruption of the new media of communication that emulate, modify or replace both the oral and the written. For some, traditions are handed down uninterrupted and faithfully from generation to generation, or from master to disciple; for others, traditions are continuously changing and may, from time to time, be in need of refurbishing. Some perceive traditions as disappearing and in need to be salvaged or revitalised, others believe in their resilience. There is also no consensus on the value of traditions: if for some traditions are the pillars of individual and collective identities, others perceive traditions as fusty, or conservative or oppressive.

All constituencies though seem to agree that traditional and modern are mutually defined, or that in order for the traditional to be meaningful as a quality there should be another quality – usually articulated as modern – to serve as a foil. This consensus might attest to the success of past Europe-born sociological theories of 'great divides.' It may also just remind us that social actors are cognitive misers, and dichotomies – no matter how much decried by scholars – help social actors get around and make sense of their worlds. What should not be overlooked somehow is that while the dichotomic relationship between traditional and modern remains widely used, the understandings or meanings of traditional and modern are constantly changing.

The sources that allow us to have an idea of how local actors reflect upon their own traditions are unequal. More sporadic or still less known, in the past, most of these reflections or discussions have taken place in relation to Islam and the various local manifestations of religiosity it could or could not accommodate (DeWeese 2016). In the present, since the dawn of independences, local talk on traditions is plentiful and the amount of publications in the national languages on

DOI: 10.4324/9780429057977-23

traditions, or customs or rituals is impressive. These publications take the shape of more or less elaborate inventories and more or less detailed descriptions of traditions in all walks of life, from the family to the nation; they foreground regional or local variations and ponder on their age or authenticity; they lament lost traditions or disappearing ones; or, they teach ordinary citizens how to perform them properly. Traditions, customs and rituals are abundantly discussed in the local news media as well as on social media, both approvingly and disapprovingly.

In the past as in the present, traditions in Central Asia have been abundantly described and discussed by outsiders. This written corpus stretches nearly uninterrupted as far back as the thirteenth century and includes, among others, travellers' accounts, a huge collection of colonial documents, the archives and ethnographies produced during the Soviet period and, last but not least, a robust body of scholarship created once the region became accessible to foreign scholars after the fall of the Soviet Union.

This chapter cannot offer but a snapshot of the past and present of traditions in Central Asia and of the ways they have been studied hitherto. It focuses on traditions as collective performances which symbolise the link between past and present generations. Ritual is central to performed traditions. By foregrounding performances, the chapter distinguishes traditions from a more diffuse process of cultural transmission of received opinions, of patterns of thought and behaviour. When traditions are performed, the sense of continuity with the past generations resides not in the attempt to repeat, reproduce or revive 'their traditions' but in the mere commitment to perform, and thus preserve. It is through performed traditions therefore that communities acquire and maintain a sense of social continuity and collective identity.

When traditions are distinguished from other processes of cultural transmission as being enacted or embodied, it is hardly a surprise that discourses on them are as plentiful as performances and communities. With the advent of nation-states, official regimes tend to lay hegemonic claims on discourses on traditions. Historians and sociologists emphasise that no matter how diverse its manifestations and meanings can be, modernity could certainly stand for this moment in history when for the first time a set of folk traditions may come to be selected and conceived of not only as being shared by an imagined community – the nation – but also as symbolising an ineffable 'national spirit' or 'national values' (Babadzan 2000). This instrumentalisation of traditions rarely happens unchallenged and the disagreement between officials and folk on the meaning and value of traditions is an outstanding feature of the contemporary world.

The chapter starts with a brief overview of the Soviet period as a key period when the relationship between nation, culture and identity was defined and when ordinary citizens in Central Asia developed various 'tactics' allowing them to maintain their commitment to local traditions without renouncing to the benefits offered by the socialist state. Next it describes how the official authorities of the newly independent states attempted to scrap the Soviet legacy and harness traditions in their attempts to nurture post-Soviet national subjectivities. The chapter then zooms in on life-cycle celebrations (Kyrgyz: *toy*; Uzbek: *to'y*; Tajik: *tūy*), in particular marriages and funerals, as a case that illustrates the rhetoric of current official condemnations of ritual excess. It analyses the latest laws and regulations on life-cycle celebrations as national traditions and the impact of the latter on ordinary citizens' practices and discourses. The chapter concludes by some observations on the ways in which the study of traditions in Central Asia contributes to the understanding of contemporary identity dilemmas and the frequent failures of the nation-state to accommodate them.

Though the study of contemporary Central Asia is an international field, this chapter foregrounds scholarly works in English as one of the leading languages in the field. This is not to deny the value of research on traditions published in other languages, those of Central Asia included. It is a consciously endorsed drawback for the sake of a coherent though limited introduction to the study of traditions in the region. It is because of the personal expertise of the author and the geographical scope of recent research that Kyrgyzstan, Uzbekistan and Tajikistan are discussed in more detail than the rest of Central Asia.

Nation building without national traditions

Scholars emphasise that both the Russian Empire and the Soviet Union were challenged by Central Asia's 'uniqueness' and that in both the imperial and Soviet jargons 'uniqueness' rhymed with otherness and backwardness (Brower 2003; Campbell 2017). And while Tsarist Russia did undertake some 'civilising' actions in its colony, these actions appear as merely palliative when compared to the policies and practices of the Soviet Union. The latter acquiesced to otherness, less so to backwardness. The otherness was tamed by identifying, naming and describing languages and lifestyles, and organising their bearers into ethnically defined nations (Hirsch 2005; Reeves 2014). Each Soviet nation then was granted a 'homeland' or a state to which it was linked by a newly minted national history and where a national culture was produced in the national language by a set of modern institutions (Adams 2010; Iğmen 2012).

As different from official national cultures, national traditions – in the sense of folk traditions that are recontextualised as symbols of the values or spirit of the new nations – seem to have had a very modest role in the design of Soviet republics. In Central Asia the only official holiday with a folk background seemed to have been Nowruz (Iranian/Islamic New Year) and its official recognition was achieved only in the 1970s after it was reshaped as Zoroastrian/pre-Islamic Spring Holiday (Kandiyoti 1996; Adams 2007). The landslide of newly introduced all-Union Soviet celebrations, or all-Union Soviet 'invented traditions,'[2] sought to distract local actors from communal traditions and get them involved in the celebration or performance of new Soviet identities, communities and lifestyles (Binns 1980). As early as 1929 the Soviet regime introduced all-Union secular life-cycle ceremonies which did enjoy some popularity in Central Asia (Kamp 2007) though by the late Soviet period, the official rules and ceremonies in weddings and funerals were being overwhelmed by local rites and rituals (Jacquesson 2008; Roche and Hohmann 2011). Scholars emphasise that it is by comparison with and in opposition to the standardised Soviet ceremonies that life-cycle celebrations in the Central Asian republics were reinterpreted as 'ethnic' or 'national.' It is also during the late Soviet period that local elites started using the notion of national traditions to refer to Islamic observances (DeWeese 2002; Khalid 2007). While these claims seem to have been welcomed and endorsed by the public in large, it is worth underlying that the official category of national traditions remained empty throughout the Soviet period.

The Soviet regime viewed most local traditions as flagrant manifestations of backwardness and an obstacle to development (Hirsch 2005; Edgar 2006). Initially, accusations of subversion were heaped on 'class enemies' (religious and community leaders) who were scapegoated for acting as patrons of anti-Soviet behaviours and practices. Yet even after the large-scale purges of the 1930s, the adoption of modern socialist lifestyles proved far from smooth. In the next 50 years or so, Soviet policy makers and scholars would be kept busy by 'survivals,' or beliefs and practices that were 'relics' of the past. It can hardly be a coincidence that among the many survivals infesting Soviet life in Central Asia the so-called 'clan survivals' (Schatz 2004; Collins 2006) – the mutual rights and duties within extended kinship groups purportedly sharing the same ancestor in the male line – and 'religious survivals' (DeWeese 2012; Schoeberlein 2012) – local religious practices that did not fit into the Soviet vision of Islam as a religion – were among the most loathed and closely scrutinised. Both perpetuated the importance – and, somehow ironically, the survival – of identities and communities incompatible with the Soviet ideology and both undermined the ongoing attempts to establish modern and secular Soviet nations.

Based on observations and fieldwork conducted after independence, most scholars agree that Soviet-style 'modernisation' in Central Asia was shallow. The region remained overwhelmingly agricultural and the canvas of local communal life was little affected by Soviet policies, notwithstanding the shock of collectivisation and the ensuing mass famine and exile. Moreover, the Soviet economy of shortages favoured the establishment of informal networks to facilitate the access to rare goods and services (Schatz 2004; Collins 2006). Being denied the right to claim private property and to accumulate it, local actors invested surplus income in lavish life-cycle celebrations and religious rituals in search of social recognition, moral satisfaction and spiritual fulfilment (Roche and Hohmann 2011; Trevisani 2016; Roberts 2017). Both networks of support and ritual networks were rooted in 'traditional identities' or 'traditional communities' that were kinship/clan or locality-based and helped the maintenance and reproduction of these identities and communities throughout the Soviet period. Based on evidence from different periods and different regions of Central Asia, scholars foreground the capacity of local actors to customise Soviet institutions – i.e., to subvert these institutions and make them serve local communal purposes (Roy 2000; Roberts 2017; cf. Beyer 2016) – and nurture layered identities or multiples subjectivities (Kandiyoti 1996; Phillips and James 2001; Sartori 2010; 2019) empowering them to move smoothly between Soviet, ethnic, religious, and subethnic registers. Soviet rule though did not go unnoticed. Scholars have consistently argued that it is through Soviet narratives that the 'naturalness' of the nation as the supreme expression of ethnic identity as well as the notion of ethnicity itself took sure hold of the minds of many Central Asians, and especially of those who belonged to the urbanised elites and the *nomenklatura* (DeWeese 2002).

Traditionalising the post-Soviet nations

At independence, the new regimes never questioned the distinctiveness and uniqueness – or 'cultural authenticity' (Rasanayagam 2011) – of the Soviet-cum-independent nations. Instead they deployed efforts to explain them and make sure that they are preserved for the future generations by being codified in state ideologies. In the process, however, the now-sovereign nations were scaled down to the so-called 'titular ethnic majorities' and large swaths of 'non-titular' citizens turned away from the pathos of independence. This is what happened in Uzbekistan and Kyrgyzstan, for example. Notwithstanding the fact that long-lived president Islam Karimov (1991–2016) was scorned for his authoritarianism while president Askar Akayev(1991–2005) was hailed as a beacon of democracy, both of them made ample use of 'ancient' national culture borne by 'ancestral' traditions to explain the uniqueness of their nations and charter the future. President Askar Akayev never tired of claiming that Kyrgyz history spanned thousands of years and was embodied in a long line of ancestors whose legacy comprised 'the most precious of precious relics,' the Manas epic (Akayev2002). He described the epic successively as 'a bearer of the national idea,' 'a prototype of the national constitution,' and 'a social genome' containing 'the genetic pool of national identity, national spirit and national culture' (Akayev2003). Since the Manas epic as 'the most precious of precious relics' was both the creation and the legacy of the ancestors, the traditions and values purportedly contained in it were not only the genuine Kyrgyz traditions and values but every Kyrgyz – by the virtue of having Kyrgyz ancestors – had these traditions and values in 'the blood and flesh' (Akayev2002).

Islam Karimov's office as a president was much longer than Akaev's. Scholars have emphasised that not only Karimov was exceptionally diligent in laying the foundations of an Uzbek national ideology but that he kept perfecting it throughout his career (Kurzman 1999; March

2003). In the early 2000s, Karimov's attention was also focused on 'the values' of the Uzbek nation. At that time, he equated these values with 'traditions and customs that have been formed over the millennia.' Like Akaev, he praised the ancestors for begetting 'noble values' and 'worthy traditions' and invited contemporary Uzbeks to preserve them as 'a precious wealth' for the future generations. The Uzbeks, Karimov noted, did not have a 'written record' of these values and traditions though, exactly like the Kyrgyz, every Uzbek recognises and respects them because they have been absorbed by Uzbek 'blood and flesh' (Karimov 2002).

Central Asians then entered the independence period with their leaders loudly assuring them that each nation or each state 'bears' an ethnic distinctiveness. By praising the ancestors as state builders and nation begetters both presidents transformed the somehow anonymous historical continuity of Soviet-style national histories into an ethnic continuity that was embodied by these ancestors. Several scholars (March 2003; Gullette 2010) have insightfully emphasised that by locating the nation and its values in the ancestors and their traditions, the new regimes attempted to deploy a new type of post-Soviet neo-traditional governmentality whereby ordinary citizens would identify with the glorious national heritage and self-discipline so as to preserve and transmit it to the future generations.

Problematising traditions

The official attempts to traditionalise the nation and the rhetoric of national ideologies may leave the wrong impression that with independence Central Asian citizens became estranged from their traditions. This is not what scholars discovered in the field that opened for investigations at that time. Just on the contrary: the commitment to traditions by social actors who have struggled with the transition from centralised socialist to market-driven systems and who kept navigating in domestic economies mined by inflation, unemployment and corruption drew the attention of scholars right away and has remained on their research agenda ever since. Among many a commitments, weddings and funerals stood out because of the extended social networks involved in their preparation and celebration and their ritualised feasting and gift exchange. Scholars have documented how these social networks from being localised have become translocal, spanning the urban–rural divide and, since the early 2000s, transnational, connecting labour migrants abroad to their home communities (Werner 1998; Reeves 2012; Ilkhamov 2013). They have noted the growing amount of expenditures on life-cycle celebrations and emphasised that while local inflation rates were not to be ignored, these expenditures were also incurred by new consumption patterns: food and fabric as ceremonial gifts have been replaced by bundles of flat bread, carpets, coats and banknotes; festive meals – based on meat, rice or dough – are being embellished with salads and pickles, confectionary from all over the world, homemade and manufactured pastries, huge wedding cakes, and elaborate displays of exotic fruit; from houses and courtyards the parties have moved to cafes, restaurants or especially built 'feastaurants' (*toykana*) capable of seating up to 2,000 persons, lavishly decorated and fitted out with the latest sound equipment and lighting systems; the wedding corteges have seen limousines, Range Rovers and Geländewagens replace Volgas, Moskviches and Zhigulis. Suffice it to add here that in the otherwise bleak domestic economies, the so-called 'toy economy' – or the production and consumption of goods and services related to life-cycle celebrations (Werner 2000; Trevisani 2016; Turdalieva and Provis 2017) – may be one of the few sure indicators of Central Asia's successful transition to the market economy.

New patterns of economic activities and consumption, scholars conclude, have been 'customised' and are used to sustain gifting and feasting that are understood and problematised by local actors as traditional or traditions (Werner 2000; Reeves 2012; Ilkhamov 2013). All scholars also note that those who hold weddings and funerals strive to a 'proper way' of conducting them and some studies explore the complex family strategies of consumption and accumulations or the hardships families face in their attempts to sustain the tradition and meet the expectations of kith and kin (Abashin 2003; Light 2015; Botoeva 2015; Trevisani 2016; Beyer 2016).

One could have expected that such a commitment to tradition and community would have fallen straight to the point of the neo-traditionalist aspirations of the new regimes and would have been welcomed by them. Instead, it drew their ire. As early as October 1998, Islam Karimov publicly expressed his disapproval of how citizens were holding life-cycle celebrations. At that time Karimov penned down a decree in which he claimed that these celebrations were infested by 'survivals of the past' such as profligacy, vanity, and extravagance. In their current manifestations, Karimov continued, life-cycle celebrations were an affront to 'folk customs and traditions.' He blamed 'arrogant officials' for 'unseemly behaviour' that hurts the self-esteem of ordinary citizens and undermines the faith of the latter in justice and in the authority of the state. In this very first decree, Karimov condemned in particular the 'lavish holding of events dedicated to the memory of the deceased' and claimed that current commemorations 'distort the national customs left to the Uzbeks by their ancestors and profane Uzbek sacred traditions.'[3] The ordinary people, according to Karimov, were not only revolted by such excess but also required that surplus income be used – 'according to ancient customs' – for charity (Karimov 1998 as quoted in Abashin 2003). Four years later, in 2002, Karimov restated that both 'modern traditions' and 'backward rites' damaged 'the centuries-old values of the nation and people.' He also specified that by 'modern traditions' and 'backward rites' he was referring to 'the misdemeanours that are increasingly invading life under the guise of traditions and customs and turning weddings and ceremonies into lavish celebrations and feasts' (Karimov 2002).

Karimov's argumentation has been repeated, borrowed, rehearsed and adapted ever since the early 2000s. Thus, in May 2007, while criticising expenditures on weddings and funerals, Tajikistan's president Emomali Rahmon mocked the amount of wedding rituals, described them as 'unnecessary and unaffordable' and blamed government officials, businesspeople and religious figures for 'showing off their wealth' and giving a bad example to those who have only modest incomes (Farangis 2007). And in March 2010, in his last public speech, Kyrgyzstan's president Kurmanbek Bakiyev acknowledged that large funerals and weddings are Kyrgyz traditions – 'without which the Kyrgyz would not be Kyrgyz' – but also argued that 'rites and rituals that entail unjustified and even inconceivable expenses' lack 'relevance' in the twenty-first century. Though indirectly, Bakiyev too accused state and government officials for spoiling the 'national values' and invited them to practice modesty and prudence (Bakiyev 2010).

Similar condemnations – using the rhetoric of excess, subsuming both elaborate rituals and high expenditures – have a long history in Central Asia (DeWeese 2012 2016). They are relatively well documented during the tide of local reformist projects in the last years of the Russian empire and the first decade of the Soviet period, and throughout the latter (Abashin 2003; Khalid 2007; Jacquesson 2008; Roberts 2017). From one period to another, 'excess' has been framed either as wrong from a religious point of view or as incompatible with ever-evolving notions of 'modernity,' 'development,' 'progress' or 'justice.' In the independence period, however, official criticisms hammer home the damage that 'excess' brings to 'ancient customs,' 'sacred traditions,' and 'national values.' When excess is scorned as a survival, it is a survival from the Soviet period, under the guise of bad Soviet habits. Though excess can still be framed as an obstacle to development, as in the 2005 statement of Kyrgyzstan's president Bakiyev, it is as regularly denounced as a corollary of development, i.e. post-Soviet economic liberalisation and growing consumerism, as in the 2002 argumentation of Karimov. In both cases, in a willing or unwilling repetition of the early Soviet argumentation, local elites – state and government officials, politicians, businesspeople, and religious figures – are either scapegoated as carriers of Soviet survivals or as patrons of alien consumerist habits. Ordinary citizens instead are depicted either as being misled in their understanding of authentic ancestral customs and traditions, or as outright suffering from the distortion of these customs and traditions. Since neither edifying discourses nor elaborate national ideologies seemed to have the desired effect, either on the elites or on the folk, it is by state regulations that the new regimes decided to strip the ancestral traditions of Soviet and other modern accretions, turn them into truly national ones and, by the same move, protect the ordinary citizens against ritual excess.

Nationalising traditions

Twenty-one years after the 1998 decree of Karimov, in September 2019, the parliament of Uzbekistan approved a new bill 'On further improving the regulations of weddings, family events,[4] funerals, and commemorations of the dead' (Senat Olij Mazhlisa Respibliki Uzbekistan 2019; Xalq so'zi 2019). During the same span of time, in 2007, Tajikistan's parliament, upon the order of the president, adopted a law on 'The regulations of traditions, celebrations, and rituals' (Prezident respubliki Tadzhikistan E. Rahmonov 2007) while Kyrgyzstan's MPs drafted several similar laws – in 2002–2011 (Zhogorku Kengesh Kyrgyzskoi respublike 2011) and 2016 (Zhogorku Kengesh Kyrgyzskoi respublike 2016) – but failed to have them voted.[5]

These regulations are extremely meticulous in sorting out the 'excessive' from the 'ancient,' the 'sacred' and the 'national' in contemporary practices. In the case of weddings,[6] for example, the 2011 Tajikistan law discusses the wedding feast – for which the number of guests is capped at 200 – as well as 18 other rituals preceding or following the feast. It bans no less than 16 of these rituals, among them the celebration of the betrothal; the pilaf meal offered to the men of the neighbourhood ahead of the wedding; the gathering upon the reception by the bride of the chests of gifts from the bridegroom's family; the gatherings upon the display of the bride's and bridegroom's wedding outfits; the meal offered during the first visit of the bride's parents to their in-laws; and the welcoming meals for the bride when she first visits the relatives of the bridegroom. Two other rituals – the first visit of the bride's family by the bridegroom and the welcoming party for the bride by the bridegroom's family – are allowed only if held 'in a family circle,' i.e. with the number of guests capped at 15. Regarding funerals, the Tajikistan law mentions 10 rituals and bans as 'extra' or 'superfluous' the offering of food or the slaughter of animals for 9 among them and, most notably, for the commemorations of the third and fortieth days, and the year of the death.

The 2011 Kyrgyzstan draft law is in many ways a reversed version of the 2007 Tajikistan law. Its section on weddings is as concise as the Tajik section on funerals: it only notes that it is forbidden to exchange clothes as gifts during the wedding celebrations, that the wedding feast should not be attended by more than 200 guests, and that the rituals following the wedding must be conducted 'in a family circle' and attended by no more than 15 people.[7] When it comes to the regulation of funerals, the Kyrgyzstan draft law is as detailed and as severe as the Tajikistan law in the case of weddings.[8] It bans 10 rituals or customs: the slaughtering of livestock by the household of the deceased in the three days following the death; the giving out of the personal belongings of the deceased; the wearing of mourning; the sacrifices to the soul of the deceased; the handing out of memory gifts; the ritual lamentation of women; the ritual lamentation of men; the use of a crook while performing the latter; the erection of a graveyard monument; and the offering and drinking of alcohol. The draft law puts restrictions – without offering food – on another four rituals: the commemorations of the third, seventh and fortieth days of the death and the prayers for the deceased on Thursdays. It offers a reformed rite for the commemoration of the year of the death: an attendance limited to 70 people, the sacrifice of a sheep or a goat, and the reading of the Koran.⁹

Official regulations claim to reduce 'unnecessary expenses' and, at the same time, 'protect national culture and folk traditions' (2007 Tajikistan law) or 'strengthen the adherence to authentic national values and the respect for folk traditions' (2011 Kyrgyzstan draft law). In the spirit of the official ideologies in which authentic national culture and folk traditions are begotten by the ancestors and thus located in the past, these regulations spare some rituals as symbols of the claimed historical continuity of the nation and its traditions but severely cut gifting and feasting practices as the basis for the social reproduction of local communities or ritual networks. It is not too far-fetched to suggest that beyond their official rhetoric these regulations seek to undermine any community other than the nation and any identity other than the national, in particular the so-called 'traditional identities' based on kinship or locality. Though some scholars suggest that these official attempts to nationalise life-cycle celebrations may signal the birth of ritual nationalisms in Central Asia – when social actors are uprooted from their local communities not by industrialisation but by the instrumentalisation of rituals' capacity to create feelings of belonging and loyalty – it is also worth emphasising that, for all practical reasons, once stripped of ritual excess, national values as embodied in the reformed celebrations become undistinguishable from strict Islamic precepts.

Conclusion

Some of these regulations are recent, and they still await investigations. Depending on the period and the country, the existing analyses assess their impact very differently. In Tajikistan, due to the traumas of the civil war (1992–1997) and the commitment to 'harmony' endorsed by both authorities and citizens, official regulations are either welcomed – because of the opportunity they offer to marry at a small expense – or circumvented, by bribing local authorities or by informalising (conducting secretly) some of the gifting and feasting practices. Scholars claim that in its present shape the law impacts only the 'public performances' of weddings (by capping the number of participants in the wedding feast and, in subsequent regulations, defining the days, durations and places where it can be held) while leaving their 'cultural performances' (the customs and rituals outside of the wedding feast) unaffected, because of the subversive tactics developed by social actors or because of the state's incapacity to enforce its own laws (Roche and Hohmann 2011). These 'cultural performances' offer various local enactments of the proper Tajik wedding, from gatherings celebrating ostentatious gifting and conspicuous consumption made possible by labour migrants' remittances to feasting- and gifting-free religious marriages where ritual excess is brought about by local mullahs who not only check 'every single ritual' for compliance with Islam but also introduce new ones claimed to date back to pre-Soviet times, 'when people were 'good Muslims'' (ibid.). In Tajikistan, ritual nationalism in an Islamic guise seems to be least resisted and broadly endorsed with 'traditional' being most often applied to religious wedding celebration while 'modern' refers to 'a consumerist feast in which status is displayed through wealth' (ibid.).

To stay within the wedding atmosphere, in Uzbekistan, past and recent official regulations – very similar in content and shape to the 2007 Tajikistan law discussed in the previous section – have led to an 'inequality in ritual' (Trevisani 2016) with those at the upper end patronising a prospering ceremonial economy and holding 'modern' marriages while those at the lower end are exposed to the zeal and whims of state-appointed neighbourhood committees that decide on the size and style of the celebration. On the one hand, these regulations have not put an end to ostentatious spending and conspicuous consumption which, contrary to the claims of the president, are not perceived as 'Soviet survivals' but as sure tokens of being 'modern.' On the other hand, recent regulations, coupled with a rampant inflation, have occasioned what many social actors perceive as a 'loss in ritual wealth' or 'traditions rotting from inside' (ibid.). So much so, that after more than 20 years of fighting excess, the official authorities have eventually taken up the duty to protect the traditions themselves: in 2018, the city state administration of the capital Tashkent started offering ready-made 'scenarios' for weddings that are modest but also nationally traditional (Orlova 2019).

In Kyrgyzstan, as mentioned above, the government and parliament have been unable to impose any regulation or law on life-cycle celebrations. The religious authorities have nevertheless been issuing regular *fatwas* (non-binding religious opinions) on the proper funeral rite for Muslims. In some places, local state administrations, with or without collaboration with local religious authorities, have introduced village charters that curtail the expenditures on life-cycle rituals. Elsewhere, decisions at the local level have been more drastic and a ban on funerary feasts has been implemented. Yet, Kyrgyzstan is also the only Central Asian country where a real counter-offensive to defend local funerary rites as pillars of Kyrgyz ethnic-national identity has been launched. In a nutshell, local state regulations, as well as the three draft laws that have been offered to the attention of the public, pigeonhole funeral rituals as 'allowed' and 'banned' in the same way as the religious *fatwas* divide them into 'right' and 'wrong' from the standpoint of a rigid Islamic norm (Jacquesson 2008; Beyer 2016; Pembeci 2017). Cultural elite figures as well as ordinary Kyrgyz in many places argue that official attempts to reform the funeral rite are jeopardising the ethnic and national traditions of the Kyrgyz and opening the way to the 'Arabisation' of the state. Being a 'bad' Muslim when conducting the funeral rite has been promoted by places into an ancestral Kyrgyz national tradition (Pembeci 2017).

In contemporary Central Asia then, both official regimes and ordinary citizens seem well established in their understandings of what traditions are and why they matter.[10] On the one side, official regimes still attempt to promote national identity as both the most ancient and the most modern form of belonging and instrumentalise traditions – unfailingly represented as ancient and ancestral – not only as the ultimate expression of national identity but also as the only way to authenticate it. The regimes themselves build their legitimacy as the custodians of these ancient national traditions and as the ultimate authorities over their authenticity or spuriousness. Traditions are thus not only the connection to glorious national pasts but, as importantly, a connection that can be claimed only if traditions remain authentic. However, as already noticed above, in all three countries the officially reformed wedding and funerary traditions are universally Islamic rather than distinctively national.

On the other side, for rank and file citizens, marriage and funeral celebrations are traditional not because of their conformity to ancient or ancestral models but because they have been held before or, to put it differently, because it is a tradition to hold them, and to hold them 'properly.' Yet the 'properly' in folk talk have a meaning quite different from the 'properly' in official talk or from the 'proper ways' imposed by laws and regulations. The folk does not define 'proper' by a ritual template that is supposedly ancient and ancestral, or right by Islam. The folk 'proper' is contingent on both private – individual and family – aspirations and public or community expectations, or the expectations of these same extended social networks that make life-cycle celebrations in the region so outstanding. As different from the historical continuity so valorised in official discourses, social actors are then concerned with social continuity, or with being recognised by and integrated within a community, or a ritual or social network. These networks have remained vital in the post-Soviet context for social, economic, and political support. They have been reconfigured to fit or, more rarely, cross the social boundaries occasioned by the end of the centralised socialist economies. Different communities or networks nurture and nourish different lifestyles, different imaginations, and different expectations. Currently, therefore, it can be a tradition to hold extravagant marriages or, on the opposite, modest ones, secular ones or, on the opposite, religious ones. It can even be a tradition to be a good Muslim or a bad one.

By their very nature of being official, recent regulations not only oblige citizens to adopt a position – either approving or disapproving – but they also equate loyalty to the nation and its values with compliance to easily controlled rules. As such these regulations and the categories produced or reproduced in them – allowed, banned, ethnic, national, modern, backward, authentic, spurious, wasteful, modest – either promote or stigmatise lifestyles and life choices and make more conflict-ridden the complex articulations of subjectivities and identities in contemporary Central Asia.

Notes

1 Even the titles of scholarly discussions contemporaneous with or following the magisterial work of Shils (1981) are revealing, i.e. Eugenia Shanklin (1981) 'Two meanings and uses of traditions,' Dan Ben-Amos (1984) 'The Seven strands of tradition: varieties in its meaning in American folklore studies' or Dorothy Noyes (2009) 'Tradition: three traditions.'
2 This chapter follows the suggestion of Hizky Shoham (2011) that modern invented traditions can be distinguished from folk traditions by the different modes of temporality they espouse: while folk traditions create a sense of continuity with the past, invented traditions are openly future-oriented to the extent that their inventors hope them to continue well into the future. Henceforth, invented traditions are overwhelmingly linked to official calendars and what Shoham calls 'quantitative chronology' (jubilees, anniversaries etc.) and they depend on repetition rather than transmission.
3 On Uzbek funerary rites, see Dağyeli 2015.
4 'Family events' are mentioned in all three regulations discussed in this section and they include circumcisions and birthday parties.
5 By 'celebrations' Tajikistan's and Kyrgyzstan's regulations refer to the newly established national holidays. In both cases, the latter have to be held 'in compliance with the existing laws.'
6 Tajik wedding rituals are described in Roche and Hohmann 2011; on Uzbek wedding rituals, see Trevisani 2016.
7 On Kyrgyz weddings, see McBrien 2017; Turdalieva and Provis 2017.
8 On Kyrgyz funerary rites, see Hardenberg 2010; Beyer 2016.
9 On the importance of this commemoration, see Jacquesson 2008; 2013.
10 For further examples of traditionalisation 'from below,' see Beyer and Finke 2019.

Bibliography

Abashin, S. (2003). Vopreki 'zdarovomu smyslu'? K voprosu o 'ratsional'nosti/irratsional'nosti' ritual'nykh raskhodov v srednei Azii. In: S. Panarin, ed. *Evraziia: Liudi i mify*. Moskva: Natalis, pp. 217–238.
Adams, L. (2007). Public and private celebrations: Uzbekistan's national holidays. In: J. Sahadeo and R. Zanca, eds. *Everyday Life in Central Asia: Past and Present*. Bloomington, IN: Indiana University Press, pp. 198–212.
Adams, L. (2010). *The Spectacular State: Culture and National Identity in Uzbekistan*. Durham, NC: Duke University Press.
Akaev, A. (2002). *Kyrgyzskaia gosudarstvennost' i narodnyi epos 'Manas.'* Bishkek: Uchkun.
Akaev, A. (2003). *Looking to the Future with Optimism: Reflections on Foreign Policy and the Universe*. New York: Global Scholarly Publications.
Babadzan, A. (2000). Anthropology, nationalism and 'the invention of tradition.' *Anthropological Forum* 10(2), pp. 131–155.
Bakiyev, K. (2010). Prezident K. Bakiyevdin Yntymak kurultaiyna kairyluusu. *Radio Free Europe/Radio Liberty*, 24 March.
Ben-Amos, D. (1984). The seven strands of tradition: Varieties in its meaning in American folklore studies. *Journal of Folklore Research* 21(2/3), pp. 97–131.

Beyer, J. (2016). *The Force of Custom: Law and the Ordering of Everyday Life in Kyrgyzstan*. Pittsburgh, PA: University of Pittsburgh Press.
Beyer, J. and P. Finke, eds. (2019). Practices of traditionalization in Central Asia. *Central Asian Survey* 38(3), pp. 310–328.
Binns, C. (1980). The changing face of power: Revolution and accommodation in the development of the Soviet ceremonial system: Part II. *Man* 15(1), pp. 170–187.
Botoeva, G. (2015). The monetization of social celebrations in rural Kyrgyzstan: On the uses of hashish money. *Central Asian Survey* 34(4), pp. 531–548.
Brower, D. (2003). *Turkestan and the Fate of the Russian Empire*. London: Taylor & Francis Group.
Bustanov, A.K. (2015). *Soviet Orientalism and the Creation of Central Asian Nations*. Abingdon: Routledge.
Campbell, I. (2017). *Knowledge and the Ends of Empire: Kazak Intermediaries and Russian Rule on the Steppe 1731–1917*. Ithaca, NY: Cornell University Press.
Collins, K. (2006). *Clan Politics and Regime Transition in Central Asia*. New York: Cambridge University Press.
Dağyeli, J.E. (2015). Contested mourning: Central Asian funerary practices in local and global Islam. *Anthropology of the Contemporary Middle East and Central Eurasia* 2(2), pp. 131–154.
DeWeese, D. (2002). Islam and the legacy of Sovietology: A review essay on Yaacov Ro'i's 'Islam in the Soviet Union.' *Journal of Islamic Studies* 13(3), pp. 298–330.
DeWeese, D. (2012). Survival strategies: Reflections on the notion of religious 'survivals' in Soviet ethnographic studies of Muslim religious life in Central Asia. In: F. Muehlfried and S. Sokolovski, eds. *Exploring the Edge of Empire: Soviet Era Anthropology in the Caucasus and Central Asia*. Muenster: LIT, pp. 35–58.
DeWeese, D. (2016). It was a dark and stagnant night ('til the Jadids brought the light): Clichés, biases, and false dichotomies in the intellectual history of Central Asia. *Journal of the Economic and Social History of the Orient* 59(1/2), pp. 37–92.
Edgar, A.L. (2006). *Tribal Nation: The Making of Soviet Turkmenistan*. Princeton, NJ: Princeton University Press.
Farangis, N. (2007). Tajikistan: President seeks limits on wedding, funeral spending. *Radio Free Europe/Radio Liberty*, 29 May.
Gullette, D. (2010). *The Genealogical Construction of the Kyrgyz Republic: Kinship, State and 'Tribalism.'* Kent: Global Oriental.
Hardenberg, R. (2010). How to overcome death? The efficacy of funeral rituals in Kyrgyzstan. *Journal of Ritual Studies* 24(1), pp. 29–43.
Hirsch, F. (2005). *Empire of Nations: Ethnographic Knowledge and the Making of the Soviet Union*. Ithaca, NY: Cornell University Press.
Iğmen, A. (2012). *Speaking Soviet with an Accent: Culture and Power in Kyrgyzstan*. Pittsburgh, PA: University of Pittsburgh Press.
Ilkhamov, A. (2013). Labour migration and the ritual economy of the Uzbek extended family. *Zeitschrift Für Ethnologie* 138(2), pp. 259–284.
Jacquesson, S. (2008). The sore zones of identity: Past and present debates on funerals in Kyrgyzstan. *Inner Asia* 10(2), pp. 281–303.
Jacquesson, S. (2013). Performance and poetics in Kyrgyz memorial feasts: The discursive construction of identity categories. In: P. Sartori, ed. *Explorations in the Social History of Modern Central Asia (19th - Early 20th Century)*. Leiden: Brill, pp. 181–206.
Kamp, M. (2007). The wedding feast: Living the new Uzbek life in the 1930s. In: J. Sahadeo and R. Zanca, eds. *Everyday Life in Central Asia: Past and Present*. Bloomington, IN: Indiana University Press, pp. 103–114.
Kandiyoti, D. (1996). Modernisation without the market? The case of the 'Soviet East.' *Economy and Society* 25(4), pp. 529–542.
Karimov, I. (1998). *Presidential Decree No. 2100*. 28 October.
Karimov, I. (2002). Vystuplenie prezidenta Islama Karimova na torzhestvennom sobranii posviashchennom desiatiletiiu Konstitutsii Respubliki Uzbekistan. *Centrasia*, 9 December. https://centrasia.org/newsA.php?st=1039412040, accessed on 12 December 2019.
Khalid, A. (2007). *Islam after Communism: Religion and Politics in Central Asia*. Berkeley, CA: University of California Press.
Kurzman, C. (1999). Uzbekistan: The Invention of nationalism in an invented nation. *Critique* 15, pp. 77–98.

Light, N. (2015). Self-sufficiency is not enough: Ritual intensification and household economies in a Kyrgyz village. In: S. Gudeman and C. Hann, eds. *Oikos and Market: Explorations in Self-Sufficiency after Socialism*. Oxford: Berghahn Books, pp. 101–136.

March, A.F. (2003). State ideology and the legitimation of authoritarianism: The case of post-Soviet Uzbekistan. *Journal of Political Ideologies* 8(2), pp. 209–232.

McBrien, J. (2017). *From Belonging to Belief: Modern Secularisms and the Construction of Religion in Kyrgyzstan*. Pittsburgh, PA: University of Pittsburgh Press.

Noyes, D. (2009). Tradition: Three traditions. *Journal of Folklore Research* 46(3), pp. 233–268.

Orlova, N. (2019). Pod makamy Mendel'sona: kak prokhodiat tashkentskie svad'by i pri chem tut stsenarii Ministerstva kul'tury. https://fergana.agency/articles/112427/, accessed on 12 January 2020.

Pembeci, B. (2017). Religion and the construction of ethnic identity in Kyrgyzstan. *Region* 6(1), pp. 133–152.

Phillips, A. and James, P. (2001). National identity between tradition and reflexive modernisation: The contradictions of Central Asia. *National Identities* 3(1), pp. 23–35.

Prezident respubliki Tadzhikistan E. Rahmonov. (2007). *Zakon Respubliki Tadzhikistan ob uporiadochenii traditsii, torzhestv i obriadov v respublike Tadzhikistan*. https://mfa.tj/ru/main/view/3960/zakon-respubliki-tadzhikistan-ob-uporyadochenii-traditsii-torzhestv-t-obryadov-v-respublike-tadzhikistan, accessed on 12 January 2020.

Rasanayagam, J. (2011). *Islam in Post-Soviet Uzbekistan: The Morality of Experience*. Cambridge: Cambridge University Press.

Reeves, M. (2012). Black work, green money: Remittances, ritual, and domestic economies in southern Kyrgyzstan. *Slavic Review* 71(1), pp. 108–134.

Reeves, M. (2014). *Border Work: Spatial Lives of the State in Rural Central Asia*. Ithaca, NY: Cornell University Press.

Roberts, F. (2017). A time for feasting? Autarky in the Tajik Ferghana Valley at war 1941–45. *Central Asian Survey* 36(1), pp. 37–54.

Roche, S. and Hohmann, S. (2011). Wedding rituals and the struggle over national identities. *Central Asian Survey* 30(1), pp. 113–128.

Roy, O. (2000). *The New Central Asia: The Creation of Nations*. New York: I.B. Tauris Publishers.

Sartori, P. (2010). Towards a history of the Muslims' Soviet Union: A view from Central Asia. *Die Welt Des Islams* 50(3/4), pp. 315–334.

Sartori, P. (2019). Of saints, shrines, and tractors: Untangling the meaning of Islam in Soviet Central Asia. *Journal of Islamic Studies* 30(3), pp. 367–405.

Schatz, E. (2004). *Modern Clan Politics: The Power of 'Blood' in Kazakhstan and Beyond*. Seattle, WA: University of Washington Press.

Schoeberlein, J. (2012). Heroes of theory: Central Asian Islam in post-war Soviet ethnography. In: F. Muehlfried and S. Sokolovski, eds. *Exploring the Edge of Empire: Soviet Era Anthropology in the Caucasus and Central Asia*. Muenster: LIT, pp. 59–79.

Senat Olij Mazhlisa Respibliki Uzbekistan. (2019). *Informatsionnoe soobshchenie o sovmestnom zasedanii kengashej senata i zakonodatel'noj palaty Olij Mazhlisa Respibliki Uzbekistan*. http://senat.uz/ru/lists/view/465, accessed on 12 January 2020.

Shanklin, E. (1981). Two meanings and uses of tradition. *Journal of Anthropological Research* 37(1), pp. 71–89.

Shils, E. (1981). *Tradition*. Chicago, IL: University of Chicago Press.

Shoham, H. (2011). Rethinking tradition: From ontological reality to assigned temporal meaning. *European Journal of Sociology* 52(2), pp. 313–340.

Trevisani, T. (2016). Modern weddings in Uzbekistan: Ritual change from 'above' and from 'below.' *Central Asian Survey* 35(1), pp. 61–75.

Turdalieva, C. and Provis, R. (2017). Dynamics of reciprocity and networks of the Kyrgyz through Bishkek toi making. *Central Asian Affairs* 4, pp. 197–216.

Werner, C. (1998). Household networks and the security of mutual indebtedness in rural Kazakstan. *Central Asian Survey* 17(4), pp. 597–612.

Werner, C. (2000). Consuming modernity, imagining tradition: Globalization, nationalism and wedding feasts in post-colonial Kazakstan. *Anthropology of East Europe Review* 18(2), pp. 125–134.

Xalq so'zi. (2019). *T'oylar, oylaviy tantanalar, ma'raka va marosimlar o'tkazilishini tartibga solish tizimini yanada takomillashtirish t'oghrisida*. 5 October. http://xs.uz/uzkr/post/tojlar-oilavij-tantanalar-maraka-va-marosimlar-otkazilishini-tartibga-solish-tizimini-yanada-takomillashtirish-togrisida, accessed on 12 January 2020.

Zhogorku Kengesh Kyrgyzskoi respublike. (2011). *O proekte zakona 'Ob uporiadochenii traditsii, torzhestv i obriadov v Kyrgyzskoi respublike.'* http://www.kenesh.kg/ky/draftlaw/17633/show, accessed 12 January 2020.

Zhogorku Kengesh Kyrgyzskoi respublike. (2016). *O proekte zakona 'Ob ob uporiadochenii traditsii, torzhestv i obriadov v Kyrgyzskoi respublike.'* http://www.kenesh.kg/ru/draftlaw/272694/show, accessed on 12 January 2020.

24
THINKING WITH GENDER ABOUT CENTRAL ASIA

Svetlana Peshkova

Why gender

The concept of 'gender,' which refers to a socio-cultural construction used to differentiate among individuals in a society of whether and how one is female, male or any other culturally acceptable category, is not indigenous to the Central Asian region and may not be widely embraced by local populations, scholars and governments (Khalid 2015: 361; Kamp 2009; Megoran 1999). The local use of this term is often limited to the field of international aid and development and non-governmental activism. This is not surprising. As an analytical concept, gender originated and matured in American and European academic and activist circles from the 1960s onward (Olson & Horn-Schott 2018). During the last decade of the twentieth century, international agencies introduced this term to local activists and scholars (Hoare 2016: 292). Despite this history, thinking *with* gender about local lifeways is not just replicating an analytical concept produced elsewhere. Gender as a lens on social complexity offers a way for a more nuanced understanding of human diversity in and history of the region.

Thinking with gender is not a requirement, but an option. Many of the existing works about Central Asia rely only on two, well-established, and widely accepted categories, such as 'women' and 'men.' These two categories are not the only categories present in the Central Asian context historically. They also fail to capture a contemporary diversity of meaningful and liveable human lives in the region.[1] As a result of a persistent scholarly reliance on 'women' and 'men' dichotomy assumed to be universal, humans and collectivities that do not fit neatly within these two categories are considered deviant and/or exceptions often undeserving of scholarly focus and empirical research. Despite the efforts of a handful of scholars (e.g., Buelow 2012; Wilkinson & Kirey 2010; Suyarkulova 2019), academic reliance on this dichotomy continues to create and maintain empirical and theoretical blind spots, which remain as mainly uncharted territory in scholarly work in and about the region. Hence, thinking with gender is also a call for offering thicker descriptions and analyses of local complex and complicated lives by shedding light on these blind spots. One of these spots is gender variance or a range of behaviours associated with opposite sex.

This chapter is neither a well-balanced representation of gender roles and/or gender struggles in the region, nor it is a balanced insight into each country's gender orders associated with a (geopolitical) concept of 'post-Soviet' or 'former-Soviet' Central Asia. These imbalances reflect a

DOI: 10.4324/9780429057977-24

lack of existing research and writing about femininities, masculinities and other identities in the region. Such research is often discouraged by a contextual sensitivity to (any) research on gender highly politicised in the former-Soviet space at large, precisely because of the concept's origin in Western academia and its deployment in local activist circles challenging local nationalisms, relational hierarchies, social stratification, and established normative gender roles. Gender also continues to be a tool for development-focused interventions, marketing research, and a neoliberal capitalist (inequal) exchange and extraction economy penetrating every corner of the world, leading to a local resistance to the word 'gender' (in Russian with hard G) and the concept.

At the same time, during the second decade of the twenty-first century, local youths and former-Soviet subjects' often pluranational existence – a feeling and experience of belonging to more than one community and/or society – made the concept of gender and the word 'gender' a part of some Central Asians' daily lives. The ever-growing transnational communications, exchanges of digital information, increased travel, tourism and (im)migration resulting in circulation of ideas and practices, facilitated the concept's adoption into writing by several local scholars and foreign researchers. Hence, thinking *with* gender is not unique and helps overcoming politicised and reductionist zones of theorising about the region, including 'women's question' and/or 'Islamic revival,' and an analytical scaling down of complex human relations to a dominance/submission model (as in 'men' over 'women' and 'Islam' over 'its regional subjects'). In the following paragraphs, I am holding a gender lens on social dynamics in the region by drawing on and synthesising some existing publications produced by regional and foreign scholars (Russian Colonial/Imperial, Soviet, Central Asian, and post- and de-colonial), and my ongoing ethnographic learning from and with local individuals (2001–). This analysis and synthesis are not exhaustive. I call on other local and non-Central Asian scholars to join the conversation.

Gender, enculturation and gender order

As an analytical tool, gender refers to a socio-cultural construction used to differentiate among individuals in a society of whether and how one is female, male or any other culturally acceptable category. Some human communities assume that one's behavioural and attitudinal differences and traits are determined by biology (e.g., genes and hormones), others – by transcendental powers (god, gods, creator, and/or creatrix), in yet others – by society and/or culture and/or all of the above.[2] In social sciences, these differences are taken to emerge from within and vis a vis a particular socio-cultural context rather than biology, creator(s/ix), social norms and/or cultural substances (e.g., ethnos). These differences are learned by humans while becoming gendered members of a society through *enculturation*. This learning continues throughout an individual's life with a set of different(ial) standards applied to being male or female and any other gender category. These standards include behavioural expectations, clothes, hairstyles, language, jobs, and sports thought to be appropriate for a particular gender category.

Human communities recognise two or more contextually defined gender categories. These categories can be created by a reference to sexual orientation, preference in behaviour, occupation, standards of beauty, dress-code, presence and/or combination of certain biological and physiological characteristics or any combination of some of the above criteria. One's gender is enacted always in a socio-historical context through quotidian practices of daily life. Hence, gender is not just a category or a noun, but also a verb: it has to be performed in culturally appropriate ways. One does gender on a daily basis by expressing it symbolically (e.g., dress code) vis à vis social expectations reflecting a prevalent organisation of gender relations in a society, or a local *gender order*. The gender order provides a context for dominant discourses on how to feel and act as a gendered being, including behaviours, practices, and standards of sexuality and morality (Stella 2015: 26). In Central Asia, as in other parts of the former-Soviet space, gender orders are binary, limited to two categories – 'women' and 'men.'

In the region, like everywhere, a human child learns how to become and act as a gendered member of a society through a process of enculturation, by interacting with and learning from others and experiencing first-hand human and non-human environment. Children watch, listen, reflect on, and repeat what others say and do. Although the childhood experiences directly contribute to learning about gendered behaviours, as a social process, enculturation never ends and includes the context of one's immediate family, mass media, oral traditions, educational institutions and personal networks. While learning from parents, children often pattern their behaviour on the same gendered parent and/or relative. For example, growing up as 'a girl-child,' one could (not everyone does) learn how to imitate the mother and other female relatives, including dress code, gait, bodily practices, and gendered activities, such as childcare, serving food, sewing, cooking daily meals, ritual practices, washing clothes and dishes, and tending to a garden and/or domestic plants or taking care of livestock. Since their teenage years, girls are expected to be interested in males and eventually build their own family reflective either of their and/or their families' choice of a groom. For Central Asian females, the practices pertinent to running a household, caretaking and childrearing, almost always become an important part of gendered social expectations. Based on her mother's and female relatives' experiences, a local girl-child could imagine the future as 'a daughter-in-law,' who under the supervision of the mother-in-law – whether they reside in the same household and/or town or not – is expected to love and care for the husband (and often the in-laws), birth children, prepare food, clean the house, have an agreeable disposition, be virtuous and demonstrate a modest behaviour. After giving birth, she could reassert some behavioural autonomy and independent decision-making (e.g., Ismailbekova 2014; Kudaibergenova 2018; Werner 2004).

Growing up as 'a boy-child,' one could, for example, learn from and with his father or/and other male relatives a trait of a handy man around the house, taking out garbage, shopping at a local bazar, playing soccer, going to the mosque and male-only gatherings, or attending to animals at the pastures (e.g., Montgomery 2016; Liu 2012). For Central Asian males, it is important to learn and master a trade and/or get an appropriate education to ensure a reliable income, because males are expected to provide financially for their families. Since their teenage years, the boys are anticipated to be interested in females and eventually build their own family reflective either of their and/or their families' choice of a bride. While observing their fathers and male relatives (verbal or physical) disciplining other family members and/or acquiescing to and respect decisions of the elderly relatives, teenage boys often learn how to be future heads of households. It is important to note that some of these gendered expectations and knowledges do not materialise and/or matter. Human lives in the region are as dynamic as everywhere else and no one template can fit all. The families differ from each other in terms of class, education, social position, geographic residence, and so on. Further, in contemporary socio-historical context, particular economic and existential needs of the families are often prioritised over gendered social expectations. Some families fall apart. Some husbands fail to get and hold a job. As a result, the wives have to bear the burden of providing for the families simultaneously attending to the house chores, children, and other social responsibilities. Some husbands may also become stay-at-home caretakers for their relatives and children, and sometimes those who are raised as 'a boy-child' feel and act as 'a girl-child,' and vice-versa. Despite such cases, local transmission of gendered knowledges and lifeways, including ideas about how to be a proper and virtuous human being, continue to safeguard the binary gender order.

Even though in daily conversations, many Central Asians might use such statements as 'this is how Central Asian women are,' or 'this is how Central Asian men are,' implying a homogeneity of experience within a gender category, there is a great experiential and existential variation in whether and how one is male or female: local socio-cultural expectations and degree of personal power and control differ not only between, but also *among*, females and males. For example, a mother-in-law is often in charge of her daughter(s)-in-law; a mother often controls a pre-menarche girl-child, while a father often controls his boy-child and is himself controlled by elderly male and female relatives. Therefore, in Central Asia, there is a variation of models for femininity (how one is to be and behave as a female) and masculinity (how one is to be and behave as a male). There are also power relations among these models, including a scaled ascending hierarchy among such femininities as pre-menarche girls, menstruating young women, mothers of a girl/girls, mothers of a boy/boys, and post-menopausal women. The same goes for a scaled ascending hierarchy among such masculinities as pre-circumcised boys, circumcised young men, husbands/fathers and grandfathers/elderly (e.g., *aksakals*). Realising this variation and pointing out, among other things, the importance of age, class, social position, geographic location, and one's access to information/education help to configure a far more nuanced and complex regional gender structure than the often-assumed one.

Sexuality matters

Sexual orientation describes one's sexual preferences, desires and activities, which could be felt and/or enacted toward an individual of an opposite sex/gender (heterosexual), between individuals of the same sex/gender (homosexual), toward an individual of the opposite and the same sex/gender (bisexual), or one can have no sexual desires, or feel an attraction but not act on it sexually (asexual). Some societies define gender categories by sexual preference, others by preference in behavioural practices, occupation, dress and spiritual/religious sensibilities, or a combination of any of these criteria. For example, in India, this combination underlines a tripartite gender structure, which includes 'male,' 'female' and the third gender, Kinnars (a pejorative term is *hijra*). Kinnars are 'neither male nor female;' they are conceptualised as 'special, sacred beings' and spiritual partners and/or 'consorts.' (Nanda 1997: 198–200). Germany too has a tripartite gender structure, the one reflecting human biological and physiological characteristics: 'male,' 'female' and 'other' (Nandi 2013).[3] It is important to remember that individuals do not necessarily conform to the social expectations of how one is to express one's sexuality.

Sexuality is an important component of social reproduction (how a society endures through time). Biological reproduction and birthing of humans ensure societal continuity, while social relations and various forms of capital (including social and financial) create the ties that bind a group of humans/community/society together. In Central Asia, each country's nationalist discourse fuses biological and social reproduction. As a result, deviations from established expectations of heterosexual coupling are taken as an affront to social continuity. Although it is unclear to what extent and how exactly human biology is related to gender expression, since males and females differ empirically often on a scale (e.g., height, weight, and/or voice pitch), and not every local person believes in transcendental relations between the human and divine worlds (e.g., god, creat/or/rix), many Central Asians, like inhabitants of other former-Soviet countries, continue to explain differences among humans by references to biology, tradition and/or religion. In other words, individual sexual desires and human coupling are thought to be determined by biology and ontology. These assumptions, in turn, inform and support the dominant view that 'men' and 'women' are created as different species and exist to be sexually paired. This view reinforces the local binary gender order. Same-sex desires and practices do not fit neatly into this gender order, and, as a result, are often considered to be socially deviant. Local individuals who experience such desires and participate in such practices have to find creative ways to negotiate their difference. They sometimes act *as if* they conform to the dominant binary categories, hide their sexual desires and preferences, adopt a 'don't ask, don't tell policy,' or immigrate. Others resist and confront the existing gender order through social activism and by creating networks of care and support (e.g., Buelow 2012; Wilkinson & Kirey 2010; Suyarkulova 2019).

Gender orders are dynamic and change overtime. A detour into the regional social history demonstrates that the existing gender order is but one example of what a dominant gender order in the region can be. The current gender order is informed by Russian Imperial/colonial and Soviet state-centred efforts to remake the regional Central Asian social structure.[4] Among other things, these efforts were meant to erase the existing non-binary (not limited to 'women' vs. 'men' only) gender positions – models of maleness and femaleness distinct from manhood or womanhood – such as '*bachcha*,' or young male performers (Nalivkin and Nalivkina 2016 [1886]).[5] In the following sections, I explore some of these efforts and former gender positions of young male performers, *bachcha*.

Pre-colonial gender order and colonial interventions

The pre-colonial and early colonial Turkestan's gender order was distinctly different from the Russian Imperial and later Soviet one.[6] Vestiges of this order are visible in the colonial travelogues and ethnographies about settled communities (e.g., Nalivkin and Nalivkins 2016). In addition to ontological and physiological characteristics, and/or sexual preferences, Turkestan's pre-colonial gender structure also reflected such categories as occupation, artistic ability, age and standards of beauty. While reading against their orientalist judgment masquerading as a scientific exploration, Arandarenko (1889) and Kushilevskij (1891) provide a glance into this local pre-colonial gender structure, which was markedly non-binary and included 'males,' 'females' and '*bachcha*.' Russian colonial ethnographers, Nalivkin and Nalivkina (2016 [1886]) spent considerable time describing these young, 'dolled-up' youth, often well-skilled in 'the art of seduction,' who were local entertainers performing for and serving older men at parties in private homes, *choy-xona* (local tea house) and at public celebrations (Nalivkin and Nalivkina 2016: 33, 133, 140–1; Levin 2016).[7] Some *bachcha* had sexual relations with their patrons.[8] Often described as tender, gentle, beautiful, seductive and sensual, *bachcha* received wide admiration from both men and women for their aesthetic qualities and performance skills (Schuyler 1876: 132–3). For example, in the Ferghana region, it would not be unusual to see the *bachcha* perform at a public holiday, exciting the crowd by exhibiting their artistry of dance, song and dress (Nalivkin and Nalivkina 2016: 140–1). As a social position, being a *bachcha* did not determine one's behaviour throughout life. Those identified as *bachcha* changed their social status from a 'boy' to 'bachi [sic.]' – a teen male dancer admired and desired by other older males – to 'a young man' expected to start his own family (Prischepova 2006).[9] In other words, local pre-colonial models for and of manhood were also age-dependent, whereby one could be a 'bacha [sic.]' as 'chuvon (guy)' and 'besaqol (beardless guy)' and then become an adult male (*Ibid.*). Further, pre-colonial same-sex desire and practices did not seem to fly in the face of the existing social mores. As Nalivkin and Nalivkina (2016: 178) report, khans (local rulers) themselves, were 'the main enthusiasts of introducing these fashionable things'; they had 'innumerable wives, *bachchas* and concubines.'

Many pre-colonial and early colonial sedentary communities in Turkestan observed strict gender segregation. Ontologically different – as different beings created by god in different ways and for different purposes – men and women led homosocial (socialising with the same gender identity) lives outside of the privacy of one's home. Homosocial entertainment, such as the ones offered by *bachcha*, and frequent visitations with family and friends were some of the favourite pastimes in the settled communities (Nalivkin and Nalivkina 2016, 116, 158). In that context, sensuality, generosity and kind etiquette, beauty and beautiful manners – even if these did not cohere to the Russian Colonial metric of beauty – were desirable attributes of all genders.

For the Russian Colonial authorities' local sociality and gender positions, like *bachcha*, were odd, deviant, uncivilised, and unacceptable. The colonial administration embraced feminisation of prostitution, which by the end of the nineteenth century, 'has almost completely replaced the *bachcha*,' in a sense that females, not the *bachcha*, became prominent entertainers at homosocial gatherings and offered sexual intimacy to their patrons (Nalivkina and Nalivkin 2016: 189). Other contemporary travellers observed and demonstrated a growing moral disdain expressed by the colonisers' gesture of reducing *bachcha* as a gender positionality to their sexuality only; as 'fallen men,' *bachcha's* artistry, sensuality and beautiful manners were completely screened out (e.g., Kushilevskij 1891). Still, although not without a sense of a moral judgement, several Russian colonial sources recorded the *bachcha's* performance at the Central Asian Agricultural, Industrial and Scientific Explosion in Tashkent in 1909.[10] These examples demonstrate that the *bachcha's* social position, their complex gender identity and social reception by the local communities, differed significantly from the *bachcha's* depictions and treatment as socially deviant and morally apprehensible by the late colonial, early Communist (Bolshevik), and then Soviet administrators and scholarship.

Gender orders change over time. The efforts to change local societies during the twentieth century by the Russian Imperial and later Soviet colonial authorities, often supported by local elites, led to an eventual transformation of regional gender order. The pre-colonial and early colonial gender order reflected religious sensibilities, communities' standards of reciprocity (e.g., communal work/building projects/celebrations), respect, exchange, and not equality and/or heterosexual companionship. This order was hierarchical but less centralised and dogmatic than the subsequent ones. The colonial encounter between the Russian Empire and local communities transformed local gender order into a binary; this order also became state-centred. Eventually, through the early Soviet period, this gender order came to rest on a non-liberal notion of equality, animated by men and women's active participation in wage-labour and socialisation of women and men in public space. Preoccupation with beauty, sensuality, dress, hair, accessories, and the art of seduction, came to be seen as mainly feminine traits. When local men expressed some of these traits, they came to be labelled as deviant and faced punitive measures, since such behaviours in males were pathologised (associated with illness and mental deficiency) and same-sex (or those assumed to be of the same sex) practices were criminalised in the region in the 1920s and throughout the Soviet Union in the 1930s.

Social transformations ensured by the Russian colonisation of the region brought about other changes to the existing gender order. Among sedentary local communities, the relations between women and men were guided by the religious law and local traditions, and were often based on the principle of exchange. For example, in settled communities in the Ferghana region, wives felt entitled to receive financial support from their husbands and in return would remain faithful and studious housemakers and caretakers; they were also not afraid to scold those husbands who failed to live up to such expectations (Nalivkina and Nalivkin 2016: 98). In such communities, only extreme poverty, or widowhood, would lead women to earn their living working outside the house, and prior to the colonialists' arrival, well-off families kept male and female slaves.[11] The socialising between female and male children was not restricted and their dress code did not mark their gender up till a certain age. At the age of 12, females often entered a gradual seclusion and took on a veil.[12] From that time on, their activities focused on learning how to run a household. Although parenting was expected to be shared by all members of the family, males and females alike, females were expected to be main care takers when it came to child and elderly care. Marriages were mainly arranged by the parents, and remarriage and child-marriage for both males and females were not unusual. Among regional sedentary and nomadic and semi-nomadic peoples polygyny – having multiple wives at one time – was rarely practiced for various reasons. In many cases, only well-off individuals could afford to have more than one wife.

By the 1910s, not the family, community, and/or local religious leadership in Central Asia, but the Russian colonial authorities (and later, in the 1920s, the Soviet ones) became the main arbiters of social organisation of gender relations. The colonial authorities outlawed practices such as polygyny and child-marriage and increasingly scorned local gender diversity, particularly in the settled communities. Since the Russian Empire also was a religious one, it reaffirmed ontological differences between males and females as fundamental to Central Asian gender structure, and defined same-sex desire and practices as abhorrent and abnormal. Yet, to the colonial authorities the region's economic and political viability and the establishment of the colonial regime's legitimacy vis-à-vis the existing – labelled as uncivilised, corrupt and ignorant – governing structures, including local religious leadership, took precedence over other efforts of remaking local gender order.[13] Although the effects of the Russian colonial efforts to remake the local gender structure were not as critical as the ones introduced by the Soviet period, they fostered (1) the initial racialising of native populations (*tuzemtsi*) as different, but also culturally and religiously inferior to the Russians, who were predominantly Slavs and Orthodox Christians; (2) informed local Central Asian reformers' (*jadids'*) ideas about modernising their society and changing women's social status, including promotion of heterosexual companionship (Khalid 1998, 2007; Kamp 2006); and (3) reinforced existing generational and gendered hierarchies.

Soviet transformations

Unlike the Russian Empire, the Communist organisers, and later the Soviet State, were markedly non-religious. They continued to codify gender relations in the region along the lines of binary, yet distinctly non-religious, gender structure. Eventually, through juristic means, strategic political activism, violence and education, Russian colonial Central Asia was transformed into five Soviet Socialist Republics. Each one of them had its titular nation and native leadership directly controlled by the Communist government in Moscow (Constantine 2007: 119). Adopting a binary gender structure wholesale from their Imperial predecessors, the Communist organisers' contempt for local gender diversity led to the eventual elimination of the *bachcha*, as a possible gender position. The colonial criticism of gender segregation, as an index of the natives' uncivilised ignorant behaviour, was amplified in the speeches of the Communist organisers calling for liberating local women from their dependence on their families and husbands. These calls included emphasis on heterosocialising (socialising with the opposite sex/gender) and coeducation, deemed inappropriate by many Central Asians, and served to encourage women to join wage labour necessary for the Soviet state-building. The Soviet organisers' belief that unveiling of local Muslim women would make them 'modern members of the new Soviet polity' came hand-in-hand with collectivisation, forced sedentarisation and industrialisation, the efforts requiring brutal methods and often having violent outcomes (Kamp 2016: 271). Kamp (2016) reminds that not all of the social and societal changes had negative outcomes; in the context of new possibilities and constraints, many Central Asians carved a space for meaningful lives for themselves and their families.

The Soviet efforts and domestic policies aimed at reallocating women's dependence from the family and husbands to the Soviet state had a particular political agenda behind them. By rewarding women's productive labour with wages and their reproductive labour with maternity leaves and free childcare, the Soviet state rendered women 'more amendable to the state's control'; as main caretakers, they could extend this control to their offspring and spouses (Ashwin 2000: 10). These efforts solidified a model of parental and spousal responsibilities that undermined fatherhood by distancing fathers from parental responsibilities toward children and sharing household chores with their wives. They glorified motherhood (e.g., financial assistance, preferential custody) and increased the labour force at the expense of introducing a dual burden for local women, who were already responsible for birthing, childcare, house chores and caretaking of their extended families. By placing gender roles and dependences at the centre of Central Asia's Soviet transformation, the Communist and Soviet organisers politicised women's rights, making them the centrepiece of the Soviet modernity (and the anti-Soviet resistance), but did little to challenge male primacy associated with in-family and societal leadership.

Soviet changes in Central Asian gender order were reflected in changing gender structure by gradually limiting the criteria for human differentiating to only two genders based on sexual preference and physiological, reflecting biological, differences. Since the Soviet project of modernising Central Asia purposefully (and violently) limited the power of religious leadership, ontological differences, one of the most important criteria in the pre-colonial and early colonial gender structure, was pushed to the periphery (Keller 2001).[14] The Soviet state-building had no space for the old bourgeois aesthetic and pastime activities; the Party organisers' disdain toward bourgeois etiquette, values and lifestyle, including artistic ability and beauty(full) manners, resulted in discarding these as other criteria for gender differentiation. Same-sex practices were pathologised and criminalised (see Kon 1995).[15] Sensuality, beauty and beautiful manners, including emotion and tenderness, formerly desirable attributes of all genders, came to be indexed as feminine only. Physiological, reflecting biological promoted by the Soviet sciences, differences and the concomitant sexual preferences were left as the only criteria for gender differentiation in the Soviet state. The Soviet State became a disciplinarian for the Soviet men, whereas the Soviet men were expected to be disciplinarians in the context of their families. Hence, local gender order became fully state-centred.

The Soviet reforms further racialised gender identities, whereby European or Slavic appearance and linguistic competence in Russian increased one's symbolic and economic capital and social status (Abashin 2007). These reforms also politicised women's rights as markers of national and societal development and set the stage for an uneasy relationship between Soviet ideals and national traditions, some of which were valorised (e.g., domestic, hardworking and modest 'Eastern' women) and others criticised (e.g., local religious practices as 'the remnants of the past'). Further, these reforms never challenged gendered and generational hierarchies, while adding education, class and ethnicity as other categories of unequal social differentiation. As a result of these social transformations, Central Asian societies' promotion of women's rights and social change were not inimical to male dominance; marriage viewed as companionship, which came with a possibility of divorce initiated by either spouse (either husband or wife) was practiced in extreme cases; and an ideological acceptance that anyone should have an ability to refuse polygynous marriage was confronted by an economic reality of single mothers' precarity and a persistent perception of an old maidenhood as a failure of humanhood. Local communities continued to glorify motherhood and value education and some level of individual independence and equality, if these did not clash with social gendered hierarchy, while (Central Asian) parents continued to be deeply involved in the decisions regarding the choice of one's future spouse. One of the side-effects of the Soviet social project was the entrenchment of an exaggerated dominance-oriented gender hierarchy with rigid social boundaries merging age, class, and ethnicity. Hence, local hierarchies of older verses younger, wealthy and educated verses poor and un-educated, Russians (here as Slavs) verses non-Slavs, and men verses women, continued to characterise dominant discourses on gender differences in the region. And even though Central Asian women eventually could occupy positions of power in their respective Soviet Socialist Republics, such as scientists, writers, performers, and administrators – some even became Communist Party leaders on local levels – to them, their families and communal obligations always came first (Peshkova 2014).

Post-soviet gender order and its current iteration

After the disintegration of the Soviet Union in the 1990s, gender order in Central Asian countries, just like the Soviet one, continued to be state-centred and reflected a binary gender structure.[16] Same-sex desires and practices continued to be criminalised and medicalised (e.g., Uzbekistan and Turkmenistan) and/or socially frowned upon, while motherhood continued to be glorified. Biological reproduction remained to be (minimally) rewarded by Central Asian states in the form of 'mother's capital,' paid leave for birthers and a post-natal childcare (e.g., Roche 2016).[17] As a result, caretaking and child-care and -rearing remained mainly women's responsibilities, while fathers' participation in parenthood continued to be reduced to the expectation of economic provisioning and their role as disciplinarians and families' protective patriarchs. The gender order in each one of the former-Soviet Central Asian states continued to be 'enmeshed with' changing political regimes, precarious economy and national struggles for cultural authenticity (Connell 2014: 557).

In its post-Soviet version, each Central Asian state also embarked on its own project of re-traditionalising society – a selective revival of customs and gender roles – a defining feature of post-Soviet nationalism in the former-Soviet societies. This process did not lead to a return to the pre-colonial or pre-Soviet gendered past; former gender positions, such as *bachcha*, were *not* reinstated and/or celebrated as traditional. Each post-Soviet nation-state also appealed to some religious discourses, like the one on 'safe' Islam, and to ancestral, and national heroes, like *Amir Timur* in Uzbekistan and *Manas* in Kyrgyzstan.[18] A growing importance of religious sensibilities, often explained as traditional, brought back a focus on ontological differences among humans as one of the criteria for distinguishing and establishing meaningful gender diversity among Central Asians. The ontological differences between females and males came with related duties and rights, which were equally important but radically different for each of the two genders. These duties and rights mapped well on the existing gender models that emphasise females' supportive roles and males' inter-family and financial leadership (Kamp 2016: 276). In some cases, an emphasis on such differences rolled back females' ability to pursue certain career aspirations, unless those fell within religiously sanctioned areas, such as religious education, childcare, elderly care and health care (Tokhtakhodjaeva 1995). In other cases, ambitious women were still able to achieve important levels of political power, like the former President of Kyrgyzstan, Ms. Otunbayeva (Kamp 2016: 275).

The post-Soviet transformations also created a space for the partnerships of local and foreign NGOs and introduced gender as a word, concept and as a metric for the projects' assessment. Some of these efforts offered spaces for female activism, particularly when it came to domestic violence and women's empowerment, such as providing consultancy to and support for battered women and their children.[19] These local-foreign partnerships also provided some space and resources for a local feminist and LGBTQ activism and eventually resulted in a growing visibility of local gender positions not fitting neatly into the regional binary gender order.

During the second decade of the twenty-first century, the existing gender order in Central Asian states still bears vestiges of its historical predecessors differentiating among humans on an ontological basis, just like its pre-Soviet (pre- and early Russian colonial) counterpart, and utilises biological, expressed physiologically, characteristics, as the main metric of gender designation, just like the Soviet one did. Both Soviet and current Central Asian gender orders, locate normative femininity in motherhood as the pinnacle of female humanhood. While in the Soviet gender order, motherhood was glorified as duty to the state, not only to the family, in the current one, motherhood becomes also a religious duty (as in Muslim woman's duty) for some, and a national duty to birth and raise a 'healthy nation' for others (Roche 2016: 207; Peshkova 2013). By increasing a purchase of motherhood as the dominant expectation of womanhood, the current gender order undermines previously established feminine gender models, such as women politicians, soldiers, workers and sportswomen, those making a great contribution to local communities beyond biological reproduction and birthing. In daily life, Central Asians do not blindly follow such gendered expectations but adopt some of them and adapt to others.

In the current gender order, there is also change and continuity when it comes to dominant contextual models for masculinity. Like the Soviet one, the current gender order links normative masculinity with a duty to provide for and lead the family and community. While Soviet men were expected to financially provide for their (often extended) families, as a manifestation of duty to the state and an example of active participation in social Soviet transformation through wage labour, the current Central Asian gender links masculinity and providing for the (extended) family to Muslim men's duty and traditional responsibilities toward family and nation (Kandiyoti 2007). As a result of an ideological appeal to religious or traditional sensibilities, the importance of privacy, honour, shame, purity, chastity and respectability became important moral markers of dominant masculinity and femininity alike. These potent cultural values inform models for normative gendered behaviour, leaving no space for gender-variance and obscuring relations and hierarchies among empirical variation of gender identities complicated by one's ethnicity, age, class, access to education and information, ability, social and physical mobility (e.g., migration), religiosity, and/or geographic location.[20] To negotiate dominant gendered expectations in a current complex and precarious socio-economic context, required some Central Asians to act *as if* succeeding in meeting these expectations and, as a result, reproducing the illusion of a stable gender order (Harris 2011: 99). Such paradoxes demonstrate ideological and existential dissonance between existing gendered expectations and existential reality of local people's daily lives.

Local social transformations and activism, increased mobility and information exchange, fostered a growing awareness of sexual diversity, socially constructed nature of gender discourses and order, and a government-sponsored effort to control human sexuality in each one of regional communities.[21] Human sexuality, particularly, became a salient political subject, whether through silencing public discussions and research about it, or displaying it in political activism in the region (Suyarkulova 2019). During the second decade of the twenty-first century, Russia's so-called 'Gay Propaganda Law' (2013), informed regional states' panic about 'nontraditional' sexuality, often defined as a foreign import. As a result, human sexuality became a central topic in local political debates with the introduction of local anti-LGBT Bills in the regional states.[22] It is curious to see how, while criticising and disavowing Russian colonial and Soviet past, the current gender order replicates and maps onto the Russian colonial and Soviet legacy of defining pre-colonial and early colonial same-sex desires and practices and gender variation as deviant. The Soviet ideological labour of reducing human existential diversity to a binary – a contrasting difference articulated in mutually exclusive terms – of manhood and womanhood marked biology and the concomitant binary sexuality as dominant criteria for establishing classificatory difference among humans. Yet, history reminds, that even though in the Soviet Union same-sex practices were banned *de jure*, a diversity of sexual relations and desires existed *de facto*; a law never translates neatly into meaningful changes in human daily life. Similarly, in contemporary Central Asian societies, while looking for a liveable life, local individuals and communities continue to contest the existing binary gender order and find a way to lead meaningful lives despite legal and political injunctions and social prejudice.

This gender order is contested not only through political activism, but also through the variety of personal views and attitudes toward existing gender roles in Central Asia. This variation is informed by one's class, age, location, education, religious sensibilities (or a lack of thereof) and reflects a growing access to digital information, transnational ties and information exchange. From Bollywood to Eminem, from Islamic preaching to Hollywood, from Asian martial arts and South Korean K-pop to Russian youth culture, the flows of information, including information about gender relations, are not adopted wholesale but negotiated considering familial pressures and obligations, values of moral behaviour, specific geographic and historical contexts and pragmatic considerations.

Liveable and meaningful lives

Currently, in the region, local people deploy a variety of individual strategies of challenging the existing gender order. While local feminist activists produce alternative discourses of empathy and support to those who transgress prevailing models for gendered behaviour, local artists continue questioning dominant gender roles and gender inequality through their artwork (Hoare 2016; Kudaibergenova 2016). Despite setbacks, local LGBTQ activists remain persistent in organising political struggle for becoming full 'sexual citizens' and confront 'heterosexual and cisgender status quo' of their respective societies (Buelow 2017; Wilkinson & Kirey 2010: 490).[23] In order to lead liveable and meaningful lives all locals have to be creative. Not everyone becomes an activist challenging existing social mores and normative behaviours. For those whose bodies and/or desires do not neatly fit in the existing binary gender order, a 'strategic performance '*as if* becomes one coping mechanism that helps to make their lives not only liveable but also meaningful. Performing *as if* they are heterosexual through concealment, or by trying to 'pass' by avoiding acting in a way that could be read as homosexual' allows one to prevent stigmatisation, shaming by the family, and physical violence by others and/or by the law enforcement agents (Wilkinson & Kirey 2010: 489–490).[24] Some of those who want to lead liveable meaningful lives against the grain of the normative gender order find support in personal networks and/or immigrate.

In this chapter, I offered thinking with gender about human diversity in and history of Central Asia. Thinking with gender is relevant despite (or maybe because of) various regional nationalist movements' allergy to the concepts of gender and feminism. Scholarly research informed by these two analytics is perceived as challenging and threatening to, and rightly so, the status quo and normative, often toxic, models of manhood and womanhood perceived as normative and traditional by the followers of such movements. I believe that a gender lens, although born elsewhere, allows one to see the region as more complicated, diverse and dynamic, than usually assumed by the proponents of such movements and many outside observers, scholars and travellers alike. Indigenous stories, living systems of spirituality and pre-colonial and early colonial gender order offer resources to challenge selective deployment of local traditions when it comes to the articulation and enactment of the existing gender order. Looking at Central Asia with a gender lens helps seeing that *bachcha* – as a gender position – is as traditional as values of honour, shame, and hospitality. A renewed focus on these resources, including sensuality, beauty, artistry and beautiful manners as traditional values, may help imagining a future gender order suitable for liveable and meaningful lives for all.

Notes

1. I am not a theologian and cultural and/or social determinist. I take human condition to be a complicated unfolding process including one's dynamic emotional engagement with the surrounding human and non-human environment. The word 'dynamic' is the key; it means that change and difference are irreducible parts of human daily lives anywhere in the world.
2. In the discourse on 'science,' both genetic predispositions and social experiences determine human attributes (Kottak 2010, 167, Mukherjee 2015). Differences in chromosomal makeup result in differences in male and female biology, or 'sexual dimorphism,' which are expressed physiologically and hormonally. Mukherjee (2015, 352–390) provides an accessible review of the role of genes in forming individual identity.
3. Intersex individuals are those who biologically do not fit into female/male dichotomy; some scholars estimate that '1 in 100 babies' is born with a body that differ in some way from what we consider to be a male or female body standard (Eckert and McConnell-Ginet 2013: 2).
4. Imperial Russia's own encounter with other European Empires and their taxonomies and ideas about morality, sexuality, difference and deviance, informed Russian colonial encounters in Central Asia and efforts to change local mores and lifeways (see Tlostanova 2010).
5. Gender structure among the nomadic and semi-nomadic populations of Central Asia (e.g., Turkoman, Kyrgyz and Kazakhs) might have been different from the settled communities.
6. I use 'Turkestan' – a term of reference in the Russian colonial literature and scholarly works to Central Asia .
7. At the time, local female youth from settled communities could dance only in the privacy of their courtyard.
8. For some resources on female same-sex desire and practices, see Tlostanova (2010: 81).
9. Prischepova (2006) observes that this tradition, highly admired among locals, all but disappeared by the late 1920s.
10. See Ilkin, Divayev and Comarov (1910).
11. Slavery has also complicated local gender structure in pre-colonial and early colonial Central Asia and needs further research.
12. Seclusion practices varied greatly reflecting ecological environment, family's finances, subsistence strategies and communal needs and norms.
13. For an import criticism of the existing religious elites by the local Central Asian reformers at the time, see Khalid 2007.
14. In the late 1920s, the party's famous unveiling campaign (*khijum*) symbolised women's entrance into a public space, as liberated from their dependences on families and religious sensibilities. This campaign was not limited to symbolic removal of the veil, but also included public education and vocational training.
15. For more details and discussion of Soviet treatment of same-sex practices in the Soviet Union and Central Asia, see Healey 2001, Kon 1995, and Buelow 2017, 45–51.
16. In Russia, see Zdravomislova 2007; in Central Asia, see Harris 2011 and Kudaibergenova 2016.
17. On daily lives and struggles of non-heterosexual and transgender people in Kyrgyzstan, see Wilkinson 2010; in Kyrgyzstan and Kazakhstan, see Buelow 2017.
18. On Uzbek government's selective use of cultural heritage, see Rasanayagam 2010, Adams 2010 and Tabyshalieva 2000.
19. For examples of such violence in different Central Asian contexts, see Ibraeva 2015, Sadyrbek 2015, Suyarkulova 2016.
20. For examples of a dominant masculinity termed as 'strongman' in Tajikistan, see Harris 2011.
21. I know of no scholarly works engaging gender in Turkmenistan directly.
22. The Russian Federal Law for the Purpose of Protecting Children from Information Advocating for a Denial of Traditional Family Values was signed into law, by the President of Russian Federation, Vladimir Putin, in July 2013.
23. Sicgender means that one's 'gender is congruent with assigned sex' (Wilkinson 2010: 485).
24. For 'passing' *as if* heterosexual among contemporary lesbians in Russia, see Stella 2015.

Bibliography

Abashin, S. (2007). *Natsionalizmi v Srednei Azii. V Poiskakh Identichnosti* (Nationalisms in Central Asia. In Quest for Identity). Saint-Petersburg: Aleteya.

Adams, L.L. (2010). *The Spectacular State: Culture and National Identity in Uzbekistan, Politics, History, and Culture*. Durham: Duke University Press.

Arandarenko, G.A. (1889). *Dosugi v Turkestane 1874—1889*. St. Petersburg: Tip. M. M. Stasulevicha.

Ashwin, S., ed. (2000). *Gender, State, and Society on Soviet and Post-Soviet Russia*. London: Routledge.

Buelow, S. (2012). 'Locating Kazakhstan: The Role of LGBT Voices in the Asia/Europe Debate.' *Lambda Nordica* 4 (17): 99–125.

Buelow, S. (2017). 'The Paradox of the Kyrgyz Crossdressers: Ethno-Nationalism and Gender Identity in Central Asia.' PhD dissertation. Anthropology Department, Indiana University.

Butler, J. (1990). *Gender Trouble: Feminism and the Subversion of Identity*. New York: Routledge.

Cleuziou, J. and L. Direnberger. (2016). 'Gender and Nation in Post-Soviet Central Asia: From National Narratives to Women's Practices.' *Nationalities Papers* 44 (2): 195–206.

Connell, R. (2014). 'The Sociology of Gender in Southern Perspective.' *Current Sociology* 62 (4): 550–567.

Constantine, E.A. (2007). 'Practical Consequences of Soviet Policy and Ideology for Gender in Central Asia and Contemporary Reversal.' In *Everyday Life in Central Asia: Past and Present*. Edited by Jeff Sahadeo and Russell Zanca, pp. 115–126. Bloomington: Indiana University Press.

Eckert, P. and S. McConnell-Ginet. (2013). *Language and Gender*. New York, NY: Cambridge University Press.

Goffman, E. (1956). *The Presentation of Self in Everyday Life*. New York: Doubleday.

Harris, C. (2011). 'State Business: Gender, Sex and Marriage in Tajikistan.' *Central Asian Survey* 30 (1): 97–111.

Healey, D. (2001). *Homosexual Desire in Revolutionary Russia: The Regulation of Sexual and Gender Dissent*. Chicago: University of Chicago Press.

Hoare, J.P. (2016). 'Doing Gender Activism in a Donor-Organized Framework: Constraints and Opportunities in Kyrgyzstan.' *Nationalities Papers* 44 (2): 281–298.

Ibraeva, G., A. Moldosheva, and M. Ablezova. (2015). 'We Will Kill You and We Will Be Acquitted!' – Critical Discourse Analysis of a Media Case of Violence against Female Migrants from Kyrgyzstan.' In *Gender in Modern Central Asia*. Edited by Thomas Kruessmann, pp. 3–26. Zurich: LIT VERLAG.

Ilkin, B.M., A.B. Divayev, and P. Comarov. (1910). 'Pesni Bachij.' *Kaufmanskij Sbornik, izdannij v pamyat 25 let, istekshih so dnya smerti pokoritelya Turkestanskogo kraya, general-adjutanta K.P. fon-Kaufman*. Moscow: Vostochnaya Literatura. http://www.vostlit.info/Texts/Dokumenty/M.Asien/XX/1900-1920/Kaufmann_sbornik/, accessed on 13 December 2017.

Ismailbekova, A. (2014). 'Migration and Patrilineal Descent: The Role of Women in Kyrgyzstan.' *Central Asian Survey* 33 (3): 375–389.

Kamp, M. (2006). *The New Woman in Uzbekistan: Islam, Modernity, and Unveiling under Communism*. Seattle: University of Washington Press.

Kamp, M. (2009). 'Women's Studies and Gender Studies in Central Asia: Are We Talking to One Another?' *Central Eurasian Studies Review* 8 (1): 2–12.

Kamp, M. (2016). 'The Soviet Legacy and Women's Rights in Central Asia.' *Current History* 115 (783): 270–276.

Kandiyoti, D. (2007). 'The Politics of Gender and the Soviet Paradox: Neither Colonized, Nor Modern?' *Central Asian Survey* 26 (4): 601–623.

Keller, S. (2001). *To Moscow, Not Mecca: The Soviet Campaign against Islam in Central Asia, 1917–1941*. Westport: Praeger Publishers.

Kon, I.S. (1995). *The Sexual Revolution in Russia: From the Age of the Czars to Today*. New York: Free Press.

Khalid, A. (1998). *The Politics of Muslim Cultural Reform: Jadidism in Central Asia*. Berkeley: University of California Press.

Khalid, A. (2015). *Making Uzbekistan: Nation, Empire, and Revolution in the Early USSR*. Ithaca: Cornell University Press.

Kottak, C.P. (2010). *Mirror for Humanity: A Concise Introduction to Cultural Anthropology*. New York: McGraw-Hill.

Kudaibergenova, D.T. (2016). 'Between the State and the Artist: Representations of Femininity and Masculinity in the Formation of Ideas of the Nation in Central Asia.' *Nationalities Papers* 44 (2): 225–246.

Kudaibergenova, D.T. (2018). 'Project 'Kelin:' Marriage, Women, and Re-Traditionalization in Post-Soviet Kazakhstan.' In *Women of Asia: Globalization, Development, and Social Change*. Edited by Mehrangiz Najafizadeh and Linda Lindsey, pp. 379–390. London: Routledge.

Kushilevskij, V.U. (1891). *Materiali Dlya Meditsinskoj Geografii i Sanitarnogo Opisaniya Ferghanskoj Oblasti*. Novij Margelan (Ferganskaya Oblast'):Tipographya Ferghanskogo Oblastnogo Pravlenia.

Levin, T. (2016). 'Music in Central Asia: An Overview' In *The Music of Central Asia*. Edited by Levin, Theodore and Emira Kochumkulova, pp. 3–25. Bloomington, IN: Indiana University Press.

Liu, M.Y. (2012). *Under Solomon's Throne: Uzbek Visions of Renewal in Osh*. Pittsburgh: University of Pittsburgh Press.

Megoran, N. (1999). 'Theorizing Gender, Ethnicity and the Nation-State in Central Asia.' *Central Asian Survey* 18 (1): 99–110.

Montgomery, D. (2016). *Practicing Islam: Knowledge, Experience, and Social Navigation in Kyrgyzstan*. Pittsburg, PA: University of Pittsburgh Press.

Mukherjee, S. (2015). *The Gene: An Intimate History*. New York: Scribner.

Nalivkina, M. and V. Nalivkin. (2016). *Muslim Women of the Ferghana Valley: A 19th-Century Ethnography from Central Asia*. Edited by Marianne Kamp. Translated by Marinana Markova and Marianne Kamp (based on *Ocherk bita jenshin osedlogo naseleniya Fergani* [*Observations on the Daily Lives of Women of the Sedentary Native Population of Fergana*], Published in Kazan in 1886). Indiana University Press.

Nanda, S. (1997). 'Neither Man Nor Woman: The Hijras of India.' In *Gender in Cross-Cultural Perspective*. Edited by Caroline Brettell and Carolyn Sargent, pp. 198–201. Dallas: Prentice Hall.

Nandi, J. (2013). 'Germany Got It Right by Offering a Third Gender Option on Birth Certificates.' *The Guardian*, 10th November.

Northrop, D.T. (2004). *Veiled Empire: Gender and Power in Stalinist Central Asia*. Ithaca: Cornell University Press.

Olson, G. and M. Horn-Schott. (2018). 'Introduction: 'Beyond Gender: Towards a Decolonized Queer Feminist Future.' In *Beyond Gender: Futures of Feminist and Sexuality Studies – An Advanced Introduction*. Edited by Greta Olson, Daniel Hartley, Mirjam Horn-Schott, and Leonie Schmidt, pp. 1–24. London: Routledge Press.

Peshkova, S. (2013). 'A Post-Soviet Subject in Uzbekistan: Islam, Rights, Gender and Other Desires.' *Women's Studies: An Interdisciplinary Journal* 42 (6): 1–29.

Peshkova, S. (2014). *Women, Islam, and Identity: Public Life in Private Spaces in Uzbekistan*. Syracuse: Syracuse University Press.

Prischepova, V.A. (2006). 'A View from the Outside: *Urda, Jalab, Bachcha* (By the Mae Ras Photograph Collections of 1870–1920).' *Manuscripta Orientalia* 12 (1): 43–68.

Rasanayagam, J. (2010). *Islam in Post-Soviet Uzbekistan: The Morality of Experience*. New York: Cambridge University Press.

Roche, S. (2016). 'A Sound Family for a Healthy Nation: Motherhood in Tajik National Politics and Society.' *Nationalities Papers* 44 (2): 207–224.

Sadyrbek, M. (2015). "There is No State in This Country!' Legal and Social Treatment of Martial Rape in Kyrgyzstan.' In *Gender in Modern Central Asia*. Edited by Thomas Kruessmann, pp. 105–124. Zurich: LIT VERLAG.

Schuyler, E. (1876). *Turkistan: Notes of a Journey in Russian Turkistan, Khokand, Bukhara, and Kuldja*. 2 vols. Vol. 1. New York: Scibner, Armstrong & Co. Printed by John F. Trow & Son.

Stella, F. (2015). *Lesbian Lives in Soviet and Post-Soviet Russia: Post Socialism and Gendered Sexualities*. New York: Palgrave Macmillan.

Suyarkulova, M. (2016). 'Fashioning the Nation: Gender and Politics of Dress in Contemporary Kyrgyzstan.' *Nationalities Papers* 44 (2): 247–265.

Suyarkulova, M. (2019). 'Becoming an Activist Scholar: Toward More Politically Engaged and Socially Accountable Research Practices in Central Asian Studies.' *CESS Blog*. Published December 12, 2019. http://thecessblog.com/2019/12/becoming-an-activist-scholar-towards-more-politically-engaged-and-socially-accountable-research-practices-in-central-asian-studies-by-mohira-suyarkulova-american-university-of-central-asia/, accessed on 30 May 2020.

Tabyshalieva, A. (2000). 'Revival of Traditions in Post-Soviet Central Asia.' In *Making the Transition Work for Women in Europe and Central Asia*. Edited by Marnia Lazreg, pp. 51–57. Washington, DC: World Bank.

Tlostanova, M. (2010). *Gender Epistemologies and Eurasian Borderlands*. New York: Palgrave Macmillan.

Tokhtakhodjaeva, M. (1995). *Between the Slogans of Communism and the Laws of Islam*. Lahore: Shirkat Gah Publishers.

Werner, C. (2004). 'Feminizing the New Silk Road: Women Traders in Rural Kazakhstan.' In *Post-Soviet Women Encountering Transition: Nation-Building, Economic Survival, and Civic Activism*. Edited by Kathleen Keuhnast and Carol Nechemias, pp. 105–126. Washington, DC: Woodrow Wilson Center Press.

Wilkinson, C. and A. Kirey. (2010). 'What's in a Name? The Personal and Political Meanings of 'LGBT' for Non-heterosexual and Transgender Youth in Kyrgyzstan.' *Central Asian Survey* 29 (4): 485–499.

Zdravomislova, E. and A. Temkina, eds. (2007). *Rossiiskii gendernii poriadok; sotziologicheskiy podkhod*. SPB: EUSPb: Trudy fakul'teta pol. nauk i sotsiologii vyp., 12.

25
CONTEMPORARY ART IN CENTRAL ASIA

Alexandra Tsay

Post-socialist Central Asia, a diverse region of different cultures with a shared Soviet past, diverse post-Soviet trajectories, has a small in scale, but vibrant contemporary art scene. The art scenes for each Republic is dispersed rather than united, but they share common discursive narratives and structural problems. Such problems include a lack of institutional development and support, a low quality of art education, government restrictions on media, religion and public expression and a limited of the traditional public sphere (Laruelle 2019: 3). In this context where there is a shrinking 'traditional' public sphere and limited space for public debates, contemporary art constitutes an arena for an alternative public sphere, producing new narratives and discussions, symbols and meanings and provoking debates on online platforms and social networks (Tsay 2019: 269).

This chapter introduces the reader to contemporary art and art practices in the post-socialist Central Asian countries of Kazakhstan, Kyrgyzstan and Uzbekistan. It also examines the role art and artists play in the formation of an alternative public sphere which produces narratives and meanings, reflects on social and cultural transformations, raises critical issues and generates public debate and discussion. The focus of the chapter is on the agency of independent artists in which artists establish a public space for free creative expressions, cultural protests and social critique. This chapter focuses on art and artists who create counter-narratives and new discourses in the closed societies of Central Asia, where with limited freedom of expression artists can still form an alternative artistic model of the public sphere.

The main narratives and themes of contemporary art of the Central Asian region discussed in this chapter are political performance and digital discussions around artistic gestures and performances, artistic studies of collective memory and trauma, and the reflection on post-Soviet identity. All these narratives to some extent question, study and deconstruct the official history of the Soviet period, the nature and power of the state during this time, the legacy of Soviet rule, and its role in relation to censorship and ideological construction. In drawing out these themes and practices in Central Asian contemporary art, I will utilise examples from the works of Kazakhstani artists Kanat Ibragimov, art collective 'Kyzyl Traktor,' Alexander Ugay, Assel Kadyrkhanova, Uzbek artist Vyacheslav Akhunov and Kyrgyz artistic duo Gulnara Kasmaliyeva and Muratbek Djumaliyev. This chapter is not aimed to provide an overview of the complete

DOI: 10.4324/9780429057977-25

contemporary art scene in Central Asia, but instead introduces the reader to contemporary art in the region by a focus on the way artists and artistic practices form an alternative space for debates and create counter-narratives and new meanings from those officially constructed by the state.

Art after independence: political performance in Kazakhstan

During the Soviet period, art was driven by ideological propaganda; government policy supported art as an instrument in the promotion of socialism and a socialist way of life. Socialist realism was the primary creative method used, and it combined naturalistic oil painting with scenes which were perceived as acceptable to be an idealised vision of socialist existence (Abykayeva-Tiesenhausen 2016, Ibrayeva 2014). Kazakh artists began to experiment with new forms of art media in the late 1980s and early 1990s. Vitaliy Simakov, Arystanbek Shalbayev, Moldakul Narymbetov, Smail Bayaliyev and Said Atabekov, who have lived in the southern city of Kazakhstan Shymkent, created the art collective 'Shymkent – Transavangard,' which was later renamed 'Kyzyl Tractor.' With making reference to the Russian avant-garde movement, Shymkent-based artists started to experiment with the composition of oil paintings and artistic materials. Moving away from figurative painting, group members deployed ready-made materials for their art objects and used different resources such as fabric, wood, stone and rubber.

They also experimented with photography and video art, and made performances based on Sufi's rituals and shamanistic practices. After the collapse of the Soviet Union, and various economic and socio-cultural transformations in the 1990s, practiced art forms became more experimental, intense and provocative. The traditional and official art supported by the state and the Union of Artists (UoA) was still developed within the framework of naturalistic oil painting, continuing the tradition of socialist realism. At the same time, some artists were looking for new artistic media and new art forms to reflect and react to the transformations taking place in society and the economy of the region. In the early 1990s, as a response to the radical changes taking place in Central Asian societies, a series of art groups and collectives moved away from the traditions of socialist realist painting and instead experimented with new forms, media, performances and artistic messages (Ibrayeva 2014: 69). This includes the art group and a gallery 'Kokserek' led by Kanat Ibragimov and Erbossyn Meldibekov, the art collective 'Zeleniy treugolnik,' Rustam Khalfin, Shay-Ziya, and the art collective 'Kyzyl Traktor.' Their use of different media, including video art, installations, performances reflected the ambiguity of the post-Soviet transition. This ambiguity can be seen, for example, in the work of the 'Kyzyl Tractor' collective, who deployed symbols, rituals and materials of the pre-Soviet period, using nomadic culture, the forms with the everyday culture of contemporary Kazakhstan. Living in Southern Kazakhstan, artists were surrounded by the steppe mythologies and rituals; for their first collective philosophy of Sufism, and the shamanistic practices of the people of the steppe but then connected this historical exhibition in Almaty in 1995, they filled the hall of the main Soviet-style state fine art museum with wood installations, oil paintings, graphics, traditional fabric and everyday objects. The nomadic rituals as the ancient game '*kokpar*' that gathers thousands of people in Southern Kazakhstan, the shamanistic practices, the objects of labours as '*ketmen*,' a land weeding tool, unconventional use of traditional fabric – 'Kyzyl Tractor' intertwines everyday culture with steppe myths and tales as well as with the problems of contemporary Kazakhstan as the dependence on oil export into provocative, thoughtful and unique array of artworks.

Another prominent artist, one of the founders of contemporary art in Central Asia Rustam Khalfin experimented with artistic forms and media, inventing his own concept of 'pulota' – a combination of emptiness and fullness. He illustrated the concept with making a fist and looking through the hole in the middle. The viewer is invited to look through the artist's hand and see an image of fragmented and personalised world. The tactility, the connectedness with human body is important in this artwork. 'Pulota' is often can be found in Khalfin's artworks, he used the fragments of image formed by the view through the fist in his oil paintings devoted to artist's intellectual and artistic dialogues with Henri Matisse. Khalfin, a student of Vladimir Sterligov, who himself had studied and worked with Kazimir Malevich, a groundbreaking Russian avant-garde artist and theorist, held artistic dialogues and reflected on ideas of artists of the past like Henri Matisse and Joseph Beuys, and developed his own concepts in response to their thoughts, but the ground for his experiments was the environment he lived in – the locality of Central Asia, with its philosophies, nomadic consciousness and culture. Khalfin's works, 'A skin of an artist' and 'Clay project. Zero level,' combined nomadic philosophy with the European art tradition (Sorokina 2016). 'Clay project. Zero level' is the total installation, total work of art, where viewer is invited to walk through the massive body of a clay man and the fragmented images he can see, walking through a leg or arm, makes him feel the 'pulota,' gives the fragmented world view and shows the detachment of contemporary humans from the natural life. The head of the clay man is symbolised with '*shanyrak*,' a part of the yurt, a traditional house of nomads (Ibrayeva, 2007). Walking through other parts of clay man, a viewer can see a video installation discovering the nomadic rituals and nomadic way of life. Khalfin worked within European art tradition, reflecting on the development of contemporary art, but his practice was directed into creating the local artistic frameworks built around nomadism, locality, tactility and nomadic aesthetics.

Art collectives 'Kokserek' and 'Zeleniy treugolnik,' a group led by Rustam Khalfin as well as 'Kyzyl Traktor' experimented with new art media exploring new approaches toward art practice. Such shifts of artistic practice were also taking place in Kyrgyzstan, where various contemporary artists and architects gathered around the studio-museum led by Ulan Djaparov, an artist

Figure 25.1 'Kyzyl Traktor' art collective, performance 'Dervish,' Prague 2003. Picture: courtesy of the artists.

with architectural background. The artistic performance as new medium became another filed of experiments and creative expression. Kanat Ibragimov and Erbossyn Meldibekov explored artistic performance as media to deliver political commentary on contemporary social issues.

Art performance as an act where an artist or people constitute the main medium and material gives an artist an opportunity for action and gesture and for manifestation and engagement with the audience (Bishop 2012: 8). The artist becomes an active figure and he activates the gallery space, turning it into a space of discussion, critique, contradictions and emotions. In the 1990s art performances were brought into the Kazakh art scene by artists such as Rustam Khalfin, Askhat Akhmediyarov, Sergey Maslov, Erbossyn Meldibekov, the art collective 'Kyzyl Tractor,' Kanat Ibragimov and the art group 'Kokserek.' Kanat Ibragimov was one of the first Kazakh artists who began the practice of radical art performances and later developed them into art happenings with political messages. In one of his well-known performances, 'Neue Kasachische Kunst,' that took place in 1997 in the Art Forum gallery in Moscow, Ibragimov slaughtered a sheep and drank its blood from a traditional cup used for tea, known as a *piala*. He also dropped some blood into a cauldron with milk and then exposed a canvas with bloodstains.[1] In a manifesto published after the performance, Ibragimov wrote that he was interested in brutal tough gestures and archetypes of primordial culture to be placed and situated in the big urbanised city (Ibragimov 1998). 'Neue Kasachische Kunst' references both nomadic rituals and Western art history, and by doing so the artist highlights his national identity and constructs it through a positioning of Kazakh symbols and traditions (via the sacrifice of the sheep) (Kudaibergenova 2019: 102).

In 1999, Ibragimov and the art group 'Kokserek' held a happening entitled 'The patriotic project 2030' during the annual 'Galleries Parade' at the National Fine Arts Museum to highlight widespread corruption and the distribution of natural resources revenue among Kazakhstani elites (Grishin 2019). 'Kokserek' invited museum visitors to dinner and offered glasses with a drink called 'Oil' and a big cake made as a full-height figure of the president, Nursultan Nazarbayev. The 'Kokserek' booth at the museum was closed the next day. Ibragimov was not active on the contemporary art scene from about 1999 till 2009. In 2009, he re-established his happenings and performances entering again the realm of politics and a critique of current political elites. Ibragimov continues to deploy brutalism and the use of violence in his later performances. The medium of art allowed Ibragimov to avoid legislative sanctions which were embedded in a series of laws which restricted citizens' freedom of expression in the public sphere.[2] In February 2010, Ibragimov conducted a performance named after the Russian language proverb 'The fish rots from the head' on the Republic Square in Almaty. The journalists who received notifications about the planned happening were awaiting the artist along with the police. Ibragimov brought with him a raw fish covered with newspaper. He placed the fish on the bricks of the square and chopped off its head with an axe while shouting, 'The fish rots from the head!' The happening was documented by journalists who surrounded the artist during his performance. Ibragimov was arrested for public order disturbance and taken to the police station but was later released.

In a situation where there are significant limits on the freedom of the press, substantial government censorship and where criticism of the country's first president is a crime, Kanat Ibragimov, through artistic gesture and allusion, drew attention to the long presidency of Kazakhstan's leader, whose figure and activities were never critically discussed in the official mass media. The artist used the city's square as a symbolic space for public gatherings, and the attention of the media and police to his art highlighted the closeness of contemporary agora for any public gatherings and demonstrations and the rarity of expression of protest in public space. This performance as a form of political gesture which represents a critique of contemporary

Kazakh politics, engages with the wider public through the symbolic space of the city's main square as a form of collective expression and collective action. It draws the media's attention to political concerns, breaking the silence of previously censored issues.

Various contemporary artists in Kazakhstan including Erbossyn Meldibekov, Askhat Akhmediyarov, the art collective 'Kyzyl Tractor' and others engage with political issues through their art practices. Many artists I interviewed consider contemporary art as a space for opposing official discourses, as a space of critique and critical discussions. Kanat Ibragimov was pioneering in his work in bringing political art performance into the mass media and public attention. He provoked debates and attracted attention to political issues in the press, stressing the lack of critique and public discussion. Ibragimov was also active in political protest, he supported the strikers in Zhanaozen in 2011 and criticised government reaction and the use of violence against protesters (Ibragimov 2013). Later in the 2000s, with the increasing level of Internet penetration and growing popularity of different social media platforms, digital and social media became an important area for the creation and consumption of political content (Kosnazarov 2019: 247). Contemporary artists took a prominent role in content creation and shaping the narratives of protest on digital platforms.

In April 2019, after the unexpected resignation of president Nursultan Nazarbayev after nearly 30 years in power, and following the renaming of the capital from Astana to Nur-Sultan, and the announcement of a new presidential election, groups of activists unfruled two banners 'You cannot run away from the truth' ('Ot pravdi ne ubezhish') with hashtags #adilsailayushin ('for fair elections') in Kazakh and #umenyaestvybor ('I have a choice') in Russian during the Almaty marathon. Two of the activists, Asya Tulesova and Beibarys Tolymbekov, were arrested and detained for 15 days for violation of the law on mass gatherings and demonstrations (Rickleton 2019). While other artists and those filming the event, Suinbike Suleimenova, Aidos Nurbolatov, and Aigul Nurbolatova were also arrested and fined. The group responsible for the second banner were not detected by police officers and left the marathon unnoticed, though the pictures of both banners immediately went viral on social media networks. The artistic performance instigated a wave of criticism related to the transition of power. Another young artist, Medina Bazargaliyeva filmed herself walking in the city murmuring and shouting: 'Nur-Sultan is not my city, Tokayev is not my President, I have a choice.' The video went viral on social media networks, launching a series of posts, pictures, collages, memes with the hashtag 'I have a choice.'

The disproportionate reaction of the authorities against the activists generated a wave of sympathy and solidarity on digital platforms. People started to create memes, comics, pictures, and graphics to support the detained activists, using various hashtags, including #otpravdineubezhish, #ihaveachoice, and others. The wave of art protest spread both online and offline with people across Kazakhstan participating in political acts in city squares and public spaces with banners and posters (Viktor 2019). For example, the artist Roman Zakharov hung a banner in Almaty with the statement that 'the only source of state power is the people' which came directly from the country's constitution. Zakharov was arrested by police officers and sentenced to five days in prison, although he was released the same evening. Zakharov's case illustrates the absurdity of police action and the closed nature of the public space for any agents and voices apart from official sources. Censorship is applied not to the message, but to the source and agency that reproduces it. The picture of the Zakharov's banner again circulated widely on social media generating reposting and new posts of support for the artist.

The banners 'You cannot run away from the truth' and the movement which emerged from this action is not specifically an artistic performance. Moreover, in interviews activists mentioned that they do not consider those protest activities to be art practices. Yet, these practices

Figure 25.2 'You cannot run away from the truth' banner during Almaty marathon, April 21, 2019. Picture: Tamina Ospanova.

can be described as art activism and as an expression of political and social critique using the medium of art in the public sphere. The activists take the city's public space and online public space to share critique, concerns, and emotions, they create a space for collective expression on social media platforms, embodying and uniting the voices of protest around the country. The use of creative media in this way engaged a younger audience which for the first time in the history of independent Kazakhstan became politically vocal on a large scale. The artists act as independent agents within the social and political structure, their action is an immediate and emotional response to the government's decision and action surrounding the transition of presidential power. Artists are creating dialogue, and a two-ways communication in a situation where the government is closed for dialogue, making important decisions without appealing to public opinion. Emotional and affective artistic response and performance challenge the closed and restricted system. Art activism tests the boundaries of freedom of expression, raising questions about power relations within society, opening up a space for alternative opinions and embodying collective actions and collectivity in the public space.

Reflection on the Post-Soviet

The legacy of Soviet rule, the socio-cultural transformations of the transition period and the formation of new identity are important narratives for contemporary artists in Central Asia.

Vyacheslav Akhunov, a well-known Uzbek artist, dissident and writer, works with the theme of Soviet heritage. His constructivist collages, drawings, installations and video deploy aesthetics of socialist realism, Moscow conceptualism, oriental symbols and practices. The only conceptual Uzbek artist, Akhunov's work was in opposition to official culture and art during the Soviet period. He continues to deconstruct Soviet symbols, reconstructing the aesthetics of Soviet protest and counter-culture. The political merges with the poetical in his works, he stands in opposition to the dominant ideology and praises the right to free expression. The figure of the artist is reminiscent of the romantic figure of the poet, the unknown legislator of the world, who questions the formal legislator in the political system. The tradition to monumentalise the image of the party leader and to reproduce it widely was an important narrative of Akhunov's work. He was working on a series of collages with the image of Lenin, 'Leniniana,' in the late 1970s and 1980s, deconstructing the image of the sacral figure of the communist era. In 2000, Akhunov created an installation called 'The cage for the leaders' with 250 polystyrene busts of Lenin. In doing so, Akhunov again raises the question of the sacral position of the political leader in contemporary Central Asia. Through his work Akhunov deconstructs the ideological system of the Soviet period, pointing to the closed nature and limitation of any ideology and revealing the position of the critical viewer who doubts, questions, criticises and ironises.

Kyrgyz contemporary artists Gulnara Kasmaliyeva and Muratbek Djumaliyev, who work as an artistic duo, also talk about the importance of adopting a critical view of governmental and ideological systems and the distance and detachment from official narratives. Their photo and video installations study and depict the transformations of society, the challenges ordinary people face going through social and economic transition of the post-Soviet period. The video

Figure 25.3 Vyacheslav Akhunov and his work 'Alphabet of Socialist Realism,' 2003. Picture: courtesy of the artist.

Figure 25.4 Gulnara Kasmaliyeva and Muratbek Djumaliyev, TransSiberian Amazons, installation, 2005.

installation, 'TransSiberian Amazons,' depicts the story of two women who have to leave their job and start to practicing small trade along the Silk Road. The contemporary form nomadism of labor migration reveals the break in social ties and growing social inequality. As Gulnara Kasmaliyeva noted that they, 'were looking for a post-Soviet identity, for characters that can be symbolic figures of the time. Society was going under tectonic changes that no one had analysed, no one had written about or fixated on through video and photography.'[3] The personal is central to their work along with the political and social, while the individual's hopes, dreams, fears become a vital part of their art. Ulan Djaparov, the prominent Kyrgyz contemporary artist and a founder of studio-museum in Bishkek, described contemporary art as the nerve of its time, as a practice that reveals the large, but sometimes not visible internal issues.[4] It ironises, problematises and depicts the complexity of the social, the political and the personal.

Art, trauma and memory: Artists as memory activists

The Soviet legacy, the issue of power relations and the relationship between the state and the individual leads artists to work with collective and personal memories of historic trauma associated with the early Soviet period in Kazakhstan. Soviet Kazakhstan, a vast territory of endless steppe went through radical modernisation processes brought on by the Soviet rule in the 1920–1930s. Rapid forced modernisation, collectivisation, and sedentarisation (the forced settlement of the nomadic population of Kazakhstan) led to dramatic transformations in the economic, social, and cultural spheres of society. Soviet rule considered nomadism as an unmodern, economically ineffective, form of social organisation and imposed forced sedentarisation on the nomadic population and organised them into collective farms. Modernisation was the main discourse to justify radical transformations in the social, economic and cultural aspects of people's life. Some Kazakh scholars challenge the notion of the 'primitivism' of traditional nomadic culture. For example, Zhulduzbek Abylkhozhin argues that such a system corresponded to the climate of the territory and helped nomads to preserve the balance in appropriating natural resources and preserving the inhabited territories from desertification. The nomadic population had sought the equilibrium of ecological rationale and economic efficiency (Abylkhozhin 1997, p.117). At the same time, Abylkhozhin agreed that the nomadic system had to be transformed under the 'challenges of progress,' but he writes that there had been possibilities of a gradual and slow method for sedentarisation and urbanisation. The violent break with the traditional way of life and the organisation of labour with into collective farms and villages, meant nomads suddenly had to become members of these collective farms. It caused great losses in cattle-breeding and the great famine. The great famine spread all over Kazakhstan and caused the death of nearly 2.2 million Kazakh people. Moreover, between 1931 and 1933 almost 2 million fled to neighbouring countries to escape the famine (Abylkhozhin 1992: 21). In the late 1930s Kazakhstan had become a territory of massive violent deportations of Koreans and Germans, Poles, Crimea Tatars, Chechens, and other ethnic groups.

The reflection on the early Soviet period and cultural and social transformations associated with it, meant collective and personal memory became important themes for different contemporary artists in Kazakhstan. For example, Almagul Menlibayeva reflects on the Soviet repression and Soviet legacy, while Saule Suleimenova develops her concept of residual memory of the Great Famine in Kazakhstan through a combination of cellophane as a new art medium and the usage of archival photographs. In other examples, Askhat Akhmediyarov touches on the issue of Soviet state repressions and Assel Kadyrkhanova, who represents younger generation of contemporary Kazakh artists, works with the trauma of Stalinist repressions. The artists working with memory narratives belong to different generations, including established contemporary artists and younger ones. Diaspora artists such as Alexander Ugay, a Kazakh artist of Korean descent, also work with memory issues, revealing the ambiguity of de-sovietisation and the post-memory context in post-socialist Central Asia. To some extent their position is a vision from the margins, not belonging to the 'titular ethnicity' they embody the complex approach to nation-building processes during the Soviet period. The ambiguity of nation-building process and the formation of national identity construction in Kazakhstan and how this has been reflected in cultural production via contemporary art, cinema and literature has been studied by closely by scholars (Isaacs 2018, Kudaibergenova 2016). Those scholars use contemporary art and cinema as analytical tools to study nation-building process, showing that actors in art field can challenge government policy in Kazakhstan and contributing to the discussion on the role of art and cultural protest in closed societies.

Assel Kadyrkhanova, a visual artist and a doctoral researcher, focuses her art practice on memory and trauma of the Stalinist repression. She works with concepts of post-memory and trauma, using art as a metaphor and medium to remember and to reconstruct memory. In her artwork 'Windows of Tolerance,' Kadyrkhanova offers a metaphorical comparison suggesting that the time after the USSR is a timeless space of trauma (Kadyrkhanova 2019: 244). The unbearable consciousness of trauma returns again and again to reconstruct the experience and shed light to what had been lost (Caruth 1996). 'Window of tolerance' is the reproduction, repetition of trauma that exists in the body of the city in form of window bars. Kadyrkhanova photographed steel window bars around the city and embroidered parts of them with red threads and with a seam she learnt from her mother, who learnt it from her mother (Kadyrkhanova 2019: 256). The act of embroidery becomes an attempt to reconstruct the memory and also a process of continuity and transfer of memory within family. Kadyrkhanova artworks also comment on the post-memory context in which artists work with memory narratives. 'Post-memory' describes the relationship that the 'generation after' bears to the personal, collective, and cultural trauma of those who came before – to experiences they 'remember' only by means of the stories, images, and behaviours among which they grew up (Hirsch 2012). But these experiences were transmitted to them so deeply and affectively as to *seem* to constitute memories in their own right. The central point in Hirsch's concept of post-memory is a familial transfer of memories that allows the individual to acquire 'external' memories of a group that an individual belongs to. The distance post-generation has for a traumatic experience allows it to discover the pain of others, to analyse the traumatic events from a standpoint of close attachment, but substantial detachment from the event itself that gives possibility to 'heal' the trauma, to grasp and overcome its consequences.

Alexander Ugay, a contemporary artist of Korean descent living and working in Almaty has been working with memory and trauma for many years, with a specific interest in mechanisms of memory per se, not the collective memory of a certain historical event.[5] In looking at how individual and collective memory works, Ugay produced a number of works devoted to the violent deportation of Koreans to Central Asia. Ugay, who belongs to third generation of deported people, created a series of artworks on Koreans in Kazakhstan for the project 'The future is coming from all directions.' One of the artworks of that project, a work entitled 'A model for the assembly' presents a series of collages depicting the lineage of the diaspora's history starting from the deportation from Russian Far East to Central Asia in 1937. The size of the images depended on the importance of the event for the Korean community members interviewed by artist for the project. The more important a certain event or date for people, the better they remember it, the bigger the image. Ugay emphasises that history is a series of events, and memory is a collection of individual perceptions of them, memory is an ambiguous, emotional, living substance. The work also reveals the familial transfer of memory as for some respondents the story of deportation is the story they have been told. Ugay works with respondents to study what they remember and how they remember, Ugay argues that memory is an extreme position of happiness or pain. He looks into these extremes, trying to reconstruct the traumatic experience through artistic instruments and to discover the consequences of trauma in the unconsciousness.

The lineage of collage refers to the constructivist nature of Soviet policy toward society and social structures. The utopian project of the Soviet state was to create a new type of society and a new type of a citizen. Art was considered as an instrument for that ambiguous endeavour; Boris Groys has argued how the primary interest of Socialist Realism, the main creative method during the Soviet period, was not an artwork, but the viewer, the consumer of art. As Groys notes, 'socialist realism was the attempt to create dreamers who would dream the Socialist dream' (Groys 2008: 147). Ugay's 'A model for the assembly' stylistically represents the idea of construction, of political power that created new social structures and eliminated old ones, that provided an extensive ethnic policy, completely removing selective ethnic groups from their territories. The black and white prints depict moments of the construction, the moment between the present and the future, a space between an old and a new, between an element and an object. The collage refers to a historical narrative of the Korean community, and also it consists of memories and stories of people with whom Ugay made a series of interviews. Artists also work with the personal and the private as domains of memory. This form is a reflection of the instrumental side of collective memory that is shaped by political power and also multivocal and vernacular nature of collective memory that emphasises the existence of different memories and different stories attributed to individuals and social groups. Aleida Assmann argues that multivocal and multidirectional memories allow for the performing of the fundamental human right for an independent worldview of one's own experience, and an identity for individuals and groups of people (Assman 2016: 56).

Contemporary art in Central Asia

Figure 25.5 Alexander Ugay, 'A model for the assembly,' 2013, courtesy of the artist. Photo: exhibition view, 175 Gallery, Seoul.

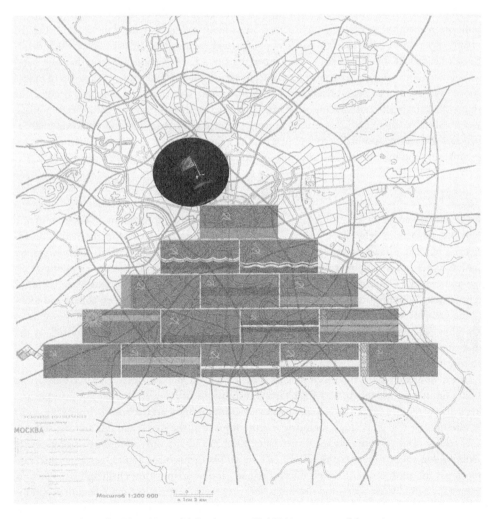

Figure 25.6 Alexander Ugay, 'A model for the assembly,' 2013, courtesy of the artist.

Ugay continued his study of memory in the work 'Memory objects - archive' devoted to the memory of political violence and the social atmosphere of the 1930s. In an artwork description Alexander points towards the impossibility of the complete transmitting of painful experience through an image and an object, even a real object. Ugay uses archival photo documents of the Karaganda Corrective Labour Camp and Akmola Camp for Wives of the Enemies of the Motherland, but he looks at the back sides of the pictures, where people left their words, signatures and ink scratches. Ugay works with the invisible side of representation, giving the viewer a real object, a document, or a photograph, but taking away the image. Ugay conceptualises the unknown, pointing towards the limits of a representation of a traumatic historical past. He does not give us an image of pain, rather saying that whatever the image the pain will not be real, and he creates a condition for us to absorb that fundamental challenge in relating to the struggles of others. His works speak to us about the inexpressibility of sufferings and pain, of difficulties in transmitting the experience of state repression, violence, fear, and distant spectacles. Ugay also reflects on the division between an object, a representation – an image, and something that always remains invisible between an object and an image. And as it is said in his own description of an artwork, looking at the back sides of pictures, he wants to discover another layer of memory; an affective, emotional, unconscious one; a memory deeply rooted in human existence.

After a period of censorship on issues of political violence and an official policy which determined what should and should not be remembered, artists act as independent agents that raise questions of remembrance and seek to revise what has been left behind by the major narratives of official history. Stories and memories of ordinary people, their fears, affections, and emotions become the subject of artistic practices. Contemporary artists problematise the instrumental and official approach toward collective memory through reflection on personal experience, on emotions and affective responses and create a possibility for cultural memory, the memory that goes beyond instrumental remembering and multivocal memories that are not afraid of contradictions (Assmann 2006: 29).

Concluding remarks

Contemporary artists in Central Asia, as demonstrated by artists in Kazakhstan, Kyrgyzstan and Uzbekistan, act as independent creative agents constructing the arena for alternative meanings and narratives against those proposed by the official government versions. Contemporary Central Asian artists are able to confront, discuss and reflect on critical issues of politics, collective memory, of trauma, and of the transformations taking place in Central Asian societies. Central Asian contemporary artists work in the context of post-memory, they collect and reenact the memory of a traumatic past, reveal the mechanism of trauma and look into possibilities of healing. The context of Central Asian contemporary art creates sites for memories, at the same time, artists question the official construction of collective 'bonding' memory and reveal the instrumental approach toward memory.

In the context where there is a lack of independent media and restricted freedom of the press, a limited public sphere and with formal institutions offering little space for critique and alternative meanings from official state discourses, contemporary art become an important arena for questioning power, politics, memory, and the impact of the social and cultural transformations taking place. Contemporary artists launch debates about the conditions of post-Soviet Central Asian society via social networks and digital platforms using artistic gestures which are emotional and unstructured, as well uncensored and non-systemic, thus challenging the system. Being a site for new narratives and meanings, for free creative expression and reflection, contemporary art of Central Asia constitutes an alternative arena for discussion and debates, provoking public attention and challenging power in the politically closed societies of Central Asia.

Notes

1 See documentation of Ibragimov's performance 'Neue Kasachischen Kunst ('Aktsiya s baranom') in Art Moscow 1997' available on Youtube, posted on July 21, 2015 by Kenneth Abraham https://www.youtube.com/watch?v=KKYPuXablXc
2 This included bans on unsanctioned public gatherings and protests proposed by the law On the organisation and conduct of peaceful protests, meetings, marches, pickets and demonstrations in the Republic of Kazakhstan 2005, the law On mass media 1999, and The Constitutional Law of the Republic of Kazakhstan No. 83-II about the First President of the Republic of Kazakhstan – Elbasy 2000 – that protects the 'honor and dignity' of Nursultan Nazarbayev.
3 Djumaliyev, M, Kasmaliyeva, G. Interview with author, September 25, 2019.
4 Djaparov, U. Interview with author, August 25, 2019.
5 Ugay, A. Interview with author, July 14, 2019.

Bibliography

Abykayeva-Tiesenhausen, A. (2016). *Central Asia in Art. Russian Orientalism*, London: IB Tauris.
Abylkhozhin, Z. (1992). *Collectivization in Kazakhstan: A Tragedy of a Peasants*, Almaty: MP Yuat.
Abylkhozhin, Z. (1997). *The Essays on Social and Economic History of Kazakhstan. Twentieth Century*, Almaty: Turan University Press.
Akhunov, V. (2018). Interview with author, 30 June 2018.
Assmann, A. (2016). *Novoye nedovol'stvo memorialnoy kulturoy*, trans. Boris Khlebnikov, Moscow: New Literary Observation.
Assmann, J. (1995). 'Collective memory and cultural identity,' *New German Critique*, 65, pp. 125–133.
Assmann, J. (2006). *Religion and Cultural Memory: Ten Studies*, transl. Rodney Livingstone, Stanford, CA: Stanford University Press.
Bishop, C. (2012). *Artificial Hells. Participatory Art and the Politics of Spectatorship*, London: Verso Book.
Caruth, C. (1996). *Unclaimed Experience: Trauma, Narrative, and History*, Baltimore: Johns Hopkins University Press.
Djaparov, U. (2019). Interview with author, 25 August 2019.
Djumaliyev, M. and G. Kasmaliyeva. (2019). Interview with authors, September 25, 2019.
Grishin, A. (2019). 'The marathon of the truth: Art activists push Kazakhstani people to protest against authoritarian system,' *Open Democracy*, 6 June.
Groys, B. (2008). *Art Power*, Cambridge, MA: MIT Press.
Hirsch, M. (2012). *The Generation of Post-Memory: Writing and Visual Culture after the Holocaust*, New York: Columbia University Press.
Ibragimov, K. (1998). 'Manifesto,' *Moscow Art Magazine*, 19–20, 1998. http://moscowartmagazine.com/issue/46/article/899, accessed on 6 September 2019.
Ibragimov, K. (2013). 'There is a period of moral famine,' *Radio Azattyq*, 12 December.
Ibrayeva, V. (2007). 'Rustam Khalfin's Art,' in N. Samman and A. Abykayeva-Tiesenhausen (eds), *Seeing through the Artist's Hand*, London: White Space Gallery, pp. 6–14.
Ibrayeva, V. (2014). *The Art of Kazakhstan. Post-Soviet Period*, Almaty: Tonkaya gran.
Isaacs, R. (2018). *Film and Identity in Kazakhstan: Soviet and Post-Soviet Culture*, London: I.B. Tauris.
Iskakov, A. (2019). Interview with author, 26 August.
Kadyrkhanova, A. (2019). 'Endless time after: Art as an instrument of reflection on cultural memory and trauma in post-Soviet Kazakhstan,' in Z. Abylkhozhin, M. Akulov, and A. Tsay (eds), *Living Memory*, Almaty: Daik Press, pp. 245–271.
Kaleeva, T. (2017). 'Amendments to law on media put an end to journalistic investigations,' *Sputnik News*, 21 December.
Kim, G. (1999). *History of Korean Immigration, Part 1: Second Half of XIX Century – 1945*, Almaty: Daik-Press.
Kosnazarov, D. (2019). '#Hashtag activism. Youth, social media, and politics,' in M. Laruelle (ed.), *The Nazarbayev Generation. Youth in Kazakhstan*, London: Lexington Books, pp. 247–267.
Kudaibergenova, D. (2016). 'Between the state and the artist: Representations of femininity and masculinity in the formation of ideas of the nation in Central Asia,' *Nationalities Papers*, 44(2), pp. 225–246.
Kudaibergenova, D. (2019). 'Mankurts, Kazakh 'Russians,' and 'Shala' Kazakhs: Language, national identity, and ethnicity revisited,' in M. Laruelle (ed.), *The Nazarbayev Generation. Youth in Kazakhstan*, London: Lexington Books, pp. 89–111.

Kulmagambetova, D. (2019). Interview with author, 3 September.
Laruelle, M. (2019). 'The Nazarbayev generation: A sociological portrait,' in M. Laruelle (ed.), *The Nazarbayev Generation. Youth in Kazakhstan*, London: Lexington Books, pp. 1–21.
Rickleton, C. (2019). 'You cannot run from the truth: Iconic art protests preface Kazakh presidential vote, Eurasia Internet,' *Global Voices*, 29 May.
Sorokina, Y. (2016). 'From evolution to growth: Central Asian video art, 1995–2015,' *Studies in Russian and Soviet Cinema*, 10(3), pp. 238–260.
Suleimenova, S. (2019). Interview with author, 10 April.
Constitutional Laws in Kazakhstan make amendments to Constitution and are adopted by Parliament (July 20, 2000). *The Constitutional Law of the Republic of Kazakhstan No. 83-II about the First President of the Republic of Kazakhstan – Elbasy*, July 20, 2000. https://online.zakon.kz/document/?doc_id=1019103, accessed on 6 September 2019.
The Law № 2126 'On the organization and conduct of peaceful protests, meetings, marches, pickets and demonstrations in the Republic of Kazakhstan,' January 1 2005. https://online.zakon.kz/document/?doc_id=1003508#pos=3;-155, accessed on 6 September 2019.
Tsay, A. (2019). 'Contemporary art as a public forum,' in M. Laruelle (ed.), *The Nazarbayev Generation. Youth in Kazakhstan*, London: Lexington Books, pp. 269–287.
Ugay, A. (2019). Interview with author, 14 July.
Viktor, D. (2019). 'A man in Kazakhstan held up a blank sign to see if he'd be detained. He was,' *The New York Times*, 9 May.
Zakharov, R. (2019). Interview with author, 31 August 2019.

26
LANGUAGE POLICY AND LANGUAGE IN CENTRAL ASIA

William Fierman

The Russian language occupied a privileged position throughout the USSR in the late Soviet era. Despite this, in different regions the division of functions between Russian and other languages varied considerably; this, in turn, fostered different patterns of diglossia. The most important factor affecting this was the status of each eponymous ethnic group in the Soviet federal system. Non-Russian languages associated with 'their own' eponymous Union Republics (henceforth UR) followed next after Russian in the hierarchy; they were followed by groups associated with 'autonomous republics,' 'autonomous regions' and, finally, 'autonomous areas.' As a rule, the Russian language had a more important role in the 'autonomous' units than in the non-Russian URs.

Although *all* UR titular languages enjoyed certain privileges, the balance of languages used in each of these units was unique. In general, Russian fulfilled certain functions in Central Asia that it did not in such areas as the Baltic and South Caucasus republics. Two fundamental reasons for this were the relatively late standardisation of Kazakh, Kyrgyz, Tajik, Turkmen and Uzbek and the associated delayed development of mass literacy in them. One of the most prominent differences between these Central Asian titular languages and titular languages in the two regions named above is that in Central Asia the languages were little used in higher education (henceforth HE). Russian-medium HE existed throughout the USSR, including in the Baltic and South Caucasus; however, by the late Soviet era, if not earlier, such training was also available in the UR titular language in many fields, and was often considered equal in quality to that in Russian. In Central Asia, titular-language HE was mostly limited to preparing teachers and to humanities disciplines with special relevance to the region. Even students accepted into 'national' groups for HE received much of their training (especially after the first year) in Russian. The less robust HE in the Central Asian languages contributed to greater reliance on Russian in a wide variety of high-prestige settings; this in turn shaped the character of local diglossia.

Despite limited domains of use for Kazakh, Kyrgyz, Tajik, Turkmen and Uzbek, the Soviet regime oversaw corpus development of these languages, including, for example, explaining and translating dictionaries as well as encyclopaedias with articles on a wide variety of subjects. Moreover, these languages were the languages of instruction in primary and secondary education for large (and in some cases overwhelming) majorities of children of titular ethnic groups. In addition, many periodical publications as well as television and radio programming were produced in these languages. Thus, although the domains of use of Central Asian languages

DOI: 10.4324/9780429057977-26

were more limited than the eponymous titular languages in the south Caucasus and Baltic, the corpus development and widespread use of the Central Asian languages in many domains during the Soviet era provided a foundation that was critical for the expanded use after the USSR's collapse. This does not imply that the respective roles of Russian and the eponymous languages were identical across the Central Asian republics.

Despite the unique nature of diglossia in each UR and the distance between Central Asia and the Baltic, the articulation of linguistic nationalism in Central Asia was profoundly influenced by events in other regions, especially the Baltic. This is evident in the adoption of language laws throughout Central Asia in 1989 and 1990. Moreover, in all cases such laws evoked both widespread hopes and fears. Those who did not know the single 'state' language identified in the laws feared that they would quickly be excluded from critical spheres of activity; many whose language repertoires included the state languages experienced exaggerated hopes that they would soon enjoy enhanced respect and rapid social mobility. Although the fears were a major stimulus to emigration from Central Asia, especially by monolingual Slavs, it would not take long for life to show that inflated expectations of those who knew the state language would be dashed. The changes that ensued in Central Asia following 1989 and especially after 1991 will be explored below.

Though easy to overlook, a critical factor affecting language throughout Central Asia was the achievement of each UR's political independence. The importance of this is evident in a comparison of the development of any Central Asian state languages and Tatar. Among ethnic groups of the USSR lacking a UR, during the Soviet era, Tatars were arguably the most successful in terms of corpus language development and breadth of domains of use. With regard to corpus development, Tatar's situation in the late Soviet era was arguably closer to that of the Central Asian UR languages than to most other languages of units with only 'autonomous' status. Today the situation of Tatar is starkly different from the Central Asian state languages. In post-Soviet Russia, the 'Republic of Tatarstan' is a subject of the Russian Federation for which Moscow continues to make major decisions. Lacking an independent state to support its eponymous language, unlike in Central Asia, the domains of use of Tatar have contracted or remained stagnant.

The above discussion has highlighted two major factors affecting diglossia in post-Soviet Central Asia, i.e., the domains of language use at the end of the Soviet era, and political independence. The analysis below of policy and language change since 1989 will examine six other factors, in particular: 1) political leaders' nation building projects, 2) language repertoires at time of independence, 3) demography, 4) international alignments 5) degree of authoritarian government and 6) financial resources. These factors are themselves intertwined and interdependent. For example, throughout the region, demography and language repertoires at the time of independence shaped leaders' approaches to nation building. Likewise, alignment in international affairs appears linked to the nature of nation building.

Because of its centrality in understanding language policy, a few words should be devoted here to the use of 'nation building project' below. I will situate each country's policy on a continuum stretching from 'civic state' to 'nation-state' projects. I will refer to civic state projects, which treat citizens and cultures of all ethnic groups equally, as 'inclusive' and 'broad;' I will contrast these to 'exclusive' or 'narrow' projects that emphasise the privileged place of the titular group. Because all Central Asian states have to some degree privileged the titular ethnic group, none of their projects are at the 'inclusive' extreme of the continuum described above. (The tendency to privilege the titular ethnic group is rooted in Soviet practices and these included the federal system, which reflected Stalin's definition of 'nationality' in a way that fostered belief in coincidence of ethnicity, language and territory.) As will be illustrated below, some Central

Asian states' projects as reflected in their language policies have been closer to the inclusive end of the continuum than others.

The quality of information needed to portray the Central Asian countries according to the six factors listed above varies considerably: it is relatively easy to determine the trajectory of each state's nation building project and international alignments. The quality of nation building is reflected (among other ways) in constitutions and laws, as well as in pronouncements and writings of each country's leaders. Similarly, leaders' statements and visits abroad, membership in international organisations and policy stands on major international issues are indicators of international alignment. Reports by local and foreign scholars and other observers as well as information compiled by international organisations offer insights into the level of authoritarian rule in each state.

Countries' financial resources are somewhat more difficult to measure; the reasons for this include the paucity of reliable data released for some countries, official and 'real' currency exchange rates and corruption. The lack of data is especially serious in the case of Turkmenistan. Even there, however, it is possible to use reports by local and foreign observers on economic life. Reports issued by domestic and international organisations provide a more accurate picture in the other four states, with less opaque indicators on poverty rates and level of international labour migration.

Although especially pertinent to diglossia, data on demography and language repertoires are particularly problematic. The primary source for information on ethnic composition is census data, which are often based on self-reporting. Even in the Soviet era, census data were likely skewed by expectations of census takers and efforts by citizens to represent themselves for official purposes in ways that differed from their own subjective identities. Consequently, many members of minority ethnic groups were counted as belonging to titular groups. Available evidence from the post-Soviet era suggests that analogous distortions have continued, if not increased. Temporary and permanent migration, which are difficult to measure and often semi-legal or illegal, further complicate compiling a complete pictures of a territory's ethnic composition.

Perhaps the most problematic indicator of the six listed above concerns language repertoires. One reason is that criteria for reporting have been loose and manipulated for political purposes. In the last Soviet censuses, citizens were supposed to be asked to name their 'native language' (родной язык) and whether they were fluent in (свободно владеть) another language. Yet we have only incomplete information on such important factors as how census takers actually prompted or recorded responses. Similar problems also apply to data from the post-Soviet states, complicated by the lack of uniformity across countries. Perhaps the most obvious case of political manipulation of language data from the Soviet era are those for Russian fluency in Uzbekistan in the censuses of 1970, 1979 and 1989. These respective censuses purportedly showed that over the relevant intercensal periods the share of Uzbeks in Uzbekistan fluent in Russian as a second language first jumped from 13.1 per cent to 52.9 per cent, and then dropped back to 22.3 per cent Another complication in measuring language repertoires is that both in the Soviet and post-Soviet eras, citizens often identify the eponymous language of their ethnic group as 'native,' even when they have little or no skills in it. This is obvious, for example, from the 1989 census results reporting that over 97 per cent of urban Kazakhs in Kazakhstan claimed Kazakh as 'native.'[1]

Since education is central to much of the discussion below, it must be noted that, with the arguable exception of Kazakhstan, the overall quality of education in Central Asia has fallen since independence. The complex reasons for this are beyond the scope of this chapter. However, because this phenomenon is closely linked to shifting domains from Russian to state languages, it should be kept in mind in considering the sketches below.

Kazakhstan

Kazakhstan has pursued a more inclusive model of nation building than any other country in Central Asia. This is apparent from numerous pronouncements by Nursultan Nazarbayev, who became leader of Kazakhstan as head of Kazakhstan's Communist Party in 1989, served as president of independent Kazakhstan for over 27 years, and even since stepping in early 2019 has remained the most powerful individual in the country. To the dismay of those who want their country to follow a narrower (Kazakhcentric) nation-building plan, Nazarbayev has consistently emphasised that the country is equally home to representatives of over 100 other ethnic groups. This inclusive approach is evident in the creation of a presidentially appointed advisory body designed to represent the country's ethnic minorities. Established by Nazarbayev's own decree in 1995, this 'Assembly of the People of Kazakhstan' (originally 'Assembly of the People**s** [plural] of Kazakhstan'), is supposed to 'foster the creation of suitable conditions for the further enhancement of interethnic harmony and tolerance in society and the unity of the people.' No such prominent organisation operates or has operated anywhere in post-1991 Central Asia (*Assambleiia*, n.d.).

Nazarbayev's nation building project has been in tension with a narrower vision of Kazakhstan's identity promoted by other members of Kazakhstan's elite. This narrower vision is visible in many places, for example the preamble to Kazakhstan's 1995 Constitution which states that the independent country has been established on 'native Kazakh land' (на исконной казахской земле/ байырғы қазақ жерінде).

Under Nazarbayev's leadership, the 'solution' to opposing views of nation building in Kazakhstan has usually been compromise and often ambiguity. This is evident in the title of Kazakhstan's first language law, adopted in 1989. The Russian name of this law clearly states that it concerns *languages* (plural) (Закон о языках); by contrast, the Kazakh title (Тіл туралы зан) 'law on language,' is not explicit whether the law concerns one language or more.[2] Another example of compromise is the same law's unambiguous reference to Kazakh as the single state language, which is nevertheless accompanied by the Russian language's designation as the 'language of inter-ethnic communication.' This same designation survived in a short-lived constitution adopted in 1993 (Fierman 1998: 179). This sort of compromise was common in URs in the last years of Soviet power and even early post-Soviet Central Asian states. However, with the exception of Kazakhstan (and to some extent, Kyrgyzstan [see below], over time, language laws and other authoritative formulations of language policy in Central Asia unambiguously reflected nation building projects privileging the titular group and its language.

Nazarbayev's support for a broad national project in Kazakhstan is also evident in his continued reference to Russian as Kazakhstan's 'official language' even though it is not (Poslanie 2007). In the debates leading up to the adoption of the 1995 Constitution, proponents of a more inclusive concept of the nation called for giving Russian status as a second state language. When this was rejected, some proponents of the broader nation retreated to the position of making Russian the 'official' language. Due to arguments of those who claimed there was no distinction between 'state' and 'official,' this was also rejected. The solution was a compromise (duplicated in the 1997 language law) stating that although Kazakh is the sole 'state' language (memlekettik til/ gosudarstvennyi iazyk), Russian was to be 'officially used on a par with Kazakh' in state organisations and organs of local administration (Art. 7). The meaning of this has been debated ever since; some interpret it to mean that Russian can be used *instead of* Kazakh, while others say this means that Kazakh is obligatory, but that in some instances Russian *may* be used instead. The fact that Nazarbayev continues to refer to Russian as the 'official' language, like his continued use of the term 'language of cross-ethnic communication' is symptomatic of the fact that the president's words and actions have been more important than law.[3]

Both the 1989 and 1997 language laws promised to raise the status of Kazakh in many domains, including the courts, public signage, mass media, onomastics, provision of public services and government offices' internal communications. Even 30 years after adoption of the first language law, implementation is far from complete.

Despite the problems outlined above regarding measurement of language repertoires, at the time of the USSR's collapse, Russian's dominance was clearly greater in Kazakhstan than anywhere else in the region. According to the 1989 census, 83.1 per cent of Kazakhstan's entire population (and 64.2 per cent of its Kazakhs) claimed to be either native Russian speakers or fluent in it as a second language. At the same time, only 1.6 per cent of non-Kazakhs claimed Kazakh as a native or second language. One of the primary reasons for the high share of Russian speakers in Kazakhstan was its demographic composition. According to the 1989 census, Kazakhstan had by far the region's smallest share of the titular group (only 39.7 per cent) and a much larger share of Russians (37.8 per cent). Russian dominance was augmented by about 6.5 per cent Ukrainians and Belorussians, a large share of whom were linguistically and culturally Russified. Slavic dominance was particularly great in urban areas, where Slavs (constituting close to 60 per cent of the population) far outnumbered the 26.7 per cent for Kazakhs. In the capital city, Kazakhs were a minority comprising just 22.5 per cent.

The ethnic composition of Kazakhstan has radically changed since 1989. By the beginning of 1999, the Kazakh and Russian shares were 53.4 per cent and 30.0 per cent, respectively; and six years later, in 2005, Kazakhs already outnumbered Russians more than two to one, comprising 57.9 per cent and 26.7 per cent of the population, respectively (Bondartsova 2011). As of the beginning of 2019, the shares were reported to be 68.0 and 19.3 per cent, respectively (Etnicheskaia 2019).

Nazarbayev's linguistic accommodation of Kazakhstan's Slavs has harmonised with the country's close international alignment with Russia. Nazarbayev has called Russia Kazakhstan's 'most important and reliable ally' (Nazarbayev: Rossiia 2017) and characterised relations between the two countries as 'exemplary' (Nazarbayev nazval 2018). The close alliance between Russia and Kazakhstan is reflected in Kazakhstan's being one of the initial signatories to the 1992 treaty creating the Collective Security Treaty Organization (CSTO); Kazakhstan was also one of the founding members of the Eurasian Economic Union (initially including only Russia, Belarus and Kazakhstan). Despite this, following Russia's 2014 occupation of Crimea and consequent increased fears in Kazakhstan that Russia had designs on parts of Kazakhstan's territory, Nazarbayev took steps that slightly distanced Kazakhstan from Russia.

In the authoritarian system overseen by Nazarbayev, major decisions on language policy have clearly been made by the president himself. That said, Kazakhstan has not witnessed levels of repression characteristic of Turkmenistan, Uzbekistan (under Islam Karimov), or Tajikistan. Thus, successive versions of the Latin alphabet that Kazakh is on course to adopt suggest that Nazarbayev's decisions on language have been influenced by linguists and even popular opinion.

Kazakhstan, with a per capital GDP of around $11,000 in 2010, is a far richer country than the other Central Asian states. The 2010 Kazakhstan per capita GDP was approximately one and one-half the amount in Turkmenistan, and three to five times analogous amounts in Uzbekistan, Kyrgyzstan and Tajikistan (*Nationmaster,* (n.d.)). Kazakhstan's relative wealth has allowed it to direct resources to support development of the state language.

The expansion of Kazakh's use in higher education (HE) is a function of more ample financial resources that have permitted much greater investment in language corpus development and textbook development than elsewhere in Central Asia. Corpus development is evident in publication of numerous dictionaries, including a thirty-one-volume series of Russian-Kazakh and Kazakh-Russian bilingual terminological dictionaries created over 1999–2000; each volume contained about 5,000 terms. Another thirty-volume set was published in 2012–2014, each volume containing between 9,000 and 12,000 words (Lysenko 2015). Equally important, the government has invested resources to develop Kazakh-language education and mass media, and to train government employees in use of the state language in the workplace.

Despite all of this, the pace of shift from Russian to Kazakh has been much, much slower than both dreamed of and dreaded in 1989, when the first language law was adopted. As of 1988, Kazakh was being used in only 25 soviet (council) executive committees of various levels in the Kazakh SSR, and was not used at all in the republic-level offices of ministries or agencies (министерства, ведомства) (Kaziev 2015). Yet, in 1990, a breathtakingly unrealistic language program was published for the republic, outlining steps to shift the language of government office work *throughout Kazakhstan* by 1995 (Fierman 2011). Following very little except symbolic progress during the next decade, in 1998 Kazakhstan's government issued a decree (postanovlenie). 'On Broadening the Spheres of Use of the State Language in State Organs.' Still, when a new language program was adopted in 2001 covering the period to 2010, it explained that most documents in government offices were still being produced in Russian. In the five years after adoption of the language program, individual oblasts began to announce that their government office work had shifted to Kazakh; however, a 2007 government 'concept paper' dedicated to expanding Kazakh's spheres of functioning reported 'even in regions with an overwhelming majority of Kazakh population' the indicators of office work in Kazakh were 'not positive'; and in central government organs 'only 20% to 30% of documents' were being prepared in Kazakh (Fierman 2009). About the same time, Kazakhstan's state secretary announced that even in oblasts where Kazakhs comprised large majorities and many assumed that government documents were entirely in Kazakh, in fact the share was only about one half (Panarin 2015).

It is impossible to give an accurate figure of the share of written office work today in Kazakh in government offices. Nevertheless, anecdotal reports suggest it is much higher than it was 10 or 15 years ago. In 2018, Quat Dombay, a Kazakh blogger with considerable experience in personnel management, claimed that between 40 and 60 per cent of ministries were operating in Kazakh; furthermore, according to Dombay, 80 per cent of court decisions were in Kazakh only, with the same being true of correspondence between the president's office and ministries (Tatilia 2018).

Perhaps the most important change from the early years of independence is the much greater capacity in government offices to conduct business in Kazakh. Kazakhs comprise an increasing share of government workers, and the share of the population who cannot at least understand spoken Kazakh is shrinking. Changes in language of education suggest that Kazakh will play an increasingly dominant role in the workplace, especially in government, where Kazakhs are overrepresented. In 1988, slightly over 30 per cent of Kazakhstan's school children were attending Kazakh-medium classes (Fierman 2005: 106). By 2004, the share had reached 56 per cent (Fierman, 2005: 106) and by 2008, approximately 60 per cent (Fierman 2011: 159); in 2015, it reached 65.8 per cent (*Statistika* 2016: 77), but fell to 64.3 per cent the following year (*Statistika* 2018: 291). Kazakhs are not just an increasing share of the country's population but are increasingly enrolling their children in Kazakh-medium education. This proportion jumped from 66.1 per cent in 1990 to 81.3 per cent in 1999, and reached over 87 per cent in 2015.

The share of Kazakhstan's HE enrolment has also rapidly increased. In 1989–1990, those in Kazakh-medium groups constituted only 17.9 per cent of all students in the republic. By 2001–2002, the share had grown to 31.5 per cent, and by 2005–2006 it had grown to 42.6 per cent. By 2014, 60.4 of the country's students in HE were studying in Kazakh, and over the next three years the share reached 62.7, 63.2 and 64.3 per cent (*Statistika* 2016: 283).⁴

Although these data suggest that in the coming years the work environment for citizens with higher education will consist of individuals educated in Kazakh, these data must be treated with caution. One reason is that many students from Kazakhstan study abroad, especially in Russia. Thus, for example, in the 2015–2016 academic year, 73,455 Kazakhstani students were enrolled in HE in Russia (Kazakhstanskie 2017). This was equivalent to almost 16 per cent of students enrolled in HE in Kazakhstan itself. (That said, this number includes many students, especially Slavs, who are unlikely to return to Kazakhstan following their studies.) Another reason for caution in projecting the language of the future work environment is that, based on anecdotal reports, students recorded as studying in one language often take individual subjects in another language or need to use literature in another language (most commonly Russian) in their studies. Thus, many students in 'Kazakh groups' of HE have at least passive reading skills in Russian and will be able to use them in their jobs. Even with this qualification, the trend of increasing use of Kazakh in HE is evident, and this will affect the language used in government and other work settings in the future.

Brief mention should be made here of English. Despite Kazakhstan's international alignment with Russia, it has followed a foreign policy promoting ties with other major world powers, including China, the European Union and the United States. Along with this, from the 1990s on, Kazakhstan sent large numbers of students abroad, where they studied a variety of disciplines in English and other foreign languages beyond Russian. In 2006, President Nazarbayev unveiled a policy of teaching English (along with Kazakh and Russian) throughout the country (Triedinstvo 2015), and in 2010, a new elite university was established with English as the sole language of instruction. The most dramatic evidence of promoting English was a policy overseen by Yerlan Sagadiyev, who became Minister of Education and Science in early 2016. Almost immediately, Sagadiyev announced a policy that was (among other things) supposed to lead, just over three years later, to teaching biology, physics, chemistry and computer science in English in all tenth and eleventh grade classes (Erlan 2016). From the outset, this policy was broadly criticised; Sagadiyev was removed as minister in February 2019 and, although the idea of teaching school pupils three languages has not been abandoned, it appears that the goal of teaching all science subjects in all schools in English in the near future is no longer on the agenda.

Despite lowering expectations for introducing English as a language of instruction in non-elite secondary schools, the continuing policy to shift Kazakh from Cyrillic to Latin letters is often justified with arguments that the change will facilitate learning English. Although such a shift had been discussed in the very earliest years of independence, it was largely ignored until the same 2006 speech in which Nazarbayev spoke about the need for citizens to know three languages. In December 2012, Nazarbayev spoke of the need to 'embark on' (приступить к) the shift to Latin letters (Poslanie 2012), but five years later he shortened the timetable for the shift, announcing that it should be completed by 2025 (Rysaliev 2017). Since then, work has been proceeding in a rapid fashion to determine the letters to be selected, defining orthographic rules, and introducing the alphabet to the population.

Kyrgyzstan

Although Kyrgyzstan's approach to nation building was inclusive in the early years of Askar Akayev's presidency (Huskey Unpublished manuscript), over time (in part due to the shifting ethnic balance discussed below), Kyrgyz dominance in the nation-building project became more marked (Karimov 2011). Furthermore, from the beginning, the role of Russians in the nation building project was much more ambiguous than in Kazakhstan. For Kyrgyzstan, which lacks a border with Russia, Russians were not the dominant ethnic group with a 'historical homeland' in a powerful neighbour that might have historical claims to its territory. Indeed, especially in Kyrgyzstan's south, Russians have arguably been viewed as a balance to Uzbeks, the one ethnic group whose representatives have sought autonomy and thus been viewed as threatening territorial integrity.

Kyrgyzstan's legal documents on language have reflected a slightly more explicit reference than Kazakhstan's to Russian's special status. Since 1989, Kyrgyz has been the only state language. However, a 2001 amendment to the 1993 constitution states that Russian should be used as the official language (в качестве официального языка) (Zakon 2001); despite periodic calls to remove this status (Tagaev & Protassova 2020), this same wording was preserved in the constitutions of 2010 and 2016 (Articles 5 and 10, respectively).

At the time of the 1989 census, 56.7 per cent of Kyrgyzstan's total and 37.3 per cent of the titular ethnic population claimed to be native speakers or fluent in Russian. Comparable figures for a later date are not available, but one estimate from around 2015 indicates that only 36 per cent of the entire population 'could read and write' Russian (Tagaev & Protassova 2020: 134).

One reason for this drop was the dramatic demographic shift. At the time of the 1989 Soviet census, Russians comprised 21.5 per cent of Kyrgyzstan's population, while Kyrgyz and Uzbeks comprised 52.4 and 12.9 per cent, respectively. Russians at the time accounted for over half of the Kyrgyz capital's population, whereas Kyrgyz comprised only about one-quarter. By 2018, Russians had plummeted to 16.6 per cent in the capital, while Kyrgyz had jumped to 73.7 per cent. At the beginning of 2018, Kyrgyz comprised 73.1 per cent of the country's total population, with Uzbeks accounting for 14.7 per cent, and Russians comprising just 5.6 per cent (Natsional'nyi ... *Demograficheskii* 2018: 101).

Despite these shifts, Russian retains a strong position in Kyrgyzstan. This is supported by Kyrgyzstan's close alignment with Russia in international relations. Kyrgyzstan has been a member of both the CSTO and EEU and hosts a Russian military base. Kyrgyzstan is also closely tied to Russia economically. Russia (and to a lesser extent other parts of the former Soviet Union) where Russian language skills are important are primary destinations of Kyrgyzstan's labour migrants. For almost a decade, these labourers have contributed between one-quarter and one-third of total GNP (World Bank, n.d.). These funds are especially important in a country where, according to the Asian Development Bank, in 2017, approximately one-fourth of the population lived below the national poverty line (Asian Development 2019).

Kyrgyzstan's poverty underlies its lack of investment in language corpus development, translation, mass media as well as education that would be required for high-status domains to shift from Russian to Kyrgyz. Thus, although regulations have repeatedly called for shifting government office work (deloproizvodstvo) from Russian to Kyrgyz, regulations have sometimes been ignored or shifts to Kyrgyz reversed (Azhymatov 2017).

In 2018, 73.1 per cent of Kyrgyzstan's school children were reportedly in Kyrgyz-medium classes (Bengard 2018). Although in 2010/2011, over 27 per cent were studying in Russian (Aref'ev 2012), by early 2018 the share had fallen to 17.9 per cent (Kukhtenova 2018). Although the drop reflected continuing Slavic emigration, the still relatively large share for Russian medium reflects the popularity of Russian education among ethnic Kyrgyz (especially in Bishkek and other cities of the north) and among Uzbeks, for whom native language education opportunities have decreased. In 2018, 8.3 per cent of Kyrgyzstan's children were studying in Uzbek. This reflects a government policy to contract Uzbek-medium education, as also reflected in the elimination of HE entrance exams in that language (Ivashchenko 2013).

Russian plays a dominant role in Kyrgyzstan's HE. According to official data, in 2017–2018, 66.7 per cent of HE students were studying in Russian groups, 24.7 per cent in Kyrgyz, 3.8 per cent in English, with the remainder in Turkish and other languages (Natsional'nyi … *Obrazovanie* 2018, p *123*). Russian's dominance in Kyrgyzstan likely reflects the lack of investment in national-language education that has occurred in Kazakhstan. In addition to Russian-medium HE inside Kyrgyzstan, approximately 15,000 HE students from Kyrgyzstan study in the Russian Federation. This equals almost 10 per cent of the total number of HE students inside Kyrgyzstan.[5]

Tajikistan

Tajikistan's nation building project has been based on a history claimed in the name of those who today identify as ethnic Tajiks; today's Tajiks are said to be the heirs of a golden age of Tajik-Persian civilisation that predates the arrival of Turks in the region. The question of 'Who was here first?' has occupied a central place in debates between historians of Tajikistan and Uzbekistan and underlies a nation-building project that disparages Uzbeks achievements and denigrates their culture and language (Hughes 2017).

Tajikistan's Constitution designates Russian as the 'language of inter-ethnic communication' (Art. 2).[6] Although Tajikistan's 1989 language law referred to the Pamiri languages as well as Uzbek, Kyrgyz and Turkmen, the references to the last three were omitted in the law adopted 20 years later.

In comparison to Kazakhstan or even Kyrgyzstan, Russian's role as a first or dominant language in Tajikistan is very small. A major reason for this is demographic. At the time of the 1989 census, 62.3 per cent of Tajikistan's population were Tajiks while the remainder were mostly Uzbeks (23.5 per cent) or Russians (7.3 per cent). In Dushanbe, Tajikistan's capital, Tajiks comprised 38.2 per cent of the population, Russians 32.9 per cent and Uzbeks 10.6 per cent. This was a fundamentally different picture from the capitals of Kazakhstan or Kyrgyzstan, where Russians dominated.

As a result of Tajikistan's devastating civil war, by 2000, the Russian share of the country's population had fallen to about 1 per cent (and a decade later it was under 0.5 per cent) (Shcherbakova 2013). The precise share of Russians in Dushanbe today is unclear but even if all of Tajikistan's Russians lived in the capital, their share would be only slightly over 5 per cent.

The change in the reported Uzbek share of Tajikistan's population and the fate of the Uzbek language vividly illustrate Tajikistan's narrow nation building project. Although, as noted above, in 1989, Uzbeks comprised almost one-quarter of the population, the reported share in 2015 was around 12 per cent. The drop was largely an artefact not of immigration, but reclassification. Some individual groups previously counted as 'Uzbeks' were encouraged by the government to claim 'tribal' identities, (e.g., Lakays and Karluks) (Mingbaev 2015). Moreover, because of the advantage of membership in the titular group, Uzbek parents who cannot even speak Tajik are reported sometimes to register their children as 'Tajiks' (Ergasheva & Shams 2014).

Partly due to demographic factors, the share of Tajikistan's population claiming fluency in Russian in 1989 (36.4 per cent) was substantially lower than in Kazakhstan or Kyrgyzstan. However, even among Tajiks, 30.5 per cent claimed to be fluent in Russian. It is noteworthy that 16.9 per cent of Tajikistan's Uzbeks claimed fluency in Tajik (compared to 3.5 per cent of Russians).

With the collapse of the USSR, civil war, emigration of native Russian speakers and deterioration of education, the share of Tajikistan's population fluent in Russian has dropped dramatically. In 1989/90, 10.8 per cent of school children in Tajikistan were in Russian-medium classes (Aref'ev 2012: 137). This dropped to just 1.2 per cent in 1999/2000 before beginning to increase again. As of early 2019 the share had grown to 4.4 per cent (V Tadzhikistane obrazovanie 2019). There is a severe shortage of teachers of Russian language and subject teachers in Russian.

Some data suggest a sharply reduced level of Russian use in Tajikistan's HE. Official government data show that in 1991–92, 40.3 per cent of Tajikistan's HE students were receiving their education in Russian, with shares for 2000–2001 and 2015–2016 – 30.4 per cent and 15.8 per cent, respectively. The same data show the share in Tajik-medium groups growing from 54.0 per cent in 1991–92 to 83.4 per cent in 2015/2016 (Agenstvo Tadzhikistan 2016: 109).

These data, however, likely understate the role of Russian: in 1991–92, students in Tajik groups almost certainly took some subjects in Russian and/or used some Russian educational materials. Despite the decline in Russian skills, it is likely that at least many better students use Russian materials today. In addition to students enrolled domestically, many of Tajikistan's students study abroad, especially in Russia. In 2016–17, the number enrolled in Russia was approximately 10 per cent the number enrolled inside Tajikistan.[7]

Russian's true role is also suggested by anecdotal reports that instructors who teach in Tajik often use Russian print or electronic sources in preparing their lectures. The continuing niche for Russian in education and scholarship is also illustrated by a 2017 decision of Tajikistan's Ministry of Education and Science that requires most dissertations to be defended in Russian or English.[8]

Russian's position in Tajikistan is reinforced by Tajikistan's international alignment with Russia and labour migration rooted in poverty. Although Tajikistan is not a member of the EEU, it joined the CSTO, and Russia maintains a military base in Tajikistan.

The Asian Development Bank estimated that in 2015, 31.3 per cent of Tajikistan's population was living below the national poverty line (Tajikistan: Remittances 2019). Russian-language skills can help find better job opportunities both in Tajikistan as well as in Russia, or other former Soviet republics. Although Tajikistan has received loans and aid from a variety of countries (particularly China) it remains dependent on Russia. As of early 2018, an estimated 1 million Tajikistan labour migrants were working in Russia; and in 2017, a total of 2.5 billion dollars were reportedly sent by money transfer from Russia to Tajikistan (Labour Migrants' Remittances 2018). Between 2002 and 2013 an average of 31.3 per cent of Tajikistan's GDP came from remittances (Tajikistan: Remittances 2019).

Tajik dominates as the language of most government offices. Despite a law reinstating Russian's status as 'language of cross-ethnic communication' in 2011 and allowing its use in 'law making' (законотворчество), the same legislation mandated that all applicants for government work pass a Tajik language test (Russkomu 2011).

Uzbekistan

Uzbekistan's nation-building project, like Tajikistan's, has concentrated narrowly on the titular nationality. Writing in 1997, Morgan Liu noted that despite rhetoric about pluralism, the Uzbek government had set out 'to build an essentially monoethnic territorial nation-state' that excluded members of other ethnic groups (Liu 1997). In a fashion that mirrors Tajikistan's marginalisation of Uzbeks, Uzbekistan's narrative has downplayed the role of Tajiks in history and the Tajik language in contemporary society.

Although Uzbekistan's 1989 language law identified Russian as the 'language of cross-ethnic communication,' it was given no such status in the 1992 Constitution. Other legislation identifies very limited use of Russian for legal purposes (e.g., in notarised documents) (Zakon Uzbekistan o vnesenii 1995).

Demographic changes in Uzbekistan since 1989 have contributed to Uzbek displacing Russian language, but considerably less than in Tajikistan. At the time of the 1989 census, Russians comprised 8.3 per cent of the republic population but 34.0 per cent in Tashkent, the capital. By 2017, the Russian share of the republic population had dropped to 2.3 per cent (Gosudarstvennyi Komitet Uzbekistan Demograficheskaia 2017), though in Tashkent, the capital, in 2014 the share was estimated to be 18 per cent (Krupnye 2015). From 1989 to 2017 the Uzbek share of the republic population increased from 71.4 per cent to 83.8 per cent (Gosudarstvennyi Komitet Uzbekistan Demograficheskaia 2017), and in Tashkent from 44.2 in 1989 to an estimated 65 per cent in 2014 (Krupnye 2015).

As noted above, data on mastery of Russian as a second language in late-Soviet Uzbekistan are particularly suspect. Clearly, though, the vast majority of Uzbekistan's inhabitants spoke Uzbek. In 1989/90, when ethnic Russians comprised over 8 per cent of the total population, only 14.8 per cent of secondary school pupils were in Russian-medium classes (Aref'ev 2012: 123).[9]

Emigration undoubtedly contributed to the decline in Russian-medium enrolments from 14.8 1989/1990 to 4.3 per cent in 2010/2011 (Aref'ev 2012: 123). Recovery of the Russian share to 10.0 per cent in 2018/2019 likely reflects the importance of Russian for labour migrants and the reductions in Tajik, Kazakh, Kyrgyz and Turkmen enrolments (O'zbekiston Khalq ta'limi 2019).[10]

As in Tajikistan, the overwhelming majority of HE students are enrolled in groups in the state language. Although in 2001/2002 the share in Russian-medium groups in Uzbekistan was 20.0 per cent, by 2010/2011 (the latest year for which data are available), it had dropped to 9.1 per cent (Aref'ev 2012: 126). Also, as in Tajikistan, these percentages likely understate the importance of Russian. Even if basic textbooks exist in Uzbek, students in national language groups at times likely need to access additional materials available only in another language (most often Russian). In order to improve their language skills, students who come from the provinces to study in Tashkent (and other cities?), reportedly often pay to study Russian in private language centres (Khurramov 2015). Uzbekistan's Russian-medium HE students also include those in Russian Federation institutions, approximately equal to 5 per cent of Uzbekistan HE enrolments.[11] Over the past two years, numerous branches of foreign HE institutions have been planned or opened in Uzbekistan; most use Russian or English for instruction.

Sergei Abashin (2015) has noted that it is 'precisely in Uzbekistan that the ideological narrative of obtaining independence has come closest to classical models of decolonisation.' This has contributed to Uzbekistan's relative disengagement from Russia and has also likely meant a weaker position for Russian language in Uzbekistan than Kazakhstan, Kyrgyzstan or Tajikistan. Uzbekistan has not joined the EAEC; although it was a member of the CSTO, it withdrew in 1999, rejoined in 2006 and then quit again in 2012 (Uzbekistan Steps 2012).

The lack of employment opportunities in Uzbekistan has stimulated large numbers of labour migrants to seek work abroad. Over 2006–2016, foreign remittances comprised an average of 6.8 per cent of Uzbekistan's GDP (Nationmaster, n.d.). Russian language skills are particularly valuable for workers in other former Soviet republics, especially the estimated 2 million in Russia who in recent years have comprised 80 per cent of all labour migrants from Uzbekistan (Ezhegodno 2019).

The mix of Uzbek and Russian in government office work appears to depend greatly on location and level of government organisation; although the use of Uzbek is increasing, Russian still remains important in this domain. According to one report, outside of the capital, Uzbek is the primary language for local government communications and office work. However, Russian is often used by local government units to send reports to higher levels (Alimdzhanov 2019). The persistence of Russian is also supported by many of the country's political and economic elites, who were educated in Russian and are most comfortable in that language.

Uzbekistan's announcement already in 1993 that it would shift Uzbek writing from the Cyrillic to Latin alphabet is evidence of the country's symbolic turning away from Russia. Beginning in 1996, children in first grade of Uzbek-medium schools learned to read in Latin letters, and subsequently, one year at a time, school textbooks for higher grades were shifted to Latin. Yet even today most non-textbook Uzbek publications are in Cyrillic and public signage is often still in Cyrillic, though sometimes duplicated in Latin. Uzbekistan, with one of the region's more authoritarian regimes, has declined to invest scarce resources in alphabet change beyond textbook preparation. (Likewise, the government does not appear to have made significant investments in other language projects, such as corpus development.)

The regime appears to view alphabet change as a problem that generation shift will resolve. However, the inattention to completing alphabet shift, corpus development and other aspects of language development in the most populous country of the region may prompt continued greater reliance on Russian.

Turkmenistan

Turkmenistan's extremely narrow nation-building project is evident in the cults of personality created by the country's authoritarian presidents. The first president, Saparmurat Niyazov, who took on the title 'Turkmenbashi' (leader of the Turkmens)[12] is credited with authorship of *Ruhnama* (Book of the Soul); this work became the cornerstone of Turkmenistan's ideology under Turkmenbashi's rule. The book became a central component of the school curriculum and was displayed in mosques alongside the Koran. *Ruhnama* consists of autobiographical elements and various thoughts on Turkmen culture, history and morality. Following the Turkmenbashi's death in 2006, his successor, Gurbanguly Berdymuhamedov, continued to rule in autocratic fashion and promoted a similar ethnically-based ideology privileging Turkmens. The extreme concentration of power in the presidents' hands has profoundly affected language policy by insulating it from public opinion, and facilitating extreme shifts.

Both presidents of Turkmenistan have aligned their country with Russia far less than any other post-Soviet Central Asian leader. In 1995, Turkmenistan declared itself 'permanently neutral' and even submitted a resolution endorsing this to the United Nations. Turkmenistan is the only Central Asian state never to have joined the CSTO and, like Uzbekistan, it has not joined the EAEU. Turkmenistan's economic relations with Russia, especially its gas exports, have been troubled, marked by periodic disputes over price and even halts of deliveries. Reliance on gas export to Russia was greatly reduced and its dependence on China increased when the Central Asia–China pipeline opened in 2009 (Stronski 2017). In large part due to this pipeline, in 2017, 83.5 per cent of Turkmenistan's exports went to China (Observatory 2019). Another indication of Turkmenistan's orientation away from Moscow and its broader isolation is that in 2002 it became impossible for Turkmenistan citizens to subscribe to periodical publications from Russia (Aref'ev 2012: 148). This remained in effect until late 2011 (Aref'ev 2012: 152).

Thanks to Turkmenistan's vast hydrocarbon resources, in the early years of independence Turkmenbashi aspired to turn his country into a new Kuwait (Dream On 2000). The high price of natural gas and Turkmenistan's relatively small population allowed the government to subsidise goods for its citizens (Stronski 2017). Later, however, due to falling hydrocarbon prices, widespread corruption, and a wasteful economic system, citizens' quality of life seriously deteriorated. Hyper-ideologisation and lack of strategic planning have made for chaotic language development. (See brief illustrations below regarding script and vocabulary.)

In May 1990, Turkmenistan became the very last Soviet republic to adopt a language law. This law named Turkmen as the single state language but identified Russian as the 'language of interethnic communication' (Zakon Turkmenskoi 1990). Independent Turkmenistan's 1992 Constitution maintained Turkmen as the state language and dropped reference to Russian (Constitution of Turkmenistan 1992).[13]

As elsewhere, Turkmenistan's language change has been both cause and result of demographic change. At the time of the 1989 census, Turkmenistan's ethnic composition resembled Uzbekistan's, i.e., over 70 per cent belonged to the titular nationality, between 8 and 10 per cent were Russians, and about half the remaining 20 per cent belonged to Central Asian minorities.[14] No reliable data on Turkmenistan's current ethnic composition are available. However, based on a CIA Factbook estimate of 85 per cent Turkmen in 2003 and reports of continued emigration by minorities, it is likely that the Turkmen share today approaches 90 per cent and the Russian share is 3 per cent or less. Already in 1989, 50.9 per cent of the population of Ashgabat (Turkmenistan's capital) were Turkmen; Russians comprised another 32.9 per cent, and about 16 per cent belonged to other ethnic groups (Fierman, 2012: 1088). According to Aref'ev (2012: 147), as of 2012, over half of Turkmenistan's Russians lived in Ashgabat, but even there comprised only about 7 per cent of the population. Today the Russian share is likely significantly less.

The share of Turkmenistan's population claiming Russian fluency in 1989 was 38.6 per cent, that is, close to Tajikistan's 36.3 per cent and far below the shares in Kazakhstan or Kyrgyzstan. Data derived from a 2010 census suggest the share of the population fluent in Russian had fallen to under 12 per cent (Aref'ev 2012: 146).

After independence, Turkmen became the overwhelming language of school instruction. According to Aref'ev (2012: 149), in 1989/90, 16 per cent of the republic's school pupils were enrolled in Russian-medium education; in 2000/2001 the share was 4.6 per cent, and in 2009/2010, only 0.6 per cent. Aref'ev (2012: 152) suggests that in the early 2010s this number began to increase. Today just one secondary school provides instruction exclusively in Russian; this institution is jointly administered with Russia's Ministry of Science and Education. Beginning in 1995, all HE in Turkmenistan was in Turkmen (Aref'ev 2012: 151). More recently, branches of Russia-based institutions (with instruction in Russian) have opened, as well as Turkmenistan's International University with English-medium instruction.

Although in 1999 Turkmenistan still had 99 Uzbek-medium schools, 49 Kazakh-medium schools, 55 Russian-medium schools, and 138 schools with more than one language of instruction, by around 2003/2004, all instruction in Uzbek and Kazakh had ceased. As a rule, Russian-medium schools were not closed, but rather either partly or mostly converted to Turkmen (Clement 2018: 151).[15]

Russian's prestige is greatly understated in the above data. Around 2012, the director of the jointly administered school cited above reportedly said that applications to his school exceeded available places by a factor of ten. Aref'ev reports that most of this school's pupils were from families of Turkmen *nomenklatura* (Aref'ev 2012: 150). Other reports contend that parents often pay large bribes to place their children in Russian-medium classes of mixed schools (V Turkmenistane 2018).

Most Turkmenistan HE students study outside their country, particularly in Russia, Belarus, Ukraine and Turkey. For the 2016/2017 academic year Turkmenistan anticipated enrolling a total of 7,256 students in HE inside the country; in 2014, over 10,000 students began studies abroad (Bairamova 2017). In 2014, when the total HE enrolment in Turkmenistan was 32,427, another 15,631 were studying in Russia and approximately 7,000 in Turkey (Obrazovanie v

Turkmenistane 2017); in 2016–2017, 9,806 students from Turkmenistan were in Ukraine (Studenty 2016) and the following year, 7,749 in Belarus (Turchina 2019).

In harmony with Turkmenistan's narrow nation building project, it appears that already in the late 1990s, Turkmen was in wide use in government communications. According to Clement, the greatest push for replacing Russian with Turkmen occurred in the first years of the new millennium (Clement 2018: Chapter 6). Nevertheless, Russian continued to be used at least informally in government offices. According to one informant, at times government workers without adequate Turkmen skills would compose correspondence intended for another office in Russian. This would be translated into Turkmen before transmission, but perhaps be re-translated back into Russian for the official on the other end. It appears that today this is no longer necessary, and that only Turkmen is used.

During the rule of Turkmenbashi, numerous terms and even common Turkmen words were replaced. Mostly, though not exclusively, the changes involved replacements for words 'borrowed' into Turkmen from Russian, though originating in Greek, Latin or other languages. One particularly bold set of new 'nationalised' words involved the names of the months. Thus, for example, the Russian words previously used in Turkmen for January, April, September and December (ianvar', aprel', sentiabr' and dekabr') became Türkmenbaşy, Gurbansoltan (name of Türkmenbaşy's mother), Ruhnama and Bitaraplyk (neutrality). Many of the other lexical replacements involved broader or new related meanings for words that were already in Turkmen dictionaries.

The quality of Turkmenistan's language planning is also evident in its alphabet shift. Implementation of a 1993 decree to shift to Latin was slow until December 29, 1999, when Turkmenistan's parliament adopted a resolution mandating that beginning in the new millennium, Turkmen would be written in Latin letters. Within days, all central newspapers began to appear only in Latin. Lack of strategic planning is also evident in the letter symbols. The initial version of the Turkmen Latin alphabet included Ññ, $¢, ¥ÿ, Žž and £ſ. In January 2000, however, four of these symbols – Ññ, $¢, ¥ÿ, and £ſ – were replaced with Ňň, Şş, Ýý and Žž (Fierman & Garibova 2010: 443).

Notes

1. Unless otherwise indicated, all Soviet census data on nationality and language are taken from pages of *Perepisi naseleniia* …
2. It would have been possible to make the plural nature explicit by calling the document 'Тілдер туралы зaң' in Kazakh, but this was not done.
3. The precedence of a president's words or actions over law is the rule rather than the exception throughout the region.
4. Data for some years are given for the academic year and in others for calendar year. This is unavoidable, since the data in sources are not consistently given for the same period. For the years provided above (through 2005–2006, all students not studying in Kazakh were studying in Russian. For 2014 through 2017, besides Russian, between 3 and 4 per cent were studying in other languages, with English accounting for all but a handful.
5. In 2017–18 the total number of higher education students in Kyrgyzstan was over 162,000 (Chislo, 2018), whereas the number of Kyrgyzstan students in RF *vuzes* in early 2019 was 15,800 (Bolee, 2019).
6. A 2009 law had removed this status, but another law in 2011 reinstated it (V Tadzhikistane russkomu …, 2011).
7. In 2016–2017, 17,043 students from Tajikistan were studying in Russia (Aref'ev 2018: 313), compared to 176,500 in Tajikistan in 2015–2016 (Agenstvo Tadzhikistan 2016: 91). 1
8. Some scholars claimed that this contradicted the regulations of the VAK (Higher Degree Commission), which implied that dissertations could be defended in Tajik (V Tadzhikistane zashchitit', 2017).

9 Even if 10 per cent were studying in classes with tuition in other Central Asian languages, three-fourths of pupils of all ethnic groups would have been studying in Uzbek.
10 Besides Russian and Uzbek, in 2018/2019 pupils were enrolled in Karakalpak-medium classes (2.0 per cent), Tajik (1.2 per cent), Kazakh (0.9 per cent), Turkmen (0.2 per cent) and Kyrgyz (0.1 per cent) (O'zbekiston Respublikasi Khalq ta'limi, 2019). Numerous reports attest to closure of Kazakh (Lakhanuly, 2015) and Tajik schools (Rukhullo, 2018).
11 This calculation is based on Aref'ev's data showing 14,161 students from Uzbekistan studying in Russia (2018: 313) and data from and O'zbekiston Khalq Ta'limi (2019), stating that there were 268,300 students in Uzbekistan.
12 An official English-language Turkmenistan website apparently posted around 2000 or 2001 states that 'As founder and president of the Association of Turkmens of the World, Mr. Niyazov holds the official title of Turkmenbashi, Leader of all Ethnic Turkmens' (Embassy of Turkmenistan, 2001?).
13 Aref'ev (2012, p, 147), however, indicates that Russian retained its status as 'interethnic' under Niyazov.
14 Most members of other geographically concentrated Central Asian groups were Uzbeks (9.0 per cent) and Kazakhs (2.5 per cent) who lived primarily in areas bordering their respective titular republic homelands.
15 Clement implies there were no pure Uzbek-medium schools remaining by this time.

Bibliography

Abashin, S. (2015). 'Uzbekistan posle SSSR,' *Zvezda*, No. 8 (August). https://zvezdaspb.ru/index.php?page=8andnput=2563.

Agenstvo po statistike pri Prezidente Respubliki Tadzhikistan. (2016). *Obrazovanie v Respublike Tadzhikistan. 25 let gosudarstvennoi nezavisimosti. Statisticheskii sbornik*. Dushanbe. http://oldstat.ww.tj/ru/img/c1464007cb84f4e545746a409ba5794c_1467094723.pdf, accessed on 22 November 2019.

AKIpress. (2019). 'Bolee 15 tys. kyrgyzstantsev obuchaiutsia v vuzakh Rossii,' 26 March.

Alimdzhanov, B. (2019). 'Uzbekistan: pochemu uzbekskii ne stal iazykom politiki i nauki?' *CABAR*, 2 February.

Aref'ev, A.L. (2012). *Russkii iazyk na rubezhe XX-XXI vekov*. Moscow: Tsentr sotsial'nogo prognozirovaniia i marketinga. https://www.civisbook.ru/files/File/russkij_yazyk.pdf, accessed on 17 November 2019.

Aref'ev, A.L. (2018). 'Mezhdunarodnoe obrazovanie v global'nom izmererenii,' in *Obrazovanie i nauka v Rossii: Sostoianiee i potentsial razvitiia. Sbornik nauchnykh statei*, Vol 3, Moscow: Tsentr Sotsial'nogo prognozirovaniia i marketinga.

Asian Development Bank. (2019). *Poverty in the Kyrgyz Republic*. https://www.adb.org/countries/kyrgyz-republic/poverty, accessed 17 November 2019.

Asia-Plus. (2018). 'Labor migrants' remittances from Russia to banks in Tajikistan reportedly increasing,' 17 April.

Assambleia naroda Kazakhstana. (n.d.). *Ofitsial'nyi sait Prezidenta Respubliki Kazakhstan*. http://www.akorda.kz/ru/national_projects/assambleya-naroda-kazahstana, accessed 15 November 2019.

Azhymatov, Z. (2017). 'Pravitel'stvo meniaet otnoshenie k kyrgyzskomu iazyku,' *Azattyk*, 28 November.

Bairamova, N. (2017). 'Staryi vuz luchshe novykh dvukh,' *Gundogar*, 13 August.

Bengard, A. (2018). 'Tol'ko 216 shkol v Kyrgyzstane s russkim iazykom obucheniia,' *24.kg*, 27 February.

Bondartsova, T.M. (2011). 'K probleme chislennogo i natsional'nogo sostava Respubliki Kazakhstan,' *Vestnik Karagandinskogo universiteta*. https://articlekz.com/article/5872, accessed on 15 November 2019.

Clement, V. (2018). *Learning to Become Turkmen: Literacy, Language, and Power, 1914–2014*. Pittsburgh: University of Pittsburgh Press.

Constitution of Turkmenistan. (1992). https://www.uta.edu/cpsees/TURKCON.htm, accessed on 27 November 2019.

Edufiles.net. 'Obrazovanie v Turkmenistane.' https://edufiles.net/2762947, accessed 27 November 2019.

EEDaily. (2017). 'Nazarbaev: Rossiia dlia Kazakhstana—samyi glavnyi i nadezhnyi soiuznik,' 12 October.

Embassy of Turkmenistan. (2001). 'His Excellency Sapamurat Niyazov Webpage from Library of Congress Web Archives Collection, 'His Excellency Saparmurat Niyazov 'Turkmenbashi',' 'Turkmenbashi,' President of Turkmenistan and Chairman of the Cabinet of Ministers.'

Embassy of Turkmenistan webpage from Library of Congress Web Archives Collection. 'His Excellency Saparmurat Niyazov "Turkmenbashi",' *Library of Congress Web Archives*. http://webarchive.loc.gov/all/

20020813051618/http://www.http://turkmenistanembassy.org/turkmen/gov/presbio.html, accessed on 27 November 2019.
Ergasheva, Z. and B. Shams. (2014). 'Uzbeks Face Obstacles in Increasingly Tajik State,' *RCA*, 28 July 2014, Issue 741.
Fergana. (2011). 'Russkomu iazyku vernuli status mezhnatsional'nogo obshcheniia,' 9 June.
Fierman, W. (1998). 'Language and Identity in Kazakhstan: Formulations in Policy Documents 1987–1997,' *Communist and Post-Communist Studies* 31(2), 171–186.
Fierman, W. (2009). 'Language Vitality and Paths to Revival. Contrasting Cases of Azerbaijani and Kazakh,' *International Journal of the Sociology of Language* 198, 75–104.
Fierman, W. (2011). 'Reversing Language Shift in Kazakhstan,' in Schiffman, H. and Spooner, B. (eds.), *Language Policy and Language Conflict in Afghanistan and Its Neighbors*. Leiden: Brill, 119–175.
Fierman, W. (2012). 'Russian in Post-Soviet Central Asia: A Comparison to the States of the Baltic and South Caucasus,' *Europe–Asia Studies* 64(6), 1077–1100.
Fierman, W. and J. Garibova. (2010). 'Central Asia and Azerbaijan,' in Fishman, J.A. and Garcia, O. (eds.), *Handbook of Language and Ethnicity*. New York: Oxford University Press, 423–452.
GlobalEconomy.com. (2019). 'Tajikistan: Remittances, Percent of GDP.' https://www.theglobaleconomy.com/Tajikistan/remittances_percent_GDP/, accessed on 25 November 2019.
Gosudarstvennyi Komitet Respubliki Uzbekistan po statistike. (2017). *Demograficheskaia situatsiia v Respublike Uzbekistan*, 20 July. https://stat.uz/ru/ofitsialnaya-statistika/433-analiticheskie-materialy-ru/2055-demograficheskaya-situatsiya-v-respublike-uzbekistan, accessed on 25 November 2019.
Gosudarstvennyi Komitet Respubliki Uzbekistan po statistike. (2019). *Statistika obrazovaniia v Respublike Uzbekistan*. https://stat.uz/ru/433-analiticheskie-materialy-ru/4881-statistika-obrazovaniya-v-respublike-uzbekistan, accessed on 26 November 2019.
Hughes, K. (2017). 'From the Achaemenids to Somoni: National Identity and Iconicity in the Landscape of Dushanbe's Capitol Complex,' *Central Asian Survey* 36(4), 511–533.
Huskey, E. 'Competing Visions of Nation in Kyrgyzstan.' (Unpublished manuscript).
Informatsionno-analaticheskii tsentr. (2016). *Statistika sistemy obrazovaniia Respubliki Kazakhstan. Natsional'nyi sbornik*. http://iac.kz/ru/analytics/statistika-sistemy-obrazovaniya-respubliki-kazakhstan-nacionalnyy-sbornik-2015-2016, accessed on 16 November 2019.
Informatsionno-analaticheskii tsentr. (2018). *Statistika sistemy obrazovaniia Respubliki Kazakhstan. Natsional'nyi sbornik*. http://iac.kz/sites/default/files/nacionalnyy_sbornik_2017-2018.pdf, accessed on 16 November 2019.
Ivashchenko, E. (2013). 'Kyrgyzstan: Komu nuzhno obrazovanie na uzbekskom iazyke?' *Fergana*, 13 February.
Karimov, D. (2011). 'Kyrgyzstan. "Osobennosti natsional'noi politiki",' *24.kg*, 30 May.
Kaziev, S.S. (2015). 'Sovetskaia natsional'naia politika i prpblemy doveriia v mezhetnicheskikh otnosheniiakh v Kazakhstane (1917–1991 gody),' Dissertation for Doktor istoricheskikh nauk, Institute of Ethnology and Anthropology, Russian Academy of Sciences, Moscow. http://static.iea.ras.ru/obrazovanie_dissovet/Kaziev/%D0%9A%D0%B0%D0%B7%D0%B8%D0%B5%D0%B2%20%D0%A1.%D0%A8.pdf, accessed on 16 November 2019.
Kazinform. (2015). 'Triedinstvo iqzykov,' 5 August.
Kazinform. (2016). 'Erlan Sagadiev: Smysl vnedreniia trekh!iazychiia v Kazakhstane –total'noe znanie kazakhskogo iazyka naseleniem,' 27 April.
Khronika Turkmenistana. (2018). 'V Turkmenistane razmer vziatki za ustroistvo rebenka v russkii klass dostigaet tysiachi dollarov,' 24 October.
Khurramov, Sh. (2015). 'Pochemu russkii iazyk nuzhen uzbekam,' *365info.kz*, 11 September.
Kukhtenkova, E. (2018). 'Na russkom iazyke poluchaiut obrazovanie 90 protsentov studentov Kirgizii,' *Rossiiskaia gazeta*, 5 October.
Lakhanuly, N. (2015). 'V Uzbekistane zakryli bolee 100 kazakhskikh shkol,' *Rus.Azattyq*, 15 September.
Lenta.Ru. (2011). 'V Tadzhikistane russkomu iazyku vernuli prezhnii status,' 9 June.
Lex.Uz. (1995). 'Zakon Respubliki Uzbekistan. O vnesenii izmenenii i dopolnenii v zakon'o gosudarstvennom iazyke Respubliki Uzbekistan,' 21 December.
Liu, M. (1997). *The Perils of Nationalism in Independent Uzbekistan*. Ann Arbor, MI: MPublishing, University of Michigan Library.
Lysenko, O. (2015). 'Sozdan terminologicheskii fond kazakhskogo iazyka,' *Liter*, 25 February.

Media Law. (1990). 'Zakon Turkmenskoi Sovetskoi Sotsialisticheskoi Respublike 'O iazyke.'' http://medialaw.asia/node/259, accessed on 27 November 2019.
Mingbaev, N. (2015). 'Kolichestvo uzbekov v Tadzhikistane umen'shilos' s 23.5% do 12% v period nezavisimosti,' *Centrasia*, 7 September 2015.
Ministry of Justice of the Kyrgyz Republic. (2001). 'O vnesenii izmenenii v stat'iu 5 Konstitutsii Kyrgyzskoi Respubliki.' http://cbd.minjust.gov.kg/act/view/ky-kg/944?cl=ky-kg, accessed 16 November 2019.
Nationmaster. (n.d.). 'Economy > GDP > Per capita: Countries Compared.' https://www.nationmaster.com/country-info/stats/Economy/GDP/Per-capita, accessed on 4 June 2019.
Natsional'nyi statisticheskii komitet Kyrgyzskoi Respubliki. (2018). *Demograficheskii ezhegodnik Kyrgyzskoi Respubliki 2013–2017*. Bishkek. http://www.stat.kg/media/publicationarchive/c98319ab-1c36-44a4-b473-90f99860b079.pdf, accessed on 17 November 2019.
Natsional'nyi statisticheskii komitet Kyrgyzskoi Respubliki. (2018). *Obrazovanie i nauka v Kyrgyzskoi Respublike, 2013–2017. Statisticheskii sbornik*. Bishkek. http://www.stat.kg/media/publicationarchive/96f08785-4102-4037-9650-bfe7315eaa68.pdf, accessed on 18 November 2019.
Observatory of Economic Complexity. (2019). 'Turkmenistan.' https://atlas.media.mit.edu/en/profile/country/tkm/, accessed on 27 November 2019.
Ofitsial'nyi sait Prezidenta Respubliki Kazakhstan. (2007). *Poslanie Prezidenta Respubliki Kazakhstan N. Nazarbaeva narodu Kazakhstana*. 28 fevralia 2007. http://www.akorda.kz/ru/addresses/addresses_of_president/poslanie-prezidenta-respubliki-kazakhstan-nnazarbaeva-narodu-kazakhstana-28-fevralya-2007-g, accessed on 15 November 2019.
Ofitsial'nyi sait Prezidenta Respubliki Kazakhstan. (2012). *Poslanie Prezidenta Respubliki Kazakhstan N.Nazarbaeva narodu Kazakhstana 14 dekabria 2012 g.*, 14 December. http://www.akorda.kz/ru/addresses/addresses_of_president/poslanie-prezidenta-respubliki-kazakhstan-nnazarbaeva-narodu-kazakhstana-14-dekabrya-2012-g, accessed on 16 November 2019.
O'zbekiston Respublikasi Xalq ta'limi vazirligi. (2019). *O'zbekiston Respublikasi Xalq ta'limi vazirligining 2018-2019 o'quv yili ko'rsatkichlari*. http://uzedu.uz/Xtv/BarchasiPage/67?tp=86, accessed on 11 April 2019.
Panarin, S. (2015). 'Sovremennyi Kazakhstan: sotsial'nye i kul'turnye factory izmenenii v polozhenii russkogo iazyka,' *Vestnik Evrazii*, 30 May.
Perepisi naseleniia Rossiiskoi Imperii, SSSR, 15 novykh nezavisimikh gosudarstv. http://www.demoscope.ru/weekly/ssp/census.php?cy=3, accessed on 14 November 2019.
Radio Azattyk. (2018). 'Chislo studentov v vuzakh Kyrgyzstana sokratilos', no vyroslo v uchilishchakh', 27 January.
Radio Ozodi. (2017). 'V Tadzhikistane zashchitit' dissertatsiiu nuzhno budet na russkom libo angliiskom iazykakh,' 9 November.
Regnum. (2019). 'V Tadzhikistane obrazovanie na russkom iazyke poluchaiut 4.4% uchashchikhsia,' 23 January.
RIA. (2018). 'Nazarbaev nazval vzaimootnosheniia Kazakhstana i Rossii obraztsovymi,' 1 November.
Rukhullo, S. (2018). 'Otkrytoe pis'mo tadzhikov Uzbekistana 'Ne zakryvaite tadzhikskie shkoly,' *Radio Ozodi*, 24 January.
Rysaliev, A. (2017). 'President Calls for Switch to Latin Alphabet by 2025,' *Eurasianet*, 12 April.
Shcherbakova, E. (2013). 'Dolia titul'noi natsional'nosti vozrastaet vo vsekh stranakh SNG, krome Rossii,' *Demoskop Weekly*, 17–30 June, Nos. 559–560.
Sputnik Uzbekistan. (2019). 'Ezhegodno uzbekskie migranty v RF perevodiat $4 mlrd na rodinu,' 8 June.
StanRadar. (2015). 'Krupnye goroda v Tsentral'noi Azii: mezhdu demografiei i politikoi,' 13 August.
Stratfor. (2012). 'Uzbekistan Steps Back From a Regional Security Alliance,' 29 June.
Stronski, P. (2017). 'Turkmenistan at Twenty-Five: The High Price of Authoritarianism,' Carnegie Endowment for International Peace, 30 January.
Tagaev, M.D. and E. Protassova. (2020). 'Russian in Kyrgyzstan. Status, functioning and collisions between languages,' in Mustajoki, A.S., Protassova, E., and Yelenevskaya, M. et al. (eds.), *The Soft Power of the Russian Language: Pluricentricity, Politics and Policies*, Routledge, pp. 134–149.
Tatilia, K. (2018). 'Smozhet li vlast' zagovorit' iskliuchiitel'no na kazakhskom, i chto eto dast?' *Central Asia Monitor*, 9 March.
Tatilia, K. (2019). 'Svet v kontse tonnelia,' *Central Asia Monitor*, 19 August.

Tengrinews.kz. (2017). 'Kazakhstanskie studenty lidiruiut po kolichestvu sredi inostrantsev v vuzakh RF,' 3 August.
The Economist. (2000). 'Dream On,' 6 January.
Turchina, I. (2019). 'Belorusskie vuzy bez turkmenskikh studentov ne ostanutsia,' *Naviny.By*, 25 April.
Vlast'. (2019). 'Etnicheskaia karta Kazakhstana: kazakhov bol'she, evropeitsev men'she, tretii mononatsional'nyi region,' 30 April 2019.
World Bank. (n.d.). *Personal Remittances, Received (% of GDP)*. Kyrgyz Republic. https://data.worldbank.org/indicator/BX.TRF.PWKR.DT.GD.ZS?locations=KG, accessed on 17 November 2019.

PART VII

Religion

27
ISLAMIC RENEWAL IN CENTRAL ASIA*

Bayram Balci

The Central Asian republics' break from the USSR was significant in religious terms. While the communist authorities had claimed to be atheist at least in theory, or non-religious, the new states on the other hand adopted a wholly new approach to religion, not opposing it but linking it with and incorporating it into the new political identity of state, nation and society. Thirty years after the end of the USSR, the renewal of Islam is a matter of history and does not in truth derive from the sociology of religion and the place of religion in the relations between the Central Asian states and the rest of the Muslim world (Balci 2003; 2019).

This chapter examines religious change in Central Asia over the last three decades from a historical perspective. Such is the complex nature of the way in which Islam is managed and experienced by state and society in Central Asia, that it should be approached not just in one way, but several. However, the approach in this chapter emphasises the interactions between internal and local dynamics and those of foreign societies, according to which each Central Asian state has empowered its own way of accommodating Islam within its society and institutions. In other words, this chapter provides an analysis of how Islam in Central Asia relates to Islamic geographical areas cut off during Russian and Soviet domination. The chapter highlights the dynamics of communication between Central Asian Islam at the end of the USSR and those of a globalised Islam, i.e., those Islamic influences from Turkey, Iran the Arab world and the Indian sub-continent. Such an approach to the topic foregrounds the different varieties of 'imported' Islam. The analysis demonstrates that the new Islam which developed in the post-Soviet period in Central Asia, is the product of a synthesis between local Islam and diverse foreign influences benefitting from the opening of frontiers which had been closed for several decades.

Concepts of and debates about Islam at the demise of the USSR and during the early years of independence

The very concept of the renewal of Islam is in some measure, problematic, since in societies where sundry approaches to and sensitivities about religion coexist, renewal can either have positive or negative connotations. Renewal might be seen as positive, innovatory or better in respect of what was there before in the Soviet era. Similarly, for some present-day Islamic

---

* Translated from French by Moya Jones   DOI: 10.4324/9780429057977-27

conservatives, the term could be unwelcome, embarrassing and annoying, since they consider that Islam has always been there and that despite the Soviet authorities' repressive anti-Islamic policies, Islam survived, and therefore to speak of Islam being renewed and imported from abroad would be a misunderstanding of Islam and of Muslims. For more wary and apprehensive circles confronting Islam's much greater visibility and especially for advocates of a strict secularism, renewal signifies a triumphal resurgence, arousing fear of a new ideological wave that will change their former secular life (Sahadeo and Zanca 2007).

The term renewal simply indicates Islam's greater visibility in the public arena, and in state educational and identity policies. This renewal indicates an increase in the number of mosques and madrassas, a more extensive practice of religion than in the past, and the enhanced discussion of the place of Islam in society and political life.

Further, liable as it is to polarisation, the debate on Islam is also marked strongly by other concepts that need defining. There has often been a confusion in discussions of Islam, between Islam as a quest for identity and Islamism in the sense of a political ideology seeking to take power and Islamise it (Farrell 2019). Likewise, political authorities confronted with managing religious inflows from abroad, often tend to associate all popular demands for Islamic practices or education with a form of Wahhabism, a pejorative term in Central Asia, deriving as it does from the precepts of Ibn 'Abd al-Wahhab in Saudi Arabia, synonymous in Central Asia with a retrograde, shadowy and radical vision of Islam. Again, it established political authorities and, generally speaking, all groups suspicious of religion have deliberately confused new demands in the religious field with Salafism and fundamentalism, with the current in Islam that pushes for a return to the true basis of Islam, to the traditions (*salaf*) of the Prophet and to the manner in which he and his close circle practised the Islamic life in the religion's early days. In order to discredit those with an alternative vision hostile to their own, established public authorities have often used such terms pejoratively, fusing legitimate new Islamic claims and radicalism, Wahhabism, Salafism and even jihadism, in order to impose the official state vision of Islam.

The context of this debate about Islam is the collapse of the USSR and the establishment of new independent republics. Indeed, one cannot understand Islamic renewal without recalling the context of Gorbachev's *glasnost* and *perestroika* (Ro'i 2000: 764). The wind of reform made possible discussions on ecology, the environment, ethnic identity and also religious issues. Even just before the end of the USSR, discussion on Islam was intense. In fact, it was well before the official end of the USSR that the first party claiming to be Islamic came to light in the *Islamic Renaissance Party* in Tajik SSR, devised by Soviet intellectuals, often Tatars, Dagestanis, Uzbeks and Tajiks (Roy 1991). However, the real renewal came with independence, with the coming together of two distinct processes: the new quest for an Islamic identity in countries where the relationship with religion was being redefined, and the arrival of various strands of Islam from abroad. While being separate in principle, these two processes fed on each other. In fact, new popular religious demands and state religious policies bring new strands, which in their turn cultivate the new way in which Central Asian societies and states think of themselves as being Muslims.

The new religious policies of the states and their main characteristics

Already underway in the context of Gorbachev's policies, the sources of Islamic renewal lay predominantly in each country itself, deep in society and in the identity policies of political elites. Even if independence was not gained in each country through revolutions or by struggles for liberation against an occupying power, established political elites acted as if this were the case, feeling the need to demonstrate a break with the old order in all fields, including religion. To accompany the phenomenon of the renewal of religion in Central Asian societies, post-Soviet regimes adopted several measures, two of which merit attention.

Firstly, the state, its leaders and institutions, particularly ministers of education, viewed intellectual and spiritual figures of the past in a new light. Literary, scientific and even religious figures of former times, long deprecated by the Soviet authorities, were rehabilitated. Taking just religious figures we can highlight three emblematic personalities. In Kazakhstan, Ahmet Yessevi, a Sufi authority who had formed the brotherhood named after him, the Yeseviyya, was no longer seen in the negative light that he had been in the Soviet period, but found himself placed by the Kazakh authorities at the centre of a policy of religious rehabilitation. His literary works were printed and distributed throughout the country, and a large Turco-Kazakh university bearing his name was established in southern Kazakhstan, in the towns of Turkistan and Chimkent. In Turkmenistan, a thirteenth-century Khwarezmian Sufi Najm al-Dîn Kubrâ became the object of a cult on the part of the Turkmen State, which wished to channel religious renewal and give it a national aspect (Clement 2020). In Uzbekistan, where Islamic heritage is richer, among the many personalities and religious figures rehabilitated and held up as new sources of inspiration or even imitation by a people seeking to rediscover their identity was Bahâ'uddin Naqshband (Khalid 2003). He was a Sufi of the fourteenth century and founder of the Naqshbendiyya brotherhood that is dispersed throughout the globe in various forms. He was restored to favour by Uzbek authorities, despite the regime being highly authoritarian when it came to managing religious matters. This mystic master's mausoleum was restored along with other Islamic sites (Zengi Atat in the Tashkent region, Termizi in Termez and Ghijduvani in Ghijduvan) to become an important place of pilgrimage within an Islam the authorities approved of, that is to say, an Islam which was more oriented towards Sufism and remote from any kind of political aspiration.

Secondly, in order to supervise or accompany the Islamic renewal in countries and societies strongly characterised by a secularism inherited from the Soviet era, states established Islamic education policies in order to forestall the emergence of a dissenting Islam which might challenge the state vision of religion. While in the Soviet period there were in total just two institutions of Islamic education in all of Central Asia, the madrassa Mir-i-Arab in Bukhara and a centre called Imam al-Bukhari Tashkent Islamic Institute, following independence each country set up several Islamic establishments in the form of Institutes, Quranic schools or Islamic universities (Kemper, Motika and Reichmuth 2009: 384). This Islamic education policy was frequently devised in the context of cooperation with a foreign nation such as Turkey or Egypt.

At present, it is important to register that the policy of supervising or encouraging the Islamic renewal was often conducted in a spirit of surveillance or policing. Establishing this was entrusted to two organisations, either newly created or inherited from the Soviet era: the Muftiat or the directorate of religious matters which was a body of religious personalities, and state committees of public servants supposedly preserving state security. Thus, the creation of any new mosque or religious association, the importing of any Islamic literature, the supervision of clergy, and also the policy of cooperation with Islam abroad, were placed under the authority of these two organisations which were then obliged to work together for the state. This contact with Islam in other countries was all the more important in that without Islam coming from abroad, the renewal of Islam in Central Asia would not have been possible, at least not on such a scale and with such speed.

Central Asia under the influence of other Islamic countries

The collapse of the USSR to some degree marked the closure of a long parenthesis in which the Muslims of Central Asia had been deprived of contact with the rest of the Muslim world and initiated the re-establishment of links between local Islam and global Islam. Furthermore, this local Islam in Central Asia was at times influenced by one or more Islamic tendencies arriving from abroad, and at times itself influenced Islam in other parts of the world, especially before Russian and Soviet domination set up a barrier between Central Asian Islam and that of the rest of the world. Since the demise of the USSR, global or external Islam, which had played a part in shaping Central Asian Islam, has come from geographical areas or countries which have always had important and varied links with Central Asia. These geographical areas are mainly Turkey–Anatolia, to a lesser degree Iran, the Indian sub-continent and the Arabian Peninsula.

In the context of the time, in the 1990s, when Turkish power and foreign policy was less marked by Islam and Islamism (which is hardly the case at present), it would have seemed paradoxical to speak of a Turkish influence on Central Asian Islam or of a Turkish contribution to the reanimation of Islam in those countries. Turkey sought to exert influence on Central Asia in order that its secularism and laicism might counterbalance other supposedly more Islamic countries, such as Iran and Saudi Arabia, which might dominate the region and turn it against Western interests (Bal 2002). Despite its secular ambitions in Central Asia, Turkey had never abandoned a real intention of influencing Central Asian Islam to make it more compatible with its own religious vision. Since the early days of their independence, in these countries, Islam has been a vital component of the Turkish policy of influence. Even if ethnic solidarity and linguistic similarity had been at the centre of Turkish policy, it was evident from the outset that if Turkey were to carry weight in this new geopolitical area it should not neglect the religious dimension as a factor in drawing closer with the Muslims of those countries. Also, Turkey, knowing that religion could be a vector of influence in Central Asia, both through official policy and by indirectly encouraging private initiatives, has established an Islamic policy in respect of those countries (Balci 2014).

For the first time in Turkish history the Diyanet, the regulatory body for religious affairs, a sort of ministry for religious affairs whose role is to manage Islam in the country, was invited to take part in Turkish foreign policy. It has been given the mission to export the Turkish vision of Islam into Central Asia, the Caucasus and the Balkan countries by way of services and concrete actions. In addition, through an attaché for religious affairs attached to each Turkish embassy, Turkey has influenced local Islam in various ways. Turkey helped form new local Islamic elites by creating theology faculties in several towns (Chymkent, Ashkhabad, Osh and Baku), invited hundreds of students of religion into Islamic establishments in Turkey, paid for their studies, and took part in building or rebuilding several mosques throughout the region, especially the biggest ones in Central Asia, those at Bishkek and Ashkhabad. Lastly, the Diyanet exported a great deal of Islamic literature in different languages to the region (Korkut 2010).

However, this official Turkish action by means of the Diyanet has not been the only Turkish contribution to the development of Islam in Central Asia. Private movements and brotherhood organisations, often coming out of the Naqshbandi formed in Central Asia, had always been an important vector of Islamic exchanges between Anatolia and the Central Asiatic region. They also played a considerable part in exporting a Turkish vision of Islam into Central Asia in the independence. In this respect, four movements must be cited for their crucial role in exporting Turkish Islam: the Mahmut Hudayi Vakfi foundation, whose present spiritual leader is Osman Nuri Topbas, the community known as the Süleymanci, which also comes out of the Naqshbendiyya and which was set up in its present form by Hilmi Süleyman Tunahan, the various associations coming out of the Sait Nursi movement, and lastly the Fethullah Gülen community which, even if it favoured a more secular education nonetheless promulgated a form of Turkish Islam, much like the other movements. In its own way each of these movements hosted students from Central Asian states in Turkey or sent own missionary educators to help the Muslims of Central Asia reanimate an Islam believed to have been destroyed by Soviet domination.

What was the impact of these various Turkish influences on Central Asian Islam? Answering this question requires a preliminary consideration of the other Islamic influences in the region, those of Iran, the Indian subcontinent, and the Arabian Peninsula.

The Irano-Persian heritage in Central Asia has been considerable and the Islamic Republic has always sought to export the ideals of its revolution. However, since the collapse of the Soviet regime, Iran failed to emerge as a major actor and political power in the region, while its contribution to the renewal of Islam in the region has been modest (Peyrouse and Ibraimov 2010). Two factors explain this weak contribution by Iran to the development of Islam in Central Asia. First, while geographically and historically close to the region, Iran practises and promulgates Shiite Islam, whereas in Central Asia Islam is predominantly Sunni. The Shiite communities of Central Asia are in the minority, such as the Ironi in the Bukhara region and Samarkand, and the "Shiites" of Tajikistan, who comprise a marginal form of Shiism since they approximate to the movement called Ismaili whose doctrine is different from the Shia of Iran. This difference in belief between Iranian Islam and that of Central Asia is not new. From the sixteenth through to the nineteenth centuries, before the region fell under the domination of Imperial Russia, there were religious wars between Shiites and Sunnis, between local dynasties, notably the Chaybanides and the Shiites of Iran, Savafid or Qadjar.

The second reason for the weak influence of Iran on Central Asian Islam was the deeply negative image of the Iranian regime in these countries whose elites have a strong aversion to all kinds of political, radical or fundamentalist Islam. Iran's poor relations with the international community as well as the US sanctions associated with Teheran's nuclear programme, prevented the establishment of Iranian influence in Central Asia. So, despite predictions made on the fall of the USSR, Iran has not carried significant weight in restructuring Islam in Central Asia. By contrast, the influence of Iran has been crucial in the rebuilding of another former Soviet country, Azerbaijan. This is not surprising, since Islam in Azerbaijan is 80% Shiite, while Iran and Azerbaijan were part of the same Iranian empire up till 1828 when Russia drew a border on the Aras River. This was the departure point for the development of a different Shiism in Iran and Azerbaijan (Balci 2004). After the collapse of the USSR, exchanges were resumed and numerous new Shiite elites from Azerbaijan were educated in Iran, particularly in the towns of Qom, Mashad and Tehran (Balci and Goyushov 2014).

In contrast with the limited influence of Iran on Central Asian Islam, contributions from the Arab world, from the Arabian Peninsula and more particularly Saudi Arabia, have been much more substantial.

The influence from across the Arab world has been as diverse and varied in kind as in geographical provenance. Various Arab states have contributed to the reorganisation of Islam in Central Asia. Two Arab countries in particular have played a crucial role in the renewal: Egypt and Saudi Arabia. Egypt's Al Azhar University for Islamic studies attracted students from across Central Asia. However, the Saudi Arabian contribution had a far greater reach. Often deemed responsible for the spread of Wahhabi, Salafist and even radical and jihadist Islam (although the reality is more complex), the Saudi influence rests on two pillars: pilgrimage to holy cities and the distinctive role of diasporic groups originating in Central Asia but long settled in Arabia.

Pilgrimages have always been a major vehicle or means of diffusing religious ideas. In the case of Islam, the *hajj* or *umrah*, the great or little pilgrimage, plays a crucial role in the religious life of Muslims in almost all countries. Its importance is such that leaders in the Muslim world, sultans, caliphs, princes, presidents and heads of state have always attached a great importance to it being well-organised and supervised. Apart from its religious role, pilgrimage can help in spreading religious and, above all, political ideas (Can 2020:271). With its potential as a site of conflict or of submission, the role of the pilgrimage was well understood by the

Western colonial powers who, in their domination of Muslims, made sure that the hajj was well organised in order to retain popular support and to guard against health risks (Chiffoleau 2015). Even before the Bolsheviks came to power, the Russian Tsars made sure the hajj was well-run, as for them it was a tool for controlling the Muslims in the Empire and satisfying their religious needs (Kane 2015).

By contrast, during the Soviet period, the pilgrimage was almost non-existent, because it was the Islamic policy of the USSR to restrict it or even make it impossible to run. However, since independence and the renewal of Muslim identity, the reopening of frontiers has fostered the revival of the hajj. While formerly, each country in Central Asia sent only 10 or so pilgrims every year, strictly selected to ensure that only those best-fitted to spread Soviet propaganda among the Muslims during the pilgrimage were allowed to visit Mecca, this number has greatly increased to 2,000–5,000 people from each country in the independence. Just how has the pilgrimage favoured Islamic renewal? The pilgrimage has been both the result of and the cause for Islamic renewal, as every pilgrimage promotes contact between local and foreign Islam in the holy cities, as well as promoting the import of foreign versions of Islam into Central Asia. Such fundamentalist ideas as Salafism, Wahhabism and even jihadism entered Central Asia by way of the pilgrimage (Balci 2003a). Some pilgrims were radicalised through encountering more revolutionary ideas on the pilgrimage. Yet this radicalisation, or rather this return to the fundamentals of religious practice, is more persuasive when viewed in conjunction with the phenomena of migration and diaspora between Central Asia and Saudi Arabia.

It is easy to forget that there are two communities with Central Asian origins that constitute distinct diasporic groups in Saudi Arabia. The less active of the two in terms of the exchange of religious ideas between Arabia and Asia is the Uyghur community, exiled from China in the 1960s during the advance of the Maoist revolution, and living in the holy cities where they sustain only limited links with their country of origin. However, they play a part in reinforcing a national Uyghur movement in exile to protest against attacks on the rights of their compatriots in Xinjiang, or as Uyghurs say, East-Turkistan. This community is assuredly strongly characterised by Islam because they are long established in the holy cities, but despite their links with the Uyghurs of Central Asia in Kazakhstan and Kyrgyzstan, they have contributed little to their re-Islamisation.

There is, however, a second community with origins in Central Asia whose role has been greater in the matter of circulating a certain type of Islam between the Arabian Peninsula and the towns of Central Asia. This comprises the descendants of two groups who, in the 1930s, departed what is today's Uzbekistan, then called Turkistan or Bukhara, and who now claim to be Uzbeks. When the Soviet Union fell apart, this small community, well integrated and even assimilated into Saudi Arabia, rapidly retied its strong links with their homeland and sundry towns in Uzbekistan. It is no exaggeration to say that this community played its part in the renewal of Islam in Uzbekistan, but not necessarily the radical or Wahhabi version as the ruling authorities asserted. Charitable organisations founded by individuals from the Uzbek diaspora in Arabia financed mosques in various towns in Uzbekistan and paved the way for students, pilgrims and businessmen to visit the holy cities. This diaspora played a substantial role in the awakening of a certain kind of Islamic consciousness in Central Asia.

To the role of pilgrims and migrants in the development of Islamic exchanges between Central Asia and Arabia, one has to add that of official Saudi Arabian diplomacy and its foundation, the *Rabita*, or World Islamic League Designed specifically to diffuse the soft power of the kingdom and which, as elsewhere in world, to promote the development of Islam by building mosques and distributing funds for the good of the religion. Central Asia, like other parts of the world, benefitted from its aid.

Being a beneficiary of the Arabian Peninsula, Turkey and to a limited extent Iran since 1991, Central Asia renewed its links with another region with which it had been closely associated historically: the Indian subcontinent, whose weight and influence on the Muslim world are often overlooked.

Before the dominance of Russia in the region, there had been strong links between the Indian sub-continent and Central Asia in all fields, including religion, notably with Buddhism, as well as with Islam (Levi 2007). It is often forgotten that even if Islam was established in India with the Sultanate of Delhi in particular, it was with the Mughal dynasty, whose founders came from Central Asia, that a genuine Islamic civilisation developed in India and was dominant until the advent of the British in the nineteenth century. Among the most notable interactions between India and Central Asia was the Naqshbandi, a brotherhood with an international span in Sunni Islam. Although it was founded in what is today's Central Asia, it moved over to India and multiplied the interchange between India and Central Asia, particularly with its *mujaddidi* branch created by Ahmad Sirhindi (Babadjanov 2020), thus creating strong links between the two regions. Yet, these important Islamic links between India and Central Asia were severely reduced by the Russian and, later, especially by Soviet domination. The relations between Central Asia and the various states of the Indian sub-continent – India, Pakistan and Bangladesh – facilitated the circulation of communist ideas, but not Islam. With the ending of the USSR, as in the rest of the Muslim world, links were forged in the religious sphere through the Tabligh Jama'at, a strong missionary proselytism of an organisation known throughout the world. The organisation was founded in a highly schematic way by an Islamic scholar, Muhammad Ilyas al-Kandhlawi in the 1920s in British India. He focused on combatting the acculturation of Muslims and the dilution of Islam in Hinduism caused by the strong demographic growth of Hindus in an India that was becoming less and less Muslim (Sikand 2006). By way of powerful preaching, the movement called Tablighi spread throughout the world, seeking above all, to Islamise Muslims and to bring non-Muslims to Islam. Emphasising religious practice in the faithful, rather than extending and deepening Islamic knowledge, it spreads an Islam that is in principle non-political but rigorous and conservative, seeking a return to the foundations of Islam. It rejects the 'modifications,' especially Sufism (Gaborieau, 2010), which, according to the organisation's view, have over time robbed Islam of its true nature.

In the 1990s the movement arrived in Central Asia where it first settled in Uzbekistan but was rapidly expelled. Even if the local Islamic authorities like the Mufti of Tashkent had found it acceptable and worthy of being active in the country, the political leadership did not see this in the same way. In Kazakhstan, Kyrgyzstan and Tajikistan, individuals trained in the precepts of the movement, after travelling to various cities of the Indian sub-continent or staying there, had developed Tablighi groups which roamed the country in order to bring Muslims back to the faith and to Islamic practices (Balci 2011). However, 10 years after these first implantations in Central Asia and in the context of post-9/11 attacks, most countries banned this movement and restricted trips by young Tablighis between towns in Central Asia and to the various centres the movement had in Pakistan, Bangladesh and India (where the international headquarters of the movement were located at Nizamuddin, a suburb of New Delhi).

As is often the case in Central Asia, Kyrgyzstan approached the religious domain differently from its neighbours, even with regard to the Tabligh Jama'at movement. As soon as it arrived in Kyrgyzstan, benefitting from the great religious liberty of which the country's authorities are so proud, the Tablighi movement was in effect, able to work in decent conditions. The individuals who said they belonged to the movement, organised themselves into groups or circles in order to travel regularly throughout the country to practise *dawa* or *bayan*, preaching in order to spread the movement's ideas. Trips were also regularly arranged from Kyrgyzstan to important Tablighi centres in the Indian sub-continent, without these movements being hampered by the country's authorities. To make sure that the activism of this movement did not take a political and adversarial turn, the authorities in Bishkek organised and channelled the movement's activities. The Kyrgyz state's view was that the action of the Tabligh Jama'at seemed beneficial to the country insofar as young drifters were taken care of and turned away from delinquency, criminal activities and drugs. This justified its support for their activities while still keeping them under the guidance of the directorate for religious affairs, known as the *muftiat* or *kaziyat* depending on the country, and of the state committee for the supervision of the country's religious affairs. The consecration of this understanding between the Kyrgyz State and the Tabligh Jama'at came in 2014 when a member of the movement, Maksatbek Toktomushev, who did his training in Pakistan, became mufti of the republic and as such he manages Islam in Kyrgyzstan (Engvall 2020).

As a conclusion to this section on the links between local and global Islam, it should be noted that it is an Islam which is above all moderate and perceived as "tolerant" by local powers. In fact, the countries of Central Asia have always been careful to place conditions on Islamic cooperation abroad, whether this is at state level or with private movements such as the brotherhoods. These conditions mainly consist of ensuring that imported Islam is compatible with traditional Islam in the country. For the religious and political leaders this means a Sunni Islam of the hanafi school, that prefers the maturidi philosophy. However, above all it is a question of this Islam remaining outside of politics and which participates with the state in shoring up the dominant ideology. This means that it should be an Islam at the service of politics, echoing Turkish-style secularity, where there is no separation between the political and the religious but where the religious is subjugated to the political. All these states view these principles in fairly much the same manner as the laicity inherited from the Soviet era. And yet, despite the policies of each country aiming to prevent the emergence of an Islam that is oppositional and radical, Central Asia has still been exposed to radical or even jihadist versions of Islam.

Central Asia – Home of radical Islam?

The very term 'jihad' is a close version of *mujahedin* which also comes from the Arabic *jhd* and which refers to work on oneself or others to reinforce Islamic faith and practices, defending or disseminating them.[1] It was, in fact, in Afghanistan, within the mujahedin resistance to the Soviet occupation that a force was built up, a jihad to combat the force of the unbelievers, the Soviet Union, with the support of the West and in particular the United States. The mutation of mujahedin fighting the USSR into jihadists fighting the West happened gradually. In Central Asia, this began as soon as the USSR collapsed, in the Ferghana Valley, an area where a small cell, *Adolat* (Justice), built itself up as a terrorist group, the Islamic Movement of Uzbekistan (IMU) (Naumkin 2003). The IMU began in Uzbekistan and was then reinforced in neighbouring Tajikistan where it found a fertile environment for its development on account of the civil war that ravaged the country from 1992 to 1997. When peace returned to Tajikistan, the jihadist movement took refuge in neighbouring Afghanistan, where it was welcomed and supported by the Taliban and Al Qaeda. However, at the same time, they turned it away somewhat from its original cause of fighting the regimes of Central Asia towards a different agenda which was a global jihad.

Even if the IMU did not have a strong impact on the societies of Central Asia and didn't pose any real threat to the security structures of the states in the region, it was nevertheless able to occupy the political agenda of the regimes. In Uzbekistan especially, the state used the movement as a pretext to justify repressive measures against the opposition and to postpone reforms. Moreover, in the context of the attacks carried out on 11 September 2001, which triggered a

US-led international military intervention in Afghanistan, the IMU had begun to cut itself off from Central Asia, its homelands, to be absorbed by Al Qaeda which mobilised the IMU for the fight against American presence in the region. This development proved fatal, since its two leaders Tahir Yoldashev and Juma Namangani were killed by American missiles. Nevertheless, their elimination, which accompanied the decline of the Islamic Movement of Uzbekistan, did not mark the end of Central Asian jihadism.

In effect, the new age of jihad and the emergence of DAESH, first in Iraqi-Syrian territory and later in different areas across the world, were not without impact in Central Asia. As in other parts of the world, for the same reasons and following the same paths of seduction, DAESH was able to acquire a certain attractiveness among young Muslims in Central Asia or those who originated from Central Asia and resided in other countries, and especially those who had emigrated to Russia (Lemon 2015). It is estimated that hundreds of fighters, sometimes with their families, wives and children, left to fight or simply just to live in the areas that DAESH controlled for a while, particularly in the Syrian towns which had escaped from the central control of Damascus. A whole battalion made up of Uzbek soldiers was formed in the region of Aleppo before being partly destroyed and then taking refuge in Idlib, where an unknown number of combatants still live. With the almost total annihilation of DAESH's territorial implantation, the question was raised about the combatants' return and the potential threat that they posed for the countries in Central Asia. Despite the deep and legitimate anxiety of the regimes, there were few uncontrolled returns; most of those who had served in Syria and Iraq and had returned to their homeland are now in prison or under strict surveillance.

Conclusion

Watching the development of Islam in Central Asia since the end of the USSR led to several observations, two of which are essential.

Firstly, contrary to all the expectations of Western analysts, the Islam of Central Asia has not drifted towards any Iranian or Saudi form of fundamentalism or radicalism. Radical cells certainly existed in some countries in Central Asia, but these have been no more active than those that we have known in some of the suburbs in France or Belgium. The marginal nature of radical Islam in Central Asia demonstrates the extent to which the secular Soviet heritage is strongly rooted amongst elites and society in the region. Arguably, those in power have carried out remarkable work in keeping these societies secular, but if they have succeeded it is also because these societies were already predisposed to secularism, a situation different from the Muslim countries of the Near and Middle East, where Islam has more of a hold over individual and collective consciences.

Secondly, after 30 years of evolution, the Islam of Central Asia is no longer what it was. This is obvious, of course, but deserves to be emphasised. Historically, Moscow exerted the political power, while the Mufti of Tashkent offered spiritual authority for Islam in Central Asia. Since the independence each Central Asian country has acquired its own government and its own spiritual authority for the management of its national Islam. In this sense, as in other parts of the world, where identity is both national and religious, it is the national part, or even the ethno-national dimension, which prevails in how one defines one's own identity. From this point of view, the Islam of Central Asia is no longer the universal and supranational Islam which it was by the end of the USSR, but has been almost specific to each country, insofar as each state has structured its own vision and management of Islam. Also, there is no longer one Islam in Central Asia, but Islams specific to each country, marked by a strong dose of nation, nationalism and ethnicity.

Note

1 This is before it adopted its current form of 'crusade' against the West, where, in the past, it enjoyed the protection of this same West.

References

Babadjanov, B. (2020) 'On the History of the Naqsbandiya-Mugaddidiya in the Central Ma'wara'an-nahr in the Late 18th and Early 19th Centuries,' in Michael Kemper, Anke von Kügelgen, and Dmitruy Yermankov (eds.), *Muslim Culture in Russia and Central Asia from the 18th to the Early 20th Century*, vol. 1. Berlin: Klaus Schwarz, 385–413.

Bal, I. (2002) 'The Turkish Model and the Turkic Republics,' in Vedat Yücel and Salomon Ruysdael (eds.), *New Trends in Turkish Foreign Affairs*. New York: Writers Club Press, 211–234.

Balci, B. (2003) *Missionnaires de l'Islam en Asie centrale: les écoles turques de Fethullah Gülen*. Paris: Maisonneuve et Larose.

Balci, B. (2003a) 'The Role of the Pilgrimage in the Establishment of Relations Between Uzbekistan and the Uzbek Community of Saudi Arabia,' *Central Eurasian Studies Review*, 2 (3): 182..

Balci, B. (2004) 'Between Sunnism and Shiism: Islam in Post-Soviet Azerbaijan', *Central Asian Survey*, 23 (2): 205–217.

Balci, B. (2011) 'JAMA'at al Tabligh in Central Asia—A Mediator in the Recreation of Islamic Relations with the Indian Subcontinent,' in Marlène Laruelle, Jean-François Huchet, Sébastien Peyrouse, and Bayram Balci (eds.), *China and India in Central Asia: A New 'Great Game.'* London: Palgrave, 235–248.

Balci, B. (2014) 'Turkey's Religious Outreach and the Turkic World', *Current Trends in Islamist Ideology*. Available at: https://www.hudson.org/research/10171-turkey-s-religious-outreach-and-the-turkic-world, accessed 30 November 2020.

Balci, B. (2019) *Islam in Central Asia and the Caucasus Since the Fall of the Soviet Union*. London: Hurst Publishers.

Balci, B. and Goyushov, A. (2014) 'Changing Islam in Post-Soviet Azerbaijan and Its Weighting on the Sunnite-Shiite Schism,' in Brigitte Maréchal and Sami Zemni (eds.), *The Dynamics of Sunni-Shia Relationships: Doctrine, Transnationalism, Intellectuals and the Media*. London: C. Hurst & Co Publishers Ltd, 193–213.

Can, L. (2020) *Spiritual Subjects, Central Asian Pilgrims and the Ottoman Hajj at the End of Empire*. Stanford: Stanford University Press.

Chiffoleau, S. (2015) *Le Voyage à La Mecque. Un pèlerinage mondial en terre d'islam*. Paris: Belin.

Clement, V. (2020) 'Religion and the Secular State in Turkmenistan,' *Silkroad Papers*. Washington, DC: Central Asia-Caucasus Institute and Silk Road Studies Program.

Engvall, J. (2020) 'Religion and the Secular State in Kyrgyzstan,' *Silk Road papers*, June. Available at: https://www.silkroadstudies.org/resources/Religion_and_the_Secular_State_in_Kyrgyzstan_-_Johan_Engvall_-_10.06.20_-_FINAL_wCover.pdf, accessed 30.11.2020.

Farrell, W.B. (2019) *Fragmentation, Fragmentation, Frustrated Revolt, and Off-Shore Opportunity: A Comparative Examination of Jihadi Mobilization in Central Asia and the South Caucasus*. PhD. Dissertation. Maine: University of Maine.

Gaborieau, M. (2010) 'The Transformation of Tablighi Jama'at into a Transnational Movement,' in Masud, Muhammad Khalid (ed.), *Travellers in Faith: Studies of the Tablighi Jama'at as a Transnational Movement for Faith Renewal*. Leiden: Brill, 121–138.

Kane, E. (2015) *Russian Hajj: Empire and Pilgrimage to Mecca*. Ithaca: Cornell University Press.

Kemper, M., Motika, R., and Reichmuth, S. (eds.). (2009) *Islamic Education in the Soviet Union and Its Successor States*. London: Routledge.

Khalid, A. (2003) 'A Secular Islam: Nation, State, and Religion in Uzbekistan', *International Journal of Middle East Studies*, 35 (4): 573–598.

Korkut, S. (2010) 'The Diyanet of Turkey and its Activities in Eurasia after the Cold War', *Acta Slavica Iaponica*, 28: 117–139.

Lemon, E. (2015) 'Daesh and Tajikistan: The Regime's (In)Security Policy', *Rusi Journal*, 160 (5): 68–76.

Levi, S. (2007) 'India, Russia, and the Eighteenth-Century Transformation of the Eighteenth-Century Transformation of the Central Asian Caravan Trade,' in Scott Levi (ed.), *India and Central Asia: Commerce and Culture, 1500–1800*. Oxford: Oxford University Press, 93–126.

Naumkin, V.V. (2003) *Militant Islam in Central Asia: The Case of the Islamic Movement of Uzbekistan*. Berkeley: Berkeley Program in Soviet and Post-Soviet Studies. Retrieved from https://escholarship.org/uc/item/7ch968cn

Peyrouse, S. and Ibraimov, S. (2010) 'Iran's Central Asia Temptations', *Current Trends in Islamist Ideology*, 10: 87–101.

Ro'i, Y. (2000) *Islam in the Soviet Union: From the Second World War to Gorbachev*. New York: Columbia University Press.

Roy, O. (1991) 'Ethnies et politique en Asie centrale,' *Revue des mondes musulmans et de la Méditerranée*, 59–60: 17–36.

Sahadeo, J. and Zanca, R. (2007) *Everyday Life in Central Asia: Past and Present*. Bloomington: Indiana University Press.

Sikand, S. (2006) 'The Tabligh Jama'at and Politics: A Critical Re-Appraisal,' *The Muslim World*, 96 (1): 175–195.

28
SECURITISATION OF RELIGION IN CENTRAL ASIA

Edward Lemon

Introduction

Although levels of religiosity vary, over 85 per cent of Central Asians claim to be Muslim (Pew 2017). But the governments of Central Asia have adopted strict secular regimes, restricting the transmission of religious knowledge and limiting religious practices. Islam came to Central Asia in the eighth century with the Arab invasion of Mā warā' an-Nahr, the land beyond the river Oxus. Society and politics were ordered by Islam until the Russian Revolution of 1917. Seventy years of Soviet rule failed to eradicate religion. As Shoshana Keller concludes 'Muslims found ways to ignore orders that they deeply opposed (especially concerning women's status), turn a blind eye as clergy served on collective farms and evaded taxes, and make sure that their children understood the rudiments of religion' (Keller 2001: xvf). Nonetheless, the Soviet period transformed Islam into a marker of identity rather than a religion requiring certain beliefs and practices (Khalid 2003). It also saw the institutionalisation of Islam, institutions that have persisted to this day to regulate and control religion (Tasar 2017).

Indeed, the independent Central Asian governments have securitised all forms of unsanctioned religious activity, labelling them as 'non-traditional' and 'extremist.' Securitisation is a speech act. In labelling certain forms of Islam a threat, the government has legitimised measures to discipline and control 'bad' forms of Islam. Although the focus of this chapter is Islam, it should be noted that the governments of Central Asia have also taken steps to restrict the activities of other religious groups, including Jehovah's Witnesses, Baptists and other Evangelical movements. These secular policies are aimed at bolstering the region's authoritarian regimes and are therefore undercut by relations of power (Lemon and Thibault 2018). Dynamics of securitisation vary across the region and within countries themselves, with Kyrgyzstan having adopted the most tolerant policies towards religion, Uzbekistan and Tajikistan creating the most restrictive environment for religion and Turkmenistan denying the very existence of an extremist threat.

This chapter covers the securitisation of religion from the Soviet Union to the present day. It is divided into four sections. The first section introduces the concept of securitisation and its links to secularism. The second section traces the origins of the understanding of Islam as potentially dangerous that remains hegemonic among Central Asia's governments back to the Soviet period. The third section examines how the threat of radical Islam and violent extremism

DOI: 10.4324/9780429057977-28

has manifested itself in Central Asia since 1991. The final section looks at how Islam has been securitised in post-Soviet Central Asia and the implications this has had in terms of state policies.

Securitisation of Islam

Developed in the years following the Cold War, securitisation theorists focus on the *process* by which actors frame phenomena as security threats (Waever et al 1993; Waever 1995; Buzan, Waever & de Wilde 1998; Balzacq 2011).[1] In the words of the leading thinkers of the 'Copenhagen School,' as the theory has come to be known, 'security is thus a self-referential practice because it is in this practice that the issue becomes a security issue – not necessarily because a real existential threat exists' (Buzan, Waever and de Wilde 1998: 24). Security threats exist insofar as they are labelled 'threats' by actors.

A number of scholars associated with the 'second generation' of securitisation theory have criticised, modified and enhanced the 'Copenhagen School's' approach (Stritzel 2014; Balzacq 2005; 2011; Donnelly 2013; McDonald 2008; Vuori 2008). First, the 'Copenhagen School's' definition of security, which focuses on the Schmittian concept of the 'politics of exception,' is too restrictive (Huysmans 1998; Williams 2007).[2] It neglects the importance of the social context in which the speech act takes place and the role of the audience in accepting or rejecting the securitisation move (Bigo 2002; Balzacq 2005; Stritzel 2011; Eriksson 1999). Second, earlier analyses failed to fully appreciate the co-constitutive relationship between the speech act and the speaker's power (Foucault 1994b). Not everyone is in a position within the social structure to label something a security threat. Indeed, the ability to label something as a security threat has specific consequences – it is a 'political technology in the hegemonic project of various agents' (Jackson 2007: 421). Lastly, although securitisation theory usefully highlights the process by which actors label security threats and begins to link such labelling to security practices, as Shahar Hamieri and Lee Jones observe, 'very little of this literature explores how security problems, once identified, are managed in practice or how the systems established to manage them actually operate. That is, they neglect security *governance*' (Hamieri and Jones 2015: 3).

In conjunction with this critique, scholars associated with the 'Paris School' of security studies have led the way in theorising security practices (Bigo 1996; Bigo and Walker 2007; Guzzini 2000; Huysmans 2006; Adler and Pouilot 2011; Leander 2005; Adler-Nissen 2008).[3] For them, studying securitisation discourses is not sufficient. Instead, 'representational practice has to be studied in terms of its imbrication within a range of practices that are not reducible to the linguistic model' (Walters 2010: 219). The securitisation of Islam in Central Asia must be understood in this context.

Assertive secularism

A number of scholars have explored the securitisation of Islam within the context of Europe. Since 9/11, the focus of public debates on migration and security has shifted towards a focus on Muslim migrant groups (Croft 2012; Huysmans and Buofino 2008; Mavelli 2013; Birt 2006). Scholars have examined the ways in which politicians (Huysmans and Buofino 2008) and the media (Croft 2012) have securitised Islam.

This securitisation of Islam and the way actors tend to contrast religious violence against secular order have provoked a discussion about the relationship between secularism and security. Put simply, secularism is a 'public settlement of the relation between politics and religion' (Hurd 2008: 12). Secularism denotes discourses and policies which attempt to construct consensus on the 'proper' relations between the state and religion. Often defined against religion, secularism involves a human-centred epistemology, emphasis on scientific reason, the prioritisation of the immanent over transcendent and a morality that lies outside of religion. Scholars have demonstrated how the 'secular' and 'religious' are not fixed, clearly defined categories; the boundaries between the two fluctuate across space and through time. Maia Carter Hallward outlines a 'boundary-focused approach' to secularism and religion which analyses the processes by which 'categories of belonging emerge and are sustained' through actors' attempts to fix the meaning of the 'secular' around certain signifiers (Hallward 2008: 8).

If secularism is not fixed, then it can take different forms in varying contexts. Secularism may involve the absence, control over, equal treatment of or replacement of religions. Through an examination of state–religion relations in Turkey, France and the United States, Ahmed Kuru outlines two forms of secularism: passive and assertive. Where the governments of France and Turkey pursue assertive secularism, attempting to banish religion from the public sphere, the United States tolerates public religious expressions and therefore adopts passive secularism (Kuru 2007). Assertive secularism is used by the authoritarian governments of Central Asia to counter potential forms of religious-based resistance. Instead of a space for tolerance of other opinions, the assertive secularist 'construction of "religious fanaticism" can promote secular rationales for violence' (Cavanagh 2011: 227).

Underlying the securitisation of religion are underlying assumptions about the need to preserve the secular order (Bilgin 2007; Gutkowski 2011). Luca Mavelli examines how European governments have implemented secular policies in order to govern religion. He focuses on the 'practice of transnational governmentality that by distinguishing between "moderate" and "radical" Islam, contributes to create a category of threatening "others" which calls for a more "interventionist" and disciplining state' (Mavelli 2013: 160). Mavelli concludes that 'the securitisation of religion is thus an exceptional measure that removes religion from "the realm of normal politics" in order to preserve the latter's secular character' (Mavelli 2012: 191).

Securitisation of religion during the Soviet Union

To understand the contemporary securitisation of Islam in Central Asia, it is necessary to study the Soviet, particularly late-Soviet period (Khalid 2003). As historian Adeeb Khalid argues 'the way in which Central Asians relate to Islam, what Islam means to them; can only be understood by taking into account seventy years of Soviet rule' (Khalid 2007: 2). The way religion is understood by elites within the region, including the association of religion with violence, and security with secularism, originated during the Soviet Union. Such a genealogical approach involves delving into the past in order to examine how hegemonic discourses and practices emerge. It involves 'working back from our present to the contingencies that have come together to give us our certainties' (Asad 2003: 16).

During the Soviet period, the ways in which Central Asians conceived of and related to Islam fundamentally changed. Soviet rule, particularly in the final 25 years, rendered Islam a key part of identity (Khalid 2003). Islam became a 'cultural marker'; religious identity did not entail a set of fixed beliefs (orthodoxy) or practices (orthopraxy). The Soviet authorities viewed Muslims, who constituted the vast majority of the Central Asian population in 1917, as a feudal society in need of rapid modernisation (Malashenko & Polanskaya 1994). Religion was an ideology in the negative sense, a false consciousness held by the masses which legitimised capitalist domination (Pospielovsky 1987).

But views on the way to achieve this modernisation and the place religion should have in society changed over time. It is impossible to talk of one Soviet policy on religion; in reality, policies diverged during different periods. An ad hoc and accommodating policy towards Islam characterised the years between the October 1917 Revolution and the founding of the USSR in 1924 (Yemelianova 2002). Under Josef Stalin, the government attempted to enforce its atheistic worldview on the Tajik population and expunge Islam from the public sphere. This assault included the banning of the hajj (1928), the *hujum* (Uzb: Lit. storming or assault) against the veiling of women, the confiscation of *waqf* (land owned by mosques), closure of mosques and persecution of the *ulema* (religious establishment).[4] The change in alphabet from Arabic to Latin (1928) and then to Cyrillic (1937–40), cut Central Asian Muslims off from the rest of the *umma* (community of believers).

Nonetheless, this period of intense repression did not last for the entire duration of Soviet rule. During World War II the party temporarily halted the onslaught and an era of rapprochement followed. In 1943, the government established SADUM (Rus.: *Dukhovnoye Upravleniye Musul'man Sredney Azii I Kazakhstana*) which managed Muslim affairs in Central Asia. SADUM was headed by a dynasty of Muslim clerics; the Babakhans.[5] In addition to this, the government reopened the Mir-i-Arab madrasa in Bukhara in 1946 and legalised the *hajj* in 1944.[6] Although these institutions continued to function, Nikita Khrushchev launched a renewed propaganda campaign against the idea of Islam between 1954 and 1958.

The pendulum swung once again in favor of accommodation during the Brezhnev era of 'mature socialism' when the government framed Islam as an integral part of the Central Asian republics' identities.[7] Islam became a crucial 'identity marker' which offered a personal function of differentiation between local 'self' and Slavic 'other' (Khalid 2007). After Mikhail Gorbachev came to power in 1985, new religious freedoms resulting from *perestroika* and *glasnost*, led to the re-emergence of Islam in the public sphere. By 1988 even the Communist Party itself was admitting that religious believers constituted around 20 per cent of the Soviet Union's population.[8] As John Anderson states: 'by 1990 a de-facto and de-jure freedom of consciousness had emerged in the USSR' (1999: 216). This culminated in the re-opening of madrassas and the formation of the Islamic Renaissance Party of Tajikistan in 1990.

Despite these changing attitudes to the role of religion, four underlying assumptions about Islam persisted during the period. These include the idea that Islam is monolithic and opposed to modernity, the rigid dichotomy between official and 'parallel' Islam, and the conclusion that Islam constituted an inevitable threat to the Soviet Union. Drawing on similar sources, many similarities exist between the way the two dominant approaches to religion in the Soviet Union – the Soviet and the Western-based Sovietological – treated the relationship between religion, politics and security (Kristeva 1986; Saroyan 1997; DeWeese 2002).

Both Soviet and Sovietological accounts framed Islam as a threat to national security. For the Soviets, it constituted tool in the hands of 'enemies' of the state – imperialists and capitalists – which could be used to manipulate local populations into threatening the state (Ashirov 1979). Sovietologists separated the Soviet state from Muslim society, pitting the two in opposition to one another. The dominant view held by the Sovietologists contended that 'the Muslim community is prepared for the inevitable showdown with its Russian rulers' (Bennigsen and Broxup 1983: 87). Sovietolotists viewed Muslims as resistant en-masse to the Soviet efforts at integration, which formed the cornerstone of the Soviet nationalities policy (Bennigsen and Wimbush 1985). Many Soviet analysts and Sovietologists assumed that a causal link existed between adherence to Islam and resistance to the regime; Islam by its very nature is inherently political and opposed to secularism (Heathershaw and Montgomery 2016). Most analysts assumed that any violence in Central Asia must *ipso facto* be religious in nature. Amir Taheri, for example, framed the 1986 protests in Alma-Ata, in which residents protested against the removal of Kazakh Communist Party leader Dinmukhamed Kunayev and his replacement by ethnic-Russian Gennady Kolbin, as being religious in nature (1989). But ultimately, as Myers argued, 'the concept of an Islamic threat to Central Asia is in itself a largely Western construct, serving Western interests' (Myer 2002: 3). Violent upheaval, such as the 1986 protests in Almaty, the 1990 riots in Dushanbe and 1990 ethnic violence in Osh and Uzgen, were rooted in local, secular grievances. Despite the prevailing view that 'it was in the Muslim republics that most clouds appear on the Soviet horizon,' the collapse of the Soviet Union in 1991 was not driven by factors within Central Asia (Taheri 1989: 272). In fact, the Central Asian republics had independence thrust upon them.

Both accounts tended to dichotomise parallel, dangerous Islam with benign, state-controlled Islam. The Soviet policy on religion had not successfully eradicated Islam from society. Instead, according to analysts, Islam had been pushed 'underground' where it was represented by Islamic teachers, Sufi *ishans* and 'Wahhabi' fanatics (Malashenko and Polonskaya 1994). For many Sovietologists, 'the primary threat to the Soviet state was an Islamically-inspired, Sufi-led led revolt' (Myer 2002: 162). They dedicated entire books, most notably Bennigsen and Wimbush's *Mystics and Commissars*, to measuring the number of Sufis in the Soviet Union and analysing the nature of the anti-Russian, fanatical Sufi threat (1985).

Beyond the idea Islam was dangerous, Soviet officials framed Islam as 'foreign,' something that proceeded spatially from the Middle East and was temporally, a *perezhitok*, a vestige of a feudal society common to all 'eastern people' (Smirnov 1954). Within this discourse of Islamic danger numerous authors argued that the Muslim threat was exogenous, imported to the region after the 1979 Revolution in Iran and the USSR's invasion of Afghanistan. Upon closer inspection, however, Islam in the Soviet Union appears to be more complex than such reductionist analyses contended. In this view the official/unofficial dichotomy is more of a continuum, upon which actors move with relative fluidity (Kemper et al 2009). Many Soviet citizens did not see Islam and Communism in such mutually exclusive terms. Instead many identified themselves as both Soviet and Muslim (Tett 1994; Khalid 2003).

The threat of terrorism in contemporary Central Asia

Although there was instability, no terrorist attacks occurred within Central Asia during the Soviet period. The region's transition from the Soviet Union was somewhat more turbulent. Tajikistan quickly slipped into civil war, harbouring a number of warlords, foreign fighters and terrorist groups that conducted a string of attacks in the country even after the Peace Accord ended the civil war in 1997. While none of the darkest predictions came to pass, during the first 15 years of Central Asian independence, the Islamic Movement of Uzbekistan (IMU) and its offshoot the Islamic Jihad Union (IJU) posed the most significant terrorist threat to the region. Between 1999 and 2000, the IMU led armed incursions from its base in war-torn Tajikistan into Kyrgyzstan and Uzbekistan, taking hostages. After these failed, the IMU retreated to Afghanistan, where it suffered heavy losses in the 2001 U.S.-led invasion and relocated to Waziristan. The Uzbek government blamed the IMU for bombings in Tashkent in 1999 and the IJU claimed responsibility for attacks in Bukhara and Tashkent in 2004. By 2013, the IMU and IJU had an estimated 3,000 fighters (Lang 2017). Excluding incidents during Tajikistan's civil war, at least 145 individuals were killed as a result of this violence across the region (Lemon 2018a).

In the second phase of the evolving jihadist threat, Central Asia became an exporter of foreign fighters to Syria and Iraq. Since 2011, between 4,000 and 9,000 Central Asian citizens went to fight with militant groups in the Middle East, with the height of recruitment between 2013 and 2015. Rather than returning to conduct attacks in Central Asia, the Central Asian terrorist threat has mostly manifested itself outside of the region. During this period, citizens of Central

Asia were involved in attacks in Karachi, Stockholm, New York and Istanbul have resulted in 104 casualties (Lemon, Mironova and Tobey 2018).

Yet despite the terrorist threat manifesting itself beyond Central Asia's borders, the threat within the region itself has remained limited. Between 2008 and 2019, terrorists organised 19 deadly attacks in Central Asia (Lemon 2018a). This figure includes attacks that resulted in one or more deaths, including the terrorists themselves; were labelled terrorism by government officials; and were instigated by a terrorist group or individual rather than by state forces as part of a counter-terrorism operation. Between 2008 and 2018, 138 individuals died in terrorist attacks, the majority being representatives of law enforcement (78) and terrorist groups (49), with 11 civilian casualties. Half of these incidents occurred in the region's most prosperous state, Kazakhstan, with over half of deaths occurring in Tajikistan. Only one of these attacks, targeting Western cyclists in Tajikistan in 2018, was irrefutably linked to Islamic State. Overall, the threat of terrorism in the region has been minimal, dwarfed by deaths due to traffic accidents, repression and weak public healthcare.

Despite the government and many observers being focused on the Islamic threat, most violence in the region cannot be explained by religion. Central Asia has experienced one civil war, driven by a struggle for power among local groups in a situation of state collapse, which killed between 20,000 and 50,000 people. Kyrgyzstan has experienced two successful revolutions and ethnic violence in Osh in 2010 in which over 500 died. Government forces have violently quelled protests in Andijon, Uzbekistan, in 2005 and Zhanoezen, Kazakhstan, in 2011. In Tajikistan, the process of 'authoritarian conflict management,' by which the government of Emomali Rahmon has purged the government of former warlords and extended its control over former opposition-controlled areas, has produced episodic violence in the Rasht Valley between 2008 and 2011, Khorog in 2012 and Dushanbe in 2015 (Heathershaw and Mullojonov 2018).

Mobilisation to violent extremist organisations and terrorism cannot be explained solely by Islam either, despite the idea that Islamisation leads to radicalisation permeating official and popular imaginaries in Central Asia. In fact, 'long-term religious practice—or past religious affiliation—is a poor or even negative predictor for extremist recruiting at the individual level' (Tucker 2019: 3). Most of those who joined had limited religious knowledge, with many taking an interest in Islam within a year of being recruited (Lemon 2018b). Islam is at best a secondary factor then, used as a tool to mobilise individuals to offer them community and a solution to their grievances (Nasritdinov et al 2018). As Noah Tucker demonstrates in his research on Aravan, one of the most prominent areas of mobilisation to Syria and Iraq in the region, many were pulled into terrorist groups through their social networks; many were recruited by people who knew them personally (Tucker 2018).

The post-Soviet discourse of Islamic danger

Despite the Islamic threat being limited in Central Asia, the governments of the region and external observers in Russia and the West, have framed the region as a 'hotbed' of Islamic extremism (Rashid, 2001; Brzezinski, 1997; Naumkin 1994; Lubin and Rubin, 1999; Slim 2002), in the 'whirlwind of jihad' (Olcott 2012) and 'the next jihadi stronghold' (Rashid 2010). Government discourses on religion continue to contain the same broad themes as Soviet discourses, framing Islam as potentially dangerous, foreign and backwards. The way governments of Central Asia conceptualise and approach Islam remains deeply post-*Soviet*. This rests on the construction of a division between 'good,' acceptable Islam and 'bad,' deviant Islam (Rasanayagam 2010). 'Bad' Muslims have been labelled 'extremists,' 'Wahabbis' or followers of 'non-traditional Islam' in the Kazakh case. As developed below, this is crucial to the way religion is managed in the region.

A degree of intertextuality continues to exist between the accounts of the links between Islam and security offered by the governments of the region and by external observers. In their analysis of the discourses produced by leading think tank the International Crisis Group, John Heathershaw and David Montgomery argue that the discourse of danger on Islam in Central Asia consists of four claims (Heathershaw and Montgomery 2016). First, there is an assumption that the post-Soviet period has been a radical break from the past, with society becoming more Islamic since 1991. While religious practices have proliferated particularly in public spaces since 1991, the notion of revival downplays the continued role Islam had during the Soviet Union. Second, like Soviet-era discourses there is a conflation between this societal Islamisation and political radicalisation. This idea pervades the local and external understandings of radicalisation, yet the evidence presented in the previous section has challenged the idea that rising religiosity has played a role in mobilisation to violent groups. Third, governments and analysts argue that groups that have been pushed 'underground' by local governments, like Hizb ut-Tarhir, are extremist or radical by nature. Fourth, these groups are globally networked via virtual and social networks. Lastly, political Islam *ipso facto* is opposed to the state. This framing legitimates a regime of practices to control and discipline religion.

Assertive secularism in Central Asia

While the extent to which the governments of Central Asia restrict and control religion differs from country to country, and region to region, there are certain commonalities to the way assertive secularism is practiced in Central Asia. In prior research with Helene Thibault, I argued that the securitisation of Islam and the authoritarian practices that have been adopted to manage religion are best understood through the prism of Michel Foucault's analytics of power (Lemon and Thibault 2018). Power lies at the centre's efforts to manage Islam in Central Asia. For Foucault, 'power comes from below; that is, there is no binary and all-encompassing opposition between rulers and ruled at the root of power relations, and serving as a general matrix' (Foucault 1981: 94). In other words, power is not something that rulers possess and wield over their subjects; power is exercised at every level of society. It is decentralised and dispersed. Most importantly, power is not always destructive. It is not only about exercising the right to take life; it can be productive too. Foucault was concerned with uncovering how practices of power produce political subjects.

Foucault theorised three different, but overlapping, forms of power: sovereign power, disciplinary power and biopower (Dean 2010; Foucault 1981). Sovereign power concerns the 'safety (sûreté) of the Prince and his territory' which is secured through the right to take life (Foucault 2003: 65). Sovereign power limits and bans certain behaviours; disciplinary power is exercised based on the socially constructed division between 'normal' and 'abnormal.' Those who are abnormal – the homosexual, the vagrant and the extremist – are subject to disciplinary measures to help them to conform. Where disciplinary power is about forcing deviants to conform, biopower promotes the life of the population, focused on administering, developing, fostering and securing life (Foucault 1981). Elites promote certain forms of life, but it is up to subjects themselves to adopt practices which conform with this vision. State-led counter-extremism in Central Asia involves disciplining 'bad' Muslims and exercises of biopower which promote 'good,' secularised forms of Islam.

The securitisation of Islam and the counter-extremist policies that they legitimise are tools for the governments of the region to exercise power. Policies towards religion have evolved over time. When they adopted constitutions in the early 1990s, each Central Asian state declared in Article 1 that the state was 'sovereign,' 'democratic' and 'secular.' After a period of relative tolerance in the early years after the Soviet Union, state policies towards Islam started to become more hostile in the mid-1990s. This can be attributed initially to external factors, including the civil war in Tajikistan and the gaining of power of the Taliban in Afghanistan in 1998 (Khalid 2007: 132). But attacks in Tashkent in 1999 and Kyrgyzstan in 2000 ushered in more restrictive policies. Over the next two decades the governments have used the spectre of Islamic extremism to justify crackdowns on a range of political opponents, journalists and civil society representatives. This has occurred against the backdrop of authoritarian consolidation across the region. Externally, by taking part in the 'War on Terror' Central Asian countries consolidated their power 'by tying all domestic opposition to "international terrorism," even when no links actually exist' (Khalid 2007: 169).

At the local level, as Marintha Miles has demonstrated, these policies are unevenly enforced and selectively targeted (Miles 2017). Discourses of Islamic danger have seeped into citizens' understandings of Islam and danger, and shape everyday life. A number of anthropologists have pointed to the way community members in Central Asia use accusations of extremism to defame members of their community with whom they have personal or business rivalries (McBrien 2006; Pelkmans and McBrien 2008; Mostowlansky 2017). In other cases, it is merely a fear of that which is unknown to them (McBrien 2006). In Uzbekistan, for example, Johann Rasanayagam (2006, 115) has examined how community members used the label 'Wahhabi' 'to direct the attention of law enforcement bodies to any religious activities that are unfamiliar.'

Sovereign power

Central Asian governments have exercised sovereign power in two ways. First, they have created a restrictive legal environment, creating the conditions for the arrest and imprisonment of those deemed threatening. To re-enforce this, second, they have banned certain groups deemed 'extremist' and 'terrorist.'

Uzbekistan was the first Central Asian state to declare Islamic extremism a major threat to national security when it introduced a new law on religion in 1998. The law required all religious associations to have to register with the state. Similarly, restrictive laws were introduced in Kyrgyzstan in 2009, Tajikistan in 2009, Kazakhstan in 2011 and Turkmenistan in 2016. Uzbekistan and Tajikistan have created the two most hostile legal environments towards religion in the region. Laws on religion place restrictions on who can register a religious group and where mosques can operate. Using these regulations, the governments have closed down mosques and madrassas. In 2011, Tajikistan passed a Law on Parental Responsibility, which banned those under the age of 18 from attending mosques under most circumstances and made it illegal to study Islam abroad without government permission. Three of the Central Asian countries, Tajikistan, Turkmenistan and Uzbekistan, are classified as 'countries of particular concern' by the Department of State under the International Religious Freedom Act.

Following Russia's lead, the Central Asian governments introduced laws on extremism and terrorism (Omelicheva 2010). Each regime has adopted similar broad and amorphous definitions of terrorism and extremism (Horsman 2005; Lemon and Antonov forthcoming). Uzbekistan, for example, defines terrorism as a 'socially dangerous act.' Crimes that are considered 'extremist' under the 2003 Law on Extremism in Tajikistan include insulting national dignity, unsanctioned rallies and calling for the overthrow of the government (Government of Tajikistan 2003). Using these definitions, each country has compiled lists of groups that they deem 'extremist,' stipulating punishment for members in their Criminal Codes (Table 28.1).

As Table 28.1 shows Tajikistan has banned most of the groups. Having adopted the country's first specific legislation on extremism in 2018, Uzbekistan's Ministry of Justice published a list

Table 28.1 Table of Banned Extremist Groups in Central Asia[a]

Group	Kazakhstan	Kyrgyzstan	Tajikistan	Turkmenistan	Uzbekistan
Hizb ut Tahrir	2005	2004	2004		
Tablighi Jamoat	2013		2006		2004
Salafi movement			2008		
Muslim Brotherhood	2005		2006		
Jehovah's Witnesses			2007		

[a] The governments of Uzbekistan and Turkmenistan have not published a list of banned extremist organisations. But they do use extremism and terrorism laws for political reasons.

of extremist websites and social media profiles in May 2019 (Gazeta.uz 2019). The list included sources linked to Uzbek-led terrorist groups Imam Bukhari Jamaat and Tavhid va Jihod, and various Salafi sites. But it is Tajikistan that has gone the furthest with the Supreme Court classifying the Islamic Renaissance Party, which until 2015 held two seats in parliament, a terrorist organisation in September 2015.

Suspected extremists and terrorists are particularly susceptible to torture in the criminal justice system. During the rule of Islam Karimov, there were 15,000 in prison who were convicted of extremism, with many being mistreated and tortured in prison. An estimated 100 prisoners of conscience are currently being held in the high-security Ovadan Depe Prison in Turkmenistan (State Department 2018). Such torture and imprisonment serve as a stark, visual warning to deter others from contemplating behaviour that could be deemed suspicious or deviant.

Disciplinary power

But the governments have not only framed the actions of those accused of 'extremism' as illegal, it has also framed their actions as deviant and abnormal, legitimating the use of disciplinary power against them (Megoran 2008). Disciplinary power shapes and normalises subjects. Those who adhere to 'bad' Islam become the objects of discipline. In order to be normal, secular subjects, men with beards need to be shaved; women with hijabs need to de-veil; mosques need to be tightly regulated; Islamic education must be restricted.

In order to disrupt the flow of religious knowledge to their citizens, the Central Asian states regulate the production, import, export, distribution and content of religious literature to different extents. As the use of the internet has become more widespread, governments have increasingly blocked religious websites and social media profiles. Religious education and proselytism are also restricted. In 2010, Tajikistan's president called on all students studying Islam abroad, estimated to be around 2,500 individuals, to return home, stating that they were in danger of becoming terrorists (Ergasheva 2010; Abramson 2010). Quotas for those who want to go on the pilgrimage to Mecca are enforced in each country.

Clothing features prominently in state discourses on religion (Nozimova 2016; Miles 2015; McBrien 2006). Officials frame signs of piety, such as beards and hijabs, as being alien to national culture and potential indicators of radicalisation. Uzbekistan's 1998 religion law outlaws 'cult robes' (religious clothing) in public places by all except 'those serving in religious organisations.' An imam lost his job after he called for President Mirziyoyev to revoke the ban (RFE/RL 2018). Other countries have adopted more limited legal measures. Tajikistan banned hijabs in schools in 2007 and Kazakhstan banned them in 2017. Beyond these legal measures, a more informal campaign against religious appearances is ongoing. Bearded men under 40 years of age in Turkmenistan, Uzbekistan and Tajikistan were forcibly shaved by police.

Names are another sight where the struggle over national values is taking place. In 2016, the government of Tajikistan banned Arabic-sounding names such as those ending with 'mullah,' 'khalifa,' 'shaikh,' 'amir' and 'sufi.'[9] The State Committee for Language and Terminology at the Academy of Sciences published a list of 4,000 appropriate names that fit with 'national values' (RFE/RL 2016).

Such policies are not all implemented from the top-down by representatives of the state. Officials repeatedly call on citizens to monitor other community members and to consciously work on themselves to ensure that they are not straying into extremism (Lemon and Thibault 2018). As Kharkhordin concludes, in such a system of panopticism, 'there is no single Big Brother, but there are many bigger brothers' (1999: 122).

Biopower

The goal of state secularism in Central Asia is not to obliterate religion from the public sphere. Instead, what we have seen since independence is 're-Islamisation "from the top"' (Fathi 2011: 174). Ultimately, the governments of Central Asia trying to create political subjects that are loyal, secularised and therefore unlikely to join radical Islamic groups in the first place. Efforts to define national identity along pre-Islamic lines, such as Tajikistan's attempts to frame identity around its Aryan past, president of Turkmenistan Sapurmuat Niyazov's promotion of his spiritual guide *The Ruhnama* (Book of the Soul), or Kyrgyzstan's flirtation with Tengrism, have given way to an attempt to frame Islam as a key part of national identity (Laruelle 2007a, Laruelle 2007b). The 'good' Islam promoted by the state is framed as peaceful, benign and non-political. Tajikistan declared 2009 the year of Imam Azam, the founder of the Hanafi madhab. Kyrgyzstan has promoted the idea of the Maturidi *aqida* (creed), referring to an obscure Central Asian cleric in the eighth century who they argue created a unique local interpretation of Islam, although few people seem to understand what this is (Tucker 2019).

Each country has established successors to the Soviet institutions designed to discipline 'bad' religion and promote 'good' religion. Each country has its own State Committee, Ministry or Department to manage religious affairs. Kazakhstan set up a Ministry of Religious Affairs in 2016 (Yermekbayev 2016). These work with the Ministry of Justice to register religious organisations. Muftiates and Sharia Councils, although nominally independent, are heavily influenced by the state (Wolters 2014: 11–13). In Tajikistan, the Islamic Centre has come to dominate the religious field, adopting positions that are highly conservative, in turn reinforcing patriarchal values and legitimising authoritarian rule (Epkenhans and Nozimova 2018). Imams in Tajikistan have been paid a salary by the state since 2014, and read sermons prepared by the Committee on Religious Affairs.

As well as promoting their own version of religion through these institutions, the governments have promoted other 'appropriate' forms of life in line with 'national' values. This includes visual appearances. Each country promotes traditional national dress as a way to express patriotism and conformity. Tajikistan introduced a dress code for its students in 2018. Uzbekistan introduced a similar code the same year. Both were viewed by analysts as an attempt to promote secular lifestyles over religious ones, and both drew criticism from families raising their children in a religious way (EurasiaNet 2018).

Conclusion

For many years after the fall of the Soviet Union, observers framed countries emerging from communism as in 'transition' to democracy and capitalism (Carrothers 2002). Almost 30 years since the emergence of independent states in Central Asia, this is clearly not the case. Instead, the region remains post-Soviet; legacies of communist rule continue to shape political, social and economic dynamics in important ways (Beissenger and Kotkin 2014). Although the Central Asian governments have moved away from the ideological trappings of Communism, they have maintained adapted versions of the Soviet-era division between 'good' and 'bad' Islam. The securitisation of 'bad' Islam continues to frame it as foreign to the region and dangerous to stability. Elites continue to view certain forms of religion as a threat to regime security. As such, they have adopted assertively secular policies that give the state the right to regulate religion, but independent religion no right to influence politics. Such policies have served to marginalise and alienate many believers, who have restricted space to express their religious beliefs.

De-securitisation involves moving an issue out of the security realm, essentially undoing the securitisation process. Lene Hansen has identified four forms of desecuritisation: 'change through stabilisation,' where an issue is no longer framed as a security threat; 'replacement,' in which it is substituted by another issue; 'rearticulation,' which occurs when an issue is moved to the realm of 'normal politics' due to a resolution of the threats and risks that caused it to be securitised in the first place, and 'silencing,' which happens when an issue is non-politicised and marginalises potentially insecure subjects (Hansen 2012). De-securitising Islam would involve breaking down the governments' dichotomy between 'good' and 'bad' Islam, de-criminalising vaguely-defined extremism and recognising that not all unsanctioned religious activity threatens social order. On the contrary, increasing the space for religious expression would allow citizens to gain the knowledge necessary to become resilient to the simplistic narratives of terrorist organisations. Rather than being a danger to be controlled, de-securitising Islam and making it part of 'normal politics' would bolster pluralism and reduce repression in Central Asia.

De-securitisation of Islam in Central Asia remains unlikely for a number of reasons. As terrorism and instability continue to occasionally manifest itself, as external powers such as Russia, China and the United States continue to place concerns over security and stability over human rights, and as the region continues to be ruled by authoritarian governments that prioritise regime security and see Islam as a threat, Islam in Central Asia will continue to be securitised for the foreseeable future.

Notes

1 For an overview of the development of securitisation theory, see Thierry Balzacq's introduction to *Securitization Theory* (2011).
2 Carl Schmitt, a German political theorist, who wrote that politics is centred on the division between friends and enemies. As such, 'the sovereign is he who decides on the exception' (Schmitt, 1985: 5).
3 The term 'Paris School' was coined by Ole Waever in 2004. It centres around the journal *Cultures et Conflits* and its editor Didier Bigo.
4 For a detailed analysis of early Soviet religious policy in Central Asia, see Northrop 2004 or Khalid 2007 (Chapter 3) and Khalid 2015.
5 The Babakhan family was a prominent Tashkent religious family who had followed the Naqshbandiyya Sufi order. Ishan Babakhan (1861–1957) ws mufti, or leader, of SADUM until his death. He was succeeded by his son Ziyauddin (1908–1982), who also led the administration until his death. His son Shamsiddin became mufti in 1982 and led until 1989.
6 Founded in the sixteenth century, the madrassa was a centre of Islamic learning across Central Asia.
7 A number of studies of the late Soviet institutionalisation of religion exist. See Tasar 2017; Khalid 2007.

8 Achildiyev, I. 'Garantii Svobody,' [Guarantees of Freedom], *Nauka i religia*, 11, November 1988, pp. 21–23.
9 In early 2016, officials suggested banning Russian names as well, replacing suffixes 'ov,' 'ev,' 'ova' and 'eva' with Tajik endings such as 'zoda,' 'zod,' 'on,' 'yon,' 'ien,' 'yor,' 'niyo' or 'far.' After the Russian government's opposition to this, they quickly backed down.

Bibliography

Abramson, D. (2010) *Foreign Religious Education and the Central Asian Islamic Revival: Impact and Prospects for Stability*. Washington, DC: Central Asia-Caucasus Institute.

Adler, E. and Pouilot, V. (2011) International Practices. *International Theory*, 3 (1): 1–36.

Adler-Nissen, R. (2008) The Diplomacy of Opting Out: A Bourdieudian Approach to National Integration Strategies. *Journal of Common Market Studies*, 46 (3): 663–684.

Anderson, J. (1999) *Kyrgyzstan: Central Asia's Island of Democracy?* London: Taylor and Francis.

Asad, T. (2003) *Formations of the Secular: Christianity, Islam, Modernity*. Stanford, CA: Stanford University Press.

Ashirov, N. (1979) *Islam i natsii* [Islam and Nations]. Moscow: Izdatel'stvo Politicheskoi Literatury.

Balzacq, T. (2005) The Three Faces of Securitization: Political Agency, Audience and Context. *European Journal of International Relations*, 11 (2): 171–201.

Balzacq, T. (2011) *Securitization Theory: How Security Problems Emerge and Dissolve*. London: Routledge.

Beissinger, M. and Kotkin, S., eds. (2014) *Historical Legacies of Communism in Russia and Eastern Europe*. Cambridge: Cambridge University Press.

Bennigsen, A. and Broxup, M. (1983) *The Islamic Threat to the Soviet State*. London: Routledge.

Bennigsen, A. and Wimbush, E. (1985) *Mystics and Commissars, Sufism in the Soviet Union*. London: Hurst & Co.

Bigo, D. (1996) *Polices en Reseaux. L'experience Europenne* [Networked Policing: The European Experience]. Paris: Presses de Sciences Po.

Bigo, D. (2001) Internal and External Security(ies): The Möbius Ribbon. In: Albert, M., Jacobson, D., and Lapid, Y. (eds.), *Identities, Borders, Orders*. Minneapolis, MN: University of Minnesota Press, pp. 91–116.

Bigo, D. (2002) Security and Immigration: Toward a Critique of the Governmentality of Unease. *Alternatives*, 27: 63–92.

Bigo, D. and Walker, R. (2007) Political Sociology and the Problem of the International. *Millenium Journal of International Studies*, 35 (3): 725–739.

Bilgin, P. (2007) The Securityness of Secularism? The Case of Turkey. *Security Dialogue*, 39 (6): 593–614.

Birt, J. (2006) Good Imam, Bad Imam: Civic Religion and National Integration in post-911 Britain. *The Muslim World*, 96 (4): 687–705.

Brzezinski, Z. (1997) *The Grand Chessboard*. New York: Basic Books.

Buzan, B., Waever, O. and de Wilde, J. (1998) *Security: A New Framework for Analysis*. Boulder, CO: Lynne Rienner.

Carrothers, T. (2002) The End of the Transition Paradigm. *Journal of Democracy*, 13 (1): 5–21.

Cavanagh, W. (2011) The Invention of Fanaticism. *Modern Theology*, 27 (2): 226–237.

Cooley, A. (2012) *Great Games, Local Rules: The New Great Power Contest in Central Asia*. Oxford: Oxford University Press.

Croft, S. (2012) *Securitising Islam: Identity and the Search for Security*. Cambridge: Cambridge University Press.

Dean, M. (2010) *Governmentality: Power and Rule in Modern Society*. London: SAGE.

DeWeese, D. (2002) Islam and the Legacy of Sovietology: A Review Essay on Yaacov Ro'i's Islam in the Soviet Union. *Journal of Islamic Studies*, 13 (3): 298–330.

Donnelly, F. (2013) *Securitization and the Iraq War: The Rules of Engagement*. London: Routledge.

Epkenhans, T. and Nozimova, S. (2018) The Transformation of Tajikistan's Religious Field: From Religious Pluralism to Authoritarian Inertia. *Central Asian Affairs*, 6: 133–165.

Ergasheva, Z. (2010) Tajikistan: Islamic Students Told to Come Home. *IWPR*, 24 November. Available at: https://iwpr.net/global-voices/tajikistan-islamic-students-told-come-home, accessed 16.12.2020.

Eriksson, J. (1999) Observers or Advocates? On the Political Role of Security Analysts. *Cooperation and Conflict*, 34 (3): 311–30.

EurasiaNet. (2018) Uzbekistan: School Uniform Rules Draw Fire from All Sides. *EurasiaNet*, 24 November. Available at: https://eurasianet.org/uzbekistan-school-uniform-rules-draw-fire-from-all-sides, accessed 16.12.2020.
Fathi, H. (2011) Female Mullahs, Healers, and Leaders of Central Asian Islam. Gendering the Old and New Religious Roles in Post-Communist Communities. In: R. Canfield and G. Rasuly-Paleczek (eds.), *Ethnicity, Authority and Power in Central Asia. New Games Great and Small*. New York: Routledge, pp. 174–195.
Foucault, M. (1981) *History of Sexuality, Volume 1: The Will to Knowledge*. Harmondsworth: Penguin.
Foucault, M. (2003) *Society Must Be Defended: Lectures at the College de France, 1975–6*. London: Penguin.
Gazeta.uz. (2019) Minust Ob'yavil Spisok Ekstremistskikh Materialov [The Ministry of Justice Published a List of Extremist Materials]. *Gazeta.uz*, 8 May. Available at: https://www.gazeta.uz/ru/2019/05/08/prohibited/, accessed 16.12.2020.
Government of Tajikistan. (2003) Konun dar boroi Muboriza bar Ziddi Ekstremism [Law on Combating Extremism]. https://mvd.tj/index.php/tj/konun/92-onuni-umkhurii-toikiston-qdar-borai-muboriza-bar-ziddi-ekstremizm-ifrotgaroq, accessed 16.12.2020.
Gutkowski, S. (2011) Secularism and the Politics of Risk Britain's Prevent Agenda, 2005–2009. *International Relations*, 25 (3): 346–362.
Guzzini, S. (2000) Reconstruction of Constructivism in International Relations. *European Journal of International Relations*, 6: 147–179.
Hallward, M. (2008) Situating the 'Secular:' Negotiating the Boundary between Religion and Politics. *International Political Sociology*, 2 (1): 1–20.
Hamieri, S. and Jones, L. (2015) *Governing Borderless Threats: Non-Traditional Security and the Politics of State Transformation*. Cambridge: Cambridge University Press.
Hansen, L. (2012) Reconstructing De-securitization: The Normative-Political in the Copenhagen School and Directions for How to Apply It. *Review of International Studies*, 38 (3): 525–546.
Heathershaw, J. and Mullojonov, P. (2018) Rebels without a Cause? Authoritarian Conflict Management in Tajikistan, 2008–2015. In: Marlene Laruelle (ed.), *Tajikistan on the Move: Statebuilding and Societal Transformations*. Lanham, MD: Lexington.
Horsman, S. (2005) Themes in Official Discourses on Terrorism in Central Asia. *Third World Quarterly*, 26 (1): 199–213.
Hurd, E. (2008) *The Politics of Secularism in International Relations*. Princeton, NJ: Princeton University Press.
Huysmans, J. (1998) Revisiting Copenhagen: Or, On the Creative Development of a Security Studies Agenda in Europe. *European Journal of International Relations*, 4 (4): 479–505.
Huysmans, J. (2006) *The Politics of Insecurity: Fear, Migration and Asylum in the EU*. London: Routledge.
Huysmans, J. and Buonfino, A. (2008) Politics of Exception and Unease: Immigration, Asylum and Terrorism in Parliamentary Debates in the UK. *Political Studies*, 56 (4): 766–788.
Jackson, R. (2007) Constructing Enemies: 'Islamic Terrorism' in Political and Academic Discourse. *Government and Opposition*, 42 (3): 394–426.
Keller, S. (2001) *To Moscow, Not Mecca: The Soviet Campaign against Islam in Central Asia, 1917–1941*. Westport, CT: Praeger Publishers.
Kemper, M., Kemper, M., Motika, R. and Reichmuth, S. eds. (2009) *Islamic Education in the Soviet Union and Its Successor States*. London: Routledge.
Khalid, A. (2003) A Secular Islam: Nation, State and Religion in Uzbekistan. *International Journal of Middle East Studies*, 35: 573–98.
Khalid, A. (2007) *Islam after Communism: Religion and Politics in Central Asia*. Berkeley, CA: University of California Press.
Kharkhordin, O. (1999) *The Collective and the Individual in Russia*. Berkeley, CA: University of California Press.
Kristeva, J. (1986) Word, Dialogue and Novel. In: T. Moi (ed.), *The Julia Kristeva Reader*. New York: Columbia University Press, pp. 35–61.
Kuru, A. (2007) Passive and Assertive Secularism: Historical Conditions, Ideological Struggles, and State Policies toward Religion. *World Politics*, 59 (4): 568–594.
Lang, J. (2017) Exporting Jihad – Islamic Terrorism from Central Asia. *OSW Commentary*, No. 236. https://www.osw.waw.pl/en/publikacje/osw-commentary/2017-04-12/exporting-jihad-islamic-terrorism-central-asia, accessed 16.12.2020.
Laruelle, M. (2007a) The Return of the Aryan Myth: Tajikistan in Search of a Secularized National Ideology. *Nationalities Papers*, 35 (1): 51–70.

Laruelle, M. (2007b) Religious Revival, Nationalism and the 'Invention of Tradition': Political Tengrism in Central Asia and Tatarstan. *Central Asian Survey*, 26: 203–216.

Leander, A. (2005) The Power to Construct International Security: On the Significance of Private Military Companies. *Millennium*, 33 (3): 803–825.

Lemon, E. (2018a) Talking Up Terrorism in Central Asia. *Kennan Cable No. 38*.

Lemon, E. (June 2018b) Pathways to Violent Extremism: Evidence from Tajik Recruits to Islamic State. *Harriman Magazine*.

Lemon, E., Mironova, V. and Tobey, W. (December 2018) Jihadists from Ex-Soviet Central Asia: Where Are They? Why Did They Radicalize? What Next? *Russia Matters*.

Lemon, E. and Thibault, H. (2018) Counter-Extremism, Power and Authoritarian Governance in Tajikistan. *Central Asian Survey*, 37 (1): 137–159.

Lubin, N. and Rubin, B. (1999) *Calming the Ferghana Valley: Development and Dialogue in the Heart of Central Asia*. Washington, DC: Council of Foreign Relations.

Malashenko, A. and Polanskaya, A. (1994) *Islam in Central Asia*. Reading: Garnet.

Mavelli, L. (2012) Security and Secularization in International Relations. *European Journal of International Relations*, 18: 177–199.

Mavelli, L. (2013) Between Normalisation and Exception: The Securitisation of Islam and the Construction of the Secular Subject. *Millennium: Journal of International Studies*, 41: 159–181.

McBrien, J. (2006) Extreme Conversations: Secularism, Religious Pluralism, and the Rhetoric of Islamic Extremism in Southern Kyrgyzstan. In: C. Hann (ed.), *The Postsocialist Religious Question: Faith and Power in Central Asia and East-Central Europe*. Merin: LIT, pp. 47–73.

McDonald, M. (2008) Securitization and the Construction of Security. *European Journal of International Relations*, 14 (4): 563–587.

Megoran, N. (2008) Framing Andijon, Narrating the Nation: Islam Karimov's Account of the Events of 13 May 2005. *Central Asian Survey*, 27 (1): 15–31.

Miles, M. (2015) Switching to Satr: An Ethnography of the Particular in Women's Choices in Head Coverings in Tajikistan. *Central Asian Affairs*, 2: 367–387.

Miles, M. (2017) Nuances of Religious Laws and Enforcement in Tajikistan. *CAP Papers*, 187.

Montgomery, D. and Heathershaw, J. (2016) Islam, Secularism and Danger: A Reconsideration of the Link between Religiosity, Radicalism and Rebellion in Central Asia. *Religion, State and Society*, 44 (3): 192–218.

Mostowlansky, T. (2017) *Azan on the Moon: Entangling Modernities on the Pamir Highway*. Pittsburgh, PA: University of Pittsburgh Press.

Myer, W. (2002) *Islam and Colonialism: Western Perspectives on Soviet Asia*. Abingdon: Routledge.

Nasritdinov, E., Urmanbetova, Z., Murzakhalilov, K. and Myrzabaev, M. (2018) Vulnerability and Resilience of Young People in Kyrgyzstan to Radicalization, Violence and Extremism: Analysis Across Five Domains. *Central Asia Program Paper*, 203.

Naumkin, V. (ed.). (1994) *Central Asia and Caucasia: Ethnicity and Conflict*. Westport, CT: Greenwood.

Northrop, D. (2004) *Veiled Empire: Gender and Power in Stalinist Central Asia*. Ithaca, NY: Cornell University Press.

Nozimova, S. (2016) Hijab in a Changing Tajik Society. *Central Asian Affairs*, 3 (2): 95–116.

Olcott, M. (2012) *In the Whirlwind of Jihad*. Washington, DC: Carnegie Endowment.

Omelicheva, Mariya (2010) *Counterterrorism Policies in Central Asia*. Routledge.

Pelkmans, M. and McBrien, J. (2008) Turning Marx on His Head: Missionaries, 'Extremists' and Archaic Secularists in Post-Soviet Kyrgyzstan. *Critique of Anthropology*, 28 (1): 87–103.

Pew. (2017) Muslims and Islam: Key Findings in the U.S. and around the World. *Pew Research Center*, August. Available at: https://www.pewresearch.org/fact-tank/2017/08/09/muslims-and-islam-key-findings-in-the-u-s-and-around-the-world/, accessed 16.12.2020.

Pospielovsky, D. (1987) *A History of Marxist-Leninist Atheism and Soviet Anti-Religious Policies*. New York: St. Martin's Press.

Rasanayagam, J. (2006) I'm not a Wahhabi: State Power and Muslim Orthodoxy in Uzbekistan. In: C. Hann (ed.), *The Postsocialist Religious Question: Faith and Power in Central Asia and East-Central Europe*. Munich: Lit Verlag, 99–124.

Rasanayagam, J. (2010) *Islam in Post-Soviet Uzbekistan: The Morality of Experience Islam in Post-Soviet Uzbekistan*. Cambridge: Cambridge University Press.

Rashid, A. (2001) *Jihad: The Rise of Militant Islam in Central Asia*. London: Penguin.

Rashid, A. (2010) Tajikistan: The Next Jihadi Stronghold? *New York Review of Books*, 29 November. Available at: https://www.nybooks.com/daily/2010/11/29/tajikistan-next-jihadi-stronghold/, accessed 16.12.2020.

RFE/RL. (2016) Tajikistan Moves to Ban Arabic Names, Marriages between Cousins. *RFE/RL*, 13 January. Available at: http://www.rferl.org/content/tajikistan-ban-arabic-names-marriage-between-cousins/27486012.html, accessed 16.12.2020.

RFE/RL. (2018) Uzbek Imam Fired after 'Deviating from the Script.' *RFE/RL*, 10 September. Available at: https://www.rferl.org/a/uzbek-imam-parpiev-fired-deviating-from-the-script-/29482370.html, accessed 16.12.2020.

Saroyan, M. (1997) *Minorities, Mullahs and Modernity: Reshaping Community in the Former Soviet Union*. Los Angeles, CA: University of California Press.

Schmitt, C. (1985) *Political Theology: Four Chapters on the Concept of Sovereignty*. Cambridge, MA: MIT Press.

Slim, R. (2002) The Ferghana Valley: In the Midst of a Host of Crises. In: van Tongeren, P., van de Veen, H. and Verhoeven, J. (eds.), *Searching for Peace in Europe and Eurasia: An Overview of Conflict Prevention and Peace-Building*. Boulder, CO: Lynne Riener, pp. 489–515.

Smirnov, N. (1954) *Ocherki Izucheniia Islama v SSSR*. [Overview of Islamic Education in the USSR]. Moscow: AN SSSR.

State Department. (2018) *Turkmenistan 2018 International Religious Freedom Report*. Bureau of Democracy, Human Rights, and Labor.

Stritzel, H. (2011) Security, the Translation. *Security Dialogue*, 42 (4): 343–355.

Stritzel, H. (2014) *Security in Translation: Securitization Theory and the Localization of Threat*. London: Palgrave.

Taheri, A. (1989) *Crescent in a Red Sky: The Future of Islam in the Soviet Union*. London: Hutchinson.

Tasar, E. (2017) *Soviet and Muslim: The Institutionalization of Islam in Central Asia*. Oxford: Oxford University Press.

Tett, G. (1994) 'Guardians of the Faith'?: Gender and Religion in an (ex) Soviet Tajik Village. In: C. Fawzi El-Solh and J. Mabro (eds.), *Muslim Women's Choices: Religious Belief and Social Reality*. Oxford: Bloomsbury, pp. 128–151.

Tucker, N. (2018) What Happens When Your Town Becomes an ISIS Recruiting Ground? *CAP Paper*, 207.

Tucker, N. (2019) Terrorism without a God. *CAP Paper*, 225.

Vuori, J. (2008) Illocutionary Logic and Strands of Securitization: Applying the Theory of Securitization to the Study of Non-Democratic Political Orders. *European Journal of International Relations*, 14 (1): 65–99.

Wæver, O. (2004) *Aberystwyth, Paris, Copenhagen: New 'Schools' in Security Theory and Their Origins between Core and Periphery*. Paper presented at the 45th Annual Convention of the International Studies Association, Montreal, Canada, 17–20 March.

Wæver, O. (1995) Securitization and Desecuritization. In: R. Lipschutz (ed.), *On Security*. New York: Columbia University Press, pp. 46–86.

Waever, O., Buzan, B., Kelstrup, M. and Lemaitre, P. (1993) *Identity, Migration, and the New Security Agenda in Europe*. London: Pinter.

Walters, W. (2010) Migration and Security. In: Burgess, P. (ed.), *The Handbook of New Security Studies*, London: Routledge, pp. 217–228.

Williams, M. (2007) *Culture and Security: Symbolic Power and the Politics of International Security*. London: Routledge.

Wolters, A. (2014) The State and Islam in Central Asia: Administering the Religious Threat or Engaging Muslim Communities? *PFH Forschungspapiere/Research Papers*, No. 2014/03.

Yemelianova, G. (2002) *Russia and Islam: A Historical Survey*. Abingdon: Routledge.

Yermekbayev, N. (2016) Why Kazakhstan Created the Ministry for Religious and Civil Society Affairs. *The Diplomat*, 10 November. Available at: https://thediplomat.com/2016/11/why-kazakhstan-created-the-ministry-for-religious-and-civil-society-affairs/, accessed 16.12.2020.

29
LIBERALISM AND ISLAM IN CENTRAL ASIA

Galym Zhussipbek

Introduction

This chapter presents an overview of the relationship between liberalism and Islam in Central Asia, two allegedly contradictory, even oxymoronic, concepts.

The resurgence of Islam in post-Soviet Central Asia since the final years of the Soviet regime has taken strong roots, and the impact of religious resurgence on the social life of Central Asian people has increased significantly. Islam has long occupied a fundamental space in Central Asian societies for more than a millennium. Nonetheless, Central Asian Muslim communities differ from other Muslim societies around the world specifically because of the 70-year-long transformative *Homo Sovieticus* experience. The Soviet experience makes Central Asian society unlike any other in the Islamic realm (Hanks 2015: 72), since virtually all forms of Islamic expression came under sustained assault by the Soviet system (Khalid 2014: 2) and the Soviet regime transformed the nature of being Muslim from a religious to an ethnically-defined cultural one (Ranasayagam 2011), particularly as part of an ethnically-defined national and secular identity, (Heathershaw and Montgomery 2014: 5). In other words, contemporary Central Asian societies were shaped by Soviet apparatchiks and a Sovietised native intelligentsia that was working under the guidance of Moscow.

On the other hand, all Central Asian states are characterised by clan-based authoritarian regimes, weak rule of law and democratic formal institutions. Islam and liberalism are seen as an 'odd couple' in post-Soviet Central Asia because of the following: (1) democratisation and political liberalisation in Central Asia tends to be perceived by many scholars and analysts as stalled processes or, at best, yielding only mixed results; (2) an on-going process of re-traditionalisation which sought to revive and legitimise paternalistic and patriarchal norms was cogent with the process of religious revival; (3) negative perceptions of liberalism adopted by the citizens of Central Asian countries; (4) the phenomenon of a 'de-modern Central Asian Islam' inherited from Soviet period (this so-called 'traditional Islam' in Central Asian countries appears to be a largely ultra-orthodox version of Sunni-Hanafi Islam and institutionalised as *Muftiyats*)[1]; (5) the securitisation of 'non-controllable' Islam by the ruling regimes. Moreover, the prevalent security-oriented literature produced in the West and by Russian scholars perceives and portrays Islamic revivalism in Central Asia as a potentially dangerous phenomenon (Heathershaw and Montgomery 2014: pp. 1–2).

DOI: 10.4324/9780429057977-29

However, the main goal of this chapter is to draw a different perspective on the relationship between Islam and the development of liberalism and liberal values in Central Asia. To do this, I aim to present an overview of the relationship between liberalism and Islam in Central Asia by analysing the phenomenon of Islamic revival and the development of liberal values and ideas in Central Asia from the region's socio-historic-institutional context, and by dwelling on the main theological views of the historically dominant Islamic school in Central Asia, Maturidism, whose epistemology was inherently rationalistic, but became largely lost and forgotten. In this respect the rationalistic approach to Islam and the development of liberal ideas are closely interrelated (see, for example, Duderija 2017; Johnston 2007).

It should be highlighted that there is the necessity of differentiating between the concepts of 'liberalism' – the models of which can range from market fundamentalist neo-liberalism and utilitarian liberalism to social-welfare Rawlsian liberalism defending the benign big government and equality of opportunity – and 'core liberal values,' which include justice, the rule of law, freedom of choice (respect for individual freedom and respect for pluralism) and accountable government. Drawing on this distinction reveals the interesting paradox of 'misperceived and unwanted' liberalism but 'wanted and not alien' core liberal values which can be observed in Central Asian countries (Zhussipbek and Moldashev 2018). Interestingly, the core liberal values tend to be seen by a majority of Central Asian people as the values emanating from their national cultural and religious heritage.

By and large, this chapter, by demonstrating the potential synergies between Islam and liberalism in the region, intends to make an important correction to much of the scholarship and policy analysis on Islam in Central Asia.

The synergy between Islam, liberalism and human rights

The underdevelopment of Islamic discourses on liberalism, or liberal values or human rights is not a problem of Islam as such, in fact, it is implausible to view Islam, like any other religion, as monolithic and static. Rationalistic Islamic theology,[2] by which in this chapter is meant the Maturidite theology, has the potential to be compatible with core liberal values.

A majority of Central Asian Muslims, at least nominally, belong to the regime's 'semi-official' Maturidite–Hanafite school of Islam. In creed (*aqeeda*) Central Asian Muslims belong to the Maturidite school and in jurisprudence (*fiqh*) to the Hanafite school[3].

One of the paradoxes of Islamic history and theology is that, although Maturidism is theoretically accepted as one of the two Sunni-Islamic schools in creed and theology (*kalam*), in reality, it has been overshadowed for many centuries by Asharism (Abdallah 1974: 7). Consequently, its rationalistic epistemology has become largely lost.

Rationalistic Islamic theology and liberalism are mutually supportive phenomena. Particularly, the two rationalistic principles of Maturidite theology can be used to produce interpretations compatible with the universal principles and values of human rights and liberal values. However, it is important to not absolutise either the Maturidite theology or the Hanafite school. For example, while it is suggested that rationalistic Maturidism may help produce inclusive[4] Islamic interpretations, in fact, Al-Maturidi's views per se can hardly be described as inclusive (Zhussipbek and Satershinov 2019). What is important is the rationalistic approach to religious sources and counting the effects of social and other phenomena on the individual and social lives. However, the denial of rationalism, even anti-rationalism, which appeared especially as a response to the challenges posed to Islamic thought by modernity, constitutes an important signpost of an epistemological crisis of traditional conservative Islamic scholarship (see, for example, Cornell, 2010: 26).

To paraphrase Marcus Borg (2001), reason is necessary to be able to read Islamic sources from a historical–metaphorical point of view, which means that they are taken seriously without being taken literally. Furthermore, reason can be seen as the human capacity to shape reality in a humane way (Sandkühler 1998), including the development of progressive religious interpretations and teachings. However, some of the contemporary philosophers warn that the use of reason never leads to agreement on moral issues (MacIntyre 1988).

Progressive religious teachings are contextual, interpretive, inductive and goal-oriented, and they speak to the current time and context and thus implicitly they are rationalistic (see, for example, Safi 2008 and Duderija 2017). Therefore, there is a direct connection between a theologically rationalistic religious doctrine and upholding of core liberal values. Any discussion about liberal values is directly related to the question of human rights. Normally, those who object to liberal values, also tend to question the universality of the notion of human rights. As such, universality of human rights is much contested by the advocates of a relativist or particularist approach (which ensues either from moral relativism or cultural relativism depending on the understanding of cultural relativism, since the 'moderate' forms of cultural relativism still recognise the universal principles and values of human rights, like respect for the inherent dignity of every human being) to human rights which rejects the idea that universal principles of human rights exist.

There is a tendency among conservative Muslims to doubt the universal nature of the concept of human rights, as it is defined by the Universal Declaration of Human Rights and it concomitant documents, which have secular Western origins (An-Naim 2000: 96). However, this critique, particularly by some conservative Muslims, is a result of denial or, at least, a result of confinement of the role of reason within strict limits and mostly in relation to secondary issues of jurisprudence (see, for example, Hunter 2009: 24-25), which is a sign of an epistemological crisis denoting the inability of conservative Islamic scholarship to answer the questions of, and adapt to, the transformative realties of the 21st century.

As progressive religious thinkers assert, a religion that is oblivious to human rights is not tenable in the modern world (Soroush 2000: 128), the universality of the modern notion of human rights cannot be realised among believers unless they accept it as consistent with their religious beliefs. And 'this process of religious legitimation requires creative approaches to theological questions' (An-Naim 2000: 100) which are, inter alia, based on an ethically objectivist approach (ethical objectivism) to Islamic ethics (Duderija 2017: 120) ensuing from a rationalistic epistemology. Overall, the conceptual compatibility between Islamic doctrine and the modern human rights scheme is affirmed by the leading progressive Muslim thinkers (Duderija 2017: 99).

In post-Soviet Central Asia, a religious doctrine based on rationalistic epistemology in a secular post-atheistic society can be a key concept to reconcile the development of liberal values and religious revival. However, there are two paradoxes which prevent this development and, in opposite, may engender the ground for the clash between them.

First paradox: unwanted liberalism but wanted core liberal values in Central Asia

According to research undertaken by scholars from Moscow's Higher School of Economics no one among self-identified 'practicing' Muslims in three Central Asian countries, Kazakhstan, Kyrgyzstan and Uzbekistan, identified themselves as 'liberal' (Lopatina et al. 2016). Therefore, it seems that especially religious Muslims are most negatively predisposed to the concept of liberalism in Central Asia. However, liberalism and liberal ideas, in general, should not be seen as paradigmatically rejected by Central Asian people.

As available research suggests, it can be argued that there is a paradox between a misperceived and, therefore, 'unwanted liberalism,' but a desire for 'non-alien core liberal values.' For example, a majority of the people, at least, who live in four Central Asian countries, covered by an online survey want the same things as people in the West, namely, justice, the rule of law, freedom of choice (respect for individual freedoms and respect for pluralism), and accountable government, i.e. they want 'core liberal' values (Zhussipbek and Moldashev 2018: 100–102; Zhussipbek and Nagayeva 2019b: 140–141).

The negative perception of liberalism in Central Asia can be seen as a result of misperceptions and stereotypes, which have been exacerbated by the information war between the West and Russia, the failures of American policy in Afghanistan and Iraq, the rise of right-wing populism around the world and fake news industry. Also, the effects of national identity-building launched by ruling elites and the ongoing process of retraditionalisation should be counted in this respect. As such, all Central Asian 'national ideologies,' which are premised on a conservative discourse (at least, informally going hand in hand with retraditionalisation[5]) stress the prevalence of 'national' interests over all other aspects of economic, political and public lives which serves as a legitimisation of restrictions of human rights and freedoms, if required by 'supreme' national interests (Mullojanov 2019: 136). In other words, it can be argued that 'conservatism' constitutes a major trend in identity-building in all Central Asian states, which inevitably contributes to downplaying of the importance of the notions of liberalism and liberal values.

Nonetheless, liberalism and liberal ideas are not paradigmatically rejected by Central Asian people, moreover the majority of Central Asian people do not reject as a principle the notions of democracy, democratic rule, and a democratic republic, although, they may have more 'nuanced interpretations' of democracy. As well, the majority of Central Asians do not regard secularism as anti-religious or tantamount to faithlessness; rather, many of them have already naturalised a secular way of life and secular perceptions of state–religion relations (Zhussipbek and Moldashev 2018: 99). In contrast to Middle Eastern societies or many Asian societies, Central Asian people, particularly in Kazakhstan and Kyrgyzstan, do not feel significant anti-Westernism (EUCAM 2014: 5–6).

In the end, it can be argued that a strategy to develop social-welfare liberalism advocating benign big government and genuine equality of opportunity, as it was conceptualised by John Rawls, could be well received in Central Asia.

The second paradox: 'De-modern' Central Asian Islam versus rationalistic Maturidism

Another paradox presents us with the dichotomisation between 'de-modern' (implying anti-rationalism) Central Asian Islam and historically dominant in Central Asian rationalistic Maturidism.

The rationalistic position assuming that God is knowable by natural means is the cornerstone of Al-Maturidi's entire intellectual edifice. As well, the acceptance of a human's rational capacity occupies a central position in his definition of the human being (Rudolph 2015: 300). In essence, Maturidism holds that there is no basic incompatibility between reason and faith/revelation. Both revelation and reason occupy a prominent place in the theological system of Al-Maturidi. Nonetheless, he assumed that in many cases only reason can reveal the truth (Ali 1963: 263). Therefore, it can be argued that the rationalistic Maturidite epistemology is premised upon two main principles. The first is the belief that reason can find what is good and what is bad independently from revelation (Al-Maturidi 1970: 9–10). The second is 'ethical objectivism' implying that God does not order to do what is known by reason as bad or evil.

As such, Al-Maturidi accepted the rationality of ethical norms, although not in absolute terms (Al-Maturidi 1970: 9-10). In other words, Maturidite theology teaches that human rational knowledge extends over various domains and, in distinction to the Ashari school, human rational knowledge encompasses ethical norms (Rudolph 2015: 300). Therefore, contrary to the Asharite theology, which accepts what is good and what is bad is based only on God's will, Maturidites and Mutazilates accept that the basis of God's commands are objective standards (Deen 2016).

Also, the Hanafite jurists, basing themselves largely on Al-Maturidi's work, argued that belief does not genuinely increase or decrease, does not depend on action, and can survive sin. Even the worst sinner cannot be treated as an unbeliever, and the decision as to whether he or she is really a believer should be left to God (Leaman 2008: 86).

By and large, Soviet policy in the realm of religion, after its combative atheistic policy decreased, produced 'de-modern' and 'ethnicised' Islam. Based on Khalid's (2007 and 2014) conceptualisation 'de-modern Islam' is the understanding of Islam which is devoid of rationality, even anti-rationalistic, closed and deaf to current theological, social and political debates and strongly tied to custom, which, in its turn, may be either superstitious or retrograde, or both. Additionally, Central Asian Muslim societies are characterised by the 'ethnicisation' of religion, i.e. accepting Islam as part of a modern secular national identity. The instrumentalisation of Islam for the purpose of building ethnocentric identities turned out to be a common theme in the identity-building processes in Central Asia, as such 'de-modern' Central Asian Islam facilitates this process.

De-modern Central Asian Islam turned out to be a major trait of Central Asian Islamic tradition in the post-independence period. The form of Islam in Central Asia which survived the Soviet period, can be depicted as representing the Hanafite–Maturidite dogmatic and ossified 'hardware,' which in some crucial aspect contradicts the dynamic Hanafite–Maturidite theology or 'rationalistic software.'

On the other hand, the lack of rationalism in Central Asian Islamic tradition can also be attributed to the influence of the theological legacy of Al-Tahawi, an Hanafite scholar from Egypt. This was spread in recent years by Central Asian *Muftiyats* as representing an inherently 'Hanafite,' i.e. 'traditional Islamic' view. However, the difference between the theological methods of Al-Maturidi and Al-Tahawi is quite evident. While Al-Maturidi was a thorough dialectician who employed rationalistic methods to discover a philosophical basis for his views, al-Tahawi was a true traditionist, who did not favour any rational discussion or speculative thinking on the pillars of faith accepting them without any questioning. As such Al-Tahawi's system may be conceptualised as dogmatic, while that of Al-Maturidi as critical. Although both scholars belong to the same Hanafi school, they considerably differ in epistemology and trends of thought (Ali 1963: 245-246). In the post-independence period, many Central Asian Muslims, who went to study Islam, specifically Hanafism, to Arabic countries (e.g. in Al-Azhar University in Egypt) or Pakistan, became exposed to the teachings which are presented as 'inherently Hanafite' but, in fact, lacking Hanafite rationalistic epistemology systematised by Al-Maturidi.

On the whole, it can be argued that the semi-official *Muftiyats* (religious bureaucracy), representing 'traditional Hanafi-Maturidi Islam,' and Central Asian Islamic education centres represent what can be depicted as 'de-modern and ultra-conservative Islam.'[6] It can be assumed that reformist *Jadids*, the progressive Muslim intellectuals of the late 19th and early 20th centuries, who wanted to revive the dynamic Hanafite–Maturidite theology, would describe today's religious bureaucracy, institutionalised in *Muftiyats*, as the followers of 'Qadimism.'[7]

Building synergy between Islam and liberalism: The theological grounds

The key epistemological premises of Maturidism (widely lost and unknown by the Central Asian religious scholars), are: the acceptance that human reason can find goodness and badness independently from revelation; the non-acceptance of 'ethical voluntarism,' but in opposite the acceptance of 'ethical objectivism'; views on free will and the fate of people who did not hear of the Prophetic mission (who were not exposed to a divine mission). These can be understood as the theological grounds to develop a synergy between liberalism and Islam in Central Asia. Some of these theological views will be discussed below.

A. Rationalistic epistemology

There are two main rationalistic Maturidite principles. Firstly, that reason, independently from revelation, can arrive at religious truths. Secondly, that God does not order to do what is known by reason/intellect as miserly and ugly ('ethical objectivism') (Al-Maturidi 1970: 9–10). Both are necessary theological tools for laying the ground for developing a progressive and liberal interpretation of Islam. By and large, in accordance with Maturidism, reason and faith should not be mutually exclusive. It can be claimed that the non-acceptance of key democratic and core liberal values, and universal principles and values of human rights and justice contradicts sound human reason. Therefore, for Muslims to reject these values and principles would mean to accept the existence of contradiction and incompatibility between reason and faith.

At the same time, the rejection of the key democratic and core liberal values and the universal principles and values of human rights and justice, means non-acceptance, even denial of unlimited wisdom, mercy and the justice of God. This is because the rejection of these values and principles means the deprivation of the rights of entire groups of people. This is what is known as *zulm*, 'the great oppression and injustice'[8] and the denial of progress leading to degradation and non-development of people. On the other hand, from the above-mentioned assumption, the argument based on 'ethical objectivism' can be inferred. To put it differently, it is 'ugly and miserable' not to accept the key democratic and core liberal values, and universal principles and values of human rights; however, according to Maturidite theology, God does not order to do and believe in what is known by reason as bad and evil.

As such, the epistemological principle assuming that reason and faith are compatible will induce Muslims to adopt key democratic values, and universal principles and values of human rights, and they do not have to feel alienated by them. In the end, the development of progressive religious interpretations, compatible with core liberal values and universal principles of human rights, can be understood as the Rawlsian notion of 'reasonableness.' Reasonableness according to Rawls is not an epistemological idea, it is a characteristic of political or religious doctrines conducive to producing agreement and consensus for public purposes (Rawls 2005: 61–62; Bilgin 2006: 5).

B. Theological views to develop inclusive interpretations of Islam

There is a nexus between the rationalistic Maturidite principle maintaining that there is a compatibility of reason and faith/revelation and inclusive interpretations of Islam.

It can be argued that the Maturidite logic accepts that religious beliefs incompatible with a narrowly-defined 'Islam' (denoting the name of specific religion) may lead to salvation. Basically, by recognising the primary role of human reason in having faith and not confining faith to specific attributes (accepting that the people may reach faith, which is similar to valid, through their reason), Maturidite logic lays the foundations to develop inclusive Islamic teachings. In other words, from rationalistic Maturidite theology it can be inferred that anyone who rationally comes to a belief in the 'Maker' (not 'Allah') is as good as Muslim in the eyes of God (Zhussipbek and Satershinov 2019: 6; Matsuyama 2013: 4–7).

The development of an inclusive interpretation of Islam and a synergy between Islam and liberalism are mutually supportive phenomena. For example, the synergy between Islam and liberal values can be observed in the theological legacy of the progressive Tatar Islamic scholar Musa Jarullah Bigiev who was an eloquent advocate of religious inclusivism. Specifically, the rationalistic principles of compatibility of reason and faith induced him to formulate an inclusive Islamic discourse which evolved into the theory of the universality of God's forgiveness (Bigiif 1911; Bigiev 2005: 78). The rationalistic approach led Bigiev also to an interpretation of Islam which included gender equality, since it is not compatible with reason if females are seen inferior than males, and it is ugly to subjugate half of humankind to another.

C. The Maturidite position on free will and Islamic individualism

The foundations of the phenomenon which can be tentatively called 'Islamic individualism' can be inferred from Maturidite theological views on free will and predestination. 'Islamic individualism' is a notion which is vital to develop liberal values and liberalism in a Muslim context and a pluralistic culture.

One of the alleged inherent incompatibilities between Islam and liberal values is centred on the criticisms of Islam that it denies the right of individual choice because of its inherent fatalism. However, while this can be true for traditionalistic conservative doctrines, a closer analysis of rationalistic Maturidism demonstrates this is not the case.

If we take into account the rationalistic epistemology of Maturidism, it is not surprising that the main Maturidite main principle is the idea of cooperation between God and human beings. Actions are attributed to God and also to human beings, they are created (*khalq*) by God, but chosen (*ikhtiyar*), acquired (*kasb*) and done (*fiil*) by human beings. In other words, each human act comprises several aspects, some of which are attributed to God, and some of which are attributed to human beings (Rudolph 2015: 211, 305). As such, human beings are the true author of their acts and, although they are subject to God's will, in the case of evil acts, they did not occur with the pleasure of God (Shah 2006: 640). In brief, Al-Maturidi developed a doctrine which accepts that a human being is an actor in the real sense, though God is the sole creator of everything. Specifically, some later Maturidite scholars taught that while God creates the act, humans add specific qualifications to the act, which are uncreated (Lucas 2006: 809). Acting and creating are two different types of activities involving different aspects of the same human act (Stefon 2010: 138–9). As such the idea of fatalism is rejected.

However, since scholars of other Islamic schools (such as Asharite, and, of course, Ahl al-Hadith) place an increasing emphasis on divine omnipotence at the expense of human's free will, their view can be regarded as excessively deterministic in substance (Shah 2006: 640). Asharite theology denies that human beings are actors in a real sense (Stefon 2010: 138). Therefore, for the notion of Islamic rationalism, the Asharite line of reasoning, which in the last centuries heavily affected the Hanafite–Maturidite doctrine, makes nonsense of the fundamental idea that man is individually responsible for his acts (Thiele 2016: 228). Reformist *Jadid* scholar Bigiev heavily criticised the excessively deterministic views on free will and predestination inspired by traditionalistic scholarship and argued that the notions of fate and predestination were not properly understood and as a consequence led Muslims to poverty, underdevelopment and depression (Bigi 1975: vii).

Furthermore, another way in which free will and individualism are promoted according to Hanafite–Maturidite theology is that performing prayers in congregation is only 'preferable.' Instead, believers can perform their prayer alone feeling herself/himself quite comfortable, and it is sufficient to have three people to perform Friday prayer.

To conclude, the Maturidite position on free will and predestination provides a ground to develop the notion of 'Islamic individualism,' which is based foremost on the belief that human beings are an actor in a real sense. As such individualism is a key factor in developing synergy between rationalistic Islam and the development of liberalism in Central Asia.

Societal grounds

Although the Soviet period was a critical juncture which profoundly influenced post-independence religious development in all Central Asian countries, ranging from the instrumentalisation of Islam in ethno-centric identity-building and regime legitimisation to the securitisation of 'non-controllable' Islam, the Soviet past might have had some positive effects to foster progressive Islamic understanding. In particular the Soviet past might help develop a 'reasonable,' in John Rawls's terms, religion and contribute to a synergy between Islam and the development of liberal values in Central Asia. As Froese asserts, the Soviet regime unwittingly brought about a more diverse religious market, for example, in addition to introducing an atheistic alternative into mainly monopolistic religious markets, the Soviets broke the hold major religious groups had over more innovative sects and also integrated people with different religious backgrounds (Froese 2004: 72–73).

As such, the secular and modernist legacy of Soviet period, coupled with the rationalistic premises of the historically-dominant Maturidism in Central Asia, may help develop progressive understandings of Islam in the region and develop a synergy between Islam and liberalism.

It is argued that, by invoking rationalistic Islamic theology, Muslims are expected to go beyond normative *fiqh* (Islamic law) towards the horizons of 'post-legal' (March 2010: 273) to build a pluralistic and human-centric society of the 21st century. The Muslims of post-atheistic Central Asia, who in their recent histories became exposed to decades-long atheism, the most comprehensive form of secularism, in comparison to the Muslims in other parts of the world, are in a more advantaged position to go beyond the normative *fiqh* and to reach the 'post-legal.' For example, according to statistics, contrary to Middle Eastern, South and South-East Asian Muslims, only 12% of Central Asian Muslims think that Islamic law should be endorsed by their governments to be made official law (Pew 2013a). Additionally, Central Asian Muslims, particularly in Kazakhstan, have a more inclusive interpretation which is illustrative of a developing religious pluralism and commitment to inter-faith dialogue (Pew 2013b).

Both the path-dependency of the Soviet past and cultural and historical factors shaped by the theological character of Islamic teachings in Central Asia, such as the legacy and popularity of Central Asian Sufism and moderate Hanafite theology, can be counted in the analysis of factors which may help develop synergy between Islam and liberalism. However, the increased interest in moderate Islam by Central Asian Muslims has been largely ignored by policy makers and commentators in the West, who tend to focus on the rise of radicalism, fundamentalism and associated acts of insurgency perpetrated by violent, but small fringe groups (Hanks 2015: 72–73).

On the whole, the effects of the atheistic and modernist Soviet past can positively contribute to develop theologically rationalistic Islamic understandings in Central Asia. However, this modernist quality of Central Asian societies is overshadowed by authoritarian politics, the process of re-traditionalisation and an inability of local Muslim actors to respond to the demands of their societies, particularly young people. The attitudes and expectations of young people constitute another important social factor to be considered in the discussion on the synergy between Islam and liberalism.

The attitudes of youth: Generation Z and the need for progressive Islam

Even after three decades since the collapse of the Soviet system, local Muslim actors, foremost Muftyats, cannot accommodate the needs of modern Central Asian societies, particularly the needs of younger generations, who have become either increasingly vulnerable to the influence of online-puritanical Salafism-inspired teachings or seriously disenchanted with Islam in general. The important signs of an epistemological crisis of Central Asian Islam are the local de-modern Islamic tradition's inability to satiate the religious demands of Central Asian people, the blind acceptance of injustices in social and political lives, and its approval of retrograde traditions including its approach to questions of gender inequality.

While Islam's revival in Central Asia is unfolding, and research emphasises young people as the most vulnerable to religious radicalisation (Nasritdinov, et al. 2019), there is an emerging parallel phenomenon – which is young people's disenchantment with the institutionalised, dogmatic and de-modern form of Islam. This phenomenon does not necessarily induce Central Asian youth to embrace the so-called non-traditional Islam, but makes them increasingly critical to Islam and religion, in general, if not open to agnostic ideas. An example of this can be found in research findings from a set of in-depth interviews conducted with the students which indicates the powerful tendencies among Kazakhstani youth to opposing, questioning and critically evaluating de-modern Islam and its conservative customs (Zhussipbek and Nagayeva 2019b). We may assume that a similar attitude to the custom and traditions linked to or supported by de-modern Central Asian Islam can be observed among young people in other Central Asian countries, at least, among the youth who are more exposed to global information and education.[9] Tellingly, according to a survey by the Frederich Ebert Foundation in Kazakhstan, the Kazakh youth trusts religious leaders the least, after politicians (Rakisheva 2017: 60).

By and large, the increasing acquaintance of Central Asian youth with the universal principles and values of human rights via different educational programs, youth activism and the Internet can be a crucial factor in developing progressive Islamic views and liberalism.

Jadidism

Jadidism was a short-lived Muslim reformist movement which emerged in the late Tsarist period and it illustrates the potential for rationalistic Maturidite theology to produce a pro-liberal interpretation of Islam. A majority of prominent *Jadids* from Central Asia and the Volga region adhered to Hanafism–Maturidism and tried to revive Islamic rationalism. In general, *Jadidism* is still one of the most understudied and largely misunderstood progressive Islamic movements.

In essence, *Jadidism* was the first pro-liberal (in political and social terms) and rationalistic (in Islamic theological terms) reformist movement among Eurasian Muslims. *Jadids* believed that the juristic and scholastic articulations of Islam must be open to evolution and reform. Therefore, although many of them were devoted Muslims, they were against polygamy and defended the legal equality between men and women. For example, the First Muslim Congress held under the leadership of *Jadids* in 1917 prohibited polygamy, declared the political equality of genders and the overall education of girls and the active participation of Muslim women in public life (Daulet 1989: 25).

A prominent Russian-Tatar reformist Hanafi-Maturidite scholar, Musa Jarullah Bigiev, (1875–1941), who was referred to as a reformist *mutakallim* (dialectical theologian) (Dudoignon 2006: 89), adopted a rationalistic and liberal approach to Islam. Emphasising that human reason cannot be limited (Bigi 1975: 192). Bigiev deeply condemned the dogmatic 'ossified' *kalam*. Instead Bigiev attempted to develop not only an inclusive interpretation of Islam which holds that non-Muslims would be saved in the Hereafter, since the belief in eternal punishment of non-Muslims contradicts reason (Bigiif 1911; Bigiev 2005: 78), but also a human-centric understanding of Islam. According to Bigiev, Islam is everything that the believer does in bringing goodness to people and to make the life of people happy, safe and comfortable (Khayrutdinov 2015: 78–80).

Gumar Karash, a largely unknown Kazakh *Jadid* scholar, and Alash-Orda, an activist, played a considerable role in the religious, social and political life of Western Kazakhstan. By employing a rationalistic methodology, Karash produced a number of *fatwas* that caused a strong backlash from conservative Muslims. For example, he argued against the ritual of male circumcision and animal sacrificing during *Eid Al-Adha*. Instead of shedding the blood of animals, he proposed to donate money to charity (Shabley 2017: 18–20).

Progressive Islam as a legitimate and authentic vehicle of cultural upgrading and societal liberalisation from inside

As it has been emphasised elsewhere, the democratisation and liberalisation efforts in Central Asia are stalled processes. As well, the process of retraditionalisation, and in general, the national and religious revival unfolding since the late Soviet years and accelerated with independence, inter alia, has led to the revival of archaic, feudal, obscurant traditions, norms and religious interpretations. As such, the proponents of this negative phenomenon refer to Islam, which in Central Asia has turned out to be 'de-modern, cultural and ethnicised.'

In view of the fact that in Central Asian countries many retrograde, patriarchal and obscurantistic traditions, custom and social norms are both based and legitimised by appeals to 'de-modern Islam,' the rationalistic Islamic theology by critically approaching and reinterpreting pre-modern, male-dominated and contradictory to universal principles and values of human rights Islamic norms,[10] may be a locomotive for social transformation. The theological and intellectual legacy of *Jadid* intellectuals, who aimed to transform their societies by developing progressive Islamic teachings, confirms this opportunity.

As it has been touched upon, the employment of Maturidite principles, that human reason, unaided by scripture, can find goodness and badness and, that there cannot be a contradiction between reason and faith/revelation, can show that the common achievements of humankind (which cannot be literally found in Quran), such as the notions of fundamental human rights, democracy, gender equality and the right of individual choice are not alien to Islam. Therefore, an obscurant pre-modern Islam can be critically analysed and reinterpreted. In other words, through employing the rationalistic principles of Maturidism, the cultural upgrading or societal liberalisation can be achieved in Central Asia, which is probably one of the most important components necessary in developing a synergy between Islam and liberalism.

To conclude, the rationalistic approach to Islam may serve as one of most transformative, but at the same time legitimate and authentic forces to reform and upgrade Central Asia Muslim societies.

Conclusion

Even though under current conditions it seems that Islam and liberalism are contradictory even oxymoronic concepts in post-Soviet Central Asia, as in many parts of the world, their co-existence, moreover a synergy between rationalistic Islam and liberal values can be conceptualised. As Haj (2009) highlights there is a neglected power of rationalistic tradition in Islam to launch reform of a Muslim mind. The negative predisposition of Central Asian peoples towards liberalism, as it is suggested by recent research, should not be seen as a paradigmatic rejection of core liberal values.

Although, the so-called 'traditional Islam' in Central Asian countries appears to be distant to rationalism, an inherent quality of Matutridism is rationalism. Specifically, two rationalistic Maturidite principles can be used to produce an interpretation of Islam compatible with liberal and democratic values. This chapter points to how the rationalistic Maturidite school has the potential to produce a progressive interpretation of Islam congruent with core liberal values and which can tentatively be called 'pro-liberal,' or at least, 'proto-liberal.'

There are some formidable obstacles to the building of a synergy between Islam and liberalism in Central Asia.

Foremost, the existence of a de-modern form of Islam in the region, which is upheld by an ongoing process of re-traditionalisation and instrumentalised by political and religious elites for national identity-building, along with the form of political authoritarianism in Central Asia, and the underdevelopment of democratic political institutions, are all factors which undermine this potential.

Youth attitudes are becoming increasingly critical of conservative interpretations of Islam. The youth represent an important social factor in the development of a progressive form of Central Asian Islam. Young people are open to new ideas and the outside world and they can be vehicles for the reconceptualisation of current anti-liberal/pro-clerical/de-modern and archaic interpretations of Islam in Central Asia.

Rationalistic Islam, being one of most transformative, but at the same time, legitimate forces to reform and 'upgrade' Central Asia Muslim societies may offer a good ground to build a synergy between liberalism and Islam in Central Asia. The views of either largely forgotten or unknown *Jadid* and Alash-Orda intellectuals, reformist Islamic scholars, such as Musa Bigiev, Gumar Karash, who followed the Maturidite rationalistic epistemology, seem to be important in presenting the claims to create a synergy between liberalism and Islam and to help transform Central Asian societies.

In the end, it is not impossible from an 'epistemological point of view' of rationalistic Maturidite Islam, to reconcile the Islamic revival and the development of liberalism and find a synergy between Islam and liberalism in Central Asia.

Notes

1 Spiritual Associations of Muslims or Muftiyats are, on paper, civil society bodies representing local 'traditional' Sunni-Hanafi Muslims in Uzbekistan, Kyrgyzstan, Kazakhstan and Tajikistan (in Tajikistan this institution is called 'Islamic Center of Tajikistan's Ulems (Islamic scholars) Council').
2 The concept rationalistic in Islamic tradition predominantly and wrongly, has become associated with Mutazilate school (Zhussipbek and Nagayeva 2019a: 357). As a result of association of rationalism in Islam with Mutazilism, rationalism obtained negative connotations for a great majority of Muslims, who tend to denounce Mutazilism as heretical.
3 A scholar from Samarqand, Al-Maturidi (eponym of Maturidite school in creed) was the first who systematised and conceptualised reason-based intellectual legacy of Abu Hanifa (eponym of the Hanafite school of jurisprudence) through coherent epistemology (Ali 1963: 261).
4 Inclusive religious interpretations accept that a salvation beyond their teachings, faith and belief system can be found
5 It can be argued that retraditionalisation is perceived by many in Central Asian countries as a 'return' to the authentic 'national identity,' and specifically by local intellectuals as a kind of 'de-sovietisation.'

6 In Spring 2019 I visited a scholar at Nur-Mubarak Islamic University in Almaty. He deplored that in his university located on Al-Farabi avenue, he and his colleague secretly read the works of Islamic philosopher Ibn-Rushd (Averroes), who commented the views of Al-Farabi, because of the fear of being accused of heresy, that they are followers of rationalistic Mutazilism. This view is held by a majority of faculty members at this university and religious bureaucracy organised by Muftyat. The same situation, the denial of Islamic rationalism and wholesale depiction of it as 'heretical Mutalizism' exists in all Central Asian states. It should be reminded that on the basis of his rationalist epistemology Al-Maturidi, on some crucial points, is close to the Mutazilate school and stands generally between the Mutazilats and Asharites (Rahman 2000: 62). In particular, the early presentations of Maturidism had positioned themselves together with Mutazilates on one side and Asharites on the other.
7 *Qadim* literally means old, or old-style, *qadimits* were the defenders of scholastic and devoid of reason, old-style Muslim education, which *Jadids* wanted to transform fundamentally.
8 For example, as the prominent Muslim feminist scholar Amina Wadud emphasises, gender inequality resultant from male-dominated conservative Islamic interpretations, means subjugation of one half of humanity to another, which is, for sure, oppression; however, God does not order to do this injustice (Wadud 2013)
9 Personal observation and communication with the students from Kyrgyzstan, Tajikistan and Turkmenistan who study in Almaty universities and the USA, Canada and the European countries.
10 For example, the development of gender egalitarian interpretations of Islam is a part of a bigger problem, the epistemological crisis of conservative Islamic thought and tradition. In general, the Muslim community as a whole cannot achieve justice unless justice is guaranteed for women and there can be no progressive interpretation of Islam without gender justice. Gender justice is crucial, indispensable and essential (Safi 2008: 10–11).

References

Abdallah, U. (1974) *The Doctrines of the Maturidite School with Special Reference to As-Sawad Al-Azam of Al-Hakim As-Samarqandi'*. Ph.D. Dissertation, University of Edinburgh.
al-Maturidi, A. (1970) *Kitab al-Tawhid*, Fathalla Kholeif (ed.). Beirut: Dar el-Machreq.
Ali, A. (1963) 'Maturidism,' in M. Sharif (ed.), *A History of Muslim Philosophy*. Weisbaden: Otto Harrassowitz, pp. 259–274.
An-Naim, A. (2000) 'Islam and Human Rights: Beyond the Universality Debate,' *Proceedings of the Annual Meeting (American Society of International Law)*, 94: 95–103.
Bigi, M. (1975) *Uzun Günlerde Oruç: Ictihad Kitabi* (in Turkish). Kazan Turkleri Ankara: Yardımlasma Dernegi.
Bigiev, M. (2005) *Dokazatelstva bojestvennogo miloserdiya* (in Russian). Kazan: Tatarskoye Knizhnoye Izdatelstvo.
Bigiif, M. (1911) *Rahmat Ilahiyya Burhanlari* (in Tatar). Orenburg. Available at: https://darul-kutub.com/uploads/books/f048f73b7675c2b7e8109bbd62f06ef69650d7e4.pdf, accessed 05.11.2019.
Bilgin, F. (2006) 'Political Liberalism and Inclusion of Religion,' *Rutgers JL & Religion*, 7 (4): 1–30.
Borg, M. (2001) *Reading the Bible Again for the First Time*. New York: Harper Collins.
Cornell, V. (2010) 'Reasons Public and Divine: Liberal Democracy, Sharia Fundamentalism, and the Epistemological Crisis of Islam,' in C. Ernst and R. Martin (eds.), *Rethinking Islamic Studies From Orientalism to Cosmopolitanism*. Columbia: University of South Carolina, pp. 23–52.
Daulet, S. (1989) 'The First All Muslim Congress of Russia Moscow 1–11 May 1917,' *Central Asian Survey*, 8 (1) 21–47.
Deen, A. (2016) *A Response to Claims of Unorthodoxy of My Theological Claims*. London: Quilliam Foundation. Available at https://www.quilliaminternational.com/a-response-to-claims-of-unorthodoxy-of-my-theological-claims-within-my-reasons-for-joining-the-quilliam-foundation-piece/, accessed 05.11.2019.
Duderija, A. (2017) *The Imperatives of Progressive Islam*. New York, NY: Routledge.
Dudoignon, S. (2006) 'Echoes to Al-Manar among the Muslims of the Russian Empire,' in S.Dudoignon, K. Hisao, and K.Yasushi (eds.), *Intellectuals in the Modern Islamic World*. New York: Routledge, pp. 85–117.
EUCAM. (2014) 'How Does Central Asia View the EU,' in S. Peyrouse (ed.), *EUCAM Working Paper 18*. Available at: https://www.files.ethz.ch/isn/180819/EUCAM-WP18-How-does-Central-Asia-view-the-EU.pdf, accessed 05.11.2019.

Froese, P. (2004) 'After Atheism: An Analysis of Religious Monopolies in the Post-Communist World,' *Sociology of Religion*, 65 (1): 57–75.

Haj, S. (2009) *Reconfiguring Islamic Tradition. Reform, Rationality and Modernity*. Stanford: Stanford University Press.

Hanks, R. (2015) 'Islamization and Civil Society in Central Asia: Religion as Substrate in Conflict Management and Social Stability,' in Ziegler, C. (ed.), *Civil Society and Politics in Central Asia*. Lexington: University Press of Kentucky, pp. 59–79.

Heathershaw, J. and Montgomery, D. (2014) 'The Myth of Post-Soviet Muslim Radicalization in the Central Asian Republics,' Chatham House. Available at: https://www.chathamhouse.org/sites/files/chathamhouse/publications/research/20141111PostSovietRadicalizationHeathershawMontgomeryFinal.pdf, accessed 05.11.2019.

Hunter, S. (2009) 'Introduction,' in Shireen Hunter (ed.), *Reformist Voices of Islam. Mediating Islam and Modernity*. New York: M. E. Sharpe, pp. 3–33.

Johnston, D. (2007) 'Maqasid al-Sharia: Epistemology and Hermeneutics of Muslim Theologies of Human Rights,' *Die Welt des Islams*, 47 (2): 149–187.

Khalid, A. (2007) 'Being Muslim in Soviet Central Asia, or an Alternative History of Muslim Modernity,' *Journal of the Canadian Historical Association*, 18 (2): 123–143.

Khalid, A. (2014) *Islam after Communism: Religion and Politics in Central Asia*. Berkeley: University of California Press.

Khayrutdinov, A. (2015) 'Bigiev on the Renewal of Muslim Legal System,' in I. Zaripov and D. Mukhetdinov (eds.), *Bigiev Symposium: Theological Thought of Russian Muslims in the 19th - early 20th centuries*. Moscow: Medina.

Leaman, O. (2008) 'The developed kalam tradition,' in T. Winter (ed.), *The Cambridge Companion to Classical Islamic Theology*. Cambridge: Cambridge University Press, pp. 77–97.

Lopatina, S., Kostenko, V. and Ponarin, E. (2016) 'Family Behavior and Sexual Liberalization in Eight Post-Soviet Societies,' *CESS Regional Conference*, Kazan Federal University, June 2–4, unpublished conference proceeding.

Lucas, S. (2006) 'Sunni Theological Schools,' in Josef W. Meri (ed.), *Medieval Islamic Civilization: An Encyclopedia*, vol. 1. New York: Routledge, pp. 808–810.

MacIntyre, A. (1988) *Whose Justice? Whose Rationality*. Notre Dame, IN: University of Notre Dame Press.

March, A. (2010) 'The Post-Legal Ethics of Tariq Ramadan: Persuasion and Performance in Radical Reform: Islamic Ethics and Liberation,' *Middle East Law and Governance*, 2 (2): 253–273.

Matsuyama, Y. (2013) 'Boundary between Believers and Non-Believers in Lands of Infidelity: Theological Basis for Interfaith Dialogue in Maturidism,' in Yohei Matsuyama (ed.), *Interrelations and Dialogue among Monotheistic Religions in the Multicultural Age*. Kyoto: Center for Interdisciplinary Study of Monotheistic Religions (CISMOR), Doshisha University.

Mullojanov, P. (2019) 'In Search of 'National Purpose': In Theory and Practice. Formation and Main Features of National Ideologies in Post-Soviet Central Asia,' in R. Isaacs and A. Frigerio (eds.), *Theorizing Central Asian Politics: The State, Ideology and Power*. Hampshire: Palgrave Macmillan, pp. 121–145.

Nasritdinov, E., Urmanbetova, Z., Murzakhalilov, K. and Myrzabaev, M. (2019) 'Vulnerability and Resilience of Young People in Kyrgyzstan to Radicalization, Violence and Extremism: Analysis across Five Domains,' *CAP Paper*, No. 213.

Pew Research. (2013b) 'Chapter 6: Interfaith Relations,' 30 April. Available at: https://www.pewforum.org/2013/04/30/the-worlds-muslims-religion-politics-society-interfaith-relations/, accessed 05.11.2019.

Pew Research. (2013a) 'The World's Muslims: Religion, Politics and Society,' 30 August. Available at: https://www.pewforum.org/2013/04/30/the-worlds-muslims-religion-politics-society-overview/, accessed 05.11 2019.

Rahman, F. (2000) *Revival and Reform in Islam*. Oxford: One World.

Rakisheva, B. (2017) *Molodezh Tsentralnoy Azii. Sravnitleniy Obzor*. Almaty: Friedrich Ebert Foundation Kazakhstan.

Rasanayagam, J. (2011) *Islam in Post-Soviet Uzbekistan: The Morality of Experience*. New York: Cambridge University Press.

Rawls, J. (2005) *Political Liberalism* (Expanded Ed.). New York: Columbia University Press.

Rudolph, U. (2015) *Al-Maturidi and the Development of Sunni Theology in Samarqand*, Rodrigo Adem (trans). Leiden: Brill.

Safi, O. (2008). 'Introduction: A Muslim Quest for Justice, Gender Equality, and Pluralism,' In O. Safi (ed.), *Progressive Muslims: on Justice, Gender, and Pluralism*. Oxford: One World, pp. 1–33.

Sandkühler, H.J. (1998) 'Pluralism and the Universality of Rights,' *20th World Congress of Philosophy*. Available at: https://www.bu.edu/wcp/Papers/Law/LawSand.htm 05.112019.

Shabley, P. (2017) 'Fatwas of Akhun Gumar Karash: Muftiyat and Legal Clashes in the Inner Kazakh Horde at the Beginning of the 20th Century,' *Islamology, Moscow, Mardjani Foundation*, 7 (2): 10–28.

Shah, M. (2006) 'Predestination,' in Josef Meri (ed.), *Medieval Islamic Civilization: An Encyclopedia*, vol. 1. New York: Routledge, pp. 638–641.

Soroush, A. (2000) 'Reason, Freedom, and Democracy in Islam: Essential Writings of Abdolkarim Soroush,' in M. Sadri and A. Sadri (eds. and trans.), New York, NY: Oxford University Press.

Stefon, M. (2010) *Islamic Beliefs and Practices*. New York: Britannica Educational.

Thiele, J. (2016) 'Between Cordoba and Nisapur: The Emergence and Consolidation of Asharism,' in S. Schmidtke (ed.), *The Oxford Handbook of Islamic Theology*. Oxford: Oxford University Press, pp. 225–241.

Wadud, A. (2013) *Inside the Gender Jihad: Women's Reform in Islam*. Oxford: Oneworld Publications.

Zhussipbek, G. and Moldashev, K. (2018) 'Rawlsian Liberalism and Rationalistic Maturidi Islam in Central Asia,' in R. Isaacs and A. Frigerio (eds.), *Theorizing Central Asia: Power and Politics: State, Ideology and Power*. Hampshire: Palgrave Macmillan, pp. 95–118.

Zhussipbek, G. and Nagayeva, Z. (2019a) 'Epistemological Reform and Embracement of Human Rights. What Can Be Inferred from Islamic Rationalistic Maturidite Theology?' *Open Theology*, 5 (1): 347–365.

Zhussipbek, G. and Nagayeva, Z. (2019b) 'The Core Liberal Values in the Context of National Identity of Kazakhstani Students,' in M. Laruelle (ed.), *Nazarbayev Generation. Studies on Youth Studies*. Lanham: Rowman and Littlefield, 133–152.

Zhussipbek, G. and Satershinov, B. (2019) 'Search for the Theological Grounds to Develop Inclusive Islamic Interpretations: Some Insights from Rationalistic Islamic Maturidite Theology,' *Religions*, 10 (11): 609.

30
TENGRISM

Rico Isaacs

The study of religion in Central Asian studies has been dominated by a focus on Islam. Notwithstanding Islam's historical role in the region, at least in terms of proto-state-building, everyday norms, social and cultural development and contemporaneously its political position within the five republics, the centrality of the study of Islam has often been at the expense of paying attention to other religions and their practices which have also played a prominent role in the history and development of the peoples of Central Asia. This chapter will introduce the reader to one such religion: Tengrism. Tengrism has had a much longer presence in the region among the Turkic people than Islam but has had less focus both academically and in terms of its practice. There is an on-going debate as to whether Tenrgrism is understood a religion, philosophy, ideology or even cult. But in this chapter, focusing on the cases of Kazakhstan and Kyrgyzstan Tengrism is understood as a religious philosophical worldview rooted in the psychogeographical relationship between the Turkic peoples of the region and the land. This chapter provides an introductory overview of Tengrism by firstly explaining its main features, before then outlining the psychogeography of this religious philosophical worldview, its history, political significance and place in contemporary Central Asian culture through Kazakh cinematic works.

What is Tengrism?

Featuring elements of shamanism, totemism, animism and the veneration of ancestors, Tengrism is characterised by both mono- and polytheism. The religion is monotheistic in that Tengri, the sky God, represents the supreme deity who determines the fate of all peoples including powerful leaders. The eighth-century Göktürk-erected inscriptions, located in the Orkhon Valley in Central Mongolia, note the all-powerful and overseeing eye of Tengri where 'all human sons are born to die in time, as determined by *Tengri*' (Bezertinov, 2000:72). At the same time, Tengrism is polytheistic, deploying multiple deities in its discourse of worship all of which have some connection to natural and/or biological phenomenon. This includes, *Umai* as mother earth and the goddess of fertility and virginity, and the Gods of Earth, Water, Fire, Sun, Moon, Star, Air, Clouds, Wind, Storm, Thunder and Lightning, and Rain and Rainbow (Shamakhay, Sarkulova, Adayeva and Tursunbaeva 2014). How many Gods there were precisely varied from population

DOI: 10.4324/9780429057977-30

to population. According to Rafael Bezertinov, Turkic groups believed there to be 17 Gods and Mongols believed there were 99 (Bezertinov, 2000: 71).

The Tengrist cosmological worldview is threefold. *Tengri*, as the God of the Sky, and the ultimate deity, represents the celestial level, or the heavenly world as it is sometimes referred to. *Yer Sub*, meaning earth water, signifies the earthly natural world of mountains, lakes, trees and plantation, that it is believed that the spirits of ancestors reside within. The Turkic people who inhabited the modern-day Kazakhs steppe viewed *Yer Sub* as forces of nature who were 'genies or spirits dwelling in hills of springs that were considered to be *iduk* (sacred) places' (Kundakbayeva 2016: 45). *Yer Sub*, therefore, is the middle earth, a central place between the celestial sphere of Tengri and the subterranean realm of *Erlik*, the third level of the cosmological worldview. *Erlik* was believed to be a son of Tengri, and was the lord of the underground, the judge of the dead and the harbinger of darkness, misfortune and evil (Odigan and Stewart 1997). What *Erlik* further represented was the plurality of spirits within the Tengrist worldview. Not only were there many, they were also diverse in character and morality, good and bad.

The worship of ancestors was and remains central to Tengrist philosophy and practice, and as we will read further, also to Kazakh and Kyrgyz political and cultural understanding of the religion. The worship of nature is also the worship of ancestors, as we noted above, because *Yer Sub* represented the sprits of those who have passed but who lived on in the trees, hills and rivers of the natural earth. Turkic nomads believed that a soul remained after death, what Kazakh folklore refers to as *aruak*, in which the dead remain among the living and can see everything (Sarsambekova et al, 2016: 110–111). Therefore, ancestors remain in the form of *aruak* to guide those living in the middle earth. Therefore, according to local scholars, 'the basis of the cult of the ancestors is to educate on the immortality of the soul, a belief in the afterlife of the souls of the dead, who are interested in family life and have an impact in their affairs' (Sarsambekova et al, 2016: 111). The Kyrgyz too 'also honoured and worshipped natural objects such as healing springs, holy sites, graves and mazars' (Ashymov 2003: 134).

It was the role of *Baksy* (Shaman) to act as the conduit between the earthly world and the spirit world of ancestors, or as one local scholar puts it, 'the bridge between heaven and earth' (Penkala-Gawęcka 2014:37). The cult of ancestors remains writ large in the post-nomadic life of Kazakhs and Kyrgyz. The long-standing tradition dating at least back to the Kazakh Khanate is that Kazakhs should be able to recite back seven generations (*Zheti ata*) of their forefathers (it is exclusively a patrilineal task). A similar practice persists amongst Kyrgyz too where the cult of ancestors, referred to as *arbak* features the cult of animism as the spirits of the dead take on holy meaning and where candles burn in honour of the dead and animals are brought as sacrifices (Ashymov 2003: 135; Gullette 2010: 52).

Tengrism is also notable for its self-proclaimed tolerance of other religions. The philosophy of Tengrism accepts there is/are many paths to God and Tengrism is but just one. In this way it is a non-dogmatic religion. This was as much the case during the reign of the powerful Mongols who ruled over believers of other religions, as it is today with modern followers of Tengrism. To some extent, it is also a non-hierarchical religion. As Marlene Laurelle has noted 'it is individualistic, does not have a holy text, and the religion is without a clergy, without dogma and interdictions' (Laurelle 2006). Moreover, the concept of prayer is also unknown (Laurelle 2006).

While Tengrism can be understood principally as a religion in which there are various deities and practices to follow, even if it is a loose, flexible and pluralistic set of practices, Tengrism can also be characterised as a deep-seated philosophy which is rooted in the relationship which Turkic peoples have had with the land. This is especially the case for the Kazakh and Kyrgyz and their historical nomadic way of life.

The psychogeography of Tengrism

Psychogeography was originally defined by French philosopher Guy Debord as 'the study of the precise laws and specific effects of the geographical environment, consciously organised or not, on the emotions and behaviour of individuals' (Debord 1955: 23). Psychogeography is typically deployed in the study of urban geography, but it should not be limited as such, and as evidenced by the wide scope of literature and literary studies which seek to examine the influence of geographical environment beyond the city on the mindset and actions of peoples, it can be used to explore the relationship between the Kazakhs and Kyrgyz and the Eurasian steppe.

It is not hard to see why Tengrism is the interlocutor between the Central Asians of the steppe and their natural environment. Tengrism as both a philosophical and cosmological worldview and a form of religious practice is inherently tied to peoples' relationship with nature and all living beings. For example, within Tengrism animals are totemistic symbols for particular Gods. Sheep are associated with fire, camels with the earth, horses with the wind and cows with water (Shamakhay, Sarkulova, Adayeva, and Tursunbaeva 2014: 382). Animals are pivotal to folktales of Turkic mythology, taking on important roles in aiding and guiding heroes (Kaskabassov 1972). This is most notable with the 'heavenly wolf,' imbued with the spirit of ancestors and revered as an intelligent, selfless and loyal friend, always on hand to lead and guide (Isaacs 2018: 177).

But Tengrism also denotes a much deeper relationship between the Turkic nomadic mentality of the Eurasian steppe and their geographical environment. The ancient relationship between nomadic humankind, the geography of the landscape, the natural world and all living beings has served to cement a distinct understanding of the Turkic nomadic self (what Kazakhs often refer to as *tusinik*). As one Kazakh scholar has highlighted in relation to the Kazakh mentality 'the understanding of mutual relations with nature served as a bridge in understanding reality. Kazakhs always understood nature and did not contrast himself to it and always aspired to be in harmony with it' (Ismagulova and Nazarbayev 2015). Tengrism was the philosophy and religious practice which underpinned this symbiotic relationship with nature which was also central to the patterns of migration practiced by the nomadic population of the steppe. Migration was cyclical and followed the path of the sun. Nomads did not fall behind the circulation of the sun. 'They were there, where the sun was … they surround time with the circle and drove it with their sheep. This circle, the circulation of the sun, distinguished nomads from settled people' (Shamakhay, Sarkulova, Adayeva, and Tursunbaeva 2014: 382). It was shamanistic figures who acted as the bridge between the nomads and different deities, although as Devin DeWeese has argued the inner life of Central Asian peoples was 'much richer' than the label shamanism suggests (DeWeese cited in Thrower 2004: 55). Shamanistic figures performed a central function in the normative reproduction of communal rites which served, in the words of James Thrower, to 'maintain material and social life – that is, with success in the hunt or agriculture, with fertility, and with the preservation of social identity and social cohesion' (Thrower 2004: 56).

In sum, Tengrism provided a belief system which gave meaning to life through a psychogeographical relationship with nature and the vast open Central Asian steppe and which guided day-to-day practices that provided the basis of material and social life for the nomadic populations of the Eurasian steppe.

The history of Tengrism

Historians know very little of the earliest religions and religious practices of the peoples of the Eurasian Steppe, but there is evidence of Hindu and Zoroastraian practices (Thrower 2004: 50). As for Tengrism, a precise date for its founding has alluded historians and scholars. It is believed to have originated sometime between the end of the second and beginning of the first millennium BC in the Xiongnu Empire, a confederation of tribal nomadic peoples who inhabited the Eastern portion of the Eurasian steppe (Beckwith 2009). It was believed then to have been later practiced by other semi-nomadic populations such as the Huns, Bulgars and various Turkic-Mongol populations of the Eurasian steppe from at least the sixth to eighth centuries AD onwards, all ancestors of modern-day Central Asians (Bonnefoy 1993: 331, Man 2006: 62, de la Vaissière, 2015, Zhaksybekov, Nurzhanov and Kadirkulov 2013). Some have gone much further in dating the origins of Tengrism. Kazakh writer Olzhas Suleimenov has argued that Tengrism is in fact one of the oldest religions in the world dating its practice back as far as ancient Sumer. In his seminal work from the 1970s, *Az i ya,* Suleimenov argues that the proof of the practice of Tengrism among ancient Sumerians lay in the linguistic connection between the word Tengri, which means sky god in Turkic and the Sumerian Dingir which in its cuneiform is a star and is understood to mean the supreme father of gods and the sky (Suleimenov 1975). This has been an interpretation which has gained currency amongst some committed specialists on the roots of Turkic civilisation who argue that Turkic people migrated to the Eurasian steppe from ancient Summer, including Murad Aji who argued that Tengrism was the historical basis of all religions in the world and whose books gained popularity in Kazakhstan in the 2000s (Kurtkaya 2016; Kudaibergenov 2017).

While it is hard to trace the earliest developments of the practice of Tengrism, and moreover, it is even harder to describe Tengrism as a single unified religious movement (it was often practiced differently by the various groups across the Eurasian steppe), it was clear that by the time of Göktürk rule in the sixth and seventh centuries Tengrism had become the political basis for the legitimacy of rulers. The prominent Soviet archaeologist and ethnologist Lev Gumilev indicated from his research that Tengrism was recorded on the Orkhon inscriptions (Gumilev 1967).[1] And it is believed that the political power of the Göktürk khans was premised on a mandate from Tengri. Among the wider population such Khans were understood to be the sons of Tengri and the sky God's representatives on Earth (Abaev 2013: 4). After the fall of the Göktürk Empire, Tengrism as the religious basis of state and political power declined as the Uighuric Khaganate grew in influence across Eurasia (Kovalev 2016).[2] During the period of the Khaganate, the Uyghur Khagans practiced various religions, including Tengrism and Buddhism, but it was generally Manichaeism that was the state religion (Abaev 2013: 4). It was also during this period of the seventh to ninth centuries that Central Asia witnessed the first Arab incursions into the Eurasian steppe. However, it was the settled populations of modern-day Uzbekistan where Islam first took hold, rather than the more difficult to reach pastoral nomads of the vast steppe in the north and east of the region (Gibb 1923). Tengrism became the focus again of state power with the rise of the Mongolian Khans which reached its pinnacle with the rule of Chinggis Khan. In *The Secret History of the Mongols,*[3] Tengri is referred to as the Eternal Blue Heaven. It is the Eternal Blue Heaven 'that appears to be guiding Chinggis Khan throughout the story, and all of his successes are attributed by him to Heaven's will' (Kahn 1984: xx). Thus, Chinggis' power, position, and political and military success was understood to be the will of Tengri. It was the Sky God who ruled the fate of the great Mongolian leader.

Since the initial Arab incursion in the Central Asian region from AD 649 onwards under Usman, Tengrism gradually became marginalised vis-à-vis the growing popularity and conversion of peoples to Islam (Hagheyeghi 1995: 75). The demographic fault line between sedentary and nomadic populations was important for the way in which Islam developed in Central Asia, and this can explain why even after large swathes of the region had converted to Islam, Tengrism remained the official state sanctioned religion of the Mongolian Empire. It is also testament to the Tengrian pluralistic approach to other religions, given Islam was permitted and flourished under the Mongolian yoke. As noted above, there were no sacred texts within Tengrism and was in fact a religion that was passed down through oral traditions (Ayupov 2012). The lack of sacred text meant the religion was always open to interpretation of how it was practiced and followed – thus it could be more accommodating and flexible in relation to alternative belief systems.

Tengrism remained the official religion of four of Chinggis Khan's successors until Öz Beg Khan pursued the conversion of the Horde to Islam in the early fourteenth century. Nevertheless, despite the conversion of most Central Asian peoples and proto-states of the region to Islam by the fourteenth century through the peaceful promotion of Islam in the Oxus Valley by missionaries and merchants, Tengrian ideas, philosophy and practices remained. The conversion of the nomadic peoples to Islam was gradual and incomplete, not least because of the sheer distances for missionaries to travel and the frequent migration of peoples across the steppe made the more sedentary practices of Islam difficult to embed. Thus, the types of Islam which developed in Central Asia were the more moderate and liberal Hanafi school and a mystical version of Sufism (Bennigsen and Wimbush 1985). Rituals of Tengrism, and the shamanistic practices associated with it, continued to co-exist alongside, if not become synthesised with, Islam once it became the dominant religion in the region (Hagheyeghi, 1995: 77).[4] For instance, it has been noted by scholars from the region that 'Sufi missionaries who proselytised Islam among the nomads through missionary activities had to be very careful in not rejecting outright the Tengrian traditions, and dealt with them very carefully' (Abazov and Kurganskaya 2015: 407).

The contemporary politics of Tengrism

There has been little published research on the contemporary politics of Tengrism. To date, the most significant study in English has been undertaken by Marlene Laruelle. In her 2007 article published in *Central Asian Survey*, Laruelle found Tengrism to have been re-born in the post-Soviet period in Kyrgyzstan, Tatarstan and Kazakhstan as an ideological movement which professed a form of post-Soviet nationalism for Turkic-Mongol peoples (Laruelle 2007: 203). This can be observed in the form of a series of specialised, and arguably marginal, intellectual movements such as the Kyrgyz movement *Tengir-Ordo*. It may be difficult to trace a direct linage between the Tengrism practiced centuries ago by the nomads of the Eurasian steppe and those that have adopted its practice once again in recent decades. As Laruelle and her colleague Aurélie Biard have argued, 'although contemporary Tengrism asserts historical connections to an ancient cult of the Sky, it has been unable to demonstrate that "Tengrist" practices have in fact been maintained throughout the centuries' (Biard and Laruelle 2010 57).

The emergence of Tengrism as a form of 'national' revival in Central Asia can be dated back to the 1970s and the work of famed Kazakh poet, Olzhas Suleimenov. Suleimenov's 1975 book *Az i Ya*, among other things, sought to trace and re-describe the Tengrian religion and its relationship to the peoples who historically roamed the steppe (Suleimenov 1975). Suleimenov re-introduced the concept of Tengrism into Russian (*Tengrianstvo*) claiming it to be one of the oldest and most ancient religions of the world (Laruelle 2012: 324).

But in the 1990s, with newfound independence, in some intellectual circles, Tengrism became a source of inspiration in both religious and political terms. According to the writer Arman Kudaibergenov, a significant part of the Kazakh intelligentsia sympathise with Tengrian ideas (Kudaibergenov 2017). Historians, journalists and cultural philosophers such as Kurmangazi Karamanuhli and Akseleu Seidimbek venerated Tengrism as the 'native tradition' of the Kazakhs. They stressed that Tengrism was the natural religion of the Kazakh people and Islam was a foreign belief system which had been aggressively forced upon the peoples of the Eurasian steppe for centuries (Weller 2014: 139). Likewise, even the Chairman of the Union of Muslims of

Kazakhstan had noted that 'that Tengrian, pagan traditions are organically woven into the fabric of Muslim ideology' (Kudaibergenov 2017). Such sentiments have also seeped out of these narrow intellectual circles into mainstream politics in Kazakhstan. Former leader of the Party of Patriots, and ex-presidential candidate, Gani Kasymov, came out in support of Tengrism in 2010 making the case that the religion had a 5,000-year history in Kazakhstan, while Islam was more recent, with the Kazakh people only having been subject to it for 800 years (Kasymov 2010). In Kazakhstan, Tengrism received some state support. In 2017, the Ministry of Culture organised and sponsored a conference for the Astana Expo on the theme of Tengrism and heritage of the Eurasian peoples. It illustrates the way in which Tengrism is being used, albeit in a minor way, as the potential philosophical, historical and religious basis to reconfigure state, national and regional identity.

Similar evocations of Tengrism as the 'national religion' have also found voice in movements in Kyrgyzstan. The promotion of Tenrgism is Kyrgyzstan has been principally led by Dastan Sarygulov (Montgomery 2016). Sarygulov, a protégé of former Kyrgyz president Askar Akayev, was a former secretary of the Talas Communist Party, state secretary under Akayev's successor Kurmanbek Bakiyev and chair of the Kyrgyz state gold mining company, *Kyrgyzaltyn* (Marat 2005). Often portrayed as 'anti-Muslim,' and an 'ethno-nationalist' (Laruelle 2007: 176), Sarygulov set up *Tengir Ordo* in 2005 as a way to promote the philosophy, values and practices of Tengrism. For Sarygulov, Tengrism is 'the genuine religion of the Kyrgyz and helped the people to survive throughout the centuries' and 'in his interpretation, Tengrism promotes an anti-capitalist lifestyle and is a natural response to the problems caused by globalization' (Marat 2005). During the 2000s, because of his high position within the state, Sarygulov was in a position to try and put forward a new ideology premised upon the principles of Tengrism. Sarygulov's position towards the apex of Kyrgyz politics did not last. He was jailed in 2017 along with other members of the political opposition in an alleged plot to overthrow the government (Djanibekova 2017). Tengrism has never been officially recognised as a religion in Kyrgyzstan and there is a deep scepticism within the corridors of power regarding the religion (Toktonaliev 2014). As we have seen above, leaders within the Tengrian movement have found themselves on the wrong side of the law in Kyrgyzstan. In 2011 one Tengrian activist, Kubanychbek Tezekbaev, was put on trial for inciting religious hatred because of comments he made regarding the growing influence of fundamentalist Islam in Kyrgyzstan (Ringmar 2019: 104). Like Sarygulov, Tezekbaev has often been accused of being anti-Muslim because of his claims that the growth of Islam is a danger to the Kyrgyz nation, although he has described himself as 'half-Muslim' he believes that Islam and Tengrism can coexist peacefully and feels that most Kyrgyz perform both Islamic and Tengrist practices (Ashakeeva and Najibullah 2012). Indeed, in anthropologist David Montgomery's work of Islamic practices in Kyrgyzstan he notes how Tengrism, while not widespread, does show ways in which religion has been revived and conceptualised in the post-Soviet period as something which is much more locally centred, rooted in the traditions and experience of the ancestors whom came before (Montgomery 2016).

There is a tension, however, in how contemporary Tengrism is understood in political terms in post-Soviet Central Asia. The type of national ideology which has been proposed by both Kazakh and Kyrgyz Tengrian leaders and their movements have been argued by some scholars to be ethno-national and exclusive in nature (Laruelle 2017). Laruelle highlights the claims of Raphael Bezertinov in this respect that, 'the spirit of a nation is oriented along three main lines: the unity of blood, language and religion' (Laruelle 2007: 213). This of course is an appeal to an exclusionary form of national identity which espouses biological primordialism and a commitment to ethnic purity. This sits uneasily with the universal principles which have guided

Tengrian thought for centuries and especially the open, non-dogmatic and pragmatic approach which had been adopted by the Mongolian Khanate when Tengrism was the state religion.

Tengrism in Central Asian culture: Kazakh cinema

It is not clear how many people in either Kazakhstan or Kyrgyzstan follow Tengrism. In Kyrgyzstan it is rumoured that the figure is around 50,000 (Ibraimov 2014), for Kazakhstan there is no estimate, yet there are a few organisations, such as the Public Foundation 'The Legacy of Nomad Civilization,' but they are not registered as religious organisation and the head of the organisation, Batyrzhan Seydomar, believes Tengrism is not a religion, but rather a philosophy and a way of life (Kudaibergenov 2017). Nevertheless, one area where Tengrism has filtered through into the wider public consciousness in Central Asia is via cinematic works. Tengrian myths, symbols, folk tales and rituals have appeared in films such as Akhat Ibryaev's children's film, *The Book of Legends: the mysterious forest* (2012), Sergei Bodrov's *Mongol* (2007) about the young Chinggis Khan and Guka Omarova's film about an old shaman folk-healer, *Baksy* (2008). However, it is the work of Kazakh film director, poet and writer Ermek Tursunov where Tengrism has been most prominent in Kazakh art and culture, especially the trilogy of films he made: *Kelin (Daughter-in-law)* (2009), *Shal* (Old Man) (2012) and *Kenzhe* (Young Brother) (2015). And, like Seydomar, Tursunov views Tengrism as a philosophical world view which is expressed in the psychogeographical relationship the peoples of the Eurasian Steppe have with nature and the environment. As the director, himself has stressed in an interview:

> nomads had their own system of values which was completely different from those of a settled population. Nomads didn't have an idea of a state, because they were constantly moving. A settled way of life implies having some territory: some limited spaces where he grows his crop. The nomad was tied to his cattle: he followed his cattle wherever it went. This is why for the nomad the land is infinite, he does not know where it ends, and he is not even asking himself this question, he just follows his cattle. This is a source of the nomad's worldview and religiousness. We did not have Islam here, we were pagans, Tengrians. It was a cult of fire, a cult of the mountain and a cult of ancestors.[5]

Like those who have expressed Tengrism as the national basis of either Kazakh or Kyrgyz identity, Tursunov sees Tengrism as a return to the philosophical roots of the Turkic peoples. It is a return to the ideas and practices traditionally held by the ancestors of modern-day Kazakhs and Kyrgyz. Tengrism expresses the belief of humankind needing to live in harmony with nature and with animals. In Tursunov's work this worldview is most clearly seen in the film *Shal*. The underlying theme of Shal focuses on the symbiosis between humans and nature and the need for people to live in an organic way with their environment rather than being a destructive force towards it. The film centres on an elderly Shepherd, Kasym, who loses his way in the cold and misty steppe while taking a flock of sheep to new pasture. During his wandering Kasym needs to protect the flock from the wolves which roam the land. Nature in the film is represented 'by the wolves, and in particular the mother of the pack (another example of the way in which the film is influenced by Tengrist ideas of Totemism)' (Isaacs 2018). The film concerns Kasym's resilience, quiet spirit and respect for nature as he manages to survive in the steppe. As the director noted, 'the steppe can either be a caring mother, or act as a stepmother … it all depends on how you treat it – as a big dumpster or as your own god.'[6]

Tursunov's films speak directly to themes inherent within Tengrism. The veneration of ancestors is a central aspect of *Shal*, observed in the relationship between Kasym and his grandson.

Kelin, on the other hand, features more concretely the practices and rituals of Tengrism, through the shamanistic mother-in-law character. Tengrian symbols, artwork and rituals are depicted throughout the film. The film also philosophically addresses the cyclical nature of Tengrism with the theme of birth, life and death – with the focus on biological reproduction a central element to the substance of life, family and nature. Tursunov's films are important in the way in which they link the philosophy and cosmological world view of Tengrism to a reinterpretation of modern-day Kazakh and broader Turkic identity. Underpinning the films is the argument that Tengrism, as a pagan religion, is the true religious identity of the people of the Eurasian steppe. And that in the confusion of post-Soviet transition and the encroachment of global capitalism, it is the spiritual ideas and framework of Tengrism which Turkic people should return to (Isaacs 2018). Tengrism as present in arts and culture in these films is about trying to reconnect Turkic people with the spiritual values of their past before the emergence of Islam in the region, the onset of Soviet rule and now global capitalism.

Conclusion

A Tengrian revival is not limited to just Kazakhstan and Kyrgyzstan. Across the broader Eurasian space other Turkic peoples have also begun to reconnect with a Tengrian belief system including in Bashkortostan, Tatarstan and the Kumyks (who are prominently based in Northern Dagestan). Tengrism is not widespread in Kazakhstan or Kyrgyzstan. But its rituals, ideas and beliefs can be observed in many Islamic practices today and there has been a resurgence in interest of Tengrian ideas. But its power in contemporary terms is less in the symbolic power it can provide in terms of arts and culture, or its residual influence in Islamic practice, or the way it has been used discursively to present and ethnic and exclusive discourse about post-Soviet identity based on blood and lineage, rather its importance lies in the cosmological worldview it provides. In Kazakhstan and Kyrgyzstan Tengrism has offered a framework and belief system which seeks to connect Turkic peoples with nature, with the vast steppe of the Kazakh landscape or the glorious mountain peaks in Kyrgyzstan. It connects the material world of the peoples of the Eurasian steppe with the eternal sky and the natural world. It is predominantly, therefore, not a religious creed as such, nor the basis of an exclusive identity, but rather a psychogeographical worldview.

Notes

1 The Orkhon inscriptions are two memorial stones located in the Orkhon Valley in Mongolia erected during the time of the Göktürk Empire and written in the Old Turkic alphabet.
2 The Uighuric Khaganate was a large state established by Turkic-speaking Uyghur pastoral nomads, which at its height in the ninth century stretched from Western Central Asian to the Korean Peninsula.
3 *The Secret History of the Mongols* details the rise of Temijun to his position as Chingis Khan. It was written in the thirteenth century after the death of Chingis in 1227.
4 Tursin Hafiz Gabitov also argues something similar that the different forms of religion which have appeared in among the Kazakh people should not be seen as sequentially replacing one after the other. Rather they exist in a dialectical process of co-existence and synthesis. For more on the work of Gabitov, see Charles Weller's (2014) review of the religious cultural historical debate in Kazakhstan.
5 Author's interview with Ermek Tursunov, Almaty, Kazakhstan, 9 November 2012.
6 Author's interview with Ermek Tursunov

References

Abaev, N. (2013) 'Tengraianstvo as the National and State Religion of the Turko-Mongolia People of Inner Asia,' *Kültür Ajans Tanıtım ve Organizasyon*, 19: 1–8.

Abazov, R. and Kurganskaya, V. (2015) 'Mukhanmadiar S. Orynbekov, Genezis religioznosti v Kazakhstane [The Genesis of Religiosity in Kazakhstan] Aleksei U. Nikonov, Tengriyanstvo: u istokov dukhovnosti chelovechestva [Tengrianism: At the Roots of Human Spirituality],' *Religion, State & Society*, 43 (4): 406–408.

Ashakeeva, G. and Najibullah, F. (2012) 'Kyrgyz Religious Hatred Trial Throws Spotlight on Ancient Creed,' *Radio Free Europe/Radio Liberty*, 31 January. Available at: https://www.rferl.org/a/kyrgyz_religious_hatred_trial_throws_spotlight_on_ancient_creed/24469022.html, accessed 15.07.2019.

Ashymov, D. (2003) 'The Religious Faith of the Kyrgyz,' *Religion, State & Society*, 31 (2): 133–138.

Ayupov, N.G. (2012) *Tengrianstvo kak otkrytoe mirovozzrenie*. Almaty: KazNPU imeni Abaya.

Beckwith, Christopher. (2009) *Empires of the Silk Road: A History of Central Eurasia from the Bronze Age to the Present*. Princeton, NJ: Princeton University Press.

Bennigsen, A. and Wimbush, S. (1985) *Mystics and Commissars: Sufism in the Soviet Union*. Berkley, CA: University of California Press.

Bezertinov, R. (2000) *Tengrianstvo – religiya turkov i mongolov*. Naberezhnye Chelny: Tatarstan, Russian Federation.

Biard, A. and Laruelle, M. (2010) '"Tengrism" in Kyrgyzstan: In Search of New Religious and Political Legitimacy,' in Delaplace, G., Hamayon, R., and Pearce, S. (eds.), *Representing Power in Modern Inner Asia: Conventions, Alternatives and Oppositions*. Bellingham, WA: Western Washington University, pp. 55–96.

Bonnefoy, Yves. (1993) *Asian Mythologies*. Chicago: University of Chicago Press, p. 331

de la Vaissière, Étienne. (2015) 'The Steppe World and the Rise of the Huns,' in Maas, Michael (ed.), *The Cambridge Companion to the Age of Attila*. Cambridge: Cambridge University Press, pp. 175–192.

Debord, G. (1955) 'Introduction to a Critique of Urban Geography' (trans. Ken Knabb), in Harald Bauderand Salvatore Engel-Di Mauro (eds.), *Critical Geographies: A Collection*. Kelowna: Praxis (e)Press, pp. 23–27.

Djanibekova, N. (2017) 'Kyrgyzstan: Four Opposition Politicians Jailed for "Coup Attempt",' *Eurasianet*, 18 April. Available at: https://eurasianet.org/kyrgyzstan-four-opposition-politicians-jailed-coup-attempt, accessed 20.08.2019.

Gibb, H. (1923) *The Arab conquests in Central Asia*. London: Royal Asiatic Society.

Gullette, D. (2010) *The Genealogical Construction of the Kyrgyz Republic: Kinship, State and "Tribalism"*. Folkstone: Global Oriental.

Gumilev, L. (1967 [2007]) *Drevnie Tyurki*. Moscow: Ayris-Press.

Hagheyeghi, M. (1995) *Islam and Politics in Central Asia*. London: Palgrave Macmillan.

Ibraimov, B. (2014) 'Kyrgyzstan's Sky Worshippers Seek Recognition', *Eurasianet*, 8 May. Available at: https://eurasianet.org/kyrgyzstans-sky-worshippers-seek-recognition, accessed 14.06.2019.

Isaacs, R. (2018) *Film and Identity in Kazakhstan: Soviet and Post-Soviet Culture*. London: I.B. Tauris.

Ismagulova, B.K. and Bazarbayeva, A.S. (2015) *Mindset and Mentality of the Kazakh Ethnos*. Available at: http://portal.kazntu.kz/files/publicate/2014-12-15-2020.pdf, accessed 14.12.2015.

Kahn, P. (1984) 'Introduction,' in Paul Khan (ed.), *The Secret History of the Mongols: The Origins of Chingis Khan* (expanded addition). Boston: Cheng & Tsui Company, pp. xi–xxvi.

Kaskabassov, S.A. (1972) *Kazakhskaya volshebnaya skazka*. Alma-ata: Nauka.

Kasymov, G. (2010) 'Ob"yavil sebya priverzhentsem tengrianstva,' nur.kz, 13th October 2010. Available at: http://www.nur.kz/165368-gani-kasymov-obyavil-sebya-priverzhenczem-tengrianstva.html, accessed 14.01.2016.

Kovalev, R. (2016) 'Uyghur Khaganate,' in John Mackenzie (ed.), *The Encyclopedia of Empire*. Oxford: Wiley Publishers, pp. 1–6.

Kudaibergenov, A. (2017) 'Inovertsy,' *Esquire.kz*, 9 February. Accessed 28 November 2019 https://esquire.kz/inoverts/

Kundakbayeva, Z. (2016) *The History of Kazakhstan from the Earliest Period to the Present Time*, Vol. 1. Almaty: Kazakhstan University.

Kurtkaya, M. (2016) *Sumerian Turks*. Ankara: Independent Publisher.

Larurelle, M. (2006) 'Tengrism: In Search for Central Asia's Spiritual Roots,' *The Central Asia-Caucasus Analyst*,' 22 March. Available at: https://www.cacianalyst.org/publications/analytical-articles/item/10734-analytical-articles-caci-analyst-2006-3-22-art-10734.html, accessed 14.07.2019.

Laruelle, M. (2007) 'Religious Revival, Nationalism and the "Invention of Tradition": Political Tengrism in Central Asia and Tatarstan,' *Central Asian Survey*, 26 (2): 203–216.

Laruelle, M. (2012) 'Olzhas Suleimenov,' in S. Norris and W. Sunderland (eds.), *Russia's People of Empire: Life Stories from Eurasia, 1500 to the Present*. Bloomington: Indiana University Press, pp. 319–326.

Laruelle, M. (2017) 'Kyrgyzstan's Nationhood: From a Monopoly of Production to a Plural Market,' in M. Laruelle and J. Engvall (eds.), *Kyrgyzstan Beyond "Democracy Island" and "Failing State"*. Lanham: Lexington Books, pp. 165–184.

Man, John. (2006) *Attila: The Barbarian King Who Challenged Rome*. New York: St. Martin Press.

Marat, E. (2005) 'High-Ranking Kyrgyz Official Proposes New National Ideology', Jamestown Foundation, 2 (226). Available at: https://jamestown.org/program/high-ranking-kyrgyz-official-proposes-new-national-ideology/, accessed 15.10.2014.

Montgomery, D. (2016) *Practicing Islam: Knowledge, Experience, and Social Navigation in Kyrgyzstan*. Pittsburgh: Pittsburgh University Press.

Odigan, S. and Stewart, J. (1997) *A Course in Mongolian Shamanism*. Ulaanbaatar: Golomt Center for Shamanist Studies.

Penkala-Gawęcka, D. (2014) 'The Way of the Shaman and the Revival of Spiritual Healing in Post-Soviet Kazakhstan and Kyrgyzstan,' *Shaman*, 22 (1–2): 35–61.

Ringmar, E. (2019) *History of International Relations: A Non-European Perspective*. Cambridge: Open Book Publishers.

Sarsambekova, A., Berdagulova, S., Arzayeva, M., Mustafayeva, A., Kokeyeva, D., Diana Ayapova, D. and Maslov, H. (2016) 'Holy Places in Kazakhstan,' *Anthropologist*, 26: 110–113.

Shamakhay, S., Sarkulova, M., Adayeva, G. and Tursunbaeva, A. (2014) 'Image of a Man and the Universe in Kazakh and Mongol Myths,' *Procedia: Social and Behavioral Sciences*, 159: 381–386.

Suleimenov, Olzhas. (1975) *Az i ya*. Alma-Ata: Zhasushy.

Thrower, James. (2004) *The Religious History of Central Asia from the Earliest Times to the Present Day*. Lewiston: Edwin Mellon Press.

Toktonaliev, T. (2014) 'No Legal Status for Ancient Kyrgyz Creed,' *Global Voices Central Asia*, 24 September. Available at:https://iwpr.net/global-voices/no-legal-status-ancient-kyrgyz-creed, accessed 22.11.

Weller, C. (2014) 'Religious-Cultural Revivalism as Historiographical Debate: Contending Claims in the Post-Soviet Kazakh Context,' *Journal of Islamic Studies*, 25 (2), pp. 138–177.

Zhaksybekov, K., Nurzhanov, A. and Kadirkulov, G. (2013) 'Kul't Tengri u drevnykh tyurok,' *Vestnik Akademii Znanii*, 1 (4): 160–164.

INDEX

3-i's framework 241, 242
9/11 terrorist attacks *see* September 11 attacks
100 New Faces 103
100 new textbooks 103
201st Military Base 125
201st Motor Rifle Division 250
1989 commission 123
2015 Corruption Perceptions Index 300n16
2018 Report on International Religious Freedom 226

Abdullayev, Ikhtiyor 253
Ablai Khan 27, 203
Ablyazov, Mukhtar 77, 80, 81, 299n12, 319
Abu'l-Fayz Khan (r. 1711–1747) 22
Abu'l-Ghazi (1603–1663) 21
Abulkhair (khan) 26
Abu'l-Khayr 19, 20
Aburrakhman Avtobachi 29
Abylkhozhin, Zhulduzbek 385
Achaemenids 15
activism: art 382; urban 6, 180
adat 31, 32
administrative reforms 27
Adolat (Justice) 418
afforded semi-autonomous (ASSR) territorial status 144
Afghan campaign (1979–1989) 249
Afghanistan 47, 125, 138, 195, 211, 218, 221–3, 225–7, 228, 249, 250, 251, 254, 258–60, 292, 296, 297, 418, 429, 440
Afghanistan-China-Pakistan-Tajikistan Armed Forces 259
Agreement on the Coordination Mechanism in Counterterrorism 259

agriculture 6, 14, 18, 21, 41, 42, 44, 45, 49, 58, 60, 64, 66, 67, 82, 116, 117, 119, 120, 123, 124, 138, 145, 154–9, 162–5, 290
Ahl al-Hadith 443
Ahmadboyev, Adham 253
Ahmad Mirza 20
Ahura Mazda 14
Aid Data 339
Aid Management Platform 339
air pollution 183, 187–8
Aitmatov, Chingiz 105
Akayev, Askar 75, 88, 89–93, 95, 97, 125, 126, 204, 220, 222, 242, 291, 322, 326, 333, 352, 353, 397, 456
Akhmediyarov, Askhat 380, 381, 385
Akhunov, Vyacheslav 377, 383
Ak Jol party 75, 96
Akmataliev, Tynchtykbek 91
Akmatbaev, Ryspek 91
Akmola Camp for Wives of the Enemies of the Motherland 388
Akmolinsk 168
aksakals 128, 365
AktobeMunaiGas Company 207
Ak Zhol party 253
Alamanov, Salamat 115, 116, 125
Alash-Orda 37, 446, 447
Al Azhar University 415
Alexander 15
Alga Kyrgyzstan party 75
Aliev, Rakhat 81
Alma-Ata protests (1986) 425, 426
Almaty 23, 28, 77, 80, 140, 206, 310
Almaty Stock Exchange 312
Al Qaeda 418, 419
al-Qanun fi'l-Tibb (*The Canon,* Ibn Sina) 18

Index

Altaic Hephthalites 16
Altynsarin, Ibrai 33
Aluminium Plant, Tursunzade 59
American foreign policy 218–28; fatigue and disillusionment 224–6; security dominates 221–4; transitioning from communism 218–21
American War on Terror 221, 228, 251
Amu Darya 19, 56, 144, 154–8, 160–4
analytical eclecticism 232, 233, 239–42
Ancient Silk Road 1, 157
Andijan massacre (2005) 219, 253
Andijan revolt (1898) 31, 33, 222, 223, 234, 253
Anglo-Russian Convention (1907) 138
Anna Ioannovna (Empress) 26
anti-*bai* campaign 47
anticolonial uprising (1916) 44
anticorruption programs 326
Anti-Corruption Service 96
anti-LGBT Bills 371
Antiochus 15
anti-religious campaign 48, 139
anti-Russian movement 29
anti-Semitism 199
Aqmola 168
Aqsakals 203
Aquinas, Thomas 18
Arabian Peninsula 1, 169, 176, 414–17
Arab Islamic American summit 225
Arab spring 211
Aral Sea 64, 65, 144, 154–6, 158, 160, 161, 163, 336
'Aral Sea Syndrome' 154
Archa Foundation 185–7, 190n10
architectural forms 175
architectural transformation 171
Armenia 212, 265, 296
Arsacid Parthians 16
art forms 378
Art Forum gallery 380
Article 5, NATO 254
Article 10, Constitution of Turkmenistan 106
artistic practices 377–9, 388
artists as memory activists 384–8
art performance 380
Artykbaev, Osmonbek 97
aruak 452
Aryan civilisation 108
A schast'e riadom (Happiness Is Nearby, 1978) 62
asexual 365
Asharism 438, 441, 443
Ashoka (c. 304–232 BCE) 15
Asian Development Bank 300n19, 398, 400
Asian Infrastructure Investment Bank (AIIB) 213
Askarov, Azimjan 224
Assembly of People of Kazakhstan 101–3, 394
assertive secularism 423–4, 428–31; biopower 431; disciplinary power 430–1; sovereign power 429–30

Assmann, Aleida 386
Astana 73, 77, 80, 81, 103, 140, 168–76, 206, 381
Astana Economic Forum 337
Atabekov, Said 378
Atambayev, Almazbek 88, 91–2, 94, 96, 97, 181, 190, 326
Ata-Meken party 94, 96
Ata-Zhurt party 94
authoritarianism 2, 73–84, 177, 198, 219, 220, 270, 306–8, 321, 393, 395, 424, 428, 431, 432, 437, 447; controlling political economy 81–3; discourse 76–9; and elections 74–5; monopolising space 79–81; practices and regimes 76
avant-garde movement 378
Ay Khanum 15
Azattyk 94
Azerbaijan 144, 169, 258, 285, 308, 415
Az i Ya (Suleimenov) 455

Babur 20
bachcha 366–8, 370, 372
backward rites 354
Baez-Camargo, C. 88
Bahovadinova, Malika 331
*bai*s 43, 47, 50, 52
Bakiyev, Kurmanbek 75, 88–91, 93, 95–7, 105, 241, 253, 254, 323, 326, 354, 456
Bakiyev, Maksim 90
Baksy (2008) 457
Baku-Tbilisi-Ceyhan pipeline 220, 223
Balkh 15
Baptists 422
Bartol'd, Vasilii 120
Basmachi 38, 46, 47, 50, 249
Battle of Talas 17
Batukaev, Aziz 97
Baudrillard, Jean 172
Bayaliyev, Smail 378
bazaars 3, 264, 267, 285, 291, 292, 322
Bazargaliyeva, Medina 381
Bazhkenova, Gul'nara 310
beauty 363, 366, 367, 369, 372
Beijing 202, 204–8, 211–13, 222, 227, 228, 251, 255, 258–60, 296
Beknazarov, Azimbek 204
Bekovich party 21
Belarus 194, 212, 250, 265, 283, 292, 296
Belt and Road Initiative (BRI) 208, 212, 213, 224–8, 259, 271, 272, 296, 336, 338, 339; *see also* Eurasian rail Landbridge
Berdimuhamedow, Gurbanguly 75, 78–80, 83, 105–7, 250, 253, 289, 290, 402
Beuys, Joseph 379
Beyneu-Shymkent Gas Pipeline 309
Bezertinov, Raphael 456
Biden, Joe 227, 228

Index

Bigiev, Musa Jarullah 443, 446, 447
bilateralism 141, 163, 194, 195, 198, 200, 203, 208, 213, 266, 272, 336
biomedical practice 63
BIOM movement 185, 187, 190n6
biopower 428, 431
Bir-Bol 91
bisexual 365
Bishkek 180, 182–9, 199, 222, 226, 258
Bishkek Thermal Power Plant 97, 325
Bissenova, Alima 199
biy court 32
*biy*s 31, 32
Bodrov, Sergei 457
Bokeikhanov, A.N. 36
Bolashak International Scholarships 297
Bolsheviks 2, 23, 37, 38, 42, 44, 45, 52, 121, 138, 162, 249, 331, 416
Bolsheviks' revolution (1917) 37
Book of Legends: the mysterious forest, The (2012) 457
borderland dynamics 143–4
Border Management Programme in Central Asia (BOMCA) 336
border(s) 139–40, 147, 148; China–Kyrgyzstan–Tajikistan 143–4; delimitation 116, 119, 125, 127, 146; disputes 117, 119–20, 143; issue 125–7; Kazakhstan–Russia 140–2; Kyrgyzstan–Tajikistan 119, 124, 129 nn.1(4), 146; management 254; maritime 144–5; security 139; Tajikistan–Afghanistan 259; Uzbekistan–Kazakhstan 144; Uzbekistan–Kyrgyzstan 124, 125, 142–3
border-talk 126
Border Work (Reeves) 143
Botanical Garden 181, 184–6, 190
Botanika 180
boundaries 117, 120, 139–40, 146, 148
boundary-focused approach 424
Brezhnev, Leonid 320
British Empire 29, 138
Brower, Daniel 137
Brubaker, Rogers 2
BTA Bank 319
Buddhism 14, 417
Bukhara 28, 29, 138
Bukhara Emirate 46
bureaucratisation 30–2
Bush, George H.W. 218, 219
Bush, George W. 218, 220, 222–4, 228
Business Environment and Enterprise Performance Survey (BEEPS) 320

C5+1 dialogue format 224, 225, 227
'The cage for the leaders' (Akhunov) 383
camouflage 88; anti-corruption (Atambayev) 96; anti-corruption (Jeenbekov) 96–7; elite consensus and party politics (Bakiyev) 95–6; inclusive democracy and charitable contributions (Akayev) 95
CAMP Ala-Too Foundation 187
Campbell, Ian 24
capital accumulation 307–9, 313
capital city projects 170, 176
capitalism 188, 189, 458
capital–labour relations 304, 313
capital relocation 171–3
Caroe, Olaf 20
Carthaginian Empire 16
Caspian Pipeline Consortium 220, 223
Caspian region 303–6, 308
Caspian Sea 144, 158, 160–3, 195
Catharism 16
Catherinian institution 32
Caucasoid types 14
CCP's Central Committee on China 205
censorship 76, 226, 238, 377, 380, 381, 388
Central Asia, definition 135
'Central Asia' as mutable regional imaginary 136–9
Central Asia–China Gas Pipeline 207, 208, 402
Central Asia Drug Action Programme (CADAP) 336
Central Asian Agricultural, Industrial and Scientific Explosion 367
Central Asian artists 377–9, 381–6, 388
Central Asian Battalion (CENTRASBAT) 220
Central Asian Bureau of the Communist Party 49, 50
Central Asian Railroad 160
Central Asian Regional Economic Cooperation (CAREC) 300n19
Central Asian Survey 455
Central Asian titular languages 391
Central Asian youth 445
Central Asian Youth Environmental Network (CAVEN) 187
Central Eurasia 136, 138
Central Executive Committee of the USSR 121
central planning 281, 283, 285
ceremonial gifts 353
Chaghatayids 19
Chek 142
Cheng Guoping 211
Chen Quanguo 26
Chevron 219, 220, 223, 225, 307, 308
childhood mortality 63
child labour 285
child-marriage 368
China 6, 67, 83, 125, 136, 141, 184, 193–6, 218, 221–4, 226–8, 233, 248, 251, 254, 259–60, 263, 269, 272, 289, 292, 296, 336, 338, 339, 340, 397, 402, 432
China-Central Asia relations 202–14, 271–2; global order 212–13; imbalance of power 208–10;

Index

regional order 211–12; Russian and Chinese empires 202–5; Xinjiang as pivot of 205–8
China National Institute for SCO International Exchange and Judicial Cooperation 258
China Road 182
China–Tajikistan cooperation 212
China–Uzbekistan relations 210
Chinese government 180, 182, 189, 202, 206
Chinese migration 272
Chinese military education 255, 258
Chinese National Petroleum Company 207, 312
Chinese People's Armed Police 211
Chinese Peoples' Liberation Army Navy 259
Chinese road construction company 182, 183
Chinggis Khan (Genghis Khan, c. 1167–1227) 18, 19, 22, 148n5, 158
Chodiev, Patokh 289
choy-xona 366
Christianity 14, 17
citizenship 106, 109, 331
City Council 181
city streets reconstruction 183
civic identity 103, 110
civic state projects 392
civil-military relations 252–4
Civil Registry offices (ZAGS) 51
civil war 41, 44, 58, 74, 78, 162, 321, 334; 1992–1997 125, 252, 356, 426; 2000 399
clan politics 5, 87
clan survivals 351
class consciousness 120, 249
'Clay project. Zero level' (Khalfin) 379
Clinton, Bill 219, 220
Clinton, Hillary 223
Clowes, Edith 135
CNPC 210, 307
'Code of Conduct for Information Security' (2015) 213
Cold War 56, 74, 121, 219, 423
collective farming/farms 43, 48, 52, 53, 59, 60, 66, 67, 121–3, 127, 385
collective identity 200, 349, 350
collective memory 377, 386, 388
Collective Security Treaty Organization (CSTO) 194, 222, 224, 227, 248, 251, 252, 254, 255, 260, 395, 398, 400–2
collectivisation 5, 53, 102, 121, 138, 162, 163, 197, 249, 331, 352, 368, 384; Central Asian agriculturalists (*dehqons*) before 45–7; Central Asian herdsmen before 44–5; in *dehqon* farming lands 49–52; in nomadic Central Asia 47–9; policies 41–3
colonial interventions 366–8
colonial schools 34
colonisation 197, 199; agricultural 47; Chinese 205; peasant 42; Russian 5, 36, 367, 368, 371
colour revolutions 211, 222, 234, 335

Combating Terrorism Fellowship Program (CTFP) 258
COMECON system 138
commemorations 354–6
Commissariat for Agriculture 43
Committee on Religious Affairs 431
The Committee on the Siberian Railroad 36
Commonwealth of Independent States (CIS) 250, 264, 300n19
Communism 41, 432
Communist Party 41, 43, 46–8, 52, 62, 74, 161, 237, 249, 297, 320, 370, 394, 425
Communist Party activists 42, 43, 50
comparative politics 232
Compatriots Living Abroad 336
competitive authoritarianism *see* electoral authoritarianism
Comprehensive Power Index 208
Conflict Could have Been Avoided (Konflikta moglo ne byt') 124
Confucian concepts in Chinese foreign policy 209
Confucianism 205, 209
Constitutional Council 146
Constitution of Kazakhstan 102, 394
Constitution of Kyrgyzstan 398
Constitution of Tajikistan 399
Constitution of Uzbekistan 400
Construction Corps 205
consumerism 354
contemporary art 6, 7, 377–88; political performance in Kazakhstan 378–82; reflection on Post-Soviet 382–4; trauma and memory 377, 384–8
control mechanisms 88, 92–5; demonstrative punishment, selective law enforcement and GKNB (Jeenbekov) 94–5; demonstrative punishment, selective law enforcement and *kompromat* (Atambayev) 94; social sanctions, demonstrative punishment, selective law enforcement and assassinations (Bakiyev) 93; social sanctions, demonstrative punishment and selective law enforcement (Akayev) 92–3
Cooley, Alexander 324
co-optation 88–92, 97, 205, 209, 213; Akayev's political family networks 90; under Atambayev 91–2; Bakiyev's political-family networks 90–1; Jeenbekov's informal networks 92
Copenhagen School 423
core liberal values 438–40, 442, 447
corpus development 391, 392, 395–6, 398, 402
corruption 3, 4, 6, 77, 87–98, 119, 180, 185, 221, 222, 237, 253, 260, 287, 290, 291, 297, 300n16, 305, 306, 308, 312, 319–27, 380; anti-corruption efforts 326–7; authorised and non-authorised 322; elite 320, 323; petty 319, 323; political economy as mode of governance 323–6; roots and evolution 320–3; systemic 323, 327

Corruption Perception Index 2018 320
cosmopolitanism *see* global citizenship
cotton: cultivation and production 42, 47, 51, 56, 58–9, 64, 160, 163, 164; monoculture 36, 67, 160
Council of People's Commissar of the USSR 47
counter-extremism 270, 428
counterterrorism 211, 226, 254, 259, 269, 272, 427
Crews, Robert 32
Crimea 141, 144, 197, 234, 296, 395
Crimean War 28
cross-border entrepreneurship 267
cross-border mixing 127, 128, 141
Crude Accountability 314
CSR Central Asia 187
cultural production 62
cultural revolution 48
cultural transformation 377, 385
cultural transmission 350, 382
culturedness and economic production 61
currency 115, 118, 125, 143, 212, 283, 285, 307, 311, 393, 454; *see also* foreign-exchange controls
Customs Union 212

DAESH 419
Dalai Lama 21
dam construction 64
Datka, Kurmanjan 105
*deava*s 14
Debord, Guy 453
decision making 238, 239, 241, 242, 263, 269, 307
decolonialism/decolonization 41, 44, 56, 331
de facto border 125, 127
Defense Logistics Agency-Energy 222
dekulakisation *see* liquidation
democracy promotion 218, 220, 221, 223, 224, 226–8
Democratic Choice of Kazakhstan (QDT) 80, 289, 299n12, 319
democratic elections 73, 76–8, 83
Democratic Party of Turkmenistan (DPT) 75
democratic processes 73, 87
democratisation 2, 73, 74, 89, 228, 260, 332–3, 335, 341, 437, 446
de-modern Islam 440–1, 445–7
demography 58, 63, 171, 195, 392, 393, 398, 399, 401, 403
Deng Xiaoping 203, 206, 213, 222
deportations 43, 45, 53, 102, 138, 268, 385, 386
de-securitisation 432
Development Assistance Committee (DAC) 333
Development Partners' Coordination Council 340
diaspora 81, 143, 386, 415, 416
Dictators without Borders (Cooley and Heathershaw) 324
digital platforms 381, 388

disciplinary power 428, 430–1
district schools 34
'divide and rule' 2, 121, 142
Diyanet 414
Djaparov, Ulan 379–80, 384
Djumaliyev, Muratbek 377, 383, 384
Dombay, Quat 396
domestic violence 370
donor agencies 337, 339
dual citizenship 106, 108
'dual sector' model 58
Dukhovskoi, S.M. 33
Durrani Empire 22
Dushanbe clothing factory 60
Dushanbinka (Dushanbinskaya) street 180–1, 183–5, 187–90
Dzhakishev, Mukhtar 81

Early Modern period 23
Earth System theory 154
EBRD Transition Indicators 283, 285
Ecological Information Services (ECOIS) 187
Ecological Movement of Kyrgyzstan 'Aleine' 187
economic consolidation 81
Economic Cooperation Organization 300n19
economic crisis (2009) 211
economic imbalance 209–10
economic reform and development 5, 6, 57, 63, 77, 82, 83, 171, 189, 206, 207, 211, 225, 252, 273, 281–98, 305, 332, 340, 341; end of oil boom 292, 296; political economy 297–8; resource boom 287, 289–92; transition from central planning 283, 285
economic rents 324
education 58, 61, 289, 393
Egypt 415
Eid Al-Adha 446
electoral authoritarianism 73
electricity production 57–8
El Nino Southern Oscillation 154
Emomali, Rustam 326
Enduring Freedom 334
energy 57, 67, 77, 186, 195, 207, 208, 212, 218, 220, 221, 223, 228, 260, 290, 292, 304, 307, 319, 322, 324
English language 397
English-medium instruction 403
Engvall, Johan 87, 88
Enlightenment 57
ENRC 81
environmental activists 187–8
Erlik 452
Ermekbayev, Nurlan 255
Esimde project 199
ethical objectivism 440, 442
ethnic cleansing 53
ethnic identity 102–3, 352, 412

Index

ethnicity 2, 110, 122, 196–7, 249, 252, 352, 369, 419
ethnic Kazakhs 102, 197, 206, 312
ethnic Kyrgyz 105, 122, 206
ethnic Russians 22, 95, 140, 171, 173, 197
ethnic Tajiks 122
ethnic Uzbeks 105, 254
ethnography 117, 142, 143, 173, 176, 177, 249, 268
Eurasia 136, 194
Eurasian Commission 266–7
Eurasian Economic Commission 266
Eurasian Economic Union (EEU) 141, 188, 194, 195, 212, 227, 263–7, 273, 290, 292, 296, 340, 395, 398, 402
Eurasian identity 103, 111
Eurasianism 199
Eurasian National Resources Corporation (ENRC) 289
Eurasian Natural Resources Corporation 322
Eurasian rail Landbridge 296
Eurasian Resources Group 289
Europe 195, 196, 270
European art 379
European Bank for Reconstruction and Development (EBRD) 320, 321
European colonialism/colonisation 57, 199
European culture 103
European Orientalists 21
European Union (EU) 194, 233, 326, 333–6, 397
Evangelical movement 422
event-based filtering 145
Excess Defense Articles (EDA) programme 258
EXIM Bank 210
extra-territoriality 123
ExxonMobil 220, 223, 225, 308, 314n5

facade trees 186
Facebook 145
face-to-face interaction 349
family planning 63
famines 43–5, 47–9, 51–3, 58, 65, 138, 352, 385
fatwas 357, 446
February Revolution 37
Federal Agency for the Commonwealth of Independent States 336
Federation of Independent Trade Unions 310
femininity 5, 363, 365, 371
feminisation 290, 367
Feng Zhang 209
Ferdowsi (c. 940–1020) 18
Ferghana basin 116, 117, 120, 121, 124, 129n2, 160, 164, 334
Fethullah Gulen 414
financialisation 304, 306, 308, 309
financial resources 91, 227, 312, 392, 393, 395
fiqh (Islamic law) 444
First Five-Year Plan (1928–1932) 42, 45, 56

'Five Principles of Peaceful Coexistence' 208
Florin, Moritz 62
folk traditions 350, 351, 354, 356, 358n2
forced labour 82, 156, 162, 297
foreign-exchange controls 258
Foreign Military Financing (FMF) 258
foreign policy 6, 203, 208–10, 213, 218, 232–42, 397, 414; analytical eclecticism 239–42; domestic matters 234–8; institutions in 238–9; international relations 233–4
foreign policy analysis (FPA) 232, 233–5, 237–9, 241, 242
formal governance 88
formal political systems 88–9, 97
Fortieth Army 249
Foster, Norman 80
Foucault, Michel 170, 173, 428
Frank, Andre Gunder 57, 137
Fravel, M. Taylor 204, 205
Frederich Ebert Foundation 445
Freedom Agenda 222
Freedom House 73, 220, 321
Freedom Support Act (1992) 219, 220
free market 332–3
free will 443–4
Friends of the Earth Europe 314
Frye, Richard N. 14
fundamentalism 269, 412, 415, 416, 419, 444
funerals 142, 268, 350, 351, 353–5, 357
'The future is coming from all directions' (Ugay) 386

G8 Summit 335
Gaipkulov, Iskender 190n10
Galdan Boshugtu Khan (1644–1697) 21
Galleries Parade 380
Gallup survey 195, 196
Gasprinskii, Ismail Bey 34
gatekeeping mechanisms 81, 82
Gavrilis, George 139
gay 146
Gay Propaganda Law 371
Gazprom 223
GDP 66, 77, 139, 264, 283, 285, 287, 290–2, 395, 400, 401
gender 6, 7, 362–72; concept of 362–3, 372; enculturation and order 363–7, 369, 371, 372; equality/inequality 372, 443, 445, 446, 448n8; identity 367, 369, 371; liveable and meaningful lives 372; post-soviet gender order 370–2; relations 363, 368, 372; segregation 366, 368; sexual orientation 365–8; soviet transformations 368–70
geographical imaginary 135, 143
Geographic Information Systems (GIS) 186
geopolitics 4, 116, 117, 126, 128, 135, 137, 138, 141–3, 176–8, 189, 232–4

Georgia 258
Georgian-Russian war (2008) 234
'ghost class' 309–13
Giffen, James 325
GKNB 94–5
glasnost' (openness) 123, 412, 425
global citizenship 146, 177
globalisation and migration 6, 20, 189, 199, 263–73; institutional integration 265–7; labour migration and remittances 264–5; threat perception 269–72; transnational life and work 267–9
'global war on terror' 77, 125, 205, 334
Gokturks (Celestial Turks) 16
Golden Age of Islam 18
gold prices 287
'good' and 'bad' Islam 432
Gorbachev, Mikhail 123, 203, 281, 412, 425
Gorchakov, A.M. 28
Gore-Chernomyrdin Commission 220
Gorno-Badakhshan Autonomous Oblast (GBAO) 79, 148n10
Gorno-Badakhshan region 143
Gosplan *see* State Planning Committee
Gosudarstvennyi Komitet Uzbekistan Demograficheskaia 401
government-subsidised housing 171
governor-generalships 30–1
Gradostroitelnyi Soviet (Urban Design Council) 184
grain procurement 48, 52
grain production 42, 51
grand corruption 319, 323
Grand Duke Nikolai Konstantinovich Romanov 161
'grassroots absolutism' 80
Great Chessboard, The (Brzezinski) 233
Great Chinese Fire Wall 145
Greater Middle East 136
'the Great Game' 138
'Great/New Renaissance' concept 106–7
Great Patriotic War 64
Great Seljuks 18
Great Silk Route 16
Greco-Bactrian Empire 15
Greco-Bactrian war 16
Greco-Persian Empire 15
green development politics 180–90; Chinese grant and local politics 182–3; Dushanbinka 180–1; Vetoshkin, Dima and apocalypses 181–2
Green Mobilisations 187
Green Party 187
green spaces 183–8, 190n10
Gregory, Derek 135
Groys, Boris 386
Gundogdyev, Begench 253
Gunpowder Empires 20

hajj 415, 416
Halyk kurultayi movement 210
Hanafi madhab 108, 431
Hanafism 438, 441, 444
Hanafite–Maturidite theology 438, 441, 443–5
Hanafite school 438
Hannibal 15, 16
health 31, 58, 60, 62, 63, 144, 145, 221, 268, 291, 309, 313, 334, 336, 339, 340, 341, 370
Heathershaw, John 324, 428
hegemony 76, 189, 236, 422, 424
heterosexual 365, 367, 368, 372
heterosocialising 368
high culture 61
Higher School of Economics 439
Hinduism 417
Hittites 15
Hizb-ut Tahrir 222, 428
home labour 67
homosexual 365, 372, 428
homosocial entertainment 366, 367
Hopkirk, Peter 22
hospitalisation 63
Hu Jingtao 211, 222
human diversity 362, 372
humanitarian aid 335
human rights 73, 102, 106, 189, 198, 213, 222–4, 226–8, 253, 332, 334, 438–46
hunger strike (2017) 310, 311
Hungry Steppe 64, 161
hydrocarbon reserves 307–9
hydroelectricity 290, 296, 299n13
hydropower 4, 57, 58, 162, 338
hyperinflation 283

Ibn Sina (c. 980–1037) 18
Ibragimov, Alijan 289
Ibragimov, Kanat 377, 378, 380, 381
Ibraimov, Albek 97, 180, 181, 183, 188–90
Ibryaev, Akhat 457
ideational approaches 235
Igelström, Otto Heinrich 27
ignorirovanie 34
Il'minskii, N.I. 33
imaginative geographies 135
Imam al-Bukhari Tashkent Islamic Institute 413
Imam Azam 431
Imam Bukhari Jamaat 430
Imanov, Amangeldi 37
Independent Ecological Expertise 187
India 16, 20, 22, 160, 199, 223, 228, 338, 365, 417
Indo-European language 14
industrialisation 41, 56, 58, 61, 62, 64, 66, 67, 138, 160, 331, 332, 368
informal–formal political relations 3
informal governance 87, 88, 97
informal politics 87–9, 98

informal rule 95, 322, 327
infrastructure projects 127, 128
Inkeles, Alex 60
'Inner Asia' 136
Innoyatov, Rustam 253
institutionalisation 2, 102, 146, 321, 322, 422
inter-communal conflict 119, 123, 127
interethnic relations 109
inter-governmental border negotiations 124
Interior Ministry 253
international alignment 393, 395, 397, 400
international anti-terrorism campaign 254
international borders 118, 119, 125, 128, 139, 140, 142
International Consortium of Investigative Journalists (ICIJ) 309
international development 6, 332–7, 341
International Development Finance Corporation (IDFC) 227
international financial crisis (2007–2008) 319, 336–7
international financial institutions (IFIs) 305–8
International Humanitarian Cooperation 336
international identity 236
international military education 255, 258
International Military Education and Training (IMET) programme 251, 258
International Monetary Fund (IMF) 283, 308, 332
International Narcotics Control and Law Enforcement 258
international organisations (IOs) 337, 393
International Organization for Migration 270
international peacekeeping operations 248, 260
international relations 6, 232–4, 235, 237, 239, 240, 242, 298, 398
International Religious Freedom Act 429
International Republican Institute 220
International Security Assistance Force 251
international trade 157, 292
International University 403
internet blackouts 145
Inter-regional Court 184
intersex individuals 373n3
inter-state relations 119, 124
inter-village disputes 128
intra-regional cooperation 292
Introduction of the Uzbek Alphabet Based on the Latin Script law (1993) 109
Iran 18, 144, 219, 225, 227, 292, 296, 297, 414, 415, 417
Iranian Islam 415
Irano-Persian heritage 415
Iraq 222, 223, 270, 419, 426, 427, 440
irrigated zones 41–3, 46
irrigation 155–9, 160–5, 183, 290
Isakov, Sapar 97, 325
Isfara valley 121, 123, 124, 126–8

Islam 1, 14–15, 17, 104, 107, 198, 351, 356, 425–7, 429, 431, 451, 456; conversion to 32; education 33, 34, 413; legitimisation 48; *vs.* Maturidism 440–1; practices 32, 35; securitisation of 4, 5, 7, 269, 423, 444; *see also* liberalism and Islam
Islamic Centre 431
Islamic extremism 427, 429
Islamic identity 412
Islamic individualism 443–4
Islamic Jihad Union (IJU) 426
Islamic Movement of Uzbekistan (IMU) 125, 220, 222, 252, 334, 418–19, 426
Islamic period 17–24; arrival of Mongols 18–20; arrival of Muscovy 21–4; decline 20
Islamic radicalism 219, 220, 412, 415, 416, 418–19, 423, 444
Islamic Renaissance Party of Tajikistan (IRPT) 74, 412, 425, 430
Islamic renewal 411–19; concepts and debates 411–12; influence of Islamic countries 413–18; radical Islam 418–19; religious policies and their main characteristics 412–13
Islamic State 270
Islamism 412, 414
Islamophobia 32
Islomidinov, Mirzosharif 129n4
Ismaili 415
Ismail Safavi 20
Ivanov, Sergei 221

Jadidism 445–6
Jadid movement 34, 35
Jadids 441, 445–7
Japan 337, 338
Japarov, Sadyr 75, 88
Jeenbekov, Asylbek 92
Jeenbekov, Sooronbai 88, 92, 94–7, 180, 322, 326
Jehovah's Witnesses 422
Jiang Zemin 204, 209, 221
jihadism 412, 416, 418, 419
Jochid Khans 20
Judaism 14, 17
Jungar rulers 21

Kadyrkhanova, Assel 377, 385
Kalinovsky, Artemy 331
Kalyev, Bakytbek 253
al-Kandhlawi, Muhammad Ilyas 417
Kangxi Emperor 22
Karaganda Corrective Labour Camp 388
Karakalpaks 17, 47, 144
Karamanuhli, Kurmangazi 455
Karash, Gumar 446, 447
Karimov, Islam 74, 77, 79, 82, 83, 125, 219, 220–2, 224, 225, 242, 251–3, 291, 297, 300n23, 325, 352–5, 395, 430

Karimova, Gulnara 291, 300n17, 325
Kashagan offshore oilfield 287, 308
Kasmaliyeva, Gulnara 377, 383, 384
Kasymov, Gani 456
Kazakh artists 378, 380, 385
Kazakh cinema 457–8
Kazakhgate scandal 325
Kazakh in higher education 395–7, 403
Kazakh Khanate 21, 203, 204, 452
Kazakh language 394–7
Kazakhmys (Kazakh Copper) 289
Kazakhs *see* Uzbek-Qazaqs
Kazakh SSR 168, 203, 207, 396
Kazakhstan 4–7, 17, 26, 42–5, 47–9, 51–3, 56, 57, 64, 65, 73, 74, 76–83, 110, 111, 140, 141, 144, 146, 168, 169, 172, 173, 176, 177, 193–7, 199, 200, 202, 203–10, 212–14, 219–21, 225, 226, 228, 236, 248, 250–2, 254, 258, 260, 263–6, 271, 272, 283, 284, 287, 289, 291, 292, 296–8, 303, 304, 307, 308, 310, 319, 321, 322, 331, 333, 335, 377, 381, 384, 385, 393–7, 417, 427, 429–31, 439, 440, 451, 456–8; nation-building policies 102–4; political performance in 378–82
Kazakhstan 2030 Strategy 287
Kazakhstan Congress of Soviets VII 47
Kazakhstan Engineering (KE) 251
Kazakhstani Security Council 271
Kazakhstan Temir Zholy (KTZ) 210
Kazakhstan Way, The (Nazarbayev) 303
Kazan' Theological Academy 33
Kazatomprom 82
KAZBRIG 251
kaziyat see muftiat
Kazkommertsbank 322
KazMunayGas Exploration and Production (KMG EP) 81, 289, 309, 312
Kelin (*Daughter-in-law*, 2009) 457, 458
Kenesari (Sultan, fl. 1836–1847) 22
Kengesh, Jogorku 97
Kenisary Qasimov 27
Kenzhe (*Young Brother*, 2015) 457
Kerry, John 224
'*ketmen*' 378
Khairulloyev, Sherali 252
Khalfin, Rustam 378–80
Khalid, Adeeb 34
Khalilzad, Zalmay 227
Khanate of Bukhara 21, 23, 203
Khanate of Khiva 21, 23, 27, 29, 46, 158–61, 203
Khanate of Kokand 21, 23, 27, 29, 203
Khiva People's Republic 46
khlebnye mesta (lucrative jobs) 323, 324
Khoqand Autonomy 37
Khorezm 155–64
Khorezmian Archaeological-Ethnographic Expedition 156, 164

Khrushchev, Nikita 58, 168, 175, 320, 331, 425
Khudoiar 29
khung-tayiji 21
Khwarezm Shah 18, 19
Kidarite Huns 16
Kim, Vladimir 289, 322
Kim Jong-il 177
Kinnars (*hijra*) 365
kinship 87–93, 97
kinship-based patronage networks 89, 97, 98
Kloop 92
Kobet, Konstantin 250
Koch, Natalie 76, 169, 176
'*kokpar*' 378
'Kokserek' 378–80
Kolbin, Gennady 425
kolkhozes 50, 51
Kolkhoz Model Statute (1935) 53
Kompromat 93, 94
Komsomol 331
Kongantiyev, Moldomusa 253
Korean community 386
koshelki 322
Koshe Partiyasy (Party of the Street) 80
KPO 308
Kriuchkov, Iu. 123
krysha 324
Kubrâ, Najm al-Din 413
Kuchluk 18, 19
Kudaibergenov, Arman 455
kulaks 43, 50
Kulibayev, Timur 81, 322
Kulmatov, Kubanychbek 97, 183
kulturnost' (culturedness) 61
Kunayev, Dinmukhamed 425
Kyrgyz 5, 17, 21, 28–30, 32, 37, 43–5, 47, 49, 51, 52, 104
Kyrgyzaltyn 456
Kyrgyz language 398
Kyrgyz-medium education 398
Kyrgyz parliament 95
Kyrgyz SSR 94, 118, 121, 122
Kyrgyzstan 4–7, 17, 26, 42, 44, 45, 47, 56, 57, 62, 64, 68, 74, 75, 79, 83, 84, 88, 90, 92, 93, 95–8, 110, 116, 118, 119, 124–6, 146, 180, 184, 187, 188, 195, 196, 202–10, 212–14, 218, 220, 221, 222, 224, 226, 228, 233, 234, 236, 239, 241, 248–50, 253, 254, 259, 260, 263–6, 271, 272, 283, 284, 287, 290–2, 296–8, 321–3, 325, 326, 331, 333–5, 337, 339–41, 351, 352, 354, 355, 357, 377, 379, 397–9, 417, 418, 422, 426, 427, 429, 431, 439, 440, 451, 456–8; nation-building policies 104–5; politics 87, 88, 91, 97; revolutions and corruption in 89
Kyrgyzstan draft law (2011) 355
'Kyrgyzstan Used to Be China's Land' 204
'Kyzyl Traktor' 377–81

labour: dispute 313; force 61, 67, 311, 369; market 264, 267, 310; migration and remittances 264–5; precarious 311
Labour Code 310
Land and Water Reform 46
land reform 45–7, 49, 50
language and language policy 6, 7, 391–404; Kazakhstan 394–7; Kyrgyzstan 397–9; Tajikistan 399–400; Turkmenistan 402–4; Uzbekistan 400–2
language law 392, 395; 1989 109, 394, 396, 399, 400; 1990 403; 1997 394
language repertoires 393, 395
Laruelle, Marlene 141, 196, 197, 236, 455, 456
Laszczkowski, Mateusz 169, 173–7
Latifi, Otahon 66
Lattimore, Owen 136
Lavrov, Sergey 197
Law on Citizenship (2017) 106, 108, 109
Law on Extremism (2003) 429
Law on Parental Responsibility (2011) 429
Law on Political Parties 75
Law on Technical Regulation 185
Law on the State Language 108, 109
Law on Trade Unions (2014) 310
Lee Kuan Yew 76
'The Legacy of Nomad Civilization' 457
legislative rents 324
legitimacy discourse 78–80, 82, 83
Leninabadskaya Pravda 123
Lerner, Daniel 60
Lewis, Arthur 58, 236
Lewis developmental model 66
LGBTQ+ 146, 370, 372
liberal democracy 95, 177
liberalisation 283, 297, 305, 307, 321, 322, 333, 354, 437
liberalism and Islam 7, 437–47; generation Z and progressive Islam 445–6; human rights 438–44; societal grounds 444–5
life-cycle celebrations 350–4, 356, 357
lifestyle 156, 175, 351, 358, 369
Li Lanqing 207
lineage associations 87
linguistic nationalism 392
liquidation 43, 50, 51
Liu, Morgan 135
livestock 42, 44, 45, 48, 49, 52, 53
London Stock Exchange 289, 312
Lord Curzon *see* Nathaniel, George
Luong, Pauline Jones 306

Magtymkuly 106
mahallas 79, 80, 127, 326
Mahayana Buddhism 16
Mahmud Hotaki 22
Mahmut Hudayi Vakfi foundation 414

Main Administration of Agriculture and Land Management 36
Malabayev, Muratbek 322
Malevich, Kazimir 379
Mamasheva, Aisuluu 190n10
Manas 221, 222, 238, 254, 258
Manas Transit Center 300n18
'Mangilik Yel' Patriotic Act 103
Mani (216–277) 16
Manichaeism 16
manpower agencies 310, 311
Manz, B. F. 20
Maoist revolution 416
market access 290, 340
market-based economies 281, 283, 285, 297, 298, 305, 339
Marshall European Center for Security Studies 258
Marxism 45, 56, 57, 120
Marxism-Leninism 2, 163
masculinity 5, 363, 365, 371
Mashkevich, Alexander 289
Maslov, Sergey 380
mass protests 79
mastermind scheme 170–3, 177, 178
Master Plan 184
material practices 175
Matisse, Henri 379
Matraimov, Iskender 92
Matraimov, Raim 97
Matraimov, Rayimbek 322
Mattis, Jim 224
Al-Maturidi 438, 440–1, 443
Maturidism 7, 418, 438, 440–7
mawali 17
Mā warā' an-Nahr 422
Mayor's Office 184–6, 189
Mazzarella, William 177
McCain, John 222
McChesney, Robert 20
McNamara, Robert 66
McNeill, William 14
meat procurements 48, 49
meat production 42
Medes 15
Megoran, Nick 117, 125, 126, 142, 143
Meldibekov, Erbossyn 378, 380, 381
memorialisation 80
'Memory objects – archive' (Ugay) 388
Menlibayeva, Almagul 385
Merv 15, 23, 29
métis 121
metrocentricity 177
Middle East 221, 222, 296, 426
migrant workers 264, 267, 270, 281, 290; *see also* labour, migration and remittances
militarisation 119, 124, 203

Military Academy of the General Staff of the Armed Forces of Russia 255
military-popular administration 31
'military-popular administration' (*voenno-narodnoe upravlenie*) 31
military power and capacity 248–60; early independence 250–5, 258–60; Soviet legacy 248–50
Mina 221
Ministry of Agriculture 287
Ministry of Culture 456
Ministry of Defense 253
Ministry of Economics 185
Ministry of Education and Science 400, 403
Ministry of Foreign Affairs (MFA) 204
Ministry of Internal Affairs 36
Ministry of Justice 185, 429, 431
Ministry of Religious Affairs 431
Mir-i-Arab 413, 425
Mirziyoyev, Shavkat 74, 77, 109, 110, 212, 226, 251–3, 258, 296–8, 300n23, 430
Mirzo, Sherali 255
Mirzoyev, Miraghlam 253
Mirzyoyev, Shavkat 198
Mithridates I (c. 171–138 BCE) 16
mobility 79, 118, 126–8, 136, 138, 145, 146, 157, 164, 263, 267, 371, 392
'A model for the assembly' (Ugay) 386
modernisation and development 325, 330–41, 352, 384, 424; donors and changing aid landscapes 335–7; Kyrgyzstan 339–41; one-size-fits-all support for democratisation and free market 332–3; security, growing scrutiny and donor-recipient relations 333–5; Soviet modernisation and its legacies 331–2; Tajikistan 337–9
modernity 3, 53, 61, 162, 171, 173, 175–7, 350, 369, 425, 438
modern marriages 356–7
modern traditions 354
modular labour 309–13
Modumarov, Adakhan 253
Mongol (2007) 457
Mongoloid types 14
Mongols 14, 15, 18–20, 158
monocausal approaches 232, 239–41
Montgomery, David 428, 456
Moore, Donald 117
Morrison, Alexander 28, 31
Moscow 23, 42, 45–9, 56–9, 63–5, 67, 121, 138, 141, 142, 194, 195, 197, 199, 207, 211, 212, 219, 222, 223, 227, 228, 233, 236, 249, 259, 260, 321, 331, 335, 341, 392, 402, 419, 439
motherhood 369–71
MoveGreen 187
muftiat 413, 418
Mufti of Tashkent 417, 419
Muftiyats 431, 441

Mughal Empire 20, 22
Muhammad (Prophet) 45
Muhammad (the Khorezmshah) 18
Muhammad Shah (r. 1719–1748) 22
Muhammad Shahi Bek 20
mujaddidi 417
mujahedin 418
multiparty democracy 74, 75
multi-vector foreign policy 203, 209, 210, 214
Murodov, Otabek 253
Muscovy 21–4
Muslim 'fanaticism' 33
Muslim identity 139, 416
Muslims of Central Asia 414, 419, 437, 444, 447
mutakallim 446
Mynbayev, Sauat 309
Mystics and Commissars (Bennigsen and Wimbush) 426

Nadir Shah Afshar (1688–1747) 21, 22
Naimans 18
Namangani, Juma 419
Naqshband, Baha'uddin 413
Naqshbandi 414, 417
Naqshbendiyya brotherhood 413, 414
Narymbetov, Moldakul 378
Nathaniel, George 22
national consciousness 120, 249
national culture 351, 352, 356
National Defense Strategy (2018) 224
national delimitation (*razmezhivanie*) 139
National Democratic Institute 220
national discourse 77, 79
National Fine Arts Museum 380
National Fund of the Republic of Kazakhstan (NFRK) 287
national identity 2, 5, 7, 78, 101, 104, 105, 108, 109, 139, 142, 235, 236, 352, 357, 380, 385, 419, 431, 437, 440, 447, 456
national ideology 115, 330, 352, 353, 355, 440, 456
national interest 237
nationalisation of traditions 349–58; nation building 351–2; post-Soviet nations 352–3; problematising 353–5
nationalism 88, 105, 108, 154, 236, 241, 289, 370, 419
national security 221, 252, 255, 429
National Security Service (NSS) 77, 251, 253
National Security Strategy (2002) 221
National Strategy for Sustainable Development (NSSD) 96
national-territorial delimitation (*natsional'no-territorialnoe razmezhevanie*) 120, 121, 124, 129, 161, 162
national traditions 351–2
nation-building 2, 5, 7, 101–11, 143, 234, 281, 296, 331, 338, 340, 385, 392–4, 397–400,

404; Kazakhstan 102–4; Kyrgyzstan 104–5; Tajikistan 107–9; Turkmenistan 105–7; Uzbekistan 109–10; without national traditions 351–2
nation-state 116, 119, 120, 138–40, 213, 350, 370, 392, 400
'native son,' concept of 93
NATO 194, 220, 221, 223, 225, 248, 258, 260
natural gas 188, 304, 308, 314
Navoi, Alisher 109
Nazarbayev, Nursultan 74, 76, 80, 81, 168, 171–3, 176, 204, 207, 219, 220, 225, 242, 251, 271, 285, 287, 289, 297, 298, 303–5, 307, 309, 319, 322, 325, 380, 381, 394–5, 397
Nazarbayeva, Dariga 81, 289
Nazarbayev University 297
Nazarov, Obid-kori 81
neoliberalism 189, 306, 335, 339, 438
'Neue Kasachische Kunst' (Ibragimov) 380
'New Great Game' 306
New Lawsan canal 161
New Silk Road 223
New Tajikistan Party 82
New World European colonisation 20
Ni, Vladimir 289, 299n11
Nicholas II 33, 36, 37
Niyazov, Saparmurat 75, 78, 83, 105–7, 221, 250, 285, 289, 333, 402, 431
nomadic culture 378, 379, 384–5
nomadism 379, 384, 385; horizontal 44; pastoral 14, 15
nomads 15–17, 20, 41, 43, 44, 53, 56, 457; pastoral 14, 19, 45, 48; steppe 32
nomenklatura 352
non-democratic electoral system 74, 76
non-governmental organisations (NGOs) 68, 187, 220, 304, 306, 314, 332, 335, 337
non-Russian languages 391
non-traditional Islam 445
non-Western-centric financial system 337
North Caspian Operating Company (NCOC) 308
Northern Distribution Network (NDN) 223, 224, 251
North Korea 225
novostroikas 188
Nowruz 351
Nuclear Non-Proliferation Treaty (NPT) 219
nuclear weapons 218–20, 225, 228
Nunn-Lugar Threat Reduction Program 219
Nurali (khan) 27
Nurbolatov, Aidos 381
Nurbolatova, Aigul 381
Nurek Dam 59
'Nurly Zhol' economic development plan 212
Nur Otan 74
Nur-Sultan 6, 195, 251, 310, 381 *see* Astana

Obama, Barack 218, 223, 224, 228, 258
October Revolution (1917) 331, 425
Office of Democratic Institutions and Human Rights (ODIHR) 73
official development assistance (ODA) 333
offshore 228, 238, 291, 308, 309, 311, 312, 319, 320, 325
Ogedei 19
Oghuz Khan 106
OGPU *see* Soviet Political Police
oil 303, 304; complex 305, 307, 308, 310, 311, 313, 314; contracts 307–9, 325; extraction 313, 314; and gas deposits 305; industries 218, 307, 314; politics 6; prices 287, 308; rents 303; reserves 308
Oil Is Not a Curse (Luong and Weinthal) 306
oil paintings 378, 379
'the oligarchic parliament' *see* Kyrgyz parliament
Omarova, Guka 457
Omelicheva, Mariya 76
Omurkulov, Isa 183
'On Broadening the Spheres of Use of the State Language in State Organs' 396
One Belt One Road (OBOR) *see* Belt and Road Initiative (BRI)
One Village 337
'On Language' 106
online content blocking 145
ontology 365, 366, 368, 369, 370
'Open Up the West' programme 207, 208
Operation Enduring Freedom 223
oral transmission 349
Orenburg Islamic Spiritual Assembly 32
Orenburg Kazaks 30
Orenburg-Tashkent Railroad 36, 160
Organisation for Economic Co-operation and Development (OECD) 333
Organisation for Security and Cooperation in Europe (OSCE) 73, 75, 186, 270
Organised Crime and Corruption Reporting Project (OCCRP) 92
Oriental despotism 168
otkat (kickbacks) 324
Otunbayeva, Roza 88, 96, 254, 291, 370
Ovadan Depe Prison 430
OzenMunayGas 312

Pakistan 211, 223, 292, 296
Pamiri Highway 331
Pamiri languages 399
Pantucci, Rafaello 211
Parham, Steven 143, 147
Paris School 423
parity commissions (*paritetnye kommissii*) 123
Parthians 15–17
Partnership for Peace initiative 220
Party of Industrialists and Entrepreneurs 75

passive secularism 424
pastoral economy 44
pastoralism 45, 155, 157–9, 164
patron–client networks 140, 321, 327
Peace Accord 426
peace-building 334, 340
People's Democratic Party 75
People's Liberation Army 205
People's Soviet Republic of Khorezm 161, 162
people with disabilities 145
perestroika 122–4, 412, 425
'Period of Might and Happiness' 107
'personality cult' hypothesis 173
Peter the Great (1672–1725) 21, 22
Petronas 210, 307
photography 378
piala 380
pilgrimages 415, 416
PLA National Defense University (PLA NDU) 255
planned economy 283, 321
plenipotentiaries *see* Communist Party activists
pluralism 32, 74–6, 84, 220, 332, 400, 432
Politburo 48
political activism 34, 368, 371, 372
political control strategy 327
political economy 6, 81–3, 127, 297–8, 304, 313, 319, 321, 323–6
political environmental history 155, 164
political family networks: of Bakiyev 90–1; of Kayev 90
political geography 3, 118, 137, 139, 140, 145
political violence 388
polygamy 445
polygyny 368, 369
Polytechnic Institute 59
Pompeo, Mike 225
Popular Front 252
population growth 58, 122, 123, 126, 127, 171
postcolonial perspectives 198–9
post-memory 385–6, 388
post-soviet gender order 370–2
post-war Central Asia development 56–68; afterlives 67–8; culture 60–2; environment 64–5; models 57–9; practices 59–60; resistance 65–6; revisions 66–7; welfare 62–4
poverty 57, 66, 78, 81, 82, 89, 142, 189, 214, 232, 252, 263, 268, 285, 339–41, 367, 393, 398, 400
pre-colonial gender order 366–8
pre-Islamic period 14–17; Parthia and silk routes 15–17; Persia and Alexander 15
price liberalisation 283
primitivism 384
pripiski 321
private property 41, 53, 95
private–public partnerships 340

privatisation 89, 95, 117, 283, 289, 297, 305, 307, 323, 332
procurement campaigns 43
professionals military education (PME) 258
professional-technical schools (PTUs) 58
progressive Islam 444–6
progressive religious teachings 439
Prosecutor General's Office 80
Prospect Mira 181
prostitution 367
protection rents 324
Protocol of Chuguchak/Tarbagatai (1884) 203
Protocol on Counterterrorism Information Coordination Center 259
Provisional Government 37
'Provisional Statute' *see* Turkestan Statute (1867)
Public Foundation 457
public intellectuals 198, 199
public offices 6, 90, 291, 319, 323
public space 377, 380, 382, 388
Pugachev uprising (1773–1774) 27
'pulota,' concept of 378–9
Putin, Vladimir 141, 197, 198, 212, 221, 222, 233, 250, 251, 259, 260, 292
pyramid systems 320, 323

Qadimism 441
Qara-Khitai 18, 19
Qaraqalpaqs 159, 162
qazi court 32
*qazi*s 32
Qing Empire 203, 205
Qipchaq 17
Qodirov, Rashid 253
Qongrat Khans 158, 159, 162
Quadrilateral Cooperation and Coordination Mechanism (QCCM) 211, 259
Quality of Government (QoG) 320
Qutaiba b. Muslim 17

Rabita (World Islamic League) 416
radical art performances 380
radicalisation 269–71, 341, 428
Rahmon, Emomali 74, 75, 78, 108, 109, 290, 354, 355, 427
Rakhmon, Imomali 252, 254
Rasanayagam, Johan 80
rastrat (embezzlement) 324
rationalistic epistemology 438, 439, 442, 447
rationalistic Islamic theology 438, 443, 444, 446, 447, 447n2
Rawls, John 7, 444
Rawlsian liberalism 438
"rayons" (regions) 180
Red Army 45, 46, 48, 249, 255
Red Banner Military Institute of the USSR Ministry of Defense 255

Red Guards 37
Red Star Enterprises 221
re-education centres 26
Reeves, Madeleine 143
regimes–foreign policy linkage 237, 238
Regional Anti-terrorist Structure (RATS) 205
regional cooperation 195, 198, 212, 220, 292, 296, 298; *see also* Eurasian Economic Union (EEU)
regionalism 107, 109, 240
registration (*propiska*) policies 271
'Regulations on the Siberian Kirgiz' 27
"Rehabilitation of city streets" 182
religious practices 4, 48, 61, 139, 351, 412, 416, 417, 422, 427, 453
Renaissance Period 107
rent-seeking 90, 91, 285, 290, 305, 322, 324
Reporters Without Borders 78
Republic Square 380
resettlement 35–7, 51, 59, 61, 62, 64, 65, 80
'Resettlement Action plan' 127
Resettlement Administration 36
'resource curse' hypothesis 303–6
Res Publica 126
Respublika 91
retraditionalisation 437, 440, 444, 446, 447, 447n5
revenge nationalism 101
Rice, Condoleezza 222
right-wing populism 440
ritual economy 60
rituals 350–2, 354–7, 378–80, 458
road construction 183, 210
Rodney, Walter 57
Roghun dam 66, 67, 338
Rossotrudnichestvo see International Humanitarian Cooperation
Ruhnama (*The Holy Book of all Turkmen,* Niyazov) 78, 106, 107, 402, 431
'Rukhani Zhangyru' ('Spiritual Modernisation') 103
Rumsfeld, Donald 221, 222
rural health networks 63
Russia 4, 6, 41, 42, 44, 47, 49, 51–3, 81, 82, 108, 118, 125, 126, 135–8, 140, 141, 144, 146, 160, 193, 199, 200, 209, 211–14, 218–24, 226–8, 233, 234, 236, 241, 248, 250, 254, 255, 258–60, 263–6, 268–71, 281, 283, 285, 287, 289, 290, 292, 296, 322, 335–7, 339, 395, 397, 398, 400, 402, 415, 417, 419, 429, 432; Central Asia's perceptions of 195–8; colonialism 5, 36, 160–1; cotton textile industry 45, 46; economy 193; imperialism 23; perceptions of Central Asia 194–5
Russia–Central Asia relationship 193
Russian Civil War (1917–22) 138
Russian Empire 20, 23, 26, 29, 137, 138, 160, 197, 202–5, 331, 351, 354, 367, 368
Russian Federation 108, 140, 250

Russian financial crisis (1998) 285
Russian Imperial Orientalists 249
Russian-Kyrgyz Development Fund (RKDF) 336, 340
Russian language 391, 392, 394–404
Russian media 145
Russian-medium higher education (HE) 391, 399, 401, 403
Russian Revolution (1917) 422
Russian rule 26–38; conquest of Turkestan 28–9; cultural and religious policy 32–5; economic change and resettlement 35–6; incorporation of Kazak hordes 26–8; law and governance 30–2; revolt and collapse 36–8; territory and laws 29–30
Russians in Kazakhstan 140
'Russo-Kazak' schools 33
Russo-native schools 33, 34
Russo-Turkish War 29

Sacred Geography 103
SADUM (*Dukhovnoye Upravleniye Musul'man Sredney Azii I Kazakhstana*) 425
Sagadiyev, Yerlan 397
Saidov, Zaid 82
Saipov, Alisher 81
Sait Nursi movement 414
Saka 15
Salafism 412, 416, 445
Salih, Mohammed 74
Salyanova, Aida 94
Samanid Dynasty (819–999) 108, 111
Samarkand 1, 15, 20, 29, 138, 321
same-sex desires 365, 366, 368, 370, 371
same-sex practices 365–71
samovol'tsy 35
Samruk-Kazyna 82
sanitary norms 185
Saroyan, Mark 139
Sarsenbaev, Altynbek 299n12
Sarts 24, 159
Sarygulov, Dastan 456
Satpaev, Dosym 82
Saudi Arabia 219, 305, 335, 412, 414, 415, 416
scholasticism 18
SCO Peace Mission 211
Scythians 15
Search for a Common Ground 270
Second Five-Year Plan 51
Second Punic War 16
Section 1004 Counter-Drug Assistance 258
secularism 198, 412–14, 422–5, 440
securitisation of religion 4, 5, 7, 124–6, 128, 142, 195, 269, 310, 422–32, 444; assertive secularism 423–4, 428–31; Islam 423; post-Soviet discourse of Islamic danger 427–8; during Soviet Union 424–6; threat of terrorism 426–7

sedentarisation 5, 41, 43, 45, 47, 52, 53, 56, 138, 155, 159, 163, 165, 331, 368, 384, 385
sedentary farmers (*dehqon*) 41–3, 45–7, 49–53
segmentary lineage societies 45
Seidimbek, Akseleu 455
Seleucid dynasty 15
Seleucus I Nikator 15
Seljuk Empire 17, 106
Semirech'e/Zhetysu/Dzhety-Suu area 44
sensuality 367, 369, 372
September 11 attacks 205, 218, 221, 223, 233, 254–5, 334
settler colonialism 43, 44, 53
sex 365, 368
sexuality 364–5, 367, 371
sexual orientation 365–8
sexual violence 146
Seydomar, Batyrzhan 457
shadow economy 60, 67, 321, 325
Shahanov, Otabek 253
Shahid-i-Mazlum Farrukhsiyar (r. 1713–1719) 22
Shahnameh (the Book of Kings) 18
Shajara-i Turk (*The Genealogy of the Turks*, Abu'l-Ghazi) 21
Shal (Old Man, 2012) 457–8
Shalbayev, Arystanbek 378
shamanistic practices 378
Shanghai Cooperation Organization (SCO) 205, 211–13, 222, 227, 248, 251, 252, 254, 255, 260, 300n19
'Shanghai Five' 251
Shaposhnikov, Marshal Yevgeny 250
shari'a 32, 33
Sharia Councils 431
Shay-Ziya 378
Shibani Khan *see* Muhammad Shahi Bek
Shiism 20, 415
shock therapy 283
Shoigu, Sergey 197
Shrine Empires 20
Shukurov, Emil 186
Shykmamatov, Almanbet 94
'Shymkent–Transavangard' *see* 'Kyzyl Traktor'
Siberia 47, 52, 199
Siberian-Aral canal 163
Siberian Water Transfer Scheme 162
Silk Road Economic Belt (SREB) 208, 212, 296
silk routes 15–17
Simakov, Vitaliy 378
Sinophobia 269, 271
Sino-Soviet border agreement (1991) 203
Sirhindi, Ahmad 417
'A skin of an artist' (Khalfin) 379
social activism 366, 371
social continuity 350
Social Democratic Party of Kyrgyzstan (SDPK) 91

socialism 49, 57, 65, 67, 162, 378
socialist modernisation 53–4, 61
socialist realism 378, 383, 386
social media 88, 145, 189, 198, 199, 204, 272, 350, 381, 382, 430
social transformation 121, 367, 369, 371, 377, 382, 385
societal liberalisation 446
sociology 66, 235, 267, 411
soft authoritarianism 76
Sohu.com 204
Sokh valley 117, 121, 124, 127
Soucek, Svat 23
South Asia 221
South Korea 335
South–South cooperation 336
sovereign power 428, 429–30
sovereignty 18, 21, 23, 120, 126, 140, 142, 198, 199, 204, 218, 219, 221, 222, 228, 263
Soviet Academy of Sciences 156
Soviet Army 250
Soviet Central Command 250
Soviet Political Police 43, 50
Soviet regime 1, 2, 4, 5, 24, 250, 351, 377, 384, 415
Soviet Socialist Republic (SSR) 2
Soviet Union 3, 4, 5, 41, 42, 43, 45, 47, 48, 49, 51–3, 56–64, 66, 67, 101, 104, 105, 110, 115, 118, 122, 125, 129, 136, 139, 140, 147, 154, 156, 162–4, 171, 181, 187, 197, 199, 205, 207, 211, 218, 219, 221, 232, 236, 248–50, 252, 260, 263, 267, 283, 285, 297, 303, 313, 330–2, 350, 351, 367–70, 377, 378, 411–16, 418, 419, 422, 424–6, 428, 429, 432
Special Advisor for Caspian Basin Energy Diplomacy 220
Special Program for the Economies of Central Asia (SPECA) 300n19
spectacular city-building 6, 168–70, 173, 174, 176
Speranskii, Mikhail 27, 31
Spiritual Administration of the Muslims of Central Asia and Kazakhstan (SADUM) 139
Srym Batyr 27
SS-18 missiles 219
Stalin, Josef 41, 48–50, 62, 64, 163, 331, 392, 425
Stalinism 41, 56
'Stalinist Great Turn' 42, 48
standard of living 66
Starr, S. Frederick 219
START I Treaty 219
State as Investment Market: Kyrgyzstan in Comparative Perspective, The (Engvall) 87
The State Committee for Language and Terminology 431
State Cotton Committee 45
State Department 220, 222, 226, 429
State Investment Committee 307

State Planning Committee 42
Steppe Eagle military exercises 220
steppe economy 44, 45
Steppe Revolt (1916) 199
Steppe Statute (1891) 30, 32–3, 35, 36
Sterligov, Vladimir 379
Stolypin, P.A. 35, 36
'Strike Hard' campaign 205, 206
structural violence 173, 176, 189
Subkhanberdin, Nurzhan 322
Sufi Empires *see* Shrine Empires
Sufieva, Gulruhsor 66
Sufism 378, 413, 417, 426, 444
Suleimenov, Olzhas 455
Suleimenova, Saule 385
Suleimenova, Suinbike 381
Suleymanci 414
Süleyman Tunahan, Hilmi 414
Sultan Sanjar 106
Sunni 418
supply chains 251, 283, 287
Surakhmatov, Aziz 183
surge in Afghanistan 218, 223, 224, 228
Suyarkulova, Mokhira 199
Suyorkulova street 183
Syr Darya 17, 19–21, 28, 30, 42, 44, 56–8, 154, 157, 163
Syria 270, 419, 426, 427

Tablighi movement 417–18
Tabligh Jama'at 417, 418
Tadjikskaya SSR 181
Al-Tahawi 441
Taheri, Amir 425
Tajikistan 4–6, 26, 42, 45, 46, 51, 56, 57, 64, 65, 67, 68, 74, 75, 78, 79, 81–3, 92, 107–9, 111, 116, 118, 119, 124, 125, 195, 196, 202–5, 208–14, 221, 222, 226, 248–50, 252, 254, 259, 260, 263–6, 268, 271, 272, 283, 285, 287, 290–2, 296, 298, 321, 325, 326, 331, 333–5, 336–9, 340, 351, 355, 356, 395, 399–400, 417, 418, 422, 426, 427, 429, 430, 431
Tajikistan–Afghanistan border 125
Tajikistan law 355, 356
Tajik-medium education 400
Tajik Muslims 107, 108
Tajiks 108, 193
Tajiks in the Mirror of History: From the Aryans to Samanids (Rahmon) 108
Taliban 227, 418, 429
Tang Chinese dynasty 16, 17
Tashkent 17, 23, 28, 30, 35, 37, 46, 51, 80, 120, 121, 125, 157, 205, 219, 222, 225, 226, 237, 240, 253, 259, 291, 321, 357, 401, 429
Tashkent State University 109
Tash Saka 162
Tatars 392

Tatar Yoke 19
Tavhid va Jihod 430
tax havens 307–9, 313, 325
'Taza Koom' 96
technocratic approach 36
technology of government 170
Teheran's nuclear programme 415
Tekebaev, Omurbek 94
TeliaSonera 325
Temujin *see* Chinggis Khan (Genghis Khan, c. 1167–1227)
Tengir-Ordo 455, 456
Tengiz oil field 287, 299n5, 307, 311, 312
Tengrism 7, 431, 451–8; contemporary politics 455–7; definition 451–2; history 453–5; Kazakh cinema 457–8; psychogeography 453
Terdikbayev, Erlis 255
territorial disputes 202–4, 269, 271; China–Kazakhstan 300n21; China–Kyrgyzstan 143–4; China–Tajikistan 212
territorial rents 324
terrorism 4, 205, 206, 222, 224, 226, 227, 251, 254, 255, 269–71, 334, 341, 426–7, 429
Tezekbaev, Kubanychbek 456
theological views 438, 442–3
Thibault, Helene 428
Tillerson, Rex 225
Timur, Amir 110
Timur Bek (Amir Timur, Tamerlane, 1336–1405) 19
Timurid civilisation 110
Timurid dynasty 19, 20
titular and non-titular ethnic majorities 352
titular languages 391, 392
Toghluq-Timur 19
Tokayev, Kassym-Jomart 74, 77, 80, 225, 242, 297, 298
Toktogul street 183
Toktomushev, Maksatbek 418
Toktonalieva Street *see* Dushanbinka (Dushanbinskaya) street
Toktonaliyev, Aliaskar 181
Tolstov, Sergei P. 156
Tolymbekov, Beibarys 381
Topbas, Osman Nuri 414
'Tournament of Shadows' (*Turniry Teney*) *see* 'the Great Game'
Toutiao.com 204
townsfolk 15
toy economy 353
traditional identities 356
traditional Islam 418, 437, 441, 447
trans-border interactions 118, 140, 142
Transcaspian region 28, 36, 38n3
transhumance 43, 44
transitional recession 283, 285
transnationalism 267–9
transnational networks 263, 265

transnational oil and gas companies (TNCs) 303, 306–10, 313, 314
transnational parenting 268
Transneft 223
Transparency International 300n16, 320
'TransSiberian Amazons' (Kasmaliyeva and Djumaliyev) 383–4
Trans-Siberian railroad 36
Treaty of Beijing (1860) 203
Treaty of Livadia (1879) 203
Treaty of St. Petersburg (1881) 203
trees 180–4, 186–9
Trevisani, T. 177
tribalism 87
Trump, D. 224–8, 258, 260
Tsarist Empire 45
Tsarist rule 26, 31, 34, 35, 41
Tselinograd *see* Akmolinsk
TselinSelMash 171
Tsewang Rabtan (1643–1727) 21
Tughan Zher (Homeland) 103
Tulesova, Asya 381
Tulip Revolution (2005) 89, 204, 222
Turan 18
Turkestan 28, 30, 32–4, 36, 38, 44, 138, 366; conquest of 28–9; Muslims of 34, 35
Turkestan–Siberia railway 42
Turkestan Statute (1867) 30–3, 36, 38n4
Turkey 19, 414, 424
Turkic identity 103, 111, 458
Turkic Qarluqs 17, 19
Turkish Islam 414
Turkistan Military District (MD) 249–50
Turkmen 403, 404
Turkmenistan 7, 26, 42, 45–7, 51, 56, 73–5, 78, 79, 80, 83, 111, 144, 145, 168, 194, 195, 202, 207, 209, 210, 213, 214, 221, 228, 248–50, 253, 258, 259, 260, 283, 285, 287, 289–90, 291, 292, 297, 298, 303, 307, 308, 310, 312, 321, 333–5, 393, 395, 402–4, 422, 429, 431; nation-building policies 105–7
Turkmenistan-Uzbekistan-Kazakhstan-China gas pipeline 292, 296
Turkmens 17, 21, 22, 29, 46, 47, 52, 105–7, 120, 159–61
Turkmen SSR 46, 162
Turk Qaghanates 16
Tursunov, Ermek 457, 458
Tursunov, Oybek 253

Ubaidullaeva, Rano 66
Ubaydullah II (r. 1702–1711) 22
Ugay, Alexander 377, 385, 386, 388
Uighur activism/activists 205, 206, 208
Uighuric Khaganate 454, 458n2
Ukraine 44, 47, 50, 194, 223, 228, 234, 250, 258, 285, 296

umrah see hajj
under-provisioned households 281; *see also* poverty
UN Ferghana Valley Development Programme 335
unfinished delimitation 117, 120–1
UN General Assembly 213
UN Human Rights Council 213
UN Interim Force 251
Union of Artists (UoA) 378
Union of Five 300n19
Union of Soviet Socialist Republics (USSR) *see* Soviet Union
Union Republics (UR) 392
Union Republics (UR) titular languages 391
Unison and Climatic Network of Kyrgyzstan 187
United Nations (UN) 212, 213, 260, 326, 402
United States 4, 6, 125, 126, 194–7, 205, 209, 211, 233, 237, 241, 251, 254, 258–60, 292, 397, 418, 424, 432
United States Agency for International Development (USAID) 332
United Tajik Opposition 252
Universal Declaration of Human Rights 439
University of Gothenburg 320
unsettled space 115–29; border disputes 119–20; delimitation deferred 121–2; Ferghana basin 117–19; living in 126–8; overview 115–17; perils of *perestroika* 122–4; unfinished delimitation 120–1; unsettled politics and 124–6
Uppdrag granskning 325
Ural Mountains 137
urban development 6, 157, 176
Urban Initiatives 187
urbanisation 58, 66, 67, 385
urban spaces 6, 79, 83, 189
Urumqi 206, 207
unuuchuluk 326
U.S. Agency for International Development (AID) 220, 221, 227
U.S. Central Command (CENTCOM) 258
U.S. Department of Defense 258
U.S.–Kyrgyzstan relations 222
U.S. National Defense Strategy 260
U.S. National Guard 254, 258
U.S.–Russian relations 227, 228
U.S. security assistance programmes 254
U.S. Special Operations Command Central 254
USSR Ministry of Health 62
Utemuratov, Bulat 322
utilitarian liberalism 438
Uyama, Tomohiko 37
Uyghur movement 416
Uzbekistan 4, 5, 7, 26, 42, 45–7, 49–51, 56, 57, 68, 74, 77–8, 81–3, 111, 116, 118, 119, 125, 126, 144, 145, 177, 194–6, 202, 203, 205, 207, 210, 212–14, 218–22, 224–8, 233, 237, 240–2, 248–51, 254, 258–60, 263–6, 272, 283, 285, 287, 290–2, 296–8, 299n15, 307, 308, 312, 321,

323, 325, 326, 334, 335, 337, 351–3, 355, 356, 377, 393, 395, 399, 413, 416–18, 422, 426, 427, 429–31, 439; nation-building policies 109–10
Uzbek Khan (r. 1313–1341) 19
Uzbek Kungrats 47
Uzbek language 109, 110, 399, 401, 402
Uzbek Lokais 47
Uzbek-medium education 398
Uzbek-medium schools 402, 403
Uzbek-Qazaqs 17, 19–21, 23, 26–8, 31–4, 36, 37, 38n2, 43–9, 51, 52, 104, 140, 171, 298
Uzbeks 19–21, 81, 159, 161, 162, 193, 198, 353, 354, 393

Vakhsh River Valley 331
Valikhanov, Ch. Ch. 33
Vassilenko, Stanislav 225
Vereikis, Juozas 120
Verevkin, N.A. 28
vernacular language 33
Verny Capital 322
Vetoshkin, Dima 181–2, 185–7, 189, 190
video art 378
video installation 379, 383–4
'Virgin Lands' campaign (1950s) 138, 331
Voda k dobry snitsa (novel) 62
von Kaufman, K.P. 29, 33, 34, 161
von Richthofen, Ferdinand 16
Votel, Joseph 226
Vozrozhdeniya Island 144

Wadud, Amina 448n8
Wahhabism 412, 416
Wakhan Corridor 138, 259
Washington 218–20, 222–8, 233, 254, 258
'Washington Consensus' 67, 283; *see also* shock therapy
water politics 6, 154–65; after Soviet Union 163–4; archaeology of irrigation 155–7; medieval period 157–8; Russian colonial rule 160–1; Soviet period 161–3; time of Khanates 158–60
Water Users Association 337
Webb Williams, N. 101
weddings 142, 268, 351, 353–8, 369
Weinthal, Erika 306
welfare and corruption 325–6
Wells, Alice 227
West–East Gas Pipeline 207
Western Europe 137

Western Liao *see* Qara-Khitai
'Why Kazakhstan Is Trying to Return to China' 204
Wikileaks 291
'Windows of Tolerance' (Kadyrkhanova) 385
Wise Thoughts and Sayings of the President of Tajikistan – the Founder of Peace and National Unity – Leader of Nation Emomali Rahmon (Rahmon) 108
Witte, S. Iu. 36
women: activism 340, 370; Central Asian 66; empowerment 340–1, 370; labour 59, 60, 67, 368, 369; in public life 445; rights 369
Women's Union of Turkmenistan 75
World Bank 66, 82, 127, 228, 283, 299n15, 305, 312, 319, 320, 332
World Development Indicators 299n15
World Trade Organization 283
World War I 41, 44
World War II 5, 53, 58, 164, 249, 425
Worldwide Governance Indicators (WGI) 320

xenophobia 194
Xi Jinping 208, 209, 211–13, 224, 338
Xinjiang/XUAR 136, 143, 202–8, 213, 254, 260, 272; economic dimension 206–8; Muslim 272; political and social dimensions 205–6
Xinjiang Production 205

Yadrintsev, Nikolai 16
Yer Sub 452
Yessevi, Ahmet 413
Yoldashev, Tahir 419
Yomut Turkmen uprising (1899) 161
youth attitudes 445–7
YouTube 145
Yrystan Foundation 187

Zakharov, Roman 381
Zanoza 94
Zarathustra (Zoroaster) 14, 15
Zarifi, Hamrokhon 204
Zelenhoz 182, 186
'Zeleniy treugolnik' 378, 379
Zhakiyanov, Galymzhan 299n12
Zhanaozen protests (2011) 77, 79, 289, 311, 312, 381
Zhogorku Kengesh Kyrgyzskoi respublike 355
Zoroastrian Sasanid state 16